Third Edition

ADOLESCENCE

Eastwood Atwater

PRENTICE HALL, Englewood Cliffs, N. J. 07632

Library of Congress Cataloging-in-Publication Data

Atwater, Eastwood, [date]
  Adolescence / Eastwood Atwater.—3rd ed.
    p. cm.
  Includes bibliographical references and index.
  ISBN 0-13-007469-1
    1. Adolescence. 2. Teenagers—United States. I. Title.
HQ796.A76   1992
305.23′5—dc20   91-23577

Acquisitions editor: *Carol Wada*
Editorial/production supervision and interior design: *Edie Riker*
Cover design: *Bruce Kenselaar*
Cover illustration: *Kathleen Keifer*
Prepress buyer: *Kelly Behr*
Manufacturing buyer: *Mary Ann Gloriande*

To **Kay, Susan,** and **Gail**

 © 1992, 1988 by Prentice-Hall, Inc.
A Simon & Schuster Company
Englewood Cliffs, New Jersey 07632

Printed in the United States of America

10 9 8 7 6 5 4 3 2 1

ISBN   0-13-007469-1

Prentice-Hall International (UK) Limited, *London*
Prentice-Hall of Australia Pty. Limited, *Sydney*
Prentice-Hall Canada Inc., *Toronto*
Prentice-Hall Hispanoamericana, S.A., *Mexico*
Prentice-Hall of India Private Limited, *New Delhi*
Prentice-Hall of Japan, Inc., *Tokyo*
Simon & Schuster Asia Pte. Ltd., *Singapore*
Editora Prentice-Hall do Brasil, Ltda., *Rio de Janeiro*

Contents

About the Author

Eastwood Atwater is professor of psychology at Montgomery County Community College and lecturer in psychology at Gwynedd-Mercy College, both in the greater Philadelphia area. He teaches a course on adolescence at both schools, and also conducts a private practice that includes adolescents. He received his Ph.D. from the University of Chicago. Dr. Atwater belongs to the American Psychological Association, the Pennsylvania Psychological Association, and The Philadelphia Society of Clinical Psychologists. He is the author of several books, including two other textbooks: *Psychology of Adjustment*, Fourth Edition, and *Human Relations*. He is married and has two grown daughters.

Preface

My aim in writing this book is to present a well-balanced account of adolescence, one based on established principles of development, research findings, and clinical data on adolescents. I have also attempted to relate adolescent development to its larger social and cultural context, including the impact of social change. My experience in teaching a course on adolescence at two- and four-year colleges, conducting therapy with older youths, and helping to rear two daughters now reaching adulthood have greatly enriched my understanding. I hope this shows through in the text, along with the personal examples I have given.

The overall arrangement of chapters reflects a mediated-effects approach to adolescence suggested by John Hill and others. In this view, the primary developmental changes of adolescence are mediated or influenced by the surroundings in which they occur, with most of adolescents' psychosocial development reflecting the combined effects of nature and nurture. Thus, after the initial chapters putting adolescence in perspective, we present the primary biological and cognitive changes in adolescence. Then we focus on the major settings in which these changes occur, including the family, peers, school, and workplace. Throughout the rest of the book, we explore the major aspects of adolescents' psychosocial development, including personal identity, sexuality, moral development, delinquency, use of drugs, psychological disorders, and the transition to adulthood. An appendix on methods of studying adolescents illustrates the various methods of study used in adolescent psychology and drawn on throughout this text.

In order to facilitate critical thought and understanding, I have endeavored to explain the material presented as well as to raise questions wherever space permits. In addition, I have provided the following pedagogical aids:

Learning objectives help to identify which aspects of learning students are expected to attain. These objectives cut across several levels of learning, especially the levels of knowledge, understanding, and application. Test questions corresponding to these three levels of learning are provided in the Instructor's Manual and labeled accordingly.

End-of-the-chapter summaries include the main points of each chapter, numbered and arranged according to the major headings, thereby helping the reader to grasp the chapter as a whole in relation to its parts.

Review questions at the end of each chapter may be useful in reviewing the chapter material, especially for short-answer and essay tests.

A glossary of terms is located at the end of the book, providing succinct definitions of basic terms and concepts used throughout the book.

Boxes, tables, and figures are used to highlight material of special interest and increase the reader's involvement with the material in the text.

I have benefited greatly from the reviews of the second edition of *Adolescence,* the most thorough and helpful reviews I've ever received. I would especially like to thank the following reviewers: Dr. Kathryn Holleque, Department of Education and Psychology, Valley City State University, North Dakota; Professor Lee Morganett, Education Department, Indiana University Southeast.

Thanks also to Carol Wada, Human Development Editor, for her commitment and support, and to Edie Riker, production editor, and Marta Steele, copy editor, for their able assistance in bringing this book into production.

I also want to thank the people in my college library as well as those in neighboring libraries who have been so cooperative in my continuing search for appropriate material for this book.

Finally, I trust that the time spent reading this book will be rewarded by a better understanding of adolescence as well as adolescents themselves.

Eastwood Atwater

Introduction to Adolescence

1

- ◆ COMING OF AGE
    - What is adolescence?
    - Boundaries of adolescence
    - Rites of passage
- ◆ ADOLESCENCE IN PERSPECTIVE
    - Early views of adolescents
    - Growing up in the United States
    - The social invention of adolescence
- ◆ ADOLESCENTS TODAY
    - Social change
    - Cultural diversity
    - Growing up faster
- ◆ SUMMARY
- ◆ REVIEW QUESTIONS

Learning Objectives

After completing this chapter, you should be able to:
1 Define the term *adolescence*.
2 List six or more different boundaries determining when adolescence begins and ends.
3 Explain the meaning of adolescence as a "social invention."
4 Describe at least five major social changes affecting adolescent development today.
5 Give an example of an adolescent being rushed into premature adulthood.

While talking with a physician friend, I asked whether he and his wife had any adolescent children. He paused, looked up as if deep in thought, and said, "Let's see, we have a 30-year-old adolescent who is getting married next month." "We also have a 27-year-old adolescent who is in medical school." Sensing the wry humor in his response, I began chuckling quietly. He continued, "And we have a 23-year-old adolescent who is still in college." "Yes," he said affirmatively, "we have *three* adolescents." By then we were both laughing, presumably at the idea of calling individuals in their twenties and thirties—accomplished ones at that—adolescents. Yet this is not a novel idea. Occasionally, we hear someone say of a grown person, "She's acting like an adolescent," meaning the person is behaving inappropriately for her age. A similar notion appealed to Harry Stack Sullivan (1953), the noted psychiatrist, who designated the final period of development "late adolescence" rather than adulthood, because he felt so few people ever fully achieve the desired goal of maturity. According to Sullivan, those who never find the right love object, who are always disappointed in love or withdrawing from close relationships exhibit the "chronic adolescent syndrome."

COMING OF AGE

Does this mean we're all doomed to an almost endless adolescence? Hopefully not. The desire to continue growing throughout our adult life is appealing. But the idea of remaining in the transitional stage of adolescence is not. Fortunately, most authorities refer to adolescence in a more conventional sense, as a designated period of development between childhood and adulthood. Accordingly, we begin this chapter by describing the meaning and boundaries of adolescence, as well as some of the "rites of passage" associated with coming of age.

What Is Adolescence?

The word *adolescence* comes from a Latin word meaning "to grow up" or "to come to maturity." In its simplest sense, then, adolescence refers to the period of rapid growth between childhood and adulthood. The traditional definition of adolescence was based largely on physical growth, as seen in the marked increase in height and weight at this age. Accordingly, adolescence became synonymous with the teenage years, roughly thirteen to eighteen years of age, and the characteristic awkwardness of this period. Indeed, Joan Newman (1985) points out that much of the obnoxiousness commonly seen among youth stems from the uneven growth process that occurs at puberty. The adolescent's awkward movements and postures stemming from uneven acquisition of physical competencies at this age are familiar enough. Even more important is the uneven development of other competencies, such as the ability to think in an adult, logical manner; the ability to see things from other people's viewpoints; and the ability to express and control one's emotions. For instance, the adolescent who has grown taller and heavier but who remains emotionally and socially immature may behave in a more extreme and offensive way than a younger child does. Instead of making noise with his toys or throwing them, he may play his stereo loudly, become violent, and throw bricks. Furthermore, his misjudgments can lead to permanent harm. He may drop out of school, jeopardize his health through the abuse of drugs, or take someone's life through careless or drunken driving. Adolescents who are *always* obnoxious need help. But even normal, healthy adolescents act this way sometimes, largely because of the uneven developmental process at this age.

At the same time, there is a growing realization that the characteristic adolescent behaviors do not result simply from the physical changes during puberty. Instead, the impact of puberty is mediated or shaped by a variety of psychological and social factors. Consequently, adolescence as we know it results from the interaction of the primary pubertal changes and the environmental settings in which they occur, such as the family, peer, school, and workplace. The realization that adolescent development depends on psychological and social influences as well as puberty has broadened the definition of adolescence. Thus, adolescence is best defined as the period of rapid growth between childhood and adulthood, including psychological and social development. As such, adolescence can begin earlier and last longer than the teenage years.

Boundaries of Adolescence

With the inclusion of psychosocial growth, adolescence has become a transitional stage with uncertain boundaries. Thus, it is difficult to tell when adolescence begins or ends, much less at what ages. For all practical purposes, the beginning of adolescence remains closely associated with the onset of puberty, though it is no longer synonymous with it. Yet, puberty itself is not a single, sudden event so much as a slow process of biological change that begins at conception and accelerates at adolescence. As such, puberty depends more on various developmental changes—such as hormonal changes, growth rate, and one's reaction to such changes—than on chronological age. Also, there are wide individual and sexual variations associated with the onset of puberty. Furthermore, because of social changes and pressures in our society, young people are beginning adolescence at earlier ages than in the past, as we shall discuss later in this chapter.

There is even less agreement about when adolescence ends, with much of the debate depending on which criteria of development are used. Those who think in terms of physical development may see the end of adolescence as synonymous with the attainment of puberty in the late teens. Yet, as we shall see in a later chapter, a small proportion of youth continue growing physically into their twenties. Those who adopt legal criteria for the termination of adolescence are inclined to view the entry into early adulthood in terms of legal privileges, such as being able to vote, obtain a marriage license without parental permission, take a drink, and work a 40-hour week. Still others may choose to define adulthood in more functional terms pertaining to the individual's ability to assume responsibility in the adult community, such as graduation from high school or college, holding a full-time job, marrying, having a family, or becoming economically self-supporting. Those who stipulate the attainment of emotional or social maturity have even greater difficulty specifying a given age marking the end of adolescence. Some people never attain full maturity in these areas. See Table 1-1.

Actually, it is difficult to specify a precise end to adolescence, because

Table 1-1   Boundaries of Adolescence

	Adolescence Begins	Adolescence Ends
Biological	Onset of puberty	Attainment of physical and sexual maturity, i.e., capability of sexual reproduction
Emotional	Beginning of adolescent autonomy from parents	Attainment of self-revised personal identity and emotional autonomy
Cognitive/Volitional	Emergence of logical reasoning, problem-solving, and decision-making skills	Establishment of adult logical reasoning and autonomous decision making
Interpersonal	Shift from parent to peer orientation	Increased capacity for intimacy with peers and adults
Social	Entry into personal, family, and work roles	Attainment of adult privileges and responsibilities
Educational	Entry into middle school or junior high school	Completion of high school or college
Religious	Preparation for confirmation, bar or bat mitzvah, and adult baptism	Attainment of adult status in religious community
Chronological	Attainment of a given age associated with adolescence (e.g., teen years)	Attainment of a given age associated with adulthood, e.g., twenties
Legal	Attainment of juvenile status	Attainment of adult legal age
Cultural	Beginning of training in preparation for ceremonial rites of passage	Completion of ceremonial rites of passage

this stage of life does not end as much as it merges into a subsequent transitional period known variously as late adolescence, youth, or early adulthood, as we'll discuss in the final chapter. For instance, one study of college students found that a majority of them were simultaneously working on at least one developmental task of middle childhood, adolescence, and early adulthood respectively, reminding us that adolescence is truly a transitional stage without sharp boundaries (Roscoe and Peterson, 1984).

At the same time, it is common to distinguish different substages of adolescence, such an early, middle, and late adolescence. Yet this is difficult because so much depends on the particular aspect of adolescence being discussed. Also, the onset and rate of growth in a particular area varies widely among adolescents, making age ranges approximate at best. In a general sense, though, early adolescence extends from the onset of puberty through the middle school or junior high school years, about 10 to 14 years. Middle adolescence corresponds to the high school years, about 15 to 17. And late adolescence includes the post-high school years, overlapping with the entry into adulthood, about 18 to the early 20s.

Rites of Passage

Partly because of the uncertainties surrounding the transition to adulthood, the attainment of adult status has been marked by formalized *rites of passage* in many preindustrial societies. These ceremonies and rites differ somewhat among boys and girls. For instance, in many primitive societies the initial rites of adolescent males involve circumcision, either in an individual or group setting. After the boy recovers, he may undergo further tests of manliness, such as surviving alone in the forest or walking across hot coals. Rites for girls are often occasioned by the experience of their menstrual period. At this time the girl may be confined to a separate part of the house for about a week. At the end of this period, she takes part in a series of ceremonies, such as spinning cotton to be used in a hammock by someone in her family. She is then dressed, adorned with jewelry, and allowed to take part in festivities of drinking, dancing, and singing. Afterward she is treated like an adult and assumes the privileges of adult women.

A major purpose of these rites of passages is to confer adult status on the young in a way that is clear both to the individual and the rest of the community. Thus, the boy who has withstood the pain of circumcision bravely may know that he is ready to join his fathers and brothers in hunting. Similarly, the newly initiated girl may continue living in her parents' home while being assured that she will be treated as an adult. Rites of passage also help pass on the appropriate male and female sex roles of a given society. However, because youth do not learn all the necessary skills for adulthood in such ceremonial activities, the rites of passage are often an integral part of a longer series of practices designed to prepare the young for adulthood.

By contrast, contemporary Western society provides no clear rites of

Rites of passage are usually an integral part of a longer series of practices designed to prepare the young for adulthood. (Eugene Gordon)

passage to adulthood, much less a sequential process that prepares the young for their adult role. Instead, adult status is achieved unevenly in one realm of life after another, and in ways that are unconnected and often in conflict with each other. For instance, religious ceremonies such as confirmation and bar or bat mitzvah denote adult status in the religious community. But there is considerable variation in the age at which such ceremonies occur, and almost half the population does not belong to any religious organization. A more common means of recognizing adult status is in the variety of laws marking legal adulthood. Yet these laws are often inconsistent. Young people may begin to drive a car at one age, marry without parental permission at another age, but not own property until still another age. Then too, young people may be eligible for military service before being allowed to buy a drink in a bar. In sum, the various rites of passage are so inconsistent it's no wonder young people have difficulty knowing when they have come of age and feeling prepared to assume an adult role in society.

ADOLESCENCE IN PERSPECTIVE

Coming of age has not always been so difficult or confusing. Up until this century, people generally held to a simpler view of human development, making the transition to adulthood relatively straightforward and swift. A brief look at some of the earlier views of adolescence—though this term was not used—along with the emergence of adolescence as a prolonged, psychosocial stage of development, will help to put our understanding of adolescence in perspective.

Early Views of Adolescents

Aristotle, the ancient Greek philosopher, recognized the importance of puberty and its impact on human development. He proposed three stages of development: infancy, which includes the first seven years of life; boyhood, from about 7 years to puberty; and young manhood, from puberty to age 21. Aristotle held that once young people reach puberty they become more capable of making voluntary and deliberate choices and thus controlling their urges and emotions. The difficulties of doing so are aptly attested to in the boxed item "Aristotle on Youth." Nevertheless, in Aristotle's view, the major developmental task for attaining adulthood is the acquisition of greater self-control and self-determination.

Much of the distinction between childhood/youth and adulthood was lost during the Middle Ages. Children became viewed mostly as miniature adults. Paintings of the *Madonna and Child* portray children with the bodily proportions of adults rather than children. That is, children's heads are comparatively small in relation to the rest of their bodies and their legs represent about half their total height, all more characteristic of adults than children. Also, children's facial expressions and dress are the same as those of adults. This portrayal of children reflects how they were regarded by adults—as little adults. After a tardy weaning, at about the age of 7, children became appren-

---

Aristotle on Youth

Young men have strong passions, and tend to gratify them indiscriminately. Of the bodily desires, it is the sexual by which they are most swayed and in which they show absence of self-control. They are changeable and fickle in their desires, which are violent while they last, but quickly over. . . . They are hot-tempered and quick-tempered, and apt to give way to their anger; bad temper often gets the better of them, for owing to their love of honor they cannot bear being slighted, and are indignant if they imagine themselves unfairly treated. . . . They have exalted notions, because they have not yet been humbled by life or learnt its neces-sary limitations; moreover, their hopeful disposition makes them think themselves equal to great things—and that means exalted notions. . . . They are fonder of their friends, intimates, and companions than older men are, because they like spending their days in the company of others, and have not yet come to value their friends or anything else by their usefulness to themselves. All their mistakes are in the direction of doing things excessively and vehemently. . . . They love too much and hate too much, and the same with everything else. They think they know everything; and are always quite sure about it; this, in fact, is why they overdo everything.

Rhetoric, Book II, chapter 12

tices in the various trades and went straight into the world of adults, readily sharing work and play with adults.

By the eighteenth century, Jean Jacques Rousseau, a French philosopher, pointed out that children are different from adults and that treating them like miniature adults is potentially harmful. Rousseau proposed that children in the infancy stage (up to 5 years) and the savage stage (5 through 12 years) lacked reasoning and should be left relatively free of restrictions to follow their innate developmental tendencies. Formal training in reading and writing are best postponed until the third stage (from 12 to 15), which is characterized by an awakening of the rational functions, including reason and self-consciousness. Youths at this stage exhibit enormous physical energy and intellectual curiosity, which the school can utilize to encourage exploratory behavior. By the fourth stage (15 to 20 years), individuals begin to mature emotionally so that they are no longer dominated by selfishness. Instead, they may exhibit a strong interest in the world and other people, with the appearance of adultlike morals.

It should be pointed out that in Rousseau's view the stages of human development correspond to similar stages in the evolution of the human race, now a discredited notion. Also, critics of Rousseau feel he overemphasized the innate factors of growth and underemphasized the importance of society and formal education. However, his views have helped us to appreciate the inherent capacities for personal growth in the developmental process and the importance of individuality and thus set the stage for later views of adolescence. See the boxed item "Images of Adolescence in Literature."

Growing Up in the United States

In the early American colonies, youth grew up in large families where they learned the skills for running the farm so necessary for family life. But as industry developed in the eighteenth and nineteenth centuries, young people began migrating from the farms to the cities. And the transition to adulthood in the United States became relatively swift.

The transition to adulthood among the working class was brief and harsh, with the exploitation of child labor a common practice. At one point in the nineteenth century, children made up 40 percent of the factory workers in New England. The decline in farming and the rise of manufacturing spurred many farmers' daughters to find work in factories. Young girls would begin work at 4:30 in the morning. Each girl would tend three or more looms in a dust-filled room until 7 o'clock in the evening, taking only a short break for breakfast and lunch. At the end of the day, the girls would return to their boardinghouses. They were usually so tired after the evening meal that they went right to bed, often sleeping six to a room, with little or no privacy.

Among the privileged classes, the passage to adulthood was equally brief but not nearly as harsh. A British visitor to nineteenth-century Boston observed that the young people were born "middle-aged." They were sent to college at 14

Images of Adolescence in Literature

Claudio Violato and Arthur Wiley (1990) examined literary works from the Middle Ages to the present to see how adolescence was portrayed. With minor exceptions, they discovered that authors such as Chaucer, Shakespeare, Milton, and Wordsworth depicted youths in similar ways. In their eyes, adolescence was a time of turbulence, excess, and passion.

Eventually this notion came to be known as the "storm and stress" view of adolescence, due partly to Goethe's works in the late eighteenth and early nineteenth centures. In the novel *The Sorrows of Young Werther,* Goethe tells about a tormented young man who is beset by many desires and dreams, not unlike the author himself. But young Werther is unable to accomplish anything. To make matters worse, the young man falls hopelessly in love with a married woman. When he is rejected, he kills himself. Thousands of teenagers were influenced by this book at the time. Some of them, reminded of their own youthful despair, committed suicide clutching the book to their breasts. Ever since, some observers have insisted that the period of adolescence is a special time of turbulence.

However, you may be interested to learn that this view is disputed by many, if not most, authorities today. A case in point is the cross-cultural study of youths in ten countries by Daniel Offer and his colleagues (1988), which will be described in the next chapter.

---

or 15 years of age and earned their degrees at 17. They were immediately launched into their careers as merchants, teachers, or physicians. Consequently they had no time for the athletic games so characteristic of the British gentleman. Instead they had only the pastimes of "chewing, smoking, drinking, driving hired horses in wretched gigs with cruel velocity." All their energies were spent on working and making money. The visitor concluded that young people in the United States were "a melancholy picture of prematurity" and that the main business of life seemed to be "to grow old as fast as possible" (Grattan, 1859/1990).

The Social Invention of Adolescence

During the same time, a number of important changes were taking place in American society that would eventually prolong the transition to adulthood. In explaining the impact of these changes, Joseph Kett (1977) suggests that adolescence became more of a "social invention" than a discovery. That is, the prolonged period of adolescence so familiar to us is essentially a conception of development that was imposed on youth in response to the needs of an emerging urban-industrial society. It was not something that arose naturally out of the way young people actually behaved. Many of the influences that led to the social invention of adolescence were already apparent by the latter part of the nineteenth century.

Three major social changes were especially important in prolonging the

What Was It Like Back Then?

If you're tired of school, think your parents are too strict, and you're the only teenager who doesn't own a car, you might talk to the students in the annual "history camp" sponsored by the Pennsylvania Historical Society.

Selected high school students spent six weeks finding out what teenage life was like in Philadelphia from 1850 to 1914. Their overall reaction can be summed up in a word, "Yuk."

By today's standards, things were bad even if your parents were well-off. Parents were really strict. Chaperones were everywhere, and girls were warned about the dangers of kissing. Young people from wealthy families were treated like kids until their social debut or "coming out."

If you were poor, it was even worse. Boys and girls became indentured workers as early as eleven years of age. Few continued in school. If you were a female or member of an ethnic, racial minority, you experienced a lot of discrimination.

The students found lots of books on etiquette, with strict social rules for practically everything. Girls who went to the beach had to be covered from head to foot. Initially, the students felt people back then were cold and stiff. But as they read young people's diaries, they realized the rules were ignored much of the time.

Now as students go through a normal day, they try to imagine what life would have been like in the old days. And they realize how fortunate they are to be teenagers today.

Adapted from "Before Adolescence Was Born," by John Corr, *The Philadephia Inquirer,* June 11, 1986.

period of adolescence: the introduction of compulsory education, child labor laws, and the concept of juvenile justice. These changes were motivated, at least on the conscious level, by humanitarian principles such as protecting young people from exploitation in the workplace and giving them a better education. But the laws also had the unintended effect of prolonging young people's dependence on adults.

Compulsory education for children and adolescents between the ages of 6 and 16 was introduced widely in the United States in the late nineteenth century. At about the same time, the period of schooling was extended to include high school. In both instances, the main reason was to give young people the necessary skills for exercising the rights and privileges of democracy. Access to public schools also provided an arena where individuals could improve themselves, thereby helping to diminish the growing gap between youths in different socioeconomic groups. At the same time, compulsory education extended the legal power of school authorities over students, thereby prolonging their dependence on adults.

The reversal of the labor shortage in the last half of the nineteenth century led to extensive child labor legislation. The newly created laws were aimed at protecting the young from exploitation and providing them with opportunities to acquire the skills needed for living in an industrial society.

However, such laws also have had the effect of isolating young people from the workplace, making it difficult for them to explore careers and find meaningful employment in their youth. Furthermore, while a delayed adolescence tends to benefit youth from affluent homes who plan to continue their education in college, it often has the opposite effect on those who seek an early entry into the workplace.

Humane considerations also led to the idea of juvenile justice. Up until the turn of the century, teenagers who broke the law were often punished as adults. Then in 1899 the Illinois legislature passed the first Juvenile Court Act, which provided for informal hearings, confidential records, and separate detention of young people. On the positive side, the juvenile justice movement has helped to protect youthful offenders from the harsher penalties of the adult law. But, as we'll see in Chapter 13, the juvenile court system has also allowed inconsistent and often unfair treatment of youth, thereby prolonging the period of life before young people can assume the rights and responsibilities of adults.

Other influences also contributed to the modern notion of adolescence. The continuing move of people from the farm to the city brought about more interaction at school and in the neighborhood among boys and girls of the same age, giving rise to the increased importance of peer groups in adolescence. Also, the increase in human longevity promoted an extended adolescence. Because the average person only lived until about 50 years of age at the turn of the century, a relatively rapid transition to adulthood made sense. But with the continuing increase in the average life expectancy, individuals could afford to spend a longer time in adolescence. Finally, the emerging scientific understanding of the growth process has led to the refinement of the developmental stages.

Largely as a result of such changes, adolescence has become a period of psychosocial growth which extends beyond the attainment of physical and sexual maturity. Erik Erikson (1980b) characterizes adolescence as a "psychosocial moratorium" granted to those who are not ready to assume adult commitments like work and marriage. Thus, adolescence has become a time when youth are given greater freedom for experimenting with their life roles. Such an extended period of development provides young people with certain advantages. First, they are able to spend longer years in school, thereby gaining a better education. Also, a larger proportion of youth than in the past may prepare for skilled careers, enabling them to rise to a higher socioeconomic level than that of their parents. Then too, the postponement of adult commitments gives young people greater freedom for exploring their life roles and values, thereby promoting a more individuated personal identity in relation to their family of origin than in the past. However, as Erikson points out, youth from affluent homes who are ambitious and interested in learning tend to make better use of these opportunities than do less privileged youth who have grown up accustomed to an early entry into the workplace.

The extension of adolescence also poses certain disadvantages. First, the extended period of formal schooling isolates young people from the workplace, except for entry level jobs, thereby complicating the task of making a wise career choice. Then too, youth who already know what they want to do, especially those who prefer to work in the manual trades, often resent having to spend long years in the classroom studying topics that do not interest them. Furthermore, a delayed adolescence prolongs young people's dependence on adults, thereby promoting needless discontent and rebelliousness. Finally, inherent in the protracted period of youth is the hazard of getting locked into adolescent roles and life-styles, with its pleasure-seeking activities and lack of responsibility.

ADOLESCENTS TODAY

Fortunately or unfortunately, as the case may be, the social invention of adolescence as a prolonged psychosocial process is undergoing further change, largely in response to the ongoing changes in society and the surrounding world. Consequently, just as youths in the 1960s and 1970s viewed their predecessors in the 1950s with a sense of amusement, so youths in the 1990s tend to regard their counterparts of the recent past with a mixture of curiosity and irrelevancy. Today's youths sense they are growing up in a different era and that their lives are being shaped by different forces that are further modifying the experience of adolescence. In this section we look at three major influences on contemporary youths: the extensive social changes affecting adolescents, the growth of cultural diversity, and the shortening of adolescence.

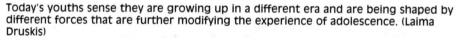

Today's youths sense they are growing up in a different era and are being shaped by different forces that are further modifying the experience of adolescence. (Laima Druskis)

Social Change

Because a comprehensive view of the social changes affecting adolescents would take us far afield, we'll focus on six areas of social change that are having a widespread impact on youth. First, the rapid rate of technological and social change has far-reaching effects on everyone, including youth. For instance, technological innovations such as space travel, computers, and television have made the world a smaller place, setting in motion a ripple effect of further changes. Because of the pervasive effects of change, adolescents soon learn that everything is temporary. The combination of technology and competition has produced planned obsolescence, giving rise to a throwaway culture. Reared in a world of constant change, youth become accustomed to change. They expect ideas and organizations to change. They also take it for granted that they will change jobs more frequently than their parents did. And they form fewer lasting ties to institutions or products. Because ideas and practices become outdated quickly, youths are learning more on their own. They are more likely to question authority, look to their peers, and sort out many things for themselves. Yet, growing up in a high-tech society, youth also are more aware of the need for a sound education to adapt in a competitive world.

Second, extensive social changes are leading to new patterns of family life, with an ever-increasing proportion of youths growing up in a greater variety of living arrangements. Today more young people are latchkey teens, runaways, exposed to parental divorce, living in single-parent homes, or coping with stepparents. Many of these youths receive less guidance from their parents and are forced to cope with greater disruption and stress at earlier ages than in the past. All of this weakens the traditional socializing, morale-building functions of the family and makes for a "less protected" adolescence.

A third area of change can be seen in the greater awareness and exercise of personal rights among youths. The civil rights movement and the youth movements that followed have given young people a greater voice in society. The student protests and demonstrations of the 1960s and 1970s arose largely out of the discrepancy between youth's aspirations and existing social and political conditions. Since then youth tend to assume a bigger role in defining their place in society. Today, youths of all ages, not simply those of legal age, feel they are entitled to certain basic rights guaranteed under the Bill of Rights, such as the rights to free speech and legal counsel.

A fourth area of social change has to do with the greater affluence in society and the impact this is having on youth's attitudes, values, and expectations. Largely because of the long period of affluence and prosperity, there has been a shift in emphasis from survival to personal fulfillment, and from a future orientation to living fully in the present. As Daniel Yankelovich (1981) points out, people of all ages are living by "new rules." Accordingly, people are less attuned to the attitudes of self-denial, loyalty to society, and working for delayed satisfactions, values that are associated with the traditional work ethic. Instead,

Adolescents growing up in a wide variety of ethnic, cultural backgrounds experience different challenges and problems in adolescence. (James Carroll)

they are more oriented to the pursuit of individual rights, desires, and happiness now, values closely associated with the emerging ethic of personal fulfillment. Although these changes are affecting people of all ages, they may be seen more clearly among the younger generation who have grown up taking the newer values for granted. Consequently, youths have higher expectations regarding the quality of their lives and what they feel entitled to.

A fifth and related influence is the greater emphasis on materialism. Today's youth now constitute a huge consumer's market, representing potential buyers of automobiles, magazines, clothes, cosmetics, sports equipment, and thousands of other items. As a result, many youths are caught up in the concern about self and how to get a good job and satisfy their material needs. Many of them have become status-conscious and, like their elders, more money-conscious. At the same time, youths from disadvantaged families have become more alienated than ever, feeling abandoned and rejected by society. However, a significant minority of youth are rebelling against the overemphasis on material things, such that crass materialism is somewhat on the wane (Gross and Scott, 1990).

Finally, there are also counterforces at work modifying the effects of the social changes described above. As a result, the current generation of youth are growing up in a world of increased competition, diminished resources, and

---

Adolescent Stress

Adolescents are experiencing greater stress than their parents did at the same age. Among the many reasons are more rapid and pervasive change in society, more disruption in family life, and greater violence. Youths 15 to 24 are more likely to die from accidents, suicide, and homicide than illness, with the rise in violent deaths more than offsetting the reduction in mortality because of disease (Diegmueller, 1987).

A major source of stress, as measured in the various stress scales for youths, is the combined effect of life changes in an individual's life, positive and negative. Death of a parent, brother or sister, or close friend is ranked at the top of most lists. Separation or divorce of parents usually comes close behind. The other leading stressors generally include accidents, major injury, or illnesses; failure at school or changing schools; disappointment in friendships or love affairs; or being cut off from others (Insel and Roth, 1985; Toler, 1983). How individuals *perceive* a given change and how well they *adapt* to it are also important but difficult to measure.

Negative events tend to be better predictors of mental and physical health than do overall stress scores. Coping with several negative life changes during a six- to twelve-month period is related to a variety of adjustment difficulties including athletic injuries, menstrual discomfort, vaginal infections, coronary disease, anxiety, academic difficulties, depression, and job dissatisfaction (Passer and Seese, 1983).

All of this suggests that adolescents must learn how to manage stress at an earlier age than in the past.

---

economic and political volatility—all of which makes for an uncertain future, frustration, and unfulfilled aspirations. Many youths feel they may be the first generation of Americans to face the real possibility of downward mobility. Consequently, as Martin Seligman (1988) points out, the widespread acceptance of soaring expectations for the self coupled with the obstacles to satisfying them in society helps to account for the sense of caution, avoidance of commitment, and increase in depression among many youths today.

Cultural Diversity

One of the major consequences of social change is the growth of cultural diversity. Social and economic upheaval throughout the world has accentuated the influx of people from different cultures into American society, making for a more culturally diversified society. People of color, such as African Americans, Hispanic Americans, Asian Americans, and Native Americans, now account for at least one-fifth of the population in the United States and will make up an even larger proportion in the future (McAdoo, 1982). This means that there are at least 8 million youths 14 to 24 years of age who come from a minority background in the United States (U.S. Bureau of the Census, 1990). African-American youths constitute the single largest group. Hispanic Americans represent the next largest group, followed by Asian Americans—Japanese, Chinese, Filipinos, and Southeast Asians—and Native American Indians.

Youths growing up in minority families experience greater stress than do those in mainstream society. They generally face more social problems, such as family disintegration, unemployment, crime, drugs, and unwed parenthood. Then too, they must often function in more than one subculture, that is, within their own ethnic and racial communities as well as the larger society from which they are alienated. As a result, minority youths are constantly being judged by others' values and, as such, found to be deficient in certain ways and labeled as inferior. Although civil rights legislation and judicial reform have helped to diminish discrimination, that is, unfair treatment, against minority youth, the struggle continues. Even more difficult to eradicate is people's prejudice, an unjustifiable and usually negative attitude toward a group and its members. Because prejudice is rooted in cognitive, emotional, and behavioral predispositions, overcoming prejudice requires the use of many resources, including education and social change as well as remaining true to democratic principles.

Fortunately, greater appreciation of cultural differences along with the continuing implementation of civil rights is helping minority groups to affirm themselves and their heritage, as well as their right to share in the entitlements of mainstream society. Also, learning to value cultural differences helps all youths to better understand each others' differences, rather than automatically equating different with inferior. An example may be seen in a study of the different meanings attached to clothing by adolescents from different backgrounds. The study included 301 adolescent girls from three ethnic, racial backgrounds—African Americans, Chicanos, and Anglo Americans—composed of third- or fourth-generation youth who identified more as "American" than Mexican American or the like. Results showed important differences in regard to clothing satisfaction and deprivation among the three different groups. African-American girls had such different values and opinions that the clothing-satisfaction instrument could not be validated with them. For Chicano girls, socioeconomic status and the number of shoes in their wardrobes proved to be most significant for satisfaction with their clothes. In contrast, the variables that affected clothing satisfaction most among Anglo Americans were feelings of social security and the number of dressy and casual dresses they owned (Kness, 1983). Given such differing attitudes toward clothing among these three groups of adolescents, one can readily see, on the one hand, the risk of peer misperception and prejudice, and, on the other hand, the potential for greater appreciation of cultural differences among girls from different ethnic backgrounds.

The emergence of cultural diversity means that American youths no longer constitute a homogenous group, if they ever did. Instead, young people are growing up in a wide variety of ethnic, cultural backgrounds that affect their attitudes, behaviors, aspirations, and values. As a result, the challenges and problems experienced by the majority of African-American youth differ from those faced by Caucasian youth from privileged backgrounds. Similarly, youth from Southeast Asian backgrounds, who are refugees from war, tend to experience different stresses than do Native American Indian youth, who grow up in one of the least visible but most deprived minority groups in American society.

Cultural diversity also generates a greater degree of cultural confusion. In a relatively stable society when everyone accepts the same ideas and values, youths feel more secure and know what is expected of them. But in today's society of differing and often conflicting beliefs, attitudes, and values, it becomes more difficult for them to know what to believe or how to live. They often feel torn between what they have learned at home and the conflicting practices and values of peers from different backgrounds. They feel forced to explore and sort out things for themselves. Consequently, adolescents reared in a culturally diverse society tend to feel insecure and uncertain of themselves and their values, which make for a more stressful transition to adulthood.

Growing Up Faster

The combined effects of these and other social changes has been to shorten adolescence. As a result, the "prolonged adolescence" of this century is being superceded by a swifter transition to adulthood. Instead of having a privileged grace period before assuming the responsibilities of adulthood as they once did, adolescents are now being rushed into what David Elkind calls "premature adulthood." In his book *All Dressed Up and No Place to Go,* Elkind (1984) discusses the disappearance of markers that teenagers could look forward to attaining as a

---

Who's Pushing?

In one newspaper ad, girls 10 to 12 were invited to a workshop on the art of makeup, skin and hair care, as well as fashion and modeling techniques, culminating in a fashion show. When the sponsors of the show were questioned about the wisdom of inviting girls this age to such a workshop, they hastened to say that they weren't "pushing" makeup for young girls. But they added that because many girls this age are already using makeup the workshop might help them to do it correctly. In contrast, critics (Gilliam, 1983) point out that the idea of holding beauty workshops for preteens appears symptomatic of a larger, deeper problem in today's society—rushing children and adolescents into adulthood.

David Elkind (1984) has voiced a similar criticism. Also, he observes that throughout his travels around the country he finds nobody *wants* to push children and adolescents into adulthood. Parents don't want to do it. The schools don't want to do it. Yet they all do it, mostly because somebody else does it or there is competition. The fact that children and adolescents are a huge consumers' market for various products advertised on television is no small part of the problem. Would you agree?

sign of their maturing. They need these markers, or rights of passage, to show that they have emerged from childhood and are assuming new responsibilities that will help them to grow and become responsible adults. Unfortunately, because many of these markers are disappearing, the transition to adulthood is becoming more abrupt.

For instance, activity markers have largely disappeared. It used to be that young children and teenagers played sandlot sports in small neighborhood pickup groups. There were no organized sports games until high school. Now everything tends to be highly organized at very early ages. The prominence and lucrativeness of professional sports have led to greater competitiveness in college sports, and in turn, high school sports. Individuals who aspire to significant accomplishments in the various sports, such as basketball, football, tennis, gymnastics, and the various Olympic sports usually must receive family support and professional guidance at an early age. The unusual amount of time and training needed for the optimal development of their skills makes them adults, at least athletically, long before their time.

Schools are also contributing to the premature onset of adulthood, mostly because they reflect the stresses and values of the larger society. Traditionally, school has been a special place where teenagers could devote their energies to academic, personal, and social growth without undue pressure from the adult world. School was a safe and secure place where it was acceptable to be a teenager. But today, many schools are victimized by drugs, sex, and violence and are no longer safe and secure places of learning. Furthermore, because schools have had to accommodate to a greater diversity of students and the pressures of society, the basic aims of education are often lost. In the minds of many, school is the place to prepare for one's career, not necessarily for learning how to think and adapt to a changing society.

Another disappearing marker is the transition to adult work roles. Traditionally, the transition occurs through a sequence that begins with the household chores of childhood and later includes the informal jobs outside the home during the teenage years and culminates in full-time jobs in the formal workplace by late adolescence and early adulthood. However, in the past couple of decades, an increasing proportion of teenagers work in adult jobs during the school years. It is not unusual for high school students to work between fifteen and twenty hours a week at an outside job. Yet, when students work longer than this, they study less, make poorer grades, and participate less in social life and extracurricular activities in school. They also increase their use of cigarettes, alcohol, marijuana, and other drugs. Because many of these jobs are monotonous and stressful and unrelated to career goals, youth risk adopting a cynical attitude toward any kind of work before they've completed school.

Adolescents who are rushed into premature adulthood do not have time to develop their emotional needs and the clear, stable sense of self they will need to be less vulnerable to stress and competent to the challenges of life. Instead, they are expected to act like adults and face adult issues in a world of unprece-

Adolescents need time to develop their emotional needs and a clear, stable sense of self in order to face the challenges of life. (Laima Druskis)

dented problems, pressures, and clashing values, all of which is confusing enough to adults themselves. Adults reared in a less stressful era sometimes envy the affluence and freedom of today's youth. They complain that today's teens are preoccupied with self, pleasure seeking, constantly testing limits, and expecting too much too fast. However, adults often fail to realize that the same adolescents are also exposed to greater hazards and stress at an earlier age. If anything, adolescents need more adult understanding and support in order to make a less pressurized, saner transition to adulthood. Accordingly, the remaining chapters in this book provide a better understanding of the developmental process of adolescence, including the characteristic influences and circumstances that affect adolescent behavior. Such understanding may help parents, teachers, and other adults who work with adolescents, as well as youths themselves, to adopt a more positive attitude toward individuals at this stage of life.

SUMMARY

Coming of Age

1. Adolescence may be defined as the period of rapid physical, psychological, and social development between childhood and adulthood.
2. Adolescence has become a transitional developmental stage with uncertain boundaries, such that it can begin earlier and last longer than the teenage years.

3. It is common to distinguish between different substages of adolescence, including early (10 to 14 years), middle (15 to 17 years), and late (18 to early 20s) adolescence, with the ages varying depending on the individual and aspect of development.

4. The transition to adulthood has been marked by formalized rites of passage in many preindustrial societies, conferring adult status on the young in a way that is clear to the individual and community. The lack of clear and consistent rites of passage makes coming of age more confusing in contemporary society.

Adolescence in Perspective

5. Earlier views of adolescence, before this term was used, were based on simpler views of human development, representing the transition to adulthood as relatively straightforward.

6. As society became more industrialized in the nineteenth century, youth grew up fast, assuming adult responsibilities at an early age.

7. The prolonged period of adolescence so familiar to us may be seen as a social invention that was imposed on youth in response to the needs of an emerging urban-industrial society that required an educated citizenry with a delayed entry into the workplace.

8. Adolescence as a prolonged psychosocial stage of development offers both advantages and disadvantages for youth; those from affluent homes make better use of this period than do less privileged youth accustomed to an early entry into the workplace.

Adolescents Today

9. Social changes continue to modify the meaning of adolescence, such that today's adolescents are keenly aware of growing up in a different world than that of their counterparts of the past.

10. Major social changes having great impact on adolescents include rapid technological and social change, greater variety of living arrangements, an emphasis on one's civil rights, heightened expectations about the quality of life, an emphasis on materialism, and the tempering of expectations by the realities of contemporary life.

11. Greater awareness of cultural diversity has helped youths of all ethnic and cultural backgrounds to affirm themselves, their heritage, and their right to share in the entitlements of mainstream society. At the same time, growing up in a society with many differing and often conflicting customs and values makes for a more stressful adolescence.

12. The overall impact of such social changes is to shorten adolescence, such that youths are being rushed into "premature adulthood" without clear markers along the way, making adolescence more stressful.

REVIEW QUESTIONS

1. To what extent does adolescence include a psychosocial and cultural process as well as physical maturation?
2. In what sense is adolescence a transitional stage without sure boundaries?
3. What are some of the functional rites of passages for adolescents today?
4. Describe the abbreviated transition to adulthood in the nineteenth-century United States.
5. How has the meaning of adolescence been affected by the introduction of compulsory education, child-labor legislation, and juvenile justice?
6. Describe some of the advantages and disadvantages of a prolonged period of adolescence.
7. What are some of the major social changes shaping adolescents today?
8. How does growing up in a more culturally diverse society affect adolescents, including those from minority groups?
9. Describe some ways adolescents are being pushed into premature adulthood.
10. What are some of the negative effects of adolescents being rushed into adulthood?

Perspectives on Adolescence

2

It was six men of Indostan
   To learning much inclined
Who went to see the Elephant
   (Though all of them were blind),
That each by observation
   Might satisfy his mind.

The First approached the Elephant
   And happening to fall
Against his broad sturdy side
   At once began to bawl:
"Bless me! but the Elephant
   Is very like a wall."

The Second, feeling of the tusk,
   Cried, "Ho! What have we here,
So very round and smooth and sharp?
   To me 'tis mighty clear
This wonder of an Elephant
   Is very like a spear."

The Third approached the animal,
   And happening to take
The squirming trunk in his hands
   Thus boldly up and spake:
"I see," quoth he, "the Elephant
   Is very like a snake."

The Fourth reached out his eager hand
   And felt about the knee.
"What most this wondrous beast is like
   Is mighty plain," quoth he;
"'Tis clear enough the Elephant
   Is very like a tree."

The Fifth, who chanced to touch the ear,
   Said, "E'en the blindest man
Can tell what this resembles most;
   Deny the fact who can,
This marvel of an Elephant
   Is very like a fan."

The Sixth no sooner had begun
   About the beast to grope
Then, seizing on the swinging tail
   That fell within his scope,
"I see," quoth he, "the Elephant
   Is very like a rope."

And so these men of Indostan
   Disputed loud and long.
Each in his own opinion
   Exceeding stiff and strong,
Though each was partly in the right,
   And all were in the wrong.

James Godfrey Saxe

A PERSPECTIVAL APPROACH

Saxe's poem about the six learned blind men of India has become a classic for a good reason. It illustrates graphically how our understanding of a thing depends largely on our view of it. This is especially appropriate for the topic of this chapter, in that scientists and clinicians approach the understanding of adolescence from different theoretical perspectives or angles of vision. That is, each of them relies on particular assumptions and concerns that focus, and by the same token, limit, what they see. In turn, their resulting theories—general explanatory statements that account for the observed phenomena—usually explain only a limited aspect of adolescent development. Accordingly, no one theory covers all aspects of adolescence. Instead, each theory offers an optimal range of explanation, explaining some aspects of adolescence better than it does others. Furthermore, few theories are fully proved or disproved. In most instances each theory continues to be modified with new discoveries and information. Thus, by examining the distinctive contributions from several major perspectives, we may arrive at a more inclusive and well-balanced understanding of adolescent development.

The representative theories of adolescence are arranged according to the various theoretical perspectives: the biological, psychoanalytical, social-cognitive, and cultural perspectives, respectively. But keep in mind there is a certain degree of overlapping between perspectives. Also, it should be noted that other major theories of adolescence have been incorporated into subsequent chapters of this book, especially Jean Piaget's theory of cognitive development, Erik Erikson's psychosocial theory of identity formation, and Lawrence Kohlberg's theory of moral reasoning.

THE BIOLOGICAL PERSPECTIVE

It has long been assumed that adolescence begins with the biological changes accompanying puberty. It should not be surprising, then, that earlier views of adolescence often assumed a direct, causal link between biological factors and the adolescent's psychological development. Some went a step further and largely equated adolescence with puberty. Stanley Hall's theory is typical of this general approach.

Hall's Critical-Stage Theory

The modern scientific study of adolescence began with the work of G. Stanley Hall. After receiving America's first Ph.D. in psychology, Hall pioneered the questionnaire method of study, publishing the results in his two-volume work *Adolescence* in 1904.

Hall, like many other thinkers in his day, was heavily influenced by the evolutionary thought of Charles Darwin, and he believed that all human development is controlled by genetically determined factors. As a result, there is a strong emphasis on the biological basis of adolescence, as seen in Hall's chapters on instincts, evolution, and physical growth. A special feature of Hall's thought is his recapitulation theory, that is, that the individual repeats or relives the major stages of evolution in the course of his or her own development. Accordingly, each individual progresses from the early animal-like past (in childhood) through periods of savagery (from later childhood and adolescence) before entering the more recent civilized ways of life characteristic of adulthood.

At the same time Hall held that adolescence is a critical stage of development, a period when biological factors are especially affected by one's environment. At no other age were evolutionary instincts so likely to give way to cultural influence. As a result, Hall taught that teenagers should be provided with an enriched environment that would aid their development. Adolescence was seen as a critical time for a "new birth," when such distinctively human traits as love and altrusim could be developed for the first time. But because these traits are the least assured by heredity and are the most dependent on individual effort, Hall believed it was important for parents and teachers to help with their adolescents' development. In the process, adults had to draw a fine line between allowing adolescents to express their own instincts and helping to socialize them. The characteristic result of this struggle was a stressful adolescence. Much of the storm and stress was caused by the abrupt and rapid rate of physical growth; but part of it was also caused by the conflict between instinctual drives and the demands for the adolescent's intellectual, emotional, and social growth. The turbulence at this stage of life was reflected in the adolescent's emotional development—including mood swings between energy and lethargy, enthusiasm and depressive gloom, selfishness and altruism, tenderness and cruelty, and curiosity and apathy. It was also evident at this age in a marked increase in crimes or delinquency as well as religious conversion.

Although Hall's views had a marked influence on the study of adolescence in his day, many of his ideas have not stood the test of time because of his reliance on now-discarded notions about evolution. Hall underestimated the extent to which adolescence is affected by child development. He also exaggerated the emotional turbulence of adolescence. Nevertheless, few would disagree with his view that adolescence is a critical stage of development.

Puberty and Adolescent Development

Hall's view reflects a persistent bias in the understanding of adolescence, namely that adolescent development is largely determined by puberty—the process of glandular and bodily changes culminating in physical and sexual maturity. By assuming that the adolescent's psychological development results from the biological changes of puberty, much of adolescent behavior is assumed to be inevitable and resistant to intervention. Fortunately, this assumption is being increasingly challenged. Anne Petersen and Brandon Taylor (1980) have suggested that propositions about the relationship between puberty and psychological development can be grouped into two broad categories, consisting of (1) the direct-effect models and (2) the mediated-effect models. Theorists such as Hall who use the direct-effect approach assume a direct causal link between the biological changes of puberty and the adolescent's psychological development. In contrast, more recent theorists who adopt the mediated-effect approach recognize that the im-

Stanley Hall's Adolescence

As a child Hall had always heard the genitals referred to as "the dirty place." Only at school did he learn otherwise. But there he was shocked at how much the boys talked about their genitals, compared them, and played with themselves.

Hall was greatly affected by a story told him by his father, about a youth who masturbated and had sexual intercourse with lewd women; as a result, the youth caught a disease that ate his nose away until there were only two flat holes in his face and he also became an idiot. For a long time after that, Hall admitted that whenever he felt sexually aroused, he carefully examined his nose to see if it was getting flat.

Hall's fears were so intense that he tried to control his sexual excitement by applying bandages to prevent an erection while he slept. Anytime he masturbated he felt intense remorse and prayed for help. At one point he felt he was so abnormal he consulted a physician. After examining him, the doctor laughed at his fears, but also warned him of the consequences of having sexual intercourse. Hall later acknowledged that he could have been spared much needless worry had "some one told me that certain experiences while I slept were as normal for boys in their teens as are the monthly phenomena for girls."

Even in his college years Hall was plagued by a sense of inferiority, especially around girls. This was a big factor in his religious conversion during his sophomore year, which in turn intensified his struggles for sexual purity. Hall also believed that his striving for academic achievement was in part a compensation for his sense of inferiority.

Hall was relieved to discover that his adolescence had been "in no sense abnormal or even exceptional." We can well understand a statement by him in 1904 that the experiences of adolescence are "extremely transitory" and are "often totally lost to the adult consciousness."

pact of puberty on the adolescent's psychological and social development is mediated by other variables. These influences consist of a variety of internalized psychological factors (such as body image) and a wide range of external factors (such as adolescent socialization practices).

It may be helpful to keep this distinction in mind as we consider the various theories of adolescence throughout this chapter and the rest of the book. For instance, in the next section you'll note that much of the early psychoanalytical thought on adolescence relied heavily on the physical changes of puberty, especially the adolescent's adaptation to the intensified sex drive and the sexual conflicts that resulted. However, more recent psychoanalytical views have reflected a greater role of the psychological and social influences in adolescence, thus moving more toward the mediated-effect model. At the same time, the social-learning theory of Albert Bandura and the cultural theory of Margaret Mead—explained in a subsequent section of this chapter—are clearly based on a mediated-effect model, in which the experience of adolescence is heavily influenced by one's social and cultural environment.

One further note concerns the increasing recognition that puberty itself is a complex process. In the past, theorists have sometimes emphasized one aspect of adolescence, such as sexual development, while neglecting others. However, it is increasingly apparent that puberty has many aspects, including complex neurological and chemical changes in the brain, hormonal changes, changes in size, height, body mass, and shape, as well as changes in the reproductive organs. Furthermore, each of these changes interacts with the others. Such distinctions are essential in that they provide functionally different forms of stimuli to the adolescent's psychological and social development.

THE PSYCHOANALYTICAL PERSPECTIVE

Sigmund Freud, the founder of psychoanalysis, was influenced by many of the biological and evolutionary ideas popular in his day. But as a clinician, Freud came to regard childhood as the most formative period of human development and as the source of adult neuroses. His daughter, Anna Freud, applied the psychoanalytical concepts to adolescence in greater detail. Although she held that adolescence is secondary to childhood, she felt that the upheavals of adolescence do not simply mirror the first few years of life but may place a decisive stamp of their own upon adult personality. The following section summarizes ideas from both Sigmund and Anna Freud.

The Freudian View of Development

According to Sigmund Freud (1964), the driving forces of personality come from the *id,* the unconscious reservoir of psychic energy derived from biological instincts; these instincts are primarily sexual and aggressive in nature. Early in the child's life, part of the id is modified through parental control to help inhibit the unruly forces of the unconscious. This part is known as the *superego,* or conscience. It serves to socialize the child before the age of rational, conscious control. Another part of personality that develops more gradually out of the id through the effects of life-long socialization is the *ego.* The ego is the center of self-consciousness and rational control which serves as the manager of the personality. As such, the ego strives to achieve psychic harmony within the personality as a whole by integrating the conflicting demands of the id, superego, and society. Freud once compared the ego to a rider on horseback, capable of guiding but not entirely controlling the underlying psychic energy from the unconscious.

Freud held that the dynamics of personality depend largely on how the sexual instinct and the ego and superego have been shaped during the formative years of childhood. Expression and control of the sexual instinct were especially crucial. Too little or too much control of the sex drive led to neurotic conflicts, if not in childhood then in adulthood. Personality development consisted of the

Sigmund Freud, the founder of psychoanalysis, formulated a major new perspective on adolescent development. (Osterreichische Nationalbibliothek, Wein)

oral, anal, and phallic stages in the first six years of life, followed by a quieter latency period (6 to 11), and then a genital stage (12 to 18).

Of special importance is the phallic stage (3 to 6 years) in which children tend to experience the *Oedipus complex*. This is named for the Greek king who unwittingly murdered his father and married his mother without realizing who she was. Similarly, preschool-aged boys and girls entertain unconscious wishes and fantasies about marrying their opposite-sex parents. The boy becomes jealous of the attention his father receives from his mother, and soon he fears his father. He also becomes fearful of his own impulses toward his mother and father. Because this conflict is intolerable to the small child, who usually loves and desires both parents, it tends to be resolved spontaneously and unconsciously by the boy's renouncing his mother as an object of special attention and identifying more strongly with his father. The girl experiences a similar sequence of events in the *Electra complex,* eventually identifying more strongly with her mother. However, when an opposite-sex parent is unduly seductive or a same-sex parent is overly critical, a boy or girl may become fixated at this stage. Some results are the Don Juan-type male who "loves 'em and leaves 'em" because of his fear of true intimacy, or the seductive female who enjoys attracting men but cannot be sexually fulfilled with them.

Adolescent Sexual Conflicts

Anna Freud (1969) held that adolescence is a turbulent time mostly because of the sexual conflicts brought on by sexual maturation, resulting in both quantitative and qualitative changes in the sex drive.

In the preadolescent years, the intensified sex drive brings about a quantitative increase in all impulse activity that has characterized childhood development. Accordingly, adolescents tend to become hungrier, more aggressive and cruel, more inquisitive, and more egocentric. These increased impulses, in turn, weaken the childhood defenses erected against them, thereby reactivating the psychosexual conflicts of childhood. Thus, adolescents may alternate between clinging dependence and exaggerated independence, taking pleasure in being messy while being preoccupied with cleanliness and orderliness, or exhibiting extreme curiosity about sex along with prudish condemnation of it. The reactivation of these conflicts helps to explain the ambivalent behavior so characteristic of early adolescents.

The general increase in impulse activity is followed shortly by a qualitative change in the sex drive—namely, the emergence of genital sexual impulses that accompany the maturation of reproductive organs and secondary sex characteristics. But here the Freuds differ in their interpretations of adolescence. Sigmund Freud held that adolescents' handling of their sexual conflicts is largely determined by the way they have resolved their Oedipal conflicts earlier in life. For example, an adolescent with an unresolved Oedipal fixation might be attracted to an older, domineering, or seductive person reminiscent of the relationship with his or her opposite-sex parent in childhood. However, Anna Freud contends that the adolescent's sexual struggles and the strategies for coping with them are also somewhat different from the child's. For one thing, the adolescent has a more developed personality and ego than the child has. In addition, the qualities of adolescent thought and emotion give them more sophisticated defenses for coping with their sexual conflicts. Furthermore, adolescents' sexual struggles must be resolved primarily in relation to their peers rather than their parents, though the latter's emotional involvement is still an important factor.

One of the biggest differences between the sexual struggles of the child and those of the adolescent is the heightened inner turmoil of the adolescent. Whereas the sexual conflicts of early childhood had been revolved largely because of such external influences as the disapproving parent, the adolescent experiences an additional inner dimension—namely, the conflict between the ego and superego in control of sexual impulses. Although adolescents may be well aware of parental disapproval in yielding to temptation, much of their conflict comes from their own feelings of guilt or concern about the loss of self-esteem. They must constantly choose a course of action between the two extremes of utter self-denial and complete self-indulgence of their sexual needs. Too much control will result in a rigid and restricted adolescent who remains cut off from his or her own sexuality; but too little control will result in impulsiveness, a low tolerance for frustration, a preoccupation with self-indulgence, and guilt.

Coping with Adolescent Sexual Conflicts

Both Sigmund and Anna Freud held that the urges and conflicts of this age arouse so much anxiety that they inevitably evoke certain ego defenses within the individual. For the most part these defenses operate automatically and unconsciously, though they may be influenced by learning. Because civilized living requires a certain degree of *repression,* in which impulses are blocked unconsciously, adolescents, like adults, are not fully aware of their sexual urges and conflicts in the first place. But the intensity of the sex drive requires other defenses as well. A major defense is *sublimation,* which is the unconscious redirection of sexual energy toward more socially acceptable goals. Common examples would be the increased curiosity, creativity, and pursuit of intellectual activity at adolescence. Another defensive strategy is *displacement,* in which sexual impulses are displaced onto other, emotionally safer objects or persons. A girl's preoccupation with physical beauty or clothes or a boy's interest in sports cars or motorcycles are examples of displacement. New *identification* with parental substitutes such as a teacher, coach, or peers also helps adolescents cope with their sexual impulses with less anxiety. The fact that such adolescent crushes are relatively short-lived probably reflects their defensive function rather than the formation of genuine object relations with others, which usually require more maturity.

Anna Freud (1969) held that two defense mechanisms especially characteristic of adolescence are *intellectualization* and *asceticism*. In intellectualization adolescents use their newly developed powers of abstract thinking to discuss sex in a relatively impersonal manner to create a certain amount of emotional distance between ideas and impulses. An example would be the typical adolescent debate on such subjects as living together versus marriage, or homosexuality versus heterosexuality. The ideas in these discussions often represent opposite sides of an adolescent's inner conflicts. In asceticism, an adolescent unconsciously denies his or her sexual urges and avoids pleasurable associations with sex. Unlike other defense mechanisms, which often express a compromise between the urge and its constraint, the ascetic response aims for a total control. An example would be the adolescent who joins a religious group that prohibits premarital sex as well as other related pleasures. Yet, because of the defensive character of asceticism, periods of restraint are often broken by periods of abandonment and sexual indulgence.

A major contribution of the psychoanalytic perspective is the developmental approach to personality. In this view, maturation, or the unfolding of the organism's genetic potential, is such that certain things are more readily learned at one stage of development than at another. Also, personality development is sequential and cumulative, so that growth at one stage necessarily depends on what has transpired at earlier stages. Thus, we've come to assume that the relationship with one's parents during the formative period of childhood affects

---

Can You Recall Your Adolescence?

Do you remember things such as taking your driver's license road test? Your most embarrassing incident? Interviewing for your first summer job?

Probably so. But chances are you can't remember your feelings at the time.

Anna Freud once observed that her adult patients suffered from an amnesia, or loss of memory, of their adolescence. But she hastened to add that this did not resemble in extent or depth the amnesia of their childhood. Adults may readily recall the events of adolescence. However, such memories are divorced from the feelings that accompanied them at the time.

What we fail to recover, as a result, is the atmosphere in which the adolescent lives, his anxieties, the height of elation or depth of despair, the quickly rising enthusiasms, the utter hopelessness, the burning—or at times sterile—intellectual and philosophical preoccupations, the yearning for freedom, the sense of loneliness, the feeling of oppression by the parents, the impotent rages or active hates directed against the adult world, the erotic crushes—whether homosexually or heterosexually directed—the suicidal fantasies, etc.

It is these transitory and elusive mood swings that loom so large during the teens. Yet they are easily forgotten and often lost to adult consciousness. Otherwise, our memories of adolescence might be more painful than they are.

Anna Freud, "Adolescence," in R.S. Eissler et al., eds., *The Psychoanalytic Study of the Child*, vol. 13 (New York: International Universities Press, 1958), pp. 259–260.

subsequent development throughout adolescence and adulthood. However, a major criticism of the psychoanalytical approach is its overemphasis on the unconscious strivings of the id and on the sexual conflicts during adolescence. As a result, many of those who followed Freud have de-emphasized the unconscious and the primacy of biological drives, especially sex. Also, they have given greater attention to the positive functions of the ego and the social, cultural influences on development. For instance, Erik Erikson has widened the potential application of the psychoanalytic perspective by transforming Freud's psychosexual theory of development within the family to a more inclusive psychosocial theory of relationships within the larger society, as discussed in Chapter 10 on adolescent identity development.

THE SOCIAL-COGNITIVE PERSPECTIVE

Theorists in this broad perspective hold that learning plays a primary role in human behavior, such that biological drives are decisively shaped by learning and environmental influences. Some, like Robert Havighurst, combine a developmental approach with a wide variety of psychological, educational, and social influences. Others, such as Albert Bandura, adopt a social learning approach, in which changes in behavior are thought to occur in a relatively smooth or continuous process. We'll begin by describing Havighurst's view of the developmental tasks of adolescence. Then we'll explore Bandura's social learning theory approach to adolescence, some recent ideas on cognition and behavior, and the implications of cognitive social learning theory for adolescent development.

Havighurst's Developmental Tasks of Adolescence

Robert Havighurst's (1972) psychosocial theory of adolescence combines a developmental understanding of individual needs with social expectations and roles. The convergence of the individual's needs and social demands gives rise to the developmental tasks of adolescence. These are the appropriate attitudes, understandings, and skills youth need to acquire at certain times in their lives through maturation, social demands, and personal growth. In Havighurst's view, there is an optimal time or "teachable moment" for learning a given task. The readiness to learn some tasks is due to biological changes, or maturation. In other instances, the appropriate time for mastering a task depends on the social expectations associated with a given age or the individual's interest and motivation to engage in a given activity at a given time.

The eight developmental tasks of adolescence are (see summary at Table 2-1):

◆ *Accepting one's body and using it effectively.* Because of the rapid changes in their bodies and the accompanying self-consciousness, adolescents need to accept their body, care for it, and use it effectively in work, sports, play, and everyday tasks.

Table 2-1   The Developmental Tasks of Adolescence

1. Accepting one's body and using it effectively
2. Achieving a masculine or feminine social role
3. Achieving new and more mature relations with peers of both sexes
4. Attaining emotional independence of parents and other adults
5. Preparing for an economic career
6. Preparing for marriage and family life
7. Desiring and achieving socially responsible behavior
8. Acquiring a set of values as a guide to behavior

♦ *Achieving a masculine or feminine social role.* Sexual maturation along with changing sex roles in society challenge youth to explore and affirm their adult sexual identity.

♦ *Achieving new and more mature relations with peers of both sexes.* With increasing emotional and personal maturity, adolescents become more capable of forming intimate and stable relationships with peers of both sexes, in friendship and love.

♦ *Attaining emotional independence of parents and other adults.* Youths need to learn how to affirm themselves as autonomous individuals in relation to their parents, other adults, and peers. This means being able to tolerate disappointment, criticism, and rejection in relation to others.

♦ *Preparing for an economic career.* Adolescents need to discover their special interests and abilities and then to choose a career goal, prepare for it educationally, and get started in it.

♦ *Preparing for marriage and family life.* Young people need to acquire the personal maturity and social skills necessary for achieving satisfying relationships with others in close living arrangements like marriage and the family.

♦ *Desiring and achieving socially responsible behavior.* Adolescents need to achieve meaningful participation in community and national affairs as well as dealing with the social and ethical issues of their day.

♦ *Acquiring a set of values as a guide to behavior.* Youths need to examine and affirm their personal and moral values. Difficulties in decision making are often due to a confusion over one's basic values.

Relative mastery of these tasks builds self-confidence, maturity, and adjustment and prepares youth for the more difficult tasks ahead. Frustration and failure give rise to anxiety, social disapproval, and a sense of personal inadequacy in the face of future tasks. However, the emphasis should be on youth's active pursuit rather than on the final achievement of these tasks, because in many instances complete mastery remains a challenge throughout one's entire lifespan.

Bandura's Cognitive Social Learning Theory

In the development of social learning theory, Albert Bandura has pioneered the view that learning and the environment play a primary role in human behavior. Accordingly, he regards human development as a lifelong process in which there is a continuous, reciprocal interaction between the individual and his or her environment, mediated by cognitive variables.

Bandura (1986) and his colleagues have demonstrated that much of what we learn and do is acquired through *observational learning*. This is the process in which we learn by observing other people, or "models," and events, and then imitating what we see without any necessary direct reinforcement. Bandura has paid special attention to how aggressive behavior may be acquired through observational learning. In one study, Bandura compared overly aggressive adolescent boys who were in trouble with the law, with better adjusted boys. He found that much of the overly aggressive boys' behavior could be explained by what they had learned at home. More specifically, he found that the fathers of overly aggressive boys were more rejecting of their sons, so that their sons became less dependent on them and spent less time with them. Parents of overly aggressive boys were also more likely to use harsh, physical punishment so that their sons were more apt to imitate their parents' aggressive behavior than their verbal warnings to the contrary. Parents of aggressive boys also tended to encourage their sons in aggressive behavior, such as standing up for their rights or leading with their fists. In contrast, parents of the better adjusted boys showed more accepting attitudes toward their sons, explained their rules and discipline, and were less likely to use physical punishment. As a result, these boys tended to develop more inner controls of their aggression, i.e., an adequate conscience and

Albert Bandura, a leading social learning theorist, has pioneered the view that cognition, learning, and environment play a primary role in human behavior. (Courtesy of Albert Bandura)

an appropriate sense of guilt, such that they kept their aggressive behavior well within the bounds of the law.

Although observational learning often occurs because of an intrinsic desire to acquire observed behaviors, such learning also may be strengthened by direct reinforcement or the consequences of a given behavior. For instance, when aggressive behavior is seen as rewarded or reinforced rather than punished, young people are more likely to imitate it. In this connection, Bandura stresses the importance of vicarious reinforcement that comes from watching socially sanctioned aggression—for instance, TV crime shows or violent sporting events. Spectators who see the advantages of aggression are more likely to engage in aggressive behavior themselves. Then, as they discover the personal payoff value of aggression in their own lives, they may administer their own reinforcement; such self-reinforcement is as effective as external reinforcement in influencing behavior. Accordingly, much of the aggressive behavior among youth, whether in vandalism or driving, largely reflects the behavior and values of American society as a whole.

Cognition and Behavior

In recent years, Bandura and others have begun exploring the impact of cognitive psychology on behavior. Essentially, cognition has to do with information processing, including attention, perception, interpretation, and memory. Bandura has turned his attention to cognition as a means of understanding those processes that mediate between the environmental stimuli and the individual's response. Thus, the adolescent's cognitive interpretation of environmental experience plays a key role in his or her behavior.

Walter Mischel (1986), another cognitive social learning theorist, has set forth five basic categories of cognitive variables that influence our response to a given event or stimulus:

1. *Competencies.* Each of us has a different combination of abilities and skills that shape our responses to events. For instance, when a car won't start, one teenager may hitch a ride with a friend or take a bus to work, while another youth, with a different set of skills, borrows battery jumper cables to get the car started.
2. *Encoding strategies.* We also have different ways of perceiving and organizing experiences that shape our responses. For example, when confronted with a long line at the school bookstore, one youth may fuss and fume with little gained, while another decides to come back later when the line is usually shorter.
3. *Expectancies.* Learning experiences lead each of us to form different expectations that help to determine our reactions to events. One student expects to do well in school, studies hard, attends class regularly, and generally makes good grades. Another student endowed with the same intelligence has an attitude problem toward school, studies intermittently, and attends class sporadically, with the expected poor results.
4. *Personal values.* Our sense of priorities and values also shapes our decisions and actions. Thus, when office politics become intolerable, one worker quits the job, but others take it in stride and stick to their work.

5. *Self-regulatory systems.* We also formulate plans, goals, and strategies that influence our actions. For instance, while some youth regard the study of foreign languages as a waste of time, others may find such knowledge useful for foreign travel or business transactions in a global market.

Cognitive variables play a vital mediating role in learning, affecting both the inner and outer determinants of behavior. Bandura (1986) refers to the mutual interaction between the three basic components of learning as "reciprocal determinism." That is, the internal personal-cognitive variables, environmental influences, and behaviors all operate as interlocking determinants of each other. For instance, adolescents' eating habits (or behaviors) are influenced by the eating patterns in the families in which they grew up (environmental factors), which are also influenced by the adolescents' past eating habits and preferences (a personal-cognitive factor). All these influences are mutual. Consequently, as adolescents learn more about nutrition (person-cognitive factor), this would affect which types of food and restaurants they would seek out (environmental factor), which in turn would shape their present eating patterns (or behavior). Such a view gives us a richer, more realistic understanding of adolescent behavior than do earlier learning theories which stress environmental control.

Implications for Adolescent Development

The basic concepts and assumptions of cognitive social learning theory have the following implications for adolescent development:

First, adolescence is not necessarily a rebellious or stormy time as depicted in traditional stage theories. Instead, much depends on the particular adolescent, his or her family, and environment. Bandura maintains that the storm-and-stress view of adolescence characterizes only the deviant minority of youth. Most youth tend to develop in a positive direction, with relative continuous changes in behavior. When there is rebelliousness, it is more likely because of what happens in the adolescent's family, school, or peer relationships.

Second, much of adolescent behavior comes from observing and imitating the behavior of parents, teachers, and peers. Thus, parents who verbally admonish their teenagers not to drink or smoke while indulging in these behaviors themselves should not be surprised to discover that youth are more influenced by what their parents *do* than what they *say.* Conversely, adults intent on teaching positive attitudes and complex skills to youth may do so more effectively through modeling the desired behavior along with appropriate verbal instruction.

Third, adolescents, like adults, are active, information-processing organisms that exert significant control over their own behavior and development. One of the most important aspects of information processing has to do with self-perception and whether youth see themselves as in control of, or controlled by, their environment. Youth high in perceived control—the belief that they can influence the occurrence of events in their environment that affect their lives—attain greater personal control over their lives. For instance, they work harder at intellectual and performance tasks, and their efforts are rewarded with better grades than are youth with less perceived control (Phares, 1988).

Fourth, adolescent development is best understood in terms of the mutual interaction between the internal and external influences on behavior. Thus, adolescents are not as strongly driven by inner forces, as suggested in some stage theories; nor are they at the mercy of environmental forces, as implied by strict behaviorists. Instead, the individual's understanding and actions (personal, cognitive variable) play a mediating role, decisively shaping the biological and social influences on adolescent development.

THE CULTURAL PERSPECTIVE

You might envision the adolescent's environment as a sequence of ever-widening concentric circles extending outward from the family, community, nation, world, and universe. Although adolescents may be well aware of those environmental influences closest to them, i.e., their families, peers, and neighborhoods, they are also influenced to a considerable extent by their more inclusive environment, including their culture. Here, culture refers to the patterns of attitudes, beliefs, behaviors, and values that are shared and passed on from one generation to another in a particular group of people. Thus, adolescents growing up in a particular society are shaped in myriad ways by their culture with little or no awareness of such influences until later in life, if at all. Anthropologists, who study cultural patterns of behavior, believe that adolescent behavior varies considerably from one culture to another, especially between traditional and industrialized societies. In this section, we'll examine Margaret Mead's study of adolescents in traditional Samoan society and her observations about adolescents in Western societies, and the impact of social change. Then we'll describe some of the findings from a cross-cultural survey of adolescents in ten countries, showing how adolescents in various parts of the world are becoming more similar to each other, largely because of social and technological changes around the world and the increasing global awareness.

Mead's Cultural Theory

Margaret Mead began her career as an anthropologist by studying adolescent girls in Samoa, in the South Pacific islands. There, Mead observed that adolescent behavior largely reflects the society in which one grows up, leading her to conclude that the experience of adolescence varies significantly from one culture to another. Her findings are published in two books, *Coming of Age in Samoa* (1950) and *Growing up in New Guinea* (1953).

Mead found that adolescence among Samoan girls was an uneventful time of life, without the emotional turbulence associated with puberty in Western societies. Adolescent girls differed from their younger sisters mostly in one respect—namely, their more mature bodies. In growing up, Samoan girls en-

Margaret Mead, an anthropologist, found that Samoan girls experience adolescence differently from American girls. (Courtesy of the American Museum of Natural History)

countered no taboo and separation at the onset of menstruation because they had learned the facts earlier. No new way of life was suddenly thrust upon them because they had been expected to share in the family work and obey their parents throughout the transition from childhood to adulthood. In fact, girls were taught dominance early in life, and six- or seven-year-old girls dominated their younger sisters just as they were dominated by their older sisters. The older the girl became, the less she was disciplined by others and the more she disciplined others. Thus, Samoan girls passed painlessly from childhood to womanhood, so that adolescence was one of the pleasantest times in their lives.

Mead explained that the tranquil adolescence of Samoan girls was due to the cultural patterns in that country. For one thing, the young passed through a succession of well-marked periods of responsibility so that they always knew what was expected of them. There was also a more casual way of life in Samoa than in Western cultures. Emotional bonds were looser, both in the family and community. There was also less conflict and competitiveness in Samoan culture. Nor were adolescents expected to make personal choices to establish their vocation or place in society. Mead pointed out that such cultural differences have their disadvantages too, especially the absence of deep feelings and little appreciation of individual differences.

Although some of these observations were later disputed by Derek Freeman (1983), who found the Samoans to be more aggressive and sexually inhibited than Mead did, her major findings remain intact. Lowell Holmes (1986),

---

Margaret Mead's Adolescence

According to her autobiography, Margaret Mead was a lively, intense, and in some ways unconventional adolescent.

She was a precocious adolescent partly because of her unusual family. Both her parents had gone to graduate school and expected her to use her mind. They insisted on treating their children in a democratic way, so that Mead always felt treated as a person, even as a child. Her mother had a strong concern for social justice and actively participated in community affairs. As a result, Mead says that "in many ways I was brought up within my own culture two generations ahead of my time" (p. 2).

Mead's paternal grandmother exercised a decisive influence on her life. She had graduated from college, become a teacher, and later a school principal, in a day when these were exceptional accomplishments for women. Grandmother lived in the Mead home, and when frequent family moves made regular school attendance impossible, she taught her granddaughter at home. Later, Mead said that it was the influence of her grandmother and mother as positive role models that inspired her to become both a professional person and a mother.

Margaret Mead became a superior student despite frequent changes in homes and schools. She not only made good grades, but was intellectually curious. She loved to read and write poetry; she kept a diary, and even began a novel. She was also physically active, playing vigorous games well beyond the age when girls were supposed to. Throughout her high-school years, Mead says, "I wanted to live out every experience that went with schooling, and so I made a best friend out of the most likely candidate, fell sentimentally in love with one of the boys, attached myself to a teacher, and organized as far as it was possible to do so, every kind of game, play, performance, May Day dance, Valentine party, and, together with Julian Gardy, a succession of clubs, in one of which we debated such subjects as 'Who was greater, Washington or Lincoln' " (p. 80). Yet, she

---

who did a restudy of Tau, the same village where Mead had worked earlier, concluded that Margaret Mead was essentially correct in her depiction of coming of age in Samoa.

The lack of continuity in coming of age in Western society largely reflects the type of society in which we live—a diverse, industrialized, technological society characterized by rapid social change. Margaret Mead (1978) described the impact of change on socialization in terms of three types of cultural patterns: postfigurative, cofigurative, and prefigurative. The prefix of each term refers to the orientation of the young toward their social models (or "figures")—to the past (post-), present (co-), or future (pre-).

The *postfigurative cultural pattern* is characteristic of very stable societies with little social change. The elders are looked up to for the wisdom needed by each generation, and adults pass on their ideas, values, and practices to the young. Young people do not ask too many questions; they take it for granted that they are going to live in a world like their parents' world. The prototype of postfigurative culture is the isolated primitive society, though much of conventional child rearing and education assumes this view.

felt she was "set apart" in school because of the educational advantages given by her family. As a result, she searched with a greater intensity than others, speculating at different times that she would become "a lawyer, a nun, a writer, or a minister's wife with six children" (p. 81).

Despite her academic excellence, Mead almost missed going to college because her father felt she should get married or become a nurse like other girls. She responded with "one of the few fits of feminist rage I have ever had" (p. 85). Her mother came to the rescue with a compromise choice, and persuaded her husband to send Mead to his own alma mater, DePauw College in Indiana. But it was a disastrous decision, because Mead's life style, with her self-designed dresses, serious books, and posters, was at odds with the prevailing social atmosphere at the college. Consequently, she was rejected by the sororities and was deeply hurt. Feeling like an "alien," she transferred to Barnard College after her first year.

Life at Barnard College in New York City was an exciting and rewarding experience for Mead. Surrounded by stimulating teachers and other bright women like herself, she became active in literary and theatrical affairs. She debated and took part in student demonstrations. She also had a mischievous streak, and ran around with a group of friends known as the "Ash Can Cats," who remained her friends for life. Although at 17 she became engaged to a seminary student with similar interests, they did not marry until several years later when Mead was 22 years old.

Like many adolescents, Margaret Mead felt unsure of herself and her career at times. She had begun college as an English major, intending to become a writer. Later, she added a minor in psychology. Then, during her senior year she took a course in anthropology under Franz Boas, and acquired a serious interest in anthropology. She also began a lifelong friendship with Boas's assistant, anthropologist Ruth Benedict.

Margaret Mead, *Blackberry Winter* (New York: William Morrow and Company, Inc., 1972).

The *cofigurative cultural pattern* is characteristic of societies with moderate social change. Young people growing up in such a society will find some of their elders' ways outdated and out of necessity will turn to their contemporaries for guidance. The elders remain dominant and set the limits within which the young learn, often regarding the differences between generations as changes in fashion rather than substance. But the young look somewhat more to their peers and less to their parents for models. An example would be the adolescent who moves to the United States from Vietnam and makes the adjustment mostly through help from his or her peers.

The *prefigurative cultural pattern* is characteristic of societies with rapid social change. The ideas, values, and skills of the adults become outdated quickly, so that the young people must learn many things for themselves. Mead calls this new style prefigurative because it is the young person and not the parent or grandparent who represents the future. Adults, in turn, take many cues from their offspring, and they value growing and learning new things from the young.

Mead (1978) thinks that we are evolving toward a prefigurative culture, although our present society retains elements of each cultural pattern. That is, although young people increasingly must chart their own way in many matters, they have much to learn from their peers and parents. But in order to socialize the young effectively, parents and adults must learn new roles. "We must create new models for adults who can teach their children not what to learn but how to learn and not what they should be committed to, but the value of commitment" (p. 72). Such a view assumes that we are evolving towards a society as an "open" rather than as a "closed" system, with a more significant positive role for social change. Even though this implies a certain degree of discontinuity in socialization, it need not result in alienation between the generations, though the potential for this is obviously greater.

A Cross-Cultural Survey of Adolescents

The impact of social change on adolescents can be seen in a cross-cultural survey of adolescents in ten countries, as reported in *The Teenage World* (Offer et al., 1988). The study was conducted by Daniel Offer, Eric Ostrov, Kenneth Howard, and Robert Atkinson, a multidisciplinary team, in cooperation with native collaborators in the various countries. Their subjects include almost six thousand adolescents in ten countries: Australia, Bangladesh, Hungary, Israel, Italy, Japan, Taiwan, Turkey, the United States and what was once called West Germany. The investigators characterize their study as cross-cultural because it includes adolescents from different cultures. But they acknowledge that all of their subjects come from industrialized, urban settings rather than traditional societies, a factor that should be kept in mind in interpreting the results.

Information was obtained through use of a structured questionnaire that measures five aspects of teenagers' self-perception, including their *psychological selves* (impulse control, emotional tone, and body image), *social selves* (social relationships, educational and career goals), *sexual selves* (sexual attitudes), *familial selves* (family relationships), and *coping selves* (psychopathology and adjustment). Adolescents' responses were registered on a six-point scale, ranging from one, "describes me very well" to six, "does not describe me at all."

A major finding is that adolescents in the various countries display broad agreement in several areas, especially in regard to family relationships, educational and career goals, coping skills, and social relationships. The vast majority of teenagers in all the countries report positive attitudes and commitment toward their families. Adolescents feel that they get along well with their parents and deny carrying a grudge against their parents. More than nine out of ten adolescents affirm the value of work and are concerned about the work they plan to do. Almost all of them (96 percent) state that a job well done brings them pleasure. They also enjoy being with other people and like to help a friend whenever they can. The majority of adolescents report good coping skills. For instance, almost nine out of ten teenagers admit that when they fail at something they try to learn from their experience. Similarly, almost all of them (88 percent) feel they will be able to assume responsibility for themselves in the future. See Table 2-2.

Table 2-2   Items Endorsed by the Majority of Adolescents Across the Ten Countries[a]

Items	Average percentage endorsement[b]
Positive Endorsements	
Social relationships	
Being together with other people gives me a good feeling.	88
Vocational and educational goals	
At times I think about what kind of work I will do in the future.	90
A job well done gives me pleasure.	96
I feel that there is plenty I can learn from others.	89
Family relationships	
Most of the time my parents get along well with each other.	82
Superior adjustment	
If I know that I will have to face a new situation, I will try in advance to find out as much as is possible about it.	85
Whenever I fail in something, I try to find out what I can do in order to avoid another failure.	87
Individual values	
I like to help a friend whenever I can.	92
Negative Endorsements	
Vocational and educational goals	
I would rather be supported for the rest of my life than work.	10
Family relationships	
My parents are ashamed of me.	7
I have been carrying a grudge against my parents for years.	9
Very often I feel that my mother is no good.	9
My parents will be disappointed in me in the future.	11
Very often I feel that my father is no good.	13
Superior adjustment	
I am certain that I will not be able to assume responsibilities for myself in the future.	12
Individual values	
Telling the truth means nothing to me.	15

[a] In order to qualify as "universal," an item must have an average endorsement of 75% or more within *each* country and none of the four groups (e.g., younger males) can have less than 67% endorsement.

[b] The percentage endorsements were averaged across all four cells (gender and age) across all countries.

Adapted from Daniel Offer, Eric Ostrov, Kenneth I. Howard, and Robert Atkinson, *The Teenage World: Adolescents' Self-Image in Ten Countries* (New York: Plenum Medical Book Company, 1988), p. 64, Table 1.

At the same time, there is little agreement with respect to such matters as impulse control, body image, and sexual attitudes, which are more a function of gender differences and socioeconomic variables in the various countries. However, boys tend to report better control of their feelings, greater pride in their bodies, and more interest in sexuality than the girls do. In contrast to the boys, girls generally report a higher degree of social awareness and commitment to others. Girls tend to be more sociable and empathetic. They also express stronger commitment to the work ethic and invest themselves more in school and studying than boys do. The investigators acknowledge the difficulty in explaining these results, but attribute many of the gender differences to the historical and social roles played by males and females in the societies studied. Age differences were also evident in many areas. In general, older adolescents 16 to 19 years of age exhibit more maturity in most matters than do younger adolescents 13 to 15 years of age. For instance, older adolescents are more self-confident than younger adolescents and are more apt to take criticism from others without resentment.

There are also numerous cross-cultural differences in various aspects of adolescent behavior. For instance, when it comes to family relationships, Israeli youth consistently report more positive family relationships than do those from other countries, with youth from the United States not far behind Israeli youth. In contrast, Australian teenagers report poorer family relationships. The relatively good feelings toward their families reported by Israeli youth may reflect the traditional Jewish emphasis on family relationships. At the same time, the relatively poor family relationships reported by Australian adolescents seems to have no ready explanation.

Attitudes toward sex vary considerably between countries. Teenagers in Turkey and Taiwan are especially apt to report more conservative sexual attitudes than do teens in other countries. Over one-fifth of the adolescents in both countries admit that "thinking or talking about sex scares me." More than three-fourths of the youth from Taiwan, who are shaped by traditional Chinese culture, do not feel that sexual experiences give them pleasure. Almost half of them feel it is not important to have a good friend of the opposite sex. In contrast, only one out of ten American youths are apprehensive in discussing sex. And more than three-fourths of them acknowledge that sexual experiences give them pleasure.

The investigators also explore the relationships between adolescent self-image and various demographic and socioeconomic variables. Many variables show little or no statistical association with the survey data on adolescents, including the number of television sets per one thousand individuals and the percent of students enrolled in secondary schools. However, several variables are statistically significant. For instance, adolescents' emotional tone and mood are positively related to the country's gross national product. Yet adolescents' body image is correlated with only one demographic variable, per capita income. The higher the country's per capita income, the more positive adolescents feel about their bodies and health. It appears that body image is a function of wealth available for individuals in contrast to mood, which seems to be more responsive to a nation's total wealth. Perhaps adolescents in countries with a high per capita income have the time, resources, and incentives to achieve physical fitness and good health, which, in turn, facilitate good body image. Social relationships also are strongly related to demographic and economic variables. For instance, youth are more apt to report good peer relationships in countries having higher educational expenditures per capita and a more positive physical quality of life. Very positive peer relationships appear to be a luxury of relatively well-advantaged adolescents.

The economic/demographic variable most highly related to adolescents' self-image is the proportion of adolescents in the total population of a given country. A high proportion of adolescents in a country's population, as is the case

Table 2-3   Population Characteristics and Demographic Economic Variables Significantly Related to Adolescents' Self-Image

Country	Population	People per square mile	Percent 14–18	PERCENT 15–19 IN LABOR FORCE		GNP[b]	Per capita income[c]	Educ. expend. per capita	Quality of life index[d]
				M	F				
Australia	16	5	8.4	48	48	142.2	9,820	505	96
Bangladesh	100	1,791	10.8	72	19	11.2	120	2	36
Hungary	10	297	6.5	41	43	45.0	4,180	167	91
Israel	4	512	8.7	35	34	17.4	4,500	389	92
Italy	57	490	7.8	44	36	368.9	6,480	259	95
Japan	120	835	7.4	33	32	1,152.9	9,890	508	98
Taiwan	19	1,530	8.8	—	—	50.6	2,579	66	88
Turkey	50	167	10.8	56	45	66.1	1,460	48	62
West Germany	61	640	8.1	57	57	827.8	13,590	566	94
United States	237	65	7.7	39	32	2,582.5	11,360	676	96

[a] Estimated population in 1984 in millions (UNESCO)

[b] GNP in billions of U.S. dollars

[c] Per capita income and educational expenditures per capita given in U.S. dollars

[d] A composite index calculated by averaging three indices—life expectancy, infant mortality, and literacy—on scale of 1 to 100.

Adapted from table 2, p. 43, and table 3, p. 44, in Daniel Offer et al., *The Teenage World: Adolescents' Self-Image in Ten Countries* (New York: Plenum Medical Book Company, 1988).

in Bangladesh and Turkey, is associated with adolescents reporting relatively poor mood, poorer social relationships, and higher psychopathology. The investigators explain that as the size of a given segment of the population increases in relation to the overall population, it produces excessive competition for existing jobs and limited resources in institutions, resulting in relative deprivation. Thus, once members of the baby-boom generation reach the labor market, they are likely to meet an unfavorable situation in the United States, such as a large number of people competing for relatively few opportunities. As a result, they may exhibit adaptive behaviors, such as attempting to improve their educational status, delaying marriage, continued employment after marriage of both spouses, and reducing the number of children they have. Such stresses also may result in greater drug and alcohol abuse as well as crime. See Table 2-3.

Emergence of the "Universal" Adolescent

A major finding of this survey is that adolescents in the different countries studied show greater similarities to one another than expected. Such a view clashes with the position of cultural relativists of earlier eras, who held that cultural differences are so pervasive there is hardly any basis for comparing adolescents of different cultures. In contrast, the investigators point out that because of extensive social and technological change, today's youth are growing up in a world of greater interdependence. The revolution in communication, in particular, is recreating the world in the image of a "global village," in which every aspect of life—every thought, every action, and every institution—is being reconsidered in light of what is happening to people in other parts of the world. Television has become a type of "significant other" on a global level. Television serves as a universal influence on the adolescent's developing self, displacing many traditional activities, such as participation in community activites, sports, dances, and parties. Consequently, instead of interacting solely with their local peers, teenagers are assimilating more of what they see in their counterparts in other parts of the world. Thus, more teenagers are being influenced by information and images having a common origin. And contemporary researchers are noticing greater similarities among adolescents in different cultures.

Daniel Offer and his colleagues (1988) contend that their findings constitute a portrait of the "universal adolescent," composed of basic similarities in adolescents' self-image across different cultures. First, teenagers are happy most of the time. They enjoy life and perceive themselves as able to control their own lives. Second, universal adolescents are caring and oriented toward others. They care about how others might be affected by their actions and derive a good feeling from being with others. Third, adolescents value work and school. They consider school and studying to be important. Also, they think about the kind of work they will do and enjoy a job well done. Fourth, adolescents express confidence about their sexuality. They are not afraid to think and talk about sex and do not feel they are boring to the opposite sex. Fifth, adolescents express positive feelings toward their families. They feel they get along well with their parents most of the time and that their parents will not be disappointed or ashamed of them. Finally, adolescents feel they are coping well with life. They are able to make decisions and make sense out of things. When faced with a problem, adolescents try to find out as much as possible about it in advance in order to cope with it more effectively. If they fail, they try to find out what can be done about that in order to avoid another failure. They are confident about themselves and feel they will be able to assume responsibility for themselves in the future.

The emergence of the universal adolescent does not deny the importance of cultural differences among adolescents. Indeed, Offer and his colleagues hasten to add that their studies reveal important gender, age, and national differences among adolescents, as noted in the previous section. However, they contend that when the apparent layers of human diversity, such as language, race, or religion, are peeled away, there appear to be core attitudes and values that motivate and guide youth in different countries. Furthermore, sources for the common adolescent experience include the biological, cognitive, and developmental aspects of adolescence. For instance, the basic physical changes at puberty that distinguish adolescence from both childhood and adulthood are universal, though the social recognition of the status of adulthood is socially determined. Cognitive development also exhibits universal constructs, such as the appearance of logical, adultlike reasoning in adolescence, which also varies among adolescents in different cultures. Then too, there are developmental tasks such as establishing a clear, coherent view of one's self and separating from one's family or origin. Finally, one universal characteristic of adolescents that is often ignored is the excitement of being an adolescent. This involves moving away from childhood, learning new skills, forming new relationships, and achieving the important role of socially accepted adult. Bearing witness to the universal adolescent are rituals marking the transition to adulthood. These rituals seem pervasive, if not universal. They differ greatly in form, but have in common the recognition and celebration of the increased physical and mental power and the elevated status that accompanies the transition to adulthood.

The portrait of the universal adolescent is also at odds with the stereotype of the rebellious, stormy adolescent that lingers in the literature of adolescence. The cross-cultural survey of adolescents shows that a clear majority (73 percent) of teenagers in the various countries exhibit a healthy self-image. This is not to deny that a significant minority of adolescents are having difficulty coping and suffer from a poor self-image. But rather, teenage maladjustment is more aptly attributed to the conditions in which teenagers are growing up than to the period of adolescence itself. A number of factors may contribute to the social alienation of teens, including poverty, deprivation, and social upheaval. Having many competing value systems also makes it difficult for adolescents to maintain a sense of sameness and continuity. Furthermore, the lack of family cohesiveness and community tradition can contribute significantly to confusion among adolescents.

Differences in age, gender, nationality, and coping ability across the various categories of adolescence do not nullify the central point of this study, that adolescents in different cultures are growing up more similar to each other than they did in the past. Despite contrary forces such as intense nationalism in many quarters, rapid social and technological changes along with the revolution in communication are bringing about greater convergence in the experience of adolescence. Whereas in the past, the local community represented the world, today the world has become a global village. Consequently, there is increasing homogenization of cultures, and in particular the experience of adolescence. Today's youth are probably more aware that the challenges and problems they face are also being experienced by other teenagers around the world, such that they are growing up with a greater sense of comradery with teenagers in other parts of the world.

SUMMARY

1. We began the chapter by noting that scientists and clinicians approach adolescence from different theoretical perspectives, and that by examining the distinctive contributions from several major perspectives, we may arrive at a more inclusive and well-balanced understanding of adolescence.

The Biological Perspective

2. The modern scientific study of adolescence is attributed to the work of Stanley Hall, who held that adolescence is a critical stage of development during which the dominant biological factors are more readily modified by one's environment than at any other time of life.

3. Although traditional theorists of adolescence, like Hall, assume a direct, causal link between puberty and the adolescent's psychological development, most current views adopt a mediated-effects approach, which recognizes that the impact of puberty on overall adolescent development is mediated by other variables.

The Psychoanalytical Perspective

4. Sigmund Freud viewed individual development as a sequence of psychosexual stages, with the personality dynamics at later stages being heavily dependent upon one's earlier development, especially childhood.

5. Anna Freud, while retaining her father's developmental approach, emphasized the additional view that adolescence is a special period of turbulence because of the sexual conflicts brought on by puberty.

6. The intensified sex drive and resulting sexual conflicts arouse considerable anxiety in adolescents, which in turn evokes a variety of ego defense mechanisms such as asceticism and intellectualization for coping with this characteristic adolescent stress.

7. Many of those who followed Freud have retained the developmental approach to adolescence, but tend to de-emphasize the unconscious strivings of the id and give greater emphasis to the positive functions of the ego and the social, cultural influences on development.

The Social-Cognitive Perspective

8. Theorists in this perspective emphasize the role of learning in human behavior, with the view that biological drives are decisively shaped by psychological and social influences.

9. Robert Havighurst combines the individual's readiness for learning with certain social demands in defining the eight developmental tasks of adolescence, which call for appropriate mastery at this stage of life.

10. Bandura has observed that much of adolescent behavior comes from observational learning, in which adolescents observe and imitate the behavior of their parents, other adults, and peers.

11. Adolescent learning and behavior are significantly affected by cognitive variables, such as the adolescents' competencies, encoding strategies, expectancies, personal values, and self-regulatory systems.

12. Thus, adolescent development is best understood in terms of the mutual interaction between the internal and external influences on behavior, with relatively continuous changes in behavior. When there is rebelliousness, it is more likely because of what happens in the adolescent's family, school, or peer relationships, than due to adolescence itself.

The Cultural Perspective

13. Based on her studies of adolescents in Samoa, Margaret Mead observed that the experience of adolescence largely reflects the society in which one grows up, and thus varies somewhat from one culture to another.

14. However, a cross-cultural survey of adolescents in ten countries shows that today's adolescents are growing up more similar to one another than expected.

15. The increasing "universality of adolescence" is attributed largely to the impact of social

and technological change, especially the communication revolution, whereby youth are more aware of and influenced by their counterparts in other countries than they were in earlier eras.

16. The majority of adolescents in different countries exhibit a healthy self-image and positive relationships with their parents, in striking contrast to the stereotype of the rebellious adolescent.

REVIEW QUESTIONS

1. Which major perspectives on adolescence were covered in this chapter?
2. In what sense did Stanley Hall regard adolescence as a critical stage of development?
3. Give an example of one direct-effect and one mediated-effect theory relating puberty and adolescent development covered in this chapter.
4. How do Sigmund and Anna Freud explain adolescent storm and stress?
5. What are Havighurst's eight developmental tasks of adolescence?
6. What are the most important determinants of adolescent development according to Bandura's cognitive social learning perspective?
7. What are some of the implications of the cognitive social learning perspective for adolescent storm and stress?
8. According to Margaret Mead, what causes the more tranquil adolescence of Samoan girls compared to that of American girls?
9. To what extent can adolescents benefit from learning from adults, peers, and themselves, respectively?
10. What are some similarities among adolescents in different countries described in the cross-cultural survey by Daniel Offer and his colleagues?

3

Physical Development

Learning Objectives

After completing this chapter, you should be able to:

1 Explain the meaning of puberty in both the technical and general usage of the term.
2 Identify the seven types of physical growth resulting from the combined effect of hormonal changes at puberty.
3 Give at least two examples of the secular trend toward earlier physical growth during adolescence.
4 Describe the major physical changes during a girl's growth spurt and the average age range of this period.
5 Describe the major physical changes during a boy's growth spurt and the average age range of this period.
6 List the sequence of pubertal changes in girls' sexual maturation.
7 List the sequence of pubertal changes in boys' sexual maturation.
8 Describe the advantages and disadvantages for both early and late maturers among girls and boys.

As individuals reach puberty, their bodies change dramatically in ways that may be confusing to them. Not only do girls begin to grow taller before boys their own age do, but some adolescents can be nearly finished with their growth spurt before others of their own sex even begin. Many adolescents do not understand what is happening to their bodies and feel awkward about being different. "Being so small I'm usually the last one selected when we're choosing teams," complains a ninth grade boy. "When I got my first period," says an eighth grade girl, "I was so upset I didn't want to talk about it. I stayed in my room and went to bed for a couple of days." Such experiences are typical among adolescents and illustrate the importance of pubertal changes for adolescents' psychological adjustment. Dramatic changes in one's body and appearance not only affect the ways teenagers feel about themselves; they also influence the way adolescents relate to their parents and peers. We begin this chapter by explaining the process of puberty. Then we describe the various bodily changes that occur during the growth spurt, the process of sexual maturation, and finally how adolescents cope psychologically with such changes.

PUBERTY

Puberty in the technical sense of the word means the attainment of sexual maturity—the maturation of the reproductive organs and thus the ability to reproduce, as well as the appearance of secondary sex characteristics. But the term is generally used more broadly to refer to the entire process of glandular and bodily changes that accompany sexual maturation. However, in both senses of the term puberty is more accurately understood as a process rather than a single marker event and is more complex than ordinarily portrayed.

The Process of Puberty

Puberty is part of the unfolding growth process that begins at conception. That is, all of the components for sexual maturity are present in the developing fetus, and thus the newborn infant, but are immature. The rapid maturation of reproductive capacity at puberty is part of the overall growth process. One of the major factors distinguishing puberty from the rest of the biological life cycle is the rapid *rate* of growth along with the *magnitude* of bodily changes that accompany it. The rate of growth during infancy is even more rapid than at adolescence, but it may be less important because the infant does not experience change the same way an adolescent does. Major changes also occur in late adulthood, but they are usually slower and more gradual (Petersen and Taylor, 1980).

At some time in late childhood or prepuberty, there is a rapid rise in the secretion of certain hormones, especially the sex-specific hormones, which signals the onset of puberty. This occurs at about 10 or 11 years of age in girls and at about 12 or 13 in boys. The rise in hormonal activity triggers a gradual increase in the size and secretion of the sex glands themselves, such as the ovaries in girls and the testes in boys. But because these changes are not immediately evident, the onset of puberty is often associated with the outward manifestations of puberty, such as the growth spurt in height and weight, the appearance of pubic hair, breast buds in girls, and the enlargement of the penis and testes in boys. This phase of puberty is sometimes referred to as *pubescence* (covered with hair) because of the pubic hair which appears on the pubic or genital area about the time the reproductive organs and secondary sex characteristics are reaching maturity.

Puberty in the narrower sense of the term refers to the culmination of sexual maturation or the attainment of reproductive powers. The first sign of this is the onset of *menstruation* in girls at about 12 or 13 years of age and the first seminal emission in boys (usually by *masturbation*) at about 13 or 14 years of age. However, it may take a year or more before some girls and boys are capable of sexual reproduction on a regular basis. The latter occurs as the girl's ovaries begin discharging a mature egg every twenty-eight days or so in regular menstrual cycles and the boy's testes begin producing a greater proportion of mature sperm, thus increasing fertility in both sexes. Most adolescents are well into this culmination phase of puberty by their midteens, even though their body growth continues a few years longer.

Although the sequence of growth at puberty is similar for most adolescents, the age of onset, as well as the rate and duration of growth, varies somewhat from one adolescent to another. Furthermore, the psychological impact of puberty does not necessarily parallel these physical changes. Psychological development often lags somewhat, so that while adolescence may begin with puberty it usually extends beyond it.

Hormonal Changes

The onset of puberty and the dramatic bodily changes that follow are due largely to the rise in certain hormonal secretions at this period of life. The puberty-producing hormones are either secreted for the first time or in higher amounts at adolescence, because many of the relevant glands have been functioning throughout childhood. It is also important to note that the effect of hormones is less specific in humans than in animals, so that the changes in puberty characteristically result from the combined effects of the various hormones as well as from the adolescent's subjective meaning and reaction to the physical changes.

The endocrine system, which produces and regulates the levels of hormones throughout the body, receives its instructions from the brain. Specifically, the hypothalamus, the structure at the base of the brain that governs many aspects of behavior, such as eating, drinking, and sleeping, regulates the endocrine system through a type of feedback loop, by which hormonal levels are monitored and adjusted, somewhat like a room thermostat. That is, when the various hormonal levels reach a certain "set" point, a message is sent back to the hypothalamus, which in turn instructs the various glands to secrete less. Conversely, when hormonal levels fall below the set point, the hypothalamus directs the particular glands to step up their secretion. In this way, the hypothalamus maintains very low levels of the sex hormones throughout childhood. However, at puberty there is a change in the feedback system, such that the hypothalamus loses a certain sensitivity to the level of sex hormones in particular, allowing them to rise. As a result, the hypothalamus releases higher levels of critical hormones—LH-RF (Luteinizing hormone-releasing factor) and FSH-RF (Follicle-stimulating hormone-releasing factor)—which, in turn, trigger a sequence of changes leading to dramatic rises in the sex hormones along with other hormones. Thus, the hypothalamus triggers the onset of puberty by stimulating the pituitary (or master) gland to secrete a variety of hormones, which, in turn, stimulate the thyroid, adrenal, and gonads, or sex glands, to secrete still other hormones. The combined effects of the various hormonal secretions produce the characteristic changes of puberty, including increases in height and weight, maturation of the skeletal system, growth of the muscles, increases in the size and functioning of the sex glands, maturation of the reproductive organs, and the appearance of secondary sex characteristics. See Figure 3-1.

As soon as adolescents reach physical and sexual maturity, the endocrine system stabilizes the hormonal secretions at an adult level. But much less is known about the mechanisms by which puberty subsides than how it begins. Nor is puberty a fixed, immutable process. It can occur much earlier or later than the usual age range at adolescence. See the boxed item "Precocious Puberty." Puberty can also be arrested or reversed. For instance, smoking marijuana may retard the onset of puberty. Poor nutrition may also delay puberty, with many Third World children reaching puberty much later on average than urban chil-

Figure 3-1   Sequence of Hormonal Changes at Puberty

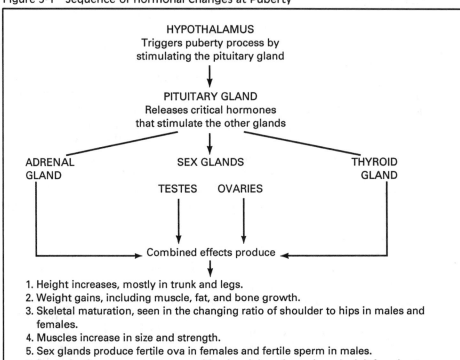

1. Height increases, mostly in trunk and legs.
2. Weight gains, including muscle, fat, and bone growth.
3. Skeletal maturation, seen in the changing ratio of shoulder to hips in males and females.
4. Muscles increase in size and strength.
5. Sex glands produce fertile ova in females and fertile sperm in males.
6. Reproductive organs mature, resulting in adult male penis and adult female uterus and vagina.
7. Secondary sex characteristics appear, such as breast development, voice change, and body hair.

dren do. Also, girls who engage in strenuous physical activity, such as cross-country runners and ballet dancers, may lose body weight and risk delay of their menarche, or first menstrual period (Rose, 1988).

Trend Toward Earlier Maturation

Interestingly, there is a trend toward earlier maturation in recent decades. It is called the *secular* (or "present") *trend* because marked evidence of it has appeared only in the last one hundred years, since about 1880. The first and most important change is that girls and boys are now beginning puberty at earlier ages. Girls now reach *menarche* at an average age of 12.8 years, which is two or three years earlier than was typical one hundred years ago (Figure 3-2). Boys are also attaining their voice change at an earlier age, in contrast to the days when boys sang soprano in Bach's choir until their late teens. During the same period, there has been an upward trend in adult height and weight, with boys and girls growing

---

Precocious Puberty

One morning in Peru, Quechua, an Indian woman, and her daughter Lina knocked at the door of the local physician. Obviously distressed, the woman explained that her child was possessed by demons. As the doctor examined the frightened girl, he observed that Lina's abdomen was greatly swollen. Discovering that Lina was carrying a child was surprising enough. But even more astonishing was that this pregnant girl was only five years old.

Several weeks later, Lina bore a healthy baby boy weighing five pounds and thirteen ounces (delivered by Caesarean section), making her the youngest mother in the world, a title she still holds.

The matter of who was the father of Lina's child was left to the local police to decide. But to the physicians and biologists who later examined her, the greater mystery was how a five-year-old girl could conceive a child. As it turned out, Lina's premature entry into womanhood—she had her first menstrual period at eight months—was apparently brought on by a tumor in one of her ovaries.

Lina's medical condition is called "precocious puberty," defined by the onset of sexual maturation before age 8 in girls and age 10 in boys. Lina's childhood was abruptly ended by sudden adolescence. In addition, she had a young son to rear, who later attended the same elementary school at the same time his mommy did.

Adapted from Kenneth Jon Rose, *The Body in Time* (New York: John Wiley & Sons, 1988). Reprinted by permission of John Wiley & Sons.

---

taller and heavier. Adult males now reach an average height of 5 feet 9 inches, and adult females an average height of 5 feet 5 inches (Tanner, 1978).

Several explanations have been offered for this trend. One is that it is part of a long-term evolutionary trend, so that we may expect adolescents to mature physically at increasingly earlier ages; yet the evidence for this is contradictory. A more plausible explanation is that the greater social mobility of recent years has resulted in more genetically varied parents producing taller children. A dramatic example is that the first generation offspring of English and Polynesian parents grew a full 2 ½ inches taller than their parents (*New York Times*, June 13, 1976).

The most widely accepted explanation for the trend toward earlier maturation is the improvement in nutrition along with better disease control which has occurred over the years. Better nutrition, in particular, has helped to lower the age at which boys and girls reach the critical body weight regarded by some, but not all, observers as a triggering event in the adolescent's growth spurt (Frisch, 1983). At the same time, it is now believed that the differences in maturation among youth in the present and past may not be as great as once thought. Instead, girls and boys may be maturing only two or three years earlier than a century ago, rather than the six years or so found by Tanner (Bullough, 1981).

In any event, the trend toward earlier maturation is slowing down, so

Figure 3-2   Declining Age of Menarche. The age of menarche, or the girl's first
             menstrual period, has declined in Western Europe and the United States so
             that today girls begin menstruation two to three years earlier than they did
             a century ago.

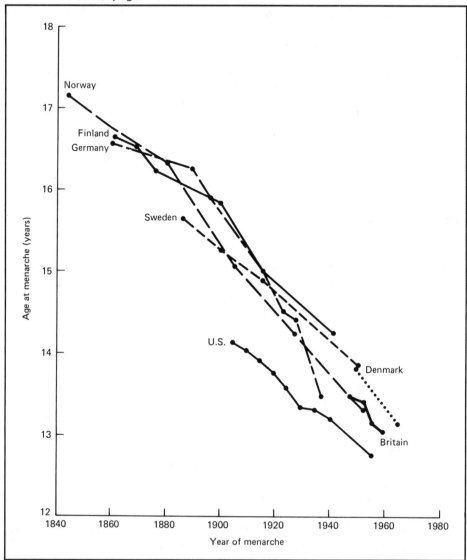

that we may expect smaller increases in earlier maturation during the coming
years. Boys born in recent years have shown no significant increase in height
over those born five to ten years earlier. Also, mothers and daughters are now
reaching their menarche at roughly the same chronological age.

THE GROWTH SPURT

Among the earliest signs that puberty has begun are dramatic changes in an adolescent's height and weight. These changes occur so quickly, for the most part, that they are commonly referred to as the growth spurt. As we mentioned earlier in this chapter, the general pattern of growth is similar for most adolescents, although the age of onset and the rate and duration of growth vary somewhat from one individual to another.

Height and Weight

The growth spurt in girls occurs, on the average, between 10 and 14 years of age. It usually begins after 10 years of age, peaks at about 11 to 12, and then declines to prepuberty rates from about 13 to 14 years. Girls continue growing at a slower rate, reaching their adult height and weight at about 15 to 16 years of age. A small proportion of girls do not reach their adult weight and height until several years later (Tanner, 1978).

The growth spurt in boys occurs, on the average, between 12 and 16 years of age. It usually begins after 12 years of age, peaks at about 13 to 14, and then declines to prepuberty rates about 15 to 16 years. Boys also continue growing at a slower rate for several more years, reaching their adult height and weight at about 17 to 18 years of age. A small proportion of boys do not reach their adult height and weight until several years later. Growth in height at this age is due more to the increase of trunk length than leg length, so that adolescent boys keep outgrowing their jackets after they have stopped outgrowing their pants (Tanner, 1978.)

Increases in height and weight tend to follow the same growth curve, though more so for girls than boys. That is, girls who grow taller than their friends also tend to be heavier, whereas shorter than average girls remain lighter. There is a greater variation among boys; some boys become tall and skinny, whereas others remain short and fat.

There is also a high correlation between prepuberty and adult height, so that adolescents who are shorter or taller than average tend to remain that way. Because the growth spurt at puberty is controlled by a different combination of hormonal secretions than in the preceding years, however, variations in the height patterns may occur among some adolescents. For example, a boy may be the runt of his class throughout childhood and then suddenly catch up with his peers at puberty; or a girl may be taller than her peers throughout childhood but then grow at a slower rate until her friends catch up with her.

Deviations in height are usually more significant than deviations in weight. The main reason is that although both may be affected by environmental factors such as malnutrition and disease, deviations in height are more likely to result from genetic or hormonal factors. In contrast, deviations in weight usually reflect other variables, such as nutrition and exercise.

A Chance to Grow Taller

Brad's friends sometimes call him a shrimp because he is so much shorter than others his age. At 13, Brad is 4 foot 8 inches tall, about 4 to 5 inches shorter than 90 percent of the kids his age. But since he began treatment with human growth hormones (HGH), the height gap between Brad and his friends is lessening. And he is picked on less because for being short (Harbison, 1990).

Treatment usually lasts six to seven years and may cost up to $20,000 a year. Up to several inches of growth in height is not unusual in the first year of treatment. But growth thereafter may be slower, due sometimes to the development of antibodies to the impure preparations of the hormone (Berkow, 1987).

In the past, injections of HGH were given only to children with serious deficiencies of the hormone, which is ordinarily secreted by the pituitary gland. But today thousands of kids who have normal levels of HGH but a family history of shortness seek out such treatment to make them taller, partly from social pressure. There is a widespread belief that taller people achieve greater success in business and get along better socially.

However, medical authorities are alarmed about the potential for abuse. Although data about the long-term effects of HGH treatment are still being gathered, there is some evidence that high doses of HGH over a long period can produce serious side effects such as arthritis, diabetes, heart disease, and joint-cartilage problems (Harbison, 1990). Meanwhile, unhappy kids who suffer because of extreme shortness feel that the prospects of growing taller outweigh the potential risks.

Skeletal and Muscular Changes

The growth spurt is accompanied by skeletal and muscular changes because both are caused by the same hormones. Since adolescents of the same chronological age may vary as much as five or six years in their maturational age, skeletal age (determined by X-ray pictures of the hands and feet) is one of the most accurate measures of maturation. Although changes in the adolescent's bone structure and muscles follow the same pattern as does the growth spurt, they follow different timetables, depending on the part of the body. For example, the head is the first to reach adult size; approximately 95 percent of the adult brain weight is attained before the growth spurt. Most changes in the head at puberty are due to growth of the jawbones and facial features, especially the nose. Growth of the hands and feet peaks soon after that of the head, leading some to observe that adolescents are "all hands and feet." As a matter of fact, arms and legs increase greatly in length during childhood and adolescence, with the arms increasing to four times their birth length and the legs to five times. Adult trunk size is achieved last and grows longer and thicker, mostly during adolescence.

One of the most noticeable differences between girls and boys during this period is the changing ratio of shoulders to hips. Even though girls reach the peak of their shoulder growth before their height spurt, the peak of their hip growth occurs after this. But just the opposite occurs in boys; the peak of their shoulder growth occurs after their height spurt. As a result, older adolescent girls have larger pelvic regions to facilitate childbearing, but older boys have larger shoulders and upper torsos necessary for the traditional male activites such as manual labor.

There is also a spurt in muscle growth during this period, though the timing is different for each sex. Although girls attain their peak muscle growth during the height spurt, boys reach their peak muscle growth about one year after the height spurt. In between, there is a short period in which girls generally have larger muscles than boys do of the same age. But boys gradually develop larger muscles and greater intensity of force, so that grown boys, on the average, exert greater muscular strength than girls do. Boys also develop larger hearts and lungs, greater capacity for carrying oxygen to the lungs, and greater power for neutralizing the chemical products of exercise. As a result, fully grown males are usually more adapted to the vigorous physical activity traditionally expected of them.

But what about the effects of changing sex roles? Because muscle development benefits from strenuous exercise, the increasing participation of girls and women in sports today promises to lessen the differences in muscular strength between the sexes. Meanwhile, bear in mind that there is considerable overlap between the sexes, such that the stronger girls are as strong as or stronger than the weaker boys. Although older boys are usually stronger than girls, they also tire more quickly, mostly because boys exert greater force. Consequently, girls may have an advantage in tasks requiring endurance, that is, exertion of moderate strength over somewhat longer periods of time.

The spurt in skeletal and muscle growth is normally accompanied by a loss of body fat, especially in boys' arms and legs; girls generally have a slower growth of body fat. But as the adolescent growth spurt ends, fat accumulation again increases in both sexes, though more so in girls.

SEXUAL MATURATION

Throughout puberty the level of sex hormones continues to rise in boys and girls. As a result, there is a sixfold increase in blood levels of estrogen in girls, though this fluctuates throughout the menstrual cycle. And there is a twentyfold increase in blood levels of androgens in boys between childhood and adulthood. However, in both sexes, bodily changes follow hormonal changes by about six months to a year. Early in puberty, the most obvious bodily changes can be seen in adolescents' growth in height and weight. But as puberty progresses, hormonal changes culminate in sexual maturation. In girls the secretion of estrogen leads to an increase in the size of the ovaries, uterus, and vagina. In boys, the secretion of testosterone leads to an increase in the testes, scrotum, and penis. Secondary sex characteristics such as body hair and breasts also mature about the same time.

How adolescents perceive and react to the changes in their bodies becomes more important psychologically than the physical changes themselves. (Laima Druskis)

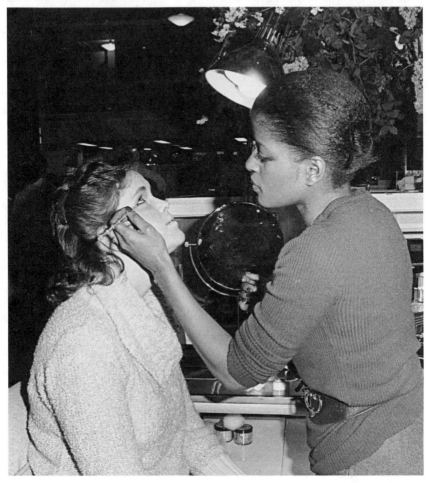

Although it was previously thought that females produce only female sex hormones and males produce only male sex hormones, recent research has shown that the bodies of boys and girls produce both sex hormones. However, at puberty the relative proportion of the respective sex hormones changes. From this point on, females have a significantly higher level of female sex hormones in proportion to male sex hormones. Similarly, males have much higher levels of the male sex hormone in proportion to female sex hormones. This dramatic shift in the proportion of sex hormones in boys and girls, combined with various psychological and social influences, gives rise to the distinctive characteristics of each sex (Money, 1980).

Girls

The typical developmental sequence in girls is as follows: the appearance of breast buds, pigmented pubic hair appears, the increase of uterus and vagina size, and the menarche—or onset of the monthly menstrual cycles—usually occurs after the girl has reached her peak rate of growth in height. At the same time, it should be clear that this pattern may vary somewhat from one girl to another (Tanner, 1978). See Table 3-1.

Breast buds appear, on the average, at about 10 or 11 years of age and take about three to four years to full breast development (Figure 3-3). Girls with rapid growth may take only one and a half years to pass through all the stages, whereas those with slow growth may take five years or even more to reach their full *breast* development. Sometimes girls worry because their breasts may develop unevenly. One girl reported, "My mother took me to the doctor because it only happened on one side at first." Some girls also worry because one breast grows slightly larger than the other or because their nipples look different from those of other girls. But, as in other parts of the body, nature rarely achieves perfect symmetry. Furthermore, breasts not only vary in size from one adolescent to another, but also in shape.

Pubic hair begins growing about the same time as the appearance of breast buds. Fine and straight at first, pubic hair gradually becomes coarser, kinkier, and more extensive. Hair soon appears on other parts of the body, especially under the arms and on the legs. The color, texture, and extent of a girl's body hair is mostly determined by heredity.

The *uterus* and vaginal canal continue growing in size throughout this period, along with the *clitoris* and labia or lips of the *vagina*. The *hymen,* or skin covering the vaginal opening, is often broken by vigorous exercise or the use of sanitary tampons before the first sexual intercourse.

The menarche occurs relatively late in the developmental sequence, at an average age of 12.8 years in the United States. It rarely occurs before 10 or after 16 years of age. Menarche usually occurs after the peak of height growth, so that the tall girl may rest assured about future height growth if her periods have begun. The menstrual cycle tends to be irregular at first, without the

Table 3-1 Sequence of Pubertal Changes in Girls

Height spurt begins.
Breast buds appear.
Straight, pigmented pubic hair appears.
Ovaries, uterus, vagina, and labia grow rapidly.
Kinky pubic hair appears.
Menarche occurs.
Auxiliary body hair grows.
Breasts develop completely.

Figure 3-3   Stages of Breast Development. Stage 1 represents preadolescence; stage 2, the appearance of breast buds; stage 3, the small pubescent breasts; stage 4, projection of the areola (pigmented area around the nipple) beyond the contour of the breast; and stage 5, the mature prepregnant breasts. Stage 4 is skipped by some girls and persists for several years in a few girls.

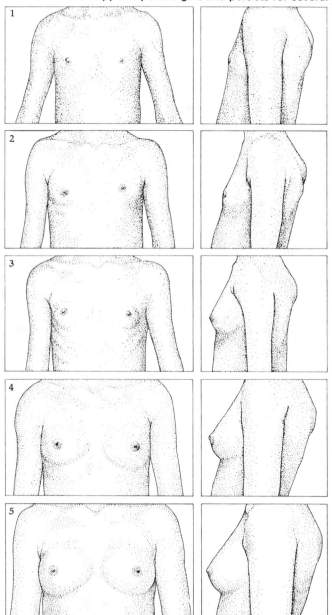

Source: H. Katchadourian, *The Biology of Adolescence* (San Francisco: W. M. Freeman, 1977), p. 55. Adapted from J. M. Tanner, *Growth at Adolescence*, 2d ed. (Oxford: Blackwell Scientific Publications, Ltd., 1962).

shedding of an ovum (egg) in some cases. However, it is usually a year or so before a girl is capable of reproduction on a regular basis.

It is important to remember that there is considerable variation in the ages at which these changes occur, as well as in the rate and extent of growth. The fact that we have cited figures for the average pattern of growth means that as many girls experience the changes earlier than these ages as later.

Menarche

A major marker event in the girl's passage to womanhood is the menarche or first menstrual period. The beliefs and expectations girls hold prior to the menarche and their subsequent reactions to this event can be seen in a study of 639 girls in selected grade levels from the fifth through the twelfth grades. In addition, 120 of the fifth- and sixth-grade girls who had not begun the menarche were followed longitudinally. As early as the fifth grade, the premenarcheal girls had clear expectations about the menstrual cycle which were similar to the reactions of the older adolescent girls. Yet girls who had begun to menstruate usually experienced less severe menstrual distress, such as pain and water retention, than the younger girls expected to experience. At the same time, there was a positive relationship between a girl's earlier expectations of menstrual distress and symptoms later reported. Although there was little change in the amount of information learned from the various sources as the girls reached menarche, there were significant differences in regard to the sources of information. Girls who received most of their information from women related menstruation less negatively and reported less severe symptoms of menstrual distress than did girls who learned mostly from male sources (Brooks-Gunn and Ruble, 1982).

The girls' reaction to menarche itself is generally mixed. Initially, there is a concern for secrecy, with moderate symptoms of menstrual distress. Girls who are the least prepared or who reach menarche early tend to report more negative reactions. However, the findings suggest that while menarche is initially experienced as inconvenient and somewhat confusing, the experience for most girls is not as negative or traumatic as often depicted (Brooks-Gunn and Ruble, 1982).

Generally, it takes a year or more before the girl's menstrual periods occur at regular intervals, which may be disconcerting to those who have received little or no instruction about such matters. Also, ovulation may not occur for several years, at least on a regular basis. In one study of two hundred normal girls, Apter and Vihko (1977) found that over half the menstrual cycles were not accompanied by ovulation in the first two years following menarche but only 20 percent or less of such cycles were not accompanied by ovulation by five years. Consequently, it is usually several years after menarche before the majority of girls are fertile on a regular basis.

In addition, some girls are bothered by such dysfunctions as the absence of menses or painful periods. *Amenorrhea* may be primary, meaning that it has never occurred, or secondary, meaning that the girl's periods may have begun but ceased. Either condition may be caused by a variety of congenital, hormonal, and physical conditions. Secondary amenorrhea may also be brought on by a change of climate, overwork, or emotional stress. Furthermore, the fact that adolescent anorexics who starve themselves and female athletes in training may cease menstruation suggests that such factors as critical body weight and metabolism may also be involved (Frisch, 1983). A more common problem is *dysmenorrhea*. A study of a national sample of seven thousand adolescents between 12 and 17 years of age found that six out of ten girls experienced cramps before or during menstruation. Many girls reported that the pain of menstruation increased somewhat throughout the first five years after menarche. Yet only 14 percent of them described such pain as severe. There are now several drugs that provide relief from menstrual distress by inhibiting the primary substance that produces cramps (Klein and Litt, 1983).

Boys

The typical developmental sequence in boys is as follows: The testes and scrotum begin to increase in size, pubic hair appears, the penis begins to enlarge about the same time the growth spurt starts, increasing sperm production leads to the initial seminal emission, and the voice begins to deepen as the larynx grows. At the same time, this pattern may vary somewhat from one boy to another, while remaining well within the normal sequence of events. See Table 3-2.

The *testes* begin increasing in size relatively early in the sequence of puberty. Because the testes increase several times in size and even more in weight, such growth remains in progress over a period of several years. The *scrotum* also darkens and thickens with the growth of blood vessels in this area. During puberty the mass threadlike *seminiferous tubules* in the testes become differentiated into mature male *sperm*. From puberty on, the testes generate sperm more or less continually throughout adulthood. About a year after the testes have begun increasing in size, the *penis* begins increasing in length and circumference, reaching adult size in several years.

Since urine and dirt may accumulate under the foreskin of the penis and lead to irritation or infection, *circumcision* is commonly performed in hospitals

Table 3-2 Sequence of Pubertal Changes in Boys

Testes and scrotum begin to grow.
Straight, pigmented pubic hair appears.
Height spurt begins.
Penis increases in circumference and length.
First seminal emission occurs.
Kinky pubic hair appears.
Auxiliary body hair grows.
Voice changes markedly.
Beard begins to grow.

throughout the country. Yet there are arguments against circumcision on the grounds that the foreskin may have some unknown but important function; for example, the lymphoidal tissue present in these structures may contribute to an individual's ability to fight disease (Crooks and Baur, 1987).

Although the difference in penis size among boys may be great in early adolescence, this difference becomes less so by the late teens. Some authorities contend that differences in penis sizes tend to diminish in the erect state. But contrary to folklore, the length and circumference of a male's penis is not related to his physique or ability to give or receive pleasure (Masters, Johnson & Kolodny, 1988).

Pubic hair appears soon after the onset of growth in the testes and penis. Facial hair first appears at the corners of the upper lip, then over the entire moustache area, and finally on the sides of the face and chin. Body hair also appears on the arms, legs, and chest area. The color, texture, and amount of hair growth is determined largely by heredity. As a result, some boys have extensive body and facial hair, whereas others have only slight hair growth.

A marked voice change occurs toward the end of the developmental sequence. The larynx (Adam's apple) enlarges and the vocal cords double in length, causing the voice to drop about an octave in pitch. The quality of a boy's voice also changes, mostly because of the enlargement of the resonating spaces above the larynx. The breaking of pitch may occur abruptly in some boys and very gradually in others, but it usually takes several years before boys gain control of the lower range of notes, especially when they sing.

Other changes also occur during this stage, such as the increase in size of a boy's sweat glands and skin pores. This usually leads to an increase in perspiration and the likelihood of facial acne in some boys. As with girls, there is considerable variation in the age at which these changes occur among boys. Early and late maturers are especially likely to attain their growth at ages different from those given for the average developmental pattern.

First Seminal Emission

The erection of the penis, which is basically a reflex action, may occur anytime from birth on, usually as the result of local stimulation such as bathing or a full bladder. Even though genital stimulation is pleasurable throughout childhood, it rarely carries the degree of excitability or urgency it does for adolescents. However, after the onset of puberty the penis becomes tumescent or pleasurably erect more readily because of the growing intensity of the sex drive and maturation of the genitals. Boys may experience erections spontaneously or in response to a wide variety of erotic sights and sounds. They take pleasure in their erections and may begin to masturbate, but without ejaculation. Boys generally feel excited and proud of their erections as a sign of their emerging manhood. But spontaneous erections at unwanted times may also become a source of embarrassment.

The first ejaculation of semen is often regarded as a marker event for male puberty similar to the menarche in girls. This usually occurs about a year after the onset of puberty, at 14 years or so on the average, though it may occur as early as 11 or as late as 16. The first seminal emission generally occurs during masturbation or in a nocturnal emission. The latter is frequently, though not always, accompanied by an erotic dream. Although today's adolescents are better informed and less likely to worry about such matters, younger boys and those who have not received any parental instruction may suffer from needless fears. Even the boy who has enjoyed the pleasurable sensations of masturbation without ejaculation may view his first seminal emission as a sign that something is physically wrong with him. Girls may also experience the equivalent of wet dreams, nocturnal dreams accompanied by orgasm, but only a small number of them do so and usually at an older age. At first the boy's sperm contains so few mobile semen that he is sterile for all practical purposes. It usually takes anywhere from one to three years before the boy's ejaculate has sufficient sperm to be fertile (Money, 1980).

PSYCHOLOGICAL ASPECTS OF PHYSICAL CHANGES

The rapid physical changes during puberty vitally affect the way adolescents feel about themselves and relate to their parents and peers. According to the direct-effects model of puberty and psychological development, much of the characteristic adolescent behavior is due to the process of puberty itself, especially the various hormonal changes. However, as you may recall from chapter 2, most authorities now follow the mediated-effects model, by which the biological changes are thought to indirectly influence psychological and social development. Accordingly, how adolescents *perceive* and *react* to the changes in their bodies becomes more important psychologically than the physical changes themselves. Of course, adolescents' psychological and social adjustment to puberty is also affected by many other factors, including how parents and peers respond to one's pubertal changes, cultural expectations, and the mass media, especially television. In this section we explore three aspects of puberty and psychological adjustment: body image, early and late maturation, and individual differences.

Body Image

Not surprisingly, when adolescents are asked what they most like or dislike about themselves, they mention physical characteristics far more frequently than intellectual or social ones. The most liked or disliked features tend to be those of the face and head, general appearance, size, and weight, and to a lesser extent body build—all related to body image. Traditionally, body image refers to the mental image adolescents form of their bodies. But in more recent years, the term *body image* has been expanded to include how adolescents *feel* about their bodies, how satisfied or dissatisfied adolescents are with their bodies, as the case may be.

When American teenagers 13 to 19 years of age are asked about their

Table 3-3 How American Teenagers Feel About Their Bodies

	PERCENT OF ADOLESCENTS WHO AGREE			
Statement about body image	Younger males*	Older males	Younger females	Older females
"I am proud of my body."	81	81	68	72
"I feel strong and healthy."	85	94	87	88
"I frequently feel ugly and unattractive."	21	17	40	30
"When others look at me, they must think I am poorly developed."	16	11	14	8

*Younger adolescents 13 to 15 years of age, older adolescents 16 to 19 years of age

Adapted from Daniel Offer, et al., *The Teenage World: Adolescents' Self-Images in Ten Countries* (New York: Plenum Medical Book Company, 1988), pp. 152, 155–57.

body images, three-fourths of them feel proud of their bodies. But a higher percentage of boys than girls feel this way. The disparity in body images between the sexes is even more pronounced in the response to the statement "I frequently feel ugly and unattractive," with twice as many girls as boys agreeing with this statement (Offer et al., 1988). See Table 3-3. By the time boys and girls reach their late teens, they generally enjoy a more favorable body image, though sex differences persist. However, by young adulthood when individuals are more likely to have come to terms with their appearances, sex differences have begun to diminish even more, with just slightly more women than men being dissatisfied with their looks (Cash, Winstead, and Janda, 1986).

At the same time, it appears that the relationship between maturation and body image is somewhat more complex for girls than boys, as shown in a study by Blyth, Bulcroft, and Simmons (1981). In the sixth grade, early-maturing girls reported greater satisfaction with their figures than did the late-maturing girls. But by the tenth grade a different pattern had emerged. At this stage, when most of the girls had achieved physical maturity, it was the late-maturing girls who were the most satisfied with their height, weight, and figures. The most plausible explanation is that the late-maturing girls are usually taller and slimmer than early maturing girls, thereby more closely resembling the cultural ideal of feminine beauty. Maturation had considerably less effect on body image among the boys, and when differences appeared they usually favored the early maturing boys.

Early versus Late Maturers

Being an early or late maturer may affect one's psychological and social development in several ways. First, simply reaching a marker event such as the menarche much earlier or later than one's peers do may be viewed as stressful by adolescents themselves. At the same time, many of the effects of early or late maturation may be associated with social recognition and acceptance, or the lack of it. For instance, an early-maturing adolescent who looks like an adult is more apt to be treated as such and act accordingly. But a late-maturing adolescent who lacks such recognition and acceptance may continue to act more immaturely. Another possibility is that reaching physical maturity early may put adolescents under greater pressure to act like adults, which can prove to be either an advantage or disadvantage. Teenagers who seek out or willingly assume greater responsibility, such as in a part-time or summer job, may benefit by becoming more emotionally mature for their age. However, those who feel pressured into adult roles before they are psychologically ready may react more negatively. Finally, adolescents who reach physical maturity before their peers do or lag behind them are often regarded as different. In some instances individuals may experience special consequences of being an early or late maturer. But for most adolescents, the consequences of being an early or late maturer tend to be relatively short-lived.

Early maturation generally has a more mixed effect for girls than for boys, as seen in the longitudinal study by Dale Blyth and his colleagues (1981), cited earlier. In the sixth and seventh grades, the early-maturing girls felt better about their figures, were more popular with the boys, and dated more frequently than did the late-maturing girls. They were also more independent than late-maturing girls and were more likely to be left alone while their parents were out and to be allowed to babysit. Yet early-maturing girls were less likely to get good grades and were more apt to get into trouble at school than were their peers. However, by the tenth grade, many of the differences between early- and late-maturing girls had disappeared.

Generally, early-maturing girls experience both advantages and disadvantages in their development. First, because of their physical development, early maturers are treated as more mature by adults and peers alike, so they tend to act that way. Then too, the greater acceptance from boys leads to a more active social life, which may help a girl to grow up socially, as long as she is emotionally ready for it. At the same time, some authorities point out that while early-maturing girls enjoy a well-ordered external adjustment, they also suffer from more internal crisis and confusion, mainly because of their shorter period of preparation for the changes of puberty. Yet follow-up studies have shown that by adulthood early-maturing girls exhibit a high level of cognitive mastery and coping skills, partly because of their richer experiences throughout puberty (Livson and Peskin, 1980).

An Early Maturing Girl

I began to fill out early and looked awful. Throughout grade school I was the tallest girl in the class.

I got my first bra in the fifth grade. I was humiliated to death when I was the first of my peers to start my period in the fifth grade. Actually, I was thrilled at entering womanhood since I had seen a film on menstruation at school. But I was disappointed because I couldn't share my experience with my friends.

Luckily, by the seventh grade, most of my friends had reached the same level of physical maturity.

Being an early or a late maturing girl has its characteristic advantages and disadvantages (Ken Karp)

Late-maturing girls also have the characteristic advantages and disadvantages. Because they lag behind other girls in physical development, late-maturing girls are more likely to suffer from anxiety and self-doubt. They worry about whether their bodies will ever develop properly or whether they will be as well endowed sexually as those around them. At the same time, late-maturing girls may enjoy the advantage of growing up with less social pressure than do early-maturing girls. Given the two-year lead of girls over boys, late-maturing girls may emerge from puberty at about the same time as their same-age male peers do, giving them a more favorable opportunity to develop emotionally and socially at the same rate as boys. Late-maturing girls have been described as gregarious, socially poised, and assertive. Yet by the time they reach adulthood, late-maturing girls may have failed to achieve the high level of cognitive mastery and coping skills exhibited by early-maturing girls because of a relatively "safe" adolescence—a longer period of preparation coupled with a less hazardous sense of sexuality in relation to boys (Tanner, 1978).

The psychological effects of being an early or late maturer are generally more marked for boys than for girls; there are, in addition, more advantages for early-maturing boys and more disadvantages for late-maturing ones.

A Late-Maturing Boy

Looking back, it seems to me that I was a late maturer. I never did get really big. It wasn't until college that I grew up.

I wasn't very good in sports or things like that which were very important in high school. The only thing I could do was study, which I did.

Being a late maturer made me more self-conscious and shy, with less self-esteem. But I've overcome most of these in time.

Generally, early-maturing boys enjoy several advantages. First, their physical maturity gives them a competitive edge in sports activities. They are also more attractive to girls their age, who ordinarily mature more rapidly than boys do. Because early-developing boys appear more mature, they are also more likely to be chosen as leaders by their peers and to be expected to behave in a mature way by adults. As a result, early-maturing boys exhibit more positive personality traits than do average- or late-maturing boys. At the same time, early-maturing boys risk certain disadvantages. Because they have a shorter time in which to adjust to their physical maturity, early-maturing boys sometimes fail to grow intellectually and socially, at least through midadolescence. They may appear more settled than do others their age, but sometimes at the price of shutting out adolescent experimentation and the search for personal identity.

In contrast, late-maturing boys tend to suffer far more disadvantages than do early or average-maturing boys. The lag in their physical development puts them at a disadvantage in sports and boy-girl relationships. They are also less popular with their peers and less likely to be chosen as leaders. As a result, late-maturing boys may be plagued by a negative self-concept and feelings of inadequacy, dependency, rejection, and rebelliousness. Yet the relative social neglect suffered by the late-maturing boy, together with the longer period of puberty adjustment, may also lead to greater cognitive mastery and coping skills. That is, having to struggle all the harder to cope with puberty, the late maturer tends to approach new situations with greater intellectual curiosity, social initiative, and exploratory behavior, whereas the early maturer may adopt a more restricted, conventional approach (Livson and Peskin, 1980).

Individual Differences

Some adolescents are more likely than others to be early or late maturers. Generally, those with an athletic build tend to be early maturers and those with a slim build late maturers, though this is not always so. In either case, each adolescent's growth pattern tends to remain consistent, so that a boy who reaches his growth spurt early will also have an earlier-than-average marked voice change (Tanner, 1978). Yet there is considerable variation within individual patterns, as was shown in a study analyzing the peak growth of five skeletal parts, including height, arm and leg length, and shoulder and hip width. The results showed that three-fourths of the boys and girls had unique development in some aspect of their physical growth (Faust, 1983). As one girl said, "I matured early in tallness, but got my period at the average age and was actually a bit late in my breast development."

The experience of puberty also varies among adolescents because of the difference in timing between the various aspects of their overall development. Thus, an eighth grade boy may be an early maturer physically, about average in regard to cognitive functioning, but lag behind his peers socially. Another boy in the same class may be an average maturer physically, slower than average in terms of cognitive functioning, but precocious socially. A lot depends on the particular adolescent.

Furthermore, much of the variation among adolescents in regard to the psychological effects of puberty depends on the interaction between the individual and his or her immediate environment or circumstances. Thus, one's overall development may be vitally affected by factors such as social demands, parental support or the lack of it, peer interaction, educational opportunities, and mentors in the workplace. For instance, an early-maturing girl with an understanding family may develop emotionally and socially all the sooner because of such support. Yet an early-maturing girl from an unhappy home who lacks parental support may be more at risk for problem behaviors because of an undue reliance on her peers, especially when they are into drugs. Similarly, a late-maturing girl from a problem family and without close friends may suffer intensely, whereas a late-maturing girl with a supportive family and friends may actually benefit from a slower emotional and social development. A great deal depends on the adolescent's particular life experiences and how well he or she copes with them.

SUMMARY

Puberty

1. Technically speaking, puberty refers to the attainment of sexual maturity. But the term is also used more broadly to include the entire process of glandular and bodily changes that accompany sexual maturation.

2. The sequence of growth at puberty is similar for most adolescents, though the age of onset as well as the rate and duration of growth varies somewhat from one adolescent to another.

3. The combined effect of the increased hormonal secretions at puberty results in various bodily changes, including changes in the adolescent's height, weight, bone structure, muscles, sex glands, reproductive organs, and secondary sex characteristics.

4. The secular trend toward earlier maturation is thought to be due mainly to better nutrition and appears to be slowing down in recent years.

The Growth Spurt

5. The growth spurt, which consists of dramatic changes in the adolescent's height and weight, occurs, on the average, between 10 and 14 years of age in girls and 12 and 16 years of age in boys.

6. Most of the growth in height during puberty is due to the increase of trunk length rather than leg length, so that adolescents outgrow their jackets before their jeans.

7. The growth spurt is accompanied by skeletal and muscular changes, including the changing ratio of shoulder to hips so noticeable in boys and girls at this age.

Sexual Maturation

8. The usual sequence of sexual maturation in girls is the appearance of breast buds, pigmented pubic hair, accelerated growth of the uterus and vagina, culminating in the menarche—the first menstrual period.

9. Although the menarche is initially felt to be inconvenient and somewhat confusing, most girls do not find it as negative or traumatic as it is ordinarily portrayed.

10. The usual sequence of sexual maturation in boys is the growth of the testes and scrotum, appearance of pubic hair, and enlargement of the penis; the voice begins to deepen toward the end of puberty.

11. Although the boy's first spontaneous ejaculation usually occurs a year or so after the onset of puberty, it normally takes anywhere from one to three years before the boy's ejaculate has sufficient sperm to be fertile.

Psychological Effects of Physical Changes

12. Although the rapid physical changes at puberty indirectly affect the way adolescents see themselves, more than three-fourths of American teenagers enjoy a positive body image. However, the relationship between maturation and body image is somewhat more complex for girls than boys.

13. Being an early or late maturer tends to have more mixed effects on girls than on boys. Early-maturing girls often exhibit greater psychological maturity because of their richer experience throughout puberty, while late-maturing girls may lag in achieving psychological maturity because of their relatively "safe" adolescence.

14. Generally, early-maturing boys enjoy more advantages than disadvantages in their psychological development. At the same time, late-maturing boys may because of their longer period of puberty adjustment acquire greater cognitive mastery and coping skills by early adulthood.

15. Although each individual's growth pattern tends to remain consistent, there is still considerable variation within each adolescent's growth pattern. This happens partly because most adolescents experience unique development in some aspect of their physical growth and also because of the differences in timing between the various aspects of adolescents' overall cognitive and psychological development.

16. The psychological effects of puberty also vary among adolescents because of their interaction with circumstances or their immediate environment—factors such as social demands, parental support or the lack of it, peer relations, and educational and work opportunities.

REVIEW QUESTIONS

1. What is the relationship between puberty and adolescence?
2. Describe the major types of bodily changes that occur during the adolescent's growth spurt.
3. What is meant by the secular trend?
4. What are the major bodily changes that occur during a boy's sexual maturation?
5. What are the major bodily changes that occur during a girl's sexual maturation?
6. How are girls' experiences of the menarche affected by their preparation for this marker event?

7. What is the significance of nocturnal emissions in puberty?
8. To what extent are adolescents satisfied or dissatisfied with their body image?
9. What are some the potential advantages and disadvantages of being an early-maturing girl?
10. What are some of the potential advantages and disadvantages of being an early-maturing boy?

4

Cognitive Development

While adolescents are undergoing obvious changes in their appearance, they are also experiencing important changes in their thinking. The impressive cognitive gains accompanying puberty make it possible for adolescents to think in a more adultlike way. But this doesn't happen overnight. Instead, as they move toward physical and sexual maturation, adolescents gradually become capable to thinking in a more hypothetical, rational, and problem-solving manner. An example is the different ways children and adolescents play the game "Twenty Questions." As you may recall, the purpose of the game is to determine what another person is thinking of, using as few questions as possible. At the outset, children tend to ask for very specific information, such as "Is it Abraham Lincoln?" In contrast, adolescents and adults are likely to adopt a more systematic, problem-solving approach. First, they determine the correct broad category by a process of elimination. Only then do they proceed to ask increasingly more specific questions. For instance, an adolescent may ask, "Is this a person?" If the answer is yes, the player may respond by asking, "Is this person living or dead?" Then the players ask more specific but relevant questions until they get the correct answer. As individuals reach adolescence, this type of thinking becomes increasingly important for dealing with more demanding subjects in school, more critical life choices such as which career one wants, and the intricacies of human relationships.

OVERVIEW OF COGNITIVE DEVELOPMENT

The extensive changes in thinking that occur during adolescence can be understood in different ways. Probably the most familiar way is Jean Piaget's developmental approach, in which qualitative changes in adolescents' thinking normally accompany maturation, aided by learning and the environment. However, as the cognitive perspective gains prominence in psychology, greater attention is being given to alternate ways of understanding the impact of mental processes on human behavior. One of these is social cognition, which deals with how people think about themselves in relation to other people, an important consideration during adolescence. Finally, the extensive use of computers in contemporary life has generated still another way of understanding adolescents' thinking, called the information-processing approach. This is more of an analytical or systematic approach, which views the human mind as a complex system for gathering, interpreting, and using information.

We begin this chapter by explaining Piaget's approach, which traces the emergence of adultlike thinking at adolescence and its importance for learning during this period. Then we discuss selected changes that occur in social cognition during adolescence, including adolescents' egocentricism, social relationships, and social perspective taking. Finally, we will describe the information-processing approach and some of the changes in information-processing abilities that occur during adolescence.

PIAGET'S VIEW OF COGNITIVE DEVELOPMENT

Jean Piaget (1980), more than anyone else, has pioneered in exploring the qualitative changes in intelligence that accompany maturation. Essentially, Piaget holds that lifelong cognitive development results from the interaction of biological and environmental factors and unfolds through a sequence of four stages. Although the genetic and biological factors inherent in the growth process determine the individual's readiness for learning at each stage, the individual's learning experiences and environment affect the rate and extent to which one's intelligence is developed. Piaget's explanation of cognitive development is especially helpful in understanding the distinctive characteristics of adolescent thought, such as the increased ability to think logically and the growing interest in the hypothetical, as well as much of the characteristic behavior at this age.

Piaget's Concept of Intelligence

One of Piaget's basic premises is that intelligence is more a process of understanding reality than a fixed trait. According to Piaget, the most essential characteristic of intelligence is the organizational properties of mental processes as a whole. Through extensive investigation with children and adolescents, Piaget discovered that the organization of mental processes changes predictably with maturation, in such a way that children think differently at the various stages of their development.

Cognitive development consists of a progressive reorganization of mental processes as a result of maturation and experience. That is, no sooner have children constructed a meaningful understanding of reality than they begin experiencing discrepancies between what they know and what their environment is presenting to them. It is the continuing process of resolving such discrepancies that transforms the child's intelligence into the more mature understanding of the adolescent and adult.

Cognitive growth proceeds through the interaction of two complementary processes, *assimilation* and *accommodation*. When children and adolescents

Jean Piaget based many of his findings on clinical interviews with children and adolescents. (Wayne Behling)

encounter something that is reasonably similar to what they already know, it is assimilated to their existing knowledge. When they encounter something that is quite dissimilar from what is already known, they either totally ignore it or change their way of thinking to accommodate their knowledge to the new and unfamiliar. For example, sexual maturation in adolescence brings about considerable accommodation in the way adolescents see themselves and relate to members of the opposite sex. The relationship between these two processes is governed by *equilibration,* a regulatory process inherent in the human organism that facilitates cognitive growth through maintaining a functional balance between assimilation and accommodation. Accordingly, individuals tend to be attracted to situations that are interesting enough to warrant assimilation but familiar enough to justify accommodation. In this way cognitive growth proceeds through a progressive reorganization of mental processes that facilitates adaptation to one's environment.

Piaget holds that the process of cognitive development unfolds in an unchanging sequence of stages, mostly because of the primary role played by heredity or maturation. The respective stages are: (1) *the sensorimotor stage,* 0 to 2 years; (2) *the preoperational stage,* 2 to 7 years; (3) *the concrete operational stage,* 7 to 11 years; and (4) *the formal operational stage,* from 11 to 12 years and up. The ages stated are those at which three-fourths of a given age group can master the relevant stage-related tasks; they have been determined through extensive test-

Table 4-1   Piaget's Four Stages of Cognitive Development

Stage	Approximate Ages	Characteristics of Thinking
Sensorimotor	Birth–2 years	Trial and error learning through sensory and motor behavior
Preoperational	2–7	Use of words, images, and signs to represent objects internally, but thinking remains rigid and perception-bound
Concrete operations	7–11 years	Use of operations—mental activities that are reversible—leads to more organized and rational thinking, to simple concepts such as number, space, and volume
Formal operations	11 or 12 and above	Gradual attainment of abstract, hypothetical, and logical reasoning

ing by Piaget and his followers. However, the rate at which a person progresses from one stage to another varies from one individual to another, mostly because of the different factors that affect the interaction between individuals and their environment including cultural, social class, IQ, and sex differences as well as the individual's learning experiences and social interactions.

Although we are interested primarily in the stage of formal operational thought, it needs to be considered in relation to the overall process of cognitive development. Consequently, we take a brief look at the first three stages of cognitive development in childhood before discussing the final stage of logical, abstract thought that emerges in adolescence. See Table 4-1.

Childhood Thought

Piaget characterizes the infant's cognitive development from birth to about 2 years of age as the sensorimotor stage. At this time, the infant possesses only rudimentary intelligence and functions mostly through trial-and-error learning. During the first six months or so, the infant learns through the senses, by sucking, touching, hearing, and seeing things. In the latter part of the first year, the infant begins to use the muscles more and learns through crawling, climbing, and hitting things. Then, during the second year, the child begins coordinating these sensorimotor abilities better and actively experiments with his or her environment.

The maturation of mental processes and the increasing use of language enables the child to enter the preoperational stage of thought, roughly during the preschool years from about 2 to 7 years of age. *Preoperational* here means essentially prerational thought; that is, the child is thinking in the general sense of using symbols to represent external events in internal, mental processes, but it is not rational, directed thought like that of adults. Instead, throughout this period, childhood thought is characteristically rigid and perception bound, such that objects are equated with their surface appearances. Psychological realities like fantasies and dreams are easily substituted for physical realities. The child also sees events related in an associational rather than a causal way; that is, two events that accidentally occur at the same time are seen as causally related, even though they are not. Consequently throughout this period, the child's thinking remains highly egocentric and lacking in concepts, though less so with the gradual transition to the next stage of thinking.

With the further maturation of the brain and nervous system, aided by learning experiences, the child enters the concrete operational stage of thought, roughly from about 7 to 11 years of age. At this stage, the child is able to think in a more flexible, abstract way, at least in relation to concrete objects and situations. For example, the child is also able to engage in what Piaget calls *conservation*, the ability to see that certain properties remain constant despite changes in appearance. This results in the emergence of simple concepts or elementary abstractions, first in relation to subjects like number, and then gradually in relation to more complex subjects like space, time, and volume. All of this makes it possible for the older child to take part in more sophisticated learning both at school and home.

Adolescent Thought

Beginning at about 11 to 12 years of age on the average, adolescents enter the formal operational stage of thinking, provided, Piaget (1980) says, they are given the necessary cognitive stimulation. Here, the term *formal* emphasizes the *form* rather than the *content* of thought. In other words, adolescents are now capable of thinking entirely mentally or in terms of pure abstraction, as contrasted with the physically oriented concepts of concrete operational thought. Adolescents can manipulate ideas and symbols in a more abstract way, as in formal scientific and logical thought, from which the label for this stage is derived.

Two essential characteristics of thought at this stage are increased possibility and flexibility of thinking. As a result, adolescents tend to become more hypothetical in their thinking, creating possibilities in their minds. They can engage in abstract, imaginative thinking, with more of the "if-then" quality characteristic of artistic and scientific endeavors. Also, adolescents can distinguish between reality and their thoughts about reality. They become more aware of their mental processes, often "thinking about thinking" itself. The increased flexibility of thought enables adolescents to combine and reverse various mental operations in such a way that they can engage in more sophisticated adultlike thought. They can grasp more complex relationships. Also, they can comprehend all aspects of a problem and deal with it systematically, as in logical reasoning, problem-solving thought, and scientific inquiry.

An example is the way adolescents approach the pendulum problem shown in Figure 4-1. The problem is to discover which factors affect the pendulum's oscillatory speed, i.e., the speed at which it swings back and forth. The factors to be manipulated are the length of the string, weight, height from which the weight is released, and the force of the push. Adolescents who have reached formal thought tend to experiment systematically with the various factors. They soon discover that the height of the drop and force of the push have no effect on

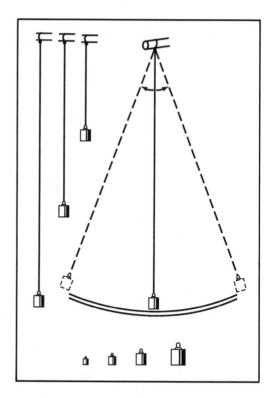

Figure 4-1 The Pendulum Problem. The pendulum problem uses a simple apparatus consisting of a string, which can be shortened or lengthened, and a set of varying weights. The other factors that at first might be considered relevant are the height of the release point and the force of the push given by the subject.

Source: *The Growth of Logical Thinking From Childhood to Adolescence,* Barbel Inhelder and Jean Piaget. Translated by Anne Parson and Stanley Milgram. Copyright © 1958 Basic Books, Inc. Reprinted by permission of Basic Books, a division of HarperCollins Publishers, Inc.

the speed of the pendulum. Once they discover that "it's got to be this or that" (length of string or weight), they experiment with each of these factors independently. A common error is the assumption that the weight makes a difference. However, once adolescents have discovered that the length of string makes a difference in speed, they usually shorten or lengthen the string several times to confirm this observation.

The attainment of formal operational thought is not an all or nothing event. Instead, it tends to emerge in two substages. Between the ages of 11 or 12 and 14 or 15 years of age, adolescents reach the first substage in which they exhibit *almost* full formal functioning. Early adolescents can handle many aspects of formal thought, but their thinking is still crude. Even when they reach the correct answer, they can't always explain why. However, by about 14 or 15 years of age, adolescents enter the second substage of formal thought, in which they exercise formal thinking more fully. Now they can formulate more elaborate concepts and offer systematic proof of their assertions, mostly because of greater awareness of the methods of logical thought. Equally important is the adolescent's justification or explanation of how he or she arrived at the correct answer (Muuss, 1988).

Also, formal thought tends to develop unevenly across different areas of

With the emergence of formal thought adolescents begin to think in a more systematic, problem-solving manner, as in scientific inquiry. (Laima Druskis)

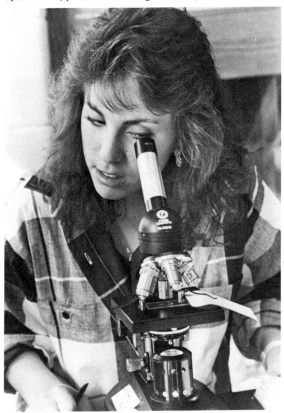

knowledge. For instance, a high school student might demonstrate formal thinking in regard to mathematics, while exhibiting less advanced thought in literature. Piaget points out that the differential development of cognitive abilities with increasing age is due largely to differences in personal interests, motivation, and stimulation. At the same time, many of Piaget's illustrations of formal thought are couched in scientific terms mostly because he has tested his theory in the adolescent range primarily with content material in mathematics and the sciences. He has shown little concern with how formal thought manifests itself in artistic and literary endeavors.

ADOLESCENT THOUGHT AND LEARNING

The emergence of formal thought, or the lack of it, becomes a significant factor in adolescent development. Adolescents begin to think and learn differently in school. And they begin to think about themselves and their relationships with others differently as well. Here we explore the impact of formal thought on adolescents' studies. In the next section we describe the effects of such thinking on adolescents' social cognition.

The Developmental Gap

Because not everyone reaches the stage of formal thought at the same age, we would expect to find some high school students who have not yet attained the capacity for abstract thought and logical reasoning. Now studies confirm what many teachers and students have long suspected—that a large proportion of high school students are not ready for high school-level work.

A comprehensive study of secondary school students' ability to utilize abstract thought was conducted by John Renner and Donald Stafford (1976). Their subjects were 588 students in grades 7 through 12 in 25 public schools in Oklahoma. Schools were randomly selected within different sectors of the state to include rural, urban, and ghetto populations. Students were interviewed on six types of Piagetian tasks designed to assess their abilities in concrete and formal operational thought. The results showed that only about 10 percent of the students had reached the level of formal thinking, and not all of those had fully attained formal thought. Even by the senior year, only one-third of the students had reached formal thought, with the remaining two-thirds still relying on concrete operational thought. See Table 4-2. Such studies confirm that many students this age are consolidating the gains of concrete thinking. Most have not begun using formal thought.

Such studies also raise the question whether everyone is potentially capable of attaining formal thought. In spite of all the critical evidence, Piaget main-

Table 4-2   Distribution of Students at the Level of Concrete Operational Thought

Grade	Sample Size	Percentage of Sample at Level of Concrete Operational Thought
7	96	83
8	108	77
9	94	82
10	94	73
11	99	72
12	97	66

Source: J. W. Renner and D. G. Stafford, "The Operational Levels of Secondary School Students," in J. W. Renner et al., eds., *Research, Teaching, and Learning with the Piaget Model* (Norman, OK: University of Oklahoma Press, 1976), p. 97, Copyright 1976 University of Oklahoma Press, Publishing Division of the University.

tains that "all normal individuals are capable of reaching the level of formal operation" (1980, p. 75), as long as their environment provides the necessary cognitive stimulation. Piaget readily admits that most of his subjects come from "the better schools of Geneva," and that his conclusions are based on a "privileged population." But Dulit (1972), utilizing Piaget's approach, claims that only about 20 to 35 percent of his group of older average adolescents had reached full formal thought. Even among a group of scientifically gifted students, the figure was only 75 percent. Reviewing the relevant literature on the subject, other authorities such as Kuhn (1979) cite the widely demonstrated estimate according to which only about 50 percent of the adult population actually fully attain formal thought. Consequently, it may be more realistic to view formal thought as a cognitive potential for people that sometimes becomes actualized. However, formal thought is far from being normal or typical among all adolescents (Muuss, 1988).

Facilitating Formal Thought

Although Piaget acknowledges that the *speed* at which adolescents develop formal thought is affected by their learning environment, he retains a maturational bias with the emphasis on the individual's natural readiness for learning. Thus, even when children and adolescents are guided to the correct answers and given explicit explanations for the same, Piaget believes they tend to return to their own level of cognitive functioning as indicated by earlier responses rather than show any generalized cognitive growth transcending their earlier levels. Apparently, the knowledge that children and adolescents might acquire before they develop the corresponding cognitive structures either disappears very rapidly, or, if retained, is kept as rote memorization without real understanding (Muuss, 1988). However, an increasing number of critics disagree with Piaget on this point. They contend there is a difference between the spontaneous demonstration of formal thought and evidence of such thinking after appropriate intervention designed to facilitate it. It is not that formal skills can be taught directly. But adolescents' thinking can be advanced by an enriched learning environment, especially one in which a reasonable degree of cognitive disequilibrium or cognitive conflict stimulates rational, problem-solving thinking. Thus, many educators are discovering that adolescents' development of formal thought may be shaped more significantly by their learning environment than Piaget acknowledges (Neimark, 1982).

Individual Differences

So far we've seen that not everyone attains formal thought by adolescence, but that many more individuals could do so with appropriate intervention. At the same time, the discrepancy between the potential for formal thought and its attainment raises questions about the wide variations in cognitive development

Youths' thinking may develop in many different directions, depending on their special interests and fields of knowledge. (Laima Druskis)

among individuals. Many authorities hold that because Piaget's primary concern has been to demonstrate the existence of universal and consistent patterns of cognitive development, he has paid little attention to how this process is affected by variables such as intelligence, socioeconomic class, age, sex, and individual differences—all of which are of greater interest to developmental psychologists and educators. Many of them feel Piaget fails to take sufficient account of individual differences in cognitive development (Muuss, 1988).

Realizing that most people do not attain formal thought, Dulit (1972) has formulated the branch model of cognitive development. In this view, progress through Piaget's first three stages of thought occurs fairly consistently across different environments. However, as children reach adolescence, their thinking becomes more sensitive to their learning environments such that they have access to alternate cognitive paths. Thus, thinking may develop in many different directions, depending on people's special career interests and fields of knowledge. In Dulit's view, formal thought is seen as intermediate between the earlier concrete stage, when individuals entertain specific thought about universal skills, and the reasoning that subsequently develops in the pursuit of one's special talents, such as literature, business, and law. Such a model provides greater allowance for the inconsistencies in cognitive abilities found among adolescents.

People engaged in highly creative endeavors, in particular, may exhibit the faculty that Arlin (1975) calls "problem-finding" thought, which is characteristic of creative thinking and discovery. In contrast to the "problem-solving" thought of the formal operational stage, problem-finding thought requires a more advanced level of reasoning in which individuals generate questions from poorly defined problems, formulate new questions, and discover new problems. Arlin holds that problem-finding thinking might constitute a fifth stage beyond formal thought, suggesting that the progressive changes in cognitive structures may continue into adulthood. Interestingly, while Arlin found that all of the college seniors who exhibited problem-finding thought had attained formal thinking, not everyone who had reached formal thought progressed to problem-finding thinking.

Even for the majority of adolescents and adults who are not engaged in highly creative endeavors, much less in the fields of science and mathematics so familiar to Piaget's research, formal thinking may not be the most useful type of adult thought. According to this view, as individuals reach adulthood in most cultures, they become increasingly involved in practical concerns that in turn help to shape their thought. That is, individuals assume greater responsibility for themselves and invest themselves more fully in their work and family lives. Largely because of such experiences, adults' thinking tends to become more pragmatic, specialized, and reality-oriented (Labouvie-Vief, 1982). This may be especially evident among people who are preoccupied with the mundane affairs necessary for survival in everyday life. But even those who are highly trained in formal thought and use it in their work, soon learn to put such thought in perspective, employing a wide range of cognitive abilities to deal with people and problems in everyday life.

CHANGES IN SOCIAL COGNITION DURING ADOLESCENCE

The emergence of formal thought, or the lack of it, not only affects the way adolescents learn at school; it also has an important impact on their personal and social lives. As a result, increasing attention is being given to a new area of study labeled social cognition, the way adolescents think about themselves, their relationships with others, and their participation in groups and larger society (Flavell, 1981). Changes in social cognition are so pervasive that they affect many of the topics covered in the remaining chapters of this book, including parent-adolescent relationships, friendships, peer groups, self-concept, and moral reasoning. In this section, we focus on several aspects of social cognition not covered elsewhere, such as egocentricism, social relationships, and social perspective taking.

Egocentrism

The emergence of formal thought at early to mid adolescence is accompanied by a marked increase in *egocentrism,* an inadequate differentiation between one's own thoughts and feelings and those of others. Being temporarily overwhelmed by the heightened self-consciousness and abstract thought at this stage, adolescents become noticeably more self-centered. The effects of adolescent egocentrism are spelled out in two related concepts—the *imaginary audience* and the *personal fable*—which account for a wide variety of typical adolescent behaviors (Elkind, 1978).

One consequence of adolescent egocentrism is the failure to differentiate between one's own thoughts and those of others, which can lead to the belief that others are preoccupied with one's thoughts and behaviors. As a result, adolescents feel as if they are constantly on stage anticipating the reactions of an "imaginary audience." It is an audience in that adolescents feel they are the focus of attention, but it is imaginary in the sense that others are actually not that concerned with the adolescent. Anticipating the reactions of this imaginary audience helps to account for the heightened self-consciousness and excessive concern for one's appearance at this age. The boy or girl who stands in front of the mirror combing his or her hair for an hour is probably thinking of how he or she will look to others. Preoccupation with others' reactions also helps to explain why *shame* rather than *guilt* is the characteristic emotional reaction—that is, reaction to an audience—at adolescence. This also explains adolescents' intense desire for privacy and their shyness or reluctance to reveal themselves. Intense awareness of others' reactions also causes adolescents to overreact to criticism and blame, as every parent has discovered. One of the most common manifestations of the imaginary audience is the adolescents' anticipation of how others will react to their deaths, hopefully with a belated recognition of their good qualities.

A complementary process to the imaginary audience is the *over*differentiation of one's feelings from those of others, leading adolescents to exaggerate their own uniqueness. Perhaps partly because they feel that they are so important to many people, adolescents tend to regard themselves as more special and unique than they really are. This is known as the personal fable, a subjective story they tell themselves that is not true. The concept of the personal fable helps to account for the typical adolescent phrase "You don't understand," which every parent has heard at one time or another. Evidence of the personal fable is also prominent in adolescent diaries, in which they express feelings that "nobody understands me" and that their loves and frustrations are of universal significance. The belief in their uniqueness often becomes a conviction that they will not die, leading some adolescents to feel they are not subject to the dangers or

"It Won't Happen to Me"

According to Peter Blos (1979), part of the personal fable is the belief in one's own indestructibility. In turn, this gives adolescents a false sense of power and invincibility. This attitude may be expressed in the following convictions:

Accidents will never happen to me.
Alcohol addiction will never happen to me.
AIDS will never happen to me.
An unwanted pregnancy will never happen to me.
Divorce will never happen to us.
Death will never happen to me.

In one study, students were given actuarial tables on life expectancies and asked to estimate how long they expected to live. Most students estimated that they would live ten to twenty years longer than their projected ages. When asked to explain why, typical remarks were "It won't happen to me," "I'm not like other people," and "I'm unique" (Snyder, 1984).

While a modest sense of our uniqueness may help us to sustain a zestful, optimistic outlook on life, an unrealistic belief in our own indestructibility impairs our judgment in regard to health and safety habits, sometimes with devastating consequences.

fate commonly suffered by others. Consequently, they may fail to use their seat belts, drive too fast, or dispense with contraceptives out of the conviction that "it won't happen to me." The personal fable is also illustrated in the adolescents' search for superhuman powers, whether in ESP, romantic love, technology, superstitions, or religion.

Piaget observes that the egocentrism of early adolescence generally declines as formal thought becomes firmly established in the late teens. At this point, adolescents have begun to modify their imaginary audience in the direction of actual peer groups, increasingly recognizing the difference between their own thoughts and the thoughts and reactions of others. The personal fable, though perhaps never entirely overcome, is also progressively modified through intimate exchanges with others. At the same time, other investigators have shown that the overall picture of cognitive and social maturity is somewhat more complex than pictured by Piaget. Enright, Lapsley, and Slukla (1979) administered several instruments to sixty students, twenty each in the sixth grade, eighth grade, and college in order to assess different aspects of adolescent egocentrism, including the imaginary audience, personal fable, and a general focusing on the self. Their results showed that different aspects of egocentrism decline at varying rates in adolescence. That is, whereas the notion of the imaginary audience declines significantly at each age level, the notion of personal fable declines in a much more gradual way. But contrary to expectations, the general focusing on self shows a significant increase with age. Part of the explanation for this is the adolescent's increasing concern with understanding and solving conflicts that come with late adolescence. The increase in self-awareness without the self-conscious expectation of others' reactions (imaginary

As the egocentrism of early adolescence declines, youths begin to modify their imaginary audience in the direction of actual peer groups, increasingly recognizing the difference between their thoughts and those of others. (Laima Druskis)

audience) and with less insistence on one's own uniqueness (personal fable) most likely represents an *un*self-conscious striving for betterment of self in the college years.

Social Relationships

During this early period adolescents generally become more perceptive of others and form somewhat more realistic impressions of them. Partly because of the faculty of formal thought, adolescents are able to use a wider variety of categories in understanding people, including the implicit or commonsense theories of personality that emerge at this age (Barenboim, 1985). That is, adolescents intuitively construct a generalized idea of what makes people think and act the way they do. Then they make inferences about other people's thoughts and feelings and compare their present and past behavior. They can also distinguish between people's characteristic behaviors and situational influences on them. For instance, an adolescent encounters a store clerk who is friendly one time but abrupt the next. Unlike children, who might simply view this person as rude, adolescents may interpret such inconsistency in different ways. They too might regard the clerk as a rude person. But they also might realize the clerk is a friendly person who is simply having a bad day.

Adolescents also engage in a great deal of social comparisons with their peers. They constantly monitor their behavior and compare themselves to their friends, striving to affirm themselves without becoming so different or similar to their friends that they risk criticism or rejection. The process of social comparison becomes a major way of establishing one's identity at this age (Seltzer, 1989). One particularly interesting consideration in social comparison is hypocrisy. Now that adolescents can distinguish between the ideal and actual, they become more adept at perceiving the discrepancy between what a person says and what he/she does. But as with adults, adolescents may be quicker to perceive hypocrisy in others than in themselves. For instance, an adolescent may belong to an environmental group that opposes large companies that pollute the air and water. Yet that same youth may fail to realize he is among the chief offenders whenever he litters the hallways and streets with discarded cups and candy wrappers.

Adolescents are also better able to cope with the anxiety that arises from relationships, mostly through the use of defense mechanisms, that is, automatic, unconscious ways of defending themselves against psychological threat. At this age, a common defense mechanism is *intellectualization* in which unacceptable feelings are hidden behind a highly intellectual but heated discussion on the subject in question. Another characteristic defense at adolescence is *rationalization,* seen in the adolescents' readiness to "explain" away socially unacceptable behavior such as being late for work. Still another defense seen at this age is *fantasy*, the tendency to resolve unfulfilled desires through imaginative action. Although fantasy is not in itself defensive, it easily becomes so when unrealistic aspirations and romantic longings are substituted for action, as they often are at this age.

Changes in social cognition may help to bring about, though by no means guarantee, the attainment of greater socialization and social competence. Adolescents are better able to understand and fulfil a variety of social roles, shifting easily between their roles as students, friends, and workers. Those who become socially competent usually have access to a wide social support network. Also, they may employ a greater variety of social skills, such as anticipating the consequences of their actions as well as those of others, managing interpersonal conflict, and trying to understand other people's views.

Social Perspective Taking

One of the most valuable social skills is the ability to become aware of other people's viewpoints and take these into consideration along with one's own views in dealing with people. Robert Selman (1980), who has studied this process, holds that the ability of social perspective taking tends to emerge in a given sequence of stages throughout childhood and adolescence. Such growth comes partly because of maturation and parallels one's overall cognitive development as in Piaget's theory, to which Selman's views are related. However, Selman puts a greater emphasis on the role of experience and learning, such that advances in social perspective taking depend heavily on the individual's experiences with others, including appropriate social stimulation and education.

Selman has investigated the development of social reasoning by telling children and adolescents stories that illustrate a challenge or a problem demanding a response. Here is one of the stories Selman uses:

> Tom is thinking of what to buy his friend Mike for his birthday. By chance, Tom meets Mike on the street and learns that Mike is upset because his dog Pepper has been lost for two weeks. In fact, Mike is so upset he tells Tom, "I never want to look at another dog again." Later, while walking home Tom passes a store that has a sale on puppies. Only two are left and those will be gone soon. What should Tom do? What would you do if you were Tom? Why?

Like Piaget, Selman is more interested in the *reasons* adolescents give for their answers than the content of their responses. We'll give some characteristic responses to this sample story as a means of illustrating adolescents' reasoning in the various stages of social perspective taking. See Table 4-3.

Stage 0. *Egocentric, undifferentiated social perspective taking* (age 3 to 6). At this stage, which corresponds roughly to Piaget's preoperational thought, children cannot distinguish clearly between their own interpretation of a situation and another person's point of view. Nor can they realize that their own view may not be the correct one. An example would be the child who responds to the sample story by saying, "I'd buy him a puppy because I like puppies." This is a simple, egocentric response, showing the child can't distinguish between his views and those of the other person.

Table 4-3 Selman's Five Stages of Social Perspective Taking

Stage	Approximate ages	Characteristic social reasoning
0. Egocentric, undifferentiated social perspective taking	3–6 years	Children cannot distinguish clearly between their views and others' views.
1. Differentiated, subjective perspective taking	5–9 years	Although children realize others may have different views than their own, they are unable to understand such views accurately.
2. Self-reflective, reciprocal perspective taking	7–12 years	Older children and preadolescents can reflect on their thoughts and feelings from another person's viewpoint, but they cannot hold both perspectives simultaneously.
3. Third-person or mutual perspective taking	10–15 years	Adolescents can step outside their own viewpoints and those of others and assume the perspective of a neutral third person.
4. In-depth and societal perspective taking	Adolescence to adulthood	Individuals can now understand their thoughts and behaviors from a more abstract level that is capable of a generalized, societal perspective.

Stage 1. *Differentiated, subjective perspective taking* (age 5 to 9). Now children begin to realize that others may have different views than their own. But they are unable to understand such views accurately. An example would be the child who says, "If Mike says he doesn't want a dog, then I won't give him one because he'll get mad." This is a subjective response because the person fails to realize that Mike's attitude might be affected by the giver's intentions. Such thinking reflects the transitional phase from preoperational to concrete thought.

Stage 2. *Self-reflective, reciprocal perspective taking* (age 7 to 12). Older children and preadolescents can reflect on their own thoughts and feelings from another person's perspective. But they cannot hold both perspectives simultaneously, as in the next stage. An example would be the following response to the sample story: "Even though Mike says he doesn't want a dog, he may change his mind when he receives a cuddly little puppy." This type of response shows awareness that Mike's attitude might be affected by his realization of the other person's intentions in giving the puppy. Such thinking reflects the usage of simple concepts as in Piaget's concrete operational thought.

Stage 3. *Third-person or mutual perspective taking* (age 10 to 15). Adolescents are able to step outside their own viewpoints and those of others and assume the perspective of a neutral third person. Thus, friendships become more than mutual back scratching and conflicts may be viewed in terms of mutual differences. An example would be an adolescent who responds to the sample story by saying, "Mike will understand what I'm trying to do. He'll realize that the best way to get over losing his dog is having a new puppy to take care of." Such thinking shows awareness of both adolescents' perspectives simultaneously and that Mike is capable of appreciating Tom's intentions in giving the puppy. This type of thought tends to occur in the transitional phase that appears in the early part of the formal operational stage.

Stage 4. *In-depth and societal perspective taking* (adolescence to adulthood). During late adolescence individuals may reach a higher and more advanced level of abstraction and social perspective taking which involves the coordination of all possible third-person perspectives—A societal perspective. The adolescent now realizes that each person can consider the shared point of view of the "generalized other" or group consensus. In turn, this leads to more accurate communication and problem-solving with others. At this level, in regard to the sample story, gift giving is understood and appreciated within the larger social perspective and includes the meaning and thought associated with gift giving and receiving. Stage 4 of social perspective taking corresponds to Piaget's formal thought. But because some people do not attain the level of formal thought, all adolescents or adults do not reach this final stage of social cognition.

Selman emphasizes that the progression to higher levels of social perspective taking depends greatly on the appropriate social experiences, with the age ranges associated with the various stages being approximate only. For instance, in a sample of ninty-two males and females of varying ages, he found that the subgroup of 15 to 18 year olds exhibited stage 3 thought of mutual perspective taking, whereas those in their twenties were more likely to be at the fourth stage of societal perspective taking. At all stages, males and females tend to function at about the same level of social reasoning. However, individuals from severely dysfunctional families or emotionally deprived social backgrounds may lag in their social understanding. Also, social awareness develops unevenly across different areas of social cognition, such that an adolescent may have a reasonably mature understanding of friendship among like-minded people but lag in regard to his or her ability to manage conflicts with people from different social and cultural backgrounds (Selman et al., 1986).

THE INFORMATION-PROCESSING APPROACH TO COGNITIVE DEVELOPMENT

During the past decade, still another perspective on cognition has emerged, largely as a result of the widespread work with computers. This is called the information-processing approach. We'll give a brief overview of this approach and then describe several of the important changes in information-processing abilities that occur during adolescence.

The Information-processing Approach

Essentially, the information-processing approach is a systematic, psychological approach to studying cognition, based on different assumptions than Piaget's developmental theory. The human mind is viewed as a complex system for gathering, interpreting, and using information. Information processing is broken down into very small parts that are then studied empirically. Scientists hope to identify which components are most essential to a particular type of reasoning, as a means of improving our ability to process information.

Human information processing is often compared to that of computers, which have become widely used in society. A helpful distinction can be made between the hardware and software aspects of computers. In computers, hardware refers to the physical equipment, such as the memory, console, monitor, and printer. Software refers to the programs used for storing and retrieving information. Similarly, adolescents' mental activities involve both hardware and software components. The adolescent's brain and nervous system constitutes the hardware. And the software consists of the adolescent's intentions, plans, mental strategies, and goals that activate the mental hardware. Cognitive development involves changes in both dimensions. But because the brain and nervous system are relatively well developed by late adolescence, much of the improvement in information processing capacity is thought to result from experience and learning.

Changes During Adolescence

Although this not a developmental approach, some studies have shown age-related changes in cognition. Studies involving children and adolescents suggest that several basic changes in information-processing abilities occur during this period, including (1) faster, automatic processing; (2) more complex, organized thought; (3) greater knowledge; and (4) improved memory capacity.

1. *Faster, automatic processing of information.* Human memory involves two different strategies for encoding or processing information into the memory system—effortful processing and automatic processing. For instance, whenever we meet a new person, we make a special effort to learn the person's name and often do something to retain it, such as repeating it in conversation or writing it down. This is effortful processing. At the same time, while we're talking with this person, we're also taking in various impressions, such as the person's appearance, tone of voice, and body language. Much of this information is processed automatically. In fact, the more information we can process automatically, the more energy and time we can spend talking with the person. The distinction between effortful and automatic processing is especially relevant to adolescence because individuals this age are able to go through the steps of selecting, encoding, and storing information more quickly than they did at younger ages. Because the brain and nervous system are largely mature at this age, it is unlikely that the increased speed is due entirely to biological growth. A more likely explanation involves the encoding strategies used, with adolescents relying more on automatic processing (Flavell, 1985). In turn, such gains in speed may help adolescents to function more competently in a time-oriented society. For instance, a student who carries a heavy schedule in school must be able to read, understand, and retain information efficiently in order to keep up with her academic work and have time for an outside job and social life. Similarly, when driving one must be able to read and understand signs quickly.

2. *More complex, organized thought.* An even more striking difference between children and adolescents is the latter's ability to think in a more complex, organized way that enables them to engage in logical, problem-solving activity. It appears that adolescents not only have a greater awareness of their minds or cognitive processes as a whole, but they are able to employ different mental strategies more selectively. A case in point involves Robert Sternberg's (1985) distinction between the "executive" learning strategies and the "performance" strategies of the mind. The executive strategies are used in selecting which performance components are needed for the task at hand, in monitoring ourselves throughout the process of carrying it out, and evaluating the consequences. For instance, a student in an English composition class is asked to write a short paper in class on some memorable experience from the past summer. As the student begins to think of all the possibilities, various procedural questions arise, such as

"what is my most interesting experience? Which is the easiest to write about? Which one is most appropriate for this assignment?" Once a decision is made at this level, the student may begin to write. However, if the student encounters difficulty or resistance in expressing himself, he may review his initial choice. After he has finished the paper, he may read it over to see how well he has communicated what he intended to.

Such flexible, sophisticated thought becomes more important as adolescents face more complex subjects in high school. Also, such thinking is useful in handling the intricate problems of social relationships; in balancing the various aspects of one's life at school, home, and work; and in making important life choices. While Piaget's developmental approach stresses the maturational readiness for this type of thinking at adolescence, i.e., formal thinking, Sternberg holds that the executive learning strategies can be taught to a greater degree, though not as easily or as directly by instruction alone as performance components can.

3. *Greater knowledge.* There's an old adage, "The more you know, the faster you can learn," which suggests that knowledge itself might play an important role in processing information. Accordingly, as adolescents come to know more than children do by virtue of their more extensive learning experiences, they can learn more rapidly. Knowledge may facilitate learning in several ways. Because people tend to "see" what they are prepared to see, knowledge may sensitize adolescents such that they pay more selective attention to things children would ordinarily miss. Then too, knowledge provides the necessary terms, concepts, and factual data to which new information can be related more readily. However, studies suggest that this principle applies mostly to the possession of relevant knowledge. For instance, students who have a greater knowledge of a given field, such as chemistry, are better able to draw relationships between the various concepts in chemistry than are people less knowledgeable in this field. By the same token, professional chemists or experts in the field, partly because of their greater knowledge of chemistry, have more pathways to follow than novices do (Flavell, 1985).

4. *Improved memory capacity.* In order to become useful, information must be remembered long enough to undergo additional processing. The initial act of paying attention or selecting information from the variety of stimuli available to us is labeled "short-term memory." This is our momentary attention span. The additional process of encoding information so that it can be stored for long-term retrieval is called "long-term memory." Many studies have confirmed that adolescents have greater memory capacity than children do in both types of memory. For instance, adolescents are superior to children in matters such as their attention span and use of selective attention, e.g., being able to concentrate on their studies while a radio is playing in the background. In a series of studies, Sternberg (1980, 1987) and his colleagues compared the problem-solving abilities of various age groups, including third, sixth, and ninth graders and college students. The major difference occurred between the younger adolescents in the third and sixth grades and the older youth in the ninth grade and college. Younger children often stop processing information before they have considered all the necessary steps to solve the problem. By contrast, older youth were more likely to persist until they had processed all the information needed to solve the task. Sternberg reasons that the older youth are more successful at such tasks because they can hold more information in their immediate memory.

Even more important gains occur in long-term memory, with adolescents being able to encode, store, and retrieve more information for long-term use. One explanation may be that long-term memory involves the entire process of selective attention, thinking, and interpretation as well as the mechanisms of memory itself. For instance, the better students understand something in terms of their existing knowledge and themselves, the better they can retain it (Kuiper and Rogers, 1979). In turn, the improved memory capacity becomes an integral part of the adolescent's ability to process information more quickly and automatically, and to think in a more complex, organized way than children do.

Implications for Cognitive Development

It is difficult to evaluate such contributions to cognitive development, mostly because the information-processing viewpoint is so new. However, this approach, along with the more inclusive field of cognitive psychology, does broaden and enrich our perspective on cognitive development. A basic goal is to create a scientifically valid knowledge base for educational theory and practice. At present, the information-processing approach rivals, and perhaps exceeds, the developmental approach in studying cognitive changes in children and adolescents. There are at least several important implications of this approach for cognitive development in adolescence.

First, cognitive development is significantly affected by adolescents' learning experiences and educational environment. Although Piaget acknowledges the necessary role of cognitive stimulation, he clearly subordinates learning to the maturational process, emphasizing adolescents' readiness for learning. In contrast, the information-processing approach stresses the learning process and the potential for improving cognitive development through the use of more effective learning strategies. Such an approach does not rule out the maturational basis of learning. But investigators oriented to the information-processing approach tend to study the physical basis of learning in a more empirical and scientific way, as seen in the experimental studies of the brain and memory. The result is a more scientifically differentiated knowledge aimed at identifying the specific cognitive components associated with different types of reasoning. Thus, the information-processing approach may help to identity *how* adolescents think in more advanced ways as well as *what* makes their thinking more advanced and refined than that of children.

Second, formal thought is associated with adolescents' use of more complex, better-

organized information-processing strategies. Some empirical studies have shown a positive correlation between formal operational thinking and the use of more complex, organized information-processing strategies (Wyatt and Geis, 1978). Thus, by studying the cognitive components of more organized information-processing, investigators hope to devise intervention strategies that might facilitate formal thought. Even when investigators discover discrepancies between Piaget's theory and adolescents' actual thought patterns, they often do not deny the existence of such characteristics as formal thought, imaginary audience, and personal fable, but hold that the developmental basis for such thinking remains unidentified (Buis and Thompson, 1989). In both instances, the information-processing approach aims to identify the appropriate cognitive components involved.

Finally, effective teaching and learning involve a knowledge of the learning process as well as the subject-specific knowledge being imparted. Traditionally, the educational focus has been on the content of knowledge imparted and intelligence testing as a means of assessing students' capacity for learning. In contrast, the information-processing approach distinguishes between adolescents' knowledge and the process by which it is acquired, holding that both are interrelated. Thus, investigators in this area are studying how students actually learn and how we may improve instruction based on this knowledge. They hold that advances in the psychology of learning need to be considered in the redesign of intelligence and achievement tests. Furthermore, a number of studies have already demonstrated the effectiveness of information-processing strategies for improving academic performance in the basic areas of reading, writing, and science (Glaser and Takanishi, 1986). All of this implies that a fundamental goal of education is to help students learn *how* to learn and that learning is an active process that continues throughout one's entire lifespan.

SUMMARY

Piaget's View of Cognitive Development

1. We began the chapter by explaining Piaget's view of cognitive development which emphasizes the qualitative changes in intelligence accompanying maturation.
2. Piaget holds that cognitive development normally unfolds in an unchanging sequence of four stages, culminating in the attainment of the level of formal thought at adolescence.
3. Adolescents who have reached the stage of formal thought are capable of thinking in a more abstract, hypothetical, and logical manner.

Adolescent Thought and Learning

4. At the same time, surveys have shown that a large proportion of high school students have not reached the stage of formal thinking, and there is a notable gap between the average student's cognitive abilities and the typical school curriculum.
5. However, studies suggest that the use of appropriate teaching strategies such as coaching and discovery learning may facilitate the attainment of formal thought, especially among those who have reached midadolescence.

6. The discrepancy between the potential for formal thought and the widespread lag in achieving it suggests that Piaget's theory fails to take sufficient account of individual differences in cognitive development.

Changes in Social Cognition During Adolescence

7. The emergence of formal thought also has an important impact on adolescents' social cognition—the way they think about themselves and their relationships with others.

8. The characteristic egocentrism that accompanies the emergence of formal thought may be seen in the adolescent's experience of the imaginary audience and personal fable, which tend to diminish with experience and maturation.

9. Adolescents also come to perceive people in a more refined and realistic way and to engage in a great deal of social comparisons with their peers during this period.

10. The ability of social perspective taking tends to emerge in a sequence of stages not unlike that of formal thought. However, Selman emphasizes that such ability depends much more on the individual's social experience than on the degree of maturity.

Information-processing Approach to Cognitive Development

11. This is a systematic approach in which the psychological components of information processing are studied empirically.

12. Several important changes in information-processing abilities tend to occur during adolescence, including faster, more automatic processing; more complex, organized thought; greater knowledge; and improved memory capacity.

13. The information-processing approach broadens our perspective on cognition, confirming some aspects of the developmental approach and challenging others, but in both instances helping to identify *what* changes occur, as well as *why* and *how* they occur.

REVIEW QUESTIONS

1. How does formal thinking differ from concrete operational thought?
2. In what sense does the high school curriculum presuppose formal thought?
3. To what extent does the attainment of formal thinking depend on the adolescent's learning experiences?
4. Which teaching strategies promote the development of formal thought?
5. What are some limitations of Piaget's theory of cognitive development?
6. What are some of the hazards of the "personal fable" for adolescent development?
7. How do adolescents achieve cognitive maturity?
8. How do adolescents' perceptions of social relationships change at adolescence?
9. What are the characteristics of adolescents' social reasoning at Selman's stage of mutual perspective taking?
10. What are the characteristic cognitive changes during adolescence according to the information-processing approach?

5

Adolescents in Their Families

Learning Objectives

After completing this chapter, you should be able to:
1 Identify three major changes that have occurred in the American family in recent decades.
2 Describe the four parenting styles and their impact on adolescent development.
3 Describe how adolescents and their parents are affected when both parents work.
4 Discuss the effects of parental divorce on adolescent development.
5 Describe adolescent development in single-parent and stepparent families.

Each of us grows up in some sort of family, which is defined as a group of two or more persons related by birth, marriage, or adoption who share a common household. Some people are fortunate enough to spend their entire childhood and youth with both of their natural parents, along with any brothers or sisters in the family. Others may grow up in strife-ridden homes that are eventually dissolved by divorce and will spend much of their youth in a single-parent or remarried family. Either way, the family becomes a major influence in the adolescent's life. Just take a look at the teens who excel in school and get along well with their peers. More often than not, they receive a lot of love and support at home. On the other hand, those who are doing poorly at school and tend to get into trouble are likely to be abused or neglected at home. In each case, it is the *quality* of family life rather than the type of living arrangement which exerts the decisive influence on the adolescent's development. But today, the quality of family life is being vitally affected by a variety of changes occurring in the American family. In this chapter, we look at some of the important changes in American family life. Then we will explore several major aspects of family life affecting adolescents' development, including the family environment, dual-income families, and the impact of divorce along with single-parent and remarried families. In the next chapter, the focus will be on family relationships and communication and how this affects the adolescent's achievement of independence.

CHANGES IN THE AMERICAN FAMILY

Much is said about the changes in American family life. Yet a look at the past shows that the family has always been changing. In previous eras, the family has been modified by such events as the influx of immigrant families from other countries and the migration of families from the farm to the cities. Today, the family continues to change because of rapid social changes throughout society. Some of the changes, such as the increase in one- and two-child families tend to have a positive influence on the quality of family life. Other changes, such as the increase of divorce and single-parent families, have a more mixed impact on family life and are still being evaluated.

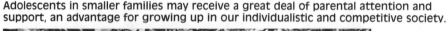
Adolescents in smaller families may receive a great deal of parental attention and support, an advantage for growing up in our individualistic and competitive society.

A major change is that families are becoming smaller than they were in the past. During colonial times, families had an average of eight children, partly because children were needed to run the family farm. But by the 1950s, families had an average of only four children. The major explanation was that most people lived in cities and had no need for a large family. Today, people are marrying mostly for companionship and personal fulfillment and it is more expensive to rear children. Consequently, families are having fewer children. The typical couple with children now has only one or two children. Although adolescents in small families may receive more parental attention, they also tend to become more dependent on their parents and ambivalent about leaving home.

Families also move around more than they formerly did. It has been estimated that about one-half of all families moves once every five years (U.S. Bureau of the Census, 1990). Most of the long-distance moves are made by families at the upper end of the socioeconomic scale, for example, professionals and executives, and those at the lower end of the scale, for example, farm laborers and the unemployed. Adolescents growing up in more mobile families tend to meet a greater number and variety of people than their parents did as adolescents. But they form fewer lasting ties with any of them. Adolescents also see their grandparents less often, sometimes not at all. As a result, many adolescents are plagued by a sense of rootlessness and loneliness, which may in part account for the high value contemporary youth place on personal relationships.

More women are entering the work force than in the past, with about three-fourths of the mothers of adolescents who still live at home being employed in the workplace. The mother's employment outside the home, in turn, triggers a ripple effect of changes in the family, including the redistribution of family responsibilities, the assignment of household chores, and the increase in latchkey teens, as we discuss later in this chapter.

Adolescents are also growing up in a greater variety of families than in the past. Married couples make up little more than one-half of all households with children and adolescents today, compared to three-fourths of households in 1960. The remaining households are composed of an increasing number of never-married singles, cohabiting couples, single-parent families, and remarried families. Furthermore, a greater proportion of adolescents come from families with varied ethnic and cultural backgrounds which, in turn, affects their attitudes, behaviors, and values. As a result, adolescents often feel torn between what they have learned at home and the conflicting practices and values of peers from different backgrounds.

Families are smaller and more mobile partly because the family fulfils different functions than it did in the past. Gone are the days when families were economically productive units, building their homes and raising their own food. Instead, with the rise of manufacturing and modern labor-saving devices, families have become primarily consumers. Now they are economically dependent on builders for their houses and merchants for their food and clothing. Along with these economic changes, the family has surrendered many of its traditional functions to other agencies. Education has become the primary responsibility of the schools. Moral and religious instruction have become the function of churches and synagogues. And care of the sick and aged is now shared with physicians, hospitals, and other agencies.

At the same time, the family has retained some vital functions and strengthened others. The family remains the approved group for the fulfillment of affectional and sexual needs, despite the emergence of alternative living arrangements. The family also sanctions the biological function of having children. Responsibility for the socialization and support of children remains with the family, in cooperation with other agencies. The family also provides for the financial and psychological support of the adolescent's education, which has become increasingly important in recent decades. Furthermore, life in an individualistic and competitive society accentuates the adolescent's need for acceptance and guidance within the family.

THE FAMILY ENVIRONMENT

How well the family fulfils its responsibilities depends largely on the family environment—the conditions surrounding and affecting the developing adolescent. The family environment depends on the combined influence of many factors, such as the emotional and social climate of the home, marital adjustment, and family cohesiveness and cooperation. Accordingly, the family environment is affected by most of the influences described in this and the next chapter. In this section, we focus on several aspects of the family environment that are especially important for the adolescent's development, namely, the particular style of parenting used in the home and its effects on the adolescent, how adolescents perceive their parents, and the influence of siblings.

Parenting Styles

This refers to the *way* parents relate to their adolescents, especially in socializing them. Parenting styles include many behaviors traditionally labeled as child-rearing methods, discipline, and parental control. Yet *parenting styles* is a more inclusive term. For instance, parenting styles include the giving of affection, guidance, and teaching as well as the use of parental control. Then too, as children reach adolescence, parents need to shift their styles of parenting, easing up on the parental control exercised throughout childhood. Wise parents not only expect but will actively encourage a greater independence on the adolescent's part.

Eleanor Maccoby and John Martin (1983) have identified four basic styles of parenting that involve different combinations of the key variables of acceptance and control, as shown in Figure 5–1. Each parenting style is associated with certain behaviors on the part of adolescents as follows:

Authoritative parenting is the preferred type of parenting, mostly because it combines a high level of parental acceptance with a reasonable degree of parental control. Authoritative parents relate to their adolescents in a warm and

Figure 5-1 The Four Parenting Styles.

PARENTAL DEMAND AND CONTROL	PARENTAL ACCEPTANCE AND RESPONSIVENESS	
	Accepting, Responsive	Rejecting, Unresponsive
Demanding, Controlling	Authoritative	Authoritarian
Undemanding, Uncontrolling	Permissive Indulgent	Permissive Indifferent

Adapted from E.E. Maccoby and J.A. Martin, "Socialization in the context of the family: Parent-child interaction." In P.H. Mussen, ed., *Handbook of Child Psychology*, 4th ed., vol. 4 (New York: John Wiley), 1983. Reprinted by permission of John Wiley & Sons.

responsive way that encourages the development of age-appropriate independence. At the same time, adults do not hesitate to use their legitimate authority as parents, especially in matters pertaining to the adolescent's health and safety. Such parents typically engage in a great deal of verbal give-and-take with youths, explaining parental rules and demonstrating a willingness to negotiate controversial matters. Adolescents growing up in such families tend to develop a high degree of self-acceptance and personal control. Feeling loved and respected by their parents, these adolescents have less need for approval from authorities or their peers. Through regular participation in the decision-making process, adolescents learn to act in a reasonable and responsible manner.

Authoritarian parenting emphasizes parental control at the expense of acceptance and responsiveness. Parents using this approach attempt to control adolescents by relying on physical power. Generally, this includes the use of threats, physical punishment, and control over the adolescent's material resources. These parents virtually ignore the adolescent's growing need for self-determination. When the parents' authority is challenged, the parents rarely explain their demands. Instead, they resort to ultimatums accompanied by threatening looks and gestures. Youths reared this way tend to become dependent, submissive, and overly conforming on the one hand, and rebellious and hostile on the other. They may act compliant and evasive in the presence of their parents or other authorities, but become defiant and resentful behind their backs. In either case, adolescents reared this way remain excessively dependent on external authority.

Parents who rely on the *permissive indulgent style* tend to be accepting and responsive toward adolescents but in a way that allows them excessive freedom. Consequently, permissive parents may fail to curtail negative, unreasonable behavior on the adolescent's part. At the same time, permissive parents may attempt to influence adolescents by the withdrawal of love, including nonphysical expressions of their anger and disapproval. They may give adolescents the "silent treatment" and turn their backs on them. Although love withdrawal poses no immediate physical threat to teenagers, it may be more punitive—because of the implicit threat of abandonment—and more prolonged than the authoritarian approach, lasting for hours or days. Adolescents growing up in permissive indulgent families learn they can get away with anything and often disregard rules and regulations. Yet they may inhibit expressions of anger for fear of being rejected and go through life with a strong need for approval. Also, they are usually low in self-acceptance and self-control.

Permissive indifferent parenting refers to a style in which parents are unresponsive and neglectful toward their young. As you might expect, adolescents growing up in these dysfunctional families suffer the most of all. They may be plagued by a sense of inferiority and self-rejection, lacking a sense of direction in their lives. The negative effects of permissive indifferent parenting are accentuated when combined with parental inconsistency. For instance, parents may turn a "blind eye" toward a youth's drug problem and yet become autocratic when he or she gets into trouble at school, evoking even greater confusion and resent-

Table 5-1   Parenting Styles and Adolescent Development

Parenting style	Parental behavior	Characteristic impact on adolescent development
Authoritative parenting	Parents warm and accepting while retaining moderate parental control, with extensive verbal give-and-take.	Adolescents acquire high degree of self-acceptance and self-control, acting in independent, responsible manner.
Authoritarian parenting	Parents emphasize parental control at the expense of acceptance and warmth, relying mostly on threats and physical punishment.	Adolescents become dependent on authority, generally anxious and compliant in presence of authority but often mixed with defiance and resentment.
Permissive indulgent parenting	Parents are accepting and responsive toward adolescents but only rarely placing limits on their behavior.	Adolescents usually exhibit low self-control, often disregarding rules and regulations.
Permissive indifferent parenting	Parents are unresponsive and neglectful of their adolescents.	Adolescents have a sense of inferiority and self-rejection.

ment on the youth's part. Furthermore, when parental rejection involves verbal or physical abuse, as it often does, adolescents experience a great deal of anger toward their parents. They often run away or leave home earlier than usual.

In practice, of course, many parents and couples use a mixture of parenting styles, with even more varied results. Also, much depends on each parent's personality and his or her consistency in the use of a particular approach. For instance, undemonstrative parents relying on the authoritative parenting style may be perceived as being distant, making adolescents feel insecure. Or conversely, warm, accepting parents who rely on authoritarian control may have a less restrictive impact on adolescents than would colder, harsher parents using the same approach. Then too, investigators increasingly find that parents' persuasive strategies are much more complex than implied in the traditional categories of authoritative, authoritarian, and permissive. Mark deTurck and Gerald Miller (1983) found that adolescents' perceptions of parenting styles vary considerably by age and sex of both participants as well as the particular situation involved. For instance, when parents attempt to get their adolescents to help with spring cleaning, they use at least sixteen different persuasive-message strategies, with significant age-by-sex interactions, including the following:

♦ Aversive stimulation: "If you don't help out this Saturday, you will have to do the dishes every night until you learn to do your share of work around here."
♦ Positive moral appeal: "As a member of this family, it is morally right for you to help out with the work."

In sum, it appears that parents use a wide range of persuasive strategies with their adolescents, varying them by the age and sex of both parent and adolescent as well as the particular context involved.

How Adolescents Feel about Their Parents

The way parents *intend* to rear their young is one thing. How adolescents *perceive* parents and their approach is another, as shown in numerous surveys on the subject.

As you might expect, adolescents' attitudes toward their parents are strongly affected by the various parenting styles as described in the previous section. To find out how teenagers feel about their mother and father's parenting style, Cay Kelly and Gail Goodwin (1983) obtained data from 100 high school students representing different social, cultural, and racial groups. They were surprised to find that more than 3 out of 4 adolescents feel their parents adopt an authoritative or democratic approach. Others feel their parents are either authoritarian or permissive. When students were asked, "Would you discipline your children in much the same way as your parents are disciplining you?" two-thirds of those with authoritative parents said yes. Fewer than half of those with permissive parents and even fewer of those with authoritarian parents indicated they would treat their children the same way their own parents treated them. Again, in response to the question "Would you like to be the kind of person your mother/father is?" the majority of teenagers with authoritative parents said they would, whereas only a minority of those with authoritarian or permissive parents responded favorably.

Such results confirm the widely accepted notion that youth growing up in families using an authoritative approach are more apt to have positive feelings toward their parents and conform with parental rules than are those with domineering or permissive parents. Furthermore, there is ample evidence that youths who have positive family relationships, as promoted in authoritative parenting styles, tend to associate with peer groups that confirm rather than contradict their parents' values (Hill, 1980). In contrast, adolescents reared in homes characterized by high parental control and frequent family conflict tend to experience a high degree of *perceived* parental rejection and exhibit a variety of negative characteristics, such as low self-esteem, depression, and suicide (Stivers, 1988; Robertson and Simons, 1989).

Adolescents' overall attitudes toward their parents are shaped by a variety of other factors as well. Numerous studies have shown that adolescents' attitudes toward their parents are vitally affected by such diverse factors as the parents' marital adjustment, family cohesiveness and cooperation, and the prevailing mood of happiness or criticism in the home (Burman, John, and Margolin, 1987). At the same time, the adolescent's own adjustment colors her attitude toward her parents. While Daniel Offer and his colleagues (1981, 1988) found that the vast majority of adolescents report positive feelings toward their parents most of the time, a disproportionate number of depressed and maladjusted adolescents exhibit negative feelings and are apt to hold a grudge against their parents. Yet, as we all know, attitudes also vary as a function of specific subjects and situations and change over time, as we discuss in the next chapter.

Sibling Relationships

About three-fourths of adolescents have one or more siblings—those having a common parent—with sibling relationships being a significant influence in the adolescent's family environment. When nearly 2,500 high school students were asked to list the important people in their lives—people they sought out for advice, cared about, and did things with—9 out of 10 of them listed a sister or brother. More than two-thirds of them listed all of their siblings as important influences in their lives. Adolescents typically rate the relationships with their favorite brother or sister at about the same level of closeness they enjoy with their best friend (Blyth, Hill, and Thiel, 1982).

Vivian Seltzer (1989) finds that siblings occupy a unique position in the family environment. On the one hand, siblings are family members and thus participate in family practices and socialization. Yet they are of a different generation than their parents and are more similar in age and outlook with their brothers and sisters. Consequently, siblings play a pivotal role in the family, sometimes supporting the parents and at other times siding with their brothers and sisters against their parents. Sibling influence tends to be greatest in those areas less dominated by parents, such as peer-oriented activities, physical problems, sexual behavior, and forbidden subjects. At the same time, adolescents relate to their siblings differently than to their parents. Children and their parents enjoy more positive and varied relationships than children do with each other. They talk, joke, and comfort each other more often than siblings do. Youths are also more likely to follow the advice of their parents than that of their siblings. In contrast, young people generally behave more negatively and punitively toward their siblings than toward their parents (Baskett and Johnston, 1982).

The quality of sibling relationships varies depending on such factors as family size, age, and sex of siblings. For instance, two same-sexed adolescents born a year or so apart may feel very competitive toward each other, especially in a small family. In contrast, two opposite-sexed adolescents born further apart would feel much less competitive toward each other, especially in a larger family. However, the trend toward smaller families, the rising divorce rate, and the decreased availability of parents during the day may intensify sibling relationships in many families. Sibling rivalry is more apt to occur in those families in which parents openly compare siblings, favoring one more than another. In many instances, sibling rivalry may be initiated by the adolescents themselves, by competing for their parents' love and attention or by juggling for power and position among themselves. Sibling relationships are also affected by adolescents' personality and adjustment. In one study (Daniels et al., 1985), both parents and siblings reported that adolescents who are psychologically well-adjusted display more friendliness toward their siblings than do those who are less well-adjusted.

Sibling relationships are also affected by birth order or the adolescent's position within the family. The effects of birth order tend to be more pronounced among firstborns. Adolescents who are the oldest in the family generally are more conscientious, responsible, and higher in achievement motivation than are later borns, mostly because of the greater parental attention and expectations directed toward firstborns. But firstborns have their downside too. Because parents of the oldest child are inexperienced in their child-rearing practices, firstborns are rewarded more generously and punished more severely than are later borns, which may account for the strong need for approval among older children. Then too, as other children are born into the family, the oldest child must share the parents' attention and often feels in competition with younger siblings. As a result, firstborns exhibit both positive and negative behaviors toward younger siblings. On the one hand, firstborns tend to be dominant in sibling relationships, nurturing, teaching, and assisting their younger siblings. But on the other hand, they are also antagonistic and jealous of younger siblings and generally feel less close to their brothers and sisters than the latter do to them (Minnett, Vandell, and Santrock, 1983).

Birth order effects tend to be less marked and even more contradictory for later-born children. In the past, the middle-born child was thought to be at a

---

Sibling Violence

Have you ever been pushed, shoved, or hit by a brother or sister? Or perhaps you've done this to a sibling. Either way, you may be surprised to learn how often this happens in other homes.

Sibling violence constitutes the most common form of family violence. In a review of the literature, O'Neill (1983) found that violence among siblings took place more often than between a husband and wife or parent and child.

Megan Goodwin and Bruce Roscoe (1990) conducted an extensive survey on sibling violence among 272 adolescents 16 to 19 years of age from different racial groups and types of families. They found that about two-thirds of the adolescents of both sexes reported being either a victim or perpetrator of sibling violence during the preceding year.

Physical violence was viewed as an integral part of conflict resolution among siblings. Most of the conflicts arose out of something said to the subject by a sibling or vice versa. Other sources of conflict were teasing, unauthorized use of possessions, shirking duties, name-calling, and invasion of privacy. For females, conflicts frequently involved a third party, such as special treatment by parents or being embarrassed in front of friends. Most of the time, teenagers attempted to resolve their conflicts by arguing, screaming, ignoring, compromising, discussing, or use of physical force and threats, in descending order. Males were more likely than females to hit with their fists or with objects, especially during arguments with their brothers.

As adolescents acquire greater language and cognitive skills, they are less likely to resort to physical force than children are. As a result, sibling violence declines among middle and older adolescents. However, because sibling violence is a significant predictor of domestic violence among adults, it is important to provide children and adolescents with alternative, more productive ways of dealing with conflict.

disadvantage, having greater difficulties finding his or her identity and being more prone to maladaptive behavior. However, because of their unique position, middle-born children have to learn multiple roles and thus may be better prepared for a variety of relationships as adults. Younger children and adolescents generally are less achievement-oriented and more sociable and peer-oriented than their older brothers and sisters. As you might suspect, birth-order effects interact with a host of other influences, such that the above characteristics are highly relative. Furthermore, birth-order effects tend to diminish as children reach adolescence and adulthood.

What about the only child? Is he/she always self-centered? Not necessarily, according to most research. It appears that only children do not fit their negative stereotype, but instead resemble firstborns in many ways. As such, they tend to be highly responsible and achievement-oriented and display desirable personality characteristics for the most part (Falbo and Polit, 1986). Again, much depends on the particular adolescent and his or her family environment.

Sibling relationships tend to persist into adulthood, such that siblings who were close to each other in childhood and adolescence continue to feel this way as adults. Many of those who did not feel close to their brothers or sisters may work through their own feelings of sibling rivalry as they mature, marry,

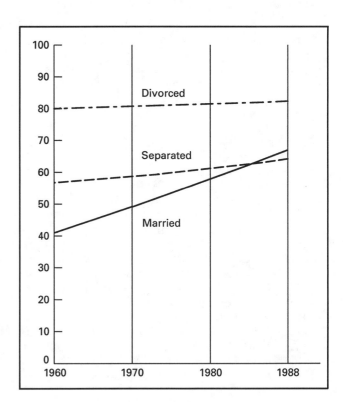

Figure 5-2 Women in the Workplace By Marital Status, with Children 6–17 Years of Age.

U.S. Bureau of the Census, *statistical abstract of the United States: 1990*, 110th ed (Washington, D.C.: U.S. Government Printing Office, 1990), p. 385.

and establish families of their own. However, some individuals are bothered by sibling rivalry throughout their entire lives (Dunn, 1984).

DUAL-INCOME FAMILIES

One of the most significant changes in the American family affecting adolescents is the dramatic increase in families in which both husbands and wives are employed in the workplace. More than half of all married women and three-fourths of separated and divorced women now work outside the home. An even larger proportion of mothers with older children and adolescents leave the home each day for a full- or part-time job in the workplace. See Figure 5-2. The additional demands of time and effort required in dual-income families affect everyone in the home, including the division of labor between husbands and wives and adolescents' help with household chores. Dual-income families as well as single-parent families also face the challenge of latchkey teens—adolescents who are left on their own for several hours each day after school.

Mothers in the Workplace

How the mother's working outside the home affects a particular family depends on many factors, including the woman's attitude toward her job, her husband's support as well as his work situation, their marital happiness, the division of labor within the home, and time spent with children and adolescents.

The attitude of both partners toward wives in the workplace is an important factor. As you might expect, an increasing number of couples agree that both partners have a right to work, yet a substantial minority feel otherwise. In Blumstein and Schwartz's (1983) in-depth study of couples, one-third of the husbands are opposed to both partners working, compared to only one-fourth of wives who feel this way. The survey also shows that married couples who disagree about the wife's right to work are less happy with their relationships. Furthermore, when the wife works, couples tend to fight more about how young children and adolescents are being raised. Much of this stems from the conventional wisdom that children grow up best with their mothers at home. Although there are studies demonstrating that this may not be true, many husbands and wives are not convinced. Interviews with such couples disclose two major reasons why men and, in some instances, women, feel it is important for the woman to stay at home. One is the belief that women are better at "mothering" than men are. The second is that because one parent is needed at home, it makes more sense that the woman be the one because she is likely to earn less than her husband can. Unfortunately, the concentration of women in low-paying, service-oriented jobs tends to add fuel to such an argument. However much of this argument may be based on the assumption that money is power in a marriage. But if so, some troublesome power struggles loom ahead as the inequality in pay between the sexes is corrected. Currently, almost 1 out of 5 working wives earns more than her husband does (Smolowe, 1990).

Partly because of such attitudes, the mother in dual-income families bears a great deal of the responsibility for reconciling the couple's work schedule and family life. According to a study of dual-income families by Kingston and Nock (1985), neither the combined number of hours a couple works nor the amount of time one or both spouses work strongly affects the quality of family life. However, the couple's work schedule generally has a stronger effect on the attitudes and behaviors of the wife than on those of the husband. As the total time parents work increases, they spend less time with their children and adolescents. Yet women feel they lose more time with their children than men do, as most husbands realize. Again, much of the reason is that in many homes women continue to bear the primary responsibility for childrearing and domestic tasks. Although Baila Miller (1990) found few differences between mothers and fathers in the actual stress level of nurturing children and adolescents, mothers do tend to suffer more health strain than fathers do.

Anne Kalleberg and Rachel Rosenfeld (1990) find that women with children and adolescents in dual-income families do most of the child care and even more of the household chores. When the wife works outside the home, the husband spends, on the average, only a small amount of additional time on housework, if any. Men are most likely to help with the grocery shopping, cleaning up after meals, and housecleaning, in this order. They are less apt to help prepare the meals and assist with the laundry. Women spend twice as much time as men do on child care each week. And they spend three and a half times as many hours on household tasks as their husbands do, averaging about seventy-eight hours a week compared to twenty-two for men.

At the same time, the division of labor within the home depends on many variables, including the education and income of the couple, their use of support systems, and the age and number of their children and adolescents. Interestingly, even though the women from Canada, Norway, and Sweden in the Kalleberg and Rosenfeld study spent fewer hours in the workplace than did American women, their husbands rendered only about the same amount of help at home as did American husbands—thereby contradicting the stereotype of the more egalitarian Scandinavian husband. Actually, education appears to play a more important role, with younger and better-educated couples in all countries sharing household chores more evenly.

Adolescents' Household Chores

How much do adolescents help out around the house? And is it true that girls continue to do more housework than boys do? In an effort to find answers to such questions, a number of studies have focused on adolescents' household chores within various types of families.

In one such study, Mary Benin and Debra Edwards (1990) found that the

Sons in full-time, dual-income families spend less time on household chores than daughters do, mostly because of the lack of parental supervision. (Marc Anderson)

combination of the adolescents' sex and family type is far more significant for adolescents' work at home than other influences, such as the number of teenage siblings, parents' education, and the father's participation at work. Two of their findings are especially surprising. First, parents in full-time dual-income families get less help from their teenagers at home than do parents in traditional families, in which the mother stays at home. Parents in families in which the mother works part-time get virtually no help from their teens. See Table 5-2. But the major reasons for these disparities are even more striking. The investigators found that full-time, dual-income families tend to be more sexist than traditional families in regard to the *time* on chores demanded of sons and daughters. Specifically, sons in full-time, dual-income families spend only one-third as much time on chores as do sons in traditional families. In contrast, daughters in full-time, dual-income families spend one-fourth more time on chores than do daughters in traditional families. However, traditional families—in which the mother is a full-time homemaker—generally require equal amounts of chore time from sons and daughters, although such chores are assigned along more sex-stereotyped divisions of labor than in full-time, dual-income families. The investigators offer several explanations for their results. First, in full-time, dual-income families,

Table 5-2   Weekly Time Spent on Household Chores by Sex of Adolescent and Current
            Family Type

Adolescent's sex	CURRENT FAMILY TYPE		
	Full-time dual-income families	Part-time dual-income families	Traditional families
Male	2.75 hours (N=34)	2.40 hours (N=10)	7.25 hours (N=17)
Female	10.21 hours (N=42)	2.50 hours (N=6)	8.19 hours (N=14)
Total time per week	12.96 hours	4.90 hours	15.44 hours

Adapted from Table 1 in Mary Holland Benin and Debra A. Edwards, "Adolescents' chores: The difference
between dual- and single-earner families," *Journal of Marriage and the Family,* May 1990, p. 368.

mothers may tend to assign the more important tasks to daughters, on the
stereotyped assumption that only daughters can perform such tasks well. Also, in
traditional families, the mother may get more work from sons through closer
supervision.

The authors also point out a bright note, namely that current work
involvement of the parents is more important than past employment during the
teenager's childhood for shaping an adolescent's attitudes and practices around
the home. Thus, by adolescence it is not too late to teach a fairer approach by
demanding equal amounts of work from sons and daughters in full-time, dual-
income families.

Margaret Sanik and Kathryn Stafford (1985) studied 1,031 adolescents
in two-parent, two-child families and found many of the same practices but with
a different twist. Adolescents of full-time employed mothers contribute more
housework than did adolescents of part-time employed mothers. And daughters
do more housework than sons. But they also discovered that firstborn adolescents of both sexes perform more household chores than second borns do. Thus,
firstborn daughters contribute about 60 percent more housework than do firstborn sons. It also appears that the sibling structure of the family or the number
or proportion of boys and girls in all sized families is a significant factor. Generally, as the number of sons increases in a family, the sex-typing of traditionally
feminine tasks decreases. But as the number of daughters increases in a family,
the sex-typing of traditionally feminine tasks becomes more pronounced. Only
in families with no sons does an increase in the number of daughters reduce the
sex-typing of traditionally male tasks (Brody and Steelman, 1985).

One of the most important but often overlooked factors affecting adolescents' help around the house is the school day. It appears that adolescents perform less housework on school days than on weekends, not unlike parents themselves. Also, teenagers spend less time on housework as they grow older. Yet,
when they take outside employment, they generally increase their contribution at

home. One explanation is that parents may give their permission conditionally, that is, "You can accept the job only if you do your home chores first" (Sanik and Stafford, 1985). Then too, there is a link between responsibilities at home and adolescent autonomy. Although home chores can be taken as another form of parental control, being responsible for your self—washing your own clothes and cooking your own food—can be viewed as training for independence. In addition, sharing responsibilities for household labor may be a trade-off for a certain amount of decision-making authority. This is especially likely to occur among adolescents who perceive the parenting styles in the home to include a balance of high parental support with moderate parental control, as is true of authoritative parenting (Amato, 1990).

Latchkey Teens

The growing number of mothers employed in the workplace has given rise to another change in the home, more teenagers returning to empty houses two to four hours each day and often entire days during the summer. These are often called "latchkey children" or "latchkey teens," because they are given the key to their front door lock (latch) so that they may use it to let themselves in the home while their parents are still at work. There are now more than 2 million school-age children under the age of 13 on their own after school, with the largest share in white, upper-income households. The proportion of latchkey teens among those 14 to 18 years of age is even higher. Furthermore, these numbers are expected to increase steadily in the coming years (Schmid, 1987).

Teenagers 12 to 15 years old are of special concern to parents, teachers, and social workers, primarily because they are too old for day care and too young to take part-time jobs. Joan Lipsitz (1986) points out that when teenagers this age are left home alone bad things are not necessarily happening. But neither are good things. Latchkey teens are losing opportunities to interact positively with their peers and adults, to be culturally enriched, and to make contributions to their communities. Lipsitz refers to latchkey teens as the "three to six o'clock problem," because these are the peak hours of referral for clinical help for adolescents this age.

Being forced to fend for yourself at such an early age can be a lonely and stressful experience. Many younger adolescents feel isolated because they are ordered to stay inside or have to limit the friends they can have over to the house. Then there is the stress of not having anyone to help when things go wrong. Physical and sexual abuse by older brothers and sisters is higher among unsupervised children and adolescents. And about one-fourth of fires in the homes are caused by unsupervised children (McCrary, 1984). Teenagers who are left to themselves in the afternoons are also more susceptible to peer pressure in regard to experimenting with alcohol and drugs. Sexual encounters between teens are more likely to happen at home while the parents are away than was the case in the past. And parents often discover what is happening the hard way. For instance, a mother returned home unexpectedly one afternoon to find a full-scale party involving drugs and sex among 14 and 15 year olds. Shocked and disillusioned by the experience, she and her husband laid down firmer guidelines for their 15-year-old son.

After interviewing more than 1,500 latchkey children, Thomas and Lynette Long (1983) conclude that most of them have negative experiences while left home alone after school. Often they are simply overwhelmed by so much responsibility so soon. The Longs found that 90 percent of the delinquents taken to juvenile court in Montgomery County, Maryland, outside Washington, D.C., are latchkey teens. And in a 1987 poll, teachers cited children and teens being home after school by themselves and social isolation as major reasons for difficulties at school. Such difficulties are less likely when homework is monitored by parents, who are often too tired to do so in the evenings (Long, 1989).

At the same time, the experiences of latchkey teens vary greatly. A lot depends on the particular teenager as well as his or her family. Authoritative parenting and parental monitoring may help latchkey teens to cope more effectively, especially in resisting negative peer pressure (Steinberg, 1986).

In some communities, parents and school administrators are cooperating to set up after-school programs for children and supervised activities for teens. In addition, Lynette Long (1989) suggests other possible approaches. Educators can establish classes to assist parents with their latchkey teens and to make better use of the various types of family support groups. Then too, couples need to see this as a family matter, rather than simply something else mothers may feel guilty about. Parents need to ask, "How can I tell if my child or teenager is mature enough to stay home alone?" "How to tell if he or she is coping well with self-care?" Many parents are doing a better job preparing their teens to cope with this situation by providing emergency telephone numbers, designating backup places for teens to go if they lose their house keys, and setting ground rules about who may be invited over to the house and under what conditions teens may go out in the neighborhood, much less to the shopping malls. Parents may also find it helpful to keep in better touch with their teenagers by telephone during the afternoon. Few parents or educators advocate leaving teenagers completely on their own after school, though more of them are accepting it as a fact of life. However, properly prepared, latchkey teenagers may learn a sense of responsibility and gain more confidence in looking after themselves.

DIVORCE AND SINGLE-PARENT AND STEPPARENT FAMILIES

Returning home from school to an empty house during the weekdays is one thing; living in a home with only one parent week after week, seeing the other parent only occasionally, if at all, is another. Yet this has become a familiar experience to more and more teenagers because of the rising divorce rate. The United States now has the highest divorce rate in the world, with one out of every two marriages ending in divorce (U.S. Bureau of the Census, 1990). As a result, it is now predicted that of every one hundred children born today, about half will be born to parents who separate or divorce before the child reaches 18. Divorce is generally a time of social and emotional disruption for both children and adolescents. Many of them will live the rest of their adolescence in single-parent families, often enduring a significant drop in their standard of living. At the same time, an increasing number of youths will make an additional adjustment to a stepparent in remarried families. Unfortunately, about half of the adolescents who experience a parental divorce will see their mother or father undergo a second divorce, with even more devastating results. Only 1 in 7 will see both their biological mothers and fathers happily remarried (Wallerstein, 1989).

Divorce

Because of the concern about divorce, we frequently overlook the fact that adolescents suffer as much, if not more, from the family dissension or "emotional divorce" in the home preceding the actual legal divorce. The latter usually comes only after a lengthy period of emotional strife in the home which inevitably affects adolescents to some degree, either directly or indirectly. In one study, the home environments of adolescents were observed as much as six years before the divorce occurred. As you might expect, these families were less stable and more conflict-ridden than other families. The parents expressed less warmth and concern for their adolescents and emphasized stricter discipline, creating a home atmosphere in which adolescents suffered from degrees of emotional deprivation. Physical violence was not uncommon. Adolescents would avoid bringing home friends out of fear of being embarrassed by a family feud. Understandably, some of them view the eventual divorce with a sense of relief (Morrison, Gjerde, and Block, 1984).

Although divorce may come as a relief in strife-ridden families, the great majority of adolescents find their parents' separation and divorce a very painful experience. Divorce usually has a disruptive effect on family life, which at best requires several years to overcome. In a long-term study of sixty divorced families, Wallerstein and Kelly (1980) found that young children and adolescents were affected somewhat differently by divorce. Young children often felt they were to blame for their parents' divorce and became very anxious about the future. Teenagers were more likely to suffer from the stress when parents put pressure on them to take sides in the marital dispute. However, because they were older and more socialized, teenagers were more apt to hide their feelings, thus intensifying their emotional suffering. In this study, adolescents reported the greatest stress during the first year or two following the announcement of their parents' divorce. But a check on these adolescents a year or so later found that over half of them had made a reasonably good adjustment and had returned to a normal developmental pattern. One-fourth of the adolescents who had shown trouble at home or school before the separation were about the same a year afterward. But another one-fourth of them, who had histories of long-standing difficulties in their families, became even more troubled after their parents' separation, exhibiting lowered self-esteem and superficial and unrewarding relationships with others.

Divorce generally has a more disruptive effect on adolescents when the parental divorce occurs during adolescence than when it occurs during childhood (Needle, Su, and Doherty, 1990). But boys and girls tend to suffer somewhat differently from parental divorce. Boys, especially, suffer from the absence of a male model and exhibit greater difficulties at school, more delinquent behavior, greater use of alcohol and drugs, and sexual experimentation. Boys who are fortunate enough to maintain a close relationship with their fathers may fare considerably better. Although girls are thought to have a less difficult adjustment to divorce because of the presence and support of their mothers, this is not always true. Girls who report a great deal of conflict with their mothers and whose mothers are experiencing a lot of conflict with their ex-spouses in front of the adolescent tend to have a lower GPA in school than do other girls (McCombs and Forehand, 1989). Also, parental divorce has an adverse effect on drug use among girls as well as boys (Needle, Su, and Doherty, 1990). Then too, youth of both sexes engage in somewhat greater dating activity and sexual intercourse. But they tend to have difficulties forming long-term relationships with their opposite-sex peers. The increase in dating activity is even greater if the parental divorce has been accompanied by acrimony during and after the divorce, by a deterioration of the parent-adolescent relationship, and by the custodial parent remaining single (Booth, Brinkerhoff, and White, 1984).

What about the long-term effects of divorce on adults? Are adults from divorced families more maladjusted and unhappy than those from intact families? Are they more apt to become divorced themselves? In a ten-year follow-up study, Judith Wallerstein (1984) interviewed thirty adolescents 12 to 18 years of age whose parents had divorced when they were children. Forty of their parents were also interviewed. She found that adolescents had few conscious memories of the intact families or the marital rupture that ensued. Most of them had made a reasonably good personal and social adjustment and were doing well in school. However, a significant number spoke of the emotional and financial deprivation that had resulted from the divorce. Half of the adolescents reported fantasies that their parents would get back together. Relationships with custodial mothers often reflected closeness, and the relationship with the noncustodial father continued to be of central concern.

Adults whose parents divorced when they were young may continue to bear emotional scars from the divorce, or they may have benefited from the experience, with a great deal depending on the individual and family involved. In her later follow-up studies, Wallerstein (1989) found that overall about half of the adults were doing well. They had emerged from a parental divorce as competent, compassionate, and courageous people. But almost as many were doing poorly. They were entering adulthood as worried, underachieving, self-deprecating, and sometimes angry young men and women. The rest exhibited an uneven adjustment to the world, making it too soon to know how they will turn out.

Wallerstein's follow-up studies with adults have yielded two surprising results. The first is what she calls the "sleeper effect"—the eventual surfacing of pent-up emotions associated with the parental divorce. Lisa is an example. As a teenager, she was viewed as a prime candidate for a full recovery from parental divorce. But now in her 20s, Lisa is troubled by anger and depression. She has also become anorexic, dropping to 94 pounds from 128, and has not menstruated for a year and a half. Curiously, most of her troubles surfaced when she fell in love with a young man. She had decided to consummate the affair by accepting his invitation to spend the summer vacation with him. But on her way there, her courage failed. Instead, she found herself hitchhiking across the country, not knowing where she was headed. Yet it was no coincidence that Lisa's problems occurred just as she was seriously in love, because she was entering the kind of relationship in which her parents had failed. For the first time, she confronted the fears, anxieties, guilt, and concerns she had suppressed over the years. The sleeper effect generally occurs at a time when youths are making decisions with long-term implications for their lives. Overcome by fears and anxieties, they begin to make connections between these feelings and their parents' divorce.

A second major unexpected finding is that fully one-fourth of the mothers and one-fifth of the fathers experience a diminished capacity to parent in their own marriages. The diminished capacity seriously disrupts the child-rearing functions of the family. These parents are chronically disorganized, are unable to meet the challenges of being a parent, and often lean heavily on their children, thereby perpetuating their unresolved difficulties on the next generation.

However, the effects of divorce are not always bad. In some instances, youth from divorced parents may experience less anguish and maladjustment than do those growing up with intact but conflict-ridden marriages (Bane, 1979). Also, because of their situation, youth of divorced families may become more responsible and self-reliant at an earlier age (Pope and Mueller, 1979). Otherwise, surveys do not indicate any clear differences in personal adjustment between those who grow up in single-parent homes and those who come from intact marriages (Kulka and Weingarten, 1979). At the same time, it is true that youths and adults from divorced families eventually are more likely to get divorced themselves, probably because they have learned that divorce is a viable solution to marital conflict.

Single-Parent Families

The rising divorce rate is an integral part of the wider changes taking part in society which include a greater variety of living arrangements, such that an ever-decreasing proportion of children and adolescents live in the traditional family with both natural parents. Although married couples made up three-fourths of all households in 1960, they constitute a little over half of such households today.

The remaining households are composed of an increasing number of never-married singles, cohabiting couples, single-parent families, and remarried families. See Figure 5-3.

About one out of every five of those under 18 lives in a female-headed single-parent family. In the majority of these families, the mother is separated or divorced. A much smaller number of such families are headed by a widow. At the same time, the number of households headed by single mothers who have never married has doubled in the past few years. Robert Weiss (1984) observes that separation and divorce almost always bring drastic changes in the amounts and sources of income. As a result, the typical single-parent family tends to suffer from financial deprivation, though there is a wide range of income in these families. Single-parent families at higher income levels rely on earnings of the new household head, and, increasingly with time, on the earnings of others, supplemented in the early years by alimony and child support. However, single-parent families at lower income levels rely much less on earnings of the new household, much less on alimony and child support, and much more on public assistance.

The quality of life for adolescents in single-parent families depends on the combined influence of many factors. Because most single-parent families are

Figure 5-3   Children Under 18 Years Old By Presence of Parents.

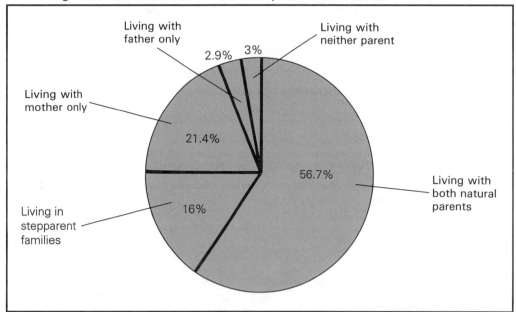

Sources: U.S. Bureau of the Census, *Statistical Abstract of the United States: 1990*, 110th ed., Washington, D.C: U.S. Government Printing Office, 1990, p. 53. Andrew Cherlin and James McCarthy, "Remarried Couple Households," *Journal of Marriage and the Family* 47, (Feb. 1985), 23–30.

headed by women, the absence of the father and/or diminished support by the father becomes an important factor as shown in Amato's (1987) study of children and adolescents in single-parent, stepparent, and intact families. Compared to adolescents in intact families, those in single-parent families generally report less father support, less family cohesion, more sibling conflict, and more household responsibility. Another study by Stern, Northman, and Van Slyck (1984) found that boys are generally affected more adversely by the absence of the father than girls are. The absence of the father resulted in a greater number of problem behaviors, such as alcohol consumption, drug use, and sexual activity, for both sexes. But this was especially true for boys. Over half the boys in father-absent homes were high-rate alcohol users, compared to about one-third of the boys in father-present homes. Furthermore, half of the boys in father-absent homes reported very high rates of sexual activity, compared to only a fifth of the boys in father-present homes. The finding that boys from father-absent homes are at greater risk for such problems should be given greater consideration by community agencies.

Girls who grow up without fathers tend to have greater anxiety and difficulty in relating to boys, as was shown in an extensive study by Mavis Hetherington (1981). Three groups of 13- to 17-year-old girls were compared: those from homes with both parents, those who had lost their fathers because of death, and those who had lost their fathers because of divorce. Daughters of widows were tense and shy around boys. As a result, they began dating at a later age and remained more sexually inhibited. Even though daughters of divorced women were somewhat insecure around boys, they compensated for their loss by becoming more flirtatious and aggressive with the opposite sex. They usually began dating at an earlier age and became more sexually active than did girls in the other two groups. Girls with divorced parents also had more conflicts with their mothers and held more negative attitudes toward their fathers.

As these girls reached young adulthood, a follow-up study focused on their sexual behavior, marital choices, and marital behavior. The daughters of divorced women generally marry at a younger age and tend to select marriage partners with inconsistent work histories as well as alcohol and drug problems. Daughters of widows are more apt to marry men with a stable but somewhat straight-laced makeup. Both daughters of widows and divorced women tend to have greater sexual adjustment problems, such as fewer orgasms. In contrast, daughters from two-parent families exhibited greater variation in their sex-role behavior and marital adjustment. They also seemed more at ease in their marital roles, suggesting that they had worked through their father-daughter relationships more successfully.

Adolescents of African-American background are especially likely to grow up in single-parent families, with the dramatic rise in female-headed homes a significant change among African-American families in the past generation. As a result, about half of all African-Americans under 18 live in single-mother families. The most widely cited reason for this is the increase in out-of-wedlock births to African-Americans, many of them attributable to teenage pregnancies. In turn, the high rate of out-of-wedlock births combined with the greater proportion of women who never marry and those who remain single after divorce all contribute to the increase in female-headed homes among African-Americans. Yet, as many authorities on this subject observe, this is an integral part of a larger, more complex pattern attributable to a combination of social, economic, and cultural factors (Staples, 1985; Tucker and Taylor, 1989). A major factor is the high rate of unemployment among African-American males, rendering many unable to assume the responsibilities of husband and father. In addition, many African-American women, faced with such circumstances, strive to be independent, thereby encouraging the trend toward single-parent families. Yet many African-American women are in dead-end jobs, lack alimony and child support, and require public assistance. The median income of single-parent African-American families is less than one-half of the average income of two-parent African-American families. By contrast, African-American families who have achieved middle- or upper-class standards may derive even greater satisfaction from family life than from their jobs. Adolescents in these homes are much more likely to be living with two parents and share many of the opportunities and values of their Caucasian counterparts. Meanwhile, an even larger number of African-American teenagers are growing up in father-absent, economically deprived homes, thereby setting the stage for problem behavior such as dropping out of school, delinquency, alcohol and drug abuse, and teenage pregnancy. Male teenagers are especially at risk.

Another significant change in family life is the dramatic increase in single fathers rearing children, with such families having tripled since 1970. According to a survey by Geoffrey Greif (1985), single fathers tend to be white, well-educated, and successful in their careers. Most of them are in middle-level positions such as managers, administrators, buyers, and store owners, and have higher-than-average incomes. More than three-fourths of them have one or two children. But a small proportion of single fathers are rearing three or more children. Male children outnumber females four to three, with most of them having reached adolescence. In most instances, the men didn't want their marriages to end, didn't initiate the divorce, and find their current situation very stressful. They usually gained custody through mutual consent or were picked by the children, mostly because the mothers were either unstable, had alcohol and drug problems, or were incapacitated. In some cases, the mothers had left the marriage. Men who were deserted by their wives had the least confidence in themselves, gave themselves the worst rating as fathers, and found the experience of being a single parent most stressful. Yet two-thirds of the single fathers wanted custody very much, felt they were prepared for it, and experienced satisfaction in many areas of parenting.

How well adolescents of either sex fare in single-parent families depends on a variety of factors, such as the custodial parent's personality and maturity, parenting skills, use of support systems, the ongoing relationship between the ex-spouses, and how consistently they behave with their adolescents. A great deal depends on the particular adolescent and single-parent family. But an extensive investigation of children of both sexes by Santrock and Warshak (1986) growing up in mother-custody, father-custody, and intact homes showed that children and adolescents of both sexes manifested more social competence when they were being reared by a same-sex custodial parent and less social competence when reared by an opposite-sex custodial parent. There are probably several explanations for this. First, adolescents have greater opportunity to identify with the same-sex parent. There is the possibility that the child in an opposite-sex custodial parent home may be pushed into adult roles too soon by substituting for the absent spouse. Of course, a lot depends on the relationship and cooperation between custodial parents and their ex-spouses. Then too, adolescents in single-parent homes may benefit from other factors, such as the custodial parent's use of available support systems, including household help and relatives, which help adolescents to form a favorable self-concept.

Stepparent Families

Because more than three-fourths of divorced people remarry, usually within a few years, adolescents are as likely to grow up in stepparent families as in single-parent families. Today, almost 10 million children and adolescents under 18 years of age, or 16 percent of the nation's youth, live in stepparent families. The most common type of stepparent family consists of a parent, more often the woman, who has custody of the children, together with a stepparent, with stepfathers outnumbering stepmothers six to one. Only in a handful of marriages do remarried couples have children or adolescents from both previous marriages *and* the new marriage (Cherlin and McCarthy, 1985).

Many of the problems in stepparent families revolve around the presence of the stepparent, partly because of the lack of clear roles for stepparents and stepchildren. How do you relate to an adolescent whose development has been heavily influenced by someone with a different personality and outlook? Or how do you behave toward a stepfather or stepmother when you already have a biological father or mother? Not surprisingly, children and adolescents generally have more adjustment problems when they are in a complex stepfamily, one in which both parents have brought children and adolescents from a previous marriage, than when they are in a simple stepfamily, in which the stepparent has not brought children (Hetherington, Hagan, and Anderson, 1988). Also, studies comparing single-parent, stepparent, and intact families have shown more strained relationships between adolescents and their parents in stepparent families. Generally, relationships between children or adolescents and their stepparents are more strained than those between adolescents and their biological parents. The relationship between the child and stepfather tends to be distant and unpleasant, while the relationship between the child and stepmother often involves a series of antagonistic interactions (Santrock, Sitterle, and Warshak, 1988).

Adolescents generally have difficulty accepting new stepparents. One reason may be that adolescents feel their primary loyalty is toward their biological parents, and they regard the stepparent as an outsider. Or adolescents may feel jealous of the attention given to the stepparent by their biological parent. A common observation is that girls have more adjustment problems with stepparents, especially with stepmothers, than boys do (Sauer and Fine, 1988). Perhaps this has something to do with mothers traditionally being more emotionally involved with their children, especially their adolescents. However, adolescents of both sexes are especially vulnerable to the effects of divorce and stepparent families, mostly because of their stage of development. At adolescence they are actively seeking their personal identity and exploring close and sexual relationships outside the family. An outsider in the family at this time makes things even more complicated. As a result, adolescents, especially males, may react to the stress of stepparent families in many of the same ways as they do in the event of parental divorce, i.e., by engaging in higher alcohol and drug use, ill-advised sexual activity, and delinquency. Adolescents in stepparent families are also more likely to be involved in family violence and become victims of sexual abuse or neglect than are those in intact families. It appears that adolescents are at high risk for abuse in families that have undergone a series of stressful changes in the preceding year (often the parents' divorce), have stepparents, and lack a flexible, appropriate family structure (Garbarino, Sebes, and Schellenbach, 1982).

Many of these problems can be minimized or avoided when parents and stepparents face up to the challenges and prepare for them appropriately. Generally, it is wise for prospective partners to give adolescents ample opportunity to get to know the future stepparent and to explore the changes remarriage will bring, such as new living arrangements and relationships with the noncustodial parent. It is also best not to force relationships with stepchildren but to let them develop gradually. Stepparents may find it more appropriate, especially at first, to become an "additional" parent rather than a replacement for an absent parent. Comparisons with the absent parent are inevitable, and stepparents should be prepared to be tested, manipulated, and challenged in their new role. At the same time, parents and stepparents should keep in mind that stepparent families, like other families, generally function as their members make them function and have vast resources for cooperation and growth. When parents and stepparents do their utmost to establish good communication in the family, show consideration and fairness for the adolescents involved, and model cooperation, stepparent families may function as well, if not better, than do many intact familes.

SUMMARY

Changes in the American Family

1. We began the chapter by pointing out some of the important changes occurring in American family life, especially the fact that adolescents are growing up in a greater variety of family types.

2. Although the family no longer fulfils all the functions it did in the past, it retains some important functions such as providing guidance and emotional support for children and adolescents.

The Family Environment

3. How well the family fulfils its responsibilities depends largely on the family environment—the overall conditions surrounding and affecting the developing adolescent.

4. Parents may adopt one of several basic parenting styles. However, authoritative parenting is the preferred style, mostly because it combines a high level of parental acceptance with moderate control, thereby fostering the growth of autonomy and responsibility in adolescents.

5. Most teenagers have positive attitudes toward their parents, especially those who perceive their parents as authoritative rather than authoritarian or permissive.

6. The quality of sibling relationships in the family depends on many factors, such as family size and age and sex of the siblings, with two adolescents of the same sex in a small family experiencing more intense sibling rivalry than do several adolescents of both sexes in a large family.

7. Birth-order effects are usually more evident among firstborns and only children, who tend to be more conscientious and achievement-oriented, largely because of greater parental attention and expectations.

Dual-Income Families

8. One of the most significant changes in family life affecting adolescents is the dramatic increase in the number of dual-income families, in which both husbands and wives are employed in the workplace.

9. As the total time that parents work increases, they spend less time with their adolescents, though the overall quality of family life depends on many other factors as well.

10. Women in dual-income families continue to bear a great deal of responsibility for reconciling the couple's work schedule and family life and do most of the household chores and nurturing of adolescents.

11. Adolescents generally spend the least time doing household chores when the mother is employed part-time, considerably more time on chores when she is employed full-time, and the most time of all in traditional families, mostly because of the closer supervision of adolescents in these families.

12. The growing number of mothers employed outside the home has given rise to more latchkey teenagers, who are susceptible to social isolation, physical and sexual abuse by older siblings, and negative peer pressure.

Divorce, Single-Parent, and Stepparent Families

13. An increasing proportion of teenagers experience a parental divorce and live in a single-parent or stepparent family.

14. Even though divorce is a stressful experience for everyone in the family, about half of the adolescents involved make a reasonably good adjustment after a year or so following the divorce.

15. Divorce generally has a more disruptive effect on adolescents when it occurs during adolescence than childhood, with adolescents being especially vulnerable to parental pressure to take sides during a marital dispute.

16. About one out of every five of those under 18 lives in a single-parent family. Although the quality of life for adolescents in these families depends on the combined influence of

many factors, adolescents demonstrate more social competence when they are reared by the same-sex custodial parent.

17. Many of the problems in stepparent families revolve around the presence of the stepparent, with adolescent-stepparent relationships being more strained than those with one's biological parents.

18. At the same time, many of these problems can be minimized or avoided when parents and stepparents face up to the challenges and prepare for them appropriately.

REVIEW QUESTIONS

1. How has American family life changed in recent decades?
2. What is the major difference between the authoritative and authoritarian parenting style?
3. How are sibling relationships affected by the adolescent's family size, birth order, and sex?
4. In what sense do mothers bear a disproportionate share of responsibility for family life?
5. How much do boys and girls help around the house when their mothers work full-time?
6. Think of some potential advantages and disadvantages of being a latchkey teen.
7. What is the "sleeper effect" of divorce?
8. How do single-parent families affect boys and girls differently?
9. What are some of the major problems adolescents face in stepparent families?
10. What suggestions would you offer to someone who is becoming a stepparent to an adolescent?

Family Relationships and Adolescent Autonomy

6

Learning Objectives

After completing this chapter, you should be able to:
1 Describe the family as a social system.
2 Identify three potential problems in parent-adolescent communication.
3 Describe how parent-adolescent conflicts change during adolescent development.
4 List the four components of an "I" message.
5 Explain the distinction between behavioral and emotional autonomy.

It has been said that the two greatest gifts the family can give its young are "roots" and "wings." By roots we mean the child's sense of being loved and accepted, and thus secure enough to develop as a person. Wings refers to the adolescent's eventual attainment of independence. Like young birds ready to try out their wings, adolescents seek greater autonomy from their parents. Wise parents not only permit but will actively encourage such independence on the adolescent's part. Yet a great deal depends on what has occurred throughout the individual's development. Adolescents with authoritative parents—who relate to their young in a warm, accepting way while setting reasonable limits—grow up participating in many of the decisions governing their lives, thereby exhibiting a high level of personal control and responsibility. Other adolescents are not so fortunate. Reared by troubled or domineering parents, often in strife-ridden homes, they may leave home early or get stuck in a lifelong pattern of rebelliousness, all of which delays their attainment of healthy autonomy.

We begin this chapter by describing family relationships and adolescent development. Then the focus shifts to parent-adolescent communication and conflict as well as how to improve family communication. The last part of the chapter describes the process by which adolescents move toward autonomy.

FAMILY RELATIONSHIPS AND ADOLESCENT DEVELOPMENT

There is increasing recognition that each family is a complex and constantly changing social system. We begin by explaining how the family functions as a social system, such that changes in one family member usually affect each of the other members. Then the impact of puberty on adolescent-parent relationships will be examined. We also consider how developmental changes in each of the parents as well as their marital relationship affect the adolescent's development.

The Family as a Social System

In recent years, many professsionals have adopted the systems approach, viewing the adolescent as an integral part of the family as a social system. In this context, each member's behavior is considered in relation to that of all the other members. Like other systems, each family develops its own identity, including certain rules and internal organization. For instance, families differ in regard to their degree of family cohesion. At one end of the continuum are *disengaged* families, in which family members have little connection with each other. Individual identity is held supreme; family identity is de-emphasized. Each family member's activities are planned and carried out without consultation or consideration of other family members. Group activity is a rare occurrence. At the other extreme are the *enmeshed* families. In these families the total family unit is elevated to the highest priority, with individual identities being relegated to a low priority. Family activities and values are emphasized over those of each family member. A family therapist once illustrated this by squeezing the wrist of the teenage daughter and asking how many others in the family felt the pain. All but one raised their hands, and that person apologized for not feeling the pain (Minuchin and Fishman, 1981). Adolescents in these families may subordinate their own needs and preferences and compete with siblings to fulfil family expectations and traditions. Youths who feel at odds with the family pattern may become even more alienated than those in other families. Healthy families fall somewhere in between these two extremes, exhibiting an optimal rather than a maximum degree of family cohesion. In these families, there is a balance in the degree of emotional closeness and support, on the one hand, and allowing each person to develop as an individual, on the other hand. See Figure 6-1.

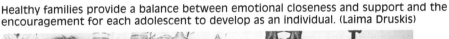

Healthy families provide a balance between emotional closeness and support and the encouragement for each adolescent to develop as an individual. (Laima Druskis)

Figure 6–1 Relationship Between Family Cohesion and Healthy Family Functioning.

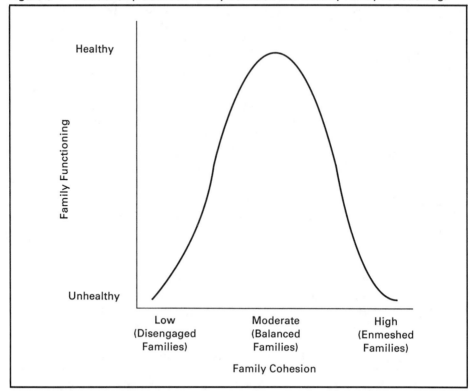

Adapted from K.M. Galvin and B.J. Brommel, *Family Communication: Cohesion and Change.* Copyright © 1982 by Scott, Foresman and Company. Reprinted by permission of HarperCollins Publishers.

A major principle of the systems approach is that whenever one person changes or develops, each other family member is also affected. Thus, an adolescent's problems with drugs or at school not only reflect the family dynamics but also affect the entire family to some degree, either directly or indirectly.

For instance, Eric, a 17 year old, reluctantly consulted a psychologist because of pressure from his parents. Eric was doing poorly in school and was running around with a group that used drugs. He had already gotten in trouble with the law. The therapist, who was trained in the systems approach, soon discovered that Eric's problems were fueled in part by a serious marital problem at home. It seems that Eric was caught up in the problems of "split loyalty" between his parents. Eric's mother resented her husband's working long hours and blamed much of Eric's problem on his father's absence from home. She also complained of the father's marital infidelity and went to great efforts to make certain Eric knew about his father's disloyalty to the family. As a result, Eric felt pressured, mostly unconsciously, to take his mother's side in the family feud.

However, in doing so, he became cut off from his father's positive influence and support. Eric responded by withdrawing from both his parents, pretending he "didn't care" about his parents' problem. Instead, he chose to escape the unhappiness at home and spend a greater than usual amount of time with his friends.

The therapist, realizing this represented not simply Eric's problems, called both parents in. At first the parents resisted, claiming that Eric was simply trying to escape responsibility for his problems. But as the therapist pointed out how the couple's marital conflict was contributing to their son's problems, and how Eric's problems, in turn, were further dividing the parents, they became more cooperative. Once the parents realized what they were inadvertently doing to their son, both of them made a greater effort to cooperate, partly for their son's welfare. Eric, in turn, reassured of his father's love and concern, focused more of his energies on resolving his own problems at school and with drugs.

Impact of Adolescents' Development

Because the family functions as a social system, we might expect that the adolescent's coming of age would affect the entire family. Now there is evidence to support this. It appears that the onset of puberty not only leads to extensive changes in the adolescent's development, but also affects the adolescent's interactions with his or her parents. In one study, Lawrence Steinberg (1988) observed family interactions at three phases of the son's development; before the onset of puberty, midway through puberty, and after puberty. He found that family interactions changed significantly as the boys matured physically. Generally, the boys became more assertive, especially in relation to their mothers. During family discussions, boys deferred less to their mothers than before. They interrupted their mothers more frequently and offered fewer explanations for their opinions than before the onset of puberty. Mothers, in turn, reasserted their authority, interrupted their sons more frequently, and gave fewer reasons for their opinions. As a result, family interaction became more tense and polarized. Both parents and adolescents paid less attention to each other's opinions. However, fathers tended to provide a balance for the interaction between mothers and sons, with adolescents deferring to their fathers more than to their mothers. As adolescents attained puberty, family interactions became more responsive and flexible. Sons offered more justification for their opinions and interrupted their parents less. Also, the son's relative influence on family decisions increased.

Similar changes occur in the relationships between girls and their parents during puberty. In one study, John Hill (1985) and his colleagues compared girls whose menstruation had not begun with girls who had begun menstruation in the past six months, those who had begun within the past twelve months, and those who had begun more than twelve months earlier. They found that girls who had experienced menarche very recently, within less than six months, exhibited more difficulty with their parents. The girls were less likely to participate in family activities and more likely to resist family rules and to feel that their

The Demand for Privacy

At what age do young people start closing the bedroom door behind them for privacy? Ross Parke and Douglas Sawin (1979) investigated this among 112 middle-class children and adolescents aged 2 to 17. The demand for privacy was determined by how readily the subjects let other people into occupied bedrooms and bathrooms.

A big factor in the demand for privacy was family density—the ratio between the size of the house and the number of people living in it. The strongest desire for privacy occurred at the extremes: those living in smaller houses (less than 1,600 square feet) with more than five people and those living in larger houses with four people or less. Children and adolescents in moderately crowded houses were less likely to keep bedroom and bathroom doors closed. The researchers explained that individuals who grow up in overly crowded homes may feel the deprivation more severely and insist on privacy whenever they can, whereas those who grow up in more spacious homes get accustomed to privacy and expect it.

The desire for privacy generally increases with age, with the biggest change occurring just before and during adolescence. Whereas boys and girls aged 2 to 5 closed bedroom doors behind them only 29 percent of the time and bathroom doors only 64 percent of the time, the 10-to-13-year olds closed bedroom doors 46 percent of the time and bathroom doors 96 percent of the time. Those aged 14 to 17 closed bedroom doors 58 percent of the time and bathroom doors 100 percent of the time.

The only group that stood out as an exception to the general rule was the 6-to-9-year olds—those in Freud's latency stage of sexual development. Boys and girls this age were less inhibited than at any time before or after. Most of them allowed anyone to come in regardless of what they were doing, whether dressing, bathing, or using the toilet. In contrast, adolescents demand more privacy partly because of their greater physical and sexual maturity, their growing independence from other family members, and their need for self-reflection.

mothers did not accept them. By contrast, girls who had begun to menstruate between six and twelve months before the study seemed to have settled into a more harmonious pattern of family relationships. As with boys, the greatest period of disruption in family relationships occurred about the time of extensive pubertal changes. However, in contrast to boys, the influence of girls in family decision making did not seem to increase over the course of pubertal changes. Furthermore, girls who had begun to menstruate more than twelve months before the study exhibited behavior and difficulties similar to those who had only recently begun menstruation. One explanation is that their precocious puberty had led to problems, such as associating with older girls, which in turn evoked conflicts at home.

It appears that the rapid physical maturation at puberty brings about psychological and social changes in boys' and girls' development which, in turn, vitally affects the relationships with their parents. For instance, physical maturity ordinarily leads to greater assertiveness on the adolescent's part. Then too, the emergence of formal thought is associated with idealistic, egocentric thinking, creating new expectations in regard to how adolescents feel they should be treated by their parents. Also, greater association with peers and adults outside the family may intensify adolescents' demands on their parents. Initially, all of this tends to have a disruptive effect on family relationships. But with the passage of time, especially in those families with authoritative parenting, family members gradually achieve greater cooperation and more adequate ways of resolving conflicts.

Changes in Family Development

Not only do adolescents change, but each of the parents and their marriage relationship and thus the entire family unit also changes over time. In turn, the combined impact of all these changes affects the adolescent's development (Cohler and Boxer, 1984). In the first few years of marriage, couples are busy establishing their households and strengthening their marriage. Then during the child-bearing stage, parental concerns shift to taking care of their young children. But by the time the children reach adolescence, important changes are taking place in the parents and their marriage as well as in the developing adolescent, all of which must be taken into account in order to understand how the family functions and influences the adolescent's development.

When the family's first child reaches adolescence, the parents are usually in their thirties and forties, the period of the midlife transition. Some parents find this such a stressful time of life that it becomes a midlife "crisis." Consequently, there is increasing recognition that the parents as well as their adolescents are going through a type of identity crisis, which involves many of the same issues but with a different meaning for each generation. For instance, both generations are undergoing extensive biological changes. Adolescents are entering a period of rapid physical growth and sexual maturation that is characterized by increasing physical attractiveness and sex appeal. Adults, on the other hand, are experiencing the bodily changes associated with middle age, accompanied by rising concerns about health, decreased energy, and diminished physical and sexual attractiveness. Also, both adults and adolescents are experiencing changes in regard to status and power. But adolescents are entering a stage in which they are moving up in status, depending on the choices they make in regard to their education, careers, and marriage. In contrast, their middle-aged parents are busy taking stock of choices already made, including the gap between their initial aspirations and actual achievements. In sum, while both adolescents and their parents are at a critical stage in their respective developments, they are going in

Middle-aged parents as well as their adolescents are going through an identity crisis which, in turn, affects parent-adolescent relationships. (Richard Hutchings/Photo Researchers)

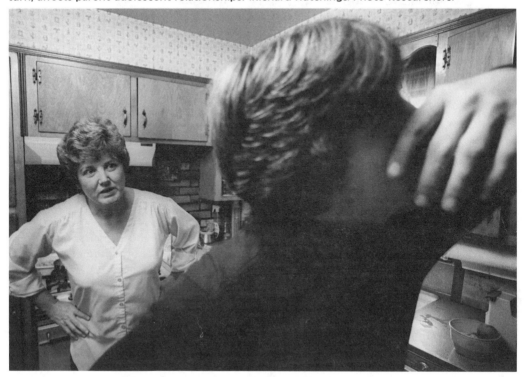

opposite directions. Adolescents are moving into early adulthood, which is often regarded as the "best time" of life; however, adults have passed the midpoint of their lives and are coming to terms with the choices made when they were younger.

Family life is also affected by the couple's marital relationship and adjustment. Studies have shown that marital satisfaction tends to be at a low point during middle age (Greeley, 1981). This probably has something to do with the length of marriage as well as the changes brought by middle age. But it also may have to do with the presence of teenagers in the home and the burden of paying for college education. A lot depends on the particular couple and their situation. When couples feel frustrated and unhappy in their marriages, this usually rubs off on their adolescents. Parents in strife-ridden homes express less warmth and concern for their children and emphasize stricter discipline, thereby creating greater emotional deprivation among adolescents (Block, Block, and Gjerde, 1986). By contrast, partners who enjoy each other and their marriage are more likely to spend pleasurable time with their adolescents and emphasize family cooperation (Burman, John, and Margolin, 1987).

The combined effect of all these changes in middle-aged parents and their marriages, along with those of the developing adolescent, affects the way the family unit functions. Consequently, the family with older adolescents and the parents well into middle age functions in different ways than it did when the children were just reaching puberty and the parents themselves were still young adults. A major change occurs in regard to the financial aspects of family life. Family finances are especially strained as children reach adolescence. Parents become concerned about increased educational needs, often coupled with care of elderly parents. Mothers often return to the workplace to help with family finances. Then too, families must accommodate to the greater maturity and independence of the growing adolescent. Adolescents are making more decisions on their own and spending more time with their peers. Parents must provide transportation and monitor peer activity, with occasional arguments about the priorities of family and peer activities. For instance, adolescents now spend more time on part-time jobs after school, which itself calls for greater adjustment at home. Then too, teenagers who work after school spend less time studying and have dinner with their families less frequently, all of which can become a problem (Steinberg et al., 1982).

PARENT-ADOLESCENT COMMUNICATION AND CONFLICT

Nowhere do family relationships have a greater impact on adolescent development than the way family members communicate with each other and manage conflict. But communication involves more than the verbal exchange of information, as important as this is. Even more important are attitudinal factors such as trust, being comfortable enough to express one's ideas and feelings, empathy, and the willingness to listen to another's ideas and feelings, especially during disagreements. Relatively normal adolescents tend to come from homes in which there is reasonably good communication between themselves and their parents, to the extent they can express disagreement without threatening family cohesion. By contrast, troubled adolescents tend to come from homes characterized by faulty communication. Parents and adolescents tend to talk past each other, without recognizing each other's needs or feelings, and thus fail to become responsive to each other.

Parent-Adolescent Communication

When family members interact in characteristic ways time and time again, families develop their own style and patterns of communication (Galvin and Brommel, 1982). In turn, these communication patterns become important not only for conveying information, but also for defining relationships, boundaries, and networks within families. For instance, families tend to develop their own characteristic communication networks that determine the flow of messages and feedback between family members and others outside the system. Key issues include who controls information in the family, with whom others talk, if and how particular individuals are included, and how much information each member receives. Communication networks are often based on the degree of cohesion between family members. A common network resembles a wheel, with a central person, often the mother in the traditional family, connecting to all the others as a hub on the wheel. An even more desirable type of communication is the all-channel pattern, in which all family members tend to communicate with each other. See Figure 6-2. The all-channel network allows for greater flow of communication and maximum use of feedback. Although this type of network requires more time and effort to work effectively, it is more satisfying to everyone in the family (Leigh and Peterson, 1986).

Generally, clear and effective communication is associated with moderate levels of family cohesion and adolescent individuation. Communication tends to be positive and supportive and includes such communication skills as genuine information giving and receiving, empathetic understanding of the other's ideas and feelings, and effective problem solving. For instance, suppose a parent com-

Figure 6–2 Two Common Communication Networks.

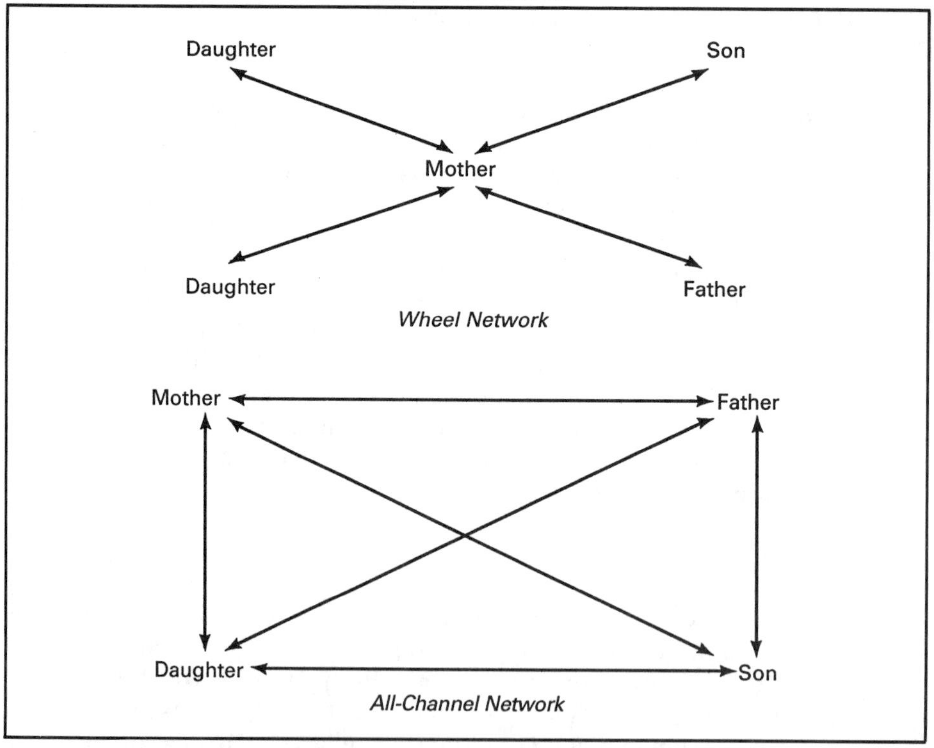

Adapted from K. M. Galvin and B.J. Brommel, *Family Communication: Cohesion and Change*. Copyright © 1982 by Scott, Foresman and Company. Reprinted by permission of HarperCollins Publishers.

mands a 13 year old, "Go to bed!" This conveys the desired information clearly. But it does so in a way that defines an authoritarian relationship between the parent and adolescent. However, this message would take on a different meaning if the parent would say, "It's late, and I would like you to go to bed. What do you think?" This conveys the desired information but in a way that defines a more positive relationship between the parent and adolescent, as associated with the authoritative style of parenting. Ordinarily, this is a more preferred type of communication because it encourages the adolescent's participation, feedback, and taking responsibility for his or her behavior.

Ineffective communication tends to be negative and defensive. Such communication involves an attitude of superiority, overcontrol, judgmental dogmatism, name-calling, and blaming. Parents are apt to express harsh criticism, act intrusively, and induce guilt in their teenagers. A troubled adolescent once said to me, "People in our family are always blaming somebody." Teenagers generally respond by expressing a greater frequency of negative or contrary responses. Also, they experience lowered self-esteem and a sense of isolation (Fischer, 1980). Defensive communication is typically related to lower conflict resolution and more frequent threatening and punishing experiences. Not surprisingly, families that are more likely to use defensive communication and less likely to use supportive communication have a higher than average number of teenage runaways (Leigh and Peterson, 1986)

A common type of problem is *underresponsible* communication, in which the speaker fails to claim ownership of the message. Typically, the speaker uses words like *people* and *nobody* rather than *I* or *me*. For instance, when asked to cut the grass on Sunday, 16-year-old Bob replies, "Nobody cuts grass on Sunday." His remark may or may not convey Bob's intention of avoiding responsibility, but it can be construed this way. Bob might facilitate clearer communication by taking responsibility for the message by saying, "I don't like to cut grass on Sunday, I'd rather cut it on a weekday."

Another type of problem communication is *disqualification*, in which family members invalidate their own messages by disguising their true emotions, contradicting themselves, switching subjects, pursuing tangents, and using incomplete sentences. An example might be the teenager who says to his father, "You probably wouldn't want to loan me money for my car insurance." "Are you asking for a loan?" replies his father. "Well, maybe, but I already know what you're going to say—'If you want a car, you've got to pay for it.' " "I'm not clear, are you asking me for a loan?" "Well, not actually a loan, just some short-term temporary help until I get paid next month. Of course, I could borrow it from a bank, but I don't have enough collateral." A clearer message might be, "Dad, I need a loan to avoid losing my car insurance."

Still another type of problem is *incongruent* or *paradoxical* communication in which a family member sends mixed signals. This may involve a verbal message accompanied by a sarcastic facial expression or gesture that amounts to a mixed message. The most famous type of incongruence is the "double-bind" communication involving two inconsistent messages. For instance, parents might tell their teenager, "You're free to go out with anyone, as long as we don't disapprove of him." The real message is that the teenager is not fully free to select his or her friends. A clearer message might be: "We aren't going to dictate your friends. But we are concerned about some of the people at your school and the things they're doing and we reserve the right to limit your association with them for your own well-being."

Parent-Adolescent Conflict

No matter how well parents communicate with their children, conflict generally increases in the home as children reach adolescence. Typically, parent-adolescent conflict increases during early adolescence, remains stable throughout middle adolescence, and then declines as adolescents leave home. Most of the conflicts during early adolescence revolve around everyday matters such as schoolwork, home chores, dress, sibling conflicts, and disobedience. Older adolescents pose more serious conflicts involving the use of the car, alcohol, drugs, and sex. Parents are more likely to argue with their sons about taking care of family property or the use of the car. Parents tend to disagree with their daughters more about dating and sex. Teenagers and their parents argue about once every three days, with each disagreement lasting about eleven minutes on the average. Most of the disagreements are moderately upsetting to the teenagers. Conflicts are more likely to involve the mother rather than father, and the majority of conflicts occur between girls and their mothers (Montemayor and Hanson, 1985).

A moderate degree of parent-adolescent conflict is not only inevitable but may be helpful in promoting independence and identity exploration on the part of adolescents. As we have discussed earlier, it is normal for growing adolescents to assert their independence, such that some clash of wills is to be expected. Then too, parents' lives have been shaped by a different era than that of their adolescents, thereby increasing the potential for disagreements between generations. However, there is a tendency for parents to feel their authority is being challenged and put even more pressure on adolescents than on children to conform to parental standards (Collins, 1987). In contrast, wise parents are more likely to recognize the adolescent's need for greater independence and to respond by easing up on parental control, appealing more to reason and negotiation. All of this encourages adolescents to assume more responsibility for their behavior. As we might expect, adolescents who are actively exploring their own identity tend to experience a moderate degree of disagreement with their parents (Cooper et al., 1982). The lack of such disagreements may reflect an adolescent's undue dependence, anxiety over separation, and fear of independence.

At the same time, chronic or intense conflict at home is detrimental to the adolescent's development. Prolonged parent-adolescent conflict is associated with many factors. Rapid social change increases the differences between genera-

---

Family Violence

Are you aware that parents are just as likely to abuse adolescents as they are children? A survey by the National Center on Child Abuse shows that mistreatment of adolescents accounts for almost half of all cases involving the abuse and neglect of children, even though adolescents account for only 38 percent of the population under 18 years of age. Adolescents in families at risk for abuse are more apt to have undergone a series of stressful changes in the past year and have stepparents and a less structured family pattern (Garbarino, 1985). Abusive parents often have suffered from child abuse themselves, and as parents have unrealistic expectations of their youth. Then they overreact when their adolescents do not conform to these expectations, mistakenly attributing teenagers' reactions to intentional and negative motivation and thus setting the stage for abusive behavior (Twentyman, et al., 1988).

You may be equally surprised to discover that parental assault by adolescents is no longer uncommon. In a national survey based on a representative sample of American youth, Robert Agnew and Sandra Huguley (1989) found that 5 percent of the adolescents 11 to 18 years of age admitted to hitting one or both parents in the past year. But the authors estimate the true rate is about twice this figure. Overall rates of parental assault bear little or no relation to such factors as the size or sex of the adolescent, family type, socioeconomic factors, or drug use. However, males are somewhat less likely to hit their mothers and more likely to hit their fathers as they age, while females are more likely to hit both parents as they age. Generally, mothers are more often hit than fathers. Also, for some reason, Caucasians are more likely than African-Americans to hit their parents. Although there is a wide range of potential causes of parental assault, adolescents who assault their parents have several things in common: namely, they are more likely to be weakly attached to their parents, have friends who assault their parents, and approve of such behavior.

---

tions. Then too, excessive parental control and delay of adult status aggravates parent-adolescent conflict (Ellis, 1986). Also, adolescents' problem behaviors, such as drug use, school dropout, delinquency, and premature marriage, are often a factor. In many cases, the turmoil at home may contribute to the adolescent's problem behaviors. But in some instances, problem behaviors have developed prior to adolescence and may occasion many of the arguments at home. In any case, it is estimated that about one in every five or six adolescents experiences intense or prolonged conflict with his or her parents and thus is at greater risk for problem behaviors (Montemayor and Hanson, 1985).

Improving Parent-Adolescent Communication

A major way of ensuring that family disagreements focus on genuine issues rather than on misunderstanding is to establish some basic rules or guidelines for effective family communication. Such rules might include the agreement to send clear messages, such as speaking in the first person singular and speaking directly to the person for whom the communication is directed. Equally important is the willingness to listen to the other person in an empathic, nonjudgmental way.

The "I" message is a valuable communication skill for expressing your ideas and feelings to others (Gordon, 1988). Essentially, this is a way of expressing yourself in an honest way without putting the other person on the defensive. "I" messages can be especially helpful when you have strong feelings about someone's behavior that has become a problem for you. The "I" message consists of four components: (1) an objective, nonjudgmental description of the other person's behavior; (2) the tangible effects on me; (3) How I feel about it; and (4) what I'd prefer the person do about it. See Table 6-1. For instance, suppose you are a parent and your daughter comes home several hours later than promised. You may instinctively say angrily, "Where have you been?" Chances are your daughter may hear only the judgmental anger and feel she has to defend herself, with an unproductive argument ensuing. But suppose you were to say something like, "When you come home much later than you told us, we worry about you. We'd like to know when you're coming home." Your daughter is more likely to get your main message, which is, "We worry about you," rather than reacting to your anger at her.

Equally important is the ability to listen accurately to someone else. After many years in clinical practice, Carl Rogers (1980) concluded that one of the major reasons we do not hear very well is our natural tendency to judge, to approve or disapprove the statements of the other person. Consequently, Rogers advocated the use of empathic listening, which involves listening to someone in a nonjudgmental way and providing objective feedback to the person as a way of checking on the accuracy of what has been heard. For instance, suppose you are a parent and your son complains, "I hate my math class." Instead of criticizing him or giving him some advice, which usually falls on deaf ears, you might respond in

Table 6-1 Examples of "I" Messages

Nonjudgmental description of person's behavior	Tangible effects on me	My feelings about it	What I'd prefer the person do about it
1. If you don't come home when you promise	then I don't know where you are	and I worry about you	I wish you'd call us when you're going to be late.
2. Each time you put off doing your share of the house chores	I don't know if we can count on your help	and I feel angry	I'd prefer that you set a specific deadline for doing your part and keep it.
3. When you want help with your homework, don't wait until the last minute	because I'm often busy with other things	and I feel frustrated and resentful	Give me more advance warning when you want my help—okay?

a more empathic way by saying, "You really dislike that class intensely." The teenager who feels that you're really listening might continue to express his feelings, including the deeper reasons he doesn't like the class. "Yeah," he might say, "the teacher gives us too much homework to do." An understanding parent might then say, "Then it's mostly the excessive amount of homework you object to rather than the subject of math." "Yeah." This type of communication usually leads to a more fruitful conversation in which both the parent and the adolescent may explore the real issues involved, thereby setting the stage for a more constructive solution to their differences.

ADOLESCENT AUTONOMY

No matter how skilled in communication parents are, there is always the risk they will become so preoccupied with the daily skirmishes with their adolescents that they lose sight of the more important goal, namely helping adolescents to achieve their "wings," or independence. For instance, one mother said, "I don't know what's come over Matt recently. He's constantly arguing with us. He's always been such a cooperative kid. I don't understand what's gotten into him." The fact that Matt is 13 years old and probably has begun puberty may have a lot to do with it. His argumentative stance may be the outer manifestation of an inner need for more autonomy. That is, he wants to be treated in a more grown-up manner and to be given more opportunities to control his life.

Making more choices on one's own is an important means of achieving autonomy. (Barbara Rios/Photo Researchers)

The Process of Achieving Autonomy

At the same time, the adolescent's achievement of autonomy is more of a gradual process than people usually assume. A major reason is the discontinuity between dependence and independence in the developmental process. A helpful way of understanding the transition to independence at adolescence is Ausubel's satellization theory of development (Ausubel, Montemayor, and Svajian, 1977).

Young children are seen as satellites who, in the normal course of development, become dependent on their parents for an extensive period of socialization before becoming relatively autonomous at adolescence. Successful development implies that individuals eventually become self-governing and form families of their own. Yet the quality of the dependency relationship throughout childhood has a significant bearing on the eventual attainment of autonomy. Children growing up with warm, loving parents with an authoritative stance tend to internalize their parents' acceptance as a lasting basis of self-worth, thereby facilitating the eventual attainment of autonomy (Pardeck and Pardeck, 1990). But children with cold, domineering or permissive, neglectful parents tend to feel undervalued in such a way that they remain unduly dependent on the approval of others or rebellious, which impedes the eventual attainment of autonomy.

At adolescence, satellization is gradually replaced by desatellization. That is, adolescents usually break away and gain more distance and autonomy from their parents at this stage of life. But adolescence does not bring total self-rule. Instead, adolescent autonomy becomes another, albeit critical, step in the eventual attainment of full autonomy. For instance, adolescent desatellization normally involves resatellization, or the transfer of dependency from parents to others. This can be seen in adolescent crushes on teachers or coaches or in the slavish conformity to peers at this age. It can also be seen in the intense emotional identification in adolescent friendships and romances. Although the element of dependency in these relationships is usually rather obvious to parents, from the adolescent's view such relationships help to diminish their dependence on their parents.

Ausubel explains that desatellization is a gradual process involving the transformation rather than the severance of emotional ties with parents. Throughout this process the attitude and behavior of parents may either help or hurt the attainment of independence. Parents who are reasonably satisfied and fulfilled in their marriage and careers, especially if they are independent people themselves, may be more willing to let go of their adolescents and encourage them in their pursuit of age-appropriate autonomy. But parents who are frustrated and unfulfilled in their own lives may attempt to hold on too tightly, thus thwarting the adolescent's development of autonomy.

It is important that parents continue to have an accepting attitude toward their adolescents and that they be willing to modify their supervision and control in a way that encourages autonomy. They must expect more responsible behavior from their youth but within appropriate limits. That is, they must not tolerate childish excuses for unacceptable behavior nor demand adult behavior

too quickly. Parents who abdicate their authority in the face of adolescent defiance may undermine the adolescents' attainment of autonomy by permitting
immature or self-defeating behavior, however "adult" such behavior may seem to
adolescents themselves. It is wise to realize that teenagers have a right to make
their own mistakes, but at the same time to set reasonable limits in regard to
matters of health and personal safety.

Types of Autonomy

So far we have referred to autonomy as if it were a unitary trait signifying self-
direction. Yet, upon closer inspection, autonomy appears to be a complex mixture of different traits and skills. Furthermore, these qualities may be more
evident in some aspects of behaviors more than others within the same person.
For instance, one teenager readily learns how to drive a car but is still fearful of
his parents' disapproval. By contrast, another teenager has not obtained her
driver's license but feels free to make decisions without her parents' approval.
We might say that the first teenager has moved toward behavioral autonomy
faster than emotional autonomy, with the sequence being just the reverse for the
second teenager. Accordingly, we can distinguish various types of autonomy,
such as behavioral autonomy, emotional autonomy, as well as value autonomy
and moral autonomy, to name some of the more important types of autonomy.

The distinction between behavioral and emotional autonomy is especially important. *Behavioral autonomy* refers to the ability to perform age-
appropriate tasks in a relatively autonomous manner, including the ability to
make responsible decisions on one's own. Such autonomous behavior is already
evident by the second year of life, when small children begin taking a more active
role in their eating and toilet habits. Even though children's ability to act in a self-
reliant way generally increases with maturation, they continue to need help in
mastering many of the skills necessary for everyday living. However, with the
rapid growth at adolescence, there is a marked increase in behavioral autonomy
between 11 and 18 years of age. Adolescents not only want to do more things for
themselves but are increasingly able to. By the late teens, most adolescents can
take care of themselves in terms of their daily needs, such as eating, dressing, and
learning the appropriate skills needed in school, sports, and social activities.
Adolescents who take jobs outside the home also learn how to handle responsibility in the workplace, manage money, and get along with people. At the same
time, most parents recognize that on occasion adolescents are likely to need
assistance in matters requiring more seasoned judgment, such as the choice of an
appropriate college or career.

An important part of behavioral autonomy is the ability to make decisions on one's own. This generally increases during adolescence largely because
of the cognitive changes that occur at this age. For instance, one study comparing
the decision-making abilities of children and adolescents 9 through 21 years of
age showed a significant increase by about 14 years of age, the age at which

formal thought emerges (Weithorn and Campbell, 1982). Such thinking permits adolescents to compare various views simultaneously. Also, the capacity to take the role of another person, which increases during this period, enables adolescents to consider divergent views in light of other people's perspectives. Then too, the adolescent's hypothetical reasoning permits him or her to consider the possible consequences of a given course of action. The capacity for autonomous decision making is also aided by the emergence of a self-chosen identity, emotional maturity, value autonomy, as well as increased peer involvement and support. See the boxed item on decision making.

Emotional autonomy usually develops later and more gradually than does behavioral autonomy, largely because it involves a transformation of the affectional ties that have been so important to both the child and parent. Basically, emotional autonomy is more relationship-oriented and involves learning to rely more on one's own inner reserves of self-esteem and self-confidence in the give-and-take of relationships. This includes the capacity to form adultlike close ties with friends of one's own choosing and the ability to survive disappointments, criticism, failure, and rejection at the hands of others. Adolescents who have received a reasonable degree of acceptance at home feel free to choose close friends and confidants, including those their parents might not approve of. On the other hand, teenagers who feel they have been neglected or unloved at home may remain unduly dependent on the approval and support of others, whether

---

Decision Making

To find out whether adolescents improve their decision-making skills as they mature, Catherine Lewis (1981) presented one-hundred adolescents 12 to 18 years of age with a series of problems in which a teenager needed help making a difficult decision. For instance, in one problem a teenager who was undecided whether to have cosmetic surgery asked, "Do you think I should have the operation?" (Lewis, 1981, p. 540)

Adolescents' responses were then examined in regard to five aspects of decision making, including (1) the awareness of future consequences, (2) the awareness of potential risks, (3) whether parents, peers, or outside experts were recommended as consultants, (4) whether they considered the vested interests of those giving advice, and (5) whether adolescents revised their views in light of new information.

For example, in response to the problem of cosmetic surgery, an eighth grader was primarily concerned about being teased at school and being turned down for a date by girls. In contrast, a twelfth grader observed that "you have to look at different things . . . that might be more important later on in your life" (Lewis, pp. 541–542), showing more awareness of the long implications of having cosmetic surgery.

Overall, the results showed that decision-making abilities generally improve throughout adolescence in four of the five areas. The sole exception is adolescents' willingness to revise their views in light of new information, something that may come with greater maturity.

they are parents or peers. Sometimes teenagers as well as adults mistakenly think adolescents have achieved their independence when they have done so only in a behavioral way. For example, Brad has a job after school, has bought his own car, and gets along well with his friends. Yet he is very touchy whenever his performance is criticized at school or at work. He also becomes very defensive and moody whenever he is disappointed in his close relationships. Consequently, even though Brad has achieved a significant degree of behavioral autonomy, he lags in the development of emotional autonomy, which is potentially as important as behavioral autonomy throughout one's life.

Personal Control and Responsibility

Another way of understanding autonomy has to do with the relationship between personal control and responsibility. Ordinarily, we assign responsibility to those who are perceived to have the most control over their lives or autonomy. But how realistic is it to expect individuals to assume greater responsibility for their behavior when they feel they have so little control over their lives, as is often the case among adolescents?

Curious about this matter, Patricia Ortman (1988) did in-depth interviews with high school students to find out how they felt about personal control and responsibility in their lives. Her subjects included an equal number of males and females, half of whom were ninth graders and half seniors.

Ortman found that teenagers feel more in control of their lives and more responsible as they advance in age and school grade. Accordingly, high school seniors generally feel they have greater personal control and accountability than they did in the ninth grade. However, boys report greater gains in both areas than girls do. That is, while ninth grade girls feel more responsible and in control of their lives than ninth grade boys do, the reverse is true among twelfth graders. There are also sex differences in specific areas. Boys report greater control in regard to their jobs, while girls feel more control in the personal and interpersonal realms.

At the same time, Ortman found little agreement among teenagers regarding the meaning of personal control and responsibility. All teenagers agree that feeling in control is good, such as feeling strong, powerful, stable, comfortable, normal, and confident. Not being in control is synonymous with feeling powerless, uneasy, insecure, and panicky in a way that leads to feelings of anger. But there is less clarity in regard to the meaning of responsibility and its relation to personal control. Students tend to define responsibility in terms of personal accountability, in a way that relates behavior to one's choices and self. Yet they acknowledge external sources of accountability that are more dependent on adults and peers, such as being trusted by others, being given responsibility, and being made to feel guilty. Overall, teenagers agree that personal control and responsibility are closely related but not synonymous. Thus, only the relationship between personal control and life satisfaction proved significant among all teenagers. The link between responsibility and life satisfaction was closely related only for the high school seniors.

Taking a cue from these findings, Ortman observes that parents and teachers alike may have little success in getting adolescents to take greater responsibility for their lives because they ignore students' perceptions that feeling responsible goes hand in hand with feeling in control of your life. Yet adults tend to disempower adolescents at precisely the time they demand greater responsibility of youth. In contrast, what is needed is to give adolescents greater opportunities and practice in sharing control and responsibility. Furthermore, it should come as no surprise that Ortman found that parent-adolescent relationships are a significant factor, and those who had authoritative parenting report the greatest gains in both personal control and responsibility.

SUMMARY

Family Relationships and Adolescent Development

1. There is increasing recognition that each family functions as a complex and constantly changing social system, such that a change or development in one person affects other family members as well.

2. Accordingly, the onset of puberty not only leads to extensive changes in adolescents but affects the interactions with their parents as well, as seen in increased parent-adolescent conflict during puberty.

3. Also, changes in other family members, especially the parents' midlife transition and their marital adjustment, modify the family's overall interactions, which, in turn, affect the adolescent's development.

Parent-Adolescent Communication and Conflict

4. Each family develops their own style and pattern of communication, and moderate levels of family cohesion are associated with healthy family functioning and adolescent individuation.

5. Effective family communication tends to be positive and supportive and includes communication skills such as genuine giving and receiving of information, empathy, and effective problem solving. Ineffective communication generally is negative and defensive, involving judgmental attitudes and underresponsible communication.

6. Parent-adolescent conflict usually increases during adolescence, initially involving disagreements about daily issues such as homework and later involving more heated discussions over controversial topics such as drugs and sex among older adolescents.

7. Whereas moderate parent-adolescent conflict tends to promote adolescent identity exploration and autonomy, prolonged intense conflict is detrimental to the adolescent's growth.

8. A major means of improving family communication is to establish basic rules that involve sending clear messages, as in the "I" message, and the willingness to listen to others in a nonjudgmental way.

Adolescent Autonomy

9. Adolescents' achievement of independence or autonomy occurs throughout a gradual process of desatellization, involving the transformation rather than the severance of emotional ties with parents.

10. Autonomy is a complex mixture of different traits and skills, such that there are several

types of autonomy, including behavioral, emotional, value, and moral autonomy, among others.

11. It is especially important to distinguish between behavioral autonomy, which refers to task-related and decision-making abilities, and emotional autonomy, which involves one's inner reserves of esteem in the give-and-take of personal relationships.

12. Finally, we pointed out that parents and teachers may have little success in getting adolescents to take greater responsibility for their lives because adults ignore adolescents' perception that feelings of responsibility go hand in hand with feelings of being in control of their lives. What adolescents need is consistent opportunities and practice in sharing control and responsibility, as exemplified by authoritative parenting.

REVIEW QUESTIONS

1. In what sense is the family a social system?
2. How does an adolescent's coming of age affect his or her family?
3. To what extent do adolescents and their parents both face an identity crisis?
4. How would you characterize effective family communication?
5. What is *underresponsible* communication?
6. Would you agree that some conflict between the generations is not only inevitable but desirable for the adolescent's development?
7. What is meant by an "I" message?
8. Can you give an example of behavioral autonomy?
9. Which is usually more difficult to achieve—behavioral or emotional autonomy?
10. How realistic is it to expect adolescents to assume greater responsibility if they do not also possess a high degree of personal control?

7

Peers

Learning Objectives

After completing this chapter, you should be able to:
1 Identify at least three issues on which adolescents prefer peer advice to parental advice.
2 Explain the process of social comparison in adolescent peer relationships.
3 Describe the sequence of changes in the relationship between cliques and crowds throughout adolescence.
4 Discuss the variables affecting peer conformity during adolescence.
5 Describe adolescent friendship patterns in regard to age and sex differences.
6 Discuss social dating among adolescents.
7 Describe the hazards of adolescent marriages and parenting.

To get an idea of what adolescents do in a typical week, two researchers gave high school students electronic pagers that beeped at various times throughout the day from early morning to late evening (Csikszentmihalyi and Larson, 1984). Each time the students were beeped, they were asked *where* they were, *what* they were doing, and *who* they were with.

About half the time, adolescents were at home, usually in their bedrooms. One-third of the time they were at school, primarily in the classroom. The rest of their time was spent in other places, such as at work, at a friend's house, or in an automobile. What were they doing? Slightly over one-fourth of the time adolescents were engaged in productive activities, mainly related to school. Somewhat more time was spent on maintenance activities, such as doing chores, eating, or personal care. Almost half of the time they were engaged in leisure activities, whether socializing or watching television.

An analysis of the people they were with showed that adolescents spend considerably less time with adults than they do with their peers. Adolescents spend only about one-fifth of their waking time with their families, whether parents or siblings. As much as one-fourth of the time is spent in solitude. But fully half of the time is spent with peers, about equally divided between classmates and friends. In fact, as adolescents move from the ninth to the twelfth grade, they spend an increasing proportion of their time with their peers. When talking with their peers, adolescents tend to feel friendly, sociable, happy, and free. But when talking with adults, adolescents report feeling passive and constrained in the relationship.

PEER RELATIONS

The "beeper" survey confirms the familiar observation that as children reach adolescence they spend more time with their peers. Although this is often taken to mean that parents and other adults are being displaced by the adolescent's friends, this is not necessarily the case. Instead, most adolescents continue to identify strongly with their parents and look to them for advice on important matters. At the same time, peers exert increasing influence on other matters, such as how to dress and social relationships. Thus, it would be more accurate to say that adolescents regard their parents and peers as different reference groups for different aspects of their lives.

Parent and Peer Influence

The degree of influence parents retain over their adolescents depends partly on how well they get along with their offspring. Although parental influence generally decreases as students advance from the sixth to the twelfth grade, mostly because of the growing independence of adolescents themselves, the decrease tends to be much less in some families than others. Parents who retain a great deal of influence in the lives of their adolescents generally show a higher level of interest, understanding, and helpfulness toward their teenagers than do other parents (Larson, 1980). When teenagers become unduly influenced by their peers, it is more likely because of something lacking in the parent-adolescent relationship than because of the greater attractiveness of peers. Parents who do not know what to expect of their adolescents or who fear being displaced by their adolescent's peers are engaging in a self-fulfilling prophecy, helping to make it so. Parents who neglect or mistreat their adolescents also leave them more vulnerable to undue peer influence. It is also important to realize that adolescents differ greatly among themselves. Some teenagers habitually conform to their parents' wishes, whereas others are more oriented toward their peers.

The relative influence parents and peers exert on the lives of adolescents depends heavily on the particular issue involved. This was brought out in a study by Hans Sebald (1989) that determined the extent to which adolescents sought advice from their parents or peers on a number of issues. Sebald found that adolescents are more likely to seek parental advice on such matters as finances, education, career plans, and to a lesser extent for such matters as personal problems. By contrast, adolescents are more inclined to seek out their peers for advice on such matters as which club to join, whom to date, and which social events to attend. See Table 7–1.

Sebald also compared adolescents' responses to similar questions over a twenty-year period and found significant changes in parent/peer orientation. Peer orientation increased between the 1963 and 1976 surveys, probably reflecting the dramatic social changes among youth during this period. Although there was a slight decline in peer influence during the early 1980s, this modified rather than reversed the earlier trend, resulting in a net increase in peer orientation among adolescents in the 1980s. At the same time, there were important differences between boys and girls. Whereas girls were more parent-oriented and boys were more peer-oriented in the 1960s, this pattern became more balanced, if not reversed, to some extent by the 1980s. Girls now exceeded boys in peer orientation in many matters.

Table 7–1   Percentages of Teenagers Seeking Peer Advice

Issues	Girls (N = 110)	Boys (N = 110)
1. On what to spend money	2	19
2. Whom to date	47	41
3. Which clubs to join	60	54
4. Advice on personal problems	53	27
5. How to dress	53	43
6. Which courses to take at school	16	8
7. Which hobbies to take up	36	46
8. In choosing the future occupation	2	0
9. Which social events to attend	60	66
10. Whether to go or not go to college	0	0
11. What books to read	40	38
12. What magazines to buy	51	46
13. How often to date	24	35
14. Participating in drinking parties	40	46
15. In choosing future spouse	9	8
16. Whether to go steady or not	29	30
17. How intimate to be on a date	24	35
18. Information about sex	44	30

Adapted from Hans Sebald, "Adolescents' Peer Orientation: Changes in the Support System During the Past Three Decades," *Adolescence*, Winter 1989, pp. 940–941.

In addition, there was an increase in a fourth category, the extent to which teenagers rely primarily on their own decisions. The questionnaire provided three categories for each of the issues: parents, peers, or undecided. Whereas all responses of the 1963 sample fell within these categories, a number of respondents in the 1976 and 1982 surveys spontaneously added comments such as "myself," "personal opinion," and "figure it out myself." In 1982 there was a marked increase of such unsolicited responses, especially among girls, probably reflecting the impact of the women's movement. Such responses suggest that neither parent nor peer orientation precludes adolescents' ability to make their own decision. It appears that the majority of adolescents decide many things for themselves, judging mostly by the situation itself. Whether they seek help from their parents or peers depends largely on which they regard as the most competent guide for the matter at hand.

Social Comparison

Adolescents are influenced by their peers primarily through the process of social comparison, that is, seeking out peers with whom to evaluate one's self, abilities, characteristics, or reactions. Social comparison is a lifelong process that everyone engages in, children as well as adults. But social comparison becomes especially critical during adolescence when individuals are busy *establishing* themselves, not simply refining themselves as in adulthood. To make childhood comparisons at this period would be regressive. To compare oneself with adults would be inappropriate. Consequently, adolescents turn to their peers as the primary reference group for defining themselves and their social identities. Social comparison becomes an intense, all-encompassing process that occurs constantly—on the school bus, especially during school, at parties, and even in the privacy of one's room at home.

Vivian Seltzer (1989) conducted an extensive investigation with twenty five hundred adolescents in Pennsylvania, Ohio, and New York over a ten-year period and found that adolescents engage in the process of social comparison somewhat differently during early and late adolescence. During early adolescence, when the slate of self is primarily blank, teenagers need a large number and variety of peers with whom to compare themselves. As a result, Seltzer suggests that "peer arena" is a more appropriate concept than peer group, because adolescents seek out peers in many different groups to explore different aspects of themselves. Adolescents are especially interested in how others view their physical appearance, their clothes, and their appeal to the opposite sex. Personality attributes generally take on more significance than do learned abilities; and friendliness, a sense of humor, popularity with the opposite sex, honesty, and loyalty to friends are important with adolescents of both sexes. Such social comparisons may have positive and negative results. For instance, Lisa may gain self-confidence from having her social abilities recognized by her friends. But Mark may experience self-doubt because of the social alienation occasioned by his shyness.

Seltzer points out that during early and mid-adolescence, teenagers are busily defining themselves rather than seeking out close relationships. Thus, they may have a wide circle of acquaintances, but few close friends. Activity level is high; intimacy level is low. Actually, during this period, adolescents need time alone in order to absorb and integrate insights discovered through social comparison. Then too, true intimacy is not possible until the individual has a sufficiently secure sense of self with which to truly engage others. Furthermore, intimacy also involves time commitments. In contrast, lack of intimacy helps adolescents to conserve their energies and consolidate their identities. Thus, much of the aloneness in early and mid-adolescence is generally not loneliness, but a functional necessity of the period.

By late adolescence, youth enter into a new phase of social comparison, in which they are more concerned with refining their sense of self. Friendships may change as the need for social comparison narrows. Now it is the type of peer, not the quantity, that matters most. At this stage, adolescents tend to select peers more like themselves, with whom to share themselves more fully. During this stage also, adolescents tend to affirm the worth of each self-selected element of self, integrating their identified abilities and characteristics into a coherent sense of self. At the same time, adolescents begin to experience greater intimacy with their peers, initially with those of the same sex. During this period adolescents are greatly influenced by their close friends. As they grow older, adolescents consult their special friends more often and their parents less often. Interestingly, Seltzer found that adolescents tend to underestimate peer influence, while overestimating parent influence. Apparently, it is more socially acceptable for adolescents to admit their dependence on parents than to acknowledge a new dependence on peers.

Acceptance and Popularity

Despite this, adolescents are greatly concerned about how they stand with their peers—the degree to which they are accepted or rejected by others. Although the value of social acceptance has declined somewhat in the past two decades, most teenagers feel it is important or very important to be liked and accepted by their peers. Generally, social acceptance has to do with adolescents being regarded as members of the various peer groups, such as school clubs or neighborhood pick-up groups. At the same time, the emphasis on ethnic pride and cultural diversity in our society has made acceptance within one's own ethnic group even more important than in the larger society. Popularity, a more restricted

Being in the right crowd becomes especially important for young women's popularity. (Laima Druskis)

term, refers to that degree of social acceptance in which adolescents are especially well liked and actively sought after by their peers.

Group acceptance and popularity depend mostly on the adolescents' personal qualities, especially those that affect their interpersonal relationships. Generally, adolescents who are well liked are at ease with themselves and make others feel accepted and involved in social activities. Thus, well-liked adolescents tend to be friendly and outgoing. They are also apt to have a moderately high level of self-acceptance and self-esteem, so that they can interact with a variety of adolescents, not just those like themselves. Having a good sense of humor, being cheerful, and being fun to be with usually increases one's popularity. Physical attractiveness, intelligence, and social skills also count for a lot (Tedesco and Gaier, 1988; Hartup, 1983).

Teenagers who are not well liked tend to exhibit personal traits opposite to those of their more popular counterparts. That is, they tend to be shy and in some cases aloof. Although habitual "loners" are generally unpopular, teenagers who spend up to a third of their waking time alone tend to get along better with their peers than do those who spend either too much time alone or too much time socializing with others (Csikszentmihalyi and Larson, 1984). Adolescents with a low level of self-acceptance tend to be self-centered, anxious, and defensive, all of which alienates others. In some instances, such individuals may attempt to compensate for their marginal status by acting sarcastic, aggressive, or conceited, thereby compounding their problems of rejection.

The relative importance of adolescents' activities and accomplishments to being popular with their peers varies somewhat depending on the type of school, community, and dominant values. However, the criteria for peer popularity have remained remarkably consistent in different eras. Joel Thirer and Stephen Wright (1985) surveyed six-hundred high school students in six states. They found that men and women rated being an athlete as the leading criterion for men's popularity and being in the "leading crowd" as the main criterion for women's popularity. But on most other items, men and women were ranked somewhat differently by their same-sex and opposite-sex peers. (See Table 7-2) For instance, both men and women ranked being a "leader in activities" higher for their own sex than for the opposite sex. Similarly, both sexes ranked "coming from the right family" dead last for their own sex, but not for the opposite sex. This suggests that teenagers are especially concerned to be judged by their own accomplishments, which they have more control over than "coming from the right family." Yet they are not always so understanding when judging their opposite-sex peers.

PEER GROUPS

Many of the relations between peers occur in groups. Some groups are characterized by an official organization, with rules for how members may be admitted and function within the group. Examples would be the various types of social

Table 7–2   Peer Popularity According to Same Sex and
             Opposite Sex

MEN	
Rated by women	Rated by men
Be an athlete	Be an athlete
Be in leading crowd	Be in leading crowd
Come from the right family	Lead in activities
Have a nice car	Make high grades, honor roll
Make high grades, honor roll	Come from the right family

WOMEN	
Rated by men	Rated by women
Be in leading crowd	Be in leading crowd
Make high grades, honor roll	Lead in activities
Come from the right family	Be a cheerleader
Be an athlete	Make high grades, honor roll
Have a nice car	Be an athlete
	Come from the right family

Source: Adapted from Joel Thirer and Stephen D. Wright, "Sport and
   Social Status for Adolescent Males and Females," *Sociology of Sport
   Journal* 2 (1985); pp. 167 and 169.

and interest groups—drama club, yearbook staff, honor society, athletic teams, and religious groups. But adolescents probably spend an even greater amount of time in informal groups, which are characterized by less formal organization and stability. For instance, two or more teenagers may share lunch daily during the week or telephone each other regularly.

Cliques and Crowds

In a well-known study, Dunphy (1980) found that the majority of adolescents belong to two types of groups, cliques and crowds, which differ both in their size and function.

Cliques are essentially small groups (less than ten members in Dunphy's study) that meet mostly for personal communication and sharing. Activity in cliques tends to occur spontaneously, such as meeting in the hallway at school. Members are attracted to each other on the basis of similar interests, personalities, schools, neighborhoods, or religious affiliations. Although adolescents tend to form same-sex cliques in early adolescence, they participate more in opposite-sex cliques as they grow into middle and late adolescence.

Crowds are larger-size groups (more than ten persons in Dunphy's study) that meet primarily for organized social activities, such as parties or dances. Crowd activities occur mostly on the weekends, in contrast to clique activities, two-thirds of which occur during the week. Most crowd activity includes both sexes. Dunphy also found that the crowd was essentially a collection of cliques, with membership in the latter required for belonging to the crowd.

About 30 percent of the boys and 20 percent of the girls in Dunphy's study did not belong to either type of group. These adolescents are often referred to as the "outsiders" or "loners," though the particular individuals so labeled may change from year to year. Some loners do not join groups because they have been rejected by their peers. Others deliberately choose not to join group activities, even when offered opportunities to do so; an example is the habitually shy adolescent who feels more comfortable with ideas, things, or nature than with people. Sometimes, marginal individuals may get together in groups of their own. Interestingly, the more creative and gifted adolescents are less likely to join groups, or even if they do, they are less conformist in them during high school and college. All this reminds us that although membership in peer groups is desirable, it is not essential for normal development in every instance.

Changes in Peer Groups

Dunphy found that the relationship between adolescent cliques and crowds changes throughout adolescence and that the sequence of changes is somewhat predictable. Furthermore, it appears that these changes are an integral part of the adolescent's socialization, especially in the transition from preadolescent, same-sex roles to the opposite-sex roles characteristic of adults. See Figure 7–1.

In Stage 1, boys and girls are still active in the same-sex peer groups characteristic of preadolescence. Boys tend to join each other mostly to do things together, and they form somewhat larger and more stable groups than girls do. The latter get together more for personal sharing and form smaller and more intimate groups than boys do.

Stage 2, characterized by more interaction between same-sex cliques, often takes place during the junior high school years. Teenagers now spend more time away from their homes and neighborhoods and have a wider selection of friends to choose from. Because girls are often taller and more mature than boys at this stage, most opposite-sex relationships occur in group activities. Individual dating tends to be the exception at this stage. Group parties and dances offer boys and girls more security, mostly because of the awkwardness and superficial antagonism between the sexes at this period.

In Stage 3, the upper-status members of the same-sex cliques begin interacting in more personal, boy-girl relationships. Adolescents begin dating at this stage, with the earlier-maturing boys and girls usually taking the lead. Teenagers now form opposite-sex cliques, which become the core of the adolescent crowd. The latter is denoted by the dotted line rectangle in Figure 7-1. Notice that these adolescents retain membership in both opposite-sex and same-sex cliques.

By Stage 4, the majority of adolescents have begun dating, which leads to a transformation in the clique system. Now the crowd becomes composed mostly of opposite-sex cliques, with a great deal of close association between them. Although Dunphy refers to this stage as the fully developed crowd, he also notes

Figure 7–1 Stages of Peer-Group Development in Adolescence. Dunphy found that the sequence of changes in adolescent peer-group formation remains remarkably persistent despite variations of time and place. But he deliberately avoided specifying an average age for the onset of each stage because of the wide variation in ages among different groups of adolescents

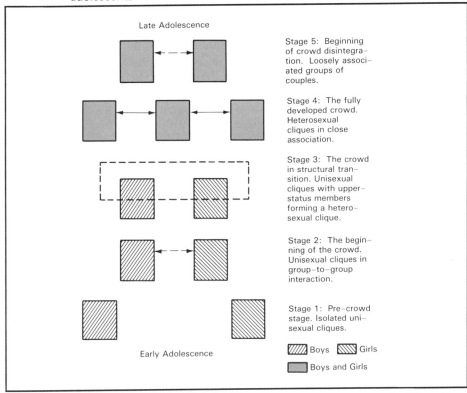

Source: D. C. Dunphy, "The Social Structure of Urban Adolescent Peer Groups," *Sociometry* 26 (1963), p. 236. Used by permission of the publisher and author.

that the crowd structure tends to last only long enough to ensure that its members have acquired the basic sex-role characteristics necessary for adult heterosexual relationships.

Stage 5 is designated as the beginning of crowd disintegration. Upon graduation from high school, individuals tend to take different paths; some leave school to work and others to attend college. More couples are also going steady, becoming engaged, or getting married. All of this makes for less need for the support of the old adolescent cliques and crowd.

Dunphy (1980) found that this sequence of changes in adolescent peer groups tends to persist despite the variations of time and place. He also found that teenagers enter the respective stages at increasingly earlier ages, mostly because of earlier maturation and the beginning of adolescence.

Conformity

The way in which adolescents relate to each other in groups is significantly affected by the social process of conformity—changing one's thinking or behavior to coincide with the group norm because of real or imagined social influence. Sometimes peer conformity may be rather obvious, such as the gang member who engages in a delinquent behavior mostly because of pressure from his buddies. But teenagers are often influenced by their peers in more subtle ways, especially in the need for approval. A common example is the adolescent who experiments with alcohol or street drugs, partly to win the approval of his or her friends. In other instances individuals may modify their behavior because of a real change in attitude, such as the teenager who stops smoking because of the conviction that it is hazardous to one's health. More often than not, conformity to peers reflects a combination of these influences.

Peer conformity generally increases throughout childhood, peaking in early to midadolescence and declining slowly afterward. The developmental trend in peer conformity can be seen in a study by Thomas Berndt (1979) that included students from the third through the twelfth grades. Students were administered a questionnaire measuring three types of conformity—prosocial, neutral, and antisocial. One prosocial item consisted of agreeing to a peer group's request to help a classmate with a project when one really wanted to do something else. A neutral item consisted of agreeing with peers to engage in an activity the student was not really interested in. An antisocial item consisted of the adolescent's response to a peer's request to engage in a delinquent act. The results showed that the average conformity score for prosocial and neutral items rose to a peak in early adolescence (grade six for prosocial, grade nine for neutral items) with a gradual decline thereafter. One possible explanation may be teenagers' increasing awareness of others' reactions, as in the imaginary audience, such that they conform to gain approval, or at the least avoid looking foolish. However, the average conformity score for antisocial behavior continued to rise, peaking in the ninth grade and then declining to the twelfth grade. The later age in peak conformity to antisocial peer behavior corresponds to the increased socialization to the peer culture and incidence of delinquency generally seen at this age.

At the same time, peer conformity varies widely among adolescents as well as within a particular individual's behavior according to a number of influences. A major factor is the age and maturity of the adolescent, especially because the cognitive capacity to internalize social rules increases with age throughout school. The attainment of formal thought or adult-type reasoning in late adolescence usually brings a greater understanding of the complexity of social behavior, along with a corresponding decrease in automatic compliance with the rules (Polovy, 1980). Then too, adolescents with high self-esteem and low self-blame are much less likely to conform to their peers than are those with low self-esteem and high self-blame (Hartup, 1983). Also, the particular issue at hand, as discussed earlier, is a very important consideration. Accordingly, adolescents are especially likely to conform to their peers in matters pertaining to personal taste and social relations, including dress, music, dating, and club memberships (Sebald, 1989). Then too, there are a number of characteristics about peer groups which influence the extent of peer conformity. Generally, the more cohesive the group, the greater the proportion of conformers in the group. Yet the presence of individuals who resist conformity tends to reduce the proportion of conformers. However, the newer and less experienced an individual is in the group, the more likely he or she is to conform to the group. Also, the more difficult the task the group is engaged in and the less knowledgeable and competent the adolescent feels in this area, the greater the tendency to conform to one's peers (Feldman, 1985).

Traditionally, girls have been portrayed as more prone to peer conformity than boys, partly because of girls' greater concern about peer acceptance. Yet it is becoming increasingly evident that such differences have been greatly exaggerated. A major reason has to do with the degree to which a particular situation reflects stereotyped male or female attitudes and behavior. Thus, a female who stops at the service station for gas may be especially susceptible to social influence in regard to the need for motor oil, for example, mostly because service stations and cars have been traditionally oriented to males. At the same time, the male who goes shopping to buy his girlfriend a blouse without knowing much about women's clothing sizes may be highly susceptible to the clerk's suggestions as to which size blouse he should buy, largely because men customarily lack knowledge about buying women's clothes. In both instances, it is the lack of relevant knowledge and experience rather than gender that is the crucial issue in conformity. Obviously, women who are experienced in taking care of cars and men who are knowledgeable about buying women's clothes would act more independently than would those in the above examples. Alice Eagly (1983) suggests yet another biasing factor, namely the sex of the researcher. Eagly found that 80 percent of the studies on conformity are conducted by men, who tend to obtain larger sex differences than do women researchers. Generally, experiments conducted by women find few, if any, sex differences, suggesting the need for continuing research in this area.

FRIENDSHIP AND DATING

Among the most important aspects of adolescents' lives are the close relationships with their friends. Although friendship is important at all ages, it is not until middle or late adolescence that friendships take the form of intimate relationships characterized by trust, self-disclosure, and loyalty. A major factor during this stage of development is the adolescent's emerging autonomy, or sense of being a separate person with a firm identity, which is necessary for healthy intimacy. Another important consideration involves the cognitive changes that enable adolescents to understand situations from another person's point of view, thereby increasing their empathy and helpfulness toward others. As a result, from this stage on, youth experience a greater need for intimacy with their peers as well as an increased capacity to form close relationships with those outside their families.

Adolescent Friendships

The meaning and quality of friendships tends to change throughout adolescence, mostly because of the developmental and social changes that are occurring during this period. Friendship gradually evolves from superficial, activity-centered relationships in early adolescence to more emotional intense and intimate relationships in late adolescence.

When boys or girls in early adolescence, around 10 to 14 years of age, speak of a friend, he or she is likely to be someone they enjoy doing things with. And because boys and girls this age have different interests and engage in different sorts of peer activities, most of their friends are of the same sex. The actual relationship between friends tends to be rather superficial, with qualities such as self-disclosure and loyalty just beginning to be evident at this stage of adolescence, especially among girls (Berndt, 1982).

During midadolescence friendships become more emotionally intense and relationship-oriented and also more unstable. (Shirley Zeiberg)

By midadolescence, around 15 to 17 years of age, friendships become more emotionally intense and relationship-oriented, and also more unstable. For one thing, adolescents are becoming more independent of their parents and more emotionally involved with their peers. Then too, feeling anxious and confused about their bodily changes and intensified sexual feelings, teenagers are looking for someone they can confide in, who will be trustworthy and can offer emotional support. As a result, friendships become more mutual, emotionally intense, and characterized by greater intimacy with peers than that shared with parents (Hunter and Youniss, 1982). The greater degree of emotional dependency and identification in relationships at this age brings more satisfaction in friendship but also greater vulnerability than in earlier stages. Consequently, midadolescent friendships tend to blow hot and cold, with sudden, dramatic changes and bitter feelings when friends break up. Even when adolescents dream of their friends, such dreams are often marked by negative fears of separation and abandonment, attesting to the intense emotional involvement of adolescent friends (Roll and Millen, 1979).

By late adolescence, from 18 years of age on, the passionate quality of friendship gives way to a calmer, more stable relationship. On the one hand, individuals are capable of forming close, meaningful relationships characterized by trust, self-disclosure, and loyalty. For instance, one study found that between the fifth and eleventh grades adolescents were increasingly apt to say they knew what their friends "feel" about things even when not told, and also, "felt freer" to talk to their friends about anything (Sharabany, Gershoni, and Hofman, 1981). At the same time, late adolescents have greater intellectual and emotional maturity, bringing them greater understanding of the complexity of human relationships. Having had more experience in making friends by this age, they tend to be more realistic about what to expect from a friendship. They are also more tolerant of individual differences and can appreciate what others bring to a relationship without the need to have their friends be "just like themselves." As a result, friendships between late adolescents tend to be emotionally close and stable relationships resembling adult friendships.

Another developmental pattern has to do with the emergence of opposite-sex friendships. Although opposite-sex friendships increase throughout adolescence, they don't become common until late adolescence, toward the end of high school. During early adolescence, boys and girls keep pretty much to friends of their own sex, mostly because they have different interests and activities at this age. Boys and girls tend to feel uncomfortable in each other's presence, as reflected in the joking and teasing so characteristic of this stage. For instance, if a boy is seen talking with a girl in the school cafeteria, each of them is apt to be teased about it by his or her same-sex friends. However, by midadolescence, a greater proportion of 15 and 16 year olds are choosing friends of the opposite sex, with girls generally choosing a larger number of them than boys. The transition from same-sex to opposite-sex friends occurs about the same time boys and girls are beginning to socialize in mixed crowds. Thus

By midadolescence a greater proportion of boys and girls are choosing opposite-sex friendships. (Laima Druskis)

opposite-sex friends are more common in dating situations, parties, and the crowd activities at school.

Opposite-sex friendships generally supplement rather than displace same-sex friendships. For instance, in one study the likelihood of opposite-sex friendships increased throughout high school, while the number of same-sex friendships remained constant. Of opposite-sex friends, girls reported an average of two while boys reported an average of only one; of same-sex friends, girls reported an average of five and boys reported an average of four (Sharabany, Gershoni, and Hofman, 1981). Girls are also more apt to report close friendships with boys who are older, often at another school, whereas boys generally list girls the same age or younger. All of this suggests that friendships among late adolescents flourish in the context of dating (Blyth, Hill, and Thiel, 1982).

Although friendship is not necessarily more important for one sex than the other, it tends to have a different meaning for girls than for boys. More specifically, intimacy appears to play a more central role in girls' friendships. Girls report higher levels of intimacy both in their same-sex and opposite-sex friendships, especially from midadolescence on. Girls also express greater anxiety over intimate relationships at all age levels. Tensions, jealousies, and conflicts between close friends are more common among girls than boys. A greater proportion of the negative themes among girls involves rejection or exclusion from friendship, whereas those of boys involve outright disputes over property, leisure

Loneliness

Throughout adolescence and the transition to adulthood, individuals are especially susceptible to loneliness, the state of unhappiness at being alone accompanied by a longing for companionship. According to a survey among people of all ages, 18 to 25 year olds suffer the most from loneliness. The intensity of loneliness decreases steadily by age, with people over 70 being the least lonely. A major reason is that loneliness is largely a state of mind resulting from the gap between one's desires for closeness and the failure to find it. Having loosened the ties with their parents, youths are actively seeking intimacy with their peers. Yet, many of them still lack the social skills and relationships to satisfy their intimacy needs (Rubenstein, Shaver, and Peplau, 1982).

Some adolescents are more likely than others to suffer from loneliness, especially those who come from broken homes, are alienated from their families, have marginal social status, lack meaningful goals, have low self-esteem, suffer from severe shyness, and have unrealistic expectations of popularity (Mijuskovic, 1986).

Youths who blame their loneliness on their personal inadequacies ("I'm so lonely because I'm unattractive") make themselves even lonelier. They are more apt to alleviate their loneliness by focusing on their own efforts ("I'll stop studying so much and get out and meet more people."). Young people usually benefit from social-skills training, learning how to initiate a relationship and conduct a meaningful conversation with others. Carolyn Cutrona (1982) points out that people who are habitually bothered by loneliness may also need to change their attitudes. She found that college students who overcame their initial loneliness at school were no more likely to initiate a conversation with strangers, join groups, or attend parties than students who remained lonely. The biggest difference between the two groups was in their attitudes. Students who eventually overcame their loneliness persisted in their efforts to socialize with others despite some initial loneliness at the beginning of the school year. In contrast, those who suffered the most from loneliness lowered their goals and rationalized their loneliness. Yet their efforts to convince themselves they didn't need friends or that they were too busy with school to pursue a more active social life made them even lonelier. Consequently, it may not be enough to encourage young people to join groups and acquire social skills. We must also help them deal with their pessimistic attitudes about making friends.

activities, and girlfriends. All of this does not mean that intimacy is absent from boys' friendships. Rather, boys tend to express their intimacy needs in more subtle ways, through shared activities rather than the direct satisfaction of emotional needs.

Dating

Many of the friendships with the opposite sex occur in the context of dating—the practice by which a boy and a girl agree to meet at a specific time and place, either alone or in a group, for a social engagement. Dating differs from opposite-sex friendships in that dating relationships are somewhat less flexible and more subject to social rules (Paul and White, 1990). Dating begins earlier and plays a more important role among young people in the United States than in many other parts of the world. This may be accounted for in part by the relatively longer adolescence of modern youth plus the characteristic emphasis on choosing one's own friends and marriage partners in Western society. In any event, youth now reach physical and sexual maturity at an earlier age and tend to marry at a later age than in the past, giving them considerably greater experience in dating than their counterparts in earlier eras had.

Dating serves several purposes in the lives of young people. First, the practice of dating provides youth with opportunities for sharing leisure activities, such as attending a concert or a party. Dating is also an important means of learning the social and interpersonal skills needed to get along with members of the other sex, such as how to initiate a relationship and how to end an unwanted relationship. One of the most important functions of dating is establishing and maintaining mutually satisfying close relationships. Dating also provides an opportunity for sexual experimentation within mutually acceptable limits. Although a certain amount of testing behavior occurs in dating, most sexual intercourse among young people occurs within close, steady relationships rather than casual dating. Finally, dating also provides valuable experience for mate selection. By the time young people reach their early to midtwenties, most have had at least one serious relationship with the other sex, and the majority have had several or more such relationships (Paul and White, 1990).

How soon teenagers begin dating depends largely on the particular adolescent, his or her parents, and peer influence. However, several studies indicate that adolescents generally begin dating when members of their particular clique have begun to date, regardless of the adolescent's age or maturity. Adolescents from single-parent families and unhappy intact families begin dating at an earlier age than do those from happy intact families, at about 14 years of age. But they are no more likely to have a greater number of partners or go steady than their counterparts from happy, intact families (Coleman, Ganong, and Ellis, 1985). At the same time, dating relationships among early adolescents differ from those among late adolescents. Early and mid adolescents tend to hold an egocentric and immediate-gratification orientation toward dating, with the emphasis on recreation and gaining others' approval. In contrast, older adolescents focus more on a reciprocal orientation, with the emphasis on intimacy and companionship, along with a future orientation. That is, early and mid adolescents tend to be *self*-focused, whereas late adolescents are focused more on mutuality, or what dating is "supposed to be like" (Roscoe, Diana, and Brooks, 1987).

Going steady has its advantages and disadvantages. On the positive side, going steady brings a sense of intimacy that is associated with heightened self-esteem and enhanced sex-role identity among both partners. Having a steady partner also provides a sense of security to many adolescents. On the negative side, many youth, especially early and mid adolescents, are not emotionally ready

What About the Bashful, Shy Adolescent?

Chances are he or she has a more difficult time making friends, especially with the opposite sex.

Shyness is the tendency to avoid contact or familiarity with others. It is especially acute at adolescence, mostly because of the rapid body changes as well as the increasing capacity for self-consciousness and abstract thought which appears at this stage.

In a study of shyness among high-school and college students Philip Zimbardo and his colleagues (1974) found that 82 percent of the students regarded themselves as shy at some point in their lives. Although about half this number felt they had outgrown shyness, over 40 percent of them labeled themselves as presently shy. Most of them did not like being shy.

Shy adolescents have more trouble making friends because they are often misperceived by others in a negative way. Shy persons tend to be regarded as aloof, bored, disinterested, condescending, cold, and hostile. When treated accordingly, they may feel even more isolated, lonely, and depressed. As a result, they overindulge in the normal process of self-monitoring, thus increasing their self-criticalness, their concern for the impression they make on others, and their shyness.

Zimbardo found that shyness covers a wide range of behaviors. At one end of the spectrum are those who are not especially apprehensive about being with people when necessary, but who prefer being alone most of the time. These are the adolescents who feel more comfortable with ideas, nature, or working with things. In the middle range are those who are easily embarrassed, reflecting their lack of self-confidence and social skills. An example would be the awkward, socially inept adolescent who hesitates to ask for a favor or a date. At the other extreme are adolescents whose shyness serves as a kind of neurotic self-imprisonment. These are the individuals who judge themselves with impossible rules, leading them to avoid unfamiliar situations and people and the possibility of rejection.

Our society aggravates shyness by the emphasis on competition, individual success, and personal responsibility for failure. Parents unintentionally encourage shyness by stressing individual achievement and social approval as the primary measures of an adolescent's self-worth.

Shyness can be overcome partly through getting teenagers involved in something outside themselves, like total absorption in a task, role playing, or dramatics. It may help to identify specific situations that elicit shyness, and to provide opportunities for practicing the social skills needed in them, as in assertiveness training. It also helps to realize that shyness is entirely "normal" for adolescents and will be outgrown in most instances.

Did you ever have any trouble with shyness in adolescence? If so, have you mostly outgrown it?

P. Zimbardo, P. Pilkonis, and R. Norwood, *The Silent Prison of Shyness* (Glenview, IL: Scott, Foresman and Company, 1974). Copyright © 1974 by Scott, Foresman and Company. Reprinted by permission.

to handle the intense give-and-take of intimate relationships. Going steady also encourages premature sexual involvement, with the increased risks of an unwanted pregnancy and adolescent marriage. Another disadvantage of going steady is that adolescents will experience a "premature crystallization" of their personal identities—or a foreclosed identity—rather than exploring more of their potential with a wider variety of people before settling on a single partner (Samet and Kelly, 1987).

Common problems in dating can be seen in a study of several hundred university students (Knox and Wilson, 1983). The single biggest problem reported by women was unwanted pressure to engage in sex. Other common problems were what to do and where to go on dates, along with establishing good communication and avoiding misunderstanding, especially in regard to sex. The most frequent problem mentioned by men was communication with their dates. Other problems, in descending order, were places to date, shyness, money, and honesty/openness. Part of the problem in dating is that older youth of both sexes value honesty and openness as an integral part of establishing close, mutually satisfying relationships. Yet initially both partners are concerned to present themselves in the best possible manner, such that it usually takes time to develop intimacy and satisfying companionship.

Adolescent Marriage

Although dating is less closely linked with courtship or mate selection than in the past, the majority of youth eventually marry, most of them in their twenties. But a significant proportion of them marry early, with one in five marriages having at least one partner, usually the woman, in his or her teens (U.S. Bureau of the Census, 1990).

The single biggest reason for adolescent marriage is that the girl is pregnant. In fact, the younger the bride, the more likely she is to be pregnant. About half the time teenage girls with a premaritally conceived pregnancy marry the father of their child. A disproportionate number of teenage pregnancies occur among those in the lower socioeconomic groups, in many of which the girl already has another child. Even when there is no pregnancy involved, teenage marriages occur more frequently among those in the lower socioeconomic groups—accompanied by lower education, higher rate of school dropouts, and lower incomes—all of which lessens a couple's chances for a successful marriage.

Unfortunately, marrying to legitimize the birth of the child reduces the likelihood that the mother will return to school after pregnancy. Such marriages also exhibit greater marital instability and chances of eventual divorce. Those who delay their marriage until after the birth of the child are even more apt to separate and divorce in later years. Alan Booth and John Edwards (1985) find that a major factor in the greater marital instability of teenage marriages is "inadequate role performance." That is, those who marry in their teens tend to have less than an adequate role model in the home as well as insufficient time

It's like being grounded for eighteen years.

Having a baby when you're a teenager takes away more than your freedom, it takes away your dreams.

The Children's Defense Fund.

Adolescent marriage reduces the chances that the girl will complete school after the birth of her child. (Children's Defense Fund)

and exposure to family life to fulfill the spouse role. One woman who grew up in a home seeing her father beat her mother was encouraged by her mother to marry early. The message was, "Find a husband, get married, get out of here." Many of these young people lack the personal maturity for marriage, especially at that age. Boys are unready to assume the responsibility of marriage and parenthood. And teenage girls often resent the loss of freedom. Moreover, the ability to enter into satisfying emotional intimacy depends on the attainment of a strong sense of personal identity. Individuals must know who they are before they can share themselves meaningfully in a marriage relationship. However, in exceptional cases individuals who marry in their teens may grow together and achieve an even more meaningful marriage because of the extra struggles they have shared.

Children of teenage parents, in turn, do less well on average than their peers do on measures of cognitive and social adjustment. At the same time, there is a wide variation in adjustment depending on several measures. Eric Dubow and Tom Luster (1990) found that children are more at risk if the mother was younger than 17 at the time of the birth, was not married, had not completed high school, and was on welfare. Also, children are at greater risk where there was little emotional support and cognitive stimulation in the home. By contrast, children of teenage parents are more likely to make a good adjustment when they are intelligent, have high self-esteem, and a supportive family background. Contrary to popular belief, most children of teenage mothers do not become adolescent parents themselves. According to one study, nearly two-thirds of the daughters of teenage mothers delayed their first birth until 19 years or later. Yet the minority of those who did have a teenage birth were more vulnerable than their mothers to economic dependence. These teen mothers were even less likely to ever become married or overcome the handicaps of early childbearing, thereby contributing to the growth of an urban underclass (Furstenberg, Levine, and Brooks-Gunn, 1990).

SUMMARY

Peer Relations

1. As children reach adolescence, they spend an increasing proportion of time with their peers—those of their own age.
2. Adolescents' orientation toward their peers tends to supplement rather than displace the orientation toward their parents, so that peers and parents serve as alternative reference groups for different matters.
3. However, there has been a net increase in peer influence among adolescents during the past two decades, especially among girls.
4. Adolescents seek out their peers as the primary reference group for defining themselves, mostly through the process of social comparison—seeking out peers with which to evaluate one's self, abilities, characteristics, or reactions.
5. Acceptance and popularity with peers depend primarily on adolescents' personal qualities, and to a lesser extent on their physical characteristics and accomplishments.

Peer Groups

6. The majority of adolescents belong to two types of peer groups: cliques (small groups that meet mostly for personal sharing) and crowds (larger-sized groups that meet primarily for organized social activities).
7. Throughout adolescence, the pattern of participation in peer groups changes from isolated same-sex cliques to crowds composed of mixed-sex cliques, thereby helping adolescents to make the transition to adult-like heterosexual roles.
8. Conformity to peers generally increases throughout childhood, peaking in early to midadolescence and declining slowly afterward, mostly because of the cognitive changes that occur during this period.

Friendship and Dating

9. Also, there is a greater need and capacity to form close relationships with one's peers during adolescence.

10. At the same time, the meaning and quality of friendships change throughout adolescence, with friendships evolving from superficial, activity-centered relationships to more emotionally intense and intimate relationships resembling adulthood friendships.

11. Although opposite-sex friendships increase throughout adolescence, they do not become common until late adolescence, toward the end of high school.

12. Much of the friendship between the sexes occurs in the context of dating—the practice by which a boy and a girl agree to meet at a specific time and place, either alone or in a group, for a social engagement.

13. Dating relationships differ among early and late adolescents, with early adolescents adopting an egocentric orientation and late adolescents having more of a reciprocal orientation emphasizing companionship.

14. Although dating is less closely linked with mate selection than in the past, about one in five marriages has one partner in his or her teens.

15. The biggest single reason for early marriage is a premarital pregnancy, which, in turn, leads to greater marital instability and chances of eventual divorce compared to other marriages.

REVIEW QUESTIONS

1. To what extent does the increased peer orientation at adolescence supplement rather than displace parental influence?
2. What is the function of peers in the lives of adolescents?
3. What generally makes an adolescent popular?
4. Can you recall your closest friends when you were an adolescent?
5. How can you explain the rise and gradual decline of peer conformity during adolescence?
6. What are the ways adolescents' friendships tend to change with age?
7. How does the meaning of friendship differ among adolescent boys and girls?
8. When do teenagers generally begin social dating?
9. What are some of the pitfalls of adolescent marriage?
10. How can we account for the greater instability of adolescent marriages?

8

Schools

Learning Objectives

After completing this chapter, you should be able to:
1 Identify the advantages and disadvantages of compulsory education.
2 Describe how middle schools are designed to meet the developmental needs of early and middle adolescents.
3 List the advantages and disadvantages of both large and small high schools.
4 Describe the characteristics of effective teachers.
5 Describe the three aspects of intelligence proposed by Robert Sternberg.
6 Identify several family, socioeconomic, and ethnic differences that affect school performance.
7 Identify the major reasons for dropping out of school.
8 Discuss the new directions for upgrading secondary education.

Kathy is a senior and an honor student at Harrisburg High School. She gets along well with her peers and is active in extracurricular activities. Kathy has been the editor-in-chief of the yearbook, has been vice-president of the student council, has taken part in several school plays, and has played on the girls' lacrosse team. She has applied to several Ivy League colleges, with an eye toward eventually studying law. Mark, also a senior, attends the same high school but associates with a different group of students. He is taking a business program and makes average grades. Mark spends the mornings in classes at school and the afternoons and weekends working at a fast-food restaurant. Although Mark's job has enabled him to buy a late-model sports car, he often feels too tired to study and does not participate in extracurricular activities. Upon graduation, Mark plans to enter the hospitality and management program at the local community college.

SECONDARY SCHOOLS

Kathy's and Mark's orientations toward school illustrate, perhaps to the extreme, some of the different types of students who attend comprehensive public high schools. Such schools are the result of a dramatic change that has taken place in public education since the 1920s. Prior to that time, the high school was essentially a voluntary institution for a minority of adolescents, mostly those who were interested in preparing for college. Since that time, the high school has become a mandatory institution for virtually all adolescents, including many students who have little or no interest in the traditional academic subjects. Consequently public high schools are expected to provide a wide variety of programs for a diverse group of students, making it difficult for educators and the public alike to agree on the goals and priorities of secondary education.

Enrollment

The biggest single reason for the change to mandatory education, of course, has been the passage of compulsory laws by the various states. By the nineteenth century, half the states had passed such laws. Today, these laws are in effect in every state, with the average cutoff age of 16. As a result, the proportion of adolescents enrolled in school has increased dramatically.

For instance, an elderly woman was telling about the high school reunion of her class of 1910 in South Philadelphia. "Out of four-hundred students who entered the ninth grade," she said, "only ninety-nine graduated from high school." She was surprised to discover this was about average for that era. Nationwide during that period, only a third of all 14 to 17 year olds were enrolled in school, with about half of them graduating from high school. Each decade since then, however, has seen a larger percentage of teenagers enrolled in school as well as graduating from high school. Today, over 94 percent of all 14 to 17 year-olds are enrolled in school, with over three-fourths of them graduating from high school. See Figure 8–1. The exact figures, of course, vary considerably from one school to another, depending largely on the socioeconomic characteristics of the students and community.

Compulsory education has both advantages and disadvantages. On the plus side, our system of compulsory education has raised the level of literacy in the general population, essential for participation in a democratic government and society. Access to free public education is also based on the ideal of providing everyone in our society with the opportunities to make the most of his or her potential, regardless of origins, race, sex, or religion. Because the median educational level is now over twelve years of schooling, graduation from high school also makes it possible to aspire to the better paying jobs, with high school dropouts having the highest rate of unemployment. On the minus side, compulsory education has not been without its problems. First and foremost, if everyone is required to attend school, then schools should be equally accountable to all types of students—gifted, disabled, socially disadvantaged, and so on—something virtually impossible to realize. Also, when students feel disinterested or uninvolved in their studies, they become bored and inclined toward problem behavior, including costly vandalism. Student discipline continues to be a leading problem in many public schools, second only to drug use. Many states have either adopted or are considering adopting even stricter standards of discipline. Meanwhile, they must continue to deal with attendance problems and school dropouts. Although one of the six national goals of education adopted by President Bush and fifty state governors is to increase the proportion of high school graduates to at least 90 percent of eligible youth by the year 2000, fewer than one in ten adults believe this goal is very likely to be attained (Elam, 1990).

Figure 8–1   Percent of 18 to 24 Year Olds Who Have Completed Four Years of High
              School.

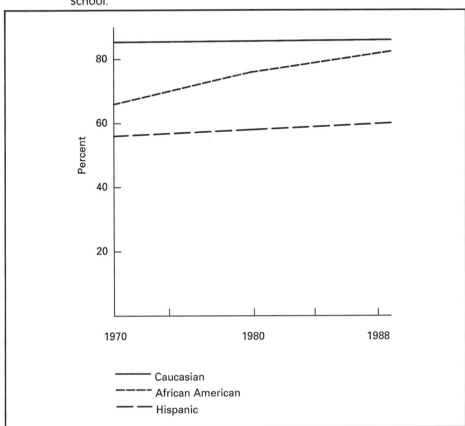

Adapted from U.S. Bureau of the Census. *Statistical Abstract of the United States: 1990*, 110th ed. (Washington,
D.C.: U.S. Government Printing Office, 1990), p. 150.

Curriculum

The comprehensive high school offers a broad range of educational programs.
These generally include an intellectually rigorous program for the most able
students who plan to attend college, a career-oriented program for those who
anticipate working immediately after high school, and general education for
other students.

   More than half of all high school students are taking courses that will
prepare them for college. Nationally, about 57 percent of all high school graduates go on to college, though many of them work for several years before enroll-
ing (U.S. Bureau of the Census, 1990). Some prestigious high schools send more

The comprehensive public high school must be equally accountable to a wide diversity of students. (Rhoda Sidney)

than this percentage of graduates to college, including the best colleges. In addition, high schools have enriched their courses to ease the transition to college-level work. More than three-fourths of all high schools now offer specialized academic courses in such subjects as anthropology, psychology, and sociology, and more than half give credit for college courses taken on college campuses.

Fewer students enroll in the career-oriented programs, though these have grown in popularity in recent years. Students in business/commercial programs may prepare for jobs in such fields as accounting, computer sciences, and secretarial services. Those in vocational/industrial programs may prepare for jobs in fields such as food services and automobile repair. Students in these programs generally spend about half their time in general education courses and the rest in special courses and on-the-job training. In addition, there are high schools devoted entirely to vocational or technical education.

Students who are not planning to attend college or not engaged in vocational training generally participate in the general education program. Traditionally, this program has attracted a larger proportion of low-achieving students, with a higher rate of dropouts. But the increased number and range of elective courses have attracted a larger proportion and a more diverse group of students in recent years. Students may also receive academic credit for work experience outside the schools as well as take a variety of courses aimed at improving life skills and personal growth (National Commission on Excellence in Education, 1983).

One of the perennial issues facing high schools is how much emphasis should be given to academic rigor and how much should be devoted to preparing students for their larger role in society. Because adolescents spend much of their waking day at school, the schools have been called upon to shoulder a disproportionate share of socializing the young. In addition to the basic academic skills, schools have added courses on an endless variety of subjects, such as drug education, sex education, health education, and the like. But with limited budgets the schools cannot accomplish everything equally well. As a result, public sentiment and educational trends tend to swing back and forth between these two emphases. For instance, since the 1960s the demand for more relevant and practical courses has resulted in a wider range of elective courses, thereby increasing the proportion of students in the general curriculum. However, in recent years there has been a move back to the "basics," partly in response to lower scores on student achievement tests and the threat that the United States is losing its competitive edge in the world market. As a result, there is a renewed emphasis on academic excellence, including the traditional academic subjects of English, mathematics, history, and science, along with basic computer skills. Yet, it remains to be seen if this trend will produce the intended results, and/or whether it will further alienate students from their own interests and needs.

Middle Schools

Another major issue in secondary education is adapting the curriculum to the different developmental needs of early and mid to late adolescents. Traditionally, the recognition that puberty begins at about 12 or 13 years of age prompted educators to separate seventh and eighth graders from elementary school students and place them in a junior high school. Yet all too often the junior high school became a scaled-down version of the high school without necessarily meeting the developmental needs of younger adolescents. Now that puberty begins earlier and educators realize that the combined effects of puberty and changing schools affect adolescents adversely, many school systems are putting early adolescents into middle schools. The characteristic groupings of the middle school tend to avoid school changes at the onset of puberty. At the same time, there is a wide variation in the age groupings, with different middle schools including students from the fifth or sixth grades through eighth or ninth grades (Lipsitz, 1984).

Students make the move to middle or junior high schools at a time when many changes are occurring in their lives simultaneously. The rapid changes taking place in their bodies lead to a new body image. The emergence of heightened consciousness and formal thought affects both their academic and social cognition. Then too, adolescents are moving from small classrooms with a few teachers to larger, more impersonal schools with many teachers. They also face an increased emphasis on academic achievement as they advance toward high

Middle schools strive to meet the developmental needs of early adolescents without sacrificing academic standards. (Ken Karp)

school. Also, adolescents confront a larger, more diverse group of peers, which calls for greater social adjustment. At this phase of their lives, adolescents are especially vulnerable to the "top-dog phenomenon." Having left a school in which they were the oldest and most powerful students (top dog), new students in a middle or junior high school find they are now the youngest and least powerful students. Consequently, they are less likely to participate in school activities and assume leadership roles during their first year. However, in the long run the advantages of middle schools far outweigh their disadvantages. Students in middle school are likely to feel more grown up, with less monitoring by teachers and parents. They have a wider selection of subjects and teachers, along with a greater challenge in their academic work. They also have more opportunities to find compatible friends. Such an environment is especially beneficial and supportive for early adolescents (Simmons et al., 1987).

At the same time, some middle schools do a better job than others in meeting the needs of early adolescents. Joan Lipsitz (1984) did a nationwide search to find the best middle schools. Eventually, four middle schools were selected for their leadership in educating early adolescents. The most outstanding feature of these schools is their ability to adapt the academic studies to the individual needs of early adolescents. More especially, they create a learning environment that fosters the social and emotional needs of each student while retaining an emphasis on academic excellence. For instance, one school was organized so that teachers could work with small groups of students in a way that varied the pace of the school day depending on students' needs. Another school developed an advisory system that gave each student daily access to an adult who would listen and provide guidance as needed. Students, parents, and teachers alike feel enthusiastic about what students are accomplishing. Such schools demonstrate that it is possible to respect the developmental needs of early adolescents without sacrificing academic standards.

THE SCHOOL ENVIRONMENT

Students entering a new school, whether a middle school or a high school, initially may be impressed by the appearance of the buildings and campus, and how spacious or crowded the hallways are. But once they have begun attending classes, they become more aware of their *human* environment—what their classes are like, how interesting and approachable their teachers are, and how friendly the other students are. These are just a few of the many factors in the school environment affecting the students' academic achievement and satisfaction in school.

School and Class Size

As mentioned earlier in this chapter, the number of students enrolled in public high schools has more than doubled in the past forty years, mostly because of the baby boom following the Second World War. At the same time the number of schools has not increased proportionately, so that large public high schools have become a familiar part of many communities. Now that the baby boomers are growing older, high school enrollment has begun to decline somewhat in many parts of the country, helping to alleviate the problem. But with much of the population living in urban communities, a significant proportion of students continues to attend large public high schools. Critics contend that large high schools are the spawning ground for many of the ills of public education, such as student passivity and boredom, violence, and dropping out of school. Smaller schools, it is claimed, would be beneficial to many students, with the optimal-sized high school being anywhere from five-hundred to one-thousand students. Although research studies have generally shown that school size does not have a major effect on academic achievement, there are other effects—such as greater prevalence of antisocial behavior in large schools—that may influence the learning climate of schools (Anderson, 1982).

Mark Grabe (1981) investigated the effects of school size among fifteen hundred adolescents of both sexes in twenty high schools of varying sizes. He found that both large and small high schools have their advantages and disadvantages, similar to earlier findings. Large schools tend to provide greater breadth and depth of course offerings, better-prepared teachers, and a greater diversity of extracurricular activities as well as auxiliary services like school counselors. Even though small schools usually have less impressive academic offerings and faculty, they tend to provide better student-teacher communication, more interaction between teachers, and greater student participation in extracurricular activities. With a greater ratio of potential activities to students in small schools, such students are generally more involved in school. Many of the advantages of small schools, such as greater improvement of the students' abilities and feelings of satisfaction, exist because the students are active performers rather than spectators. Although the more active students in large schools show many of these same benefits, a larger proportion of students are active in small schools. The difference is especially striking for marginal students, who are less likely to drop out in smaller high schools, even when they have the same intelligence, grades, and family backgrounds as do those who drop out of larger schools. At the same time Grabe found that a few students in small schools feel more alienated than do those in large schools, mostly because of the pressure to participate. When students lack the ability, motivation, or interest to meet the greater demand for participation in small schools, they may suffer from negative self-images and a loss of self-esteem.

Participation in high school activities also has important implications for one's later involvement in the adult community. A followup study of a national sample of adolescents done when the subjects were 30 years old showed that, independent of social origins, ability, or academic performance, greater involvement in high school extracurricular activities led to greater involvement in the adult community, including voting behavior (Hanks and Eckland, 1978).

The issue of class size has also received a lot of attention, though there is no consistent support for small classes. After conducting an intensive investigation of students in twelve inner-city schools, Michael Rutter (1983) maintains that variations of class size within the usual range—thirty students plus or minus ten—have no significant effect on academic achievement. Students in a class of forty tend to learn as much as do those in classes with twenty students. At the same time, there are certain situations in which small classes are especially effective, for example remedial classes with low-ability students. Some schools already have a policy of expanding many of their regular classes of twenty-five to thirty students by several students each, thereby allowing other teachers to teach small classes for students who need specialized instruction.

Teachers

Teachers play a major role in determining whether an adolescent's school experience will be rewarding or not. Although teachers do not always fare well in the media, parents consistently report favorable attitudes toward teachers. When asked, "What grade would you give the public high school teachers in this community?" 43 percent of all parents would give an A or B. See Table 8–1. Note that public school parents have somewhat more favorable attitudes toward teachers than do parents who have either no children in school or children in nonpublic schools. Apparently, the more firsthand knowledge parents have of

Table 8–1   How Parents Rate Teachers in Public High Schools

Using the A, B, C, D, FAIL scale, what grade would you give the public high school teachers in this community?

Grade	National Totals %	No Children in School %	Public School Parents %	Nonpublic School Parents %
A and B	43	42	44	37
A	8	8	8	7
B	35	34	36	30
C	28	29	28	32
D	10	10	9	12
FAIL	4	4	4	5
Don't know	15	15	15	14

Source: Stanley M. Elam, ed., *The 22nd Annual Gallup Poll of the Public's Attitudes Toward the Public Schools, Phi Delta Kappan*, September 1990, p. 52.

teachers, the better they like and respect them. At the same time, only half of today's parents (compared to three-fourths a generation ago) would like to see one of their children become a public school teacher (Elam, 1990).

When students are asked, "What do you like about a teacher?" their answers are instructive. In one national survey (Norman and Harris, 1981), this question was posed to 160,000 students aged 13 to 18 with the following results. The most common responses included: the teacher "is fair, grades fairly, and doesn't pick on students." Yet nearly three-fourths of the students felt that teachers favor bright students. After fairness, other desirable characteristics of the teacher were ranked in this order: knows his or her subject, enthusiastic about his or her subject, helpful with kids' homework, likes kids, gives few homework assignments, and can maintain adequate discipline in the classroom. According to other studies, students generally prefer warm, friendly teachers who possess sufficient self-confidence and poise to deal with students' suggestions and criticisms without making students feel inferior. Students also like teachers who are trustworthy and can set reasonable limits without being harsh. Adolescents respond best to teachers who exercise natural authority based on their greater experience and wisdom, rather than exerting arbitrary authority or abdicating their authority and trying to become "pals" with their students.

No matter how many desirable characteristics a teacher may have, there are few characteristics that are *always* effective. A great deal depends on the interaction between the teacher and students in the classroom situation, including such factors as age and grade of students, their ability and performance, and compatibility between teacher and students. As a result, recent research has focused more on the teacher's *behavior* and interactions with students.

There is greater realization that teachers tend to treat various students differently and that such treatment generally leads to different results. For instance, Rutter (1983) found that teachers who adopt a teaching style that actively involves students in the learning process tend to get more effective results than those who treat students as passive objects of learning. Teachers who are hostile and domineering tend to affect student performance and behavior adversely. Teachers often adopt more positive expectations and give more generous praise to high achievers, which in turn encourages them to give their best and continue their high achievement. However, differential treatment is sometimes based on stereotypes of race and socioeconomic and sex differences, with negative results. For instance, some studies of young adolescents have shown that girls receive less criticism than boys do but also less praise. And when girls are treated differently than boys in this way, they adopt lower expectations of their own achievements. There is also a tendency for teachers to prefer students who don't "make waves." Several studies have shown that education majors and student teachers—compared to psychology majors and teacher-corps interns—give more favorable ratings to students who are perceived as conforming, orderly, and rigid, and give unfavorable ratings to those who are seen as independent, active, and assertive (Minuchin and Shapiro, 1983).

The teacher's behavior is also influenced by the student's behavior. In a study by Natriello and Dornbush (1983), one of the more consistent findings was that the teacher's classroom behavior was shaped more by the student's *behavior* than by the student's characteristics. In contrast to many earlier studies, the student's race and sex had little effect on the teacher's standards, warmth, or helpfulness. Instead, the student's achievement record and classroom behavior had the greatest impact on the teacher's behavior, though not always as predicted. For instance, teachers sometimes gave more favorable attention to low-achieving students who were needy and receptive to help.

The Importance of the Learning Climate

What teachers do in the classroom is usually a major factor in the learning process. But there is an increasing realization that it is the interaction or combined effect of various factors that affect the student's overall learning experience. Research in this area aims at discovering the learning climate of the school or classroom and tends to focus on process variables such as teacher-student interaction rather than on structural variables such as school size. After reviewing the literature in this area, Carolyn Anderson (1982) points out that while many studies have yielded inconclusive or conflicting results, some have discovered significant factors in the learning process that are not ordinarily found in studies based on the results of standardized achievement tests.

In one approach, Edison Trickett (1978) used a questionnaire called the Classroom Environment Scale (CES). Students complete a questionnaire measuring nine variables: involvement, affiliation, order and organization, rule clarity, task orientation, competition, teacher control, teacher support, and innovation.

The learning climate in the classroom depends a lot on the interaction between teacher and students. (Laima Druskis)

The results of this line of research have shown that schools and classrooms differ markedly in their overall climate of learning.

Students generally are more satisfied in classes that combine moderate structure with high student involvement and high teacher support. Students in these classes are encouraged to participate and are given ample opportunities for innovation and responsibility. Students tend to be least satisfied in classes that are too task-oriented and tightly controlled by the teacher. Students in these classes are more likely to feel anxious, disinterested, and angry. At the same time, the desirable classroom climate varies somewhat by subject matter, with rule clarity and teacher control being considered more important in business and vocational classes than in English and social studies.

In his study of inner-city schools, Michael Rutter (1983) found several factors similar to those discussed above that were significantly related to the learning climate. That is, students did best in those classes where teachers held positive expectations of their students and reasonable, well-defined standards of academic performance and behavior. The teacher's commitment to improving student performance and time spent on lessons were important factors. Student involvement was encouraged, with students being active participants in the learning process. Although classroom-management skills were essential in creating a conducive atmosphere for learning, effective teachers emphasized a system of incentives and rewards rather than punishment. Students in classrooms exhibit-

Time Spent on Homework

How much time did you spend on homework each week when you were in high school? At least 6 hours a week?

According to a survey by the U.S. Census Bureau (1985), the median amount of time spent on homework by students in public schools is 6.5 hours a week, or about 1 hour and 20 minutes a day. Girls generally report doing more homework than boys do. But the sharpest difference is between types of schools, with students in private high schools doing 14.2 hours of homework weekly, more than twice the national average.

The National Commission on Excellence in Education has recommended that public school students be assigned far more homework. The parents of such students agree by a ratio of five to three. Parents whose teenagers have average or below-average grades and who are nonwhites, residents of inner cities, and live in the western United States are somewhat more likely to favor increased homework (Gallup, 1985).

However, homework practices haven't improved much in many schools. A government-financed survey indicates that high school teachers did assign more homework in the late 1980s but also that students were not doing much more. On average, students reported studying at most an hour each day, about the same as in 1980. Overall, 62 percent of 17 year olds did less than an hour of homework each day in 1988. Another 26 percent did 1 to 1.5 hours daily. But only 1 in 8 students (12 percent) did more than 2 hours a day (Cooper, 1990).

ing these characteristics demonstrated better academic work, attended class more regularly, and were less likely to engage in delinquency or antisocial behavior than students in other classes.

Such studies suggest that it is the *combined* effect of different variables that most influence the student's learning experience. One of the encouraging results of this approach is the discovery that many of the significant factors in the learning process are under the control of the school staff and thus can be improved.

SELECTED FACTORS AFFECTING SCHOOL ACHIEVEMENT

School achievement is also affected by many other factors not directly under the control of the school. The student's intelligence or learning ability is a very important though controversial ingredient in academic achievement. So is the educational level in the home and the encouragement and support students receive, or don't receive, from their parents. Family and socioeconomic influences shape students' attitudes toward learning before they enter school, and these become more pronounced with each passing year. Consequently, whether students do well in school and go on to college or do poorly in high school and eventually drop out frequently depends on the combined effect of these background factors and the school environment, rather than the school alone.

Learning Ability

Traditionally, learning ability has been measured by intelligence tests. Much of the reason for this has to do with the high correlations between measures of intelligence and standardized achievement test scores, which are usually consistently higher than the association between teachers' reports and achievement test scores. In recent years, however, critics of intelligence testing have pointed out that students from disadvantaged backgrounds tend to score lower on intelligence tests partly because such tests reflect the highly emphasized, traditional academic skills of white middle-class culture. Accordingly, the use of intelligence tests to place students from minority groups in slow classes or vocational programs is thought to further restrict their opportunities for learning. Largely because of the controversy surrounding intelligence testing, educators tend now to use intelligence tests much more selectively than in the past. In many schools intelligence tests are used mostly to determine if a student needs remedial help—preferably along with other measures such as teacher reports—and even then such tests should be subject to periodic review.

Much of the current interest in learning ability is based on a broader view of intelligence than implied in the traditional IQ tests. For instance, Robert Sternberg in his book *Beyond IQ* (1985) suggests that all of us are governed by three aspects of intelligence: componential, experiential, and contextual. Each aspect of intelligence is explained in a subtheory. In his *componential* subtheory, Sternberg distinguishes between "performance" components that are used in solving a problem and "metacomponents," or the executive learning strategies, used in selecting which performance components are needed to solve a given problem, how to monitor ourselves while solving it, and how to evaluate it after we're done. For example, suppose you were traveling in England and wanted to know how many English pounds you could get for 500 dollars. Metacomponents are the processes used to determine how the problem is to be solved, such as determining what each dollar is worth in pounds at the time. The performance components are the processes used in the actual solution, such as multiplying the amount a dollar is worth in pounds by 500. Although these metacomponents cannot be changed as easily or directly by instruction alone as the performance components, in the long run they are very important to one's overall intelligence and learning.

The *experiential* subtheory emphasizes the importance of insight and creativity in intelligence. It includes several abilities such as the selective encoding of knowledge and the selective combining and selective comparing of the same. As an example of selective encoding of knowledge, Sternberg cites Sir Alexander Fleming's discovery of penicillin. One of Fleming's experiments was spoiled when a sample of bacteria was contaminated by mold. Most people would have become disgusted and thrown it out. But not Fleming. Instead, he realized that the mold that killed the bacteria was more important than the bacteria, an example of selective encoding, an insight that eventually led him to the discovery of a substance in the mold he called penicillin.

Three Graduate Students

Robert Sternberg illustrates his triarchic theory of intelligence with stories of three hypothetical graduate students—Alice, Barbara, and Celia.

Alice seemed very smart according to conventional views of intelligence. She had nearly a 4.0 grade average in college, an extremely high score on the Graduate Record Exam (GRE), and excellent letters of recommendation. In the first year of graduate school, Alice did very well on multiple-choice tests and was good at analyzing arguments and criticizing other people's work. Yet, as she advanced in the program, it became apparent that Alice lacked the ability to come up with good ideas on her own, thus limiting her contribution.

Barbara, the second student, had a different kind of record. Her college grades were not exceptional and her GRE scores were low by Yale standards. However, her letters of recommendation said that Barbara was extremely creative and did superb research. Realizing that creativity is a precious quality, Sternberg wanted to accept her into the program. When Sternberg was outvoted, he hired Barbara as a research assistant. Sure enough, Barbara's work and ideas proved to be just as good as her former professors said, and in time she was admitted into the program. Furthermore, some of Sternberg's most important work was done in collaboration with her.

Celia, the third student, had grades, GRE scores, and letters of recommendation that were good but not great. Accepted into the program, she did all right. But her work was not outstanding. Later, however, she turned out to be the easiest student to place in a good job. Celia had learned how to play the game. She did the type of research that was valued in the journals and submitted her papers to the right journals. Although Celia lacked Alice's superb analytical ability and Barbara's creative ability, she possessed a high level of "street-smarts"—a valuable quality that doesn't show up in traditional IQ tests.

From Robert J. Trotter, "Profile—Robert J. Sternberg: Three Heads Are Better than One," *Psychology Today*, August 1986, p. 60. Reprinted from *Psychology Today* Magazine, Copyright © 1986 American Psychological Association.

The *contextual* subtheory emphasizes adaptation, or the practical applications of intelligence in dealing with the environment. In order to better understand this aspect of intelligence, Sternberg and Richard Wagner studied people in two careers, business and psychology. People who had achieved success and prominence in these two careers were asked what qualities were needed to be practically intelligent in their fields. One quality business executives and psychologists agreed on was something Sternberg called tacit knowledge. Sternberg and Wagner constructed a test for such knowledge and administered it to junior and senior personnel in business and psychology. Their results suggest that tacit knowledge comes through learning from experience. Business executives who scored high on this test exhibited better performance ratings, higher salaries, and more merit raises than did those who scored low. Similarly, psychologists who did well on the test, compared to those who did not, had published more research, presented more papers at conventions, and were at the better universities.

Most people combine these various aspects of intelligence in different proportions. In some cases, individuals may excel in a given aspect of intelligence but not necessarily in others. See the examples cited in the box "Three Graduate Students." Currently Sternberg is developing a multidimensional abilities test that will measure intelligence in a much broader way than the traditional IQ tests do. Instead of giving individuals a number etched in stone, a common misunderstanding of IQ tests, this test can be used as a basis for assessing one's intellectual strengths and weaknesses in the everyday world as well as in school.

Exceptional Students

A perennial challenge facing high schools is how to deal with significant differences in learning ability. Because the comprehensive high school is oriented toward the typical or average student, those who deviate from this norm are less likely to receive an education that matches their needs and interests. Of special concern are the exceptional students, those whose abilities tend to be extremely high or low in relation to their peers. At one extreme are the adolescents who are gifted in some way, whether intellectually gifted—often determined by intelligence tests—or those who have a special talent or creativeness that sets them apart from others. At the other extreme are students who suffer from some type of learning disability, whether cognitive, affective, or behavioral. For instance, some adolescents with learning disabilities have normal intelligence but show a marked discrepancy between their estimated academic potential and their performance. Although a great deal of attention has been focused on the failure to read, known as dyslexia, students may also suffer from verbal, perceptual, attention, and memory disabilities, frequently accompanied by behavior problems. Increasing recognition of the different types of learning disabilities has resulted in a larger proportion of students with these disabilities benefiting from federally supported programs. See Figure 8–2.

Many experts feel that students who differ significantly from their peers in learning ability or talent benefit from educational programs oriented toward their special needs. Yet funding for these programs is frequently limited, and the public may have mixed feelings about spending money for the gifted when so many students need training in remedial skills. Furthermore, the emphasis has turned toward mainstreaming exceptional students into regular classes whenever possible. The success of mainstreaming varies widely from one school to another and depends on such matters as the ratio of special students to the school's resources, the attitude and skill of administrators and teachers, and the understanding and acceptance of other students. Some students with mild disabilities may readily enter regular academic programs. Students with more marked learning handicaps may divide their time between special and regular classes, while still others may require special educational programs or schools. At

Figure 8–2   Percentages of Disabled Students According to Types of Disability.

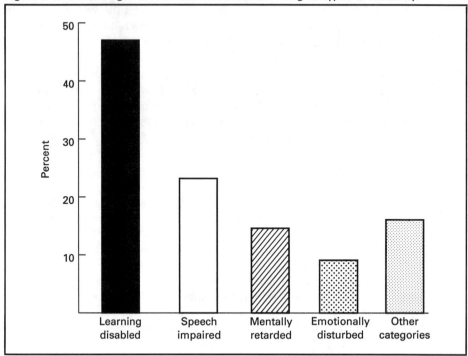

Source: U.S. Bureau of the Census, *The Statistical Abstract of the United States: 1990,* 110th ed. (Washington, D.C.:
    U. S. Government Printing Office, 1990), p. 146.

the same time, there has been a movement toward focusing on the individual
student's strengths and weaknesses rather than categorizing students into global
categories. In many places, each student who is designated exceptional must
have an individual educational program, in which the student, parents, and
teachers agree on what the student will study. In the case of gifted adolescents,
this might involve the opportunity to accelerate through the regular program at
a faster pace, possibly taking college-level courses sooner than others. Or it might
take the form of enrichment, with students having special activities and classes in
addition to their regular classes.

There are advantages and disadvantages of each approach. On the one
hand, separate classes with specially trained instructors may more readily meet
the needs of exceptional students than the regular academic programs. But
separating students solely on the basis of their learning ability may also have
negative psychological and social effects, such as the loss of self-esteem, lowered
expectations about their abilities, and social stigma among students in the lower-
ability programs (Rutter, 1983). Furthermore, there is some evidence that in
many situations mixed-ability classes may offer academic and social advantages

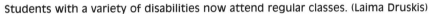
Students with a variety of disabilities now attend regular classes. (Laima Druskis)

for low-ability students without significantly limiting the progress of high-ability students. The impact of mixed-ability classes seems to be even greater on the low-ability students, who appear to be more influenced by the class norm than higher-ability students are (Veldman and Sanford, 1984).

Family and Socioeconomic Status

How well adolescents do in school has a great deal to do with the homes they come from—their parents' education, income, and values. First of all, there is a strong positive association between the parents' education and the student's achievement in school. Students whose parents never completed high school generally score below the national median on most areas of achievement tests, whereas those whose parents completed high school score at or above the median. Students with college-educated parents score even higher. To a some extent the mother's education is more significant for girls, while the father's education plays a greater role for boys (Rumberger, 1983).

Parental expectations also play a significant role in adolescents' educational achievements. Parents' educational aspirations for their adolescents appear to be as important as the students' own ability in predicting the latter's educational aspirations and achievements. But parental influence on young people's academic achievement depends partly on the extent to which adolescents identify with their parents. Adolescents growing up in a middle-class home with warm, caring parents are especially apt to identity with their parents' educational aspirations and values. However, most teachers and counselors know of students who are highly motivated to achieve in school despite negative parental models and lack of support at home.

The importance of the family is closely meshed with other socioeconomic factors, such as parental education, income, family size, ethnic, and racial background. The effects of family background are especially strong for students in the lower socioeconomic groups and accounts for much of the racial differences in educational achievement (Rumberger, 1983). Thus, adolescents from the lower socioeconomic groups generally come from homes with lower incomes, less-educated parents, and more brothers and sisters. These adolescents receive less attention and support than do those in higher socioeconomic groups. In contrast, adolescents from the middle and higher socioeconomic levels tend to come from families with higher levels of education and income, from smaller families (which is especially significant among Caucasians), and to receive greater recognition and support for their educational achievements. As a result, middle-class adolescents generally score higher on achievement tests, make higher grades in school, and complete more years of school than do their counterparts from the lower socioeconomic groups (Garbarino and Asp, 1981). Unfortunately, in many instances the school environment inadvertently widens, rather than closes, the gap between students from the various socioeconomic groups. For instance, several studies have shown that teachers expect higher achievements from middle-class students than from lower-class students (Scott-Jones and Clark, 1986).

Ethnicity

Students' school performance also may be significantly restricted by their ethnic background, a fact that should not be surprising. Because the school is a microcosm of society, the racial biases prevalent in society tend to find their way into the school. Consequently, students who are members of minority groups must adjust to a school environment that values Caucasians over minority groups.

Thus, they must not only strive to overcome language differences, when these exist, but maintain a bicultural existence, all of which makes school a more stressful experience for minority students (Scott-Jones and Clark, 1986).

When parents across the United States were asked whether minorities in their communities have the same educational opportunities as do Caucasian students, almost eight out of ten of them said yes. Yet barely half of the parents from minority groups agreed, which suggests that ethnic and racial discrimination still exists in public schools to some extent (Elam, 1990). The differential treatment of minority students involves a number of variables, including the teacher's preparation or lack of it, for working with culturally diverse students; the teacher's expectations; the presence in the school of positive role models for minority students; the quality of relations between school personnel and parents from different ethnic backgrounds; and school and community relationships (Minuchin and Shapiro, 1983).

Diane Scott-Jones and Maxine Clark (1986) point out that teacher/student interactions vary as a function of the student's race. Teachers look for and reinforce achievement-oriented behaviors in Caucasian students more often than in African-American students. Furthermore, teachers tend to attribute the achievements of Caucasian students to internal factors the students can modify, such as effort or motivation, while attributing the achievements of African-American students to factors the students have no control over, such as parental encouragement and heredity. Although gender often interacts with ethnic factors, such that African-American females suffer additional discrimination, racial differences tend to greatly exceed gender differences.

The academic success of students from minority groups is usually due to positive educational experiences as well as other factors. African-American youth who achieve a high level of academic and social success despite ethnic barriers exhibit certain characteristics, including supportive families who provide direction; strong identification with positive role models; positive educational experiences, with school providing the major social outlet; high educational and career goals; positive but realistic self-concepts; and limited ethnic consciousness, such that race is not a major factor in their social interactions (Lee, 1985).

Dropping Out

Not surprisingly, socioeconomic and ethnic factors are strongly associated with dropping out of school, with a disproportionate number of dropouts coming from the lower socioeconomic groups. Because dropping out of high school is less prevalent today than it has been in the past, many people think the problem no longer exists. Yet dropping out of school has even greater consequences today than in the past. Dropouts can expect to hold lower-level jobs and have the highest unemployment rates.

Figures on high school dropouts vary widely largely because of factors

Figure 8–3   High School Dropouts from 14 to 21 Years Old, by Race and Sex, 1990.

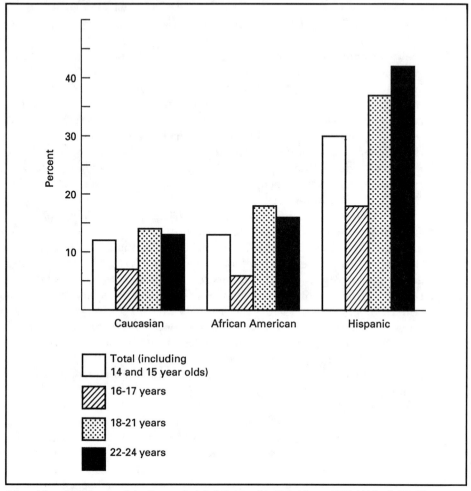

Adapted from U.S. Bureau of the Census. *Statistical Abstract of the United States: 1990,* 110th ed. (Washington, D.C.: U.S. Government Printing Office, 1990), p. 150.

such as age, sex, race, and socioeconomic variables. See Figure 8–3. For instance, the dropout rate among Caucasians aged 18 to 24 is about 14 percent but is considerably higher among Hispanic youth. At the same time, although the dropout rates have remained at the same level for Caucasians, they have decreased significantly among African Americans. Dropout rates also vary significantly among different types of schools, with many inner-city schools in poor neighborhoods having dropout rates in the 50 percent bracket or more.

Students leave school for a variety of reasons, many of them school related. Most youth who drop out of school dislike school, are doing poor academic work, or have been suspended or expelled. But students also drop out of high school for other reasons. Male tend to drop out because they would rather work or feel they must work for economic reasons. Females are more likely to drop out because of pregnancy and marriage. See Table 8–2. Family background strongly influences the adolescent's tendency to drop out of school and accounts for much of the socioeconomic differences in dropout rates. Youths with the highest dropout rates generally come from large families, have parents of low educational attainment and aspirations, are from lower socioeconomic groups in the inner city, or are youths who themselves were born outside the United States. The inability to speak and read English is a major disadvantage, as seen in the high dropout rate among Hispanic youth who are not native born (Rumberger, 1983).

The act of dropping out of school appears to be the culmination of a long process involving repeated poor performance in school, frustration and failure, and dislike for school. Youths with low intelligence tend to drop out of school in greater numbers than do those with average or higher intelligence, especially in the lower grades. Yet intelligence itself is not always a decisive factor, especially because the majority of high school dropouts have at least average intelligence. In these cases, youths have the ability to complete school but fail to do so for a variety of reasons, as explained earlier in this chapter. About half of the individuals who drop out of school do so as ninth or tenth graders (Grant and Snyder, 1984). By this time, students' poor records, school absences, and behavior problems have become painfully evident. Peer influence also weighs heavily at this age; when friends are not doing well in school or are dropouts already, potential dropouts are even more at risk. Then too, in many states, age 16 is the cutoff for enforcing compulsory education laws.

However, because the majority of high school dropouts have the ability to complete school, most school districts have developed a variety of programs to keep students from dropping out. A major aim of these programs is to make school a more rewarding experience for students, and the earlier in the student's

Table 8–2   Reasons Most Frequently Given for Dropping Out of School, by Sex

Males	Females
Disliked school	Disliked school
Desired to work	Pregnancy
Expelled or suspended	Marriage
Poor school performance	Home responsibilities
Financial difficulties	Desired to work
Home responsibilities	Poor school performance

Adapted from data in the National Longitudinal Survey of Youth Labor Market Experience, in Russel W. Rumberger, "Dropping Out of High School: The Influence of Race, Sex, and Family Background," *American Educational Research Journal* (Summer 1983), p. 201.

school experience such programs can be implemented, the better. In one program (Ruby and Law, 1982), ninth graders identified as potential dropouts were given special assistance in addition to their regular classes to improve their attitude, attendance, and academic achievement. As a result class attendance and behavior improved, with more than two-thirds of these students eventually graduating from high school compared to none of the controls who had not received such help.

IMPROVING THE SCHOOLS

High schools have become such an important part of adolescents' lives that they are expected to take on a broad range of programs and issues that have social, economic, moral, and political dimensions. Accordingly, schools have become easy targets for criticism by practically everyone, including students, parents, educators, legislators, and the media. We could easily devote an entire chapter to what people think of public high schools and what improvements they think are necessary. However, in this final section we confine our attention to the results of a national opinion poll and some of the recommendations for education reform by a national commission.

What People Think of Public Schools

One of the most reliable sources of public opinion is the Annual Gallup Poll of the Public's Attitudes toward the Public Schools. The report of the 1990 poll edited by Stanley M. Elam is based on personal interviews with a representative national sample of 1,594 adults in all areas of the nation. It includes parents of students who attend public, parochial, and private or independent schools in all types of communities (Elam, 1990).

When asked to rate the local public schools, four out of ten public school parents give the schools an A or B. Another third of the parents give the schools a C or average. See Table 8–3.

At the same time, there is a reasonable degree of discontent with existing schools. When asked about the right to choose the public school their children and adolescents would attend, regardless of residence, a majority of adults favor this idea. In choosing a new school, parents would give top priority to the quality of the teaching staff, student discipline, and the curriculum. However, parental opinion is more divided when it comes to the voucher system, by which the government allots a certain amount of money for each child's education. About four out of ten parents feel the voucher system might hurt public education. Thus, it remains to be seen whether the right to choose schools can be carried out in a way that will preserve other values that may be equally important to people. Current experiments in Minnesota, Arkansas, and Iowa might well provide some clues.

When asked which subjects should be required of students planning to

Table 8–3 Rating of the Public Schools, 1990 (in percents)

Students are often given the grades A, B, C, D, and FAIL to denote the quality of
their work. Suppose the public schools themselves, in this community, were graded
in the same way. What grade would you give the public schools here—A, B, C, D, or
FAIL?

Grade	National Totals	No Children In School	Public School Parents	Nonpublic School Parents
A	8	7	12	6
B	33	32	36	26
C	34	34	36	37
D	12	12	9	18
FAIL	5	5	4	6
Don't Know	8	10	3	7

Source: Stanley M. Elam, ed., *The 22nd Annual Gallup Poll of the Public Attitudes toward the Public Schools,*
Phi Delta Kappan (September 1990), p. 51.

attend college, public opinion has remained fairly consistent over the past decade. More than seven out of ten parents put the top priority on five basic
subjects: math, English, history, science, and computer training. They would
place less emphasis on these subjects for non-college bound students, and greater
emphasis on career education. People would also like their public schools to do
much more than teach the so-called basics. In fact, more people would require
drug abuse education in high schools than any other subject except math and
English. Alcohol abuse education, AIDS education, sex education, teen pregnancy, and environmental issues are also high on the public's list of required
subjects.

Educators are well aware that academic success in high school is important for academic success in college. Now the Gallup Poll shows that the general
public is also aware of the close connection. Three-fourths of the public school
parents believe there is a fairly close or very close relationship between high
school students' grades and their success in college. Nearly as many people
believe that high school grades correlate with career success in later life, though
this is more difficult to document because of the problems in measuring "success" in one's career. All of this shows how important people believe a good
education to be for success in one's life work.

Have the public schools been improving? Evidently, not many people
think so. When asked, "Would you say that the public schools in this community
have improved from, say, five years ago, gotten worse, or stayed about the
same?" the answers are revealing. Barely a fifth of the adults think the schools
have improved. One-third think their schools have gotten worse, and another
third feel the schools are about the same.

When parents of public school students are asked about the biggest
problems facing local schools, the use of drugs tops the list of answers. Other
leading problems include the lack of discipline, lack of proper financial support,

Table 8–4   Biggest Problems Facing the Public Schools, 1990 (in percents)

What do you think are the biggest problems with which the public schools in this community must deal?

	Public School Parents %	Nonpublic School Parents %
Use of drugs	34	39
Lack of discipline	17	25
Lack of proper financial support	17	21
Poor curriculum/poor standards	7	6
Large schools/overcrowding	10	16
Difficulty getting good teachers	10	10
Pupils' lack of interest/truancy	3	3
Low teacher pay	6	8
Crime/vandalism	4	1
Integration/busing	4	6
Parents' lack of interest	3	3
Drinking/alcoholism	4	3
Teachers' lack of interest	5	5
Moral standards	2	1
Lack of respect for teachers/other students	3	4
Lack of needed teachers	3	1
Lack of family structure	3	2
Lack of proper facilities	2	4
Parents' involvement in school activities	2	2
Mismanagement of funds/programs	2	1
Problems with administration	3	3

(Figures add to more than 100 percent because of multiple answers.)

Source: Stanley M. Elam, ed., *"The 22nd Annual Gallup Poll of the Public's Attitudes toward the Public Schools," Phi Delta Kappan* (September 1990), p. 53.

and poor academic standards. See Table 8–4. Educators can take some comfort from the responses to a question asking where the blame for the problems confronting public education should be placed. About three-fourths of all adults blame society and current social problems, not the schools. At the same time, educators themselves have a somewhat different view of the problems facing high schools. In a national survey of public school teachers sponsored by the Carnegie Foundation (1987), almost all of the teachers said that they lacked parental support and that their main problems are students' apathy, absenteeism, and disruptive behavior.

New Directions

Educators, school boards, and legislators also have plenty of ideas about the kinds of improvements needed in schools. At the national level, many of the criticisms and recommendations for educational reform have been expressed in the report of the National Commission on Excellence in Education (1983), with a major emphasis on improving the quality of public education. It appears that

Americans are now among the most educated people in the world in terms of years of school completed. More than three-fourths of those over age 25 have completed high school, with about one-third of them having some college. Yet a variety of measures, including SAT and achievement test scores indicate that the quality of education has declined since the 1970s. Furthermore, grades have risen while the amount of homework has decreased, making the rise in grades suspect. As a result a large proportion of public school students do not have the basic study skills needed for a quality education. Colleges, business, and the military are spending millions on remedial education.

Many of the commission's recommendations are aimed at upgrading the standards of education, making better use of time in school, and improving the quality of teaching.

1. Upgrading standards.   An increasing proportion of students are in the general curriculum, taking fewer academic courses and more electives in the areas of "life education" and "personal growth." As a result, the commission recommends upgrading graduation requirements to include more courses in language, math, and the sciences and improving academic rigor throughout the entire curriculum.

2. Better use of time.   Noting that American students spend less time in school than do students in many other nations, the commission proposes that students spend more time in school. This includes a longer school day, a longer school year, and a more efficient use of time in school.

3. Improving teaching.   Some of the perennial problems cited by the commission have been the difficulty of attracting talented individuals to teaching, teacher's low salaries—especially in the fields of math, sciences, languages, and special education—and teachers' lack of involvement in decision making. Among the recommendations are improving the standards of the teaching profession, better salaries, use of personnel from outside education, and greater involvement of teachers in the decision-making process.

Unfortunately, the commission didn't propose *how* these measures might be implemented. And because the public has generally opposed raising local taxes for financing public schools (Gallup, 1986), it remains to be seen how many of these recommendations will be carried out.

The goal of upgrading educational standards, as admirable as it may be, is not without its critics. Some educational researchers (Sedlack et al., 1986) point out that designing more difficult programs, raising grading standards, and eliminating the so-called frill courses only treat the symptoms rather than the underlying problems of secondary education. In their view, the basic weakness of the public schools is that the majority of students are not actively involved or motivated to learn. They estimate that only a small proportion, about one-third or more, of high school students do their homework, study for tests, and actively participate in classroom discussions. These are the students who are planning to go on to the better colleges. Most of the others actively or passively resist learning, doing just enough to get by. Much of the resistance to learning stems from the discrepancy between the school's goal of formal learning and the students' interests and developmental needs. For instance, when asked what they like best about school, students usually rank personal and social concerns at the top of the scale and academic concerns (classes, teachers, and rules) toward the bottom (Goodlad, 1984).

Such a discrepancy is a reminder of the perennial issue facing schools, that is, whether to emphasize academic rigor or relevance to life. As mentioned earlier, the pendulum of educational priorities has swung back toward an emphasis on academic excellence in recent years. But these concerns need not be so polarized. Courses that help prepare students for life beyond high school, such as drug abuse education or sex education, which are endorsed by the great majority of parents, need not be excluded. Nor should the concern for basic skills and academic excellence be pursued in such a competitive way that it discourages the love for learning itself and the value of learning in preparing students for life in a constantly changing world. Instead, the diversity of students requires that schools continue to be responsive to a wide variety of needs. What is needed is a balanced curriculum that addresses the personal and social as well as the intellectual needs of *all* adolescents.

SUMMARY

Secondary Schools

1. Largely because of compulsory education laws, secondary schools now enroll the vast majority of adolescents of school age, making for a diverse group of students.
2. A continuing challenge facing the schools is providing programs that serve the needs of all students equally well.
3. Consequently, the comprehensive high school offers a broad range of educational programs, which usually includes college preparation, career training, and general studies.
4. The development of middle schools in recent years is an attempt to design schools that more nearly reflect the physical, cognitive, and social needs of early adolescents than has the traditional organization of secondary schools.

The School Environment

5. Although both large and small schools have their advantages and disadvantages, students tend to become more involved in smaller schools, such that marginal students are less likely to drop out.
6. Teachers who are fair-minded and actively involve students in the learning process tend to be more effective than are those who treat students as passive objects.
7. While the learning climate of classrooms involves the interaction of many factors, students generally do better in classes that combine moderate structure with positive teacher expectations and support.

Selected Factors Affecting School Achievement

8. Learning ability, once measured exclusively in intelligence tests, is now approached more in terms of cognitive development along with a variety of other measures.

9. Exceptional students, ranging from gifted adolescents to those with learning disabilities, are dealt with in a variety of ways that usually combine special programs with regular classes.

10. How well students do in school depends to a great extent on their family and socioeconomic backgrounds, with students who come from middle-class homes and who have college-educated parents generally doing better than those from lower socioeconomic groups.

11. Students' school performance may also be adversely affected by their ethnic background, with some evidence that teachers look for and reinforce achievement behaviors more in Caucasian students than in African-American students.

12. Although students drop out of school for many reasons, a major factor is the dislike of school, with males inclined to go to work and females leaving school because of pregnancy or marriage.

13. Dropping out of school is generally the culmination of a long process of frustration and failure; today, many schools offer a variety of programs aimed at making school a more positive experience for those at risk.

Improving the Schools

14. The public is generally supportive of high schools. Almost half of public school parents give their adolescents' schools an above average grade.

15. At the same time, a majority of adults believe the public schools are in need of improvement, with drug abuse as the top problem facing the schools.

16. A major theme of recent education reform is the concern to improve the quality of secondary education, putting the emphasis on academic excellence.

17. However, given the diversity of students, what is needed is a balanced curriculum that will address the personal and social as well as the intellectual needs of all adolescents.

REVIEW QUESTIONS

1. At what legal age should adolescents be allowed to quit school?
2. What is meant by the comprehensive high school?
3. In theory, how are middle schools like and unlike junior high schools?
4. Which schools have the lowest rates of dropouts?
5. What is the most common response given by adolescents to the question, What do you like about a teacher?
6. How much time does the average high school student spend on homework each week?
7. What is mainstreaming?
8. In what ways are minority students treated differently in schools?
9. Which types of adolescents are most likely to drop out of school?
10. How can high schools be improved academically?

9

Work and Career Choice

Learning Objectives

After completing this chapter, you should be able to:
1 Identify the advantages and disadvantages of teenage employment.
2 Describe Don Super's stages of vocational identity.
3 Describe John Holland's six personality-occupational types.
4 Identify several ways in which an adolescent's family influences his or her career choice.
5 Discuss the socioeconomic, racial, and sex differences affecting career choice.
6 Describe the relationships between a college education and career outlook.

Looking around at parents and teachers already settled in their careers, young people may sometimes feel adults don't understand the perplexity and frustration one experiences in choosing a career. But such is usually not the case. When asked, many adults will frankly admit that settling on a career isn't as easy as it appears. Even people who achieve fame in their fields sometimes must struggle before finding their life work. Some people, like Charles Darwin, flounder throughout adolescence and give their parents a lot of worry before arriving at a firm career goal. Others, like Margaret Mead, entertain a wide variety of vocational aspirations before choosing their career. As you may recall from an earlier chapter, at one time or another, Margaret Mead wanted to be a lawyer, a nun, a writer, and a minister's wife with six children. As it turned out, she went on to get a master's degree in psychology and later became a famous anthropologist. Still other people like Erik Erikson settle on their lifework later in life. After spending much of his youth as a traveling Bohemian or "hippie," Erikson started out as an art teacher and only later in his career became a psychoanalyst.

ADOLESCENTS IN THE WORKPLACE

The experiences mentioned above remind us that the choice of a career—a purposeful life pattern of work—is an extended developmental process. As such, it involves a great deal of exploration and change before individuals settle on a firm career goal. Compared to youth in the past, young people today enjoy many advantages in selecting what they want to do in the workplace, such as greater educational opportunities, a wider variety of careers, and greater freedom of choice in career selection. At the same time, many careers in our technology-oriented society require a high degree of specialization and many years of expensive education, such that young people often feel under a lot of pressure to choose wisely. Yet they spend so many years in school isolated from career-related work experience that they usually have little basis for knowing what type of work they want to do. Furthermore, rapid shifts in the need for particular specialized skills as well as the economy generally may make one's hard-won skills obsolete rather quickly, forcing people to change careers more often. All of this makes the choice of a career a major challenge for young people.

We begin by taking a look at the changing patterns of teenage employment and the pros and cons of their work experience. Then we examine the developmental process of career choice along with the various influences on young people's decisions, such as the family, socioeconomic background, and sex differences. Finally, we discuss the matter of preparing for a career, including the value of a college education.

Teenage Employment

The individual's transition to adult work roles in the United States generally occurs throughout a sequential process that begins with household chores in childhood and culminates in a full-time job in the formal workplace by late adolescence or the early twenties. During childhood, most boys and girls are assigned jobs around the house. Although younger children are equally likely to do the same type of chores around the house, such as clearing the table after a meal, household chores become more sex-typed as children grow older. However, as we mentioned in Chapter 5, children from dual-income families tend to be more flexible about the particular tasks they perform at home than are youngsters from the traditional, one-wage-earner homes. By early adolescence, teenagers take on informal jobs outside the home, frequently for neighbors. The most common jobs at this age are babysitting, newspaper delivery, house cleaning, and lawn and garden work. As adolescents reach the age required for employment in the formal work force—anywhere from 14 to 16 years of age depending on the state—they begin taking part-time jobs in the formal workplace. Teenagers may work after school, in the evenings, on the weekends, and during the summer. By their senior year in high school, more than three-fourths of the teenagers in school are working more than fifteen hours a week on an outside job (Grant and Snyder, 1984). Full-time employment usually begins after graduation from high school or college.

The range of jobs available to adolescents in the formal workplace is rather limited. One-half of teenagers who have jobs either work in restaurants or in the retail trades. About one in five working teenagers is employed in restaurants, either preparing food, waiting on customers, clearing tables, or cleaning dishes. Many of them work in the fast-food restaurants. Another one in five teenagers works in a retail business, often as a cashier or a sales clerk. The remainder of adolescents work in a variety of jobs, such as clerical work, service station attendants, maids, and other types of service jobs or manual labor. Relatively few teenagers now work on farms or in factories. And only a small proportion of teenagers have jobs that are interesting and challenging.

Occasionally, one sees a girl delivering newspapers and a boy babysitting. But these are still exceptions to the rule. In one study of several thousand teenagers, only 9 percent of the newspaper carriers were girls and only 5 percent

Students who work 20 hours or more each week at an outside job are often too tired to study. (National Archives)

of the babysitters were boys. It appears that part-time jobs for teenagers are no less sex-typed than those for adults. Boys generally work as manual laborers, gardeners, newspaper carriers, service station attendants, and busboys. Girls are more likely to work as maids, babysitters, food counter workers, and waitresses. Furthermore, boys work longer hours than girls do and boys' jobs generally pay better than girls' jobs do (Greenberger and Steinberg, 1986).

Combining School and Work

One of the most remarkable changes in the past couple of decades is the increased proportion of teenagers who work during the school year. Prior to the 1950s, it was unusual for students to combine school and work. Today, it's unusual for students *not* to work after school. About one in three public school students in the ninth grade hold part-time jobs after school. By the senior year, more than 9 out of 10 students work after school (Grant and Snyder, 1984). A major reason for this change is the rapid expansion of those aspects of the American economy that need a large number of part-time workers, namely the

Most adolescents work in jobs that are unrelated to their career goals. (Courtesy NCR)

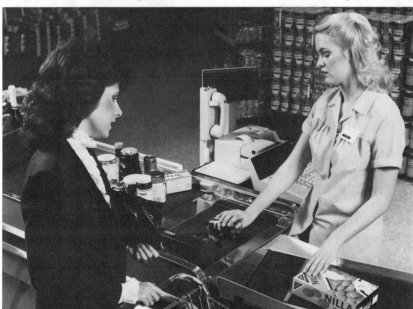

retail trades and service sectors. Employers, such as the fast-food chains, need workers who are willing to work for relatively low wages and short shifts, require- ments readily filled by teenagers. Another factor has been the dramatic increase in inflation since the 1980s—it costs more to be an American teenager than it did in the past. Practically everything teenagers buy costs more, including candy, gum, toys, records, fast food, tickets to games and movies, cars, and gas, not to mention alcohol and drugs.

Surprisingly, students from middle-class families are even more likely to work after school than are those from less privileged homes, which is just the opposite from the practice in earlier eras. The most likely explanation is that middle-class teenagers have an easier time finding jobs because they live in the suburbs where many of the newer jobs are located. One study of 4,587 high school students found that employed students were more likely to come from families in the higher socioeconomic groups with a mother or father in the higher-status careers. Unemployed students were more apt to come from fami- lies in the lower socioeconomic groups and to have parents in the lower-status, low-paying careers (Schill, McCartin, and Meyer, 1985).

Students are also working more hours than ever before. The average high school sophomore works about fifteen hours a week. Seniors average close to twenty hours a week. Almost half the seniors in public high schools work more than twenty hours a week (Grant and Synder, 1984). The sum of thirty hours per week in class plus 6.5 hours of homework a week on the average, combined with twenty hours a week at a part-time job makes the student's total work load over fifty hours a week. And many students work even more. As a result, students are often too tired to study, with school grades more likely to suffer after about fifteen to twenty hours a week. Marginal students' grades are especially likely to suffer from part-time jobs. Grades tend to increase somewhat for students with part-time jobs up to about fifteen hours a week. After that, grades steadily decrease. Furthermore, students who work long hours are less likely to participate in extracurricular activities and tend to become more distant from their families and friends (Ogle, 1990).

The Value of Work Experience

Such findings raise questions about the impact of part-time jobs on adolescent development. All too often, adults have assumed that work is "good" for teenagers. It teaches them about the value of money and the real world. Work experience also helps prepare them for adulthood. Yet it is also apparent that teenage work often exacts a price from teens' social development. More realistically, it's a matter of balancing the advantages and disadvantages of work experience.

The biggest gain from part-time work is the practical knowledge acquired. Young people learn how to find and hold a job, a valuable lifetime skill. They also learn how to budget their time. Work also develops the individual's sense of responsibility and work maturity, that is, the ability to complete a task and feel pride in a job well done. Although most adolescents work primarily for money, getting paid for what they do also brings self-reliance. But one of the most valuable lessons of all is learning how to get along with other people. One girl said, "My job as a cashier in a supermarket has helped me to be less shy and to talk to people" (Cole, 1981).

On the minus side, most adolescent jobs are dull, monotonous, and stressful. In contrast to adolescents in more traditional societies, who come into contact with adults who prepare them for their career goals—as in an apprenticeship program—today's teenagers spend most of their time with other adolescents in jobs that are unrelated to their career goals. Adolescents have few opportunities to make decisions on their own. They generally get little instruction from their supervisors, who are often only a few years older. Furthermore, adolescents in their work seldom make use of the skills they are learning in school, such as reading and writing. Also, most part-time jobs do not develop teenagers' sense of social responsibility or their concern for others. Instead, students often acquire cynical views about the business world, such as the view that there is something wrong with people who work harder then they have to. Teens are also more likely to go along with unethical business practices, such as supporting the idea that poorly paid workers are entitled to take little things from their jobs as a way of making up for their unfair treatment (Greenberger and Steinberg, 1986).

Should We Toughen Child-Labor Laws?

Federal law limits work for employees aged 14 through 17, not to begin work before 7 A.M. and work later than 7 P.M., and to work no more than three hours on any school day, or more than eight hours on a Saturday, Sunday, or holiday, for a total of eighteen hours a week. Some states set even lower limits. However, not all employees obey the law. The biggest single category of violations involves putting teens in hazardous jobs.

For instance, a 15-year-old boy was killed in operating a dough-mixing machine, in violation of state regulations. The boy had told his parents he was simply "bagging rolls." But investigators found that he had been working after permitted hours, without working papers, and paid a flat amount in cash per evening under the table. The bakery pleaded guilty to violating the state child-labor laws and was fined $200. Not satisfied, the parents called for federal action forcing states to require parental permission before adolescents could operate dangerous machinery and tougher penalties for violators (Hess, 1990).

"Are tougher government rules the answer?" asks Neil Peirce (1987). Part of the problem is that nobody pays attention to the laws on the books. How about enforcing the existing child-labor laws? Perhaps a combined strategy is needed. Some proposed legislation would impose stricter penalties for violators of child-labor laws. Other legislation would tighten the various provisions of the federal law. Also, parents need to set limits on the types of jobs their teenagers can do and the hours they work.

Such findings raise questions about the value of adolescents' work experience during school. On the one hand, the advantages of having a part-time job in high school appear to be short-lived. That is, students who have worked during high school tend to have an easier time finding full-time jobs with good pay than do those who have not worked after school. But within a few years, there is little or no difference between the two groups of students. Those who didn't work during high school are just as likely to be employed and earn just as much money as those who worked during high school (Freeman and Wise, 1982). On the other hand, students may achieve more lasting benefits from supervised work-study programs that integrate adolescents' learning experiences and their career goals. In such programs, special effort is made to match students' jobs with their interests and to provide appropriate instruction and supervision, thereby maximizing the learning experience of adolescent work. Such programs may also help adolescents to view work in a more meaningful way, increasing their sense of social responsibility and the value of feedback regarding their work performance.

EXPLORING AND CHOOSING A CAREER GOAL

Because our society places such a high value on work, there is considerable pressure on teenagers to choose a career. At first casually and then more anxiously, parents begin asking their children, "What do you want to do when you grow up?"

Schools, too, expect adolescents to make important decisions bearing on their choice of a career. Which courses do you want to take? Which activities are you most interested in? Students' choices and how well they do in their courses and extracurricular activities, in turn, help to shape their eventual choice of a career. Additional pressure to choose a career comes from within. Serious concerns about a person's life work appear by the age of 12 or so and generally increase with intensity into adulthood. Anxiety builds during the last year or so of high school, when students usually ponder such questions as "Do I want to go to college?" "If so, what will I major in?" "Or, if not, what am I going to do after graduation?"

Unfortunately, many students approach the choice of a career goal in a haphazard manner. In early adolescence, ideas about careers tend to be based on activities, interests, and fantasies, all of which are tentative at this age. During mid to late adolescence, students may consider career choices successively on the basis of their interests, abilities, and values. From late adolescence on is a time for resolving career choice more realistically on the basis of a candid self-appraisal and viable career options. Yet, throughout this period youths tend to explore a limited range of options. They may consider only those fields of work they are familiar with, such as what their parents do or the more popular careers at the time. Students who have access to well-organized career guidance programs may discover additional career possibilities, as well as valuable insights about the decision-making process itself. But all too often, when students talk with a high school guidance counselor, it is about high school courses rather than career exploration. Consequently, there is less purposeful, conscious career exploration occurring among high school students than is desirable.

Super's Developmental Theory

Career exploration tends to be a drawn-out process partly because it is so closely related to one's overall development as a person. As a result, Don Super (1980, 1985) has put forth a developmental theory of career choice that emphasizes the relationship between the individual's self-control and personal identity and his or her choice of a career. In this view, the choice of a career results largely from exploring and affirming our personal identity, i.e., how we see ourselves and what we want to become, in the world of work. The basic idea is that we tend to choose those careers that affirm our self-image and personal identity, including our interests, needs, and abilities. Problems in career choice and adjustment generally reflect the difficulties a person has in achieving a clear self-concept and positive identity.

Although adolescence is a critical period in the choice of a career, the process of affirming our vocational identity lasts throughout the lifespan. The stages of vocational identity, together with the approximate ages, are as follows:

- ◆ *Growth (up to 14 years).* Children and early adolescents get ideas about the nature and meaning of work through their play, interests, and activities.

♦ *Exploration (15 to 25 years).*   Adolescents and youths become more aware of the need to make career-related decisions, including self-assessment, career exploration, and eventually the choice of a career goal.

♦ *Establishment (26 to 45 years).*   Adults generally settle down into an appropriate career pattern, and acquire experience and further specialization in their chosen fields.

♦ *Maintenance (46 to 65 years).*   Individuals acquire further expertise, seniority, and status in their chosen careers.

♦ *Decline (66 years and over).*   People normally retire and explore new roles and new ways of understanding themselves in a way that emphasizes satisfaction outside their careers.

At the same time, a certain degree of change in one's career goal is to be expected, especially in a society characterized by frequent shifts in the supply and demand for various types of workers. Furthermore, individuals who change their careers may go through the cycle of stages more than once.

Don Super has proposed the concept of career maturity as a way of determining how well individuals are progressing toward their vocational identities. Career maturity refers to the readiness to explore career goals, make commitments, and pursue the appropriate educational preparation as called for by social expectations and by events. Super (1985) investigated the role of career maturity in achieving career success in a longitudinal study of young men over a ten-year period, from high school through early adulthood. A major finding is that the predictors of career success change between the ninth and twelfth grades. At the end of junior high school, the best predictors of career success at age 25 are the conventional ones, such as self-concept and socioeconomic status. For instance, a major factor is the career status of the father; the higher the father's career status, the more likely the son will be settled in an appropriate career at age 25. Information about careers seems to have little influence on career choice at this age. However, by the senior year of high school, the most important predictor of career success is career maturity or evidence of a purposeful, planning orientation on the part of individuals. That is, those who later achieve success in their career search are actively exploring career options as an integral part of mature decision making. They have the ability to consider alternatives, weigh the various options, and make a commitment to a career goal.

In Super's view, the high school years are best viewed as a time of wide-ranging, general, but increasingly realistic exploration of careers. Yet, as he points out, less career exploration occurs at this age than is desirable. Between 18 and 25, only about half of the individuals in his study were engaged in purposeful planning. The other half were drifting. Career exploration tends to peak in the early twenties. Between 25 and 36, the process shifts from exploration to commitment, with two-thirds of the men having stabilized their career goals by their mid-thirties.

Young women tend to experience additional challenges in their search for vocational identity. Sally Archer (1985a) studied the relation between identity formation and career exploration among adolescents from junior high school to senior high school, including males and females. On the one hand, she found no gender differences in regard to career exploration, nor in the proportion of males and females who had settled on a career goal. However, she did find a major difference between the sexes on one central issue, namely, relating family and career roles. Whereas the majority of males saw no conflict between family and career responsibilities, 90 percent of the females anticipated conflicts in this area. Furthermore, three-fourths of them expressed concern about how they would resolve this conflict. Such concern is understandable given the realities of balancing career and family responsibilities as well as the barriers to female employment in many sectors. Consequently, as Archer suggests, career counseling and support is especially critical for young women.

Holland's Occupational Environment Theory

Another approach to career choice that is widely used is John Holland's (1985) occupational environment theory. The basic idea is that individuals tend to select careers that are compatible with their personalities. Once individuals find a suitable job in a career that fits their personality, they are more likely to remain in that field. In contrast, those who work at a job that is incompatible with their personality are more likely to change careers somewhere down the road. Holland has described six basic personality types and the occupational environments that are consistent with these types. In turn, these personality-occupational types can be useful in helping individuals identify the most compatible careers for themselves. See the boxed item on Holland's six personality-occupational types.

Holland realizes that few individuals conveniently fall into any one "pure" type. Most people's personalities combine all six types to some degree, with the three top-ranked types for each person being most helpful in identifying a compatible career. Consequently, the basic idea of matching personal interests with particular careers is an important contribution to career choice. Futhermore, studies have shown some support for Holland's approach (Brown, 1987). At the same time, people may choose a career or remain in a job for a variety of reasons. For instance, people may stay in a job because of the pay, fringe benefits, job security, or status. Also, they may lack the education to get into their preferred field. Then too, people often stay in an incompatible career or job because of personal and family obligations.

Identifying a Compatible Career

Given the complexities of choosing a career, most youth would benefit from assistance in identifying a compatible career. In the first place, students spend long years in school, with their part-time and summer employment generally unrelated to their career goals. Then too, with more than twenty thousand careers to choose from, it's hard to know where to begin. As a result, students

Holland's Six Personality-Occupational Types

The following are descriptions of Holland's six personality-occupational types. These descriptions are, most emphatically, only generalizations. None will fit any one person exactly. In fact, most people's interests combine all six themes or types to some degree. Even if you rate high on a given theme, you will find that some of the statements used to characterize this theme do not apply to you.

The archetypal models of Holland's six types can be described as follows:

Realistic: Persons of this type are robust, rugged, practical, physically strong, and often athletic; have good motor coordination and skills but lack verbal and interpersonal skills, and are therefore somewhat uncomfortable in social settings; usually perceive themselves as mechanically inclined; are direct, stable, natural, and persistent; prefer concrete to abstract problems; see themselves as aggressive; have conventional political and economic goals; and rarely perform in the arts or sciences, but do like to build things with tools. Realistic types prefer such occupations as mechanic, engineer, electrician, fish and wildlife specialist, crane operator, and tool designer.

Investigative: This category includes those with a strong scientific orientation; they are usually task-oriented, introspective, and asocial; prefer to think through rather than act out problems; have a great need to understand the physical world; enjoy ambiguous tasks; prefer to work independently; have unconventional values and attitudes; usually perceive themselves as lacking in leadership or persuasive abilities but are confident of their scholarly and intellectual abilities; describe themselves as analytical, curious, independent, and reserved; and especially dislike repetitive activities. Voca-

tional preferences include astronomer, biologist, chemist, technical writer, zoologist, and psychologist.

Artistic: Persons of the artistic type prefer free unstructured situations with maximum opportunity for self-expression; resemble investigative types in being introspective and asocial but differ in having less ego strength, greater need for individual expression, and greater tendency to impulsive behavior; they are creative, especially in artistic and musical media; avoid problems that are highly structured or require gross physical skills; prefer dealing with problems through self-expression in artistic media; perform well on standard measures of creativity and value aesthetic qualities; see themselves as expressive, original, intuitive, creative, nonconforming, introspective, and independent. Vocational preferences include artist, author, composer, writer, musician, stage director, and symphony conductor.

Social: Persons of this type are sociable, responsible, humanistic, and often religious; like to work in groups, and enjoy being central in the group; have good verbal and interpersonal skills; avoid intellectual problem solving, physical exertion, and highly ordered activities; prefer to solve problems through feelings and interpersonal manipulation of others; enjoy activities that involve informing, training, developing, curing, or enlightening others; perceive themselves as understanding, responsible, idealistic, and helpful. Vocational preferences include social worker, missionary, high school teacher, marriage counselor, and speech therapist.

Enterprising: Persons of this type have verbal skills suited to selling, dominating, and leading; are strong leaders;

have a strong drive to attain organizational goals or economic aims; tend to avoid work situations requiring long periods of intellectual effort; differ from conventional types in having a greater preference for ambiguous social tasks and an even greater concern for power, status, and leadership; see themselves as aggressive, popular, self-confident, cheerful, and sociable; generally have a high energy level; and show an aversion to scientific activities. Vocational preferences include business executive, political campaign manager, real estate sales, stock and bond sales, television producer, and retail merchandising.

Conventional: Conventional people prefer well-ordered environments and like systematic verbal and numerical activities; are usually conforming and prefer subordinate roles; are effective at well-structured tasks, but avoid ambiguous situations and problems involving interpersonal relationships or physical skills; describe themselves as conscientious, efficient, obedient, calm, orderly, and practical; identify with power; and value material possessions and status. Vocational preferences include bank examiner, bookkeeper, clerical worker, financial anayalst, quality control expert, statistician, and traffic manager.

Reprinted from David P. Campbell and Jo-Ida C. Hansen, *Manual for the Strong-Campbell Interest Inventory.* Form T325 of the *Strong Vocational Interest Blank,* 3d ed., with the permission of the distributors, Consulting Psychologists Press Inc, for the publisher, Stanford University Press. © 1974, 1977, 1981, by the Board of Trustees of the Leland Stanford Junior University.

need more information about careers and how to go about identifying a compatible career goal. Most students would benefit from talking over their educational plans and career goals with an interested teacher, school or career counselor, or someone in their fields of interest. In turn, counselors at school or career guidance centers can refer students to the sources of information they need in order to engage in meaningful career exploration. Counselors also have access to a wide assortment of career inventories that may help students to identify the most compatible careers for them. Two familiar inventories are Holland's Self-Directed Search and the Strong-Campbell Interest Inventory. Both of these instruments make use of Holland's personality-occupational types or themes, which match different personality characteristics with the requirements of various careers. In addition, many career and counseling centers have computer-aided resources. There's the SIGI PLUS (System of Interractive Guidance and Information) published by the Educational Testing Service in Princeton, New Jersey, and the DISCOVER program published by the American Council of Teachers. You sit at a terminal and enter into a dialogue with the computer, examining your values, exploring career options, and making tentative choices that can be tested realistically and revised. In this way you may learn more about the process of choosing a compatible career.

Students often wonder whether such resources can really help. A lot depends on how they are used. If a person looks to them as a substitute for making a career choice, the answer is no. But if the results are used as a guide in reaching one's own decision, then the answer is decidedly more positive. Talking over the results of such inventories and programs with a counselor may furnish valuable leads for the most compatible careers for each person. These instruments will not tell people how happy or successful they will be. Such outcomes depend more on people's abilities, motivation, and available opportunities. But these resources may provide a valuable aid in determining whether an individual will persist or eventually drop out of a given career. Considering all the time and money people invest in preparing for their careers, such information can be extremely helpful.

INFLUENCES ON CAREER CHOICE

Although young people are generally encouraged to choose their own career, they rarely make such an important decision entirely on their own. In discussing their plans with a school counselor, they may be encouraged or discouraged by what the counselor says. Young people are even more likely to share their educational and career plans with their parents, and parental support or the lack of it, becomes an important factor in whether they pursue their career goals or change them (Sebald, 1986). Then too, young people tend to choose careers that are familiar to them, usually on the basis of the particular people they've known in those careers, rather than out of an objective consideration of unfamiliar careers. Sometimes they are well aware that their career preferences have been influenced by others, such as the girl who goes ahead with her plans of applying to medical school largely because her uncle, a physician, has promised to lend her part of the necessary money. But more often than not, young peoples' choices of a career have been influenced by others in more indirect, subtle ways. The degree to which young people's career choices have been influenced by their families, socioeconomic backgrounds, and sex roles has been the subject of extensive studies.

The Family

The family's influence on young people's career choices has been attributed to such factors as the parents as role models, that is, the parents' education, career, income, and degree of success. But numerous studies suggest that the impact of parental models is mediated through a variety of processes and relationships within the family, such as how satisfied parents are with their careers, how close young people are with a given parent, childrearing practices, and values in the home. As a result, the influence of the family on career choice is more complex than suggested by the findings in any one study, which is well to keep in mind throughout this section.

The father's career usually has an important bearing on the career choices of his sons, though to a lesser extent for his daughters. Although this pattern holds true across many fields, it is especially marked for sons of professionals, technical workers, and those who enter public service. Even when sons do not choose their father's career, they often choose fields with similar career characteristics, such as the extent of work autonomy involved, the complexity of work activities, and whether the rewards are intrinsic or extrinsic. At the same time, the father's influence tends to be greater when he has a high-status career and a close relationship with his son. Furthermore, sons of fathers in the professions, such as law or medicine, are more likely to hold intrinsic career values, while sons of fathers in the business world are more apt to hold extrinsic values. Sons who have a close, positive relationship with their mothers are also more likely to choose a people-oriented career than sons who remain more distant from their mothers (Mortimer and Kumka, 1982).

Although girls generally identify more strongly with their mothers, their choice of a career is also influenced by their fathers, especially the father's attitude toward women's roles. Young women whose fathers have a negative attitude toward the homemaker role are more likely to plan on a college education and to work outside the home. As you might imagine, young women's career choices are also greatly influenced by their mother's example. Young women from families in which the mother works outside the home generally have a high regard for women as competent people in the workplace, believe in more flexible sex roles, are more likely to plan on working outside the home, and aspire to higher-status careers than do women whose mothers remain in the home (Fox and Hesse-Biber, 1984). At the same time, the impact of the mother as a role model is mediated by the same type of influences discussed in relation to the father, such as the status of the mother's career, whether the mother works full- or part-time, how successful she is, and how satisfied she is in her role. When the mother is satisfied with her role, whether she is employed outside the home or not, there is a greater chance the daughter will follow the mother's role. But the opposite is true if the mother is dissatisfied with her role.

The influence of the family may also be seen in the growing proportion of women who want to combine career and family roles in their own lives. Although a college education tends to increase career aspiration among women, this need not exclude plans for marriage and a family. Ruth Fassinger (1985) found that even with college women with high ability with a feminist orientation now see both career and family roles as important in the choice of a career. In fact, college women with high ability tend to select high-prestige careers, often in nontraditional fields for women. At the same time, as mentioned earlier, most women anticipate some conflict between their career and family roles and are concerned about how they will resolve this conflict (Archer, 1985a). A major issue is child care. Most women in the workplace have children. Over half of them have preschool-age children. Consequently, child care arrangements for young children are changing, especially with the growth of more organized child care facilities. See Figure 9-1. Yet, it is difficult to find high-quality day care that is affordable, much less fully tax-deductible. Currently, only a small proportion

Figure 9-1   Changing Child Care Arrangements For Children Under Five Years of Age
with Employed Mothers, 1965 and 1985.

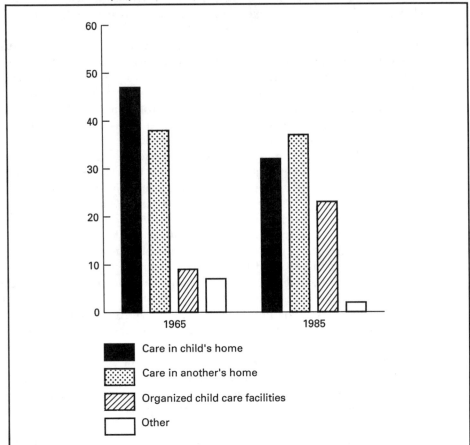

Source: U.S. Bureau of the Census, *The Statistical Abstract of the United States: 1988*, 108th ed. (Washington, D.C.:
U.S. Government Printing Office, 1987), p. 357. *Children, Youth, and Families, 1983. A year-end report*
(Washington, D.C.: U.S. Government Printing Office, 1984), p. 51.

of employers provide child care for their workers. But as an increasing proportion of women enter the workplace, issues such as maternity leave and subsidized
child care may become the valued fringe benefit of the 1990s.

Socioeconomic and Racial Influences

The socioeconomic status of the adolescent's family continues to be a powerful
predictor of career choice, primarily because it includes so many other important
factors such as parental education, income, career status, child-rearing practices,
and values. As a result, a vicious cycle often occurs, with youths tending to

remain in the same broad socioeconomic group in which they are reared. In the first place, socioeconomic status limits the opportunities available to those with different socioeconomic backgrounds. Thus, youths from the lower socioeconomic groups tend to have fewer opportunities for higher-status careers because of a combination of negative influences in their homes, neighborhoods, and schools, and the limited job market, with the reverse being true for youths from the middle and higher socioeconomic groups. Even when exposed to opportunities for higher-status careers, youths from the lower socioeconomic groups are not as likely to take advantage of them because of the way they have been socialized. For instance, parents from lower socioeconomic groups often work as part of a group or team and are more likely to stress being able to work as part of a crew, while parents from higher socioeconomic groups are more likely to work in one of the professions and stress the value of individual initiative. Also, because youths from the lower socioeconomic groups are given less encouragement for educational or social mobility, they either do not aspire to higher-status careers or think such careers are not possible for them. Consequently, there is a tendency for socioeconomic status to perpetuate itself in the next generation, with career mobility occurring more frequently among those in the middle ranges than among those in the extremely high or low socioeconomic statuses (Schulenberg, Vondracek, and Crouter, 1984).

Ethnic and racial factors, often enmeshed with socioeconomic variables, present additional hindrances to career exploration and mobility among youth from minority groups. For instance, although African-Americans comprise about 12 percent of the total population in the United States, they are concentrated in three career groups: (1) operators, fabricators, and laborers; (2) technical, sales, and administrative support; and (3) the service occupations. For example, African Americans account for about one-third of all postal clerks, cleaners, maids, and servants. In contrast, they represent fewer than 1 out of 10 nurses and teachers, and an even smaller proportion of lawyers, judges, dentists, and doctors (U.S. Bureau of this Census, 1990). As a result, the lack of appropriate work opportunities and role models becomes very frustrating in the adolescent's attempts to find a meaningful role in society. Parents from minority groups often instill in their children a strong work ethic, and, like youths of lower socioeconomic groups, minority youths may initially entertain aspirations to enter a higher status career than that of their parents. But the lack of appropriate role models and opportunities to perform roles to which they aspire often leads to negative attitudes toward school and, in turn, diminished career exploration and mobility (Bell-Scott and McKenry, 1986).

Unfortunately, school counselors often add to the problem. High school counselors spend disproportionately less time with working-class students in general, and minority students in particular, and more time helping middle-class students. To make matters worse, counselors, along with parents and teachers, tend to persuade working-class and minority youths from aspiring to higher status careers (Yogev and Roditi, 1987).

Sex Differences

Traditionally, the career choices of males and females have been highly sex-typed, with sex differences often outweighing educational, cultural, and racial differences in career aspirations and achievements. Boys have chosen from a much wider range of careers than have girls. Furthermore, boys have been more likely to choose challenging, high-status careers that offer opportunities for independence and leadership as well as high pay. Girls have been more inclined to shun competitive, high-status careers in favor of lower-status service-oriented careers with low pay (Grotevant and Thorbecke, 1982).

The traditional pattern of sexual inequality in career choice stems from a variety of factors in American society, especially the stereotyped sex roles and restricted opportunities for women in the workplace. Even with the extensive changes in the past decade or so, the majority of women are crowded into just 20 of the Labor Department's 427 job categories. Women are overrepresented in such jobs as secretary, waitress, house servant, nurse, and elementary school

A college education tends to increase career-orientation among women. (Laima Druskis)

teacher. But they are underrepresented in such jobs as auto mechanic, police officer, miner, and construction worker. Only a small proportion of women belong to unions or apprenticeship programs in the trades. Furthermore, the traditionally feminine careers are unevenly distributed throughout the socioeconomic hierarchy of careers, with most of them in the low-paying service sector. Consequently, women who choose traditionally feminine careers not only limit their career mobility but only earn about two-thirds as much as men earn with the same education and job (Lewin, 1984). See Table 9-1.

Young women are now being encouraged to raise their career aspirations through a variety of career development programs. For instance, Barbara Kerr (1983) conducted an intensive one-day program in which forty-eight gifted boys and girls in the eleventh grade visited the guidance center at the University of Nebraska. In the morning, the participants took career interest tests, visited a university class related to their career interests, and later during lunch shared their experiences with the guidance center staff and university faculty members. In the afternoon, the students participated in individual and group counseling sessions in which they discussed their test results and career interests. Then all the students participated in a life-planning group in which they discussed the possible barriers that might thwart their career aspirations, including sex-role stereotypes. Six months later, the students were interviewed about their career plans and the responses were compared with their initial interests during the one-day program. The results showed that girls chose significantly higher-status careers over the six-month period. The status level of careers chosen by boys did not appreciably change during the same period, most likely because they had such high career aspirations initially.

Table 9-1   Distribution of the Sexes in Selected Careers

Male-Dominated Careers		Percent Men
Engineers		92.7
Dentists		90.7
Police		86.6
Lawyers, Judges		80.5
Physicians		80
Female-Dominated Careers		Percent Women
Secretaries		99.1
Registered nurses		94.6
Bank tellers		91
Speech therapists		90.2
Elementary school teachers		84.8
Evenly Distributed Careers	Percent Men	Percent Women
Secondary school teachers	48.8	51.2
Real estate sales	51.5	48.5
Psychologists	44.2	55.8
Public relations	40.9	59.1
Editors, reporters	48.9	51.1

Source: U.S. Bureau of the Census, *Statistical Abstract of the United States: 1990*, 110th ed. (Washington, D.C.: U.S. Government Printing Office, 1990), p. 389.

Fortunately, the outlook for women is improving because of more flexible sex roles, social practices, and greater sexual equality in the workplace. As a result, college enrollment has increased faster for women than for men in the past decade, with the number of women attending graduate and professional school increasing by 75 percent. More women are also entering the workplace than ever before. More than nine out of ten women work outside the home sometime during their lives, with about two-thirds of them employed in the workplace at any one time. More young women are working before marriage, delaying marriage, combining work and marriage, having fewer children, and returning to work sooner after marriage. Women are also choosing from a broader range of careers, including many nontraditional careers for women. Although the *proportion* of women in the nontraditional career remains small, the *rate* of increase is dramatic. For instance, since 1960, the percentage of college professors who are women has more than doubled, the percentage of women workers in the life and physical sciences has increased two and one-half times, the percentage of women engineers has increased four times, and the percentage of lawyers and judges who are women has risen nearly five times (U.S. Department of Labor, 1982).

PREPARING FOR A CAREER

The mention of college brings us to the important matter of preparing for a career. Actually, there are a variety of ways young people may prepare for a career. Some careers are normally entered through an apprenticeship program, vocational school, or an on-the-job training program. Other careers require a two-year or a four-year college degree. Most professions like medicine and law also require an advanced degree and professional training. A very important part of the decision-making process is learning what type and how much education is needed, the entrance requirements, the expected expenses, and the job prospects. Much of this information may be acquired during talks with the school counselor or from resources such as the *Occupational Outlook Handbook*. But in many instances, students remain ill-informed and have educational plans that are not consistent with their career goals.

Career Education

Many people feel that such misunderstanding could be avoided or minimized if students had more exposure to careers earlier in their education, as in career education. The general purpose of career education is to bridge the gap between the individual's learning experience and the workplace. Career education is especially needed among today's students because of the long years spent in school isolated from the workplace, except for the part-time jobs unrelated to career goals so characteristic of teenage employment. A Gallup Poll (Elam, 1990) showed that two-thirds of public school parents believe some type of career

Students need to explore their interests and a range of careers before settling on a particular career goal. (Laima Druskis)

education should be required for all high school students, college-bound youth as well as those not planning to attend college. Some of the components of a comprehensive career education include providing information on the career implications of every learning experience, attitudes and values of a work-oriented society, career awareness, career exploration, decision-making skills, career choice, entry-level work skills, specific vocational training, and supervised work experience.

A master plan for school-based career education would involve students at all age levels. Throughout elementary school, the emphasis would be on career awareness. Children would be exposed to the different kinds of work done by adults in the community. Teachers would point out the career implications of various learning experiences, including practical problems in arithmetic, and would simulate appropriate work experience in the classroom. Beginning in middle school or junior high school and continuing into high school, the emphasis would shift to career exploration. Students would explore career clusters, or groups of related careers. After becoming familiar with all of the clusters, they would explore in more depth one or two clusters of the greatest interest to them, such as health careers. Students would then become aware of the many different jobs in these clusters and how each job relates to the larger society. As they move into high school, students would be assisted in formulating tentative career goals and become aware of the necessary preparation to achieve them. Students who are not planning to go to college would also be encouraged to develop entry-level skills useful in a variety of fields, as well as basic vocational training in a field of their choice.

A valuable part of career education is providing appropriate experience in the workplace. In contrast to the usual teenage employment, such experience should include appropriate instruction and supervision and should help integrate what is learned in school and on the job. One approach is the familiar work-study programs, in which students spend half the day in class and the other half at work on the job. In addition, some private schools have initiated internships that provide students firsthand experience in a field related to their career goals. Examples would be helping in a lawyer's office, a television studio, a dentist's office, or at a newspaper. One school requires all juniors and seniors to spend their Fridays working on a semester-long internship instead of going to class. Students are also encouraged to start their own small businesses, such as a painting company. Another option is providing students with human-services education, with supervised work experience for academic credit but without pay. This may be especially valuable for people considering professional fields such as teaching, nursing, and medicine as well as social service agencies in which entry-level, people-oriented jobs are not available on a paid basis. Still another option is volunteer work, including social service agencies, hospitals, community centers, tutoring in schools, and libraries. One way for organizations to make better use of volunteers is to arrange voluntary work around the free time in students' schedules, such as near lunch or at the end of classes. In one school, students organized a catalogue of service opportunities and made it available in a volunteer bureau as a kind of clearing house for student volunteers.

Despite the commendable goals of career education advanced since the 1970s, few comprehensive career education programs have been implemented. And now that the emphasis in educational priorities has swung toward improving basic skills and academic excellence, the funding for career education is likely to become even more competitive. Furthermore, the results of career education vary widely with the particular programs and students, and generally have been more successful in the area of increasing awareness of careers and how to go about selecting a career than substantial changes in unemployment. One study focused on the relationship between career maturity and career education practices among 2,280 students in the ninth and eleventh grades in 38 secondary schools in metropolitan areas. The results showed that students in schools with career education programs achieved higher gains in their career maturity during high school than did those in schools with no career education programs. There was also a strong association between the type of career education program and support given, such that the greatest gains in career maturity occurred among students in schools offering innovative career education programs strongly supported by the school and community (Treblico, 1984).

Going to College

Many jobs now require a college degree either from a two-year or four-year college. As a result, a larger proportion of high school graduates now go on to college. While about one-third of high school graduates attended college in 1960, over half (57 percent) do so today. About half of all students in the first two years of college are enrolled in two-year public or community colleges. Many of these students are older than the traditional college student. Some have delayed their entry into colege for a few years, hoping to earn money for their education and/or settle on a career goal. Others are adults who are returning to school after rearing a family or want to change their careers. An increasing proportion of students attend college part-time, combining school with a job or family responsibilities.

   One of the most significant changes in recent years has been the marked increase in career-minded students. Whereas barely half of the college students were enrolled in a career-oriented program in 1960, more than two-thirds of them were taking such a program by the 1980s. Much of the reason has to do with the tight job market, inflation, and increased cost of a college education. As a result, more students have been taking degrees in job-related fields such as business and management, computer science, health professions, and engineering, while fewer of them take degrees in the arts, humanities, and social sciences (See Figure 9-2.) Such changes also reflect the perceived value of a college education. When the respondents in the annual Gallup poll (1986) were asked about the advantages of a college education, 34 percent of them cited better job opportunities, 8 percent better-paying jobs, and 9 percent financial security. Relatively few Americans mentioned preparation for life (23 percent); acquiring knowledge (10 percent); acquiring thinking, learning, and understanding skills (3 percent); learning how to get along with others (4 percent); or contributing to society (3 percent). Yet, in the long run, the latter advantages of a college education might be just as valuable, if not more so, than the more obviously career-related advantages of a college education. Given the rapid changes in the job market and the fact that roughly one in nine workers changes his or her career every year, one of the most valuable but overlooked rewards of a college education is the ability to continue learning on one's own and being able to adapt to continuing change (U.S. Department of Labor, 1990).

Figure 9-2 Bachelor's Degrees Conferred, by Field of Study: 1971–1986.

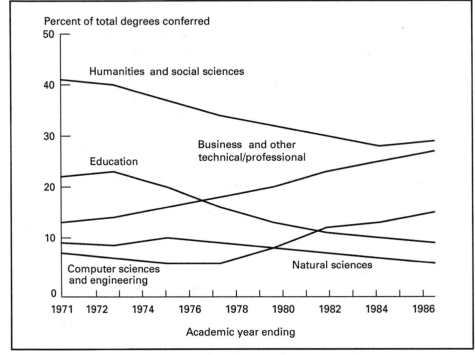

Source: Laurence T. Ogle, ed., *The Condition of Education 1990*. (Washington, D.C.: National Center for Education Statistics, U.S. Department of Education. U.S. Government Printing Office, 1990), p. 13.

Career Outlook

Individuals planning on a career should be aware of the rising educational level of the work force and the importance of a college education. Presently about four out of ten workers have had some college education. See Figure 9-3. The increasing level of education in the work force reflects both the retirement of older workers, many of whom had little formal education, and the entry into the workplace of young people who generally have a higher level of formal education. Among workers aged 25 to 34, nearly half have completed at least one year of college, and one-fourth have four or more years of college. The advantages of college-educated workers can be seen in their lower unemployment rates and higher lifetime earnings. Although earnings vary greatly among people in different careers as well as among those with different levels of experience in the same career, college graduates earn about 50 percent more than high school graduates do (Murphy & Welch, 1989).

About one out of every four jobs in the workplace requires a four-year college degree. But the rate of increase in the projected openings for college

Figure 9-3   The Proportion of Workers with a College Background has Increased Substantially Since the 1970s.

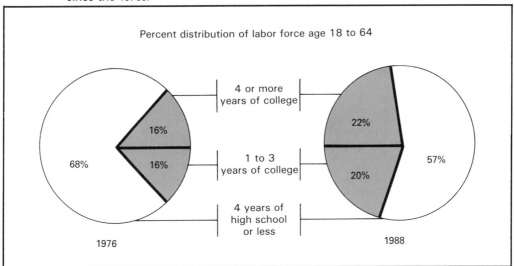

Percent distribution of labor force age 18 to 64

4 or more years of college

1 to 3 years of college

4 years of high school or less

16%

16%

68%

1976

22%

20%

57%

1988

Source: U.S. Department of Labor, *Occupational Outlook Handbook, 1990–91* (Washington, D.C.: U.S. Government Printing Office, 1990), p. 9.

graduates between now and the year 2000 will vary considerably depending on many factors. Two key factors are the projected number of openings in the different careers and the expected growth of workers looking for jobs in these fields.

Job prospects will vary considerably from one career to another because of changes in the workplace. Service-oriented industries will continue to expand at a faster rate than will other industries and will account for about one-half of all new jobs by the year 2000. The expansion of service-oriented industries reflects a number of influences, including changes in consumer tastes, legal and regulatory changes, advances in science and technology, and changes in the way businesses are organized and managed (U.S. Department of Labor, 1990). Health services, business services—including computer and data processing—and educational services will be among the fastest-growing fields. Selected careers that are expected to grow at a faster than average rate (20 to 30 percent) and a much faster than average rate (31 percent and over) are listed in Table 9-2.

Career prospects depend not only on the job openings but also on the number of people looking for these types of jobs. Generally, the labor force is expected to grow through the 1990s at a slower rate than in the past, reflecting population trends in the United States. At the same time, the American work force is becoming increasingly diverse. As a result, workers from minority groups, especially African Americans, Hispanics, and Asians, will increase by about one-third between 1990 and the year 2000. Women will account for over

Table 9-2   Selected Careers with Faster Than Average Projected Job Growth, 1988–2000 (The numerical projections are in thousands)

Career	1988 Employment Number	CHANGE IN EM- PLOYMENT 1988–2000	
		Number	Percent
Paralegals	83	62	75
Medical assistants	149	104	70
Radiologic technicians	132	87	66
Homemaker/home-health aides	327	207	63
Medical records librarians	47	28	60
Operations research analysts	55	30	55
Travel agents	142	77	54
Actuaries	16	9	54
Computer systems analysts	402	214	53
EEG technicians	6	3	50
Occupational therapists	33	16	49
Computer programmers	519	250	48
Service sales representatives	481	216	45
Human services	118	53	45
Health service managers	177	75	42
Correction officers	186	76	41
Electrical/electronic engineers	439	176	40
Employment interviewers	81	33	40
Registered nurses	1,577	613	39
Flight attendants	88	34	39
Aircraft pilots	83	26	31
Lawyers and judges	622	188	30
Meteorologists	6	2	30
Actors, directors, producers	80	24	30
Child care workers	670	186	30
Social workers	385	110	29
Physicians	535	149	28
Dieticians, nutritionists	40	11	28
Pharmacists	162	44	27
Psychologists	104	28	27
Economists	36	10	27
Visual artists	216	58	27
Biological scientists	57	15	26
Marketing, advertising, public relations	406	105	26
Writers and editors	219	55	25
Engineers	1,411	351	25
Architects	86	21	25
Accountants	963	211	23
Teachers, secondary school	1,164	224	19

Source: Shelley J. Davis, "The 1990–91 Job Outlook in Brief," *Occupational Outlook Quarterly* (Spring 1990), pp. 14–45.

half of all entrants to the workplace during the same period. Other trends reflect the changing proportions of workers in the various age groups. Because of the decline of people in the 16- to 24-year-old group, there will be fewer youth competing for entry-level jobs. However, the proportion of people in the 25- to 54-year-old group is expected to increase considerably because of the aging baby

Many of the fastest growing careers involve the use of computers. (Courtesy IBM)

boomers. Both these factors will keep the job market competitive for this age group throughout the 1990s. Most of the jobs through the year 2000 will come from replacement needs as a result of workers who retire (U.S. Department of Labor, 1990).

Finally, as mentioned earlier, there is a trend toward employing more educated workers. But because the supply of college graduates has been increasing faster than the fields that employ college-educated workers, the job market is expected to remain competitive for college graduates. In recent years, one in five college graduates has had to take a job that does not require a college education. Yet, not all careers that require a college degree will be crowded. Good opportunities are expected in a number of fields, including computer-related careers, engineering, and the health-related careers. Despite the competitive job market for college graduates, a degree is still needed for most high-status, high-paying jobs. Individuals interested in these careers should not be discouraged from pursuing a career that they believe matches their interests and abilities. But they should be aware of the job market conditions.

SUMMARY

Adolescents in the Workplace

1. The transition to adult work roles in the United States occurs gradually, with young people doing household chores and holding part-time jobs before assuming responsibility for a full-time job in the workplace.

2. One of the remarkable changes in the past decade or so has been the greater proportion of teenagers who work during the school year, with the average student-worker spending about fifteen to twenty hours a week on the job.

3. Although students gain a lot of practical knowledge from their part-time jobs, their work tends to be dull and stressful and unrelated to their career goals, with school grades being adversely affected after fifteen to twenty hours on the job.

Exploring and Choosing a Career Goal

4. Choosing a career is generally an extended developmental process that involves a great deal of exploration and tentative choices before settling on a firm career goal.

5. According to Super's developmental theory, career exploration is an extended process that involves the individual's search for a vocational identity in the workplace.

6. According to Holland's occupational environment theory, individuals tend to select careers that are compatible with their overall personalities.

7. Given the complexities of choosing a career, counselors have access to a wide assortment of career inventories that may help students to identify the careers most suitable to them.

Influences on Career Choice

8. The choice of a career is influenced by a variety of factors in adolescents' families, such as the parents' education and careers as well as the extent to which adolescents identify with their parents.

9. Socioeconomic factors also shape career choice, with youths from affluent, educated families especially likely to choose high-status careers.

10. In contrast, youth from minority groups often receive less encouragement from parents, teachers, and counselors and entertain career aspirations lower than their abilities warrant.

11. Due to stereotyped sex roles and restricted opportunities in the workplace, the majority of women have been overrepresented in low-paying service jobs.

12. At the same time, because of extensive changes in human rights and rules governing the workplace, women are aspiring to higher educational and career goals than in the past.

Preparing for a Career

13. Students who have access to career education programs, especially the innovative and well-supported ones, tend to experience greater gains in career maturity in school than do those who have little or no career education.

14. Now that many careers require a two- or four-year college degree, more than half of all high school graduates go on to college. Many of them enroll in career-oriented degree programs.

15. Although the job market is expected to remain competitive for college graduates between now and the year 2000, a college degree is still needed for most high-status, high-paying careers.

REVIEW QUESTIONS

1. What are the most common part-time jobs for 16 and 17 year olds?
2. How valuable is the typical teenager's work experience?
3. To what extent does career choice reflect how we see ourselves and who we want to become?
4. How can adolescents benefit from career inventories like Holland's Self-Directed Search?
5. To what extent does the consideration of family roles influence women's choice of a career?
6. How important are socioeconomic differences in the selection of a career?
7. What is the single biggest inequality between the sexes in the workplace?
8. How did you arrive at your present choice of a career?
9. What are the advantages of a college education for your career?
10. Which careers have the most favorable projected outlook during the 1990s?

10

The Self-Concept and Personal Identity

Learning Objectives

After completing this chapter, you should be able to:
1 Define *self-concept.*
2 Describe the characteristic changes in the self-concept during adolescence.
3 Describe how adolescents' self-esteem is influenced by their families.
4 Discuss how self-esteem may be improved.
5 Discuss Erik Erikson's view of the adolescent identity crisis.
6 Give one example for each identity status: achievement, moratorium, foreclosure, and confusion.
7 Describe the characteristic developmental changes in personal identity during adolescence.

Throughout high school, Roy Baumaster (1986) remained a straight, all-American boy. He says, "I did lots of homework, was on the swim team, and stayed away from drugs and sex and other delights." But once in college, he began experimenting with other lifestyles. "I grew a beard, played in a rock band," he says, and generally "became quite a different person." Still later, in graduate school, he changed again.

Like so many youths, Baumaster was busily exploring the kind of person he wanted to be. In the process of redefining themselves, young people like Baumaster tend to affirm some self-images and reject others, while retaining a definite connection between their past and present selves. At the same time, they're less certain of the kind of person they want to be, realizing full well that they will continue to change. However, friends and acquaintances are not always so understanding. For instance, during graduate school, Baumaster found it annoying to meet people who had known him in college, and even more irritating to interact with those who had known him in high school. He says, "These people expected me to act the way I had acted when they had known me." Such observations eventually led Baumaster, now a psychologist, to consider how the growth of one's inner, private self may become constricted by one's public self-image—the impressions others have of us.

THE SELF-CONCEPT

Baumaster's experience illustrates the importance of the self-concept and the process of exploring and reshaping one's personal identity during late adolescence and early adulthood. We begin by describing the development of the self-concept and especially how it changes during adolescence, along with the accompanying changes in self-esteem. Then in the next two sections of the chapter, we will explain Erik Erikson's view of the adolescent identity crisis and the important changes in personal identity that occur throughout adolescence and the transition to adulthood.

Formation of the Self-Concept

Essentially, the self-concept is the overall awareness we have of ourselves. As such, it includes all those perceptions of "I" and "me" together with the feelings, beliefs, and values associated with them. Even though we habitually refer to it in the singular, the self-concept is actually a collection of hundreds of selves or self-perceptions. It is also common to identity specific clusters of selves, such as the *body-image*, how I perceive my body and feel about it; the *self-image*, the self I see myself to be; the *ideal self*, the self I'd like to be, and our *social selves*, or the ways I feel others see me.

Children begin forming their self-images in response to a variety of factors. Don Hammachek (1985) has identified four types of influences that are especially important in the early formation of the self-concept:

1. *Physical sensations.* Experiences of stretching, crawling, being held tenderly, being spanked, or being left alone all stimulate the infant's sensory, bodily experiences and thus the sense of being a separate experiencing organism.

Our self-concept is made up of the many self-images we have acquired while growing up, especially in the formative years.

2. *Body image.*   As infants see, touch, and explore their bodies, they gradually build up a more coherent body image, consisting of how they perceive and feel about their bodies.
3. *Auditory cues.*   Hearing one's name, and being called good, bad, cute, or smart help to shape one's sense of self as does the tone of voice and frequency of being talked to.
4. *Personal memories.*   Early life experiences and their emotional meaning for children, especially the more significant ones such as being loved or rejected, are stored and incorporated into the child's self-image.

The contents of the self-concept are acquired mostly through the child's interaction with significant others. During this formative period, children tend to internalize the reactions and expectations of others into their self-concepts. For instance, if a parent repeatedly tells a child, "You're stupid," the child eventually sees himself or herself in this way. In a similar manner, children learn to anticipate what others expect of them and adapt the same attitude toward themselves. In this way, children build up images of themselves as a "me" or an object to themselves. As they acquire greater self-consciousness and individuation, they become aware of themselves more as an acting subject or an "I" rather than a "me." But much of their self-awareness is shaped by the reactions and expectations of others. At the same time, the self-concept is not simply a mirrorlike reflection of external reality. Instead, the self-concept, like impressions of other people and the world, involves an integration and interpretation of a tremendous amount of information and continues to change with one's personal experience (Harter, 1983). Eventually, the combination of all the self-attributes leads to the development of two core ingredients of the self,

---

Mirror Images and Self-Awareness

Some animals like the preadolescent macaque monkey show little evidence of self-recognition even after hours of viewing themselves in the mirror. In contrast, chimpanzees and orangutans show signs of self-recognition after only two or three days of mirror confrontation. Although the chimps initially treat their mirror image as another chimp, they soon recognize it as themselves and use this information to experiment with themselves somewhat like humans with a self-concept.

Similarly, one of the earliest signs of human self-awareness occurs when a child recognizes herself in a mirror. Such self-recognition emerges gradually over about a year, beginning about the sixth month, when the child reaches out to touch the mirror image as if it were another child (Damon and Hart, 1982). But how do we know the infant recognizes that the girl in the mirror is herself and not another playmate? In order to find out, Gallup and Suarez (1986) put a spot of rouge on infants's noses and then placed them in front of the mirror. Starting at about 15 to 18 months, children, upon noticing the red spot, touched their noses. It seems that by this age, children have an idea of how their faces should look, and react to the discrepancy in the mirror as if to ask, "What is this spot doing on *my* face?"

namely the *self-concept,* or ideas about one's self, and *self-esteem,* the feelings and evaluations about one's self.

By the time children reach 8 to 10 years of age, their self-concept has become relatively stable. They come to see themselves as skillful in some ways, but not in others. They also have an idea of the personal traits and skills they would like to have. Furthermore, their images of themselves affect their behavior. Children with positive self-concepts tend to be assertive, optimistic, and sociable, while those with negative self-concepts are inclined to be shy, pessimistic, and introverted.

Changes During Adolescence

The heightened self-awareness and ability to think in an abstract way that emerges during puberty leads to extensive changes in the adolescent's self-concept. First, adolescents perceive themselves in a more detailed, differentiated way than in the past, so that, for example, an adolescent may feel apprehensive about herself with her father but feel comfortable with herself in relation to her best friend. Second, adolescents acquire a more individuated view of themselves than they did as children and are more apt to affirm themselves in terms of their differences or uniqueness in relation to others in addition to their similarities to them. Third, adolescents also acquire more perspective on the self and are better able to put themselves in the shoes of others and see themselves as others see them. As a result, adolescents become very much concerned with how others react to them.

Adolescents gradually learn to view themselves in a more abstract and differentiated way than do children, as was demonstrated in a study by Montemayor and Eisen (1977). The subjects included students from preadolescence through late adolescence. Younger and older adolescents' responses to the question "Who am I?" were analyzed according to thirty different categories, such as age, sex, body image, social status, and career role. As expected, the younger adolescents were more likely to describe themselves in concrete ways, such as "I have blue eyes. I have two brothers. I like ice cream." In contrast, the older adolescents relied on more ideological statements and interpersonal characteristics, such as "I am an ambitious person. I believe in God. I'm someone other people like to tell their problems to." Such findings show that older adolescents use their growing cognitive skills to perceive themselves and the surrounding world in a more complex, differentiated way.

The self-concept gradually stabilizes by late adolescence, such that youths may experience only slight changes in their self-concepts throughout the transition to early adulthood. Accordingly, individuals who have a positive self-concept enter adulthood with similar feelings, while those with negative self-concepts tend to carry these views into adulthood (Chiam, 1987). At the same time, adolescents are quite sensitive to important changes in their lives. For instance, those who associate with the wrong crowd and engage in drugs and deviant behavior usually experience poorer self-images. Similarly, youths whose families move long distances to a new home may suffer from anxiety and self-doubt in the process of finding new friends. Changing schools about the same time as puberty begins, around 12 years of age, commonly leads to temporary drops in adolescents' self-image. Apparently, the move from the relatively safe, personal atmosphere of elementary school to the larger, more impersonal setting of middle school or junior high school, in which teachers and classmates are constantly changing, is disturbing to an adolescent's self-image (Simmons, Burgeson, and Reef, 1987).

Adolescents who have difficulty adjusting to the important events and changes in their lives may be helped in a number of ways. Educators may place students in alternative classes, programs, and schools as a way of modifying their attitudes and self-images. Summer camps and supervised work programs related to adolescents' interests can also be beneficial. Also, many investigators have found that adolescents who are introverted and timid may benefit from assertiveness training. Through role playing and other techniques, adolescents are taught how to express their needs and preferences and how to refuse unfair demands made upon them, which, in turn, may lead to more mutually satisfying relationships with the peers and adults in their lives (Wehr and Kaufman, 1987).

Self-Esteem

A critical aspect of one's self-concept is the sense of self-esteem, which consists of evaluations of about oneself or the feelings of self-worth associated with the self-concept. Adolescents' self-esteem is obviously affected by their outward successes and failures as well as their relationships with others. Yet a lot depends on how emotionally invested an adolescent becomes in a given task or relationship, such that an adolescent who does poorly in gym but doesn't care about this aspect of her life may suffer less than one who would like to do well in this subject. Ultimately, of course, adolescents judge themselves in light of their own expectations, aspirations, and ideals. Consequently, if two students make a B plus on the same test, the one with a modest self-ideal may feel reasonably satisfied with the results, while another youth with perfectionistic standards may remain highly dissatisfied.

Although people customarily speak of self-esteem as a single entity—"global esteem"—there is a growing recognition that one's self-esteem, like the self-concept, varies somewhat in relation to different situations and abilities. Thus, Mark may have high self-esteem in regard to playing certain sports, such as basketball and tennis. But he may lack confidence in himself in regard to some academic subjects, especially those requiring a high level of verbal abilities. On the other hand, Lisa may feel good about herself as a student, though this also varies somewhat from subject to subject. At the same time, she may suffer from low esteem in regard to her looks, mostly because she is overweight for her age.

Actually, adolescents of both sexes find their self-esteem is significantly affected by their body images—how they perceive their bodies and feel about

Feeling good about yourself comes partly through measuring up to standards at school, work, and home. (Ken Karp)

their appearance. When adolescents are asked what they most like or dislike about themselves, they mention physical characteristics far more frequently than any others. This is understandable in light of the many bodily changes that occur during puberty. As mentioned in Chapter 3, adolescents' feelings about their bodies, especially their general appearance, become more favorable as they reach late adolescence. And the more favorably adolescents feel about their physical appearance, attractiveness, fitness, and physical competence, the better they like themselves. However, in evaluating themselves, adolescents tend to compare their own physical development to that of their peers as well as the cultural body ideals for their sex. Then too, youths in their teens and twenties tend to be more concerned about their appearance than any other age group, with females being somewhat more dissatisfied than males with their looks. This is most likely due to the greater emphasis on physical appearance for women than men and the more stringent standards for female attractiveness. Generally, there is a mutual relationship between body image and self-esteem, so that those who like their appearance also feel good about themselves as people. But it works the other way too; youths with high self-esteem are able to accept their bodies despite their physical shortcomings (Cash, Winstead, and Janda, 1986). See Table 10-1.

Adolescents' self-esteem is especially affected by their family life. Because self-esteem is shaped by the combination of various factors, such as family structure, family interaction, and cohesiveness, among others, it is difficult to

Table 10-1 Signs of Self-Esteem

Adolescents with High Self-Esteem:	Adolescents with Low Self-Esteem:
Express their opinions readily	Do not express their views, even if asked
Listen to what others say	Criticize what others say
Initiate friendly relationships	Avoid initiating personal contacts
Cooperate with others in groups	Look around to monitor others in groups
Accept compliments graciously	Reject or qualify compliments
Give credit to others when it's due	Envy others and make sarcastic comments
Make realistic demands on themselves	Expect too much or too little of themselves
Savor their accomplishments	Brag excessively about their achievements
Give and receive affection	Withhold affection for fear of being hurt
Like their appearance in the mirror	Avoid viewing themselves in the mirror

assess the impact of any one factor. However, a review of the literature shows that some patterns are fairly well established. Thus, adolescents are more likely to have high self-esteem when they have parents (1) who love and support them, (2) who use an authoritative parenting style that encourages the adolescent's self-determination, and (3) who foster a cohesive and adaptive family unit, with effective communication (Openshaw and Thomas, 1986).

An important though controversial factor concerns the relationship between different types of family structure and adolescent self-esteem, especially differences between single-parent and two-parent families. Although there is substantial evidence that adolescents are often adversely affected by the loss of a parent through divorce or death, such factors work in combination with other influences. For instance, Joycelyn and Thomas Parish (1983) found that family structure interacts with family atmosphere, or how happy adolescents are in their respective families. Thus, an adolescent from a happy single-parent home might exhibit high esteem, whereas another adolescent of the same age and sex from an unhappy two-parent home might suffer from low esteem. Similarly, other studies have shown that the effect of family structure also depends on the age and sex of the parent and adolescents. Then too, divorce and single-parent homes bring a mixture of gains and losses. That is, while adolescents may have been hurt by their parents' divorce, they may also gain more self-confidence in their own abilities to cope with life in such a situation. All of this reminds us that the connection between family structure and self-esteem is sufficiently complex to resist simplistic generalizations.

Change and Stability in Self-Esteem

Self-esteem tends to fluctuate throughout adolescence, with girls experiencing greater drops in esteem than boys. At ages 8 and 9, about 6 out of 10 adolescents of both sexes feel confident and positive about themselves. But over the next eight years, the gap between the sexes widens, with girls more likely than boys to have their lowered esteem inhibit their abilities and actions. A major reason is thought to be that girls are systematically, though unintentionally, discouraged from a wide range of pursuits, such as math and science in schools (Freiberg, 1991).

The period of greatest fluctuation occurs during early adolescence, with 12 and 13 year olds exhibiting the highest self-consciousness and lowest self-esteem. The rapid, unpredictable changes in the body at this stage of development may have a negative impact on body image. But adolescents' self-esteem appears to suffer even more because of changing schools. This was demonstrated in a series of longitudinal studies by Blyth, Simmons, and Carlton-Ford (1983) comparing changes in adolescents' self-esteem among students attending schools using the 8-4 plan and those using the 6-3-3 plan. The results showed that school transitions generally have a temporary negative effect on adolescents' self-esteem. Girls in the 6-3-3 arrangement showed two dramatic drops in self-esteem during each of the moves to a new school, that is, between the sixth and seventh grades and between the ninth and tenth grades. Although such changes were less pronounced among the boys, the boys in the 6-3-3 arrangement experienced slight drops in self-esteem between the ninth and tenth grades. In contrast, boys and girls attending school using the 8-4 plan experienced a gradual rise in self-esteem throughout adolescence. For girls, changing schools following the sixth grade may be upsetting because it coincides with the onset of puberty and the beginning of dating. Changing schools in the ninth grade appears to have negative effects among both sexes primarily because of the presence of older youth. As a result, the younger students who have just changed schools become less active in school activities, are more prone to use alcohol and drugs, and are more likely to feel anonymous—all of which has a deleterious effect on their self-esteem.

Educators have long realized that self-esteem is a critical factor in learning, with high-esteem students forging ahead academically and low-esteem students falling behind. Consequently, as Barbara Lerner (1985) points out, since the 1960s many educators have advocated giving priority to raising students' self-esteem. To do this, teachers have provided students with constant praise and encouragement, ensuring that they experience a feeling of success in school as immediately and as often as possible. At all costs, students' self-esteem must be protected from injury through critcism or failure. An unintended result, however, has been the awarding of good grades for mediocre accomplishments, sometimes accompanied by a lack of basic competence. Lerner contends that an undue emphasis on "feel-good-now" esteem has encouraged an orientation toward instant success and a constant hunger to get more for less. An example can be seen in the contrast between students' self-confidence and their actual test performance. For instance, when a standardized math test was given to 13 year olds in six countries, Koreans did the best and Americans the worst, coming in behind Spain, Britain, Ireland, and Canada. However, when students responded to the statement "I am good at mathematics," the results were just the opposite. Koreans came last in this category, while Americans were number 1, with over two-thirds of them feeling they were good in math despite their dismal test performance (Krauthammer, 1990).

By contrast, many current approaches, inspired by the emphasis on excellence in education, aim to raise students' self-esteem through the development of competence and achievement. As Lerner (1985) points out, self-esteem is based on measuring up to standards at school, work, and home. Such esteem is hard won and develops slowly. Students must learn to persist during times of momentary unhappiness, other times when they tend to be overly self-critical, and occasional bouts of failure in order to acquire this sort of self-esteem. For teachers, self-esteem involves the stubborn determination to help students affirm their strengths, rather than the easier path of judging students and dwelling on the things they do wrong. "Tough-minded" teachers need to operate on the assumption that positive expectations accompanied by positive reinforcement for work well done are far stronger than harsh directives (Batten, 1990). This approach includes linking praise to noteworthy effort and achievement, along with setting specific standards and praising students for achieving them.

When California announced in 1987 that it was establishing a Task Force to Promote Self-esteem and Personal and Social Responsibility (Calif. State Dept. of Educ., 1990), *Doonesbury* cartoonist Gary Trudeau portrayed the idea as a flaky New Age fad. But now that the task force has completed its report, the sneers are giving way to cheers. The task force urges, among many other things, that schools offer parenting classes to high school students and require prospective teachers to receive training in teaching self-esteem and responsibility. Other recommendations include establishing peer support groups for people on welfare, combatting the destructive behavior of gangs with programs that teach self-esteem, and holding juvenile offenders accountable for their behaviors with consistent and appropriate penalties. At least twelve other states are considering similar proposals. Such concern is commendable, though the success of these efforts remains to be seen. A major hazard consists of regarding self-esteem as the primary root cause of many adolescent difficulties that, in turn, can be manipulated directly through various programs. Yet self-esteem also results from the combined effects of many influences that cannot be easily manipulated and ultimately depends on the individual's own attitudes and commitments. Also, there is the related danger of emphasizing global self-esteem in the face of increasing evidence that self-esteem depends largely on one's skills and achievements in specific situations. Consequently, as John Leo (1990) points out in his essay "The Trouble with Self-Esteem," lasting esteem is more apt to be acquired as students learn something and develop a sense of mastery. It is a byproduct of, rather than a substitute for, real education.

TOWARD A SELF-CHOSEN IDENTITY

The self-concept and related feelings of esteem or self-worth provide adolescents with their personal identity, a sense of who they are and who they are becoming. In turn, their identity gives them a sense of sameness and continuity amid constant change in their lives. This is especially important today in a society of constant change, when so many traditional ideas are changing, such as what it means to be a male or female or an adolescent or an adult.

Erikson's Psychosocial Theory

The idea that late adolescents are especially concerned with the pursuit of their personal identity has long been associated with Erik Erikson's name. Although Erikson was trained in the psychoanalytical tradition, he later modified many of the Freudian ideas in the light of his own thought and experience. Essentially, Erikson has widened the potential application of psychoanalytic theory by transforming Freud's psychosexual theory of development into a more inclusive psychosocial theory of development. Whereas Freud focused on the child's psychosexual development within the family, Erikson takes into account the individual's psychosocial relationships within the larger society. Furthermore, whereas Freud's stages covered only the years between birth and puberty, Erikson's stages extend throughout adulthood into old age.

One of Erikson's (1980b) major ideas is that development is cumulative, in the sense that each part of development has its special time of ascendancy until all the parts of development are integrated into a fundamental whole. More specifically, the individual's genetic potential unfolds throughout a lifelong sequence of eight developmental stages. Each stage of development is set by the biological readiness for a particular kind of growth, especially throughout the first four stages. In addition, each stage consists of a positive ability to be achieved along with a related threat or vulnerability. (See Table 10-2). Optimal

Table10-2   Erikson's Psychosocial Stages of Development

Approximate Ages	Developmental Tasks of Each Stage
1. Infancy (lst year)	Trust vs. mistrust As needs are met, infant develops a sense of basic trust.
2. Toddler (2nd year)	Autonomy vs. shame and doubt Toddler acquires age-appropriate autonomy and self-confidence.
3. Preschooler (3–5 Years)	Initiative vs. guilt Young child learns to initiate tasks and acquire self-control.
4. School-aged child (6 years to puberty)	Competence vs. inferiority Child learns to feel competent or inadequate through developing various skills.
5. Adolescence (teenage years)	Identity vs. role confusion Adolescents engage in self-exploration and role testing, striving for a self-chosen identity.
6. Young adulthood (20–30 years)	Intimacy vs. isolation Young adults seek to form close relationships in friendship, love, marriage, and their families.
7. Middle adulthood (40–50 years)	Generativity vs. stagnation Middle-aged adults strive to make contributions to their world through their family, work, and community.
8. Late adulthood (mid 60s and older)	Integrity vs. despair Reflecting on their lives, older adults gain a sense of life satisfaction, or a sense of failure.

Adapted from *Identity, Youth and Crisis* by Erik H. Erickson, by permission of W.W. Norton & Co., Inc. Copyright © 1968 by W.W. Norton & Co., Inc.

growth consists of the successful resolution of the developmental crises at each stage, with one's overall personality composed of the cumulative strengths and weaknesses acquired in each stage. The greater the relative stengths acquired, the stronger one's personality.

The Adolescent Identity Crisis

Erikson holds that the characteristic life crisis of adolescence is the establishing of a self-chosen identity. Actually, identity formation is a lifelong task that begins in infancy and continues into old age. What makes the search for identity so critical at adolescence is the combination of changes that occur at this age, especially the dramatic bodily changes, sexual maturation, cognitive changes, and the growing involvement with peers and emancipation from one's family.

The developmental task of this period is the achievement of a positive identity based on one's self-exploration and commitments, with the attendant danger of identity confusion. Although this is a period of great growth potential, it is also a time when individuals suffer more deeply than ever before or again from the confusion of roles. Yet Erikson holds that the disturbances of this period are more aptly regarded as an aggravated life crisis rather than a psychological disorder. A certain amount of conflict, experimentation, and self-doubt are essential for achieving a firm self-chosen identity. Otherwise, those who take

Erik Erikson is a pioneer in studying the adolescent identity crisis. (Rick Stafford)

Erikson's Youth

Erikson's own development is itself a dramatic example of the adolescent identity crisis. "No doubt," he says, "my best friends will insist that I needed to name this crisis and to see it in everybody else in order to really come to terms with it in myself." Erikson readily admits, "They could, indeed, quote a whole roster of problems related to my *personal* identity" (1975, p. 25).

Erik Erikson was born to a Danish Jewish mother and a Danish father who abandoned Erikson's mother before he was born. His father died at about the time of Erikson's birth. During his first several years, Erikson lived alone with his mother, an artist who traveled frequently. When he was 3 years old, his mother married a German-Jewish pediatrician and settled in southern Germany. His stepfather was a highly respected man who served as the leader of the local synagogue. Although the marriage provided Erikson with security, it also posed thorny problems about his identity. For example, his parents attempted to "forget" his earlier years with his mother, though Erikson always knew better. Later, as a blonde, blue-eyed youth, Erikson was called "goy" (non-Jewish outsider) at the synagogue but "Jew" by his classmates at school (Roazen, 1976).

During his teens, like other youth with artistic or literary aspirations, Erikson felt alienated from everything his family stood for. "At that point," he said, "I *set out* to be different" (1975, p. 28). After graduating from the *gymnasium* (high school), Erikson went to art school, then took to wandering. In those days art was considered more a way of life than a specific career with an acceptable niche in society. As a result, even though he had enough artistic talent to consider it a vocation, he saw himself as a traveling "Bohemian." He recalls those years as an important part of his training, however, acknowledging that highly creative people tend to resolve their identity crisis somewhat later than other youth do.

By his mid-twenties, Erikson was teaching art at a school near Vienna, where he met his wife-to-be. She was a Canadian-born American (Gentile) who was taking her training and personal work in psychoanalysis. Through her, Erikson became interested in psychoanalysis and was admitted into the circle of Freud's followers. He underwent a personal analysis by Freud's daughter, Anna Freud, who strengthened his interest in children and adolescents. By his late twenties, Erikson had become a psychoanalyst, but the lack of formal degrees left him somewhat insecure about his professional identity. After an unsuccessful attempt to practice in Denmark, he came to the United States. Upon becoming a naturalized citizen, he took the name of "Erikson," retaining his stepfather's name Homburger as his middle name. Although some authorities claim that this was Erikson's attempt to acknowledge his real father, others contend he was simply naming himself after the early Danish discoverer of America (Roazen, 1976).

Erikson's life illustrates, perhaps to an extreme, his view that adolescence is better understood as an aggravated life crisis than as a psychiatric disturbance. As he himself discovered, adolescents must often test the extremes before settling on a considered course.

up their parents' goals of success too easily may find themselves with only a weak, untested character, leaving them vulnerable to subsequent developmental crises.

Erikson deliberately uses the rather broad term *identity* to capture the overall richness of the adolescent's experience. At the same time, Erikson distinguishes at least three related meanings of the term. First, identity refers to the sense of sameness or continuity between one's past and present selves. Ordinarily, adolescents retain a fairly strong sense of continuity with their past, affirming many aspects of themselves while rejecting others. Second, identity also pertains to the integration of one's private and public selves. At this age individuals must strive to integrate the selves that they know themselves to be with the more role-oriented selves that others know them by. Otherwise, gross misperceptions and illusions about themselves may hinder adolescents' efforts to achieve realistic goals and find an acceptable place in society. Third, identity also refers to the relationship between one's present self and one's future or potential self. More often than not, it's the concern for the "self I *can* be" that evokes the most anxiety in late adolescents. After all, who fully knows his or her potential self? This must be discovered through an active process of trial and error and involves considerable anxiety. In the process adolescents must reject some existing aspects of themselves, which are known, while affirming potential aspects of themselves that are not fully known. Understandably, this is a risky process filled with promise and self-doubt. It's no wonder some young people do not fully resolve their adolescent identity crisis.

Although the search for identity may become totally preoccupying and assume dramatic forms, it tends to occur gradually and unconsciously in the lives of most adolescents. As James Marcia (1980) reminds us, the achievement of a new identity "gets done by bits and pieces." Sometimes there are major decisions to be made dealing with whether to take a job after high school or attend college. At other times, the decisions may seem trivial, such as which courses to take and whom to date. In most cases, decisions are not made once and for all but have to be made again and again. One of the hallmarks of a successful identity is flexibility. That is, having resolved one's identity crisis at adolescence doesn't preclude future crises and decisions. Rather, the successful resolution of one's identity at adolescence provides the necessary stability with which to explore subsequent revisions. As Erikson (1968) says, an optimal sense of identity is experienced as a "sense of psychological well-being, . . . a feeling [of being] at home in one's body," "knowing where one is going," and the assurance of "anticipated recognition from those who count."

Four Identity Statuses

By now, it may be apparent that adolescents cannot simply be divided into two groups—those who have achieved a positive identity and those who remain confused about themselves. Instead, it is more realistic to view the adolescent's struggle with identity along a continuum, with identity achievement at one end and identity confusion at the other end. As a result, in order to empirically test Erikson's theoretical notions about identity, James Marcia (1980) and others have used a fourfold concept of identity status—identity achieved, moratorium, foreclosure, and identity confusion. These identity statuses are best seen as four different modes of dealing with the adolescent identity crisis and provide a greater variety of styles of identity formation than does Erikson's simple dichotomy of identity versus identity confusion. Individuals are usually classified into the various identity statuses on the basis of in-depth interviews and questionnaires. The major criteria used are the presence or absence of a critical period of exploration (crisis) or and the extent of the adolescent's personal involvement or decision making (commitment) in two key areas—career and ideology, or beliefs and values. (See Table 10-3)

Individuals who are classified as *identity-achieved* have faced the identity crisis and have already resolved many of the issues involved. Typically they have chosen a career goal and have a good sense of their own values. At the same time, they are flexible and able to change their life goals depending on their experience. Also, as Harold Bernard (1981) found, these individuals are able to appraise their parents realistically so that they tend to form "part identifications" with them, that is, identifying with some aspects of their parental models they find attractive and rejecting parts they find unappealing. They also tend to choose friends and romantic partners who will help them to become less dependent on their parents. Such individuals tend to set realistic goals for themselves and perform well under stress. An example would be a young man who is majoring in engineering because he does well in subjects like math and physics and enjoys working with mechanical things. Although he disagrees with his parents on some issues, like sex and politics, he identifies with many of their middle-class values and gets along with them reasonably well.

Those classified in the *identity moratorium* status are generally experiencing a delayed or drawn-out exploration of their identity. They have made few, if

Table 10-3   The Four Statuses of Identity

		CRISIS	
		Present	Absent
COMMITMENT	Present	Identity achievement	Identity foreclosure
	Absent	Identity moratorium	Identity confusion

By providing an atmosphere for exploring ideas and roles, college tends to promote a temporary moratorium as well as the eventual attainment of a self-chosen identity. (Laima Druskis)

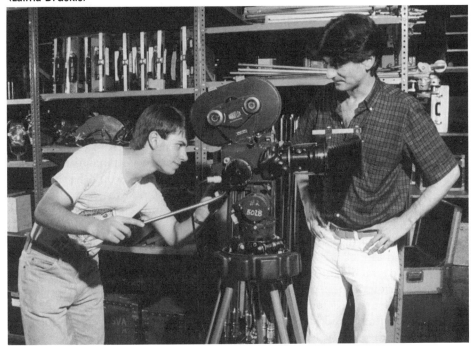

any, firm commitments to a career or personal values. Understandably, they have high levels of anxiety, suggesting the continued awareness of an unresolved life crisis. They are also less certain of their values than identity achievers and are more apt to change their minds. They may be less confident in their choice of a college major and are more likely to change it or drop out before making a firm choice. Students in this group are more likely to be experimental, rebellious, and critical of the establishment. They also have a great deal of guilt about disappointing their parents or about their potential for doing so (Bernard, 1981). An example would be a student who changes her college major several times before dropping out. Even when she returns to college, she remains undecided whether to combine marriage with a career or not.

Individuals classified in the *identity foreclosure* status have largely avoided any substantial identity exploration, usually through premature choices endorsed by their parents. On the surface, at least, they appear much like the identity achievers. But the appearance of maturity comes at a price. Inwardly, they experience a high level of anxiety, depression, and defeatist thoughts and feelings, suggesting that even though they have specific goals they are greatly concerned about fulfilling them and others' expectations of them (Rothman,

1984). By and large, individuals in identity foreclosure avoid experimentation and conflict. Instead, they show great respect for authority and tend to choose friends and romantic partners who are substitute objects of dependency (Bernard, 1981). An example would be the student who marries his high school girlfriend, takes a position in his father's company, settles down in his parents' community, and only later in life comes to regret such choices.

People classified in the *identity confusion* status have largely avoided the adolescent identity crisis. Not surprisingly, these individuals exhibit very high levels of anxiety, rigid or stereotyped behavior, and felt inadequacy (Rothman, 1984). As a result, they put off making life choices, feeling they aren't ready for them. Some lose themselves in an endless absorption with social life, sex, and drugs. Others become loners and drifters, shifting from one interest or job to another. Still others may experience a profound emotional disturbance and need hospitalization at one time or another. An example would be the young woman who attends a college with minimal academic standards, grows bored, drops out, and gets married. She soon becomes restless and unhappy and attempts suicide, eventually turning to psychotherapy.

Because some degree of role confusion is an inherent part of the adolescent identity crisis, almost every adolescent experiences occasional moments of bewilderment and self-doubt. But youths who are persistently plagued by a confusion of their personal identities are at odds with themselves and the world. Even then, such individuals can be viewed along a continuum. At one end are those with the mildest degree of confusion—the normal "lost" adolescents—who outwardly may function fairly well but inwardly have little sense of who they are or where they are headed. At the other end are youths who are severely disturbed—the schizophrenic individual who needs psychological treatment and perhaps hospitalization.

DEVELOPMENTAL CHANGES IN PERSONAL IDENTITY

Throughout the process of self-exploration and personal growth, youths tend to shift from one ego-identity status to another. Earlier, it was assumed that the pattern of development was mostly sequential, beginning with confusion and proceeding to foreclosure, then to moratorium and finally achievement. However, Alan Waterman (1985) and others have shown that these changes do not necessarily proceed in a straight line. For instance, a student who is confused about her career choice may settle on a career goal rather prematurely to alleviate her anxiety, thereby shifting to a foreclosure status. Or, she might seek consultation and counseling as a means of reaching a decision, which would put her in the moratorium status. Similarly, an individual who has already reached the moratorium status might progress to the identity achievement status, or, if confronted with additional information, might drop back to the confusion status. Thus, each individual tends to follow a different pattern of changes in regard to his or her identity status on the way to achieving a firm, satisfying identity.

Changes During Adolescence

The early adolescent years generally are not conducive to self-exploration, much less the development of a firm identity. Young adolescents need psychological time to adapt to the impact of pubertal changes. Then too, most homes and schools do not provide the atmosphere and range of alternatives that encourage adolescents to explore and experiment at this stage. If anything, most adolescents are just beginning the move into moratorium status. In one study, Sally Archer (1982) examined various aspects of identity development, including career goals, religious beliefs, political views, and sex-role preferences among students in the sixth through the twelfth grades. She found that the identity achievement status increased in frequency with each successive grade level. But the confusion and foreclosure statuses remained the most common categories at all grade levels for both sexes.

The most significant changes in identity status tend to occur during late adolescence, in the late teens and early twenties. By the time students reach their senior year in college, they are more likely to have achieved a firm sense of identity. Alan Waterman (1985) reports that college seniors of both sexes are more apt to have resolved their identity crisis and hold a stronger sense of personal identity than do those just entering college. This is especially true in regard to career goals. But it is less apparent in other areas such as religious belief. If anything, the college atmosphere tends to undermine students' traditional religious beliefs, so that students in the foreclosure status in their religious beliefs tend to move into the moratorium status. Students are most likely to remain in the confused status in regard to their political views, especially those who are unsure of their political commitments or apathetic in this area.

Several trends are evident throughout the process of identity formation, as seen in a series of studies by Waterman (1985) on identity and career choice among youths in various age groups, ranging from junior high school to college. First, there is a steady increase in the proportion of youth who reach the identity achievement status, ranging from 5 percent in junior high school to about 40 percent by the end of college. Second, there is a corresponding decrease in the percentage of those in the identity confusion status, from almost half of the students in junior high school to only 14 percent among those in the last two years of college. Third, the moratorium status tends to peak during the college years, when youth are more actively pondering their career goals and plans. Finally, for some reason, the category of foreclosure status remains remarkably stable throughout this period, and includes anywhere from one-fourth to one-third of all youth depending on the age group. Because the studies are not longitudinal, it is not clear whether these figures represent the same people. Although the foreclosure status is appropriate during early adolescence, it is less so during the latter years of high school. Individuals at this level who remain in the foreclosure status may be somewhat apprehensive about their personal development, passively accepting roles and identities from parents and others with little questioning, rather than actively exploring their choices. Such youths may fear that if they were to question the ideas and values they have grown up with, they might lose control, go adrift, or have no sense of purpose in life. Yet the lack of growth may be accompanied by undesirable characteristics, such as rigid beliefs and defensive behavior.

Factors Facilitating Identity Achievement

Youths fortunate enough to grow up in a warm, supportive family tend to move toward a self-chosen identity more readily than do those from less functional families. According to a series of studies by Harold Grotevant and Catherine Cooper (1985), families that have strong parental bonds and promote individuation are more likely to foster their adolescents' identity achievement. Family connectedness involves sensitivity to the views of others and thereby respecting and supporting the adolescent's beliefs. Individuation has to with the adolescent's separate and distinctive identity. Fathers in these families tend to encourage, or at least tolerate, their adolescents' independence and assertiveness. Mothers express their own ideas and play an active role in family affairs, rather than always acquiescing to their husbands' views.

Adolescents who grow up in troubled families characterized by family conflict, separation, and divorce are not so fortunate. Jurich and Jones (1986) point out that when parents divorce, adolescents often face three poor alternatives: (1) adopting a negative identity, (2) settling on a foreclosed or premature identity, or (3) suffering from identity confusion in a lifelong search for self. Yet this does not have to be true. At least one study of high school girls found that two-thirds of those in the achievement status came from homes disrupted by death or divorce, compared to only one-fifth of those in the other identity statuses who came from broken homes (St. Clair and Day, 1979). Although coping with a parental divorce may temporarily hurt adolescents, it may also challenge them to struggle all the harder to work out their own personal identity.

As adolescents reach puberty and acquire greater capacity for self-reflection, they become more actively engaged in the task of self-exploration. Accordingly, Lee Shain and Barry Farber (1989) found that females in their late teens and early twenties in the advanced identity statuses, achievement and moratorium, exhibited greater capacity for self-reflection than did those in the less advanced identity statuses. Yet it is not clear whether self-reflection enhances identity status or vice versa. Perhaps, as in Erikson's view, the two processes are synergistic, occurring together. Or, from Piaget's view, the emergence of abstract thinking and self-reflection may lead to increased awareness of self and a greater need to separate from one's parents and find a distinctive place in the world. In any event, the increased capacity for self-reflection normally accompanies many of the processes that enhance self-exploration, including social perspective taking.

Attending college also fosters personal development in identity formation. But again it isn't clear whether the college experience facilitates identity formation or is simply associated or correlated with it. Because college provides a socially acceptable atmosphere for gaining self-knowledge and exploring ideas and roles, it tends to promote temporary moratorium as well as the eventual attainment of a self-chosen identity. Yet it may be that smart people who are progressing well toward a clear identity are more likely to enroll in college and remain there, so that identity development encourages attendance at college, rather than the other way around. Then too, all youths this age may experience significant growth in their identity, whether they attend college or not.

At the same time, studies comparing college and non-college youth suggest that the two groups experience the identity crisis differently. Non-college youths are more apt to be in the identity-achieved and identity-confused status, while the moratorium status is more prevalent among college youth (Morash, 1980). The most likely explanation is that non-college youths go through the identity crisis in a shorter period of time, establishing their careers and basic values without benefit of the prolonged moratorium available to college students. In contrast, the college experience encourages self-reflection, the examination of ideas and roles, and the development of more complex reasoning, all of which fosters a temporary moratorium along with the eventual achievement of a self-chosen identity. Although the value of college for identity formation varies widely among individuals, as well as from one aspect of development to another, college attendance tends to be especially helpful in pursuing a career goal (Waterman, 1985).

What About Your Own Personal Development?

Looking back, how would you characterize your own experience of the adolescent identity crisis? That is, to what extent did you explore meaningful alternatives in regard to the kind of person you hoped to become? How readily did you arrive at a decision or commitment in the various aspects of your identity development, such as career goals, sexual attitudes and practices, values, and religious beliefs?

For instance, did you settle on a satisfying career goal (identity achieved) with little or no trouble? Or did you experience considerable indecision (identity moratorium and/or confusion) before achieving a firm career goal?

Reflecting on her marriage at an early age, one woman said, "At the time I felt like an achiever. But now I realize my first marriage represented more of a foreclosed pattern." One young man who changed his degree major twice during college felt he had been confused about his career goals during that period of his life. Yet, in retrospect, he said, "Actually, I think it was a moratorium experience. Now I realize it's normal to change your career goal at that age."

What about you? Which aspect of your personal development has been the least difficult in achieving a self-chosen identity? Which area has given you the most trouble? How would you account for this?

Identity and Intimacy

In Erikson's view (1980b), it is essential that individuals achieve a firm sense of identity before they are able to enter into the intimate relationships of young adulthood. Because healthy intimacy, such as friendship, love, and marriage, involve closeness without the surrender of one's personal identity, individuals who are sure of themselves are freer to enter into the give-and-take of close relationships. By contrast, those with a weak or confused identity may become so fearful of losing themselves that they can only enter into superficial, unstable, or addictive relationships. Sure enough, studies of college students and adults have shown that men and women with a firm sense of identity tend to enjoy deep and committed relationships. In contrast, those with the less advanced identity statuses generally report less intimate and committed relationships. The rationale here is that a certain degree of individuation is an important precursor for mature intimacy. Accordingly, individuals with less intimate relationships usually exhibit lower levels of individuation, self-reliance, and a high level of insecure attachment (Levitz-Jones and Orlofsky, 1985). Additional support for this view can be seen in Sally Archer's (1985) study of identity and intimacy among divorced women at several stages of their lives, including high school, marriage, divorce, and the present. At high school and marriage, most women exhibited a foreclosed identity and a romantic type of intimacy. But as they grappled more seriously both with the issue of who they were and with their marital problems, a larger proportion of the women entered a moratorium status, with this status peaking at the time of their divorce. When the women were interviewed again in their adult years, most of them reported an identity achievement status as well as more mature types of intimate relationships.

At the same time, not everyone accepts Erikson's view of the identity-before-intimacy sequence as the norm. Researchers such as John Meacham and Nicholas Santilli (1982) suggest there are other possible sequences. For instance, an individual with a foreclosed identity status is experiencing a crisis in his or her close relationships. One possibility, in line with Erikson's theory, is that the intimacy crisis will remain unresolved until the person confronts and successfully resolves the identity issue. Yet there are other possibilities. The individual might resolve the intimacy crisis in some fashion and move forward to the developmental task of middle adulthood, without fully resolving the identity crisis. Still a third possibility is that after resolving the intimacy crisis, the individual could return to the identity problem. The main point is that there is greater variation in the sequence by which individuals experience and resolve their identity and intimacy needs than in Erikson's view.

This especially true among women. As Carol Gilligan (1982) points out, the identity-before-intimacy sequence is more characteristic of males than females. Women tend to be less concerned than men with viewing themselves as separate individuals and are more concerned with intimate relationships. In fact,

Women follow a greater variety of patterns than men do in integrating their identity and intimacy needs. (U.S. Coast Guard Official Photo)

recent studies by Kahn and others (1985) suggest that women follow a greater variety of patterns than men do in integrating their identity and intimacy needs. A large proportion of young women follow the traditional pattern, resolving their needs for close relationships in love, sex, and marriage before exploring, much less resolving, their career goals. At the same time, an increasing proportion of women adopt a pattern similar to males, focusing on their educational and career goals before resolving their intimacy needs. Still others follow more of a combined or androgynous pattern, exploring their identity and intimacy needs simultaneously. Now that there are more flexible gender roles, a growing range of career options for women, and diminished obligation for women to have children, we may see greater variation in the ways both men and women go about resolving their identity and intimacy needs. Indeed, much of the research on identity development today points to greater similarities rather than differences in the ways men and women approach the identity crisis in late adolescence and young adulthood (Grotevant and Thorbecke, 1982).

SUMMARY

Self-Concept

1. The individual's self-concept—all those perceptions of "I" or "me" together with the feelings, beliefs, and values associated with them—develops mostly through interaction with significant others during the formative years of childhood.

2. Once acquired, the self-concept exerts an important influence on the individual's outlook and behavior.

3. Largely because of the cognitive changes that occur at puberty, adolescents begin to perceive themselves in a more abstract and individualized way.

4. A critical aspect of the adolescent's self-concept is self-esteem—the personal judgment and feelings of worth associated with one's self-concept.

5. Adolescents' self-esteem is influenced by many aspects of their environment, with adolescents who grow up in homes with authoritative parenting more likely to have high self-esteem.

6. The temporary drop in self-esteem often seen during early adolescence may be due to the combined effects of relocating and changing schools at the onset of puberty. Otherwise, self-esteem tends to rise steadily, especially through the development of competence and achievement in school, with late adolescents generally reporting higher levels of self-esteem.

Toward a Self-Chosen Identity

7. The particular combination of changes that occur during adolescence triggers the process of self-exploration and the pursuit of a personal identity—the sense of who one is and can become.

8. Erikson holds that the major developmental task during this period is achieving a self-chosen identity, with the attendant risk of identity confusion.

9. Adolescents may choose to resolve their identity crisis in several ways, including the four identity statuses—identity achievement, moratorium, foreclosure, and confusion.

10. Adolescents classified as identity-achieved have engaged in self-exploration and made firm commitments; those in the moratorium status are still exploring but have made few, if any, commitments.

11. Adolescents in the foreclosure status have made premature commitments, while those in the confused status have largely avoided self-exploration and making commitments.

Developmental Changes in Personal Identity

12. Each adolescent tends to follow a different pattern or sequence of changes in regard to identity status, often, but not necessarily, beginning with identity confusion proceeding to foreclosure, then to moratorium and finally achievement.

13. The early adolescent years are not conducive to self-exploration, such that the most significant changes in identity status tend to occur during late adolescence.

14. With increasing age and maturity, a larger proportion of youths fall in the identity-achieved status, with a decreasing proportion of youth in the confused status.

15. The moratorium status peaks during the college years, though the proportion of youth in the foreclosure status remains stable throughout adolescence.

16. Adolescents are more likely to achieve a firm identity when they grow up in families that foster a connectedness to parents combined with an emphasis on individuation.

17. College attendance also aids in the task of identity formation by fostering a temporary

identity moratorium, encouraging self-reflection and the exploration of ideas and roles, as well as the eventual attainment of a self-chosen identity.

18. Erikson's view that youth must achieve a firm identity before entering into the intimate relationships of early adulthood tends to be more characteristic of males than females. By contrast, females follow a greater variety of paths in integrating their identity and intimacy needs.

REVIEW QUESTIONS

1. In what sense is the adolescent's self-concept a cluster of selves?
2. How much do you think an adolescent's self-esteem varies from one situation to another?
3. Why is early adolescence characterized by heightened self-consciousness and low self-esteem?
4. How can we help adolescents improve their self-esteem?
5. In what sense do adolescents experience an identity crisis?
6. To what extent does Erikson's personal life illustrate his views of the adolescent identity crisis?
7. What does it mean for an adolescent to have achieved an identity status in regard to his or her career?
8. Which identity status, moratorium or foreclosure, represents a greater risk of adolescents failing to find themselves?
9. How does attending college affect one's resolution of the identity crisis?
10. In what ways do males and females approach the adolescent identity crisis differently?

11

Sexuality

David and Lisa, now in their junior year in high school, are going steady. For the past four months, they've been sexually active. David has been using condoms regularly, not only as a means of birth control but also to minimize the risk of contracting one of the sexually transmitted diseases. He now realizes that AIDS is a potential problem for all sexually active people—not just homosexuals and intravenous drug users. Although the couple didn't discuss birth control until after their initial act of intercourse, David was pleased to discover that Lisa was on the pill. Lisa added that she become especially concerned about the use of contraceptives after she learned that one of her girlfriends had just recently become pregnant unexpectedly.

SEXUAL ATTITUDES

David and Lisa's sexual attitudes and practices are typical of their peers in several ways, as we'll see throughout this chapter. First, they developed an affectionate relationship with each other before engaging in sex. Even then, their initial act of sex was a spur-of-the-moment thing with no discussion of birth control. Only later did they talk about the use of contraceptives. But once they discussed the matter, both of them felt equally responsible for practicing birth control. Then too, David and Lisa admitted privately that they probably began having sex at an earlier age than they think is desirable. And finally, for many reasons, David and Lisa have become more cautious and responsible in their sexual behavior than many of their counterparts were a decade ago.

Adolescents' attitudes toward sex generally reflect the times in which they live. For instance, during the 1960s only one in ten teenagers felt "sexually behind" others his or her age. But by the 1980s, one in five teenagers felt this way, largely because of the extensive changes in sexual attitudes and practices that occurred during the previous decade (Offer, Ostrov, and Howard, 1981). Today, sex among U.S. teenagers has become so common that three-fourths of the girls have intercourse by the time they reach 20. Much of the change is due to the sharp rise in sexual activity among Caucasian females in the middle and upper income groups (Forrest and Singh, 1990). Another major factor is the growing perception among teenagers that sex is no longer for adults only; sex is now a normal part of the adolescent experience (Brooks-Gunn and Furstenburg, 1989).

Changing Attitudes toward Sex

Attitudes toward sex continue to change, partly because youths in each generation face different social influences and trends, thereby growing up somewhat differently. However, attitudes toward sex generally became more liberal in the period from the late 1960s through the 1970s as an integral part of the social changes that brought about an emphasis on civil rights, racial equality, free speech, and women's rights. The impact of these changes has had several major implications for youths' attitudes toward sex.

First, there has been a greater openness and honesty in sexual matters. You can hardly pick up a newspaper or watch television without being aware that issues such as abortion, rape, and the sexual abuse of children are treated more candidly than a generation ago. Young people brought up in this atmosphere naturally talk about sex more openly and honestly with their peers, though to a lesser extent with their parents and teachers. They are also more inclined to discuss sensitive subjects, such as homosexuality, and they want better sex education.

Second, sexual intercourse outside of marriage has become more acceptable than in the past. Legal marriage is no longer required as a sanction for sex. For the majority, sex is now acceptable within a "relationship." And many youths adopt an even more liberal attitude, approving of casual sex or sex primarily for pleasure. As a result, youths are more accepting of premarital sex than their counterparts were a generation ago.

Third, youths and adults alike enjoy greater personal choice in regard to sexual matters than in the past. By the 1970s, Sorenson (1973) found that two-thirds of adolescents 13 to 19 years of age admitted that when it comes to sex "I do what I want to do" regardless of what society thinks. Such a change reflects the growing suspicion of established institutions like the school and church—if not adult authority in general—as well as the trend toward individualism and self-expression. At the same time, this approach makes greater demands on the personal judgment and maturity of the individual than did the past practice of conforming to a set standard. At what age are adolescents prepared to make such decisions? How does a particular adolescent know whether he or she is sufficiently mature to handle sex? The difficulty of answering such questions makes it harder for youth to know right from wrong in sexual matters.

Once the link between marriage and sexual activity is broken and sex becomes a matter of personal choice, the idea of timing sexual activity has practically disappeared. Now there is no particular age for sanctioning the initiation of sexual activity. Largely as the result of such changes, sexual activity is initiated at earlier ages than in the past, and by an increasing proportion of youth. At the

Adolescents are more sexually sophisticated than they were in the past but also more cautious about casual sex. (Shirley Zeiberg)

same time, sexual attitudes and practices continue to change. After talking with many leaders at schools and campuses around the country, John Leo (1984) observes that the sexual revolution has peaked, with sexual attitudes and behavior becoming somewhat more conservative. One reason is that the baby boomers are growing up and settling down into family life, thereby adopting a less adventurous attitude toward sex. Then too, there is a significant but growing minority of youths who disapprove of premarital sex mostly because of moral and religious beliefs. About one-fourth of junior and senior high school students think premarital sex is wrong. A somewhat larger proportion of 18 to 29 year olds disapprove of premarital sex. Furthermore, the growing fear of sexually transmitted diseases, especially AIDS, has a chilling effect on sexual practices, making this the second major reason for disapproving of premarital sex (Gallup, 1987).

How Consistent Are Attitudes and Behavior?

Not surprisingly, adolescents, like adults, do not always act in a manner consistent with their attitudes. In an effort to find the relationship between adolescents' sexual attitudes and behavior, Laurie Zabin and her colleagues (1984) collected data from about 3,500 junior and senior high school students attending four inner-city schools. They found that the majority of young people already hold attitudes and values that are consistent with responsible sexual conduct, but not all of them translate these attitudes into their personal behavior.

First of all, it appears that many adolescents are initiating sexual intercourse at an earlier age than they themselves regard as desirable. When students were asked "What is the best age for a woman (or man) to have sex for the first time?" 83 percent of the sexually experienced adolescents reported they had experienced their first intercourse at a younger age than they considered desirable. (See Table 11-1.) Almost half of the sexually experienced adolescents re-

Table 11-1 Percentage of Sexually Active Adolescents Whose Age at First Intercourse was Younger than, the Same as, or Older than the Age They Gave as the Best Age for First Intercourse, According to Sex, Race, and Current Age

Sex, Race, and Current Age	Younger	Same	Older	Total
Female	**86.3**	**10.6**	**3.1**	**100.0**
White	88.3	10.5	1.2	100.0
≤ 15	96.2	2.5	1.3	100.0
≥ 16	84.6	14.2	1.2	100.0
Black	85.7	10.6	3.7	100.0
≤ 15	87.5	9.6	2.9	100.0
≥ 16	84.3	11.4	4.3	100.0
Male	**80.7**	**13.6**	**5.8**	**100.0**
White	75.9	16.8	7.3	100.0
≤ 15	84.7	11.9	3.4	100.0
≥ 16	71.7	19.1	9.2	100.0
Black	83.2	11.9	4.9	100.0
≤ 15	90.0	6.2	3.8	100.0
≥ 16	75.5	18.3	6.2	100.0

Female N = 1032′   ′Male N = 1060

Source: Laurie S. Zabin, Marilyn B. Hirsch, Edward A. Smith, and Janet B. Hardy, "Adolescent Sexual Attitudes and Behavior: Are They Consistent?" *Family Planning Perspectives* (July/August 1984): p. 182.

ported a best age for first intercourse older than their current age. As you might expect, virgins of both sexes expressed a preferred age for first intercourse two or three years older than did sexually experienced adolescents: about 18 years of age compared to 16 (for women) and 15 (for men) years respectively.

Young women are much more likely than men to desire a strong relationship or marriage before engaging in sex. At the same time, about half of both sexes require no stronger ties than the dating relationship to initiate sex. Virgins of both sexes demand stronger relationships before engaging in sex than nonvirgins do, with about 30 percent of the men and 40 percent of the women virgins holding marriage as a requirement for sex. Women are also twice as likely as men to report having had a strong relationship with their last partner. In contrast, about four times as many men as women report having had casual sex, that is, sex with someone they had just met or didn't know well. Such results confirm the familiar finding that women are more concerned than men about having sex within an affectionate relationship with commitment. Yet it is noteworthy that 18 percent of the young women and 25 percent of the men saw the relationship in which they last had intercourse as weaker than they desire for engaging in sex, indicating an inconsistency between their attitudes and behavior.

Although there is considerable overlap between adolescents' beliefs and practices in regard to birth control, there are inconsistencies as well. For instance, adolescents were asked for a true or false answer to the question "I would only have sex if one of us were using some kind of birth control." Among those who answered "true" to this statement, 21 percent of the women and 26 percent of the men, or about one-fourth of the adolescents, admitted they hadn't used a contraceptive device during their last intercourse. And the failure to use a contraceptive device was even higher among those who answered "false"—more than 50 percent for men and women alike. As expected, adolescents who felt that one or both partners is responsible for birth control are much more likely to use contraceptives than those who feel neither partner is responsible. Furthermore, contraceptive use is strongly related to the strength of the couple's relationship before engaging in sex, with about 7 out of 10 adolescents of both sexes with a strong relationship using some contraceptive device compared to only 4 out of 10 of those with a weak relationship.

These findings show that although there is frequently a significant relationship between adolescents' sexual attitudes and reported behavior, there is a large minority in each area for whom attitudes and behavior are at odds. Although some adolescents may recognize that there is an inconsistency between their ideals and behavior, for the majority this is probably not the case. Some of the attitude-behavior inconsistency may be due to the influence of peers, family, community, and mass media. That is, questions about premarital sex or the best age for first intercourse may trigger a response that is influenced by these pressures. In other cases, inconsistencies may result from changes in attitude over time. But the inconsistency between general attitudes and personal behavior suggests that sex education should include helping adolescents translate their attitudes into practice, through decision making and the like, rather than assuming that changes in attitudes will automatically influence behavior.

Sex and Love

The link between sex and love—both in attitude and behavior—is an important concern among youths. Yet adolescents, like adults in our pluralistic society, differ among themselves in regard to how they feel about this issue.

As we noted earlier, only a minority of youths reserve sex for marriage. About one-fourth of junior and senior high school students disapprove of premarital sex, mostly because of moral and religious beliefs. A somewhat larger proportion of youth in their twenties disapprove of premarital sex (Gallup, 1987). But, for many, if not most, youths premarital sex is now acceptable as long as it is accompanied by affection or occurs within a relationship. However, the strength of such a relationship may vary considerably, with women more likely than men to desire a strong relationship before engaging in sex. In one study (Zelnik and Shah, 1983), about two-thirds of the female adolescents were either engaged or going steady when they had their first intercourse, compared to fewer than half of the males. More males than females had their intercourse with a casual friend or someone they had recently met.

At the same time, many youths now approve of sexual intercourse with a minimum of affection. According to one survey, three-fourths of college students of both sexes feel that although love enriches sex, it is not necessary for its enjoyment (Crooks and Baur, 1990). Consequently, as Godfrey Cobliner (1988) observes, all too often, casual encounters between the sexes are formed for the primary purpose of sexual gratification without shared intimacy or commitment. Such relationships are expected to be transient, and partners are expected to deliberately suppress any feelings of tenderness or closeness. Speaking of his relationships with women, one male college students says, "I stay cool. If any feelings well up in me, I check them at once. I am afraid of strong feelings of passion" (Cobliner, 1988, p. 103). Similarly, explaining how easy it is to get hurt when one becomes emotionally involved, a female college student says, 'You can become the victim of your own strong feelings. I have to always to be on guard. I have to curb my feelings" (Cobliner, 1988, p. 104). Yet, as Cobliner points out, the inhibition of feelings leads to depersonalization or the separation of oneself from his or her feelings. Thus, casual sex tends to involve manipulative relationships that eventually undermine the meaning and satisfaction of sex.

The different attitudes regarding the relationship of sex and love partly reflect the loosened bond between sex and marriage alluded to earlier. Thus, while an increasing majority of men and women now disapprove of marrying someone they are not in love with (Simpson, Campbell, and Berscheid, 1986), the proportion of youth that disapproves of engaging in sex without love is considerably smaller. Much of this has to do with the fact that youths now initiate sex at an earlier age than in the past and delay marriage somewhat later. Meanwhile, sexual activity is increasingly regarded as an integral rite of adolescence. Although adults are rightly concerned about the risks of increased sexual activity among adolescents, especially casual sex, they exercise less control over adolescents than they did in the past. Furthermore, because we now tolerate a variety of sexual attitudes and practices on the part of adults, it's difficult to dictate what is proper for teens without sounding hypocritical.

SEXUAL BEHAVIOR

In some ways, it's even more difficult to describe adolescents' sexual behavior than their attitudes toward sex. For one thing, sexual behavior is an intensely private matter, such that researchers have to rely on self-reports. Also, as mentioned earlier, adolescents' sexual behaviors are not always consistent with their expressed attitudes. Then too, sexual practices vary widely among different groups and such factors as socioeconomic, ethnic, and regional differences. Finally, sexual practices vary widely among individuals. Keeping these points in mind, we'll examine the typical developmental sequence of sexual activity, the incidence of sexual intercourse among youth, and homosexuality.

Physical Intimacy and Sexual Activity

With the onset of puberty, adolescents tend to engage in more intimate forms of physical and erotic contact with the opposite sex. In most instances, individuals engage in a variety of erotic and sexual activities before engaging in sexual intercourse, with the later occuring as an integral part of an extended sequence of sexual activities rather than an isolated behavior.

In one study, older adolescents ranging in age from 18 to 23 were asked which of nine sexual behaviors they had ever engaged in and, if so, the age at which they first experienced it. The results indicate that the developmental sequence in which males and females engage in various sexual activities is remarkably similar. By the midteens, 14 to 15 years of age, the great majority of adolescents of both sexes have kissed and hugged their partners and engaged in deep kissing. By 16 or 17 years of age, most boys have touched the girl's breast and both sexes have fondled the genitals of the other sex. The more intensely erotic behaviors such as rubbing one's genital area against the partner's genitals generally occur about the same time teenagers begin having sexual intercourse. Oral-genital sex is more apt to occur in the late teens, after the initiation of sexual intercourse (DeLamater and MacCorquodale, 1979).

The major exception is masturbation, which tends to become a common practice earlier among boys than girls. By 16 years of age, about three-fourths of the boys but only one-half the girls report having masturbated (Hass, 1979). However, by the time they reach college age, practically all of the men and two-thirds of the women have engaged in masturbation (Story, 1982). At the same time, the age of first masturbation varies considerably among girls. Some may begin masturbation during early adolescence; others begin the practice after they have initiated sexual intercourse. Boys tend to masturbate more regularly and frequently than girls do. But masturbation practices vary more widely among girls. Some girls masturbate regularly, others sporadically, and still others not at all. Youths of both sexes often use fantasy and, to a lesser extent, erotic pictures and stories to heighten arousal during masturbation. Although such fantasies may sometimes involve improbable feats and partners, in most instances sexual fantasies involve having sex with a loved partner (Miller and Simon, 1980).

Probably the greatest change in masturbation practice is the reduced anxiety and guilt associated with it. Yet some youths worry about whether they masturbate too frequently. Interestingly, it also appears that many youths are reluctant to discuss masturbation, largely because they have misgivings about achieving pleasure through self-stimulation. Perhaps this is true because the sense of adventure and the closeness and stimulation of a love relationship that accompanies sexual intercourse are missing in masturbation.

Sexual Intercourse

Adolescents usually engage in their first sexual intercourse rather late in the sequence of sexual activity. The specific age varies widely depending on such factors as sex, race, and socioeconomic differences. Overall, slightly over half of all girls aged 15 to 19 reported they had ever engaged in intercourse by 1988, up somewhat from the early 1980s. However, comparative differences between age groups is even more revealing. Whereas fewer than 4 out of 10 girls in the 15–17 year old group have ever had sex, three-fourths of those in the 18–19 year old group have engaged in sexual intercourse. Most of the increase between 1982 and 1988 occurred among Caucasian teenagers in the middle and upper socioeconomic groups, thereby narrowing the racial and income differences in regard to sexual behavior (Forrest and Singh, 1990). See Figure 11-1.

Although teenagers have been sexually active for only a short period of time, a disproportionate number of them have had two or more sex partners. Among girls in the 15–19-year-old group who have had sex in the past three months, 8 percent have two or more sex partners, a relatively high figure compared to women in their twenties. Furthermore, if these rates are viewed cumulatively, the figures are even more impressive. That is, assuming the same proportion of females change partners every three months or so, the proportion of females who have had more than one sex partner is likely to be considerably higher. Thus, about one-third of the females in the 15–19 year old group and one-half of the males in the same age group have had multiple sex partners in a one-year period. These teenagers are at increased risk for sexually transmitted diseases (Forrest and Singh, 1990).

Adolescent girls' first sexual intercourse generally occurs with someone toward whom they feel an emotional commitment. More than six out of ten girls

Figure 11-1   Percentage of Women Aged 15–19 Who Had Ever Had Sexual Intercourse, by Race and Age Group, 1982–1988.

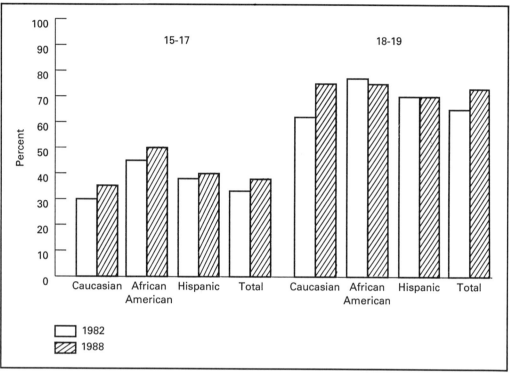

Adapted from data in Jacqueline Darroch Forrest and Susheela Singh, "The Sexual and Reproductive Behavior of American Women, 1982–1988," *Family Planning Perspectives* 22 (September-October 1990) No. 5, p. 208, Table 4. © The Alan Guttmacher Institute.

in Zelnik and Shah's study (1983) said they had been going steady or were engaged to their first sexual partner. By contrast, fewer than four out of ten boys said they had been going steady or were engaged to their first sexual partner. Males were much more likely to have had their first intercourse with a friend or someone they had just met. See Table 11-2. The degree to which adolescents' sexual activity is influenced by their peers varies somewhat with the individual. For instance, one study showed that friends of either sex had no significant influence on the sexual activity of African-American males and females or Caucasian males. However, Caucasian females were more likely to be influenced by the sexual behavior of their best friend of either sex. A Caucasian female virgin whose best friends of both sexes are sexually active ususally becomes sexually active sooner than does a virgin whose best friends are not sexually active (Billy and Udry, 1985).

The initiation of sex seems to be a spur-of-the-moment decision for most youths. Only 17 percent of the females and 25 percent of the males in Zelnik and Shah's study (1983) said they had planned their first intercourse. Females who

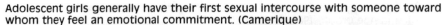

Adolescent girls generally have their first sexual intercourse with someone toward whom they feel an emotional commitment. (Camerique)

were going steady with their first partner were most likely to have planned intercourse while males who had just met their partner shortly before intercourse were the most likely to have planned the sexual act.

The proportion of young people who have ever engaged in sexual intercourse rises steadily with age. The pattern continues into the college years, with decreasing differences in the percentage of men and women who have ever engaged in sexual intercourse. It appears that sexual activity has become an integral part of the overall adolescent experience and is engaged in by all types of youths. Thus, instead of debating whether teenagers should have sex, adults should be talking about *when*. Then it's a matter of saying to adolescents, "Are you really ready for sex? If so, are you prepared to take responsibility for it?" (Brooks-Gunn and Furstenberg, 1989).

Homosexuality

Homosexuality is a topic that arouses considerable anxiety among adolescents. At earlier ages, children are exposed almost exclusively to heterosexual models, at least visibly. This, plus the assumption in our society that everyone is expected to be heterosexual unless "proved" otherwise, means that most adolescents come

Table 11-2 Percentage of Women and Men Ranked by Relationship with Their First
Sexual Partner and Age at First Intercourse

Relationship with first partner	WOMEN			MEN		
	<15 (N=273)	15–17 (N=555)	≥ 18 (N=103)	<15 (N=305)	15–17 (N=294)	≥ 18 (N=64)
Engaged	3.9	8.8	18.7	0.4	0.8	0.0
Going steady	44.4	61.9	46.1	20.0	46.2	47.9
Dating	28.9	21.6	29.0	18.6	22.4	12.6
Friends	13.2	4.3	5.4	54.4	20.0	26.7
Recently met	9.6	3.4	0.8	6.6	10.6	12.8
Total	100.0	100.0	100.0	100.0	100.0	100.0

Source: Melvin Zelnik and Farida K. Shah, "First intercourse among Young Americans," *Family Planning Perspectives* (March/April 1983): p. 66.

to think of themselves as heterosexuals. Yet the process of affirming one's sexual identity that occurs at puberty may well evoke a certain degree of self-doubt in the adolescent's mind about his or her own sexual identity. The awkwardness and frustrations in their sexual relationships with the opposite sex may also arouse anxiety and self-doubt. Consequently, it is not uncommon for adolescents to wonder, if only in passing, about their heterosexuality.

The concern about homosexuality greatly overshadows the amount of homosexual activity that occurs among adolescents. Homosexual contact tends to occur in a relatively small number of adolescents. Also, it tends to occur rather early in adolescence, usually before 15 years of age, and is more common among boys than girls (Dreyer, 1982). In one sample of 600 adolescents 15 to 18 years of age, only 14 percent of the boys and 11 percent of the girls reported having had at least one instance of homosexual activity. When asked about their attitude toward homosexual activity among other adolescents, a majority of both sexes approved. Yet boys were more accepting of homosexuality among girls than among boys, while girls were equally accepting of homosexuality activity among both sexes. At the same time, in reponse to open-ended questions about homosexuality, these same adolescents expressed more negative, judgmental attitudes toward homosexual activity, reflecting some of their underlying anxiety and insecurity in this area (Hass, 1979).

In most instances, homosexual experimentation in adolescence is a passing phase of development and does not lead to a homosexual identity. Masters, Johnson, and Kolodny (1988) report that although about two in ten men and one in ten women experience homosexual activity in some phase of their lives, relatively few individuals become exclusively homosexual. Only about 4 percent of the men and 2 to 3 percent of the women ackowledge a lifelong preference for homosexuality. An extensive study of sexual preferences among heterosexuals and homosexuals by Bell, Weinberg, and Hammersmith (1981) has cast doubt on the familiar theories regarding the cause of homosexuality. These researchers found little evidence that male homosexuality is caused by the combination of a

A gay pride march in New York City. (Ken Karp)

dominant mother and a weak father. Nor is female homosexuality caused by girls choosing their fathers as role models. Also, the stereotype that homosexuality is often caused by being seduced by an older person of the same sex is untrue. Instead, it appears that sexual preference is firmly extablished by late adolescence. As children and adolescents, homosexuals have as many heterosexual experiences as their heterosexual counterparts do, but tend to find these experiences frustrating or less satisfying. Gender noncomformity, such as boys avoiding sports like football while playing house or hopscotch, is a significant but not absolute predictor of a homosexual identity. All things considered, the lack of solid support for any of the usual theories of homosexuality plus newer research suggests that there might be a biological basis to homosexuality (Money, 1987). But at this point, the determinants of homosexuality remain mostly a mystery.

PROBLEMS IN SEXUAL BEHAVIOR

The fact that teenagers are becoming sexually active at an earlier age than in the past has intensified some of the perennial problems of adolescent sexuality. One of these is the failure to use contraceptives, a matter of increasing concern to parents and sex educators alike. A related problem is the incidence of premarital pregnancies, with American teenagers having one of the highest rates of teenage pregnancies in the world. Still another problem is the dramatic rise in sexually transmitted diseases in young people, which has become even more serious in recent years.

Use of Contraceptives

Fortunately, more teenagers are now using contraceptives than in the past. About two-thirds of the females in the 15–19-year-old group used some method of contraceptive in their first act of intercourse in 1988, up significantly from contraceptive use a few years earlier. Most of the gain is due to a marked increase in the use of condoms, along with a decreased use of the less reliable methods such as withdrawal. See Table 11-3. These changes are probably related to the increasing concern with AIDS and other types of sexually transmitted diseases. At the same time, poor female teenagers are the least likely to use contraceptives. At least one-fourth of them fail to use any method of contraception, which, in turn, results in a high rate of unintended pregnancies in this group (Forrest and Singh, 1990).

Similar gains in contraceptive use are evident among women in the 20–29-year-old group. However, women in their twenties are more likely to rely on the pill. Greater use of the pill, especially among college-educated women, may be associated with their access to regular health care required for the continued use of the pill. Marked decreases in the use of the IUD and diaphragm have also contributed to greater reliance on the pill. Another difference between women in the teens and twenties is the progressive rise in the use of sterilization among women in their twenties and thirties, though to a lesser extent among men in the same age groups. Reliance on sterilization has increased especially among single African-American women, with female sterilization becoming the second leading method in this group. However, research is needed to determine why African-American women who have given up the IUD often favor sterilization although Caucasian women tend to favor the pill. One hypothesis is that the perceptions of Caucasian women and their doctors regarding the risks of the pill may differ from those of minority women. Another possible reason has to do with the differences in access to regular health care required for use of the pill (Mosher, 1990).

The fact that one-third of all teenagers fail to use any method of contra-

Table 11-3   Percentage Distribution of Women Aged 15–19 by Contraceptive Use at First Intercourse, 1982–1988.

Contraceptive Use	1982	1988
No method used	52.1	35.0
Any method used	47.9	65.0
Pill	8.3	8.2
Condom	22.6	47.4
Withdrawl	13.0	8.4
Other	4.1	0.9

Adapted from data in Jacqueline Darroch Forrest and Susheela Singh, "The Sexual and Reproductive Behavior of American Women, 1982–1988." *Family Planning Perspectives*, 22 (September-October 1990), No. 5, p. 209, Table 5. © The Alan Guttmacher Institute.

ceptive in their first act of intercourse is a continuing concern. A major problem is the lack of communication about contraceptives among teenage sex partners. For instance, a study of sexually active couples, with young women ranging in age from 15 to 18, showed that the majority of them had discussed birth control on at least one occasion. But such discussions usually occured *after* their first intercourse. In only one-fourth of the couples did partners agree that they had discussed birth control prior to their initial act of intercourse. Among couples who disagreed, girls more commonly than boys denied prior conversation regarding birth control. Couples who agreed they had good communication were more likely to practice effective contraception. Yet one-fourth of all the respondents felt that they had not adequately discussed the use of contraceptives. And these individuals were found to be most at risk for unintended pregnancy (Polit-O'Hara and Kahn, 1985).

Young people who plan to have sex are more apt to use a contraceptive than those who engage in sex spontaneously. And this holds true for males and females, African Americans, and Caucasians. At the same time, a sizable group of those who plan to have sex go unprotected. Generally, the use of contraceptives rises for subsequent acts of intercourse. Also, as we might expect, there is a strong positive association between contraceptive use and the couple's relationship. Couples who are going steady are the most likely to use contraceptives, with dating couples somewhat less inclined to do so. Individuals who have just met or have a "weak" relationship are the least likely to use contraceptives. Furthermore, the partners' views about whose responsibility it is to use birth control have a strong impact on contraceptive use. The great majority of both sexes, especially among older teenagers, believe that both partners are equally responsible for practicing birth control. Not surprisingly, these teenagers are somewhat more likely to use a contraceptive than those who say one partner or the other should bear the entire responsibility. Just 1 percent of sexually experienced adolescents believe neither partner is responsible, and half of these teenagers say they used no contraceptive at their last intercourse (Zabin et al., 1984).

Why do young people fail to use contraceptives? The most frequently given reason is ignorance of which device to use or where to obtain them. Another common reason is the feeling that use of a contraceptive may spoil the spontaneity and pleasure of sex (Zelnik and Shah, 1983). A variety of other reasons may be seen in the study of 1,200 young women 12 to 19 years of age, which inquired into why they had delayed coming to a family planning clinic. (See Table 11-4.) Many of the reasons reflect anxieties and fears as well as widespread ignorance about birth control. The sizable number who responded that they "just didn't get around to it" also reflects immaturity and lack of responsibility in regard to sex. Consequently, there is increasing concern that sex education must include help in decision making as well as information on the availability of contraceptives.

Table 11-4   Reasons Given for Delaying Visit to Family
            Planning Clinic for Birth Control Help

Reason	Percent
Just didn't get around to it	38.1
Afraid my family would find out if I came	31.0
Waiting for a closer relationship with partner	27.6
Thought birth control dangerous	26.5
Afraid to be examined	24.8
Thought it would cost too much	18.5
Didn't think having sex often enough to get pregnant	16.5
Never thought of it	16.4
Didn't know where to get birth control help	15.3
Thought I had to be older to get birth control	13.1
Didn't expect to have sex	12.8
Thought I was too young to get pregnant	11.5
Thought birth control was wrong	9.2
Partner opposed	8.4
Thought I wanted pregnancy	8.4
Thought birth control I was using was good enough	7.8
Forced to have sex	1.4
Sex with relative	0.7
Other	9.7

Source: Adapted from L. S. Zabin and S. D. Clark, Jr "Why They Delay: A
   Study of Teenage Family Planning Clinic Patients, *Family Planning Perspectives* (September/October 1981): p. 214.

Premarital Pregnancy

The failure to use contraceptives correctly or at all greatly increases the risk of
premarital pregnancy. Consider the following statistics on premarital pregnancy
among sexually active teenagers in the United States (Forrest and Singh, 1990):

- ◆ 1 out of 5 teenagers never uses any contraceptive: Half of these teens have at
  least one unintended pregnancy
- ◆ More than one million teenage girls become pregnant each year, one of the
  highest rates in the world
- ◆ 8 out of 10 teenage pregnancies are unintended
- ◆ Females under 19 years of age account for more than one-third of all births to
  unwed mothers

About half of all pregnancies conceived in 1987 (excluding those ending
in miscarriages) were unintended, with the highest incidence of unintended
pregnancies occurring among teenagers. Among women 15 to 19 years of age,
only about 2 out of 10 pregnancies were intended, with most of these ending in
live births. In contrast, 8 out of 10 pregnancies among women in this age group
were unintended. Unmarried teenage women who find themselves pregnant
face several options.

Legal abortion is an option that has become increasingly available though controversial. As a result, about 44 percent of the unintended teenage pregnancies are terminated by abortion, accounting for about one-fourth of all legal abortions. Another 13 percent end in miscarriages (Forrest and Singh, 1990). In about half of the cases, the teenager has been pregnant less than nine weeks. However, the longer the female waits, the greater the risks become. Because adolescents often delay making a decision, they suffer more complications, not to mention the mental agony and guilt accompanying such a decision.

About 42 percent of all unintended teenage pregnancies end in live births, which combined with the unintended pregnancies among women in the 20–24-year-old group account for about two-thirds of all births to unmarried women (U.S. Bureau of the Census, 1990). Adolescent pregnancy increases the health risks of both the mother and infant. Young mothers themselves are more likely to have difficult pregnancies and deliveries, along with higher rates of birth complications. And the psychological impact of an unintended pregnancy can be quite stressful. Also, infants born to adolescent mothers are more likely to have low birth weights, a major cause of infant mortality, as well as birth complications and childhood illnesses (Hayes, 1987).

The great majority of teenage mothers choose to keep their babies. Less than 5 percent of young women put up their babies for adoption. The proportion of mothers offering their babies for adoption is highest among Caucasian women and lowest among African-American women (McGee, 1982). Many young women, especially those in the lower socioeconomic groups, raise their child as a single-parent mother. The high rate of out-of-wedlock births combined with the greater proportion of women who never marry contributes to the prevalence of single-parent families among minority groups, especially African-Americans. Unfortunately, about half of these single-parent homes live on incomes below the poverty level (Staples, 1985).

In about half the cases, teenage girls with a premarital pregnancy choose to marry the father of the child. In fact, the younger the bride, the more likely she is to be pregnant. Yet, as we've seen in an earlier chapter, adolescent marriage reduces the chances that the girl will continue school after the birth of the child. Then too, many of these marriages are entered into under pressure, with uncertainties on the part of both partners. Not surprisingly, couples who marry in their teens are more likely to have marital problems and to separate and divorce in later years than are those who delay marriage until their twenties. Those who delay marriage until after the birth of the child are at even greater risk of marital failure (McLaughlin et al., 1986). At the same time, there are exceptions to the rule. Young women who make the best adjustment are those who marry the father of the child, return to school, and delay having additional children. Within five years, these womens' lives resemble those of their counterparts who have delayed marriage and pregnancy until their twenties (Furstenberg, Brooks-Gunn, and Morgan, 1987).

Sexually Transmitted Diseases

Another consequence of increased sexual activity among youth is the rise in sexually transmitted diseases (STD), a broader and less value-laden phrase than the older term "veneral diseases." The increase in sexually transmitted diseases probably reflects the increased sexual activity among young people as well as the tendency to have multiple sex partners. The incidence of sexually transmitted diseases is highest among 20 to 24 year olds, followed by the 15 to 19 year olds, and then 25 to 29 year olds. Each year, about 6 million new cases of sexually transmitted diseases are reported in the United States (Smilgis, 1987).

Chlamydia, the "silent epidemic," which causes inflammation of the urethral tube, has rapidly become one of the most common sexually transmitted diseases. About 3 to 10 million new cases of chlamydia occur each year, afflicting up to 10 percent of all college students (Wallis, 1985). Males who contract the infection have symptoms similar to gonorrhea, with a discharge from the penis and a mild burning sensation during urination. Females with chlamydia infections may have little or no symptoms, such that they are often unaware of the disease until they are informed by an infected partner. Yet women may have the infection for a long time and, during this time they may pass it on to their sexual partners. When left untreated in women, chlamydia may result in cervial inflammation or pelvic inflammatory disease, and in cases of pregnancy may cause eye damage to infants at birth. In men, it may spread to the prostate. It is important that an infected person get laboratory diagnosis before receiving treatment because the sypmtoms of chlamydia are often confused with those of gonorrhea, though they are treated with different drugs.

Gonorrhea continues to be one of the most common sexually transmitted diseases. Although about 1 million new cases of gonorrhea are reported each year, the true incidence is estimated to be closer to 2 million. Gonorrhea may be transmitted by any form of sexual contact, from kissing to sexual intercourse. A woman who has intercourse once with an infected man has a 50 percent chance of catching gonorrhea, while a man who has intercourse with an infected woman has a lower risk, around 25 percent chance of catching the disease. The old excuse "I caught it from a toilet seat" has been shown to be theoretically possible, though rare (Masters, Johnson, and Kolodny, 1988). Despite the fact that gonorrhea is readily treatable by antibiotic drugs, many young people do not seek treatment because they have so few symptoms that they fail to realize they are infected. This is especially true among women, with as many as two out of three women infected with gonorrhea not being aware of their condition. Yet, women with untreated gonorrhea may suffer from inflammation of the fallopian tubes, infertility, birth malformations, or menstrual disorders. Although a much smaller proportion of men remain relatively free of symptoms, untreated gonorrhea may be equally devastating to males. Gonorrhea is the single most important cause of sterility among males.

Syphilis, though much less common than gonorrhea, is a more serious disease. Men are twice as likely as women to have syphilis, with half of the men infected with syphilis being homosexual or bisexual (Masters, Johnson, and Kolodny, 1988). Although syphilis is generally transmitted by sexual contact, it can also be acquired from a blood transfusion or transmitted from a pregnant mother to the fetus. Fortunately, syphilis is readily treatable, usually with injections of penicillin. But if left untreated, the disease continues into an advanced stage in which it can cause brain damage, heart failure, blindness, or paralysis.

Genital herpes, one of several herpes viral infections, has increased dramatically in recent years. Over a half million new cases of genital herpes are reported each year, with an estimated 20 million Americans now suffering from this disease. Furthermore, because of the frequent recurrence rate and lack of effective treatment, the number of cases continues to increase. Although this disease is more common among young adults, an estimated 1 in 35 adolescents has herpes (Oppenheimer, 1982). Genital herpes is generally transmitted through direct sexual contact, such as sexual intercourse or oral-genital contact. At the same time, oral herpes can be transmitted through kissing, sharing towels, or drinking out of the same cup. And, contrary to earlier notions, if someone with cold sores or fever blisters in the mouth performs oral sex on another person, the latter person may develop *genital* herpes (Peter, Bryson, and Lovett, 1982). Although there is no known cure for genital herpes so far, there are drugs that may lessen the severity of the symptoms and shorten the time for healing. In addition to the intermittent discomfort of herpes sores, genital herpes can lead to serious complications. Newborn infants exposed to herpes sores in the birth canal may be infected with herpes and can suffer physical damage and even death. Furthermore, women infected with genital herpes are eight times more likely to have cervical cancer than women not infected. (*Harvard Medical School Health Letter,* 1981).

AIDS (Acquired Immune Deficiency Syndrome) is one of the newest and most frightening sexually transmitted diseases to come to public awareness. The infection rate in the United States as a whole is about four-tenths to six-tenths of 1 percent, affecting about 1.5 million people. One-fifth of the reported AIDS cases occur in people under 29 years of age, with the great majority being males, U.S. Bureau of the Census, 1990). Individuals at greatest risk of AIDS are those who have multiple sex partners. An estimated 5 percent of the men in the 18–29-year-old group, or approximately 700,000 men, have had ten or more sex partners in the past year, putting them at considerable risk of contracting AIDS. Most teenage females contract the AIDS virus through intercourse with an infected male.

AIDS is transmitted primarily through blood or blood products containing the virus—notably semen and blood. Although homosexual men make up the largest fraction of AIDS patients in the United States, the virus can also be transmitted through vaginal intercourse, and by intravenous drug users who share needles. The risk of contracting AIDS through sexual intercourse between heterosexuals is expected to rise dramatically.

One of the most troubling aspects of AIDS is the relatively long incubation period from the time of exposure to the appearance of symptoms. The

---

AIDS Quiz

Which of the following statements are true?

1. If you think you've been exposed to the AIDS virus, you should get an AIDS test.
2. You can tell by looking that someone has the AIDS virus.
3. The AIDS virus can enter the body through the vagina, penis, rectum, or mouth.
4. Condoms are an effective but not a foolproof way to prevent the spread of AIDS virus.
5. It's possible to get the AIDS virus from kissing or from a toilet seat.
6. The AIDS virus may live in the human body for years before actual symptoms appear.

Answers: Numbers 2 and 5 are false. The others are true.

Source: *Understanding AIDS*, HHS Publication No. 88-8404 (Washington D.C.: U.S. Government Printing Office, 1988).

---

incubation period is generally 12 to 18 months, but may last up to several years. During this time a person is probably contagious to others. It is estimated that about 90 percent of the people carrying the AIDS virus do not know that they have the virus (Smilgis, 1987).

Adolescents might underestimate their risk of contracting AIDS because they are not engaging in the behaviors known to transmit the virus. However, even though you are not using intravenous drugs, you need to know if your partners have ever used them. Also, even though you are not engaging in homosexual behavior, you need to know if your partners have ever done so. Marked public awareness of AIDS in recent years may well alter the attitudes toward casual sex among heterosexuals as well as homosexuals, with "safe sex" becoming the watchword of the nineties (*Harvard Medical School Health Letter*, 1985).

Sexual Victimization

Another problem that has attracted public concern in recent years is sexual victimization. Individuals become sexually victimized when they are forced to comply with sexual acts under duress. Sexual victimization may take many forms, ranging from the sexual abuse of a child or adolescent to an adult who is coerced to engage in offensive sexual acts by his or her partner.

Ellen Bass and Laura Davis (1988), pioneers in child sexual abuse education, report that as many as one out of three girls and one out of seven boys are sexually abused by the time they reach 18 years of age. Most often the abuser is a close relative or friend, usually a middle-age or older man. No more than 5 percent of the perpetrators who molest girls and 20 percent of those who molest boys are female. It is not uncommon for the abuser to have been a victim of sexual abuse as a child. Sexual abuse is most likely to occur among older children and early adolescents, with the typical victim being a girl between 9 and 12 years of age.

In many cases, sexual abuse involves a series of abusive episodes, usually without physical force. Sexual interactions consist of touching and fondling the genitals of the child or adolescent, though sometimes molesters may engage in intercourse.

David Finkelhor (1984) has developed a list of factors that are strongly associated with sexual abuse in childhood and adolescence. The single most important predictor is having a stepfather, which more than doubles a girl's vulnerability to sexual victimization. Next in importance is having a mother who is punitive or negative about sexual matters. Six additional vulnerability factors also have been identified. In a study of 796 college students, Finkelhor found that when none of these risk factors were present in the student's background, there were virtually no reports of childhood or adolescent victimization. However, two-thirds of those with five or more of the risk factors reported they had been sexually abused. See Figure 11-2.

The long-term effects of child or adolescent sexual abuse vary considerably. Some victims of sexual abuse emerge from the experience relatively unscathed. Yet most bear some psychological scars. Child or adolescent sexual abuse

Figure 11-2 Likelihood of Girls' Sexual Victimization by Presence of Eight Vulnerability Factors in Childhood.

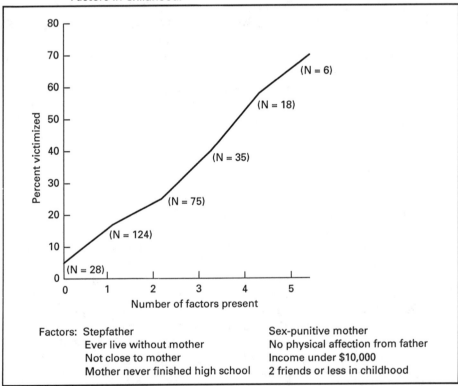

Factors: Stepfather   Sex-punitive mother
        Ever live without mother   No physical affection from father
        Not close to mother   Income under $10,000
        Mother never finished high school   2 friends or less in childhood

Source: Reprinted with permission of The Free Press, a Division of Macmillan, Inc. from *Child Sexual Abuse* by David Finkelhor. Copyright © 1984 by David Finkelhor, p. 29.

may be a contributing factor to many psychological disorders, such as multiple personality, borderline personality, and posttraumatic stress disorder. Survivors may have difficulty becoming involved with the other sex or they may compulsively engage in sex. One of the most disturbing findings is the effect on the next generation. Boys who are abused are more likely to become child molesters. And as many as two-thirds of the girls who experience child sexual abuse later become victims of rape in adulthood. One explanation is that these individuals continue to suffer from low self-esteem and a lack of assertiveness. On a more positive note, most victims of sexual abuse, as well as molesters, may benefit from psychotherapy.

Older youths may be exposed to a variety of abusive sexual activities. For instance, in a study of sexual harassment on campus, Natalie Malovich and Jayne Stake (1990) found that four out of ten women, and one out of eight men had experienced some type of sexual harassment during their first two years on campus. See Figure 11-3. They also discovered that students reacted to such incidents quite differently depending on their self-esteem and attitudes toward women. Women with high self-esteem and traditional attitudes toward women

Figure 11-3   Percent of College Students Reporting Each Type of Sexual Harassment.

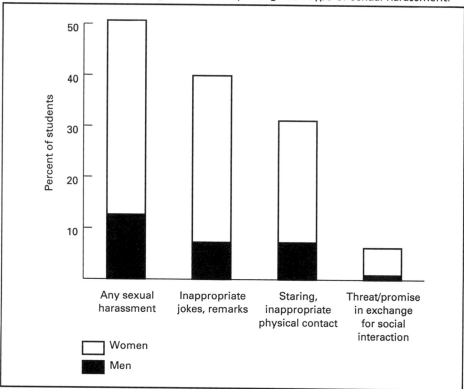

Adapted from data in Natalie J. Malovich and Jayne E. Stake, "Sexual Harassment on Campus: Individual Differences in Attitudes and Beliefs" *Psychology of Women Quarterly* (March 1990), p. 71. Reprinted with permission of Cambridge University Press.

who had been harassed were more likely to have ignored the harasser. In contrast, women with high esteem and nontraditional attitudes toward women were more likely to have used a confrontational style in handling harassment. They were also much more likely to report such incidents than were other women. However, men with low self-esteem coupled with traditional attitudes toward women were the least sensitive about sexual harassment among women.

Rape—sexual intercourse under conditions of actual or threatened force—continues to be a serious problem in American society. The vast majority of rapes continue to involve male rapists and female victims despite the increase in the rape of males in recent years. Accurate statistics on rape are difficult to obtain, mostly because people are reluctant to report such assaults. Thus, the number of forceable rapes reported each year, about 100,000, is probably less than half of those that actually occur (U.S. Bureau of the Census, 1990).

The true prevalence of rape is further complicated by the fact that most rapes are committed by someone known to the woman victim, rather than a stranger who jumps out of the bushes. These "date rapes," as they are sometimes labeled, are much less likely to be reported to authorities than those in which the women is assaulted by an intruder who breaks into the house. According to college surveys, anywhere from 15 to 20 percent of the women have experienced forceable sex sometime during their college years (Leo, 1987). However, many of them are reluctant to label such assaults as rape, mostly because of the misconception that rape must be committed by a stranger under the conditions of extreme violence. Date rapes are more likely to occur with someone who is already familiar to the woman, and when alcohol or drugs are involved. The use of alcohol or drugs not only lowers the rapist's judgment and control, but is also impairs the victim's memory of the event and clouds the issue of consent in a criminal trial.

The women's movement has been an important impetus for reform in this area, including the view that the problem of rape stems partly from the way in which society deals with it. Accordingly, in some cities and campuses men have formed groups to examine male attitudes that perpetuate rape. Some colleges have also been held legally accountable for the failure to provide adequate protection for women students who were raped on campus. Rape litigation has also prompted insurance companies to demand stricter security measures before providing coverage to property owners and institutions (Crooks and Baur, 1990). Furthermore, improvements in the police and court system may make officials more sensitive to and supportive of rape victims. Finally, the establishment of rape victim advocacy programs and centers not only increases the likelihood that victims will report the crime but also aids them in making an effective recovery.

SEX EDUCATION

Many of the problems in adolescent sexuality can be traced to the lack of an adequate sex education in our society. Despite the openness and honesty in sexual matters and relative sophistication of today's teenagers in regard to sexuality, sex education continues to be mostly a hit-or-miss affair, varying widely in content and quality in different families and schools.

Sources of Sex Information

A major problem is that teenagers continue to get most of their information about sex from the least reliable source, their peers. Evidence for this can be seen in a survey (Davis and Harris, 1982) in which several hundred adolescents of both sexes ranging in age from 11 to 18 were asked about their knowledge of sex and its sources. The subjects included Caucasians, Hispanics, and Native American Indians. As expected, friends were the most commonly cited source of sex information, followed in order by the school, parents, and books/magazines. Most students learned relatively little from movies and television. The proportion of students receiving information from the different sources is shown in Table 11-5.

Other studies have shown that the sources of sex information also vary somewhat depending on the particular topic. For instance, Thornburg's (1981) study found that adolescents were most likely to seek out their friends for information about sexual intercourse, contraceptives, and homosexuality—topics not usually discussed elsewhere. Mothers were more likely to discuss menstruation and conception, usually with their daughters, while schools were the major source of information about sexually transmitted diseases.

The Parents' Role

Informal sex education usually begins in the home. Children learn about sex the same way they learn about most other things—by observing their parents and talking about them. The manner in which parents hug, kiss, and touch each other, or fail to do so, shows the degree to which they have accepted themselves

Table 11-5 Percentages of Students Receiving Sex Information from Different Sources

Source	A Lot	A Little	None
Friends	43.5	47.4	9.1
School	36.0	47.7	16.3
Parents	26.1	50.2	23.7
Books/Magazines	25.5	51.0	23.4
Movies	18.6	51.9	29.5
Television	9.8	55.8	34.4
Brothers/Sisters	20.3	32.9	46.9
Doctors/Nurses	15.1	33.8	51.1
Church	2.8	4.6	92.6
Other	15.2	16.6	68.3

Source: Adapted from S. M. Davis and M. B. Harris, "Sexual Knowledge, Sexual Interests, and Sources of Sexual Information of Rural and Urban Adolescents from Three Cultures," *Adolescence* 17 (1982), p. 478.

and each other as sexual beings. Then too, the way parents handle their child's or adolescent's questions about sex helps to shape the latter's attitudes toward sex. Parents who are embarrassed to talk about sex may unwittingly encourage an attitude of reticence or shame toward the teenager's own sexuality. Unfortunately, it seems, this is all too often the case. When teenagers in one study (Hass, 1979) were asked if they had tried to discuss sex openly with their parents, about half of them said they had tried to do so at one time or another. Asked how their parents had responded to their questions, only a minority gave a positive response. More often than not, teenagers felt that their parents had responded negatively, either by avoidance, denial, teasing, or disapproval. As a result, about half of the teenagers either shared nothing about sex with their parents or only what they thought their parents would approve of. Only about 1 in 10 teenagers reported that they shared everything about their sex lives with their parents.

Parents may not be doing a very good job of sex education in the home for a number of reasons. First, some parents do not feel comfortable with their own sexuality because they have grown up in an era in which sex was less accepted than it is today. Hence their embarrassment in discussing sex. Then there are those parents who are either not sufficiently informed about sex or, if so, do not know how to explain sex to their adolescents. Parents need to realize that even the experts need practice in communicating sexual information to teenagers in an acceptable way. A major reason for parent's reluctance to discuss sex is their fear that exposing children and adolescents to information about sex will stimulate their curiosity and prematurely draw them into sexual activity. Yet, the reverse is often true. In the author's experience the uninformed teenagers are more likely to get into trouble. For instance, when talking with the parents of a 16-year-old boy whose girlfriend was pregnant, I asked, "Did you ever discuss the use of contraceptives with your son?" They replied, "No, because we thought he was too young to be having sex."

Sex Education in the School

Many parents are well aware that they are not doing an adequate job with sex education in the home and favor some type of sex education in the schools. According to a Gallup poll (Elam, 1990), three-fourths of the public school parents favor including sex education, including AIDS, in the school curriculum. Adolescents are even more supportive of sex education in the school, with more than eight out of ten teenagers desiring such courses (Gallup, 1985).

By contrast, only 60 percent of all adolescents receive any sex education in high school (Forrest and Silverman, 1989). The major reason is that only eighteen states required sex education as of 1988, with twenty-three other states encouraging it. Fortunately, an increasing number of schools are offering some type of sex education largely because of the AIDS crisis facing the nation (Foderaro, 1990). But the content and quality of the programs varies widely from one school to another, with many programs being remarkably incomplete. A survey of secondary schools has shown that sex education generally begins in high school, in the tenth grade on the average, with courses much more likely to be offered in grades 9 through 12 than grades 7 and 8. The most popular topics are anatomy and physiology, reproduction, pregnancy, childbirth, birth control, and sexually transmitted diseases. Less likely to be included are topics such as homosexuality and prostitution. An encouraging trend is the number of schools that offer some instruction on sex roles, love, and marriage (Newton, 1982).

Educators and parents alike have a number of concerns about sex education. First, many educators feel that waiting until high school for sex education may be waiting too long. Most sex information has been acquired by the time teenagers begin high school, a time when many teenagers have already become sexually active. Consequently, many educators believe that sex education should begin in elementary school and be taught in an age-appropriate manner throughout a child's formal education (Masters, Johnson, and Kolodny, 1988). Yet, only slightly over half of public school parents favor starting sex education in elementary school (Gallup, 1985). A second concern is what should be taught. Sex education should address more than sound factual knowledge, as important as this is. It should also include students' attitudes and help them to develop a sense of responsibility about sex, especially in regard to the use of contraceptives. Then there is the issue of who should teach sex education classes. Ideally, sex education teachers should be highly qualified and have a healthy attitude toward sex. At the least, teachers should have some special training in the field. But teachers' attitudes toward sex may be just as important as their knowledge of sex. Teachers who can answer students' questions and deal with controversial issues in a frank, fair manner encourage the development of similar attitudes among students. Also, there is the issue of teens' sexual knowledge in relation to their peers. Because teenagers tend to learn about sex from their peers, some programs have successfully used teenage discussion groups led by skilled moderators (Kisker, 1985). Finally, there is the issue of parental involvement. There is some evidence that the most successful sex education programs have involved parents in one way or another (Alexander, 1984).

A final matter pertains to the impact of sex education courses. Contrary to the fears of some adults, there is ample evidence that formal sex education does not usually lead to premature or greater sexual activity among adolescents. Instead, there are generally fewer premarital pregnancies among those who have received formal sex instruction (Dawson, 1986). Other positive gains associated with sex education programs include greater factual knowledge and accuracy of information about sexual matters, decline of fears and doubts about sex, greater awareness and use of contraceptives, better communication about sex, and, where specifically focused on, greater skill in decision making about sexual matters such as the use of contraceptives (Zelnik and Kim, 1982).

SUMMARY

Sexual Attitudes

1. We began the chapter describing the changing attitudes toward sex, including the greater openness and honesty in sex, the greater acceptance of intercourse outside marriage, and the greater personal freedom of choice in sex.

2. The majority of youths hold sexual attitudes that are consistent with responsible conduct, but they do not always apply these attitudes to their personal behavior. For instance, three-fourths of all teenagers report they had their first intercourse at an age earlier than they deem desirable.

3. Although most youths feel that love enriches sex, many of them continue to engage in casual sex.

Sexual Behavior

4. Adolescents of both sexes engage in a similar developmental sequence of sexual activities, beginning with kissing and hugging their partners by the midteens, progressing to more erotic fondling of the genitals of the opposite sex, and culminating in sexual intercourse in the late teens.

5. About three-fourths of teenagers have engaged in sexual intercourse by the time they are 18 or 19 years of age. In most instances, the initial act of sex is a spur-of-the-moment decision, especially among those who are not dating regularly or going steady.

6. Homosexual experimentation tends to occur relatively early during adolescence and especially among males. Homosexuality is generally a passing phase of development that does not lead to a lifelong preference for homosexuality.

Problems in Sexual Behavior

7. Teenagers are more likely to use a contraceptive device than in the past, partly because of the increasing concern with AIDS. About two-thirds of the females in the 15–19-year-old group use some method of contraception in their first intercourse.

8. The failure to use contraceptives correctly or at all greatly increases the risk of premarital pregnancy, with eight out of ten adolescent pregnancies being unintended. Almost half of the unintended pregnancies end in live births; most of the other unintended pregnancies result in abortions.

9. Another consequence of the increased sexual activity among youths is the rise in sexually transmitted diseases, with the highest incidence of these diseases occurring among 20–24 year olds, followed by the 15–19 year olds.

10. Because about one-fifth of the reported AIDS cases occur among people under 29 years of age, mostly males, many young people have altered their attitudes toward casual sex.

11. Another problem that has attracted public concern in recent years is sexual victimization. As many as one out of three girls and one out of seven boys are sexually abused by the time they reach 18. Older youths may be exposed to a variety of abusive sexual behaviors, with anywhere from 15 to 20 percent of college-aged-women experiencing rape or attempted rape.

Sex Education

12. Teenagers continue to get most of their information about sex from the least reliable source—their friends, followed in order by the school, parents, and books/magazines.

13. Informal sex education in the home leaves much to be desired, with teenagers sharing

very little about sex with their parents, mostly because of their dissatisfaction with parental communication in such matters.

14. Many parents are well aware that they are not doing an adequate job in sex education in the home and favor some type of formal sex education at school.

15. A major drawback to existing sex education programs is that most courses begin in high school, after many teens have already begun learning and experimenting with sex.

16. Contrary to adult fears, teenagers who receive formal instruction in sex do not engage in more premature sexual activity than do teens who receive no instruction; in addition, teens who have been taught sex education have a lower rate of premarital pregnancy.

REVIEW QUESTIONS

1. How would you characterize adolescents' attitudes toward sex?
2. What are some of the glaring inconsistencies between adolescents' sexual attitudes and their sexual behavior?
3. To what extent does the relationship between love and sex vary according to the individual's age, sex, and sexual values?
4. How much basis is there to the criticism that teenagers are having sex too early?
5. To what extent is homosexual play among adolescents a passing phase of development?
6. What are some of the common reasons teenagers fail to use contraceptives?
7. Why do American teenagers have one of the highest rates of premarital pregnancy in the world?
8. Which type of adolescents are most at risk of contracting AIDS?
9. What might account for the high rate of rape in American society?
10. What type of sex education would you like to see, including school courses and parent involvement?

12

Moral Development and Religion

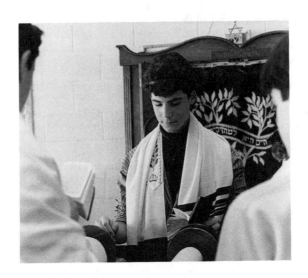

Learning Objectives

After completing this chapter, you should be able to:
1 Identify Lawrence Kohlberg's three levels and six stages of moral reasoning.
2 Discuss how the development of moral reasoning depends on the interaction between adolescents and their social environment as well as maturation.
3 Describe two approaches to reducing classroom cheating.
4 Discuss the importance of empathy for helping behavior.
5 List the three stages of decision making involved in bystander intervention.
6 Describe value-behavior inconsistency among adolescents.
7 Describe the four broad stages of religious development.

Lisa, a 16 year old who recently obtained her driver's license, has borrowed the family car for an errand at a local shopping mall. On the way over to the mall, she picks up her boyfriend, Brad. A short time later, while parking her car at the mall, Lisa accidentally scrapes the fender of a Mercedes sedan in the adjacent parking space. Inspecting the damage, Lisa discovers a small indentation in the fender of the other car along with a smear of blue paint from her parents' car. Lisa is very upset and says, "Maybe I should leave a note with my name and phone number on the windshield of the Mercedes." "I'd forget it," Brad chimes in. "The guy's insurance will cover it." Shaking her head, Lisa replies, "I'd feel better if I left a note." "Listen," says Brad, "anyone who drives an expensive car like that can afford to fix a small scratch in the fender. Come on, let's move the car to another parking place before someone finds out about this."

THE DEVELOPMENT OF MORAL REASONING

What do you think Lisa should do? Should she contact the driver of the other car? Or should she overlook the incident and move her car to another parking space? When individuals of various ages are faced with such moral dilemmas, their responses vary considerably, depending largely on their age and the maturity of their moral reasoning. Younger children tend to be concerned about the reactions of authorities, such as what would happen if Lisa were caught and punished. Older children and adolescents are capable of more complex moral reasoning and show more concern for the rules of society. Such differences reflect the characteristic types of reasoning associated with the various stages of moral development.

One of the best-known approaches to how adolescents develop their sense of right and wrong is Lawrence Kohlberg's theory of moral development, Kohlberg (1984) has formulated a comprehensive, lifespan theory of moral reasoning. Essentially, Kohlberg holds that children and adolescents progress through a sequence of six distinct stages of moral reasoning that parallel cognitive development, with higher stages of moral reasoning presupposing the attainment of formal or abstract thinking. Each stage develops out of and includes the attainments of the previous stages, so that the individual's moral reasoning becomes increasingly complex with age and experience. Similar to Piaget, Kohlberg views the sequence of stages of moral reasoning as invariant, though the rate of development varies considerably among individuals, with those thwarted in their moral development remaining at a given stage of moral development, perhaps permanently. Kohlberg holds that the attainment of each successive stage of cognitive thought is a necessary but not a sufficient condition of reaching the corresponding level of moral reasoning. That is, many adolescents who have acquired the capacity for formal, abstract thought have not yet attained the corresponding level of moral reasoning. A primary reason is that the development of moral reasoning also depends on other factors, such as the individual's learning experiences and social interaction. As a result, moral reasoning tends to lag somewhat behind cognitive development.

Kohlberg's knowledge of moral development has been acquired through twenty years of extensive research using a method of personal interviews. Individuals of various ages are presented with various moral dilemmas involving moral concepts, values, and issues. Then the subjects are asked what the actor in the situation ought to do and—more important—the reasons or justifications for doing so. For example, in one such dilemma, a woman is near death from a very bad disease. There is one drug doctors think might save her. Yet it is very expensive. After Heinz, the woman's husband, is unable to borrow the necessary money, he pleads with the druggist to let him pay for the drug in installments. But the druggist refuses. Now Heinz must decide whether to steal the drug he cannot afford in order to save his dying wife. Subjects are asked what they would do in such a situation and to explain the reasons for their decisions. On the basis of the responses to such moral dilemmas, Kohlberg and his associates have concluded that the moral reasoning of children and adolescents tends to evolve through the same sequence of stages. (See Table 12-1.)

Kohlberg's Stages of Moral Reasoning

Kohlberg (1984) has identified six successive stages of moral reasoning, divided into three major levels: preconventional, conventional, and postconventional.

At the preconventional or premoral level, which parallels Piaget's preoperational stage of thinking, the child remains highly egocentric and unable to adopt the views of others. The sense of right and wrong is understood in relation to external authority. In Stage 1, designated variously as heteronomous morality or the punishment and obedience orientation, the child obeys parental rules to avoid punishment. For example, Jeff avoids running into the street because he fears being punished by his parents. By Stage 2, a type of instrumental hedonism comes into play, such that the rules are followed to meet the child's own interest and needs with the assumption that others will do the same. The child begins to

Table 12-1 Kohlberg's Levels and Stages of Moral Reasoning

Stage Descriptions	Examples of Moral Reasoning in Support of Heinz's Stealing	Examples of Moral Reasoning Against Heinz's Stealing
Preconventional Morality Morality is based on what one has to gain or lose personally		
1. Avoidance of punishment by authorities	"If you let your wife die, you'll get in trouble."	"You shouldn't steal the drug because you'll be sent to jail."
2. Acting in one's own self-interest	"If you get caught you could give the drug back and get a lighter sentence."	"You may not get much of a jail term, but your wife will probably die before you get out."
Conventional Morality Morality is based on upholding social conventions		
3. Gaining approval/avoiding disapproval	"Your family will consider you an inhuman husband if you don't."	"It isn't just the druggist but everyone else who will think you're a criminal."
4. Doing one's duty to maintain social and legal order	"If you have any honor, you won't let your wife die because you're afraid to act in a way that will save her."	"You'll always feel guilty for breaking the law."
Postconventional Morality Morality is based on ethical principles		
5. Affirming socially agreed upon rights	"If you let your wife die, it would be out of fear rather than thinking it through."	"You'd lose respect for yourself if you get carried away by your emotions and forget the long-range point of view."
6. Adhering to universal ethical principles	"If you don't steal the drug you have obeyed the external law, but you wouldn't have lived up to your own conscience."	"If you stole the drug, you would condemn yourself because you wouldn't have lived up to your own standards of honesty."

Adaptation of Table 1.6, "Motives for Engaging in Moral Action," pp. 52–53 from *The Psychology of Moral Development*, Volume II by Lawrence Kohlberg, Copyright © 1984 by Lawrence Kohlberg. Reprinted by permission of Harper & Row, Publishers, Inc.

take into consideration the views of others, but mostly in order to get what he or she wants. At this stage, Jeff tries not to run into the street mostly because of the reward promised by his mother.

At the conventional level, which roughly parallels Piaget's stage of concrete operational thinking and the early stages of formal thought, children and adolescents are better able to grasp the views of others, so that moral reasoning is based more on internalized, socially acceptable authority. At Stage 3, characterized by mutual interpersonal expectations and relationships, children and adolescents regard right and wrong in relation to what others expect of them in terms of their roles—that is, as daughter or son, sister or brother, and friend. Motives and intentions also become more important at this stage. For example, Kathy doesn't tell her parents that her brother is smoking cigarettes because Kathy doesn't want to betray her brother's trust and friendship. Naturally, Kathy expects her brother would do the same. By Stage 4, sometimes known as the social system or "law and order" stage, the individual's moral reasoning takes into account the larger social system such as the rules of the group or laws of society. At this stage, the sense of right and wrong is based on a more generalized approach than that assumed at the level of interpersonal relationships and often involves consideration of "What if everyone does this?" An example would be Kathy's obeying the stop signs at street crossings when she drives because she feels this is necessary for everyone's safety.

The postconventional level of moral reasoning presupposes the attainment of formal operational thinking, such that moral judgment is based on abstract moral principles and a more generalized role taking. In Stage 5, moral reasoning is based on the social contract or system of principles which takes into account the individual rights agreed upon by society as a whole, such as the Constitution of the United States. Thus, a person's conviction for stealing a car (violation of laws in Stage 4) might be thrown out by a higher court because the defendant's right had not been duly respected during the process of arrest and trial. By Stage 6, the highest level of moral development, individuals follow self-chosen moral precepts based on universal ethical principles. At this level, particular laws or social agreements are held to be valid or not depending on whether they are based on certain universal principles, such as the equality of human rights and respect for the dignity of human beings as individual persons. For example, an individual might feel that people should not be denied their basic rights because of their skin color despite laws to the contrary in their particular society.

The Attainment of Moral Reasoning

Kohlberg (1984) and his colleagues have found a strong relationship between peoples' overall developmental stage, as reflected in their age, and their stage or moral reasoning. Most preschool-aged children and those in the early grades, who are in Piaget's stage of preoperational thinking and the early stages of concrete operational thought, characteristically exhibit preconventional moral reasoning. As older children and early adolescents reach the stage of concrete operational thinking and the beginning stages of formal thought, an increasing proportion of them can use conventional moral reasoning. Data from a twenty-year longitudinal study of moral development by Kohlberg and his colleagues

(Colby et al., 1983) chart the growth of moral reasoning with age, from late childhood on. During mid- to late adolescence there is a dramatic decline in the proportion of individuals using preconventional moral thought, that is, Stages 1 and 2. At the same time, there is a marked increased in the proportion of adolescents in the early stages of conventional moral thinking, that is, Stage 3, or the interpersonal orientation. Also, there is a slow but steady rise in Stage 4 thinking, or the more advanced conventional moral reasoning reflecting the more generalized viewpoint and laws of society, so that by the time individuals have reached their thirties more than six out of ten of them exhibit conventional moral understanding. Stage 5 thinking, or the early stages of postconventional moral thinking, which does not appear generally until after 20 years of age, grows much more slowly and never characterizes more than 10 to 15 percent of the early adults. (See Figure 12-1.) Apparently, because formal thinking does not always emerge in adolescence, if at all, neither do the higher stages of moral reasoning. Individuals whose characteristic moral reasoning is at the postconventional level tend to be in the distinct minority.

    The development of moral reasoning depends largely on the interaction between the individuals and their social environment and involves both cognitive and social processes as well as maturation. According to Kohlberg's cognitive-

Figure 12-1 The Percentage of People in Each Age Group Exhibiting the Various Stages of Moral Reasoning.

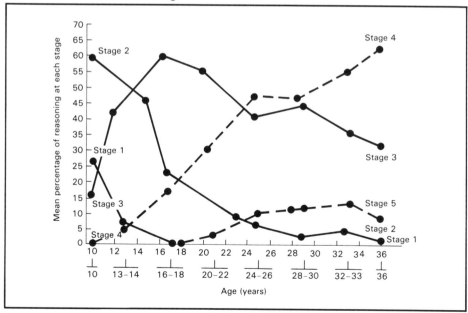

Source: A. Colby, L. Kohlberg, J. Gibbs, and M. Lieberman, "A Longitudinal Study of Moral Judgment," *Monographs of Society for Research in Child Development.* © 1983 The Society for Research in Child Development, Inc.

Discussing moral issues and conflicts
helps to deepen adolescents' moral
understanding. (Ken Karp)

disequilibrium model, individuals progress in their moral reasoning through the experience of cognitive disequilibrium. That is, when they confront new information or situations they do not fully understand, the resulting conflict or disequilibrium motivates them to reorganize their moral reasoning. Thus, individuals who continue to learn and grow in their moral development are progressively reorganizing their moral reasoning to deal with new problems and issues in their lives. Kohlberg estimates that at any time, about half of a person's moral thinking will be at a given stage, with the remainder reflecting the adjoining stages. Normally, individuals take the moral views of one stage above their own characteristic stage as their moral ideal. At the same time, there is increased awareness that the growth of moral reasoning involves more than cognitive development and is also dependent on the individual's social interactions, especially social role taking, that is, the ability to understand moral issues from another person's viewpoint. Consequently, efforts to facilitate the growth of moral reasoning must include more than the cognitive dimensions of development. For instance, in one experimental study, high school seniors 16 to 18 years of age enrolled in three psychology classes were randomly assigned either to one of two treatment groups or to a control group. Those in the treatment groups participated in a three-week unit on character development that included classroom experiences involving the development of listening and communication skills, empathy, social role taking, and assertive behavioral skills as well as the discussion of moral dilemmas. The results showed that the students who were exposed to this enriched learning environment exhibited a significant improvement in their levels of moral reasoning compared to those in the control group (Kessler, Ibrahim, and Kahn, 1986).

A Critique of Kohlberg's Theory

Despite the helpfulness of Kohlberg's approach and the extensive research it has generated, his theory has been criticized on a number of points. A recurring criticism is that relatively few people ever attain the highest stages of moral thought even in American society. The fact that even fewer people in the less-developed societies, especially those not using a democratic form of government, reach the higher stages of moral thought has been taken to mean that Kohlberg's theory is ethnically and culturally biased on the one hand, and also that his stages of moral development are not universal and invariant. At the same time, the lack of empirical verification of Kohlberg's theory in other societies may have been due partly to earlier scoring procedures, and better support may be expected from research using Kohlberg's newer, improved methods (Hoffman, 1980).

Another criticism is that many of the moral dilemmas used in Kohlberg's studies fail to deal with the issues that are most important to adolescents. In one study, Yussen (1977) asked adolescents in the seventh, ninth, and twelfth grades to write a realistic moral dilemma of their own. When Yussen analyzed the adolescents' moral dilemma, he discovered that they were quite different from those used by Kohlberg. A central issue for all adolescents was interpersonal relationships, especially among friends. There were also age differences, with seventh graders more likely to be concerned about matters of physical safety, that is, harm from threats and physical violence, whereas ninth and twelfth graders were more concerned about sexual matters, and twelfth graders were beginning to struggle with job-related difficulties. Other issues that emerged in the adolescents' own moral dilemmas included the use of alcohol and drugs, civil rights, and stealing.

Still another criticism focuses on Kohlberg's emphasis on the abstract principles of moral reasoning. Carol Gilligan (1982) holds that Kohlberg's theory reflects a male bias, with the emphasis on the abstract, impersonal principles of right and wrong superseding the interpersonal aspects of morality which are often more developed among women. Thus, when boys score higher than girls do on Kohlberg's measures of moral development, this may be more of an indication that the measures themselves are biased. A more comprehensive account of moral development should give greater consideration of right and wrong in relation to people's connectedness or relationships with others in a given situation. Gilligan contends that women think more in terms of specific people than general principles of justice and fairness. Women tend to view morality in terms of selfishness versus responsibility, with an obligation to care for others and avoid causing them harm. Gilligan uses two biblical stories to contrast her morality of nonviolence with Kohlberg's morality of rights. The abstract morality of Kohlberg's Stage 6 can be seen in Abraham's willingness to sacrifice his son's life when God demanded it as a test of faith. But Gilligan's own morality of nonviolence can be seen in the story of the woman who proved to King Solomon she was the baby's real mother by agreeing to let another woman have it rather than see it harmed.

Despite these criticisms, Kohlberg's theory remains one of the most helpful explanations of moral development available, especially in an area that has lacked serious attention from the social sciences. Even though Kohlberg's stages of moral reasoning may not be universal or invariant, Kohlberg's theory is helpful in understanding the development of moral thought, especially in our society with its democratic form of government. But we should bear in mind that Kohlberg's theory is essential a *cognitive* view of moral reasoning and that this must be seen in relation to other aspects of moral development as well.

MORAL BEHAVIOR

The ability of youths to reason about right and wrong in a mature way in a given situation is one thing; how they act in the situation is something else. For instance, faced with the possibility of getting caught for classroom cheating, 15 year olds may act out of self-serving motives rather than in accordance with their more sophisticated moral reasoning. As a result, morality is considerably more complex than moral reasoning, as important as this is.

In this section, we examine some other aspects of moral development that are especially relevant for moral behavior. We begin by discussing the resistance to wrongdoing, that is, the avoidance of such behaviors as cheating, lying, and stealing. Then we look at the development of empathy and prosocial behavior, such as coming to the aid of a stranded motorist. Finally, we consider the importance of moral values and the characteristic value-behavior conflicts that occur during adolescence as well as the development of moral values.

Resistance to Wrongdoing

Every day, adolescents and adults are faced with choices that involve doing the right thing versus taking the easy way out. That is, they may lie, cheat, steal, or do something to gain an immediate reward in an unethical or illegal way. The temptations are great, and, judging by newspaper headlines and surveys on the subject, so is the amount of unethical behavior. In one national survey, investigators (Hassett, 1981) polled over 24,000 people about a variety of moral issues. One-fourth of the subjects were between 13 and 25 years of age, another one-fourth were in their mid- to late twenties, and the rest were older. The results showed that during the year prior to the survey a majority of respondents had broken the law or engaged in some unethical behavior. (See Figure 12-2.) Furthermore, while 89 percent of them reported they feel it is unethical to drive away after scratching a car without telling the owner, 44 percent of them admitted they would probably do it. And if they were sure they wouldn't get caught,

Figure 12-2   Unethical Behavior.

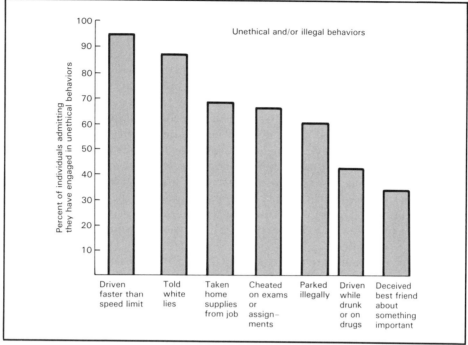

Source: Adapted from data in the Psychology Today Survey Report on unethical behavior—James Hassett, "But That Would Be Wrong . . .," *Psychology Today* (November 1981), p. 41. Reprinted from *Psychology Today* Magazine, © 1981 The American Psychological Association.

over half of them (52 percent) would be even more likely to do so. Similarly, while 85 percent of them feel it is unethical to keep $10 extra change at a local supermarket, one-fourth of them (26 percent) said they would probably do so. One-third of them (33 percent) indicated they would keep the change if they were sure they wouldn't get caught.

Some individuals are more likely than others to engage in wrongdoing. For instance, those who cheat on exams tend to be low in the ability to delay gratification, low in interpersonal trust, and low in self-esteem. Such people also tend to be high in sociopathic tendencies, high in the need for approval, and high in chronic self-destructive tendencies. Altogether, such individuals tend to be emotionally and morally immature and unable to sacrifice short-term gains in order to obtain future rewards (Baron and Byrne, 1984). At the same time, how individuals will behave at any given time also depends heavily on the particular circumstances. In nonviolent crimes, the situation seems to play a major role, with individuals deciding whether to act on the basis of the benefits to be gained, the probability of getting caught, and the costs involved if the misdeeds are discovered. For instance, with respect to stolen property, the possible benefits are often exceeded by the high risk of getting caught, convicted, and punished, such that the incidence of property crime is relatively high among young, risk-taking males. By contrast, with fraud there's often a high potential gain, with a low risk of indictment and a low penalty, so fraud is widely practiced by both men and women from age 20 to 60.

Have you ever cheated on an exam or passed off another person's paper as your own? If so, you have plenty of company. Surveys by the Institute for the Advancement of Ethics indicate that three-fourths of high school students have cheated at least once. More than half of them admit to cheating occasionally, and one out of ten of them cheat often. Between 40 and 50 percent of college students admit to cheating on exams (O'Reilly, 1990). Cheating tends to be more common among males than among females, and among those with average grades or below than those with higher grades. When asked why they cheat, some youths say that because others are doing it they have to cheat to protect themselves. Others admit they cheat because it is easier than studying and saves time (Norman and Harris, 1981). Then too, many youths simply don't see cheating as dishonest.

Attempts to reduce classroom cheating have usually relied on one of two approaches or a combination of both. First, there are attempts to alter the situation to increase the perceived probability of getting caught, such as the presence of an alert examiner in the classroom. Unfortunately, the probability of getting caught is so low that cheaters are seldom deterred by this fear. Of those who say they have cheated, only one out of five admit they have ever been caught, about the same proportion as those who ever fear getting caught (Norman and Harris, 1981). There is also some evidence that when students are placed in a situation in which a high level of effort is rewarded fairly, they are more likely to work hard and less likely to cheat when performing similar tasks at a later date (Eisenberger and Masterson, 1983).

A second approach aims at altering the individual's moral awareness and feelings of guilt. Because anywhere up to half the students report some feelings of guilt after cheating on a test or paper, especially an important one, attempts to increase ethical awareness might be effective in reducing classroom cheating. In one experiment, investigators (Dienstbier et al., 1980) administered a vocabulary test to students followed by some material with moral theories. Students in the externally oriented condition read material that emphasized the threat of punishment and fear of getting caught. Those in the internally oriented condition read material that stressed the emotional tension that resulted from violating one's own moral standards. At this point, students had the opportunity to cheat. They were given the correct answers and warned not to change their answers. During the next couple of minutes the experimenter supposedly was busy with a telephone call, making it easy for students to cheat. But there was a sheet of pressure-sensitive paper in the test booklets so that changed answers could be identified easily. The results showed that less than one-sixth of the students in the internally oriented condition cheated, compared to almost one-third of the students in the externally oriented and control groups. (See Figure 12-3.) The investigators suggested that the internally oriented approach was more effective because most of the students already possessed the appropriate moral rule but needed a slight reminder to act on their moral views. At the same time, the effectiveness of this approach was probably enhanced because of other factors, such as the reliance on free choice versus external pressure and the appeal to a positive self-image in which students like to think of themselves as honest and ethical individuals—all of which reflect democratic socialization practices.

Empathy

We might also add empathy, the ability to understand another person and to share his or her emotions as our own. Accordingly, increasing attention is being to given to empathy as a major ingredient in moral behavior, whether resisting wrongdoing or actively reaching out to help others.

Martin Hoffman (1980) asserts that empathy is the core experience required for prosocial behavior, i.e., actions intended primarily to benefit others. He explains how a person's readiness to help people usually results from a combination of empathic affect, or feelings, and the cognitive ability to take the viewpoint of others. Infants and young children may experience a kind of global empathic distress response. Yet, lacking a clear distinction between themselves and others, they may be unclear as to who is feeling the distress. As children acquire a rudimen-

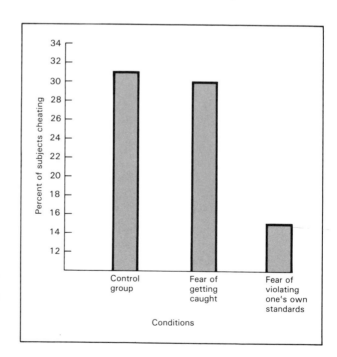

Figure 12-3 The Reduction of
              Cheating Behavior:
              Guilt versus Fear of
              Getting Caught.

Source: Based on data from R. A. Dienstbier, R. L. Kahle, K. A. Willis, and G. B. Tunnell, "The Impact of Moral Theories on Cheating: Studies of Emotion Attribution and Schema Activation," *Motivation and Emotion* 4 (1980): pp. 93–216. Used by permission of Plenum Publishing Corporation.

tary sense of self and subjective perspective taking, they may experience a more specific empathic distress response. But because they cannot yet distinguish accurately between their feelings and those of others, young childrens' efforts to help may consist in giving others what they themselves find most comforting, such as offering their teddy bear or security blanket to a troubled friend. Older children are capable of responding to signals of distress with more appropriate empathic affect and objective perspective taking, such that they can recognize signs of happiness and sadness in others in specific situations. Sometime during late childhood and early adolescence, largely because of the emergence of greater autonomy, self-identity, and more mutual perspective taking, youths can not only empathize with people's feelings in transitory situations but also imagine the other person's general condition. Thus, individuals can experience empathy together with a fairly realistic mental image of the general plight of others. As Rolf Muuss (1988) suggests, one might draw a parallel here between the emergence of the capacity for mature empathic arousal and Kohlberg's conventional level of moral reasoning as a basis for moral behavior.

Hoffman makes an important distinction between the person's subjective arousal of empathy and the related response of "sympathetic distress," with the latter including a sense of compassion and desire to help another person. Ordinarily, it is only as individuals experience sympathetic distress that they actually engage in helping behaviors. Those who simply feel empathic or sympathetic arousal and do nothing about it often blame themselves for not helping and feel guilty. Guilt over inaction has much in common with sympathetic distress, with the primary difference being that in the case of guilt observers are aware of something they could have done but didn't.

Empathy is such an important component of helping behavior that considerable attention has been directed at how it develops or fails to develop. Because identical twins are more similar in empathetic concern than are fraternal twins, the disposition to be empathetic may be partly hereditary. The child's early experiences also play an important role in the development of empathy. For instance, empathy tends to be very low in abused children as well as in those who are spanked a great deal by their parents. On the other hand, children who are high in empathy report receiving more affection from their parents and are more apt to discuss their feelings with their mothers than are children low in empathy. Prosocial behavior is also influenced by the type of play children engage in, with those exhibiting high empathy more likely to have played cooperative games than competitive ones. Furthermore, the motive to help others seems to increase with age, so that adolescents and adults value altruistic behavior more than children do. In part, this may be due to older individuals feeling a greater sense of personal responsibility and knowing what to do in situations of human need (Baron and Byrne, 1984).

Females generally score higher on measures of empathy than males do. For instance, in a recent study relating empathy to practical, everyday moral issues, females were more empathic than males, largely because of the higher levels of affective arousal of distress and perspective taking among females (Shelton and McAdams, 1990). Much of this may reflect the ways women and men are socialized. That is, traditionally women have been brought up with an emphasis on close, nurturing relationships and the expression of emotions, whereas men have been taught to emphasize active mastery of their environment. As a result, women tend to be more skilled in recognizing the nonverbal cues of other's feelings and in expressing their own emotions more freely. Then too, when surveyed, women are more likely than men to describe themselves as empathic. Yet, although women *report* stronger empathic reactions than men do, measures such as heart rate, taken during empathic arousal, do not indicate that women consistently experience more physiological arousal than men do (Berman, 1980). One explanation may be that women are more adept at expressing empathy. In any case, among children in the elementary grades, girls are often perceived as more empathic than boys, though girls are only slightly more altruistic or unselfish in their actual behavior (Shigetomi, Hartmann, and Gelfand, 1981). Thus, when it comes to moral behavior, sex difference in empathy should be considered along with many other factors, such as the particular individual and circumstances involved.

Helping Behavior

It is usually the combination of empathic feelings, the capacity for mutual perspective taking, and the desire to help that leads individuals to engage in helping behaviors. As individuals reach mid to late adolescence, they become more capable of genuine empathy for others as well as understanding people's problems more objectively. However, adolescents do not generally function at this level, largely because of the strong pressures toward social conformity to peers at this age (Selman et al., 1986). Nevertheless, youths may engage in a variety of helping behaviors in their schools, churches, and communities, ranging from one-to-one tutoring projects to social and political activism. Surveys have shown that youths today are more socially concerned than popularly portrayed. For instance, a majority of high school and college students favor strong government intervention in such areas as the control of environmental pollution, energy conservation, national health insurance, and consumer protection (Roark, 1986). Almost half of today's youths report they are concerned about the environment. However, for a generation that has witnessed so much failure in the political system, the majority of youths prefer activities that are more results-oriented and tangible in scope, such as cleaning up a park over a weekend, initiating a recycling campaign in their community, and teaching literacy to underprivileged children (Gross and Scott, 1990).

Nowhere is empathy put to test more than the willingness to intervene on behalf of others in situations of distress. So often we hear on TV that a store clerk was robbed while several customers watched and did nothing. But how typicals are such reactions? In order to find out, Harold Takooshian and Herzel

A VISTA volunteer helps an elderly
woman with home repairs.

Bodinger (1982) asked volunteers from a psychology class to simulate the burglary of a volunteer's parked car. During daylight in full view of passersby in
downtown New York City, the "burglar" would force open the car door with a
coathanger, remove a valuable object, relock the car, and hurry away. The "bur-
glars" felt uneasy throughout the experiment and wanted to quit. But their fears
were soon allayed. The more than three thousand passersby who witnessed 214
"burglaries" often paused to stare and some even offered to help. But only six
people bothered to ask what was happening, and three of them were police
officers. People's reluctance to intervene in such situations has been labeled the
bystander effect.

     Rather than blaming people's indifference, social psychologists tend to
attribute witnesses' inaction to a variety of factors. Bibb Latane and John Darley
(1970), who conducted a series of experiments in this area, have incorporated
their findings in the three-stage decision-making process involved in bystander
intervention. Accordingly, we tend to help those in need only if we (1) *notice* the
incident, (2) *interpret* it as an emergency, and (3) *assume* personal responsibility for
helping. See Figure 12-4. At each stage, the presence of other bystanders tends
to inhibit us from becoming involved, especially in a dangerous situation such as
a mugging. A major explanation is that the presence of others leads to a diffu-
sion of responsibility, so that there is less likelihood of anyone intervening. By

Figure 12-4   Decision-Making Process in Bystander Intervention.

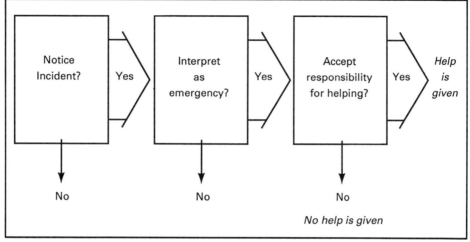

Adapted from B. Latane and J. Darley, *The Unresponsive Bystander: Why Doesn't He Help?* (New York: Prentice-Hall, 1970), p. 43.

contrast, when a lone individual observes a mugging, this person is more apt to feel responsible and come to the aid of the victim.

At the same time many other factors are involved in bystander intervention. For instance, individuals who are easily embarrassed are less likely to risk helping. On the other hand, those with a strong need for approval may be more inclined to help, especially when there is little danger involved and there are witnesses to their good deeds. The willingness to help in dangerous situations generally depends on additional factors, such as feeling competent and knowing what to do in a given situation. For instance, a comparison of individuals who had intervened in actual instances of violent crime and those who failed to intervene disclosed some important differences. Individuals who intervened were more likely to have had training in first aid, life saving, self-defense, and experience in medical or police work. They were also taller and heavier (Huston et al., 1981).

Moral Values

The tendency to act on one's moral understanding in a given situation also depends heavily on the individual's moral values—shared beliefs about what is good and right. Because our values are initially acquired in the home, there is usually a strong relationship between adolescents' values and those of their parents. Partly for the same reason, youths' values remain remarkably stable throughout adolescence. However, the passage through adolescence tends to be accompanied by a decrease in the values of obedience, cheerfulness, and helpfulness associated with childhood morality, and an increase in the sense of achievement, self-respect, broadmindedness, and responsibility associated with the growth of autonomous morality (Dudley and Dudley, 1984).

At the same time, today's younger generation is sometimes criticized for their lack of moral values. Michael Josephson, founder of the Institute for the Advancement of Ethics, observes that many youths lack the bedrock values of honesty, respect for others, and responsibility for civic duty. He characterizes them as the "I deserve it" (IDIs, pronounced *iddies*) generation, believing that getting what one wants is an inalienable right. Yet he is quick to point out that youths are not getting their values from the air. Nor does he believe that parents are failing to teach values. Parents *are* teaching values, but the wrong values, often by default. Growing up in an era of social upheaval, today's parents are uncertain about how they're supposed to act. Furthermore, parents who use drugs, scoff at monogamy, and disdain patriotism feel hypocritical about urging traditional values on their children. It is not surprising that so many youths lack firm moral values (O'Reilly, 1990).

Then too, as youths struggle with such issues as premarital sex and the use of alcohol and drugs, they often experience considerable inconsistency between their values and behaviors. A major reason is that at this stage of development, adolescents' values are still shaped more strongly by parental influences, although their behavior tends to be influenced more by peer influence (DeVaus, 1983). As a result, adolescents tend to experience a considerable degree of value-behavior inconsistency, being torn between values acquired at home and behavior more acceptable to their peers. Another source of value conflict is the discrepancy between an adolescent's existing moral values and the need to respond to new life situations, reflecting the impact of social change. The upheaval in values during the seventies and eighties brought about an emphasis on expressive, self-fulfillment values, such as personal freedom and growth. Yet the nineties are characterized by economic uncertainty, heightened competition, and political unrest in many parts of the world. It is not that self-fulfilment values are being surrendered. But they are being modified by a new realism as well as a greater concern with relationships and commitments that bring enduring satisfaction within the larger community.

Still another source of value conflicts is the relativity of values which characterizes many aspects of American society. Perceiving all values as relativistic, many youths and adults alike are inclined to adopt the view that anyone has the right to his or her own beliefs and values over and against those realms of authority where a more definite sense of right and wrong still prevails, such as the church. Ironically, this is one of the criticisms aimed at the values clarification approach, namely that even though it raises people's consciousness of their values it does so in a highly relative and individualistic way.

Fortunately, many youths feel the need for assistance in developing their values. An extensive survey of high school and college students showed that three-fourths of them felt that the family, school, clergy, and other individuals should be involved in the development of moral values to some degree (Zern, 1985). Generally, the family was regarded as the primary influence for elementary-aged children, with the family and other individuals sharing influence among adolescents in secondary school, and other individuals more influential at the college level. All groups see the school and clergy as having substantial influence but as being of lesser importance than the family and other individuals. College students in particular regard authorities such as the family, school, and clergy as less important than other individuals such as peers at this stage in life. One of the most helpful ways of assisting youths to develop their moral values is the moral-dilemma discussion method. In this approach, students are confronted with a situation involving a moral dilemma. An example might be the physician who is torn between the responsibility of preserving life and honoring the wishes of a family to disconnect the lifesupport equipment of their comatose son, when their son had never indicated his preferences in this matter. Then through a process of questions and discussion, individuals are encouraged to develop their own responses to the persons and issues involved. Students in these programs learn to think in a more complex manner, to see important issues from different points of views, and generally formulate a more coherent set of moral values (Schlaefli, Rest, and Thomas, 1985).

RELIGION

Traditionally, churches and synagogues, along with the family, have played a major role in the teaching of moral standards and values to young people. The more important religion is to the particular family and individual, the more likely it is that religion will become a significant factor in the young person's moral development. However, with the emergence of formal thinking and greater autonomy during adolescence, even religious youths tend to go through a stage of questioning their faith, accompanied by a decrease in church attendance. During this period, youths characteristically maintain an intense interest in religious matters. According to surveys, more than nine out of ten teenagers believe in God, with almost as many practicing some form of prayer or meditation. Compared to youth in the past, young people are somewhat more conservative in their religion. Almost half the Protestant teenagers and one-fifth of Catholic youth have had a religious conversion experience. At the same time, today's youths are placing more emphasis on personal and non-traditional religion. As a result, even though religious attitudes and beliefs tend to remain strong throughout the college years for many youths, there is a characteristic decline in church attendance. One study found that a smaller proportion of college seniors than first-year students attended church once a week, with a larger proportion of seniors attending church once or twice a month or not at all (McAllister, 1985).

Much depends on the particular individual and his or her religious development. We'll begin with a description of the typical developmental sequence of religious growth, including the distinction between extrinsic and intrinsic religious orientation. We'll also discuss the importance of religious cults among youths. Finally, we'll point out some of the relationships between religion and moral behavior.

The Developmental Sequence

Mary Jo Meadow and Richard Kahoe (1984) have proposed a developmental model of religious growth that incorporates many of the established principles and findings in this field. They suggest that the individual's religious development typically begins near the extrinsic pole in their model and progresses in a counterclockwise fashion toward an intrinsic religious orientation. (See Figure 12-5.) Not all religious persons experience the entire developmental sequence, as in other developmental models. But this is the general path they travel.

Psychologically significant religion, as opposed to empty habits, typically begins at the *extrinsic pole*. People with this orientation are inclined to use religion for their own ends, with religious beliefs and practices being motivated primarily by any number of human needs, such as insecurities, fears, and guilt. Examples would be the teenager who feels happier and more at peace with herself after she meditates, and the salesman who claims he can sell more cars after beginning the day with prayer. For some people, religion remains on a self-serving, extrinsic basis. But for many people—if not most—an extrinsic religious orientation becomes modified through affiliation with some type of organized religion.

Religiously oriented people characteristically identify with a religious institution or system, at least early in their religious development. *Religious observance* refers to a variety of religious matters, such as membership in a group, authority, beliefs, practices, ceremonies, and rituals. All of these aspects of organized religion are probably interrelated and may occur simultaneously, though some tend to occur before others. For instance, social belongingness usually occurs early, with the internalization of beliefs coming later. The shift toward

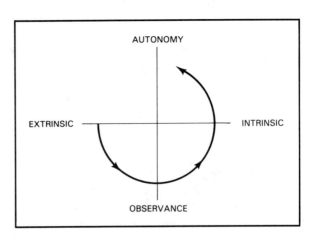

Figure 12-5 The Developmental Sequence of Personal Religiousness.

Source: From Richard D. Kahoe and Mary Jo Meadow, "A Developmental Perspective on Religious Orientation Dimensions," *Journal of Religion and Health* 20 (1981): pp. 8–17. © 1981 Human Sciences Press, Inc. In M. J. Meadow and R. D. Kahoe, *Psychology of Religion* (New York: Harper & Row, 1984), p. 321.

institutional participation requires the member or believer to turn away from purely self-serving, extrinsic religion toward causes and tasks greater than the self. However, the shift is usually relative. That is, since most people maintain many of their extrinsic motives, religious institutions cultivate loyalty by directing attention and services to individual needs. Thus, church social activities may reduce a new member's this-world loneliness while also helping to form an attachment to the church. Examples of individuals in the observance stage would be young people who join a church after attending a year long confirmation class or those who join a cult after a religious conversion experience.

The tendency to turn away from self, which is set in motion by institutional religion, is developed further in *intrinsic religiousness*. At this stage, individuals endeavor to internalize and follow religious beliefs, that is, they *live* their religion. These are the "true believers." In contrast to individuals with an extrinsic religious orientation, those with an intrinsic orientation are more likely to have an internal sense of control over their lives, greater sense of personal responsibility, less prejudice, and engage in a variety of helping behaviors (Meadow and Kahoe, 1984). Furthermore, individuals with an intrinsic religious orientation are more likely than those with an extrinsic orientation to keep active in a religious organization during college (Woodroof, 1985). Although intrinsic religion tends to grow out of the religion of observance, many people fail to achieve any great degree of intrinsic faith. In some instances, institutional leaders fail to promote intrinsic religiousness. But in other instances, individuals simply lack the personal maturity to make the transition. Most people who develop an intrinsic religious orientation also keep strong ties with organized religion, especially among mainstream religious groups. An example would be the college senior who is not only active in her own church but is also involved in campuswide humanitarian causes and is concerned about human need in other countries.

Autonomous religiousness is a step beyond an intrinsic faith and represents the most mature stage of personal religious development. Individuals who have reached this level of religious development exhibit a more advanced religious orientation characterized by greater independence of thought and practice and concern for others than that of people in earlier stages. Whereas most higher religions advocate intrinsic religion, they seldom promote a thoroughly autonomous faith because such independence of thought and behavior is generally against the vested interests of organized religion. Other forces also work against the development of autonomous religion. People who need the social support or sense of security of traditional religion may resist movement toward autonomous religion. Also, many individuals isolate religious experience, so that their faith remains less mature than other aspects of their development. In most cases, a strong personal inclination leads the occasional person to religious autonomy despite institutional discouragement. This might be an individual who is highly intelligent or educated, especially one with training in the reflective disciplines like philosophy or with a pronounced mystical outlook. An example would be a graduate student in philosophy, who, while struggling with existential questions in all their complexity, sees religion more as an open-ended quest than a system of answers (Batson and Ventis, 1982).

These stages of religious development are not tied to specific ages but probably parallel in large measure other developmental processes, such as Kohlberg's stages of moral reasoning. Thus, the extrinsic orientation generally reflects Kohlberg's level of preconventional moral reasoning, that is, the heteronomous morality of Stage 1 or the self-serving outlook of Stage 2. Involvement in organized religion reflects more conventional moral reasoning, with the social aspect that accompanies religious observances associated with the interpersonal orientation of Kohlberg's Stage 3 and the emphasis on doctrine and church law parallel to the emphasis on authority and fixed rules in Stage 4. The development of intrinsic religion tends to parallel the attainment of the social contract orientation in Stage 5 of Kohlberg's sequence. Finally, autonomous religiousness parallels Kohlberg's Stage 6 of universal ethical principles. However, just as few individuals reach Kohlberg's fifth and sixth stages of postconventional moral reasoning, so relatively few individuals, much less adolescents, achieve an intrinsic religious orientation, and even fewer an autonomous religion.

Cults

Religious cults have achieved widespread attention in recent years because they have played a more prominent role in the religious development of a substantial minority of youth than in the past. Membership in these groups is estimated to be

More young people are becoming active in nontraditional religious groups. (Charles Gatewood)

at least 2 or 3 million people in the United States. Among the groups that receive the most public attention are the Unification Church (Moonies), the Divine Light Mission of Maharaj Ji, the Institute of Krishna Consciousness, the Children of God, and the Church of Scientology (*U.S. News and World Report*, 1982).

Religious cults vary widely in their structure and orientation. Some of these groups tend to be rather informal and loosely organized and are characterized by a disillusionment with materialistic society and a concern for helping people. But an ever larger number of cults tend to be highly authoritarian and require individuals to surrender their autonomy and conform completely to the dictates of the leader. New converts are often subjected to brainwashing techniques, in which they are stripped of their previous identities, programmed with cult beliefs and practices, and made heavily dependent on the leader and the group. In some instances, individuals become converts gradually, even inadvertently, through being responsive to offers of warm, social relationships, especially during personal crises. Most groups incorporate new members through a combination of indoctrination, mind-control techniques, and an extensive system of socialization practices (Long and Hadden, 1983).

Young people may be attracted to religious cults for a variety of reasons, with such youths exhibiting one or more of the following conditions and characteristics (Swope, 1980; Dean, 1982):

1. *Insecurity.* The adolescent reared in an affluent, permissive family who remains beset by uncertainties may be a prime target for the clearly defined limits and authority of cults.
2. *Inquisitiveness.* Intellectually curious youths who are questioning old beliefs and seeking meaning to their lives may be attracted to new ideas and groups, especially when approached by attractive, enthusiastic recruiters.
3. *Idealism.* Cults also exploit youthful idealism by convincing prospective members that society's ills can be solved only through the group's particular approach.
4. *Loneliness.* Young people on their own away from home who lack close friends and support groups may be especially receptive to invitations of friendship and free meals.
5. *Disillusionment.* Many converts to cults have become disillusioned with their lives, whether in reaction to heavy addiction to alcohol or drugs, sexual experimentation, or the pressures for success.
6. *Identity crises.* Severely anxious or confused youth may be attracted to cults as a way of finding their identity in a rapidly changing society that often appears to be excessively competitive and impersonal.
7. *Naiveté.* Lonely, overprotected youths who have been reared to trust others, especially their religious leaders, are easy targets for people offering friendship and guidance.

Interestingly, the majority of young people who join cults are white, single, and middle class. Membership in such groups usually brings them a sense of less confusion in their lives, often accompanied by the avoidance of alcohol, drugs, or permissive sex. Such youths may welcome the structured environment with its ready-made beliefs and friendships. At the same time, because cults usually provide a safe, regulated environment that relieves individuals of the responsibilities of making personal decisions, membership in these groups tends to undermine healthy personal and religious development.

Critics of cults claim that members have been so radically and permanently transformed that some type of deprogramming is needed to sever ties with the cult. As one ex-cult member said, "Everything that happens is exactly parallel to what a POW experiences, and for a certain amount of time, I feel I did not have my free will" (Wright, 1984). Consequently, in their attempts to reorient former cult members, many deprogramming groups feel justified in using similar tactics of kidnapping, isolation, and intensive teaching sessions, though such practices have been criticized because they violate the civil rights of former cult members. However, most deprogramming is voluntary and consists of an intensive teaching and counseling process, in which the individual is encouraged to think, ask questions, critically evaluate his or her beliefs and practices, and make decisions. Deprogramming can last from a few hours to several weeks, though the rehabilitation process may continue for several months, usually within the home of the ex-cult member. Sometimes going shopping with an ex-cult member may take an entire afternoon, mostly because the person hasn't been making personal decisions for several years (Sifford, 1983).

At the same time, studies of young people who have voluntarily defected from cults have shown that many of them willingly participated in cults. Only a minority of voluntary defectors reported that they had been duped or brainwashed. As one voluntary defector said, "I'm not angry, you know, because it was of my own volition that I was there and I could have just walked out anytime" (Wright, 1984). Voluntary defectors explained their involvement in terms of sophisticated techniques of mind control and a combination of physical and psychological deprivations. Unlike ex-cult members who were involuntarily removed from cults, these members usually saw some redeeming value in their experience. At the same time, most of them perceived their original choice, in retrospect, as a mistake (Wright, 1984). At first, many ex-cult members are furious. They want to return to the cult and get their friends out. But after counseling and rehabilitation, many of them attain a level of achievement and personal growth that is above average compared to the general population. Eventually, most of them marry and have families (Sifford, 1983).

Religion and Moral Behavior

It might seem logical to assume that religious youth have more stringent moral standards and are less likely to cheat on tests and use illicit drugs. But is there any truth to this view? Apparently so, but a lot depends on the specific behavior and circumstances. The national survey on morality cited earlier (Hassett, 1981) showed there was a significant relationship between people's religiosity and their moral behavior. As a matter of fact, the respondents' self-ratings of their religiousness turned out to be one of the single best predictors of moral standards

Youths with a personal faith are often motivated to help others. (Courtesy of MDA)

and behavior. Moderately religious people scored significantly higher on the scale of morality than did less committed people, and very religious people scored significantly higher than did the moderate group. But the relationship between religiosity and morality was much stronger for institutional behavior than for personal issues. That is, religious people were much less likely to cheat on tests or income taxes, take home office supplies, or use a business phone for personal calls than were other people. But they were only slightly less likely to tell little white lies, deceive their best friends, or cut into line ahead of people. At the same time, religious youths did report stricter moral standards; they were much less likely to be influenced by the fear of getting caught compared to less religious people, who were more apt to say they would try to get away with what they could.

　　Other studies have shown varying degrees of relationships between such items as religious orientation and church attendance and moral attitudes and behavior. Using a random sample of 600 adolescents in grades 9 to 12, Hadaway, Elifson, and Peterson (1984) found a moderately strong relationship between religion and the use of drugs. The more important religion was to the individuals and the more active they were in organized religion, the lower their levels of alcohol consumption and drug use. However, the association was stronger between religion and the use of illicit drugs than for alcohol, probably because of the greater social acceptance of alcohol. Also, the importance of religion was more influential than church attendance itself on moral attitudes and behavior. At the same, other studies using this same sample found little or no relationship between religious orientation and aggressive behavior, theft, and truancy (Elifson, Petersen, and Hadaway, 1983). Another study of first-year college students by Woodroof (1985) found a marked relationship between religious orientation and involvement and premarital sexual activity. The more religious youths were and the more frequently they attended church, the less sexually active they were—casually or otherwise. Also, the maintenance of virginity was considerably higher among those who were very religious than among those who attended church once a week or less.

The relationship between religion and helping behavior is more complex. On the one hand, in a study using a random sample of five hundred high school students, Howard Bahr and Thomas Martin (1983) found a significant positive association between respondents' church attendance and their faith in people. Subjects who attended church regularly were much less likely to agree with such statements as "Most people can't be trusted" or "Most people don't really care what happens to the next person." However, because there is also a strong association between higher socioeconomic status and faith in people, it is not clear whether religion inclines youth to have greater faith in people or whether youths from higher socioeconomic groups are more apt to attend church and thus express greater faith in people.

Sometimes studies on the relationship between religion and helping behavior yield even more mixed results. In a review of the literature in this field, Daniel Batson and Larry Ventis (1982) found a difference in the methods used in experimental studies, especially between the use of self-ratings and behavioral measures. Studies using self-ratings of religiosity and helping behavior (as in Hassett's survey cited earlier) and rating by someone else, showed a positive, though weak, association between religious involvement and helping behavior such as coming to the aid of a stranded motorist. However, as the authors point out, such studies are more likely to be contaminated by social desirability. For instance, people who are rated as more likable and sociable tend also to be rated as more helpful, even when they are not. In contrast, none of the studies relying primarily on behavioral measures suggested that religious people are more helpful than others. Thus, more religious youth may hold more stringent moral attitudes and standards and may see themselves as more helpful and caring than others and may be so regarded by others. But when it comes to action, there is no convincing evidence that religious youth are more consistently compassionate toward others. At the same time, the further along the developmental sequence of religious growth individuals have come, especially the intrinsic and autonomous religious orientation, the more likely they are to practice their faith.

SUMMARY

The Development of Moral Reasoning

1. According to Kohlberg's theory of moral development, children and adolescents progress through a sequence of stages of moral reasoning that parallels their cognitive development.

2. Kohlberg has identified six successive stages of moral reasoning divided into three major levels—preconventional, conventional, and postconventional—with the highest level of moral judgment presupposing the attainment of formal thought.

3. During mid- to late adolescence, there is a marked rise in the proportion of individuals exhibiting conventional moral reasoning, with a slower but steady rise in the number of youths with Stage 4 thought reflecting the general rules of laws of society.

4. Kohlberg's theory has been criticized on a number of grounds, such as that relatively few people ever attain the highest stages of moral reasoning, and that it puts undue emphasis on abstract reasoning compared to the interpersonal aspects of moral development.

Moral Behavior

5. The extent to which individuals act on their moral reasoning depends on a variety of factors, such as the existence of internalized moral standards and feelings, the immediate situation, empathetic arousal, and moral values.

6. Unethical behavior such as classroom cheating is fairly widespread among youth, though such behavior tends to be less evident among those with a strong concern for obeying their internalized moral standards.

7. Prosocial behavior depends on the arousal of empathy, with the capacity for mature empathic arousal emerging during adolescence.

8. The willingness to help people in need generally requires that individuals notice their plight, interpret it as an emergency, and take responsibility for helping those in need.

9. When adolescents struggle with such issues as premarital sex and the use of alcohol and drugs, they experience a certain degree of value-behavior inconsistency, partly because of the tension between parental and peer influences and the relativity of values in American society.

10. Youths may strengthen their moral values through the moral-dilemma approach, which challenges them to think about life situations and moral issues in a more complex manner.

Religion

11. Traditionally, the churches and synagogues have played a major role in the transmission of moral standards, though many of today's youth place more emphasis on personal than institutional religion.

12. Religious development typically begins with an extrinsic religious orientation and generally progresses toward affiliation with organizational religion, with relatively fewer individuals acquiring an intrinsic religious orientation characterized by a devotion to causes and ideals beyond themselves.

13. Although religious cults have attracted a substantial minority of youth in recent years, they tend to undermine religious development because cults relieve youths of the necessity of making personal decisions.

14. Religious youths, especially those with an intrinsic orientation, tend to hold more stringent moral attitudes and standards than do nonreligious youths, though they are not necessarily more likely to engage in helping behaviors than are other youths.

REVIEW QUESTIONS

1. To what extent does Kohlberg's view of moral reasoning depend on Piaget's theory of cognitive development?
2. What is the basis of right and wrong in each of Kohlberg's three levels of moral reasoning?
3. What proportion of late adolescents have reached the conventional stage of moral reasoning?
4. What are some of the pros and cons of Kohlberg's theory of moral development?
5. What are some of the factors associated with classroom cheating and resistance to such behavior?
6. Which types of adolescents are more likely to engage in helping behaviors as they reach late adolescence?
7. How important is the experience of value-behavior inconsistency in adolescence?
8. Which stage of religious development are most adolescents in?
9. What are some of the reasons youths join religious cults?
10. To what extent do religious youths behave more morally than do nonreligious youths?

Delinquency

13

Did you ever engage in shoplifting, petty vandalism, or underage drinking when you were a teenager? If so, you were engaging in typical adolescent behavior. Studies of self-reported delinquency have shown that more than three-fourths of Americans admit to commiting one or more delinquent acts during the relatively short period of their adolescence. Most of these acts are minor infractions of the law, such as vandalism. At the same time, youths are responsible for a significant proportion of serious offenses such as arson and burglary. Strictly speaking, youthful offenders are not legally classified as "delinquent" until they have been arrested, taken to juvenile court, and labeled as such by the court. But because many more adolescents are arrested than the number who appear in juvenile court, the term *delinquency* is generally used in a broader sense. Thus, juvenile delinquency usually refers to any legally deviant behavior on the part of people under the legal age, which is set somewhere between 16 and 18 in most states, whether processed by the juvenile court or not. Consequently, throughout this chapter we will be dealing with delinquency in both senses of the term, including the broad range of behaviors resulting in juvenile arrests as well as the smaller number of more serious offenses that are taken to court.

THE EXTENT OF DELINQUENCY

Of the almost 12 million people who are arrested for all criminal activities except traffic violations in a given year, a significant proportion of them are youths. Approximately one out of six of them are under 18 years of age, one out of three of them are under 21, and one out of two of them are under 25. Teenagers under 18 commit about one-third of all acts of arson, burglary, theft, and motor vehicle theft. Youth under 25 account for two-thirds of the same crimes, plus almost one-half of violent crimes such as aggravated assault, rape, and murder (Uniform Crime Reports, 1989). See Figure 13-1.

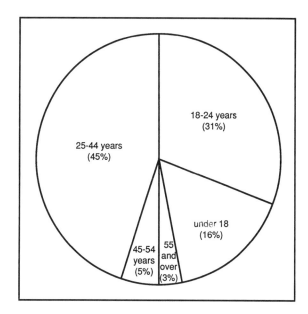

**Figure 13-1   Percentage of All People
Arrested According to Age**

Source: U.S. Bureau of the Census, *Statistical
Abstract of the United States, 1990*, 110th ed.
(Washington, D.C.: U.S. Government Printing
Office, 1990), p. 177.

Age Trends

Much of the delinquency in early adolescence involves relatively minor offenses,
such as drinking beer, smoking marijuana, petty thefts, and vandalism. But the
frequency and seriousness of delinquent behavior rises with age. For the relatively minor offenses such as vandalism, delinquency increases from late childhood throughout adolescence and then levels off somewhat in early adulthood
before subsiding. More serious offenses, such as rape, murder, and manslaughter, continue to accelerate into early adulthood.

There are also significant differences in delinquent activities among the
various age groups. Youths under 15 years of age typically engage in a great deal
of nuisance behavior, such as curfew violations, vandalism, and burglary. At the
same time, early adolescents account for almost one-third of all arson cases.
Adolescents under 18 commit a significant proportion of liquor law and drug
abuse violations, sexual offenses, and vandalism. Youths this age also get more
involved in serious offenses, such as weapons violations, burglary, and theft.
About four out of ten motor vehicle thefts are committed by youths in this age
group. Older youths under 21 are more heavily involved in drug and liquor law
violations, disorderly conduct, and sexual offenses. Youths under 21 account for
about one-half of burglaries, robberies, and thefts. In addition, they commit
almost one-third of all homicides and rapes (Uniform Crime Reports, 1989). See
Table 13-1.

At the same time, there is a changing patterns of arrests, mostly because

Table 13-1 Percent of All Arrests By Persons Under 15, 18, 21, and 25 Years of Age

	Under 15	Under 18	Under 21	Under 25
Murder	1.6	12.3	30.5	48.7
Rape	5.6	15.4	27.8	43.6
Robbery	6.6	23.0	41.2	59.7
Assault	4.0	13.3	25.4	41.3
Burglary	12.6	31.9	50.0	64.7
Larceny-theft	12.9	28.7	42.6	55.2
Motor vehicle theft	11.2	40.9	59.6	73.1
Arson	29.7	43.4	53.6	63.9
Total	10.5	26.1	41.3	56.2

Adapted from data in the U.S. Department of Justice, Federal Bureau of Investigation, *Uniform Crime Reports for the United States, 1989* (Washington, D.C.: Government Printing Office, 1989), p. 188.

of shifts in the population. There is now a decline in arrests of youths under 18 years of age, along with an increase of arrests among those over 25 years of age. Authorities believe this can be accounted for mostly by the aging of the baby boomers, resulting in a smaller proportion of youths in the traditionally high-crime group of 14 to 24 years of age.

Are adolescents who are arrested more likely to engage in crime when they become adults? Not necessarily. A lot depends on how early they become involved in delinquency, how serious their offenses are, and how often they are arrested. The earlier the age of delinquency, the more serious the offenses, the greater the number of subsequent arrests, and the more the criminal behavior involves a delinquent peer group, the more likely the individual will be to continue criminal activities as an adult. Also, the more delinquent behavior involves an antisocial pattern, such as disregard for the rights of others and failure to learn from experience, the greater the likelihood that criminal activity will continue into adulthood. In fact, evidence of antisocial tendencies is the single best predictor of a career in crime. However, the great majority of youths who engage in occasional acts of delinquency do not go on to adult crime.

Types of Offenses

Although youths in the 15–24-year-old group represent only 15 percent of the general population, they commit about one-half of all robberies, two-thirds of all cases of arson and burglary, and three-fourths of all motor vehicle thefts.

The biggest single category of offenses committed by young people comprises crimes against property. Youthful offenders under 25 account for two-thirds of all arson, burglary, motor vehicle thefts, dealing in stolen property, and vandalism. Although they commit a smaller proportion of the crimes against people, they account for about half of aggravated assaults, rape, and murder, including non-negligent manslaughter. The second biggest category of offenses committed by youth is that of the so-called victimless crimes, including drunkenness, disorderly conduct, gambling, and liquor law and drug abuse violation. See Table 13-2.

At least one-third of all delinquencies referred to juvenile court involve status offenses. These include a variety of behaviors, such as curfew violations, running away from home, truancy, incorrigible behavior, and sexual offenses. Because many of these behaviors reflect family problems rather than criminal acts, legislation in recent years has stipulated that such problems should not be the responsibility of already overburdened police departments. Also, because of their age and vulnerability, status offenders should be kept in separate physical facilities from other delinquents and adult offenders. Furthermore, status of-

Table 13-2   Number of Arrests According to Type of Crime, Age, and Sex, 1989

Offense	Males under 18	Females under 18
Crime Index		
Larceny (theft)	263,542	96,190
Burglary (breaking or entering)	104,711	9,043
Motor vehicle theft	67,118	7,611
Aggravated assault	40,050	6,959
Robbery	28,211	2,599
Forcible rape	4,599	107
Murder	2,069	139
Arson	5,738	622
Violent crimes	74,929	9,803
Property crimes	441,109	113,466
All Other Crimes		
Drug abuse violations	79,654	10,355
Liquor law violations	84,526	32,591
Disorderly conduct	80,228	19,753
Vandalism	88,754	8,732
Other assaults	87,015	25,680
Fraud	6,577	2,761
Stolen property	32,204	3,203
Weapons (carrying, possessing)	29,500	2,077
Forgery and counterfeiting	4,265	1,949
Embezzlement	601	513
Prostitution	522	778
Sex offenses (except rape and prostitution)	12,622	973
Offenses against family and children	1,416	817
Driving under the influence	13,371	2,135
Gambling	899	54
Drunkenness	14,693	2,907
Vagrancy	1,980	350
Curfew violations	48,343	16,749
Runaways	57,296	72,976
Suspicion	1,934	476
All other offense (except traffic)	200,376	52,906
Total of all crimes	1,362,814	382,004

Source: U.S. Department of Justice, Federal Bureau of Investigation, *Uniform Crime Reports for the United States*, 1989 (Washington, D.C.: Government Printing Officer, 1989), pp. 184, 186.

fenders should be given the support services that will enable them to return to a viable home environment as soon as possible. However, the actual procedures used with status offenders vary considerably from one part of the country to another, with status offenders still being kept in detention centers with serious juvenile offenders in many places.

This new approach to status offenses can be seen in regard to running away from home, which is increasingly viewed as a social problem. Older children and early adolescents are running away from home at earlier ages than in the past, with a peak incidence in runaways at 14 to 16 years of age. Girls are somewhat more likely than boys to run away from home, with girls accounting for almost six out of ten runaways. Also, it is estimated that there are several times as many actual runaways as those recorded in the official figures. One reason so few runaways appear in the statistics is that many of them run off to the home of a nearby friend or relative. Most stay within the community and return within four days.

Runaways may leave home for different reasons, as seen in Roberts's (1982) typology of runaways. Roberts arranges the various types of runaways along a continuum according to the degree of parent-adolescent conflict involved. Toward the left end of the continuum representing a low degree of parent-adolescent conflict are the *runaway explorers,* who leave home for adventure and to assert their independence. They usually leave a note informing their parents where they are going and return home on their own. In the same category are the *social pleasure seekers,* who after disagreeing with their parents on an important issue generally sneak out of the house to engage in some forbidden activity and then return home.

Runaway manipulators generally experience more serious conflict with their parents and attempt to manipulate their parents by running away and returning only on their own terms. *Runaway retreatists* come from homes with even more tension, including frequent yelling and hitting. Many of these adolescents have problems at school as well as at home and have retreated into drugs or getting drunk daily before leaving home.

Adolescents labeled *endangered runaways* are placed at the right end of the continuum because they come from homes with a maximum degree of parent-adolescent conflict as well as problem parents. These adolescents are sometimes called "throwaways," because they are either told to leave or become victims of sexual abuse or violence who feel they have no alternative but to leave. It has been estimated that throwaways account for as many as 30 to 60 percent of all runaways.

Runaways who are arrested or taken to juvenile court may feel frightened and defiant. But those who wander into the streets of the large cities may fare even more badly, with drug addiction and prostitution being a common fate for runaway girls. On the other hand, youth who are fortunate enough to find help in a temporary shelter for runaways, especially those with a network of support services, may find the assistance necessary to cope with their home situation. For example, when Cheryl's parents divorced, she went to live with her mother, who remarried a year later. When Cheryl, now a 16 year old, disagreed with her stepfather about the family rules, Cheryl's mother usually sided with her new husband. Feeling betrayed, Cheryl began staying out later, spending more time away from home, and engaging in rebellious behaviors. Finally, after an argument with her mother, Cheryl ran away with her boyfriend. But two weeks later, after a fight with her boyfriend, Cheryl sought refuge in a shelter for runaways. There she began talking about her problems at home. With the help of the counselor, Cheryl contacted her parents and agreed to return home on the condition that all of them enter family therapy.

Sex Differences

Although males continue to commit delinquent acts more frequently than do females, the gap between the sexes is narrowing. The male-female ratio of reported delinquency, which remained at 4 or 5 to 1 for many years, is now about 3½ to 1 for serious crimes. The male-female ratio of self-reported delinquency is even closer. However, the ratio between the sexes varies considerably according

Females are involved in a wider range of offenses than in the past. (Ken Karp)

to the types of offenses. Males are much more likely than females to commit violent crimes, such as aggravated assault, forcible rape, and murder. But there is less difference between the sexes in regard to status offenses and property crimes, with the greatest comparability occurring in embezzlement. Female arrests actually exceed male arrests in several status offenses, notably runaways and prostitution (*Uniform Crime Reports*, 1989).

At the same time, there are some significant, though often less noticeable, changes between the sexes occurring in regard to delinquency. First, females are involved in a wider range of offenses than in the past, with fewer differences between the sexes. Actually, female arrests are increasing at a faster *rate* in regard to some offenses, especially rape, motor vehicle thefts, weapons violations, embezzlement, liquor law violations, and sex offenses. Second, females are more active in delinquency in the under-15 age bracket than at older ages. Early-adolescent females are especially likely to engage in aggravated assaults, larceny, and murder. As Hershel Thornburg (1986) notes, this increase in delinquency among early adolescent girls is not a chance occurrence. It probably represents (1) an increasing proportion of girls who want to assume a more active female sex role and now see the opportunity to do so; (2) a growing number of girls in a transitional stage between the stereotyped traditional sex role and an emerging more active female role; and (3) girls who are simply unable to live up to role expectations at home, school, and among their peers. Third, while girls are somewhat less likely than boys to be arrested for delinquent acts, they are often treated more harshly than boys. Traditionally, girls are more apt to be turned over to authorities by their parents than arrested by police. Once in the juvenile justice system, though, girls are more likely to be institutionalized, for longer terms, and at earlier ages. Yet, compared to boys, girls tend to come from more socially disorganized families, and be less severely delinquent and less likely to become repeaters. A major reason for such discrimination is that deviant, aggressive behavior is much less acceptable among girls than among boys in our society (Rutter and Giller, 1983; Westendorp et al., 1986). Perhaps with changing sex-role expectations, females may be arrested more readily and treated more fairly in the juvenile justice system.

CONTRIBUTING FACTORS

The rapid rise in delinquency during adolescence is sometimes attributed to the onset of puberty. Yet early developers are no more delinquent at that time than those who mature later. Also, even though girls reach puberty earlier than boys on the average, the delinquency behavior of adolescent girls increases at the same time as boys. Furthermore, the relationship between age and delinquency becomes negligible when variables other than sexual development are considered. Such findings suggest that delinquency probably has more to do with the psychological and social processes of role taking and identity formation, especially negative identity, that take place during puberty, such that delinquency is intimately associated with the cultural process of adolescence itself.

All things considered, the causes of delinquency are so complex and interwoven, and thus poorly understood, that we discuss them in the context of the various contributing factors to delinquency. The list of potential contributing factors to delinquency would include such things as the rapid rate of social change in American society, social and economic inequities, the mobility of families that uproots teenagers from their schools and peers, the increase in dual income families, the importance of peer groups during adolescence, and changing sex roles. In this section, we focus on several of the major factors, such as the family, socioeconomic factors, personality, psychopathology, and drug abuse.

The Family

Youths who are arrested for delinquent behavior tend to come from families with inadequate child-rearing or socialization practices, poor adolescent-parent relationships, and little family cohesiveness.

Parents of delinquent youths tend to be ill-informed or inept in regard to rearing children to become self-respecting, law-abiding individuals. Such parents tend to rely on discipline that is too harsh, too lenient, or extremely inconsistent. They're especially apt to use physical punishment without any accompanying explanation. In their work with families of delinquent youth, Snyder and Patterson (1987) have identified four aspects of family life that are strongly associated with delinquency. First, there is a lack of "house rules," with no predictable family routines or expectations about what adolescents may or may not do. Second, there is a lack of parental supervision, so that parents don't know what adolescents are doing or feeling and tend not to respond to deviant behavior because they haven't seen it. Third, there is a lack of effective contingencies, or a system of rewards and punishment. Parents of delinquent youths are not consistent in their responses to unacceptable behavior. They tend to nag and shout but do not follow through. They also tend to punish undesirable behavior more than they reward desirable behavior. Finally, there are no effective strategies for dealing with family problems and crises. As a result, conflicts lead to tension and dispute but do not get resolved.

One of the single best predictors of delinquency is the lack of affectional ties between adolescents and their parents. Generally, the better young people get along with their parents the less likely they will engage in delinquent behavior. And conversely, the worse youth get along with their parents, the more likely they will eventually commit delinquent acts. Delinquents of both sexes tend to experience more parental indifference and rejection than do nondelinquent youth, resulting in more mutual hostility between themselves and their parents. In a series of longitudinal studies, Stott (1982) found that the breach of affectional ties between parents and their adolescents was a major factor in more than nine out of ten delinquent acts. Delinquent youth usually have been threatened with rejection or have lost the support of their preferred parent. Mothers are not seen as a dependable source of affection. Feeling rejected, these youths had little or no incentive to avoid parental punishment.

Delinquent youths are also more likely to come from homes lacking in family cohesiveness. An obvious example would be delinquent youths from families broken by parental separation, divorce, or the death of a parent. But in actuality, a lot depends on the age and sex of the adolescent as well as on which parent is absent from the home. One study found that whether an adolescent engages in delinquency or not depends more on the adolescent-mother relationship among boys and girls under 14 years of age, and more on the adolescent-father relationship among older adolescents. It appears that the father's influence assumes greater importance as young people mature and take on new roles in the larger community. Yet the absence of the father generally has greater impact on boys than on girls, with boys from father-absent homes much more likely to engage in delinquent behavior than girls from the same homes or boys in father-present homes (Stern, Northman, and Van Slyck, 1984).

It is also important not to equate the lack of family cohesiveness with the absence of a parent through marital separation, divorce, or death. A great deal depends on the adolescent-parent relationships, childrearing practices, and emotional climate within the home. There is increasing recognition that the presence of emotional turbulence and family dissension in the home does more harm to the adolescent's emotional and psychological development than the physical separation of the parents through divorce. However, because families that eventually divorce tend to have a higher-than-average level of dissension as much as six years prior to separation and divorce, it is often difficult, if not impossible, to disentangle the effects of emotional turbulence from legal separation and divorce. In some instances, an equally high or higher number of delinquents come from intact homes characterized by parental indifference, dissension, and mutual hostility, than from homes broken by divorce or death. In contrast, the absence of these factors in many single-parent homes sometimes results in greater family cohesiveness.

Inclination

I have read somewhere that children between twelve and fourteen years of age . . . are especially apt to become murderers or incendiaries. When I recall my own adolescence (and the state of mind I was in one day) I can understand the incentive to the most dreadful crimes committed without aim or purpose, without any precise desire to harm others—done simply out of curiosity, out of an unconscious need of action. There are moments when the future looks so gloomy that one fears to look forward to it.

Leo Tolstoy, *Childhood, Boyhood, Youth* (New York: John Wiley, 1904).

Socioeconomic and Racial Factors

The highest rates of delinquency, especialy for serious offenses, continue to be found among socioeconomically disadvantaged youth in the heavily populated areas of the large cities (Haskell and Yablonsky, 1982). Their families are characterized by low education, low income, high unemployment, and overcrowding and come from racial and ethnic minorities. The prevalence of delinquency among disadvantaged youths has been explained mostly on the basis of their deprived environment. Faced with fewer educational and occupational opportunities, these youths easily become frustrated with the circumstances of their lives and turn to less legitimate means of achievement. As a result, disadvantaged youths often turn to stealing cars, robbing homes and stores, and dealing drugs as a socially acceptable means of survival. Not surprisingly, predatory crimes against people, such as aggravated assault, sexual assault, and robbery, occur about three times more frequently among disadvantaged youth.

However, the presumed link between socioeconomic deprivation and delinquency has been questioned by some sociologists in recent years. Some authorities contend that the prevalence of crime in the large cities may be attrib-

Predatory crimes against people are committed more frequently by disadvantaged youth. (Marc Anderson)

uted largely to discrimination against disadvantaged youth by society, such that these youth are more likely to be arrested and institutionalized (Rutter and Giller, 1983). Furthermore, there is increasing evidence that racial factors are involved. For instance, studies have shown that African-American and Caucasian youths from a working-class background engage in delinquent behavior such as carrying weapons and participating in gang fights at about the same rate. Yet African-American youths are more likely to be arrested and charged for the same crimes (Cavan and Ferdinand, 1981). Thus, the disproportionately high rate of delinquency among minority youth may be partly attributable to racism among police and juvenile authorities as well as society in general.

At the same time, the prevalence of serious delinquency among disadvantaged, urban youth should not blind us to the increasing problem of delinquency among middle-class, suburban youth. In the first place, delinquency continues to increase at a faster rate among adolescents in the suburbs than among those in urban and rural areas. The sharpest increases in suburban delinquency have occurred in motor vehicle thefts, embezzlement, fraud, and drug abuse violations (*Uniform Crime Reports*, 1989). Then too, affluent youths are less likely to be arrested and charged with their offenses than their lower-class counterparts in the city, such that the actual rates of suburban delinquency may be even higher than reported (Tygart, 1988).

The rapid rise in delinquency among suburban youth has been attributed to various factors, including influence of peer groups, breakdowns in the family, and materialistic values. Also, despite the greater material affluence in the suburbs, middle-class youth may suffer from another type of deprivation due to deficient socialization and inadequate parenting. Suburban youth are exposed to a strange mixture of material affluence and emotional neglect. That is, parents tend to be concerned that their young people have the necessary material means to fulfill their middle-class roles. When youths feel they lack the material objects needed to continue their middle-class life-style, such as, cars, clothes, pocket money, alcohol, and drugs, they may resort to stealing, with the typical suburban delinquent more willing to rob homes in his or her own neighborhood than in the past. Yet, suburban parents are not nearly as conscientious in regard to providing the emotional nurture and guidance their teenagers need. Accordingly, a great deal of suburban delinquency occurs through default, because parents don't know what their teenagers are doing and don't want to be bothered by them. As a result, parents discover only a small proportion of their teenager's offenses. Even when parents discover that their son or daughter has engaged in delinquent behavior, many parents don't do much about it. Too many parents simply ignore, scold, or punish their young people and then try to forget about it. Few parents discuss the matter in a calm, concerned way that will diminish the chances of their young people engaging in such behavior again. Apparently, delinquency is regarded as an inevitable part of growing up, something to be taken lightly by parents and youth alike.

Personality

Youths who are arrested for delinquency, especially those who have committed serious offenses or become chronic delinquents, commonly exhibit certain personality characteristics. Delinquents generally have poor self-control, with a marked inability to delay gratification and a tendency to engage in impulsive behavior. They are usually antagonistic and defiant toward authorities, frequently displaying hostility and resentment. They also tend to be less honest and more hedonistic than other youth and generally lack a sense of social responsibility. Delinquent youth characteristically have poor emotional and social adjustment compared to their nondelinquent peers. Although chronic delinquents tend to have lower-than-average intelligence, most delinquents have at least average intelligence, such that intelligence itself may play less of a critical role in delinquency than do other psychological and social factors (Rutter and Giller, 1983).

Delinquent youths generally have poor self-images and low self-esteem. They're apt to describe themselves as bad, ignorant, lazy, and selfish, generally regarding themselves as undesirable people. It is sometimes suggested that the mere act of engaging in antisocial behavior may contribute to the delinquent's low self-esteem. But all things considered self-esteem seems to influence delinquency more than the other way around. In some instances, the delinquents' lack of self-esteem may be readily apparent in their posture and dress as well as in their deviant behavior. At other times, they may not be fully aware of their low sense of self-worth, often displaying a cockiness and toughness admired by others. The explanation seems to be that although some delinquents may exhibit high self-esteem in their surface awareness, most of them harbor a deeper sense of inferiority or low self-esteem in the unconscious level of their psyche (Rutter & Giller, 1983).

Psychopathology

Whenever you hear of teenagers shooting at passing motorists, beating up elderly people, or committing gang rapes, you may find yourself thinking, "They're sick!" And in some instances, they may be. Yet emotional disturbance varies considerably among delinquents, ranging from the milder acting-out behavior commonly seen among adolescents to the more severe psychotic disturbances like schizophrenia. One of the most common links between delinquency and psychological disturbance may be seen in the conduct disorders. These are described in the authoritative *Diagnostic and Statistical Manual of Mental Disorders* (Third Edition) published by the American Psychiatric Association (1987), generally referred to as DSM-III-R. The essential feature of these disorders is a repetitive and persistent pattern of behavior lasting at least six months in which the rights of others and/or appropriate social rules are violated. Such behavior is considerably more serious than the occasional mischief and pranks committed by children and adolescents. Not surprisingly, individuals with this disorder tend to come from homes with inconsistent child-rearing methods, harsh discipline, rejection, absence of a parent, and/or parents who themselves are addicted to alcohol, illicit drugs, and engage in criminal activities. It isn't hard to imagine how individuals growing up in such homes acquire the characteristic personality traits associated with conduct disorders, such as poor self-esteem, lack of self-control, hostility toward authorities, and poor emotional and social adjustment in the home, school, and community. Conduct disorders are more common among males than females.

The DSM-III-R specifies three subtypes of conduct disorders: group type, solitary aggressive type, and undifferentiated type (American Psychiatric Association, 1987).

Group type.   These youths exhibit socially deviant behavior mainly as a group activity with their peers. Aggressive physical behavior may or may not be present. They may engage in a wide variety of deviant activities, such as stealing cars, selling drugs, or armed robbery. Such youths trend to form normal emotional attachments to their family and friends. But they often belong to a gang and commit most of their delinquent acts as an integral part of gang activity. Group types seem to have been socialized into a deviant system of values, such that they

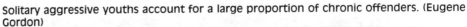
Solitary aggressive youths account for a large proportion of chronic offenders. (Eugene Gordon)

are often loyal to gang members, in contrast to the solitary, aggressive types. Most girls with conduct disorders fall into the group category, especially those involved in substance abuse and underage sexual activity (Rathus and Nevid, 1991). See box on "Gang Violence."

Solitary aggressive type. Here, the essential feature is the predominance of aggressive physical behavior toward adults and peers, usually initiated by the individual apart from any group activity. Unlike the group types, the solitary aggressive types lack emotional attachments, are quick to inform on their companions, and even try to shift the blame for their misdeeds onto their peers. These youths tend to be highly aggressive and callous and thus lacking in friends, similar to the adult antisocial personality. They grow up with parents who are often neglectful, inconsistent in discipline, and exhibit antisocial behavior themselves. The solitary aggressive types may consistently lie, steal, break into houses, rape, and murder, all with a characteristic callousness toward their victims. Such individuals are the most likely to continue their criminal careers into adulthood (Rathus and Nevid, 1991).

Gang Violence

In 1989 the House Committee on Children, Youth, and Families found that the growing violence by and against youth has become a "national emergency." Homicide is now the leading killer of African-American males 15 to 24, and the second cause for Caucasian males after automobile accidents. Most experts agree that the increased violence reflects, among other things, more organized gang activity frequently associated with the spoils of drug money (Diesenhouse, 1990). Combat has changed from bare fists and knives to high-powered pistols and automatic weapons. In Los Angeles County alone, there were 462 gang-related deaths in 1988.

Most members of gangs are in their late teens and early twenties, though early adolescents readily join. For example, "Little Ducc" was inducted into a Los Angeles gang when he was only 12, going along as an observer in a drive-by shooting. By the time he was 14 he was arrested for assault with a deadly weapon (a .38 cal. pistol), one of his many brushes with the law.

Ducc's family history is typical for his neighborhood. His mother died when he was only 5. His father has spent the past five years in prision. And his older brother, 17, is also in the gang. What little care Ducc has received comes from his grandmother. Although he was discovered by a program that pays the college tuition for gifted ghetto kids, he hasn't attended school much since the fourth grade.

Kids like Ducc join a gang as a way of obtaining "respect" and then prove themselves by punishing someone outside the gang for an act of disrespect. Once Ducc shot a rival gang member simply because he was one of the "enemy." But because it wasn't "personal," he says he felt no remorse, though he admits he later got drunk, mostly to hide his feelings (Stanley, 1990).

Undifferentiated type.   Adolescents classified with this type of conduct disorder exhibit a mixture of clinical features from the group type and the solitary aggressive type.

Treating adolescents with a conduct disorder remains a challenge for professionals in the mental health field. Generally, psychotherapy has not been effective in changing adolescents' antisocial behavior. A more helpful approach has been to place them in programs or settings that have explicit rules and clear rewards for obeying them. Even more promising is problem-solving therapy, in which aggressive adolescents are taught to perceive confrontations with others as problems to be solved, rather than cues to violence. In one approach, boys were trained to generate nonviolent solutions to conflicts and then to try out the most promising ones. The treatment led to significant decreases in aggressive behavior at school and at home. Despite such improvement, though, the majority of adolescents receiving problem-solving therapy remain poorly adjusted, which suggests the difficulty of modifying antisocial behavior (Lochman and Curry, 1986).

Drugs

Although the high crime rate is often blamed on youth's use of alcohol and illegal drugs, the association between drug use and delinquency is more complex than a simple cause-and-effect relationship. In the first place, many youths occasionally use alcohol and smoke marijuana without engaging in serious delinquency. For other youths, the use of an illegal drug is simply part of a life-style or general pattern of delinquency. That is, those teenagers most apt to break the law in using the drug are also likely to have a preexisting pattern of delinquency which is the antecedent of both drug use and criminal activity. In these cases, it is not so much that a given drug such as marijuana causes crime, but that those who use it may also be the type of people more likely to commit crime (White, 1991). Then there are those who would engage in delinquent behavior whether they used drugs or not. At the same time, there are countless youths and adults whose drug problem contributes directly or indirectly to criminal activity.

One of the strongest links between drug abuse and crime is found among heroin users. Whether they have a preexisting criminal tendency or not, many heroin users resort to crime mostly because the cost of their drug habit forces them to do so. Generally, the crime rate of heroin users increases with the beginning of their drug use and declines when they quit taking the drug. Crime rates even drop during periods of low drug use (White, 1991). It has been estimated that a heroin user has to steal three to five times the actual cost of the drug to maintain the drug habit. Because it is impossible for addicts to earn this amount of money legally, most of them resort to criminal activity. For instance, it has been estimated that three out of four prostitutes in the major cities has a serious heroin dependency problem. Furthermore, the seriousness of the criminal act grows greater with age. Whereas muggings and purse snatchings are common among youthful offenders, burglary and armed robbery are more likely among older offenders. The most frequent activity involves property crimes, which in descending order includes drug sales, burglary, and other types of thefts, forgeries, assaults, and robberies. Yet only a fraction of their crimes result in an arrest: 250 crimes to one arrest. Drug sales are the least likely to be detected, with a 761 to 1 ratio, whereas acts of assault and robbery are the most likely to result in arrest, with a 35 to 1 ratio (O'Brien and Cohen, 1984).

The proportion of alcohol-addicted youths with a record of delinquency is also heavier than average compared to that of other youth. Although the statistics involving alcohol-related delinquency vary considerably, alcohol involvement has been found in up to one-half of all rape offenders, especially those involved in gang rapes; two-thirds of all assault offenders; and three-fourths of all murderers. Alcohol also contributes to a wide variety of other deviant behaviors, such as drunk driving, vehicular homicide, and family violence. A common explanation for the link between alcohol and violence is that alcohol releases inhibitions and intensifies certain mental states, and that the release of anger may enhance the likelihood of violence. The combination of alcohol with other drugs may result in increased violent behavior. We should also note that high levels of alcohol use also predispose people to become victims of violent crime (Welte and Abel, 1989).

All things considered, it is difficult to generalize about the association of drug use and delinquency, not only because of the question of causality but also the many other factors involved. One must consider the type of drug used, the level of drug use, and the wide variation in the types of crimes the different drug users are likely to commit. Generally, small doses of drugs do not lead to aggression and criminal activity, while large doses are often incapacitating. At the same time, the setting in which individuals take a drug, along with their mood, personality, and disposition to crime, can also alter a drug's impact on their behavior and thus accentuate the possibility of criminal activity (O'Brien and Cohen, 1984).

TREATMENT AND PREVENTION OF DELINQUENCY

For hundreds of years, youthful offenders were treated much like adult criminals, with the emphasis on handing out justice for violations of the law. Older children and adolescents were sometimes subjected to unduly harsh punishment. For instance, under the old Engligh law, 12 and 13 year olds could be put to death for stealing small sums of money. Then with the increased understanding of human development that surfaced in the late nineteenth century, enlightened authorities instituted the juvenile court, with the aim of treating youthful offenders differently than adults. Unlike the criminal court with its philosophy of punitive justice, the juvenile court aimed at a more humane and appropriate treatment for immature offenders. Rather than fitting the punishment to the severity of the crime, as with adult defendants, judges in the juvenile court acted as wise parents dealing with youth according to the "best interests" of the child, with an eye toward rehabilitation. However, an unintended result was that juvenile courts acquired an almost absolute authority over youth, with glaring inconsistencies in the way they have been handled. For instance, a 16-year-old murderer who evokes the compassion of the judge might be released when witnesses don't show up for the hearing, whereas a 14 year old who steals a woman's purse might be institutionalized by another judge.

The abuses of the juvenile court system received national attention in the Gault case. In 1964, Gerald Francis Gault, a 15 year old, was arrested for making an obscene phone call to a neighbor. Had he been of legal age, he might have received a small fine and a two-month jail sentence. But being a juvenile, he was treated differently. Gault was sentenced to an institution until he reached 21 years of age. However, in the process of being convicted, Gault was denied many of his rights. Gault's parents were not notified, the neighbor who lodged the complaint never appeared in court, the judge never spoke to the complainant, and there was no record of the proceedings. Eventually, the case was taken to the U.S. Supreme Court, which in 1967 reversed the decision of the lower courts and freed Gault. The decision initiated widespread reforms in the juvenile system. As a result, youthful offenders now have the same civil rights accorded adult citizens, including the right to know the charges against them, the right not to incriminate themselves, the right to have a lawyer represent them, to have that lawyer cross-examine witnesses, and the right to appeal the decision to a higher court. The court decision also set in motion other reform measures, such as keeping status offenders in separate physical facilities (Prescott, 1981).

In this last section we'll take a look at the three main components of the juvenile justice system, including the police, juvenile court, and correctional institutions as well as some of the current approaches to treatment and prevention.

Police and the Juvenile Court

Police are among the first authorities to come into contact with juvenile offenders, with the majority of arrests resulting from citizen complaints. Police usually have a great deal of discretionary power and may choose to deal with the juvenile offender in a number of ways: (1) They can let the offender go at the scene of the offense with only a verbal warning; (2) they can do the same thing, except at the police station, perhaps accompanied by a phone call to the individual's parents; (3) they can refer the adolescent to a social agency for help; (4) they may also choose to hold the offender in temporary custody; or (5) while in custody, they may petition for a court hearing. Police generally dispose of up to one-half of all juvenile arrests themselves (*Uniform Crime Reports* 1989).

Once a petition has been made to the juvenile court, a given procedure is usually followed, though it may vary somewhat from one legal jurisdiction to another. Ordinarily, the youthful offender must be a given a preliminary hearing within a stated period, for example, seventy-two hours. Prior to the hearing juveniles may be released to the custody of their parents or kept in a juvenile detention center, depending on the individual and the offense. At the preliminary hearing, the offender may be dismissed outright, referred to a social agency, placed on informal probation, or referred to a formal hearing. When a case warrants a formal hearing in juvenile court, there is a written petition stating the charges and verification of the youth's right to counsel at the preliminary hearing. Generally, the juvenile court hearing is conducted by the judge, with the offender, his or her parents, and others, such as the offender's lawyer, present. There may be two formal hearings: an adjudication hearing, at which the offender is convicted of the charges or not, and a disposition hearing, at which the judge determines what will be done with the offender. Between the two hearings there should be ample time for a social investigation to determine which course of action will be best for the offender.

The juvenile justice system may be compared to a giant funnel with many cracks in it. Juvenile offenders who are arrested enter the system at the wide end of the funnel at the top. But as they progress through the system, the great majority of youths slip out through the "cracks" in the system. Most offenders are dealt with at the initial stages of the system, whether by the police, school authorities, or at the preliminary hearing. Once in the courtroom, many of the remaining offenders are found not guilty or dismissed, while others are placed

Youthful offender and police appear in juvenile court. (John Huber)

on probation or supervision. Only a small minority of cases proceed through the entire juvenile justice system and are placed in a residential treatment program, and for good reason, as explained below.

Current Approaches to Treatment

Once juvenile offenders are committed by the courts, they may be placed in a variety of facilities and programs. Almost two-thirds of them (60 percent) will be put in public facilities. (See Figure 13-2.) Most of these individuals are kept in detention centers and training schools, with only a small proportion of them in smaller settings like group homes or ranches. In contrast, the majority of youth placed in private facilities stay in halfway houses, group homes, ranches, forestry camps, or farms (U.S. Bureau of the Census, 1990). The programs in these institutions tend to be based on the combined goals of correction and rehabilitation. Yet, neither of these goals is accomplished very well. Instead, institutionalized youth tend to look down on themselves and are exposed to an even more unfavorable environment with a core of serious offenders who model and reinforce negative behavior. All of this results in a poor rate of rehabilitation, such that anywhere from 60 to 75 percent of juveniles held in correctional facilities are arrested again (Rutter and Giller, 1983).

The low success rate of conventional programs has led to experimentation with a variety of community-based programs. Many of these programs rely

Figure 13-2   Distribution of Juveniles In Custody By Public or Private Facility. Almost two-thirds (60 percent) of the 94,000 juveniles in custody are housed in public facilities, with the remaining third in private facilities.

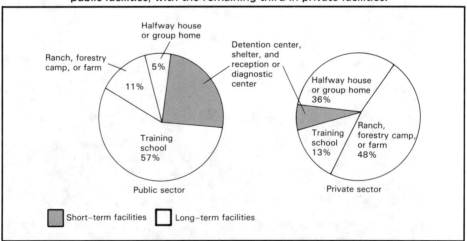

Sources: U.S. Law Enforcement Assistance Administration. *Children in Custody.* (Washington, DC: Government Printing Office, 1979), p. 6. U.S. Bureau of the Census. *The Statistical Abstract of the United States, 1990,* 110th ed. (Washington, DC: U.S. Government Printing Office, 1990), p. 186.

on a cognitive behavioral approach to the treatment of delinquency, in which appropriate behavior is systematically rewarded and deviant behavior is either not rewarded or results in unpleasant consequences, such as a "time out" period or the temporary withdrawal of some privilege. In one program, for example, the focus is on teaching positive social skills that have a wide application in everyday life, such as problem solving, communication skills, and how to get a job. A five-year follow-up study showed that the juveniles who had participated in this program while in custody were much less likely to get into trouble again than those in the control group, with a 23 percent rearrest record compared to 48 percent for other juvenile offenders (Rutter and Giller, 1983).

Authorities are also looking anew at probation, with about four juvenile offenders put on probation for every one placed in a correctional facility. Probation appears to be one of the most effective approaches to delinquency, in that individuals on probation generally have lower rearrest records than do those kept in institutions (Singer and Isralowitz, 1983). At the same time, the success rate of probation depends on certain conditions. First, it is generally more effective with individuals who are arrested the first time for minor offenses, rather than those with a record of serious offenses. Second, there should be clear conditions associated with the probation, such as school attendance, work requirements, and a curfew. Third, there must be adequate supervision and assistance, with an eye toward helping the juvenile fulfill the conditions of his or her probation. However, the latter condition usually requires a reduced workload of the probation officer or caseworker, which is not always possible in a more extensive application of this approach.

Family therapy has also become an increasingly popular approach to the treatment of delinquent youth. Time and again, youthful offenders have shown improvement on an individual basis, only to relapse once they have returned home. By dealing with the home situation, family therapy increases the probability of long-term gains in the individual's behavior. Although there are over a dozen types of family therapy, as we mentioned earlier in the book, most of them assume that each family functions as a system, in such a way that each adolescent's behavior is best understood and changed within the family unit. For example, Bill is a 16 year old who has repeatedly gotten into trouble at school with his low grades, disruptive behavior in class, and skipping school. Since the school counselor discovered that Bill doesn't get along well with his parents, family therapy was recommended. In dealing with Bill and his family, the therapist soon discovered that Bill's difficulties at school were related to the family dynamics. Unlike his older sister in college and his younger brother who was the family favorite, Bill appeared to be the "black sheep" of the family who was always getting into trouble. During the new few months the therapists pointed out several factors that contributed to Bill's problems, such as his parents' harsh discipline, lack of supervision, poor communication with Bill, and a marked tendency to make Bill the scapegoat for the family's problems. In promoting more positive behavior on Bill's part, the therapist proposed the use of a family contract, a commonly used and effective method of family therapy. Bill and his parents drew up a behavioral contract regarding his desired performance at school, including attendance, study habits, and a certain grade point average. They also agreed upon the procedures by which Bill's goals would be attained and how other family members would assist him. After six months Bill's school performance was no longer a problem. Although family therapy is not always this effective, it often serves as an alternative to institutionalizing youth and may also shorten the stay in cases when the individual is placed in a residential treatment program (Ault-Riche and Rosenthal, 1986).

Preventing Delinquency

All too often, our approach to the treatment and prevention of delinquency is distorted by two illusions. Either we think there's nothing we can do about it, or we believe that somewhere, somehow we'll find a cure for it. As we've already seen, there is no simple cure for the problem because delinquency is the combined product of so many factors, such as the kind of society and the times in which we live. Yet this does not mean that we must succumb to the opposite myth that nothing can be done about delinquency. We've already seen that some strategies work better than others. Also, anything that improves the root causes of delinquency, such as social and economic inequities and family instability, indirectly helps diminish delinquency. But there are also some direct preventive steps we can take.

First, we can encourage people to identify and provide help for youths who are at high risk for delinquency. Because delinquency begins in the early school grades and chronic delinquents get into trouble sooner than nonrepeaters do, the sooner we can intervene in the lives of such youth in a positive way, especially in school, the better.

Second, intervention strategies should focus on teaching positive social skills rather than simply suppressing deviant behavior. Troubled youths need help in feeling better about themselves and acquiring the social skills and competence to find a meaningful role for themselves in society. Yet this type of assistance is more demanding than simply controlling negative behavior.

Third, we can support the existing trend toward dealing with minor delinquency and status offenses outside the conventional juvenile justice system. Because the system's "cure" tends to worsen the problem, every effort should be made to exhaust preventive measures such as early warning and release, informal probation, counseling, and social agencies before proceeding further into the juvenile justice system.

Fourth, we can encourage better use of local police in handling juvenile offenders. Because the police are among the first to encounter delinquent youth and have great discretionary powers in handling them there's much to be gained in training police to deal with youthful offenders in the early stages of delinquency.

Fifth, we can continue the trend toward greater use of small, community-based programs such as halfway houses and group homes. In these programs youth are more likely to be given the warmth and individual attention they need as well as integration into the comunity, resulting in lower rates of repeated delinquency.

Finally, we need to realize that delinquency partly reflects the society in which we live. Consequently, anything that helps to strengthen family life; alleviate economic conditions in the urban ghettos; reduce ethnic, racial, and sexual discrimination; improve the schools; and reduce drug abuse helps, however indirectly, in the continuing struggle against delinquency.

SUMMARY

The Extent of Delinquency

1. A significant proporation of people arrested for all criminal activities except traffic violations are youths, with one out of six of them under 18, one out of three of them under 21, and one out of two of them under 25.

2. The frequency and seriousness of delinquency rises with age, such that youth under 25 account for about one-half of all serious crime.

3. The biggest single category of offenses committed by youth is property crimes. Youth under 25 are responsible for three-fourths of all burglaries, vandalism, and motor vehicle thefts.

4. At least one-third of delinquency involves status offenses, such as running away from home. Although adolescents leave home for different reasons, a significant proportion of runaways are victims of sexual abuse or violence.

5. The male-female ratio of reported delinquency is now about 3 and ½ to 1. Males are more likely than females to commit violent crimes such as assault, rape, and murder; Females are somewhat more likely to be involved in prostitution and runaways.

Contributing Factors

6. The causes of delinquency are complex and interwoven reflecting the society in which we live as well the social, cultural process of adolescence.

7. Delinquents generally come from families characterized by overly harsh or lenient discipline and lack of family structure and affectional ties between youth and their families.

8. The highest rates of delinquency, especially for serious offenses, are found among disadvantaged youth in the inner cities, though the gap between urban and suburban delinquency continues to diminish.

9. Delinquent youths tend to lack self-esteem, impulse control, and a sense of social responsibility.

10. Chronic juvenile offenders often exhibit psychopathology, especially one of the conduct disorders such as the group type, solitary aggressive type, or undifferentiated type.

11. Although the relationship between drug use and delinquency is complex, drug abuse is a significant factor in such crimes as theft, burglary, and drug dealing.

Treatment and Prevention of Delinquency

12. Police, among the first authorities to come into contract with juvenile offenders, dispose of up to one-half of juvenile arrests themselves.

13. The juvenile justice system can be compared to a giant funnel, with the great majority of juvenile offenders slipping through the cracks in the system and only a small minority being placed in residential treatment programs.

14. Although the majority of juvenile offenders committed by the courts are placed in large public correctional facilities, the low success rate of these institutions has led to experimentation with a variety of community-based programs.

15. Practical steps in preventing delinquency include identifying high-risk youth early in their development, providing positive social skills training, diverting low-risk youth from entering the juvenile justice system, and emphasizing community-based programs.

REVIEW QUESTIONS

1. To what extent does the frequency and seriousness of delinquency increase with age?
2. Which types of offenses are most frequently committed by youths under 25?
3. To what extent are there sex differences in delinquency?
4. How do families contribute to delinquent behavior?
5. How important are socioeconomic and racial factors in delinquency?
6. What is the difference between the three types of conduct disorders?
7. What role does drug use play in delinquency?
8. In what sense is the juvenile justice system like a giant funnel?
9. What are the pros and cons of putting juvenile offenders on probation?
10. How do you think we can decrease the rate of serious delinquency?

Youth and
Drugs

14

Learning Objectives

After completing this chapter, you should be able to:
1 Describe several key findings of the annual high school drug survey regarding the use of alcohol, tobacco, and illegal drugs.
2 List the five major patterns of drug use.
3 Describe the psychological and social factors associated with alcohol abuse.
4 Discuss the trends in marijuana use presented in the annual high school drug survey.
5 Discuss the trends in cocaine use presented in the annual high school drug survey.
6 List at least seven of the nine characteristics of drug abuse found in the DSM-III-R.
7 Discuss the treatment and prevention of drug abuse.

People have been experimenting with mind-altering drugs longer than most of us realize. The ancient Assyrians sucked on opium lozenges, and the Romans ate hashish sweets two thousand years ago. In the nineteenth century, the man who synthesized nitrous oxide, popularly known as laughing gas, held laughing gas parties in his home. Later, inhalations of nitrous oxide were sold at county fairs for a quarter, with individuals inhaling it for its pleasurable sensations and colorful fantasies. Although a few customers may have discovered final truths, most went away with little more than a laughing jag, dizziness, or an upset stomach (O'Brien and Cohen, 1984).

Today, however, drug use has become a far more serious matter in our technological and rapidly changing culture. We've virtually become a drug-oriented society, relying on different drugs for a variety of purposes. Youths are bombarded with commercials urging them to take this aspirin or drink a certain beer. It is no wonder that many of them experiment with illicit drugs as well. Then, too, there are more powerful drugs available through an extensive network of illegal dealers. Part of the problem is the seemingly unending capacity of pharmacological experts and amateurs to discover new substances for altering consciousness with potential for abuse. Fortunately, growing public concern over drug abuse has resulted in some significant progress. But drugs remain a serious problem among youths and adults alike.

USE OF DRUGS

Despite the improvements in recents years, this nation's high school students and other youths in their twenties still show a level of involvement with illicit drugs which is greater than that found in any other industrialized nation in the world. Even by historical standards in the United States, these rates remain extremely high. Also, youths now initiate drug use at a relatively early age. For instance, one-half of all adolescents have used alcohol and one-fourth of them have tried marijuana by the ninth grade. The lack of judgment and emotional resiliency at this age increases the risk of harm. Then too, drug abuse is having more wide-ranging harmful effects on society—from impaired performance at school and work to increased crime and substance-related accidents and death. Fortunately, there is an increased public concern over the drug problem and mobilized efforts to combat it. As a result, there is a growing awareness of the harmful effects of drugs, with the majority of high school seniors and young adults in their twenties expressing disapproval of the experimental, occasional, and regular use of any illicit drug (Johnston, O'Malley, and Bachman, 1989). Furthermore, a nation-wide Gallup poll shows that parents now regard the use of drugs as the number 1 problem facing the public schools (Elam, 1990).

We begin the chapter with an overview of drug use among youth. Then there is a discussion of alcohol and tobacco, the two most commonly used drugs among youth and adults alike. Later in the chapter, we examine the use of selected illegal drugs, such as marijuana and cocaine. Finally, we will take a look at people's relationships with drugs, along with the treatment and prevention of drug abuse.

The Extent of Drug Use

One of the most reliable sources of information about drug use among youth is the well-known annual high school survey and follow-up studies conducted by Lloyd Johnston, Patrick O'Malley, and Jerald Bachman (1989) at the University of Michigan Institute for Social Research, which is funded by the National Insti-tute on Drug Abuse. Each year they gather extensive confidential information about drug use from about 17,000 high school seniors at 130 public and private high schools across the United States. The data obtained from these surveys, together with the follow-up studies, give us a well-rounded picture of drug use among high school students, college students, and other post-high school young adults up through their late twenties. Most of the data in the following section are based on the survey of the high school class of 1988, together with follow-up studies of graduates of earlier classes now in their twenties.

As in the past, alcohol and cigarettes are used more frequently than any illegal drug. Nearly all the high school students have tried alcohol by their senior year, with the great majority having used it in the past month. More than two-thirds of the students report having tried cigarettes at some time, with almost one-third of them having smoked some during the past month. About half (54 percent) of the seniors have used an illegal drug at some time during their lives. However, a substantial majority of them have used only marijuana. At the same time, three in ten seniors have used an illegal drug other than marijuana. The most widely used illegal drugs, in descending order of the frequency of use, are marijuana, stimulants, inhalants, cocaine, tranquilizers, hallucinogens, opiates other than heroin, and sedatives. See Figure 14-1. Preliminary findings of the class of 1990 indicate that these trends continue, with slightly fewer high school seniors (48 percent) using an illegal drug and significant drops in the use of cocaine (Cooper, 1991).

Figure 14-1   Drug Use Among High School Seniors.

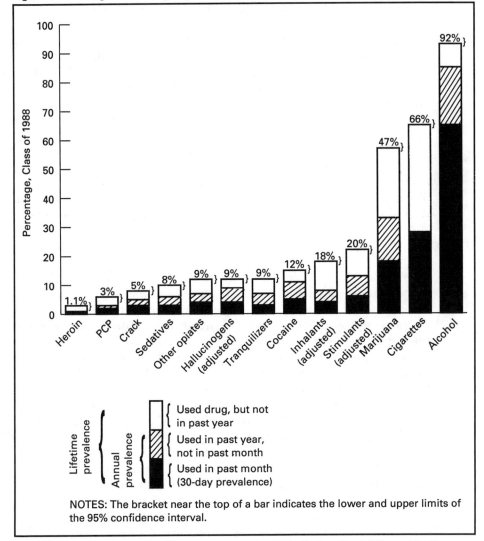

Source: Lloyd D. Johnston, Patrick M. O'Malley, and Jerald G. Bachman, *Drug Use, Drinking, and Smoking: National Survey Results from High School, College, and Young Adult Populations 1975–1988* (Washington, D.C.: National Institute on Drug Abuse, U.S. Government Printing Office, 1989), p. 33.

The high proportion of youths who have at least tried any illegal drug by their senior year in high school grows substantially as they move into their twenties. For instance, in the high school classes of 1976 through 1979, anywhere from 58 to 65 percent of students had tried an illicit drug by their senior year. But by 1988, when they were in their late twenties, roughly 80 percent of them had done so. At the same time, the *active* use of many illegal drugs, including marijuana and tranquilizers, remains at levels similar to those observed among high school seniors. In fact, compared to high school students, young adults actually have lower rates of annual use of six drugs—the inhalants, LSD, methaqualone, barbiturates, stimulants, and opiates other than heroin. The major exception, of course, is the use of cocaine, which continues to rise until about age 25, when it reaches a plateau and thereafter may decline.

Although college-bound high school seniors are less likely to use most drugs than those not planning on a four-year college degree, the differences between these two groups diminish with age. As a result, college students show usage rates for a number of drugs which are about average for all young adults their age. This "catching up" phenomenon may be explained more in terms of leaving home and getting married than any direct effects of college per se. At the same time, compared to other young adults their age, college students have lower than average rates of use for several drugs, especially LSD, stimulants, barbiturates, and tranquilzers.

Males are more likely than females to use most illegal drugs at all ages. And the differences tend to be the largest at the higher frequency level. For instance, in the class of 1988 about three times as many males (3.9 percent) as females (1.3 percent) use marijuana on a daily basis. A similar ratio exists among college students. The major exception to the rule that males are more frequently users of illegal drugs than females occurs for stimulant and tranquilizer use among high school students and other young adults, where females are at roughly the same level. However, over the years the trend is toward less difference between the sexes, with the convergency of rates due mostly to the faster drop in drug use by males.

One of the key findings on trends over the last eight years is the appreciable decline in the use of a number of illicit drugs among high seniors, and even larger declines in their use among American college students and other young adults. A major exception to these trends is the use of cocaine which didn't decline until about 1986. Crack use did not begin to decline among seniors until 1988, and its use now appears to have leveled off among the young adults in the population. However, one must keep in mind the various regional and socioeconomic differences as well as individual differences. Furthermore, bear in mind that the survey data do not include high school dropouts, who tend to have substantially higher rates of drug use than do in-school students or graduates, many of whom become part of the hard-core drug problems in the inner cities.

The Development of Drug Use

One of the disconcerting findings of the annual high school surveys is the relatively early age at which drugs are first used. This is especially important in that the time from early adolescence to the early twenties is a critical period for developing drug problems. For instance, many of the youths who try alcohol, cigarettes, and marijuana do so before they reach the tenth grade. About half of the students who try alcohol and tobacco and one-fourth of those who try marijuana have done so before reaching high school. Of the illicit drugs, marijuana and inhalants show the earliest pattern of initiation. By the time adolescents reach their senior year in high school, more than half of the eventual users of any illicit drugs have tried them. Cocaine presents a contrasting picture to nearly all the other drugs in that the initiation rates are higher in the last two years of high school and continue up through the mid-twenties. Fewer than one out of four eventual users of cocaine have initiated use of this drug prior to high school (Johnston, O'Malley, and Bachman, 1989). See Table 14-1.

The sequence in which youths try various drugs tends to follow a typical pattern. In a longitudinal study of high school students, Denise Kandel (1980) found that the majority of drug users begin with legal drugs before progressing to illegal or illicit drugs. Most teenagers who use a legal drug start with beer or wine. Two to three times as many beer and wine drinkers progress to hard liquor as progress to cigarettes. At the same time, more than half of those who smoke eventually use hard liquor. But few if any adolescents go straight from beer and wine to illicit drugs without first trying hard liquor or cigarettes. The usual sequence is from alcohol and tobacco to marijuana, which in turn is a crucial step toward the use of other illegal drugs. The sequential pattern of drug use holds true at all grades through high school and is similar for both sexes. At the same time, this is not a causal progression. Many youths stop at a particular stage of drug usage and never go any further. The most likely explanation is that different factors are related to drug usage at each stage and probably depend on cultural as well as psychological influences.

A critical factor is peer interaction, especially with drug-using friends. Many studies including that by Kandel as well as those by Johnston, O'Malley, and Bachman (1989) have shown a high correlation between an individual's illicit drug use and that of his or her friends. Such an association probably reflects several different causal patterns. A person whose friends use a drug is more likely to try the drug, especially if these friends are the same age or older. Conversely, the individual who is already using a drug is likely to introduce friends to the experience. Then too, one who is already a user is more likely to establish friendships with others who are also users.

Another important factor is the perceived availability of drugs, as well as their cost. Generally, the more widely used drugs are reported to be readily available by the highest proportion of the age group using a given drug. Yet it is important to point out that the supply reduction does not appear to have played a major role in perhaps the two most important downturns in use which have occurred to date—namely, those for cocaine and marijuana. In regard to cocaine, the perceived availability was actually rising during the period of downturn in use. In the case of marijuana, availability has remained almost universal in the high school age group over the last ten years, although the use has dropped substantially. What has changed dramatically are young people's beliefs

Table 14-1 Grade in which Drug was First Used by High School Students, Class of 1988 (in percents)

Grade in which drug was first used:	Marijuana	Inhalants	Amyl/Butyl Nitrites	Hallucinogens	LSD	PCP	Cocaine	Heroin	Other Opiates	Stimulants (adjusted)	Sedatives	Barbiturates	Methaqualone	Tranquilizers	Alcohol	Getting Drunk	Cigarettes	Cigarettes (daily)
6th	2.3	2.4	0.2	0.1	0.1	0.1	0.2	0.1	0.2	0.2	0.2	0.2	0.2	0.2	8.6	3.3	19.4	1.5
7–8th	8.8	3.0	0.3	0.7	0.6	0.3	0.7	0.2	1.1	3.2	1.3	1.2	0.7	1.1	21.9	13.5	19.5	4.2
9th	13.2	3.4	0.7	1.8	1.5	0.7	1.6	0.3	1.8	5.2	2.4	2.1	1.2	2.2	25.7	20.6	11.7	5.3
10th	10.1	2.8	0.6	2.3	2.0	0.8	3.0	0.2	2.6	5.0	1.7	1.4	0.5	1.8	18.2	16.2	7.3	4.2
11th	8.5	2.8	0.8	2.4	2.2	0.6	4.1	0.2	1.8	4.1	1.3	1.2	0.5	2.7	12.0	12.1	5.8	3.5
12th	4.3	2.2	0.6	1.5	1.3	0.3	2.5	0.2	1.1	2.0	0.9	0.7	0.3	1.3	5.6	5.6	2.6	2.1
Never used	52.8	83.3	96.8	91.1	92.3	97.1	87.9	98.9	91.4	80.2	92.2	93.3	96.7	90.6	8.0	28.8	33.6	79.3

Source: Adapted from Lloyd D. Johnston, Patrick M. O'Malley, and Jerald G. Bachman, *Drug Use, Drinking, and Smoking: National Survey Resuts from High School, College, and Young Adult Populations 1975–1988* (Washington, D. C.: National Institute on Drug Abuse, U.S. Government Printing Office, 1989), p. 94.

about the dangers of using marijuana and cocaine. These changes in attitudes have helped to bring about a decreased demand for these drugs (Johnston, O'Malley, and Bachman, 1989).

Why Youths Use Drugs

Individuals may use mind-altering drugs for any number of reasons. Given the natural curiosity of young people and the availability of drugs, young people may try a drug like alcohol or marijuana mostly "to see what it's like." An even more common reason, especially for those who continue using drugs, is to enhance social interaction or "to have a good time with my friends." The various reasons people use drugs reflect several basic patterns of drug use as follows:

Experimental use includes trying one or more drugs on a short-term basis, up to ten times per drug. Users are motivated mostly by curiosity or the desire to experience new feelings, and rarely use drugs on a daily basis or to escape personal problems.

Social-recreational use occurs more among friends and acquaintances socializing with each other. Users do not usually increase the frequency or intensity of drug use or use drugs like heroin.

Circumstantial-situational use is undertaken for a desired effect. Common examples would be students' taking stimulants to study or sedatives to go to sleep. The greatest danger is an undue reliance on drugs to the point where they become habitual.

Intensified drug use refers to a long-term pattern of daily drug use to alleviate personal problems or stressful situations. Drug use is usually integrated into the user's social and community life, and users associate mostly with other users. Behavioral change may also occur, depending on the frequency and intensity of drug use, as well as drug dependence.

Compulsive drug use generally includes frequent and intense use of drugs over a relatively long time, resulting in both physical and psychological dependence. This may include the more conventional alcohol-dependent people as well as the heroin addicts who need their daily fix to function in everyday life.

When Lloyd Johnston and Patrick O'Malley (1986) asked young people themselves why they use drugs, the responses were revealing. The reason most often given for use of *any* drug was "to have a good time with my friends." A substantial but smaller number of students indicated they use drugs "to feel good and get high." These reasons were especially characteristic of people who continued to use drugs as opposed to those who had simply tried a drug or used it occasionally. Thus, a major reason for using drugs is social-recreational. This may also help to explain the strong association between drug use and peer relationships, with those who have recently used a specific drug, such as alcohol, more likely to report that they have been with others using this drug, and that most of their friends use it. Slightly less than half (41 percent) of the seniors mentioned that they used drugs "to relax or relieve tension." The two drugs most often taken to achieve a desired effect were alcohol and marijuana, the "beer" of illegal drugs. At the same time, there has been a trend away from the social-recreational use of the amphetamines toward using them for a specific purpose, such as to lose weight or to get more energy.

Many of the self-reported reasons for using drugs clustered around coping with negative affect, such as "to deal with anger and frustration," "to get away from my problems," or "to get through the day." These reasons were mentioned by a large proportion of youth using the central nervous system depressant drugs, especially alcohol, barbiturates, and tranquilizers. Although there were few differences between the sexes in regard to the reasons for using any drug, females were slightly less likely to use drugs for social-recreational reasons, and at the high levels of frequency, somewhat more likely to mention using drugs for coping with negative affect, for self-medication, or some other functional reason. For each drug, the more frequent users gave more reasons, especially those who used a drug on a daily basis. According to the researchers, this pattern suggests that many of the heavier users, especially those who use alcohol and marijuana on a daily basis, turn to drugs for psychological coping, for example, to alleviate boredom or frustration, or to get energy.

ALCOHOL AND TOBACCO

Alcohol and nicotine (tobacco) continue to be the most commonly accepted psychoactive drugs among young people and adults, as they have been for decades. One reason is their ease of availability. Another reason is the widespread acceptance of smoking and drinking of alcoholic beverages among adults, making for less of a generation gap than in regard to other drugs. As a result, tobacco and alcohol, in that order, remain—after caffeine—the most commonly used and abused drugs among youths and adults alike. Furthermore, the two drugs tend to be used together, so that heavy drinkers are apt to be heavy smokers, and vice versa (O'Brien and Cohen, 1984).

Use of Alcohol

Alcohol acts as a depressant for the central nervous system, diminishing the degree of voluntary control over behavior. Taken in small to moderate amounts, alcohol acts as a social lubricant, making people feel less inhibited and more relaxed. It also slows the reflex actions and alters the individual's sense of time, memory, and reasoning ability. When taken in larger amounts, alcohol has a more marked effect on mood, perception, judgment, and bodily functions. It

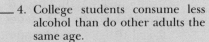

Fact or Fiction?

Indicate whether each of the following statements is true or false.

_____ 1. Taken in small amounts, alcohol is a stimulant.
_____ 2. Alcohol is less likely to make us intoxicated at 2 o'clock in the afternoon than at 2 o'clock in the morning.
_____ 3. More than nine out of ten alcoholics smoke cigarettes.

_____ 4. College students consume less alcohol than do other adults the same age.
_____ 5. The highest rate of binge drinking, defined as five or more drinks in a row, is among full-time college students.

The correct answers together with brief explanations can be found at the end of this chapter.

---

also has an adverse effect on the kidney and liver. Consumed in excessive amounts, alcohol may lead to coma and death, though individuals usually become unconscious before reaching a fatal dose. The amount of alcohol needed to become intoxicated varies with the individual, depending on body weight, personality, and previous experience with alcohol.

Although it is illegal for virtually all high school students to purchase alcoholic beverages, over one-half of them have tried alcohol by the ninth grade. Practically all of them (92 percent) have used alcohol by their senior year in high school. Beer is the most commonly used beverage, especially among boys. At the same time, partly because of the rising concern about alcohol abuse among teenagers, there has been a slight decline in adolescent drinking throughout the 1980s, both in monthly and daily use. Occasional heavy drinking, defined as five or more drinks in a row, has also declined among high school students but continues to be widespread. About one-third of high school seniors report that they engage in heavy drinking once or twice each weekend. Although only about four in ten seniors think there is great risk in such occasional heavy drinking, the vast majority of parents disagree.

The problem with alcohol generally gets worse after high school. Although college-bound seniors are somewhat less inclined to drink heavily than those without college plans, the situation becomes reversed during the post-high school years. Compared to all high school graduates, college students have an above average annual use of alcohol. The most alarming trend is the increase in occasional heavy drinking among college students, most of it at parties on weekends. About 43 percent of college students drink heavily on occasions. Much of the increase in occasional heavy drinking has occurred among college men. Also, daily use of alcohol is twice as common among males as females. Although there has been little or no decline in occasional heavy drinking among college students, there has been a decline in occasional, heavy drinking among other young adults. Such trends imply wider differences in regard to alcohol use among college

Occasional heavy drinking, especially at weekend parties, remains a big problem among college students. (Laima Druskis)

students and other young adults than in the past (Johnston, O'Malley, and Bachman, 1989).

Psychological and Social Factors

Most adolescents begin drinking at home under parental supervision, especially on holidays and special occasions. The older they become, the more likely they are to drink away from home and without adult supervision. By the senior year of high school, most drinking is done at teenage parties with no adults present, or sitting in a car or driving around at night. Once young people are away at college, as we've seen, they are even more likely to engage in occasional heavy drinking, especially at weekend parties. At the same time, some individuals are more likely than others to engage in heavy or problem drinking. In a comparison of youths who used or abused drugs, Anthony Jurich (1985) and his colleagues found that those who abuse alcohol or other drugs tend to come from troubled families. Such families are characterized by a greater degree of mother–father conflicts, parental divorce, parental absence, poor parent–adolescent communication, and parental discipline that is either overly lenient or overly harsh. Also, the person perceived to be the strongest person in the family was inclined to use psychological crutches such as denial or drugs to cope with stress. Youths who are heavy or problem drinkers also exhibit certain personality characteristics: They tend to have low self-esteem and are impulsive, irresponsible, and rebellious. They tend to have poor relationships with their parents compared to others their age. They are also less likely to value academic achievement, and make lower grades and drop out of school in greater numbers than do those without a drinking problem.

The use and abuse of alcohol is also strongly related to social and socio-economic differences, with the incidence of moderate and heavy drinking rising with education and affluence. The number of problem drinkers with a college education is more than double the number with only an elementary school education. Drinking is also related to religious and ethnic differences. People from an Asian background and from Jewish groups, especially Orthodox Jews, tend to have the lowest proportion of problem drinkers. Conservative Protestant groups have the highest proportion of abstainers, while liberal Protestants and Catholics have the higher proportion of moderate and heavy drinkers. There's also a tendency for adolescents who attend church frequently to remain abstainers.

The lowest incidence of problem drinking and alcoholism generally occurs in groups that have clear attitudes and rules regarding the use of alcohol. When children are exposed to alcohol, it is usually within a strong family or religious group. In these groups, alcohol is served in very diluted form, in small quantities, usually as an integral part of a meal. Abstinence is socially acceptable. Parents set an example of abstinence or moderate drinking and regard excessive drinking or intoxication as socially unacceptable. The use of alcohol is not viewed as proof of adulthood or virility. Finally, and most important, there is widespread and usually complete agreement on the ground rules of drinking by all members of the group (Jones-Witters and Witters, 1983).

Many of the measures aimed at curbing alcohol abuse have arisen out of concern over alcohol-related accidents among youth. Although teenagers comprise only 8 percent of the nation's drivers, they account for 15 percent of all drunken drivers involved in accidents. The leading cause of death among youth in their teens and twenties continues to be accidents, especially automobile accidents, with more than half of all fatally injured teenage drivers having alcohol in their blood. As a result, many states now have stiff penalties for drunk driving. In addition, there is greater awareness that hosts and hostesses need to watch out for guests who have been drinking and make arrangements for them to get home safely without driving. Many communities are providing teenagers with interesting and constructive social opportunities, such as alcohol- and substance-free post-prom, weekend, and graduation parties. In one school in Bucks County, Pennsylvania, high school seniors were treated to an elaborate formal prom that lasted from 7:30 P.M. to 6 A.M. the next day. It included a full-course catered dinner, live entertainment, and dancing throughout the night, with pizza at 3 A.M. and a continental breakfast at 6 A.M. Such occasions provide a good atmosphere for young people to enjoy themselves without jeopardizing their health or safety (Kennedy, 1984).

Tobacco and Smoking

Most people who smoke cigarettes begin using them during adolescence. Initiation of daily smoking most often occurs between 11 and 14 years of age, in grades 6 and 9. By the time students have reached their senior year in high school, about two-thirds of them have tried cigarettes. In fact, cigarettes are used daily by a larger proportion of teenagers (18 percent) than any other drug, despite the adverse publicity about tobacco. About one in ten seniors smokes a half-pack of cigarettes a day. College-bound seniors are much less inclined to smoke cigarettes than those not planning to attend college. And the difference between the two groups becomes more pronounced with age. Compared to college students, about three times as many other young adults the same age smoke at least a half-pack of cigarettes daily. Cigarette smoking is somewhat higher among females in high school as well as among other young adults. But cigarette smoking is considerably higher among women in college, with about 15 percent of college women versus 9 percent of college men smoking daily (Johnston, O'Malley, and Bachman, 1989).

Fortunately, many youths have become more aware of the dangers of smoking in the past decade. The proportion of teenagers who believe that smoking one or more packs of cigarettes a day entails greater harm for the user has risen slightly to 68 percent in 1988. Greater realization of the health hazards of smoking, as well as other uses of tobacco, has led to a decrease in smokers at all age levels. At the same time, these gains should not blind us to the fact that nearly a million teenagers begin smoking each year, and that about one-third of them are not yet convinced that cigarette smoking is a health hazard.

Young people smoke for a variety of reasons, many of them unclear even to themselves. Although some teenagers initially try cigarettes because of curiosity, others do so out of defiance, because it's something they are "not supposed to do." Then too, many youth feel it is sophisticated to smoke, which is not surprising in light of all the seductive advertising in newspapers and magazines. Smok-

---

Tobacco Addiction

When a prominent physician was told that his heart arrhythmia was aggravated by his heavy cigar smoking, up to twenty cigars a day, he stopped smoking for fourteen months. Later, he described the torture of not being able to smoke as "beyond human power to bear" and resumed smoking, though on a somewhat more moderate basis (Jones, 1953). Eventually, he developed cancer of the jaw and mouth that was also attributed to smoking. However, despite thirty-three operations for cancer and the construction of an artificial jaw, this physician continued to smoke until his death at the age of 83. His repeated efforts to stop smoking and the suffering he endured make him a tragic example of tobacco addiction. His name is Sigmund Freud (Altrocci, 1980).

ing is also associated with sociability—something to do after a meal, talking to friends, and at social gatherings. Teenagers are also much more likely to smoke if at least one parent smokes, especially the same-sex parent. There is also some evidence that teenage smokers are more extroverted, happy-go-lucky, and frank, but less agreeable than nonsmokers their age.

Smoking is a difficult habit to break. Even conservative estimates imply that half or more of those who quit smoking eventually resume the habit. In addition to the psychological dependence on the smoking habit, nicotine is considered to be physically addictive by many authorities. As a result, smokers build a tolerance to nicotine and need to smoke a larger number of cigarettes or ones with a higher nicotine content to get the same effect. The average smoker smokes twenty to thirty cigarettes a day—one about every thirty to forty minutes. And since the biological half-life of nicotine in humans is approximately twenty to thirty minutes, habitual smokers keep their systems primed with nicotine during most of their waking hours. Although nicotine has a variety of effects on the body, it is primarily a stimulant that increases the respiratory rate, heart rate, and blood pressure. Withdrawal from habitual smoking, and therefore nicotine, produces a variety of symptoms, including nervousness, headaches, dizziness, fatigue, insomnia, sweating, cramps, tremors, and heart palpitations (Jones-Witters and Witters, 1983).

Various antismoking programs have been studied in regard to the most effective strategies with adolescents (Perry et al., 1983). Among the more important findings are the following points:

1. *Present all the facts of smoking honestly.* Avoid half-truths that undermine the credibility of the message. Although factual knowledge alone does not usually change behavior, it can have great influence on knowledge and attitudes.
2. *Avoid scare tactics.* Use of extreme scare tactics evokes defensiveness and rejection of the message. The combination of factual material and mild to moderate arousal of anxiety is usually more effective.
3. *Emphasize the positive aspects of not smoking.* Appeal to adolescents' desire to take charge of their lives and to maintain physical fitness.
4. *Begin antismoking programs early in the educational process.* Because most adolescents who smoke the habit between grades 6 and 9, it would be better to begin antismoking education in the fourth or fifth grades than in high school.

Although antismoking education has not been very successful in changing smoking behavior of adolescents who already smoke, such programs might be more effective if initiated in the elementary grades before adolescents begin to smoke.

SELECTED ILLEGAL DRUGS

The widespread abuse of alcohol and tobacco is an apt reminder that legal drugs are still the worst killers. In fact, national drug abuse statistics show that more Americans die or suffer medical emergencies from using prescription drugs improperly than from the use of all illegal drugs combined (Ostrow, 1982). At the same time, this should not blind us to the growing menace of illegal drugs. There are now a wide variety of powerful drugs that are manufactured, distributed, and consumed apart from medical and legal supervision and without age restrictions, which multiplies the potential for drug abuse. In this section, we describe some of the effects and patterns of use of the most commonly used illegal drugs, including marijuana, the stimulants, the depressants, inhalants, hallucinogens, and heroin. But keep in mind that people who use drugs tend to use more than one of them at a time, without fully understanding the interactive effects of the drugs they are using. People use more than one drug at a time for a variety of reasons, such as to enhance the effect of one drug, to counteract the undesirable effects of another drug, or to achieve a less expensive high by combining one drug with a less expensive drug. In any event, multiple drug or polydrug use is becoming more and more popular, with single drug users being in the minority (O'Brien and Cohen, 1984).

Marijuana

Marijuana is made from the common hemp plant *Cannibis sativa*. This plant was once widely grown in the American colonies as a source of fiber for clothing and rope, and to a lesser extent for medicinal uses, and is now grown in most parts of the world. The potency of the drug varies with the content of THC (*tetrahydrocannabinol*), the main active ingredient of the Cannabis plant. The most powerful form of the drug, made from the resin of the female plant, is called hashish. The least potent form, marijuana, is made from the leaves, stems, and flowering tops, and is commonly grown in Mexico and the United States. Although marijuana is often classified as a hallucinogen, it is considerably milder than the other drugs in this class such as LSD and is used much more widely, so that it is generally discussed separately.

Marijuana is usually inhaled through smoking, though it can also be ingested. The common physical effects are a slight rise in pulse rate, lowered blood pressure, dilation of the pupils with a reddening of the eyes, dryness of the mouth and throat, and increased frequency of urination. Marijuana has an adverse effect on concentration, reading, comprehension, thinking, and short-term memory, so that habitual marijuana use may lower school performance. Marijuana also impairs vision and retards the reaction time and performance of mental and motor faculties. Although such changes are usually slight at low-dosage levels, they become more marked at higher levels. Over three-fourths of those who use marijuana say they sometimes drive while they are high, with marijuana users overrepresented in highway accidents. Driving under the combined influence of marijuana and alcohol is especially dangerous (Jones-Witters and Witters, 1983).

The psychological effects of marijuana, especially at lower dosage levels, depend largely on the personality of the user, his or her expectations of the drug,

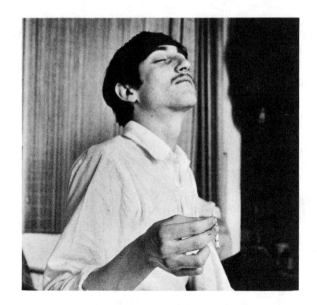

Although marijuana remains the most widely used illegal drug in the United States, marijuana use has declined because of the growing recognition of its harmful effects. (Charles Gatewood)

the circumstances in which it is used, and the user's past experience with the drug. Some common psychological effects are a feeling of relaxation, inner satisfaction, a free flow of ideas and imagination, exhilaration, and an altered sense of time and space—minutes may seem like hours and near objects appear distant. Yet much depends on the individual. New users may report little or no effect or overwhelming effects, depending on their makeup and moods. An anxious person may become more anxious or a depressed person more depressed. Marijuana is generally pleasurable at low levels, though unpleasant at very high levels. In short-term occasional use, marijuana may act as an aphrodisiac by releasing the central nervous system inhibitions on behavior. It also increases dilation of the blood vessels in the genitals and delays ejaculation in the male, though decreasing the sperm count. However, high doses over a long period of time are associated with a lowered libido and impotence.

Because marijuana cigarettes contain strong tars and some of the chemicals in marijuana are carcinogenic, chronic use of marijuana may be damaging to the lungs. However, since smokers in the United States are not exposed to as high a level of tars because marijuana is smoked less than tobacco, there may be a longer interval of time for the pathological effects of marijuana to show up. Frequent use of marijuana may lead to psychological dependence, with only mild physical addiction if at all. However, abrupt withdrawal from habitual use may produce irritability, sleep disturbance, appetite and weight loss, sweating, and gastrointestinal disturbances.

Although marijuana use declined among all age groups throughout the 1980s, it remains the most widely used illegal drug in the United States. According to the annual high school survey by Lloyd Johnston (1989) and his col-

Figure 14-2   Antimarijuana poster distributed by the Federal Bureau of Narcotics in the late 1930s.

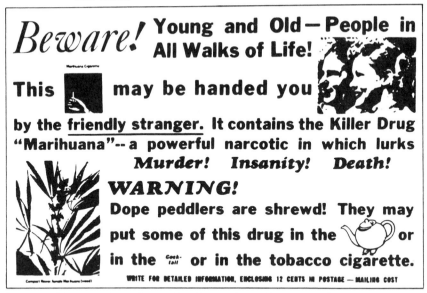

Source: Patricia Jones-Witters, Ph.D., and Weldon L. Witters, Ph.D., *Drugs and Society* (Boston, MA: Jones and Bartlett Publishers, Inc., 1983), p. 116.

leagues, about one-fourth of teenagers have tried marijuana by the time they reach the ninth grade, and almost half (47 percent) of them by their senior year. But only about one in twenty-seven seniors uses marijuana on a daily basis, down considerably from triple that number in the late 1970s. College-bound seniors are less inclined to use marijuana than their counterparts not planning to attend college. And the difference between these two groups increases throughout young adulthood, with fewer daily marijuana users among college students than others their age. Nevertheless, the proportion of individuals who try marijuana rises with age, with three-fourths of those in the 18–25 age group having used it at some time. Although occasional use of marijuana is only slightly higher among males than females, males are about twice as likely to use it on a daily basis in high school, with the differences between the sexes becoming less evident during young adulthood.

About half the marijuana users in high school get "high" for one to two hours, with one-third of them staying "high" for three to six hours. But the downward trend in the degree and duration of highs in recent years continues, with only two-thirds of the seniors in 1988 saying they get either moderately or very "high," compared to three-fourths of them a decade earlier. Not only are fewer high school students now using marijuana, but those who are doing so are using it less frequently and taking smaller amounts and doses of the active ingredient on each occasion.

A major reason marijuana use has declined among youth is the growing recognition of its harmful effects. Between the late 1970s and 1988, the proportion of high school seniors who felt that the regular use of marijuana is harmful almost doubled, from 43 to 77 percent. The increased awareness of the potential harmfulness of marijuana is probably due to the dramatic short-term changes in mood, behavior, and self-control associated with the drug in addition to the long-term physiological impact. At the same time, older youths tend to see lower risks for both regular and occasional marijuana use, which may be explained largely by "cohort effects," i.e., by effects due to their time of birth or generation rather than to the effects of age.

Attitudes toward decriminalizing marijuana have also changed among youth. The fairly tolerant attitudes of students in the late 1970s toward marijuana use have eroded considerably such that fewer youth now think marijuana use should be entirely legal. Only 15 percent of high school seniors in 1988, compared to twice that number a decade earlier, favor outright legalization of marijuana use. The great majority (81 percent) of seniors favor legally prohibiting marijuana use in public places, despite the fact that may of them have used marijuana themselves and do not judge it to be as dangerous as the other illicit drugs. But considerably fewer (52 percent) feel that marijuana use in private should be prohibited (Johnston, O'Malley, and Bachman, 1989).

Stimulants

These are substances that act on the central nervous system, causing the person who takes them to feel more lively. He or she may become more talkative and restless and be unable to sleep. With the exception of caffeine-type stimulants (coffee, tea, chocolate, and cola), the most commonly used stimulates are the amphetamines and cocaine.

There have been significant declines in the annual use of amphetamines among high school and college students, and even sharper drops among other young adults throughout the 1980s. A major reason is the increasing proportion of teenagers who disapprove of using amphetamines. Yet amphetamines remain the third most widely used class of illicit drugs among high school seniors, with about one-third of the seniors having friends who use them. Concurrent with the drop in amphetamines is an increase in the use of over-the-counter stay-awake pills, which generally contain caffeine as their active ingredient. Annual use of these pills has more than doubled in six years among high school students. Use of the other two classes of nonprescription stimulants—the "look alikes" and the over-the-counter diet pills—has fallen off some among both seniors and young adults in recent years.

Cocaine, another powerful stimulant, is similar to the amphetamines in reducing fatigue and inducing a euphoric state, though the effects of cocaine last only a short period of time. The most common reasons given for using cocaine are "to see what it's like", "to get high," and "to have a good time with my

The Coffee Cantata

Johann Sebastian Bach (1685–1750) wrote the Coffee Cantata around 1732, when the new drink began to leave the male society of coffee houses in Germany and invade private homes, where ladies began to consume it. In the cantata, the father is angry because his daughter is a coffee addict. He threatens not to provide her with a husband unless she promises to stop drinking it. Here are a few excerpts from their dialogue:

FATHER: O wicked child! Ungrateful daughter, why will you not respect my wishes and cease this coffee drinking?

DAUGHTER: Dear Father, be not so unkind; I love my cup of coffee at least three times a day, and if this pleasure you deny me, what else on earth is there to live for?

DAUGHTER: [continues in solo aria]: Far beyond all other pleasures, rarer than jewels or treasures, sweeter than grape from the vine. Yes! Yes! Greatest of pleasures! Coffee, coffee, how I love its flavor, and if you would win my favor, yes! Yes! let me have coffee, let me have my coffee strong.

FATHER: Well, pretty daughter, you must choose. If sense of duty you have none, then I must try another way. My patience is well nigh exhausted! Now listen! From your dress allowance I will take one half. Your next birthday should soon be here; no present will you get from me.

DAUGHTER: ... how cruel! But I will forgive you and consolation find in coffee ...

* * *

FATHER: Now, hearken to my last word. If coffee you must have, then a husband you shall not have.

DAUGHTER: O father! O horror! Not a husband?

FATHER: I swear it, and I mean it too.

DAUGHTER: O harsh decree! O cruel choice, between a husband and my joy. I'll strive no more; my coffee I surrender.

FATHER: At last you have regained your senses. [The daughter sings a melancholy aria of resignation.]

TENOR: And now, behold the happy father as forth he goes in search of a husband, rich and handsome, for his daughter. But the crafty little maiden has quite made up her mind, that, ere she gives consent to marriage, her lover must make a solemn promise that she may have her coffee whenever and wherever she pleases.

From Andrew Weil, M.D., and Winifred Rosen, *Chocolate to Morphine* (Boston: Houghton Mifflin Company, 1983) © by Andrew Weil, M.D., and Winifred Rosen. Reprinted by permission of Houghton Mifflin Company. All rights reserved.

friends." Compared to nonusers, individuals who use cocaine are more likely to use other illicit drugs, especially marijuana, to smoke cigarettes, and to drink heavily. It is not uncommon to use cocaine concurrently with marijuana or alcohol or both. The earlier notion that cocaine is not physically addictive has not been proved totally correct (Gawin and Kleber, 1986). But psychological dependence can become quite strong in some cases and may or may not be associated with signs of physical dependence (White, 1991).

Cocaine use has been declining among youths of all ages since about 1986. A major reason is that more youths are beginning to see that even the experimental and occasional use of this drug is more dangerous than they believed. Also, the hazards of cocaine received extensive media coverage, partly

Cocaine use has been declining among youths of all ages, mostly because even occasional use of this drug is more dangerous than previously believed. (Marc Anderson)

because of the cocaine-related deaths in 1986 of sports stars Len Bias and Don Rogers.

As a result, in 1988 only one in eight (12 percent) teenagers had tried cocaine by their senior year in high school, down from one in six (17 pecent) three years earlier. Similar declines in lifetime and annual use of cocaine occurred among college students and other young adults. However, cocaine remains unique among illicit drugs in that lifetime, annual, and current use all rise substantially with age. About 40 percent of all youths have tried cocaine by the time they reach 29 or 30 years of age. Clearly this drug is used much more frequently among people in their twenties than among those in their late teens. Although more males than females use cocaine, the sharp drop in cocaine use by males accounts for much of the decline in cocaine use in recent years. See Figure 14-3.

"Crack" is a more concentrated form of cocaine that comes in small, soap-like pellets that are smoked in pipes. Although cheaper than the usual forms of cocaine, the effects of crack are also shorter, such that crack users need more of the drug to maintain their habit. Crack is also more addictive, mostly because it is more potent and inhaled into the lungs, where it is absorbed into the bloodstream in about ten seconds. Thus, crack not only produces a higher "high" but a deeper "crash," leaving the user desperate for more.

One of the most important developments in 1988 was the drop in crack use among high school seniors for the first time. This is especially significant in that about four out of ten seniors who use cocaine use it in the form of crack.

Figure 14-3   Trends in annual cocaine use among male and female college students.

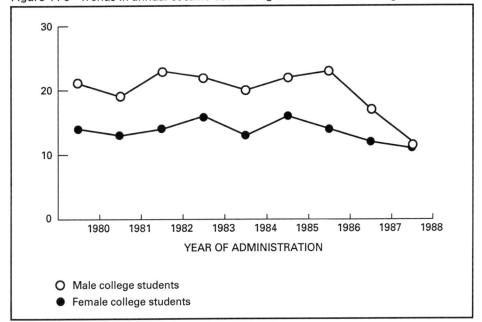

YEAR OF ADMINISTRATION

○ Male college students
● Female college students

Source: Lloyd D. Johnston, Patrick M. O'Malley, and Jerald G. Bachman, *Drug Use, Drinking, and Smoking: National Survey Results from High School, College, and Young Adult Populations 1975–1988* (Washington, D.C.: National Institute on Drug Abuse, U.S. Government Printing Office, 1989), p. 293.

Similar declines in both lifetime and annual use of cocaine were evident among college students and other young adults, mostly because of the rise in the perceived danger of using the drug. Two-thirds of youths in their twenties believe there is a risk of harming themselves in trying crack once or twice. Furthermore, nine out of ten of them disapprove of using crack regularly (Johnston, O'Malley, and Bachman, 1989).

Depressants

The depressants are a diverse group of drugs that diminish the activity of the central nervous system, producing anything from mild sedation to a coma, depending on the dosage. (See Table 14-2) The most common depressants are the barbiturates, methaqualone, and the minor tranquilizers. Along with alcohol and the stimulants, the depressants are among the most used and abused drugs in our society.

About one in twenty teenagers has taken a sedative, such as one of the barbiturates or methaqualone, by his or her senior year in high school. Although the barbiturates or "sleeping pills" are commonly prescribed to reduce anxiety and promote sleep, adolescents often use the short-acting barbiturates to lower

Table 14-2   How the Body and Mind Can React to Barbiturates and Other
              Depressants

	Body	Mind
Low dose	Drowsiness	Decreased anxiety, relaxation
	Trouble with coordination	
	Slurred speech	Decreased ability to reason and solve problems
	Dizziness	
	Staggering	Difficulty in judging distance and time
	Double vision	
	Sleep	
	Depressed breathing	Amnesia
High dose	Coma (unconscious and cannot be awakened)	Damage to brain
	Depressed blood pressure	
	Death	

Source: Patricia Jones-Witters, Ph.D., and Weldon L. Witters, Ph.D., *Drugs and Society* (Boston, MA: Jones and Bartlett Publishers, Inc., 1983), p. 175.

their tension and inhibitions, to take the edge off a pep-pill habit, or along with alcohol—an especially dangerous habit because of the additive effect of the barbiturates when combined with other drugs. Methaqualone, a sedative hypnotic that produces effects similar to those of the barbiturates, enjoyed a rapid rise in popularity during the 1970s as a recreational drug. Youths who take methaqualone tend to get very high for longer periods of time than with many of the other drugs. The most probable explanation is the youthful users' claim that methaqualone enhances sexual desire. Both the barbiturates and methaqualone have a high potential for physical and psychological dependence. Fortunately, the use of these depressants among youths of all ages has continued to decline since the mid 1970s.

The minor tranquilizers, such as those known by the trade names of Valium and Librium, are another class of depressants that alleviate anxiety. Although tranquilizers are widely used by adults, they are also used by a significant number of teenagers, with one out of ten (9 percent) of them having used a tranquilizer by his or her senior year in high school. The majority of users first try the drug in early adolescence and have used it only several times in their lives. Although these drugs are somewhat safer than the barbiturates in regard to overdosing and physical dependence, they are habit-forming and do have serious effects. Valium combined with alcohol has killed people. Use of the tranquilizers peaked in the late 1970s and has since declined substantially among young people (Johnston, O'Malley, and Bachman, 1989).

Other Drugs

There are a variety of other drugs that are used mostly on occasions by a substantial minority of youth. These include the inhalants, hallucinogens, heroin, and the other opiates. Use of these drugs is generally higher among teenagers who do not plan to go college and young adults generally than among college students. Also, the lifetime prevalence of these drugs is two and one-half times higher among males than females.

During high school, about one in five teenagers (17 percent) use inhalants—substances whose fumes are inhaled to make the user feel good or "high." The two classes of inhalants used most frequently by adolescents are the amyl and butyl nitrites. Butyl nitrite got its reputation as an aphrodisiac by its apparent effect if used during sexual relations near orgasm. However, afterward users may have a tremendous headache and feel nauseous for a while. As a result, most of those who try this inhalant do not continue to use it. The inhalants tend to be used more commonly by younger adolescents who have usually discontinued their use by late high school, often failing to report their earlier experience with the drug. Although most teenagers experiment with inhalants in transition to other drugs, some of them become chronic users. The inhalants do not lead to physical addiction, but they can cause adverse reactions and also long-term carcinogenic effects that may not appear for ten to thirty years (Jones-Witters and Witters, 1983).

About one in eleven teenagers (9 percent) have tried one of the hallucinogens during high school. This diverse group of mind-altering drugs, including LSD and PCP, is variously known as the psychedelic (consciousness-expanding) or the psychotomimetic (psychosis-mimicking) group. Taken in small amounts, these drugs bring about mild feelings of euphoria. Larger amounts produce more marked reactions, ranging from horror to ecstasy, from minor distortions of body image to loss of ego boundaries, and from intensification of color and depth to hallucinations. LSD is the most widely used hallucinogen, with the majority of users taking it only occasionally to get very high. Although LSD does not cause physical dependence, it does have moderate potential for psychological dependence and abuse. Most former users of LSD have discontinued the drug because of their fear of physical damage, psychological harm, or an emotionally upsetting experience with the drug. PCP, which is often present in other drugs sold on the streets such as mescaline, is regarded with fear by many people because it sometimes leads to intense feelings of paranoia, unpredictable violent behavior, and a complete loss of reality testing. Consequently, use of PCP by teenagers has fallen sharply (Johnston, O'Malley, and Bachman, 1989).

Heroin, generally regarded as the least frequently used illicit drug, continues to decline in use among youths of all ages. Only .5 percent of high school seniors used it in 1988. A much larger proportion of adolescents (5 percent) have used one of the other opiates such as codeine. Drugs such as heroin, codeine, and morphine are classified as opiates or narcotics, synonymous terms for drugs derived from opium, which is made from the juice of the poppy flower. Codeine, a common ingredient in cough medicines, is used by teenagers to get "high," often with beer or wine. Morphine, a standard painkiller, is sometimes obtained illicitly through fake prescriptions or drugstore robberies. When heroin was extracted from morphine and proved effective in combating opium and mor-

Steroid Use by Youth

In earlier generations, ninety-seven-pound weaklings at the beach turned to body-building exercises or pumping iron. Now they may turn to steroids—synthetic male hormones that increase muscle mass, strength, and performance.

Surveys show that about one in fifteen male high school seniors and as many as five hundred thousand adolescents nationwide have used steroids. Nearly a third of them take the drug to acquire that brawny, Rambo look (Toufexis, 1989). Other high school and college athletes as well as professional athletes use steroids to enhance their performance in weight lifting, football, wrestling, body building, and track (Fuller and LaFountain, 1987).

Yet their drug-enhanced physiques and performances may be a costly bargain. Emotional and psychological instability are common. Steroid users are especially prone to aggression, resulting in increased arguments and fights along with sexual aggression. Steroids can cause harm to the heart, liver, kidneys, stomach, connective tissue, and reproductive systems of both sexes. Also, contaminated illegal steroids can cause serious infections. Doctors suspect steroids may contribute to liver cancer and arteriosclerosis (Kruskemper, 1986).

Once on steroids, adolescents find it hard to quit. One teenager said, "I'll take them for four months until I look the way I want. Then I'll quit." But it doesn't work that way. When the drug is halted, the bulging biceps fade fast. As a result, almost every user resumes steroids (Toufexis, 1989).

phine addiction, it was received with such high hopes that it was named from the word "hero"—heroin. Yet it has turned out to be the most physically addictive and destructive of all the drugs, accounting for more drug-related deaths than any other drug except alcohol.

Heroin use occurs in two stages. In the early stages it is taken mostly for its psychological effects, which include an early surge of feelings of warmth and peace likened to a prolonged orgasm. Users feel relaxed and drowsy, with an easing of pain, fears, and worries. They also experience reduced hunger and sex drives for three to four hours. However, after becoming addicted, which may occur after using the drug daily for only several weeks, users enter a second stage of heroin use in which they take it mostly to avoid the unpleasant withdrawal symptoms, such as vomiting, diarrhea, convulsions, sweating, and twitching muscles. Largely because it is only available illegally and is expensive and addictive, heroin is the least used illegal drug and is more common among noncollege youth and males in the ghettos of the large cities.

PUTTING DRUGS IN PERSPECTIVE

The discussion of young people's use of drugs is especially difficult because of the lack of a clear and consistent approach by parents, educators, and youths alike. Some people equate the use of any illegal drug with drug abuse. As a result, what passes for drug education becomes a thinly disguised attempt to scare young people away from disapproved drugs by exaggerating their dangers. Yet the lectures, pamphlets, and filmstrips that adopt this approach often stimulate curiosity, making the prohibited substances even more attractive. In contrast, other people distinguish between the moderate recreational use of drugs and an abusive, pathological use of any drugs, including legal drugs. Drug education based on this approach tends to emphasize the importance of understanding the various types of drugs, including their potential for danger, and the value of individuals making a personal decision about the use or disuse of drugs. More in line with this latter approach, in this section we take a look at people's overall relationships with drugs, including the problem of drug dependence. Then we will examine the treatment of drug abuse and the important matter of prevention.

Relationships with Drugs

The effect of a drug is not simply a matter of what drug a person chooses to consume. It also depends on the relationship individuals form with a given drug. Many factors determine people's relationships with drugs. The drug itself is obviously a crucial factor, with the whole field of pharmacology devoted to discovering the makeup and effects of drugs. But the overall effect a drug produces also depends on many other factors, such as the person's physical and psychological makeup, his or her needs and traits, and past experiences with the drugs. The person's psychological "set" or expectations of a given drug also contribute to the psychological effect of a drug. It is common knowledge that teenagers who expect to get high on a couple of beers will begin to act that way regardless of the amount of alcohol they have consumed. Another factor that modifies the effects of a drug is the social "setting," or total environment, in which a drug is used. A few drinks of an alcoholic beverage may produce sexual arousal in one situation, whereas the same amount of alcohol consumed by the same person may lead to drowsiness and fatigue in another set of circumstances. The set and setting are thought to be of even greater importance in the use of the psychedelic and hallucinogenic drugs than in that of other drugs (Jones-Witters and Witters, 1983).

In their book *Chocolate to Morphine,* Andrew Weil, M.D., and Winifred Rosen (1983) provide some guidelines for establishing good relationships with drugs as follows:

1. *Recognition that the substance you're using is a drug and being aware of what it does to your body.* The people who develop the worst relationships with drugs have little understanding of the drugs they're using. They think that coffee is just another beverage or that cigarettes are harmless because they are sold legally, despite the warning on the package. People need to realize that *all* drugs—including prescription drugs—have the potential to cause trouble unless they control their use. A necessary first step is to understand the nature and the effects of the substances being used.

2. *Experience of a useful effect of the drug over time.* People who use drugs regularly often find that their early experiences with them were their best. The effects seem to diminish the more often a drug is used. People in bad relationships with drugs tend to use them very heavily but get the least out of them. Frequency is the most important factor in determining whether the effect of a drug will last over time. When the experience people like from a drug begins to fade, that is a sign that they are using too much. Those who ignore the warning and increase their consumption of a drug risk sliding into a worse relationship with the drug.

3. *Ease of separation from use of the drug.* People who are in a good relationship with drugs can take them or leave them. By contrast, one of the striking features of a bad relationship with drugs is dependence on a drug—psychological or physical. When people have become dependent on a drug—whether it's caffeine, nicotine, alcohol, or some illegal drug—the drug controls them more than they control the drug. Thus, drug dependence is a major factor in determining drug abuse.

4. *Freedom from adverse effects on health and behavior.* People vary in their susceptibility to the adverse effects of drugs; some people can smoke cigarettes all their lives and never develop cancer of the lung, mouth, or throat; others cannot. Some people can take a drink or two before dinner without disrupting their family lives or work, while other people's drinking contributes directly to their troubles at home or on the job. Using drugs in ways that produce adverse effects on health and behavior is another major characteristic of drug abuse.

Weil and Rosen point out that bad relationships with a drug begin with an ignorance of the substance and the loss of the desired effect with an increasing frequency of use, gradually leading to drug dependence, with the eventual impairment of one's health and social functioning. The pattern of progression from initial use of a drug to dependence on it may vary considerably among individuals depending on such factors as personality, the particular drug, frequency and intensity of use, and the extent to which physical or psychological dependence occurs.

Individuals who become dependent on a drug tend to have the characteristic symptoms of the psychoactive substance dependence disorder. Such individuals exhibit an impaired control of and continued use of a substance despite adverse consequences. The symptoms of the dependence syndrome include, but are not limited to, the physiological symptoms of tolerance and withdrawal. In addition, some symptoms must have persisted for at least one month or have occurred repeatedly over a longer period of time, as in binge drinking. Individuals may have different degrees of drug dependence, whether mild, moderate, or severe. Furthermore, the following guidelines are given for a partial or full remission: For a partial remission, during the past six months some use of the substance and some symptoms of dependence must have existed. For a full remission during the past six months either no use of the substance or use of the substance and no symptoms of dependence must have existed. See Figure 14-4.

Figure 14–4 Symptoms of Substance Abuse

According to the American Psychiatric Association's authoritative guide, DSM-III-R, at least three of the following nine characteristic symptoms are necessary to make the diagnosis of a psychoactive substance dependence disorder:

1. Substance taken in larger amounts or over a longer period than the person intended.
2. Persistent desire of one or more unsuccessful efforts to cut down or control substance use.
3. A great deal of time spent obtaining the substance, taking the substance, or recovering from its effects.
4. Frequent intoxication or withdrawal symptoms when there are major role obligations at work, school, or home, or when substance use is physically hazardous.
5. Important social, occupational, or recreational activities reduced or given up because of substance use.
6. Continued use despite persistent or recurrent social, psychological, or physical problems caused or exacerbated by use of the substance.
7. Marked tolerance, i.e., need for significantly increased amounts of the substance (at least a 50 percent increase) in order to achieve intoxication or desired effect, or markedly diminished effect with continued use of the same amount.

Note: The following items may not apply to cannabis, hallucinogens, or phencyclidine (PCP):

8. Characteristic withdrawal symptoms (vary with specific substances).
9. Substance often taken to relieve or avoid withdrawal symptoms.

Source: *Diagnostic and Statistical Manual of Mental Disorders* (DSM-III-R), 3d. ed. rev. (Washington, D.C.: American Psychiatric Association, 1987), pp. 167–68.

Treatment of Drug Abuse

There is a wide variety of programs available for treating drug abuse. The various treatment programs differ in regard to a number of issues, such as whether they are voluntary or involuntary, selective or nonselective, inpatient or outpatient, medical or nonmedical, and whether the goal is abstinence or controlled use of the substance.

A major consideration in the approach to drug abuse is whether individuals receive treatment in a residential or outpatient program. Most of these programs assume that drug abuse is a symptom of underlying psychological problems and aim at a change in life-style as well as abstinence. There are several hundred residential treatment programs, including medically oriented, hospital-based programs and therapeutic communities staffed largely by former addicts. Hospital treatment programs typically last one or two months, though some last up to a year. Therapeutic communities tend to require longer periods, from about nine to eighteen months. But both types of programs have a relatively high failure rate. Individuals may not be ready for the complete change in life-style demanded by the program. Or they become bored and frustrated, with most dropouts leaving in the first 28 days. A large proportion of people who enter these programs drop out and reenter the program at a later date, with relapse being the rule rather than the exception. In the outpatient programs, individuals visit the treatment facility at certain intervals and participate in a variety of programs including individual and family counseling, encounter groups, educational and career programs, training in life skills, and work assignments in the community. Yet overall effectiveness in outpatient drug-free programs has also been poor (Jones-Witters and Witters, 1983).

Because of the prevalence of relapse, some cognitive behavioral therapists have developed relapse-prevention training to help substance abusers cope with high-risk situations and prevent lapses from becoming full-blown relapses (Marlatt and Gordon, 1985). Trainees are taught to cope with high-risk situations by practicing relaxation and to avoid practices that might trigger a relapse, such as keeping alcohol in the house for friends. They are also taught how to avoid the abstinence violation effect—overreacting to a lapse—by reorienting their thinking. Unlike the disease model, which claims that alcoholics automatically lose control if they take a single drink, the relapse-prevention model contends a lot depends on the individual's reaction to a lapse. Use of self-defeating attributions such as "What's the use? I'm doomed to fail" evoke resignation and a resumption of problem drinking. However, individuals in a relapse-prevention training are encouraged to view lapses as temporary setbacks that they can learn from and avoid in the future. For instance, individuals are taught to think, "Okay, I had a little slip. But that doesn't mean I'm all through. I can get right back on track." Participants are trained to challenge dysfunctional thinking about lapses and substitute more adaptive coping thoughts and actions. Despite their promise, the results of relapse-prevention training have been mixed, such that more research is needed to fully evaluate the benefits of such training.

A comprehensive approach treatment suggested by Turanski (1982) would include components for youths at different stages of drug use and abuse. A preventive component, especially for teenagers whose parents abuse drugs, would include individual, group, and family therapy, as well as the availability of educational and career counseling and support groups. A second component would focus on teens at risk who are currently recreational users of drugs but are in danger of future escalation of drug use. This would include the resources mentioned above plus workshops in life-skills training and alternative activities to drug use. A third component would provide intensive and long-term residential treatment for the more severe drug abusers. A final component would include aftercare and support for youths and their families during the transition back to the community, crisis intervention if needed, and guidance in developing new activities and peer relationships. In addition, Craig Thorne and Richard DeBlassie (1985) suggest more widespread acceptance of the view that addiction is something the individual can and has to take responsibility for in order to achieve lasting improvement.

Prevention

Throughout the chapter we've alluded to the notion that it is easier to prevent adolescents from starting drugs than persuading them to quit once they've begun. If so, programs aimed at prevention should be initiated early in the educational process, prior to the ninth grade. Preventive education aimed at the use of alcohol and cigarettes should begin before the sixth grade. A variety of approaches to drug education have been and still are used (White, 1991).

One type of program provides students with information about drugs. Most of these explain how drugs affect the brain, and thus how we feel and behave, along with the adverse effects of drugs. Usually, it's more helpful to present the facts as honestly as possible, avoiding scare tactics.

Another approach is to deal with issues of health and psychological well-being that are strongly associated with drug abuse and a drug-free existence. Major topics include dysfunctional and healthy families, self-esteem, health, fitness, personal control, and stress management. Activities often consist of class or small group discussions aimed at promoting self-understanding and positive attitudes and values.

A third type of program focuses on alternatives to drug use. The aim is to discover activities that provide students with positive experiences similar to those obtained by drugs. Some have suggested that a given type of activity is needed to counteract a specific type of drug problem. For instance, people who

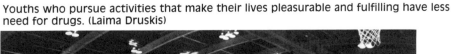

Youths who pursue activities that make their lives pleasurable and fulfilling have less need for drugs. (Laima Druskis)

seek excitement through stimulants need to seek an alternative form of excitement such as hang gliding. Yet this notion implies an oversimplified view of the effects produced by different drugs. A sounder approach would be to emphasize activities that make people's lives more pleasurable and fulfilling without the hazards of drugs (White, 1991).

Still another approach stresses the acquisition of social skills. Some skills would increase social competence, such as how to initiate a conversation. Others might focus on drug-refusal skills, such as refusing an alcoholic drink at a party. Given the importance of peer interaction during adolescence and especially in regard to drug use, this approach should not be underestimated. Evidence for reduced drug use is strongest for this approach (Tobler, 1986).

A fifth approach emphasizes the importance of personal commitment. The importance of personal decision is apparent in a study of drug use and abuse among several hundred high school students (Scott, 1978). When asked why they continued to use drugs, users frequently cited the "payoff" of drugs. To the question what might make them stop using or abusing drugs, the most common answer was "my decision." When former drug users and abusers were asked why they had stopped, a larger percentage of them indicated there was "no payoff" from drugs or they no longer had "need for drugs." And the most frequently given reason for staying off drugs was "willpower" and "self-determination," all of which underlines the importance of making a personal commitment to stay away from drugs.

SUMMARY

Use of Drugs

1. Despite the appreciable decline in illicit drug use in recent years, American youths in their teens and twenties show a level of involvement with illicit drugs which is greater than that found in any other industrialized nation in the world.
2. Practically all adolescents have tried alcohol and more than half of them have used an illegal drug by the time they have reached their senior year in high school.
3. Adolescents start to use drugs at a relatively early age, beginning with the legal drugs such as alcohol and cigarettes before progressing to the illegal drugs such as marijuana.
4. Although youths may take drugs for a variety of reasons, the most commonly mentioned ones are to have a good time with friends, to get high, and to relieve tension.

Alcohol and Tobacco

5. Alcohol and tobacco continue to be the most commonly used and abused substances, mostly because of their availability and widespread acceptance.
6. Occasional heavy drinking, mostly at weekend parties, has declined but continues to be widespread among high school and college students.
7. Many of the measures aimed at curbing alcohol abuse have arisen out of concern over alcohol-related accidents, and over half of the fatally injured teenage drivers are found to have alcohol in their blood.

8. Cigarettes are used daily by a larger proportion of teenagers than any other drug, though increased awareness of the health risk posed by smoking has led to a decline in cigarette smoking in recent years.

Selected Illegal Drugs

9. Marijuana remains the most widely used illegal drug, with three-fourths of youths having tried it by their mid-twenties.
10. The most commonly used stimulants, apart from the caffeine-type substances, are the amphetamines and cocaine.
11. Cocaine use, especially, has been declining among youths of all ages since about 1986, mostly because of the hazards associated with its use.
12. Although use of depressants such as the barbiturates, methaqualone, and tranquilizers has declined in the past decade, a minority of adolescents have used them at one time or another.
13. A variety of other illegal drugs, such as the inhalants, hallucinogens, and the various opiates, are used by a substantial minority of youth, mostly on an occasional basis.
14. Heroin, one of the most physically addictive and destructive of all the drugs, is the most infrequently used illegal drug.

Putting Drugs in Perspective

15. The effects of a drug depend on a number of factors in addition to the drug itself, including the individual's expectations, the social setting in which the drug is taken, the physical and psychological makeup of the individual, and his or her past experience with the drug.
16. Youths get into bad relationships with drugs through an ignorance of what the drug does to their bodies and minds, and the loss of effect with an increasing frequence of use, which leads gradually to greater dependence on the drug, with the eventual impairment of health and social functioning.
17. Although there is a wide variety of approaches to treating drug abuse, the overall success rate continues to be poor. Relapse-prevention training may be helpful in preventing temporary lapses from becoming full-blown relapses.
18. Educational approaches aimed at prevention include providing information about drugs, dealing with pertinent health and psychological issues, discovering alternatives to drugs, teaching social skills, and emphasizing the importance of personal commitment.

Answers to Fact or Fiction

1. False. Even in small amounts alcohol is a depressant. Alcohol may appear to enliven a drinker by slowing brain activity that controls inhibitions.
2. False. The enzymes that break down the toxins in alcohol are the slowest around 2 o'clock in the afternoon and the fastest twelve hours later, with significant sex differences. Women's enzymes tend to be faster than men's enzymes during the wee hours of the morning (Rose, 1988).
3. True. More than nine out of ten alcoholics are cigarette smokers (Istvan and Matarazzo, 1984).
4. False. College students consume more alcohol than do other adults the same age (Johnston, O'Malley, and Bachman, 1989).
5. True. The highest rate of binge drinking—43 percent—is among full-time college students (Johnston, O'Malley, and Bachman, 1989).

REVIEW QUESTIONS

1. Describe the typical developmental sequence in which teenagers begin using the various legal and illegal drugs.
2. What are the most common reasons given for using drugs?
3. In what ways has alcohol abuse become a serious problem among youths?
4. Which youths are more at risk for alcohol abuse?
5. Why is cigarette smoking such a health risk among youth?
6. Do you think marijuana should be legalized?
7. How would you account for the popularity of cocaine in recent years?
8. What are the symptoms of drug abuse?
9. How would you go about helping a friend with an alcohol problem?
10. What are some ways to prevent youths from beginning the drug habit?

Psychological Disorders

15

Learning Objectives

After completing this chapter, you should be able to:

1 Discuss the extent of psychological disorders in adolescence.
2 Identify three anxiety disorders and their major features.
3 Identify five types of depression and their major features.
4 Describe the major contributing factors to adolescent suicide.
5 Give one example each of an eating disorder and a personality disorder.
6 Identify at least six factors affecting the outlook for an adolescent suffering from schizophrenia.
7 Describe the range of therapeutic approaches used for disturbed adolescents.

Carol, a high school student, takes exactly the same route to and from school every day. Recently, while walking home with another girl, she tried walking down a different street. Midway down the unfamiliar block, Carol felt dizzy and her heart began pounding. She broke out in a cold sweat. She quickly excused herself, ran back to the corner, and went home the usual way.

Ed is a freshman at college who has been doing poorly in school. Each time he sits down to study he finds himself worrying and daydreaming. He suffers from feelings of worthlessness and makes excuses to keep from going out with his friends. Ed is also having trouble getting to sleep at night and has begun drinking several beers before bedtime. He sleeps until noon but still feels tired all the time.

Amy is an eccentric teenager who has few friends. Most of the time at home she keeps to herself in her room. For the past several months, Amy has complained that students are talking about her and calling her names behind her back. She has also begun hearing voices that accuse her of engaging in homosexual acts. Recently, after she began staying up most nights and refused to attend school, she was taken to a local mental health center for an evaluation.

PSYCHOLOGICAL DISTURBANCE IN ADOLESCENCE

All three of these youths are experiencing significant psychological disturbances. Carol is suffering from agoraphobia, one of the anxiety disorders. Ed exhibits several of the classic symptoms of depression, a common disorder that is often masked behind other problems, especially alcohol and drug abuse. Amy has been diagnosed as suffering from schizophrenia, a severe psychological disorder that is more likely to make its initial appearance during adolescence or early adulthood than at any other period of life. We discuss these and other disorders in this chapter. But first we take a look at the incidence of psychological disturbances at adolescence.

Admissions of children to clinics begin to increase gradually at 6 or 7 years of age and reach a peak at 14 or 15 years of age. The increase in admissions at 6 or 7 is probably related to the child's beginning school. Problems that have been ignored or put up with at home may no longer be tolerated in the classroom. Then too, starting school itself is often stressful and may precipitate psychological problems. The peak in psychological disturbances at midadolescence probably reflects the normal developmental problems of this age coupled with the inherent stress of adolescence. Surveys have shown that anywhere between 10 and 20 percent of adolescents in the United States are suffering from a serious psychological disturbance (Rutter and Garmezy, 1983: Bootzin & Acocella, 1988). Unfortunately, only about one-half of those who need professional help get it. An even smaller proportion of needy adolescents in less developed countries receive treatment. The implication is that there are millions of adolescents in need of treatment who do not receive it (Offer et al., 1988).

The extent to which psychological disturbances are recognized as such during adolescence depends partly on the forms in which they are manifested. Achenbach and Edelbrock (1981) make a useful distinction between adolescents who are externalizers and those who are internalizers, depending on the extent to which an adolescent's problems are expressed primarily in conflicts with the outside world or in intrapsychic conflicts. Externalizers are more likely to have

Quiet, introverted youths often have trouble expressing their problems to others. (Ken Karp)

problems with aggression, delinquency, and sex, whereas internalizers tend to have problems with depression, anxiety, obsessions, phobias, and somatic complaints. Achenbach suggests that the difference between externalizers and internalizers is partly the product of adolescents' socialization. That is, externalizers generally have parents who have more overt problems and who exhibit little concern about their adolescents. Consequently, these youths have learned to express their aggressive impulses overtly, resulting in more behavior problems in school and with the police. On the other hand, internalizers tend to come from more stable homes, with parents who have fewer overt problems and show more concern about their adolescents. As a result, these youths characteristically react to stress with inner conflicts. The fact that a greater proportion of boys are classified as externalizers and are more likely to express their difficulties in outward behavior may help to explain why about twice as many boys as girls are referred for psychological help during adolescence (Taube and Barrett, 1985). The same distinction may also help to explain the preponderance of lower-class youth referred for help. Achenbach and Edelbrock found that lower-class parents reported a greater incidence of problems and disturbances among their children and adolescents than did middle-class parents, with many of these problems involving undercontrolled, externalizing behavior.

Experienced clinicians have long realized that it is more difficult to distinguish between normal and disturbed behavior at adolescence than at any other period of life. Because adolescence is an intense period of rapid physical, cognitive, and emotional growth, symptoms that might suggest abnormality in adults often turn out to be considerably less serious in adolescents. Thus, clinicians are often reluctant to apply the more serious diagnostic labels to adolescents, lest this should make the client's situation worse. Weiner (1980) reports that a disproportionately high percentage of adolescents are classified in the less serious categories, such as one of the adjustment disorders in the DSM-III-R. This category includes relatively minor disturbances of adjustment brought on by developmental and situational factors such as stress, rather than deep or long-standing psychological conflicts.

At the same time, Weiner reports that youths diagnosed with the less serious labels are just as likely to receive psychotherapy and remain in treatment as long as those with more serious diagnoses. Nor do they easily outgrow their problems. A ten-year follow-up study showed that youths originally diagnosed with the milder situational or adjustments disorders were just as likely to reappear in therapy and for just as many subsequent periods of psychological help as those with more serious disorders. Finally, of the youths who returned for help, an almost equal number of those with the milder diagnoses (11.2 percent) were subsequently diagnosed as schizophrenic, as compared to 14 percent of those with the personality and anxiety disorders. All this suggests that youths who are sufficiently disturbed to warrant treatment are often experiencing more than just growing pains.

The close link between adolescent development and disturbance presents two opposing dangers to adults. One danger is to overinterpret signs of disturbance at adolescence, thereby undermining the youth's self-confidence and creating self-fulfilling expectancies among adolescents and adults alike. The other danger is to dismiss serious problems at adolescence, thereby avoiding the needed treatment and allowing problems to get out of hand. In order to minimize these dangers, parents and other concerned adults might assess the troubled adolescent's behavior in light of the following questions:

◆ Has the problem lasted beyond the expected age?
◆ Is it frequently displayed?
◆ Does such behavior resist ordinary efforts to change it?
◆ How seriously does it interfere with the adolescent's relationships with adults and peers?
◆ Does the behavior interfere with schoolwork?
◆ If such behavior continues, will it interfere with adult adjustment?

ANXIETY DISORDERS

Anxiety is a vague unpleasant feeling of apprehension warning us of impending danger. In a stressful situation, such as an exam, anxiety may be adaptive by motivating us to prepare ourselves accordingly. But when anxiety becomes unrealistic and excessive to the situation at hand, it has a disruptive effect. In a generalized anxiety disorder the anxiety itself becomes the predominant disturbance, with the person being chronically anxious. However, in a phobic disorder, the anxiety is evoked by some dreaded object or situation, such as riding in an elevator, and triggers avoidance behavior. In the obsessive-compulsive disorder, anxiety occurs if the person does *not* engage in some thought or behavior, such as repeatedly washing one's hands, which otherwise is senseless and embarrassing.

Generalized Anxiety Disorder

The main feature of a generalized anxiety disorder is a chronic state of diffuse, "free-floating anxiety," as Freud labeled it. Individuals are prone to unrealistic and excessive anxiety about two or more life circumstances, e.g., their grades in school and social life. Anxious youths are continually waiting for something dreadful to happen. Frequently, the subjective condition affects their thinking and bodily functioning. Individuals find it hard to concentrate and remember commitments, thereby impairing their performance. Also, they may suffer from headaches and muscle tension.

For example, a 15-year-old girl became noticeably more fearful after her family's move to a new city. Her grades in school began to suffer, she had trouble sleeping and she could not seem to make new friends. A concerned counselor discovered that the girl's anxiety reflected a disturbance in the home—namely, repeated threats of a marital separation, as well as the girl's conflicting feelings about becoming more independent of her parents. Another contributing factor was an intense rivalry with an older sister. The family's move simply precipitated the anxiety attack, which then provided the opportunity for clarifying the girl's conflicts.

A related syndrome is the panic attack. Individuals with a panic disorder are prone to attacks of intense, almost unbearable anxiety which last for several minutes. Such attacks are largely unpredictable, usually appearing suddenly, and in many instances in the absence of an identifiable stimulus. The individual may feel short of breath, dizzy, and fearful of losing control. See Figure 15-1, "Symptoms of a Panic Attack." Although the panic attack sounds like an acute version of a generalized anxiety disorder, it is a related but separate syndrome. For instance, most of the symptoms of a panic disorder will become worse if the victims hyperventilate, whereas this procedure is much less likely to increase anxiety in those with generalized anxiety disorder. This, along with other findings, suggests there is a stronger organic component in panic disorder than in generalized anxiety disorder (Rapee, 1986).

Phobias

A phobia is a persistent and irrational fear of a specific object or activity, accompanied by a compelling desire to avoid it. Most of us experience an irrational avoidance of selected objects, such as snakes and spiders, but this generally has no significant impact on our lives. By contrast, when the avoidance behavior becomes a significant source of distress to the individual and interferes with his or her everyday behavior, the diagnosis of a phobic disorder is warranted. Simple phobias generally involve a circumscribed stimulus, such as the fear of heights or the fear of closed places. Social phobias involve an irrational fear of and a compelling desire to avoid situations in which the individual may be scrutinized by others, such as the fear of speaking in public. See the boxed item on selected phobias.

Figure 15-1 Symptoms of a Panic Attack.

According to the American Psychiatric Association's authoritative guide, the DSM-III-R, at least four of the following symptoms must be present for the diagnosis of a panic disorder or panic attack:

1. Shortness of breath
2. Dizziness or faintness
3. Accelerated heart rate
4. Trembling or shaking
5. Sweating
6. Choking
7. Nausea or other abdominal distress
8. Feelings of depersonalization
9. Numbness or tingling
10. Hot flashes or chills
11. Chest pains or discomfort
12. Fear of dying
13. Fear of going crazy or losing control

Source: *Diagnostic and Statistical Manual of Mental Disorders* (DSM-III-R), 3d ed. rev. (Washington, D.C.: American Psychiatric Association, 1987), p. 238.

Selected Phobias

Androphobia—fear of men
Cyberphobia—fear of computers
Gamophobia—fear of marriage
Gynephobia—fear of women
Hypergiaphobia—fear of responsibility
Monophobia—fear of being alone
Nyctophobia—fear of darkness

Ochlophobia—fear of crowds
Ophidiophobia—fear of snakes
Phobophobia—fear of fear
Sophophobia—fear of learning
Taphophobia—fear of being buried alive
Topophobia—fear of performing ("stage fright")

Although *school phobia* is more common among children, it is more serious when it occurs at adolescence. School phobias usually reflect a dread of some aspect of school, such as an authoritarian teacher or sports. According to a dynamic view, a school phobia may reflect an internal conflict involving separation anxiety in relation to overprotective parents. In many instances, the father may fail to counteract the mother's possessiveness. Sometimes, a school phobia reflects negative experiences at school, perhaps in relation to a critical teacher or excessive competitiveness among peers. In many instances, anxiety is directed toward specific aspects of the school environment—for example, test anxiety or competition over college admissions. School phobia among adolescents is often just one aspect of chronic maladjustment with a long history of problems. Chronic phobics tend to break off contact with their friends and mope around the house without accomplishing anything. Consequently, school phobia is usually a more serious condition among adolescents than in children, a difficult condition to treat, and perhaps a prelude to poor adult adjustment in work-related situations (Weiner, 1980).

Agoraphobia is typically the most severe phobic reaction and the one for which people most often seek treatment. Agoraphobia is a cluster of different fears, all of which evoke intense anxiety about panicking in unfamiliar places. Situations commonly avoided include being in crowds, such as a crowded store, in elevators or tunnels, or on public transportation or bridges. This type of phobia tends to occur in the late teens or early twenties, though it can occur later in life. It is also much more prevalent among young women than men. During the outbreak of this phobia, individuals are often housebound. If they do go out, great care is taken to avoid certain situations such as being in an elevator or crossing a bridge.

Obsessive-Compulsive Disorder

The essential features of this disorder are recurrent obsessions or compulsions, or, as is usually the case, both. Young people afflicted with this disorder may find themselves unable to put certain unacceptable ideas out of their heads. Typically, these obsessions involve thoughts of lust and violence, partly because of their association with the individual's anxiety and guilt. Then too, the individuals may have the urge, almost against their wills, to engage in repetitive activities to ward off the imaginary threats. Most of these compulsions fall into two categories and involve checking rituals, such as making certain the door is locked, and cleaning rituals, such as changing clothes several times a day to ensure that they are spotless. Common examples would be the teenager who bathes compulsively, habitually sets fires, or engages in ritualistic acts to maintain neatness. Another example is the young man who always spent an hour checking over various parts of his car before starting it.

DEPRESSION AND SUICIDE

Depression rivals the anxiety disorders as the most widespread psychological disturbance among adolescents and adults alike. (Robins et al., 1984). Although fluctuations in mood are normal in everyone, including feelings of sadness at times, when such feelings persist and become the dominant mood, clinicians ordinarily speak of depression. Even then, the term *depression* covers a wide range of disorders, from the relatively mild feelings of sadness to the more severe melancholy associated with a major depression.

Even though fewer than 10 percent of adolescents between 10 and 17 years of age are diagnosed as being primarily depressed, as many as half of them

---

Multiple Personality

Multiple personality is one of the dissociative disorders in which the individual alternates between two or more distinct personalities. Or there may be a dominant personality with a variety of subordinate ones.

The disorder is most often diagnosed among late adolescents and young adults and is especially common among females. Many have been victims of physical or sexual abuse in childhood. It appears that when faced with overwhelming stress, such children escape emotionally by imagining separate personalities to deal with the suffering (Bass and Davis, 1988).

Most cases of multiple personality have certain features in common. First, there are marked differences in the memories and mannerisms of each personality. Also, each personality tends to emerge in response to a particular situation. Then too, each personality takes on a particular role or emotional experience for others. That is, one personality may take on a controlling role; another one may play a more rebellious role. In many cases, the dominant personality is unaware of the activities of the other personalities, which may account for the "lost time" reported by people suffering from multiple personality (Putnam, 1982).

During treatment, therapists help the person to integrate the different personalities, sometimes through the use of hypnosis. But it is usually a long and difficult process. In the famous case of Sybil, for example, it took eleven years to integrate her sixteen personalities into a stable, coherent personality (Schreiber, 1974).

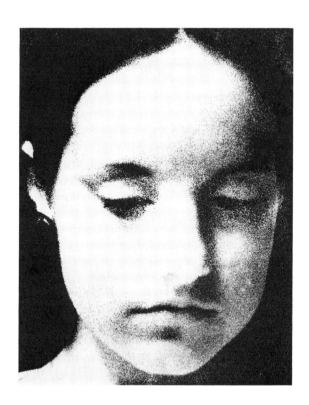

Half of all adolescents show some symptoms of depression at one time or another. (Camerique)

display some of the symptoms of depression, such as mood disturbances, self-deprecation, crying spells, and suicidal thoughts. As adolescents mature, they tend to manifest depression in more adult terms, such that the incidence of depression increases among older youth. It has been estimated that at any one time one-fourth of all college students are suffering from symptoms of depression. About half of these students will require some type of professional help. Furthermore, more than three-fourths of all college students suffer some type of depressive symptoms at one time or another during each year. Depressed students tend to experience difficulties in sleeping, loss of appetite, long periods of sadness, diminished pleasure in everyday activities, feelings of worthlessness, and in some cases suicidal thoughts (Beck and Young, 1978).

From mid- to late adolescence and up, depression tends to be much more common among females than males. One explanation is that females are closer to their emotions and can admit illness more readily than males do. But females are also twice as likely to seek help for depression, which further distorts the figures. Furthermore, it is now thought that the actual prevalence of depression among males may be closer to that of females, except that depression among males is often masked as alcoholism and drug addiction. Evidence for this can be seen in a study among the Amish people in Pennsylvania which showed that depression is equally common among men and women, largely because the Amish prohibit the use of alcohol and drugs (Egeland and Hostetter, 1983).

Manifestations of Depression

A major difficulty in recognizing depression in adolescents is the frequency with which they mask their feelings and express their depression in other symptoms. For one thing, adolescents find it difficult to admit to themselves or others self-critical attitudes or doubts about their being competent. Then too, they are inclined more toward doing things than thinking about them, so their feelings of depression frequently get expressed in substitute symptoms or behavioral equivalents of depression. Some common signs of masked depression are boredom, a preoccupation with bodily complaints, constant fatigue, and excessive complaining. Adolescents often express their depression through a lack of interest in school, difficulties in concentrating, poor performance, and dropping out of school. Depression is one of the most frequent reasons for dropping out of school, especially in college.

The masking of depression often consists of efforts to ward off depression. One common form is restlessness, which may consist of keeping busy or searching for new and stimulating activities. What may initially appear as a lively enthusiasm for life on closer inspection often turns out to be a desperate effort to keep busy so that the individual will not have sufficient time to think. Adolescents may also attempt to escape depression by a flight towards or away from people. Adolescents may exhibit a need for constant companionship or the search for more interesting friends. Or their attempts may take the form of avoiding people, spending more time by themselves, or pursuing solitary activities. Still another way of warding off depression, especially among older youth, is alcohol and drug abuse. Youth who are unable to realize a satisfying degree of excitement and companionship through more adaptive pursuits may turn to sex and drugs as a way of combatting depression. In some adolescents, depression may be expressed primarily through indirect appeals for help, usually in some type of problem behavior, such as attempted suicide, running away, stealing, truancy, and other acts of defiance or delinquency.

Types of Depression

It is important to distinguish between the mild, short-lived symptoms of depression that so often accompany adolescence and the more severe types of depression that have more serious consequences and usually require treatment.

Adolescents often experience the more transitory form of depression characterized by feelings of emptiness, uncertainty about one's personal identity, and depersonalization. Such experience is associated with the loss of childhood and the transition into adolescence. Youths with this type of depression are not so preoccupied with inward hostility, as many depressed adults are, as much as with

Case History of Donna

Donna, a 19-year-old college student, experienced a major depression, which eventually led to a suicide attempt. Donna felt that she had never been a happy person, placing much of the blame on her unhappy childhood. Her parents fought constantly before getting a divorce when Donna was 6 years old. She continued to live with her mother, but felt abandoned by her father, who had moved to California and telephoned only on her birthdays.

When Donna's mother remarried, Donna felt even more left out because of her mother's attention to her new husband and their preoccupation with the stepfather's three younger children. Her mother recalled that Donna had always been a somewhat sad person. Since childhood, Donna had remained shy and introverted, making few friends. Tall, thin, and not too attractive, Donna also suffered from a poor body image and an inferiority complex. Although she had a good mind, Donna made only mediocre grades, mostly because of her preoccupation with her inner feelings and problems.

Donna's problems intensified when she went away to college. Much of the stress came from her conflicts with an incompatible roommate, demanding studies, and a part-time job. The final blow came when Donna received a note from her boyfriend ending their tenuous relationship. A call to her mother brought only an admonition, "Grow up! Losing a boyfriend isn't the end of the world." Feeling desperate and lonely, Donna took an overdose of sleeping pills. Fortunately, she was discovered in time when her roommate returned from a date later that evening.

After a brief stay in the university hospital and several months in outpatient therapy, Donna decided to return to a less stressful environment in her hometown. With added support and encouragement from her parents, she took an apartment and enrolled part-time in a community college near her home. Donna feels she is a stronger person now and has a more positive attitude toward herself and her future.

the lack of feelings of esteem and control over their lives. They are bothered by how to evaluate and express these feelings. This is by far the most common and benign types of depression among youth and is usually outgrown as adolescents acquire a firmer self-identity, autonomy, and social skills.

A major depression is more serious and usually requires treatment. Adolescents suffering from a major depression have a long history of problems, repeated experiences of self-defeating behavior, and difficulties relating to others. A major depression during adolescence is usually related to a great deal of family stress, lack of family cohesion, and little support for coping with stress and loss. This type of depression is more marked and persistent than the characteristic adolescent depression and is more likely to lead to suicide or suicide attempts. Common symptoms of a major depression include a habitually irritable or depressed mood, diminished interest or pleasure in everyday activities, significant weight loss or gain, insomnia, fatigue, feelings of worthlessness, inability to concentrate, and recurrent thoughts of death. Youths who are chronically depressed but whose condition is not debilitating enough to warrant the diagnosis of a major depression may be suffering from a milder but related disorder—dysthymia (American Psychiatric Association, 1987).

Another type of depression that has received greater attention among youth in recent years is that in which individuals may experience an alternation of elated and depressive moods. Popularly known as manic-depression, this condition is now labeled *bipolar disorder*. This disorder generally appears in the form of a manic episode, in which the individual exhibits such symptoms as an expansive mood, increased social activity, talkativeness, sleeplessness, and reckless behavior. In due time, the initial manic episode may be followed by a period of normal activity and eventually a depressed episode, and then another normal period. Actually, the sequence of moods varies somewhat between the different types of this disorder. In addition to the manic episodes, there are other characteristics that distinguish bipolar disorder from a major depression. The bipolar disorder is much less common than depression and tends to be more equally distributed among both sexes. Unlike a major depression, which may occur at any age, bipolar disorder usually appears before age 30. It is also more likely to run in families (Hirschfield and Cross, 1982). The use of lithium carbonate is often helpful in controlling the mood swings in this disorder. However, it is difficult to find the correct dosage and to get patients to take their medication continuously. Individuals may stop taking their medication, mainly because it takes away their feelings of well-being when they are in a mildly elated state. Yet if they do not resume the medication, they may experience another manic or depressive attack as great as that experienced before they began taking medication. Individuals who chronically pass through depressed and expansive periods but whose condition is not sufficiently debilitating to warrant the diagnosis of a bipolar disorder may be suffering from a milder but related disorder—cyclothymia (American Psychiatric Association, 1987). Furthermore, clinicians recently have begun to recognize that when an episode of bipolar disorder or major depression regularly appears during a particular period of the year, such as the winter months, the individual may have a seasonal mood disorder. See the boxed item "More Than the Winter Blues."

Adolescent Suicide

Depression is also a major risk factor in suicide, with up to half of all the suicides in the United States being committed by people suffering from depression or depressive symptoms associated with other disorders (Greenberg, 1982). Suicide is relatively rare among children and early adolescents. But as youths gain more self-identity and autonomy, from midadolescence on, both the potential for suicide and the number of reported suicides rise rapidly. Furthermore, the suicide rate among youth has almost tripled in the past thirty years, though it has leveled off somewhat in recent years. See Figure 15-2. There are now about 13 reported suicides per 100,000 youths in the 15–24 age bracket in the United States, with

More Than the Winter Blues

Winter can become a dreary time for us. Darkness comes by 5 in the afternoon. Cold weather and snow call for heavy clothing and boots. Most of us learn to take it in stride. But for some people, winter is especially depressing. They may be suffering from a particular mood disorder labeled SAD—seasonal affective disorder (American Psychiatric Association, 1987).

What causes this disorder? Even the experts are not certain. Because most people with this syndrome have a close relative with a mood disorder, genetic factors are suspected (Toufexis, 1988). Also, winter weather disturbs the body's natural clock, affecting the production of chemicals such as serotonin and melatonin. The absence of light is thought to be a major factor. During darkness, the pineal gland in the brain secretes larger amounts of the hormone melatonin, which is associated with drowsiness and lethargy. Light suppresses the secretion of this chemical. Although the extra melatonin secreted in winter doesn't disturb most of us, individuals with SAD suffer from an overdose of this hormone (Bootzin and Acocella, 1988).

Youths with SAD may obtain relief with light therapy. During the winter months, they spend several hours a day in front of a sun-box, which is fitted with fluorescent lights that emit the full spectrum of natural daylight. One young woman, who suffered from severe depression and obesity each winter, gained more energy and a sense of well-being from light therapy—something she had never felt during winter.

the suicide rate among males about five times that of females. For youths this age, suicide is now the second leading cause of death among males, after accidents, and tied for the second most common cause of death along with cancer for females (U.S. Bureau of the Census, 1990).

It is widely recognized that reported suicides are greatly outnumbered by unreported suicides, attempted suicides, and other types of self-destructive behavior. For instance, David Phillips (1981) found that automobile fatalities in California increased by one-third three days after a widely publicized suicide. Many of these accidents may have been unconsciously caused by people intent on suicide. Most were single-car accidents involving people close to the age of the suicide victim. The victims also lingered fewer days before dying than did those in other car accidents.

Although adolescents are less likely than adults to take their lives, they are at least as likely to attempt suicide. Whereas there are about six to ten suicide attempts for each suicide in the general population, the ratio of attempted to actual suicides among high school and college students ranges as high as fifty to one (Goleman, 1986). And although suicide threats are several times more common among young women than men, young men are five times more likely to actually commit suicide. A major reason is that a larger proportion of men use more swift and violent means, such as a gun or hanging. By contrast, more women are likely to use pills or some form of poisoning, which often permits

Figure 15-2   Suicide Rates for 15–24 Year Olds.

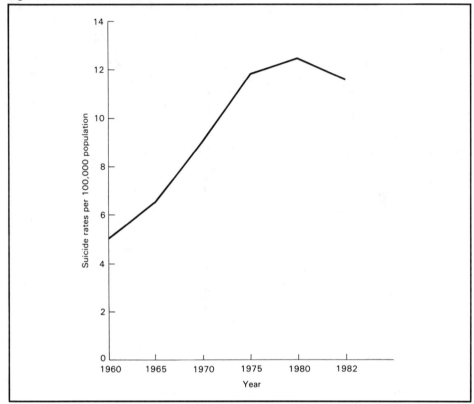

Source: National Center for Health Statistics, in Carl A. Taube and Sally A. Barrett, eds., *Mental Health, United States, 1985* (Washington, D.C.: U.S. Department of Health and Human Services, DHHS Publ. No. [ADM] 85-1378; Government Printing Office, 1985), p. 150. U.S. Bureau of the Census, *The Statistical Abstract of the United States, 1990,* 110th ed. (Washington, D.C.: U.S. Government Printing Office, 1990), p. 86.

intervention (U.S. Bureau of the Census, 1990). As a result, many of these unsuccessful suicide attempts are regarded as a cry for help. It may be that women are more able than men to cry out for help with their emotional needs, such that twice as many women students as men seek help from college counselors. Yet the higher risk is the silent and isolated college man who does not turn to anyone for help (Goleman, 1986).

Contributing Factors

In order to identify troubled youth at risk for suicide, George White (1990) and his colleagues compared twenty-five adolescents who had failed in a suicide attempt with about twice that number of adolescents who had never attempted suicide. Poor relationships with parents tops the list of factors which distinguish the two groups, with suicide attempters generally having negative relationships with their parents. Poor relationships with siblings is also an important factor, as is a family history of suicide, though to a lesser degree. Doing poorly in school as well as having few friends is also more common among the suicide attempters. One of the most significant factors is self-perception, or the way teenagers see themselves, with suicide attempters characteristically having low self-esteem compared to others their age who have never attempted suicide.

Charles Rich, Mariam Sherman, and Richard Fowler (1990) conducted a psychological autopsy and toxicological examination of 283 students, including detailed data on the fourteen adolescent suicides. They found that most of the adolescents met the criteria for at least one psychological disorder, with the most common being the Substance Use Disorder followed by the Adjustment Disorder with Depressed Mood. Over one-third of the teenagers' bodies revealed the presence of drugs, including alcohol at the time of death. Almost all of the adolescents had long histories of adjustment or behavioral problems. In addition, most of the subjects experienced an interpersonal loss or rejection that the investigators felt may have precipitated the suicide. Although about half of them had received treatment from a psychiatrist or psychologist at some time in their lives, only one was known to be in active treatment at the time of death. One-third of them had made prior attempts at suicide. Over half had communicated ideas about suicide recently. For instance, one youth had seen a suicide depicted on television four days prior to his death and had told a friend he viewed the suicide as a "courageous thing to do." On the day of his death, he asked his mother for money. After she refused he said, "After tonight I won't need anything." Also, that day he told several family members as well as his girlfriend that he intended to kill himself. But because none of them believed him, no one took action. That night he drank heavily with friends before shooting himself in the head with a rifle.

Two recurring themes in the lives of suicidal youth are the loss of love, often the loss of a parent at an early age, and a sense of hostility, guilt, and self-blame associated with this loss. Consequently, such individuals remain especially vulnerable to the loss of love in later life, with broken relationships being a major precipitating factor in suicides. Interestingly, youths who have lost a parent through divorce are more likely to attempt suicide, whereas those who have lost a parent through death are more apt to commit suicide (Sudak, 1984).

Suicide Prevention

The prevention of suicide among young people has received greater attention in recent years. One approach has been to make it more difficult to engage in self-destructive behavior, such as having tighter control over the prescription of sedatives and taking protective measures against people driving while they are intoxicated. Another approach is to increase campus and community awareness and the resources for dealing with suicide. Many communities have established

Suicidal behavior is often involved in single-car fatalities. (Irene Springer)

suicide hotlines that are available twenty-four hours a day, though these are more apt to be used by low-risk individuals. Even then, it is important to know how to respond to a suicide threat. In the first place, the old myth that those who threaten suicide seldom carry it out has been disproved. Instead, it is now believed that most suicidal individuals express some warning signs, such as an indirect or direct expression of suicidal feelings or sense of hopelessness. Then too, allowing the suicidal person to talk about his or her thoughts does not necessarily give such ideas greater force. Instead, providing these people with an opportunity to talk about their suicidal thoughts may help them to overcome such wishes and know where to turn for help. But it's important not to analyze their motives or show anger. It's usually better to express warmth and concern, without overreacting to the threats of suicide. Friends and helpers also need to distinguish between dealing with the immediate situation and helping to get the person to professional help for the longer-standing problems.

Do suicide prevention programs in school really help? There is some evidence that they do, along with a few questions. On the plus side, a two-year effort to prevent adolescent suicide in New Jersey schools concluded that school-based programs in which mental health professionals and educators work side by side can significantly reduce teenage suicide. Of the 1,140 students exposed to the program in six schools throughout the state, nine out of ten said the program should be brought to the other students. About 6 percent of the students exposed to the program were identified as high-risk individuals. Another seventy-

Warning Signals

Here are some warning signs of suicide:

Expression of suicidal thoughts or a preoc-
    cupation with death
Prior suicidal attempt
Depression over a broken love relationship
Despondency over one's situation at school
    or work

Giving away prized possessions
Abuse of alcohol or drugs
Marked personality changes
Change in eating habits
Change in sleeping habits
Sense of hopelessness

two students who had expressed suicidal feelings were referred for counseling. None of these students resented being identified. All were glad to receive help (Sullivan, 1988).

At the same time, another study evaluating the effects of a school-based suicide prevention program raises some questions. Almost one thousand students in the ninth and tenth grades were divided into two groups, with each group including about thirty suicide attempters. One group participated in a three-hour-long program designed to raise awareness of teenage suicides, describe the warning signs, and recommend counseling; the other group did not participate in the program. Previous suicide attempters exposed to the programs were much less likely to recommend such programs to other students. About one-fourth of them thought the program might stir up depressed feelings and increase suicide attempts. However, only about one in ten of the participants who had not attempted suicide felt this way. One implication of the study is that such programs must involve more than a workshop dispersing information. There's more to suicide prevention than that (Diskin, 1990).

One of the more successful suicide prevention programs is in the public schools in Fairfax County, Virginia, just outside Wasington, D.C. Every high school and intermediate school teacher is trained in the causes and symptoms of suicide. The program includes seminars for students and meetings for parents to discuss adolescents' stress-related problems with mental health professionals. Special counselors are also available at the school to work with troubled teens (On Campus, 1985). Chances are such a comprehensive program has a more positive impact, with fewer unwanted effects.

SELECTED DISORDERS

Most of the disorders discussed so far may appear at any age from adolescence through adulthood. However, there are other disorders that characteristically appear first during adolescence. Two eating disorders, anorexia and bulimia, fall into this category. Anorexia generally occurs during early and midadolescence and bulimia in late adolescence. Also, the various personality disorders are usually recognizable by adolescence or earlier, at least to clinicians, though individuals with these disorders often resist changing. Two other types of disorders, conduct disorders and substance abuse disorders, that are commonly found among troubled youth, have been discussed in Chapters 13 and 14. Although schizophrenia is classified along with the other "adult" disorders because it may begin in middle adulthood or later, the initial onset is usually during adolescence and early adulthood and will be discussed in this section.

Eating Disorders

Because feeding is such a crucial part of development among infants and children, it should not be surprising that the eating disorders often mirror emotional problems. Unlike obesity, which is common among adolescents and adults alike, anorexia and bulimia are two related eating disorders that characteristically appear at adolescence.

The essential features of *anorexia nervosa* are a fear of becoming fat or obese, accompanied by a disturbance in body image and a refusal to maintain normal weight. A loss of 25 percent of body weight, along with other physical signs such as the suspension of menstrual periods, is usually sufficient for a diagnosis of anorexia. The weight loss is usually accomplished by a reduction in total food intake, especially foods high in carbohydrates and fats, self-induced vomiting, use of laxatives or diuretics, and sometimes extensive exercise.

Anorexia tends to occur during early and midadolescence, commonly at 14 or 15 years of age. It is nine to ten times more frequent among girls than among boys, and more common in all-girl families. Parents of anorexics tend to be older than average and from the higher socioeconomic groups. The girl is characteristically overweight for her age and height. She is intelligent and makes good grades. But she is also conscientious and perfectionistic. Often, she begins restricting her food intake after being teased about her weight, either by peers or adults. Then she becomes meticulous about counting calories, what she eats, and how she eats it. When parents put pressure on the girl to eat, she may react by hiding food or throwing it away. Sometimes the girl will eat and later vomit the food. The denial of food together with a reluctance to reduce activity leads to severe physical problems.

Anorexic girls generally have emotional conflicts from growing up in strict families. Typically, they have been "model" children and are quiet and obedient. Yet they lack a firm sense of personal identity and autonomy. They also suffer from a disturbed body image, so that they do not realize they are getting dangerously thin, even when they see themselves in the mirror. The eating habits of these girls have been so regulated by their parents that they have not learned to interpret the inner cues signaling the need for food. Instead, they have an obsessional need to control their lives primarily through their eating habits, often engaging in elaborate rituals to ensure that they will not eat too much (Bruch, 1978).

Because most anorexics deny the illness and are uninterested in or resistant to treatment, they are notoriously difficult to treat. In some cases, the course of anorexia may continue in an unremitting way, leading to starvation and death. However, the mortality rate has been greatly reduced in recent years through greater recognition and prompt treatment of the illness. More commonly anorexia consists of a single episode with a full recovery. Salvador Minuchin (1981) and Fishman point out that the long-term success usually necessitates family therapy, because the anorexic symptoms are seen as an expression of the patient's attempted solution to the family dysfunction. Minuchin and Fishman report a high success rate for such patients after long-term follow-ups. Bulimia is closely related to but distinct from anorexia. Whereas the aim of the anorexic is to lose weight, the bulimic tries to eat without gaining weight. The essential features of this illness are episodic eating sprees or binges, accompanied by an awareness that the eating pattern is abnormal, a fear of not being able to stop eating voluntarily, and the depressed mood and self-disparaging thoughts that follow the eating binges.

Unlike anorexia, which occurs in early and midadolescence, bulimia typically occurs in late adolescence, most frequently at 18 years of age. However, like

---

An Anorexic Girl

Nancy, the oldest of three girls in an affluent family, began exhibiting anorexic symptoms as she approached her sixteenth birthday. Although she was only slightly overweight for her age, Nancy suffered from an intense fear of getting fat. Her fears, coupled with a desire to become socially attractive, led her to experiment with ever stricter diets.

Nancy blamed much of her troubles on her father, a well-known trial lawyer, who constantly threatened her when she wouldn't eat. At the dinner table he would start out reasoning calmly with her, but inevitably ended up yelling at her. During this same period Nancy also had numerous fights with her boyfriend, mostly because of his attempts to get her to eat. But the more her father and boyfriend pressured her to eat, the more she resisted. As a result, her weight dropped from 140 pounds to 88 pounds in less than a year.

Nancy exhibited many of the characteristic symptoms of anorexics. She was depressed, easily upset, frequently lost her temper, lost interest in her boyfriend, and ceased having her monthly periods. She also suffered from low self-esteem. Despite being one of the better students at school, she intensified her study efforts, acknowledging that even her best efforts "were never good enough."

When Nancy finally agreed to see a psychiatrist, she discovered that her poor eating habits had a lot to do with her low self-esteem and were an overreaction to strict, overcontrolling parents. After a joint consultation with Nancy's parents led them to rely more on negotiation than threats, she gained greater freedom in her daily affairs and began feeling better about herself. Later, during a two-week stay in the hospital, she was told that she would be allowed to attend her boyfriend's senior prom if she resumed sensible eating habits, which she did, and continued doing so.

Now 21, Nancy has no trouble with her eating habits or weight control, but admits she has not fully gotten over the fear of getting fat.

anorexia, bulimia is more common among girls, especially those in the middle and upper socioeconomic groups. Although the estimated frequency of the illness varies considerably, about one in five college-aged women are involved in bulimic behavior (Muuss, 1986).

Bulimia is usually triggered by an unhappy experience, whether in school, work, or close relationships. It also increases greatly at exam time. The eating patterns may vary considerably. Some girls binge and purge occasionally, while with others eating becomes a continuing obsession. The food is usually gobbled down quite rapidly, with little chewing. Once eating has begun, there is a feeling of loss of control or inability to stop eating. For instance, Maria, a 19-year-old bulimic, felt an eating spree coming on gradually but felt helpless to resist. During a short period of time, she consumed a gallon of ice creasm, a dozen doughnuts, and several boxes of brownies. Afterward she felt despondent and self-critical. Such binges are generally terminated by abdominal pain, sleep, social interruption, or induced vomiting. The vomiting decreases the physical pain, thereby allowing either continued eating or termination of the binge. Although the eating may be pleasurable, it is usually followed by disparaging self-criticism and depression (Muuss, 1986).

Individuals with bulimia show great concern about their weight and appearance and make repeated attempts to control their weight through dieting, vomiting, and the use of diuretics. Frequent weight fluctuations due to alternating binges and fasts are common. Although bulimia is not usually incapacitating, except in the few individuals who spend their entire day in binge eating and self-induced vomiting, without treatment the illness tends to get progressively worse. Also, because these individuals feel their life is dominated by conflicts about eating, therapy is usually indicated.

Personality Disorders

Personality traits are enduring patterns of thinking, feeling, acting, and relating to others that are exhibited in a wide range of situations. When people's personality traits are inflexible and maladaptive such that they cause marked impairment in their social and occupational lives or personal distress, they may have one of the personality disorders. These disorders are somewhat unique in that they often cause less distress to the individuals themselves than to others involved with them. Accordingly, such individuals often resist getting professional help and thus changing themselves. Two personality disorders of special interest are the Narcissistic Personality Disorder and the Antisocial Personality Disorder.

The narcissistic personality is thought to be the characteristic personality disorder of our time, with many otherwise normal individuals in our society exhibiting undue self-interest. People with this disorder have a grandiose sense of self-importance (in fantasy or behavior), often accompanied by a sense of inferiority. They tend to exaggerate their talents and accomplishments and expect to be recognized as "special" even without appropriate achievement. At the same time, these people are hypersensitive to the evaluation of others, reacting to criticism with arrogance and contempt. Such individuals feel unique and that they can be understood only by special people. Experts differ among themselves regarding the causes of this disorder. Psychodynamic theorists explain that narcissistic personalities are compensating for inadequate affection and approval in childhood. Lacking parental support, these children fail to develop a sense of self-esteem. Instead, they construct grandiose self-images as a way of avoiding their perceived inadequacies and need constant reassurance to maintain their inflated self-esteem. In contrast, cognitive and social learning theorists view narcissistic individuals as the products of exaggerated expectations of what children will achieve in adulthood, based on inflated views of their talents. Whatever the primary causes, narcissism may be fostered by many forces in today's society, including the "overvaluing" of children, rushing children into adulthood, heightened expectations among youth, prominence of television, and the pervasive consumer orientation in today's society.

One of the most troubling personality disorders is the antisocial personality. These individuals have a history of chronic antisocial behavior, usually beginning before age 15. Often they get in trouble with the law because of their predatory attitude toward people and their disregard for the rights of others. They characteristically act in an impulsive and reckless manner, stealing a pack of cigarettes or a car, depending on what seems the easiest at the moment. They're also irresponsible, often walking out on their jobs and betraying their friends. Antisocial personalities lack a sense of empathy and a normal conscience, such that they are callous and manipulative toward others with little or no guilt. Accordingly, many antisocial personalities become engaged in criminal activities. Those who are prone to violence can also be dangerous and can kill with little or no remorse.

For instance, Henry Lee Lucas initiated a life of crime and violence by the age of 13, when he strangled a woman who refused him sex. Later in life, he confessed to having stabbed, shot, or mutilated over three hundred women, men, and children at one time or another. His life of crime ended when he confessed to stabbing and dismembering his 15-year-old common-law wife, who was his niece. Like so many other antisocial personalities, Lucas expressed little regret over taking people's lives. He thought killing, "like smoking a cigarette," was just another habit (Darrach and Norris, 1984).

How can individuals get away with such outrageous behavior? One reason may be their superficial charm, poise, and intelligence. Then too, lacking a sense of responsibility, they can engage in spontaneous behavior, giving the appearance of being "free." Some, like the notorious Charles Manson, have spent so much time in prison that they excel in ingratiating themselves to others in order to manipulate them. In many cases, these people have grown up undersocialized. Individuals with this disorder tend to come from a home characterized by the absence of love and harsh punishment, with one or more parents exhibiting antisocial behavior. Particular patterns of brain wave activity have been found in some of these people, suggesting they have a lower arousal level than most people. Other explanations emphasize the social origins of such behavior. Western society may encourage antisocial tendencies by glamorizing fame and success, such that antisocial individuals' superficial charm and lack of concern for others may help them get ahead (Bootzin and Acocella, 1988).

Schizophrenia

Schizophrenia, one of the most severe psychological disorders, is especially apt to make its initial appearance during adolescence or early adulthood. Although schizophrenia is relatively rare, affecting about one in one hundred people in the general population, it is so disabling that as many as half of the mental hospital beds in the United States are occupied by people with this disorder. Schizophrenia literally translated means "split mind," but the split is not between a Dr. Jekyll and Mr. Hyde type of personality; rather, it's a splitting of the different psychic functions of thought, feeling, and behavior such that the person is out of touch with social reality. Even though the singular term *schizophrenia* is commonly used for the sake of convenience, it actually refers to a group of related disorders which exhibit a wide diversity of symptoms. The essential features of these disorders consist of disordered thinking, including delusions; disturbed perception, including hallucinations such as hearing voices; blunted or inappropriate emotions; and social withdrawal.

The risk of schizophrenia rises rapidly after age 15 and peaks in late adolescence and early adulthood. Males are more at risk before 25 years of age, females after 25 (Lewine, 1981). The initial onset of schizophrenia is more difficult to detect among adolescents than adults. Only about 30 to 40 percent of adolescent schizophrenics manifest the clear symptoms associated with this disorder. The rest initially show a mixed picture in which the characteristic schizophrenic symptoms, such as incoherent thinking and inappropriate emotions, are peripheral to other complaints, especially depression and behavior problems. Like depression, schizophrenia may be masked by other symptoms. Instead of appearing schizophrenic, the adolescent may exhibit behavior problems such as fighting and stealing, especially common among males, or may act depressed, as is often the case with females (Weiner, 1980).

The onset of this illness may occur abruptly, with marked changes in personality appearing in a matter of days or weeks. Or it may occur in a gradual, insidious deterioration in functioning over a period of years, usually an unfavorable sign. During the initial phase of the illness, individuals tend to have difficulty communicating with others, become socially withdrawn, and neglect personal hygiene, school work, or their jobs. The active phase of the disorder is often precipitated by intense psychological stress, such as rejection in love or the death of a parent. During this period, individuals display the characteristic symptoms of the disorder, such as delusions, hearing voices, and other bizarre behavior (American Psychiatric Association, 1987).

Despite extensive research and treatment, the causes of schizophrenia are not fully understood. However, it is generally thought that this disorder results from an interaction of the individual's inherited predisposition to the illness and environmental stress. So far, the evidence strongly suggests that there is a genetic predisposition to schizophrenia. The 100 to 1 odds of anyone becoming schizophrenic rise to 10 to 1 among those with a parent or sibling who is schizophrenic and 50:50 among those with an identical twin diagnosed schizophrenic. Furthermore, it seems that an identical twin of a schizophrenic individual is about as likely to develop this disorder whether reared apart or with the schizophrenic twin. Also, children of schizophrenic parents who are adopted by nonschizophrenic parents have an increased risk of getting this disorder, while children of nonschizophrenic parents who are adopted by someone who becomes schizophrenic are unlikely to catch the illness. Thus, there is a genetic predisposition to this illness, though the predisposition by itself is not usually sufficient for the development of schizophrenia (Nicol and Gottesman, 1983).

Although there is no environmental factor that invariably produces

Case History of Sandy

Sandy was a shy, lonely, but otherwise normal child until she suffered an acute schizophrenic breakdown at age 17. She was the last born of three children and felt inferior in comparison with her older brother and sister. Her sister, the oldest, was especially attractive and outstanding in school. Sandy, however, was rather plain in appearance and made only average grades in school. She had no real friends outside the family. She attended church with her family but felt uneasy there because of her guilt about sex. Sandy said that she masturbated under the covers for fear that God would see her.

Although she had planned on attending college away from home, she was apprehensive about being separated from her family. Late in the spring of her senior year in high school, Sandy became obsessed with some strange ideas. She felt that her mother was out to destroy her, and that only her father, who was God, could save her. She begged him to take her to work with him, but he refused, not clearly understanding her reasons. Then one day, Sandy ran out of the house screaming incoherently. At first, neighbors thought she was on drugs, even though Sandy had only smoked marijuana occasionally.

After a quick consultation with the family's clergyman, Sandy was taken to a local hospital, where she received excellent treatment in the psychiatric unit. Within several weeks she was acting normally and resumed life at home. She spent the next year at a local college, living at home. Then she went away to college, where she made several good friends and better-than-average grades.

Sandy made a good recovery because she had supportive parents, got prompt treatment, made a favorable response, and was fortunate enough to be treated by psychiatrists who had a positive attitude about the possibilities for recovery for such individuals.

schizophrenia in people who are not related to a schizophrenic, environmental factors often play a significant role in triggering the development of schizophrenia. For many years, authorities emphasized the role of overprotective but rejecting mothers and weak, ineffectual fathers in the development of the disorder. More recently, the focus of attention has been on deviant family patterns, especially faulty communication. In one study, deviant communication by parents, such as mixed messages, proved to be an accurate predictor of whether their adolescents would be diagnosed as schizophrenic five years later (Doane et al., 1981). In hopes of identifying the psychosocial triggers of schizophrenia, some researchers have begun following the "high-risk" children born to a schizophrenic parent and comparing the experiences of individuals who become schizophrenic with those who do not. In this way, eventually we may be able to detect the early warning signs and the circumstances that worsen an individual's chances of contracting this disorder. So far, it appears that children who eventually become schizophrenic are more likely to have a mother whose schizophrenia was severe and chronic and/or a mother who underwent complications at the child's birth; further, it is more likely that children who become schizophrenic have been separated from their parents and have created disturbances in school (Watt et al., 1984).

There is a considerable difference of opinion about the outlook for individuals who have suffered an acute schizophrenic episode. For a long while clinicians adhered to the principle of thirds, that is, about one-third of the individuals who have experienced a schizophrenic episode make a good recovery, another one-third make a partial recovery with occasional relapses, and still another third remain chronic schizophrenics. However, with improved methods of treatment, including the use of powerful antipsychotic drugs, more favorable attitudes toward those afflicted with the disorder, and more sophisticated research strategies, a larger proportion of schizophrenic individuals are making at least a partial recovery. For instance, an extensive follow-up study of one thousand people who suffered a schizophrenic episode by Manfred Bleuler (1978) showed that one-fourth of them resumed normal functioning, one-half to two-thirds of them alternated between normal life and a recurrence of the active phase of the illness, and only about one in ten of them remained schizophrenic for the rest of their lives. See Figure 15-3.

For example, Mark Vonnegut, son of writer Kurt Vonnegut, was an excellent student in college. While in his twenties and living in an experimental community with other youths, Mark experienced a combination of stressful events including his parents splitting up and his girlfriend running off with another man, all of which contributed to his acute schizophrenic disorder. Yet with prompt medical treatment Mark made a good recovery and later entered medical school (Vonnegut, 1975; Gorman, 1984). Mark's experience points up some of the predictive factors mentioned here: the better the person's prior adjustment, the more quickly the disorder develops; and the better the patient responds to the treatment, the more favorable the chances of recovery.

Figure 15-3 Outlook for Recovery

How well an individual recovers from an acute schizophrenic episode depends on a variety of influences, especially the following factors:

1. *Premorbid adjustment.* The more adequately the individual functioned prior to the illness, the better the outcome.
2. *Triggering event.* If the illness is triggered by a specific event, such as the death of a parent, the possibility of recovery is more favorable.
3. *Sudden onset.* The more quickly the disorder develops, the more favorable the outcome.
4. *Age of onset.* The later in life the first illness develops, the better. Men are more at risk before the age of 25; women are more at risk after 25.
5. *Affective behavior.* The presence of conscious anxiety and other emotions, including depression, are favorable signs. A state of hopelessness not ac-

companied by depression is a poor sign.

6. *Content of delusions and hallucinations.* The more the delusions involve feelings of guilt and responsibility, the better the outlook. Conversely, the more the delusions and hallucinations blame others and exonerate the individual, the more severe the illness.
7. *Type of schizophrenia.* Individuals with the diagnosis of paranoid schizophrenia have the best chance of recovery; those diagnosed undifferentiated schizophrenic have the worst chances.
8. *Response to the illness and treatment.* The more insight individuals have as to what makes them ill and the more cooperative they are with their therapists, the better their chances of recovery.
9. *Family support.* The more understanding and supportive the families of these individuals are, the better their chances for a good recovery.

THERAPY

Adolescents are often referred for help because a parent, teacher, or social worker notices that "something is wrong." Because adolescents spend much of their waking day at school, it should come as no surprise that anywhere from one-third to one-half of all adolescents referred for help have school-related problems, such as learning difficulties or behavior problems (Weiner, 1980). Among older youth 18 to 24 years of age, the primary presenting problems vary somewhat according to sex. For males, the four most common psychological disorders are alcohol abuse/dependence, drug abuse/dependence, phobia, and antisocial personality. The most frequent disorders among females are phobia, drug abuse/dependence, major depressive episode, and alcohol abuse/dependence. Troubled youths may be seen in a variety of therapeutic settings. The majority of them will be treated in one of the publicly funded community mental health centers, with a much smaller number seeing a mental heath specialist, such as a psychiatrist or psychologist in private practice. Youths with the more serious disorders, such as schizophrenia, are initially treated in an institutional setting. (Taube & Barrett, 1985).

Individual psychotherapy with adolescents is generally more difficult than with children or adults. For one thing, adolescents are still in a process of clarifying their identity and autonomy and may be uncommunicative, skeptical,

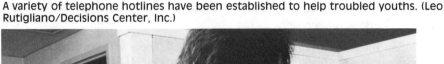

A variety of telephone hotlines have been established to help troubled youths. (Leo Rutigliano/Decisions Center, Inc.)

and uncooperative in therapy. Then too, many of them have been referred by their parents, and the therapist must establish a relationship of trust and cooperation before significant progress can be made. Also, adolescents' behavior is often unpredictable, with youthful clients feeling overwhelmed by their problems in one session and feeling little or no need for help the next. Furthermore, acting-out behavior, such as running away or vandalism, often complicates the treatment program. All things considered, it is usually best for therapists to focus on the adolescent's present situation rather than the achievement of deep insight. It is also important for the therapist not to pay undue attention to the adolescent's problem behaviors, but to look beyond the symptoms to the unfulfilled needs being expressed. In this way, the therapist can assist the adolescent to articulate more positive goals and to acquire the necessary skills to achieve them. Although it is not realistic to ask adolescents to make a long-term commitment to therapy, it appears that the greater number of sessions attended, at least up to twenty-six or so, the more specific goals are attained (Howard et al., 1986).

There is a growing realization that troubled youths may make faster progress when treated in groups. Among the major reasons are that use of the group process permits the adolescent's identification with others with similar problems and encourages conformity to group norms; in addition, there is mutual help and support among group members. Another advantage is that the therapist is able to observe directly the adolescent's behavior with others. Group therapy may take place in outpatient mental health centers or, as is frequently the case, as an integral part of a residential treatment program. Family therapy is especially valuable for observing the adolescent's behavior within the family group and for eliciting parental involvement. However, a major difficulty in explaining this type of therapy is that there are at least fourteen different schools of family therapy, which vary in their theoretical approaches, range of techniques, and procedures used (Gurman, 1983). Some family therapists see the parents for an initial session and then the adolescent with his or her parents in the remaining sessions. Other therapists prefer to see all family members together from beginning to end. Still other family therapists may see only the parents and the adolescent who is the identified patient.

Another group approach, which is especially appropriate for adolescents, is Vivian Seltzer's (1989) peer arena therapy. In contrast to family therapy, the focus of peer arena therapy is on the developmental dynamics of troubled adolescents in relation to their peers. Because peers are a major influence on the individual's personal and social development at this stage of life, problems such as shyness or substance abuse are conceptualized as symptoms of maladaptive peer relationships. Therapy is geared to uncovering and remedying the forces that caused the problems. Accordingly, in addition to the customary family history, there is an extensive peer history, which characterizes the ways an adolescent has managed his or her peer relationships. The groups to which adolescents are assigned become peer groups in microcosm, in which the difficulties originally experienced with one's peers are reexperienced and resolved in a protected setting guided by a professional. Group sessions may be supplemented by individual therapy. Help for parents may take the form of parent education classes and/or parent therapy groups. The goal is to rehabilitate troubled adolescents so that they can continue the necessary developmental work in relation to their peers.

There is also a wide range of community services available to troubled youth, including hotlines, group homes, halfway homes, shelters, and peer programs. Hundreds of hotlines have been established in the last decade or so, especially in large cities. Some hotlines are more general in scope; others specialize in a particular type of problem like drug abuse or suicide prevention. Halfway houses provide support for the young person's transition from the hospital or residential treatment program back to the community. Shelters and group homes provide a similar type of support, often for those who have not been institutionalized. Frequently, these agencies are aimed at particular types of troubled persons, such as runaways, drug abusers, or unwed mothers. Group homes are usually staffed by a professional or paraprofessional with a high involvement of young people. The aim is to provide positive adult models, while encouraging individual responsibility and self-governance. Peer programs, another innovative type of help, are springing up everywhere. Although peer programs are staffed primarily by young people—frequently those who have successfully overcome a problem similar to that being dealt with—they are closely supervised and supported by professionals in most cases. Peer programs have been established for a wide variety of problems, including smoking, alcohol and drug abuse, sexual problems, and depression. In some cases, peer programs can change behavior just as effectively, or more so, than conventional therapies can.

SUMMARY

Psychological Disturbance in Adolescence

1. Clinic admissions tend to peak at midadolescence, with anywhere between 10 and 20 percent of adolescents in the United States suffering from a serious psychological disturbance.
2. A greater proportion of boys than girls are referred for psychological help during adolescence, partly because the boys' characteristic problems with aggression and undercontrolled behavior are more likely to come to the attention of authorities.
3. It is more difficult to distinguish between normal and disturbed behavior at adolescence than at any other period of life, with parents and concerned adults likely to overinterpret signs of disturbance in adolescents or prematurely dismiss them until problems get out of hand.

Anxiety Disorders

4. In a generalized anxiety disorder, the person suffers from a chronic sense of anxiety which is excessive and unrealistic for the situation at hand.
5. Phobias are excessive, unrealistic fears, with school phobia being more serious when it occurs at adolescence than during childhood.
6. Adolescents with the obsessive-compulsive disorder are unable to put certain unacceptable ideas out of their heads and are afflicted with the urge to engage in repetitive acts to ward off the imaginary threats.

Depression and Suicide

7. The symptoms of depression are common among youth, though they are often masked in boredom, fatigue, excessive complaining, and dropping out of school.
8. Depression appears to be more common among females partly because they are more likely to seek help for their depression, whereas males are more likely to mask their depression in alcohol and drug abuse.
9. There are many types of depression, ranging from the mild, short-lived symptoms of depression often seen in adolescents, to the more severe types such as a major depression and bipolar disorder.
10. Depression is also a major risk factor in suicide, now the second leading cause of death among youths 15 to 24 years of age.
11. Youths who attempt or commit suicide tend to have a history of adaptive problems, with their self-destructive acts being triggered by a combination of stressful events, especially the loss of a love relationship.

12. Suicide prevention measures include greater campus and community awareness of the problem, recognition of the warning signs, and more resources for dealing with individuals at risk.

Selected Disorders

13. Anorexia, an eating disorder among adolescent girls, is characterized by a disturbance in body image and eating habits that result in a loss of normal body weight.
14. Bulimia, another eating disorder that is more common among older adolescent girls, involves episodic eating binges accompanied by a fear of not being able to stop eating voluntarily, eventually followed by a depressive mood.
15. Youths with a narcissistic personality have an exaggerated sense of self-importance and need constant reassurance to maintain their inflated esteem.
16. Individuals with an antisocial personality characteristically act in an impulsive and reckless manner without regard for the rights of others.
17. Schizophrenia, a severely disabling disorder, is characterized by disturbance in thought or perception, blunted inappropriate emotions, and social withdrawal.
18. Schizophrenia is thought to result from an interaction of the individual's inherited predisposition to the illness and environmental stress, with the incidence of this disorder peaking in late adolescence and early adulthood.
19. How well an individual recovers from a schizophrenic episode depends on a variety of factors, such as age and suddenness of onset.

Therapy

20. Disturbed youth may be seen in a variety of therapeutic settings and treated with individual or group therapy or both.
21. Individual therapy with adolescents is usually more difficult than with adults and usually focuses on improving practical behaviors rather than gaining deep insight.
22. Group therapy may include family therapy and/or supervised peer groups.
23. Troubled youth also have a wide range of community services available to them, including hotlines, group homes, halfway houses, shelters, and peer-oriented programs.

REVIEW QUESTIONS

1. Why is it more difficult to determine the presence of a psychological disorder during adolescence than in adulthood?
2. How can you tell when an adolescent is having a panic attack?
3. For which phobia do people most often seek treatment?
4. What are the symptoms of masked depression in adolescents?
5. What are the symptoms of a bipolar disorder?
6. Which adolescents are especially at risk for suicide?
7. What are the warning signs of suicide?
8. How is bulimia like and unlike anorexia?
9. How can you identify youths with the antisocial personality disorder?
10. Which youths with schizophrenia have a more favorable outlook for recovery?

16 Transition to Adulthood

- ◆ LEAVING HOME
    - A family matter
    - Leaving for college
    - Patterns of maturation
- ◆ TAKING HOLD IN THE ADULT WORLD
    - Autonomous decision making
    - Economic independence
    - Establishing close relationships
- ◆ CONTINUITY AND CHANGE IN DEVELOPMENT
    - Continuity
    - Change
    - Individual differences
- ◆ SUMMARY
- ◆ REVIEW QUESTIONS

Learning Objectives

After completing this chapter, you should be able to:
1. Describe the external and internal aspects of the developmental task of leaving home.
2. Identify four patterns of maturation in parent-youth relationships during the transition to adulthood.
3. Discuss how important autonomous decision making is to becoming an adult.
4. Discuss how important economic independence is to becoming an adult.
5. Describe Erik Erikson's developmental task of establishing close relationships and the attendant risk of loneliness.
6. Discuss the issues of continuity and change in personality development during youths' transition to adulthood.

As a way of determining the developmental tasks college students are currently working on, Bruce Roscoe and Karen Peterson (1984) administered a variety of inventories to 485 undergraduates at a midwestern university. They found that although the students regarded themselves as young adults, most of them were working on tasks from several developmental stages simultaneously. More than three-fourths of the students were engaged in the developmental tasks of adolescence, including acquiring emotional independence from parents, achieving mature relationships with peers, learning socially responsible behavior, and acquiring a set of values. At the same time, almost as many of them were still working on developmental tasks from even earlier periods, such as developing attitudes toward self and toward social groups, and developing concepts for everyday living. Only about half of the students were engaged in the typical developmental tasks of early adulthood, such as getting started in a career, finding congenial peers, selecting a mate, and taking on civic responsibility. Had the investigators included students at some of the large commuter universities as well as community colleges, where many of the students are well into their twenties, the results may have turned out somewhat differently. Nevertheless, the major findings suggest that individuals of this age are characteristically in *transition* to adulthood, rather than having fully arrived there.

LEAVING HOME

In their longitudinal study of adult development, Daniel Levinson (1978) and his colleagues made a similar discovery, namely, that the process of entering adulthood is more lengthy and complex than popularly portrayed. College students, like others their age, are usually in the initial stages of early adulthood. Levinson has called this period the early adult transition, which lasts roughly from the late teens to the early twenties. But the overall transition to adulthood usually lasts longer, typically throughout the twenties. During this transitional period, indi-

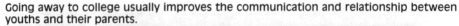
Going away to college usually improves the communication and relationship between youths and their parents.

viduals face two major developmental tasks: leaving the preadult world and entering the adult world. We'll take a look at the first developmental task in this section and the second one in the next section.

A major part of leaving the preadult world is separating from one's family of origin, popularly known as "leaving home." The external aspects of this transition involve moving out of the family home, becoming less dependent financially, and taking on new roles and responsibilities. Its internal aspects involve increasing differentiation of self from parents and reducing emotional dependence on parental authority and support. Because the separation from our families is never complete, it is generally more accurate to understand "leaving home" more in terms of the transformation of emotional ties between youths and their families which takes place during this period than a severance of ties.

A Family Matter

It's not uncommon to hear teenagers tell their friends, "I've got to get away from home. My parents are driving me crazy." But they seldom act on these feelings before 17 or 18 years of age. Most of them lack the financial resources to set out on their own and generally remain at home at least until graduation from high school. After 18, young people are more inclined to act on their convictions and begin pulling up their roots in earnest. Graduation from high school usually provides the occasion for their departure, with college, military service, jobs, and short-term trips serving as the acceptable vehicles for getting away from home. Attitudes toward parents tend to soften somewhat, with 18 to 22 year olds less likely to blame their parents for their problems, seeing them, instead, as less important in their lives.

In many instances, leaving home is a gradual, relatively peaceful affair. For instance, Kim had always gotten along well with her parents throughout high school. As a teenager, she had spent time away from home at summer camps and felt comfortable looking out for herself. During college Kim returned home regularly during holidays and part of each summer, partly to see her friends back home. However, by the time she had entered medical school at the same university where she had attended college, Kim felt more at home among her friends at school and visted home less often. Kim kept in touch with her parents regularly by phone and letters, but more as an adult who enjoyed sharing her experiences than as an adolescent in need of direction. When Kim's parents disagreed with her on occasion, they respected their daughter's right to live her life in her own way. Gradually, they not only made the adjustment to her grownup status but felt proud of having a daughter who was her "own person."

In some instances, the departure from home is a stormy one. John, who constantly fought with his father about school grades and the use of the family car, hastily moved away after graduating from high school. He worked at a service station for a year while attending a nearby community college part-time. Even when he was refused financial aid from the state because of his father's income, John preferred his independence to financial support from his father. Debbie, a 20 year old with a clerk's job, frequently argued with her mother over taking her own apartment. She was told that she should not leave home until she married. Her friends were not surprised when she suddenly moved in with her boyfriend, whom she had known for only four months. In Debbie's case, an abrupt physical departure simply added physical distance to psychological alienation and transferred emotional and financial dependence from her parents to her boyfriend. By contrast, John's stormy departure may have provided the needed opportunity for assuming responsibility and growth.

How peaceful or stormy the departure from home is depends as much on the parents as on young people themselves. In his book *Leaving Home*, Jay Haley (1980) points out that maladjustment at this age often reflects problems in separating from home as well as in the dynamics of the family itself. Separation troubles can take many forms, including drug addiction, delinquent behavior, emotional disturbance, suicide, failure at school or work, or paralyzing apathy. In many instances, troubled young people have difficulty leaving home because their parents are unwilling to "let go." Such parents may complain of a young person's problems at school or with drugs, while deriving an unconscious satisfaction from knowing that they are still needed as parents. Physical presence in the

Table 16-1   Living Arrangements of Persons 15 Years Old and Over by Age and
            Sex

| | | PERCENT LIVING | | | |
Age and Sex	Total (1,000)	Alone	With Spouse	With Parents/ Relatives	With Non-Relatives
Male					
15–19 years	9,089	.7	.9	95.9	2.5
20–24 years	9,254	6.4	19.2	58.9	15.4
25–44 years	21,320	11.1	55.5	20.6	12.9
Female					
15–19 years	8,907	.7	4.1	91.3	3.8
20–24 years	9,586	5.5	32.5	49.6	12.4
25–44 years	21,649	7.6	62.3	23.3	6.9

Source: From U.S. Bureau of the Census, *Statistical Abstract of the Unites States, 1990,* 110th ed. (Washington, D.C.: Government Printing Office, 1990), p. 49.

home is not necessary for the expression of dependence. A young person might be in a mental institution or be a member of a religious cult. The constant thread is the youth's refusal to succeed by becoming independent. It is as if the young people sacrifice their own personal growth for the sake of preserving family unity. Ironically, such problems often occur in "model" families with overprotective parents.

The healthier the family, the more parents desire, and in most cases actively promote, the disengagement of their young. For one thing, the presence of young people in the home is frequently an added source of aggravation at a time when marital satisfaction is at its lowest point in marriage. Many parents of older adolescents also express regrets over the mistakes they made in raising their children. In some instances, parents may be too eager to get rid of their children. For example, one father took over his son's room as a study as soon as the son left for college. One young woman who was married and quickly divorced expressed disappointment that "her room" was no longer available when she wanted to return home in the period following her divorce. Wiser parents may actively promote disengagement, but in a more gradual and constructive way. That is, parents may expect their young people to earn part of the money for their education, to help with chores while at home, and yet be reassured that they have a home base while they are starting out on their own.

Leaving for College

Young people understandably experience some conflict over leaving home— wanting to leave on the one hand, yet apprehensive about leaving on the other— mostly because of their uncertainty over the future. Leaving for college helps to tip the balance toward greater independence, though not without a certain degree of inner anguish. As a result, incoming college freshmen tend to experience a great deal of anxiety about leaving home, often coupled with anger toward their parents. Girls are even more likely than boys to report resentment toward their parents, perhaps because of the overprotective attitude toward girls. But as students adjust to college, they come to feel closer to their parents. The most likely explanation is that anxiety and anger toward one's parents are a normal part of the emotional disengagement of leaving for college. Only when such feelings persist long after the transition to college do they seem to indicate a deeper problem (Goleman, 1980).

Going away to college usually improves the relationship between young people and their parents. This was brought out in a study by Kenneth and Anna Sullivan (1980) which included 242 male students from twelve high schools in Pennsylvania, New Jersey, New York, and Massachusetts. The Sullivans compared two groups: those who attended residential colleges and those who remained at home and commuted to school. Students completed questionaires during high school and again during college, as did their parents. Questions were asked about affection and communication between parents and students and the students' independence. The level of the young man's independence was measured by whether he felt his family encouraged him to make his own decisions or criticized him and tried to dictate things like hairstyle, and the degree to which he made decisions without their help. Results showed marked differences between the two groups, with those who had gone away to college reporting more affection and better communication with their parents than those living at home.

Leaving home, in the more inclusive sense of making a successful psychosocial transition to adulthood, appears to be an essential part of one's ego-identity development as well as adjustment to college. In one study involving 132 students in various stages of college, Steven Anderson and William Fleming (1986) administered a variety of instruments measuring the students' home-leaving strategies, ego-identity, and college adjustment. The extent to which students had left home was measured in terms of four related variables; economic independence, living apart from one's parents, perception of personal control, and emotional attachment to parents. The results showed that all four aspects of leaving home were highly predictive of the student's ego-identity and college adjustment. Compared with other students, individuals with strong ego-identity were more likely to have attained economic independence, their own living quarters, greater personal control over their lives, and positive feelings and attachment to their parents. Results for college adjustment were similar, with higher scores for college adjustment associated with all four measures.

Patterns of Maturation

The association between leaving home and personal maturity is evident in other areas of development as well. For instance, Susan Frank, a psychologist, studied 150 men and women in their twenties in order to discover the characteristic shifts that occur in parent-youth relationships and the development of autonomy during this period of life. All of them were from middle-class suburbs and lived within a two-hour drive from their parents. Frank and her colleagues found that the real-life patterns of development did not fit one simple continuum of maturity. Instead, youths in their twenties exhibited several major patterns of maturation, with significant differences between men and women (Frank, Avery, and Laman, 1988).

Women most often fell into a pattern of "competent and connected" relationships with their parents. About 40 percent of the women but only 6 percent of the men fit this pattern. These people had a strong sense of independence and held views that differed strongly from those of their parents. But even so, they kept on good terms with their parents. Even though the women saw their mothers as demanding and critical, they understood their mother's shortcomings, which in turn helped mother-daughter conflicts from getting out of hand.

Another pattern more common among women than men was to be emotionally dependent or enmeshed with parents, especially with their mothers. These individuals felt troubled by their inability to handle life without their parent's help. Yet they also felt trapped in the relationship. As a result, childish power struggles with parents were common among these people.

The largest number of men exhibited "individuated" relationships characterized by respect for their parents and self-confidence in meeting the challenges of life on their own. About 36 percent of the men and 6 percent of the women fell into this group. Although these people felt there was a clear boundary between themselves and their parents, they also felt free to seek their parents' advice and assistance. They generally enjoyed their parents' company. Yet there was an emotional distance betweeen them and their parents, with little discussion of personal matters or conflict.

Another pattern more common among men than women can be characterized as a false autonomy. Young adults who fell into this group feigned an indifference to conflicts with their parents, which they usually managed by avoiding confrontations. The main complaint of their fathers was mutual disinterest. With their mothers, it was the need to hold off an intrusive parent. These people often held their parents in contempt, resenting their parent's offers of help and their parents' inability to accept them as they were.

The investigators concluded that a great deal of personal growth occurs throughout the twenties, with an astonishing difference between those in their early and late twenties in doing things without leaning on their parents. An important finding is that the emotionally mature young adults tend to become interdependent with their parents rather than completely independent, as mentioned earlier in regard to leaving home. For instance, the less mature young adults not only relied on their parents to help with decisions, but they were often overwhelmed by their feelings of rage and dependency. They tended to be emotionally estranged from their parents, with little understanding of the com-

Returning to the Nest

After Brad graduated from college he returned home while looking for a job. Similarly, when Marie separated from her husband she moved back with her parents temporarily. Brad and Marie are typical of a trend. Like birds flying back to the nest, more youths are moving in with their parents, sometimes after years of absence. The increase in "nesters," as some social workers call them, occurs partly because there are more people this age in our society. But much of the increase is due to economic pressures in recent years, such as inflation, a tight job market, and the high cost of housing. As a result, about half of those 18 to 24 year olds still live with their parents.

Returning home is often a mixed blessing for both generations. People like Brad and Marie may have to swallow their pride and give up some personal freedom for the safety of the nest. Then too, parents who anticipated their children would be launched by their early twenties may be annoyed to have their son or daugher back home. Parents walk a very fine line. They want to be supportive of their youth but not be overprotective. Young people, too, must be careful not to let their temporary living arrangements undermine their self-confidence and ability to take charge of their lives.

In some cases, youths and their parents may find this a satisfying time for strengthening their ties before a son or daughter leaves home again, usually for good.

plexities of their parents' lives. By contrast, the more mature young adults had more confidence in their own abilities to make decisions on their own and would risk parental disapproval by expressing values that may clash with those of their parents. At the same time, they held strong emotional ties to their parents and were able to talk with their parents about concerns and feelings of importance to them. They also were able to understand the complexities of their parents' lives, rather than painting them in stereotyped terms.

TAKING HOLD IN THE ADULT WORLD

Just as leaving home means more than simply moving out of the family house, so becoming an adult involves more than getting a job and finding a place of one's own, as important as these accomplishments are. Taking hold in the adult world—the second major developmental task in the transition to adulthood—has to do with a new level of psychosocial engagement with the world. Accordingly, individuals in their twenties characteristically are struggling to implement their personal identities and goals in the larger society, in contrast to adolescent's struggles for self-definition. This involves trying out new roles, assuming more adult responsibilities, and, in the process, finding an optimal fit between oneself and society. The major components of this developmental task include (1) making decisions more independently, (2) preparing for economic independence, and (3) forming mutually satisfying close relationships with peers.

Autonomous Decision Making

Autonomous decision making involves young people making decisions by and for themselves. That is, they must not only make their own decisions with a minimum of assistance from others, but they must also do so without an undue need for approval from their parents and other adults. Admittedly, this is a difficult goal for anyone, much less someone at this stage of life. One reason is that most young people have had only limited experience in making important life decisions. Even when they are given the opportunity to make an important decision, such as whether to attend college and, if so, which college, they usually decide jointly with their parents who often share the major burden of the expenses. Another reason has to do with the inherent difficulty of making good decisions, which requires experience and good judgment as well as vigorous information processing, weighing alternatives, and making a final choice. Then too, young people may become overwhelmed by the vast array of options in

Making more decisions on one's own is an important part of growing up. (Courtesy NCR)

regard to schools and careers, especially if they haven't clarified their goals. Lack of a sense of direction makes decision making all the more agonizing at this stage of life.

Autonomous decision making is especially crucial at this stage when so many important life decisions are being made. Three of the most important decisions of one's life generally are made during this period: deciding whether to attend college and, if so, which one; choosing a career; and selecting a marriage partner. In explaining the importance of decisions during early adulthood, Daniel Levinson (1978) has observed that one of the great paradoxes of development is that we are required to make crucial choices before we have the judgment and self-understanding to choose wisely. Yet if such choices are put off until we feel ready, the delay may produce even greater costs. This paradox is especially true in the choice of a career or starting a family.

A major problem for people in their twenties is the terrifying feeling that their choices are irrevocable. When young people decide against graduate school or against having children, or they forego travel abroad, they often have the feeling that they will have to live with that choice forever. Yet this is generally a false fear, because change is not only possible but often inevitable. In fact, one of the distinctive requirements of this period is keeping in balance two coexisting tasks: to explore options and to create a stable structure for one's life. On the one hand, young people need to explore their options, expand their horizons, and put off firmer commitments until their options are clearer. Yet they must also create an initial adult life structure giving them roots, direction, and continuity. Those who "hang loose" too long may find themselves drifting from one thing to another, while those who make rigid commitments may needlessly shut off personal and professional growth. One of the most important competencies of early adulthood is to learn to make basic life choices independently, with the realization that these may well need to be modified, without feeling one has betrayed one's "dreams."

Economic Independence

Another important developmental task is economic independence, which depends largely on one's work. However, most people this age are still engaged in *preparing* for their careers and economic independence, rather than having fully established themselves in these areas. Thus, there is great concern, change, and economic instability. Most college students are working in part-time jobs that are not related to their career goals. Also, compared to their counterparts in earlier eras, today's students express greater concern about choosing fields with good opportunities and courses that will be useful to them in their jobs; they also worry about their grades in school. Even after graduation, early adulthood continues to be a time of change and experimentation. The typical worker in his or her twenties tends to hold several brief jobs before settling into a more promising position.

People's attitudes toward finances also play an imporant role at this time. Because of increased economic pressures in society, people have become more money conscious, with those in the 18–25-year-old group the most money conscious of all. Individuals this age worry more about money and are more dissatisfied with their finances than middle-aged and older adults. Many of those under 30 are postponing some of their goals, such as returning to school, getting a place of their own to live, or buying a house (Rubenstein, 1981). At the same time, there is evidence that some of those now in their twenties disdain the emphasis on greed characteristic of the baby boomers now in their thirties and forties. Although money is still important as an indicator of career performance, crass materialism seems to be on the wane. Most of all, young workers want jobs and careers that are gratifying, meaningful, and without high risk of premature burnout (Gross and Scott, 1990).

Young women may experience added difficulties in achieving economic independence. Traditionally, the majority of women have sought economic stability primarily through marriage. Today, however, more young women are getting a college education, working before marriage, marrying later, and combining marriage and a career. A major issue for women is economic parity with men, with women on the average earning only two-thirds as much as men with the

Combining career and family
responsibilities is not easy. (Ken Karp)

same education and job. Women who choose a traditionally feminine job in the lower-paying service sector are at an even greater disadvantage. Fortunately, as we noted in chapter 9, an increasing proportion of women are choosing careers and jobs in a wider spectrum of fields.

Married women face additional challenges, such as combining the responsibilities of marriage and work. Unfortunately, as we discussed in chapter 5, women are still assuming a disproportionate amount of responsibility for house chores and child rearing. Yet women who work outside the home tend to feel greater self-esteem and share power more equally with their husbands than do other women. Furthermore, the more satisfied couples are with their joint income, the happier they are with their marriage relationship. Couples generally experience more problems in regard to how they spend their money. More than three-fourths of couples married ten years or more favor pooling their financial resources, though women are somewhat less enthusiastic about this than their husbands. A lot depends on both partners' attitudes toward their relationship. More than eight out of ten husbands and wives who believe marriage is a lifetime relationship favor pooling, whereas only five out of ten spouses who subscribe to the idea of "voluntary marriage" like the idea. Couples living together generally feel even less favorable toward pooling their money and property. Actually, couples who keep their money separate have fewer fights over money. But they also have weaker ties, making it easier for them to dissolve their relationships. The longer an unmarried couple lives together, the more likely they are to pool their resources (Blumstein and Schwartz, 1983).

Establishing Close Relationships

The link between money management and marriage touches on another important area of development, close relationships. Erik Erikson (1980b) holds that achieving intimacy or closeness with one's peers is the major developmental task of this period. The high priority of intimate relationships has been confirmed in numerous surveys, with over nine out of ten people this age regarding close relationships as very important in their lives (Rubenstein, 1983). At the same time, as Erikson points out, the need for intimacy is rarely fully satisfied, such that young people are especially prone to feelings of loneliness or social "isolation." In fact, people in the 18–25-year-old group suffer more from loneliness than does any other age group. A major explanation is that people this age, having loosened the emotional ties with their families, are acutely aware of the discrepancy between their search for intimacy and their failure to find it (Rubenstein, Shaver, and Peplau, 1982).

Individuals this age usually seek close emotional attachments with one or more special persons, such as their best friends, lovers, and, when so desired, marriage partners. But they also tend to have a wider network of less emotionally involved relationships, including casual friends and congenial people of both sexes, such as friends at work. Most individuals have little difficulty distinguishing between their close and casual friends, with the quality of the relationships being more important than the frequency of association. But what about the similarities and differences betweeen friendships and love relationships? A study comparing friendships and love relationships among a variety of young adults, including college students and other adults in the community, showed that friendships and love relationships share many similarities, such as acceptance, trust, and mutual assistance. Yet two additional clusters of characteristics make love relationships unique, namely the "caring" cluster and the "passion" cluster. Thus, love relationships generally exhibit greater exclusiveness and sexual intimacy. But lovers also experience greater ambivalence, conflict, distress, and mutual criticism. As a result, although love relationships are more satisfying, they are also more volatile and frustrating than friendships. In contrast, friendships tend toward greater mutual acceptance and stability, especially among same-sex friends (Davis, 1985).

The search for a romantic partner is especially crucial at this stage of life, as shown in a survey of love and romance. When the respondents were asked what they looked for in their romantic relationships, over half of them indicated love, followed closely by companionship. Other qualities such as romance, sex, and financial security were ranked much further down the list. Most individuals this age regard romance as the initial stage of love. In contrast, love was defined more in terms of the enduring qualities of the relationship, such as compatibility, friendship, and devotion. One of the most disturbing aspects of close relationships was said to be the uneven emotional involvement between the partners. Half of the couples felt that they had a love relationship in which one partner loved more than the other did. Furthermore, women, who are more often on the

For many adults, the search for intimacy leads to marriage and having a family. (United Nations Photo by L. Barns)

giving end of such relationships, tended to be more demanding, more critical, and less happy in their love relationships. One explanation is that women have higher expectations for intimacy and thus react more negatively to the reality of close relationships. Women also said that they wanted more verbal responsiveness from their partners, the type they have with their women friends. They complained that men, especially the strong silent types, communicate too little in their love relationships (Rubenstein, 1983).

Individuals and couples alike tend to have different priorities in regard to the importance of close relationships, as was brought out in a study by Philip Blumstein and Pepper Schwartz (1983) involving cohabiting couples as well as married couples. In about half of the married couples, one partner was relationship-centered while the other was more work-centered. In many instances the husband devoted most of his energies to the job and the wife to the needs of the relationship. Yet this was not always the case. Actually, there was a tendency for the partner most inclined to be understanding and compassionate, regardless of sex, to put the relationship first. In a few instances, the roles were reversed, with men putting the relationship first. In one-fourth of the married couples and slightly more of the cohabiting couples, both partners were relationship-centered. Generally, these were the happiest couples of all. Couples in which one partner was relationship-centered were somewhat less happy in their marriage. Couples in which both partners were work-centered were the least happy and committed to their marriages. (See Figure 16–1.) Now that work demands so much of a person's energies and there are more dual-income couples, there is an increased risk that

Figure 16-1   Relationship-centered Couples, Work-centered Couples and Mixed Couples.

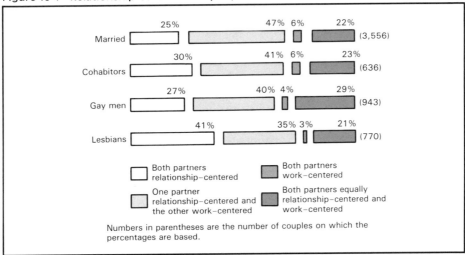

Source: From *American Couples* by Philip Blumstein, Ph.D., and Pepper Schwartz, Ph.D., (New York: William Morrow and Company, 1983), copyright © 1983 by Philip Blumstein and Pepper Schwartz. By permission of William Morrow and Company, 1983, p. 171.

the marriage relationship may easily become a secondary aspect of the individual's and couple's life.

CONTINUITY AND CHANGE IN DEVELOPMENT

As youths in their late teens and early twenties take hold in the adult world, they increasingly view themselves as adults. They tend to dress and act somewhat differently than they did at younger ages. Also, they may relate to others in a more mature way. But in the process of growing up, do young people undergo significant change or growth in their personalities? Or do they remain essentially the same kind of people they were in their youth? Although longitudinal studies do not support either extreme, they do provide some evidence for both views. That is, youths exhibit both continuity and change in their personalities as they move into adulthood.

Continuity

Apparently, there is considerable continuity in personality development between adolescence and adulthood. In one study, Jack Block (1981) has observed several hundred individuals for more than twenty years, beginning in junior high school, then again in their late teens, again in their thirties, and later when these subjects were middle-aged. Data were gathered not only from the subjects themselves but also from their parents, teachers, and spouses. The results have shown a striking pattern of stability. Block has found significant correlations between the subjects' ratings of themselves in high school and ratings of themselves in their thirties on virtually every one of the ninety rating scales. Thus, individuals who were cheerful and outgoing as teenagers continued to exhibit these same qualities as young adults. And individuals who were bothered by mood fluctuations when they were in high school were still experiencing mood swings in midlife. Similar support for the continuity of personality comes from another longitudinal study by (Bachman, O'Malley, and Johnston (1978). Their data were collected from a national sample of over two thousand boys in the tenth grade and again at varied periods throughout the next eight years. Again, the dominant picture was one of stability in various areas of development. For instance, in regard to achievement, students who had been successful in high school also tended to be successful in their careers and maintained high achievement aspirations throughout adulthood. By contrast, those who had not done well in high school experienced less success in their careers and entertained lower achievement aspirations.

In another longitudinal study, Paul Costa, and Robert McCrae (1980) discovered that some personal traits are generally more stable than others. They found the highest degree of stability on measures of introversion-extroversion, which assesses gregariousness, warmth, and assertiveness. Thus, individuals who were expressive and outgoing in their teens were apt to remain that way as adults. The researchers found almost as much consistency in some specific traits

Cheerful and outgoing youths tend to show these same qualities as they become adults.

such as anxiety, impulsiveness, hostility, and depression. Although activity levels generally decreased for everyone across time, they also remained quite stable within individuals, with those who were active in their youth remaining more active and energetic than their peers as adults.

Change

The same researchers also observed certain changes in personality in the course of development. They frequently found that with increasing age there were slight drops in activity levels, excitement-seeking behavior, hostility, and impulsiveness. But they attributed these changes to the mellowing that comes with age and experience. Thus, the relative differences between individuals remained intact, such that an impulsive 17 year old may be a bit less impulsive by the time he is 30 years old, but he is still likely to be more impulsive than his peers. Similarly, men and women tend to achieve greater feelings of self-esteem, self-control and personal mastery as they grow older, mostly because of the maturing effect of life experiences (Brim and Kagan, 1980).

Daniel Levinson (1978) and his colleagues found that many of the individuals in their study changed significantly during their transition to adulthood. One reason is that young people make so many crucial life choices at this stage. Also, most of the people in their study moved out of the family home during this period, thereby facilitating a certain degree of personal growth as well. Probably the most important reason for the change during this period has to do with the need for adapting to the extensive changes in a complex, rapidly changing society. Compared to people in the past, individuals now have a greater number of personal options and are being encouraged to forge their own way, rather than to follow in their parents' footsteps. Consequently, most of the people in Levinson's study were already moving toward lives that were quite different from those of their parents, a shift that increased throughout adulthood. Creative individuals such as artists and novelists exhibited the greatest break with their past, with professionals such as doctors and lawyers the next greatest. Factory workers and executives were somewhat less likely to make significant changes in their lives. Few individuals strongly rejected their families, but most held only tenuous ties with their family's ethnic and religious traditions.

Individual Differences

The degree to which people change with age varies even more widely among individuals as they move into adulthood. One reason is the increased importance of non-age-graded influences compared to age-graded influences (Baltes, 1979). Up through adolescence, much of our development is associated with changes that generally occur at a given age, such as puberty and high school graduation. By contrast, adult development depends more on events and influences that may occur at any age, such as the decision to change careers. Thus, the person who drops out of college permanently at 20, delays marriage until 30, and changes careers at 45 will have a different development and outlook than does someone who graduates from college at 22, marries at 25, and remains in the same career throughout middle age.

How much people change also depends on the different priorities they assign to stability or change in their lives. Thus, people with traditional values, and outlook tend to exhibit a high degree of stability in their lives *unless* something happens to them. The events that would be likely to change deeply ingrained patterns usually have to be pretty dramatic ones, such as an unwanted divorce, the death of a child, or being taken hostage in a crisis situation. In these cases, individuals may undergo marked changes in their outlook and personality. In contrast, those who put a greater value on personal growth may continue changing to a greater extent throughout their lives. Orville Brim and Jerome Kagan (1980) hold that people are dynamic organisms who continue striving to master their environment, such that they naturally change and grow, *unless* they get stuck. Brim and Kagan point out that we are now in the midst of a revolution in human development away from the traditional pattern of continuity toward greater change and growth throughout the lifespan. Medical technologies, such as plastic surgery and organ transplants, techniques of behavior modification, and the encouragement of change provided by thousands of support groups are all part of this trend. Furthermore, perhaps more than ever before, people are deliberately trying to change and improve themselves.

Reliving Those Golden Days

Have you ever attended a school reunion? Do you wonder what your former classmates are doing now? You may be interested to know that going back to school reunions gives people an opportunity to reflect on their lives and to make comparisons about themselves and others.

In order to find out who attends reunions and why, Douglas Lamb and Glenn Reeder (1986) conducted a survey among the graduates of a high school in a middle-class community on the east coast. The school held a five-day reunion that everyone who ever graduated from the school was invited to attend. From this roster, the researchers selected fifteen hundred graduates, including eight hundred returnees and seven hundred nonreturnees.

People who returned were similar to those who didn't, with the two groups being almost identical in regard to age, sex, marital status, education, and how happy they were at the present time. However, there was one important difference. The returnees rated themselves happier and more popular while in high school than did the nonreturnees.

When asked why they wanted to attend the reunion, the majority of graduates indicated it was to renew old friendships. In some cases, the likely presence of one special person was the main reason for attending. Other reasons were to reminisce, to relive the fun and feelings they experienced in high school, and to look for changes, usually in the form of comparisons between themselves and others.

The older grads were especially interested in renewing old friendships. They spent most of their time with friends and little time meeting new acquaintances. By contrast, the younger grads were more interested in seeing how "others have changed" and in having them see "the ways I have changed." Many of them were interested in comparing their progress with that of others in their graduating class. At the same time, some younger grads had a sense of cynicism and expected that people would brag about themselves and their jobs. About one in four people in all age groups admitted making a special effort to look good, such as going on a diet, starting an exercise program, or purchasing special clothes. One woman even rescheduled eye surgery to avoid wearing her thick glasses to the reunion.

When asked how they felt about the reunion, the majority of returnees were glad they attended. Three-fourths of them indicated that since the reunion they had found themselves thinking about "how I was then" and "how I am now" and were generally pleased with the changes in their lives.

From Douglas H. Lamb and Glenn D. Reeder, "Reliving Golden Days," *Psychology Today* (June 1986), pp. 22–30. Reprinted from *Psychology Today* Magazine. © 1986 The American Psychological Association.

What about yourself? Was your adolescence any indication of what you are like now? If you were a bit shy and had only a few friends, are you still this way? Or have you changed a great deal? Perhaps you feel more at ease with others and now have a wider circle of friends. What about the classmates you have known over the years? You may find yourself making such observations if you decide to attend a class reunion. See the boxed item "Reliving Those Golden Days."

It is also encouraging to remember that there is a tendency for humans to change toward adaptation and health. That is, adolescents and young adults tend to grow toward adaptation rather than away from it, and characteristics that interfere with personal and social adjustment are the most likely to change. For instance, at least one study has shown that adolescents who change the most in their transition to adulthood are those who were characterized as brittle, passive, and negativistic, traits that are valued neither by society nor by the youths themselves. Intellectually bright, productive youths tended to change the least, mostly because they had already achieved a positive adjustment (Block, 1981). Realizing this, parents and teachers as well as young people themselves might adopt a more positive attitude toward youth, especially troubled youths, thereby helping them to make the desired changes in their lives as they move into adulthood.

SUMMARY

Leaving Home

1. We began the chapter by noting that the transition to adulthood is a complex and lengthy process, usually lasting from the late teens into the twenties.
2. A major developmental task of this period is leaving home, which involves a psychosocial transition as well as moving out of the family house.
3. Whether young people make a peaceful or stormy departure from home depends partly on the parents and the dynamics of the family itself, with some parents having difficulty letting go of their young.
4. Going away to college generally promotes the emotional disengagement and autonomy associated with leaving home.
5. Individuals in their twenties mature in a variety of ways. Most women exhibit the "competent and connected" pattern characterized by close relationships with their parents; most men exhibit the "individuated relationships" pattern characterized by distant but respectful relationships with parents.

Taking Hold in the Adult World

6. A second major developmental task in the transition to adulthood has to do with taking hold in the adult world.
7. Young people must learn to make important life decisions on their own without an undue need of approval from their parents or other adults.
8. Individuals at this stage of life are generally engaged in preparing for economic independence rather than having achieved it and are in school or the early stages of their career.
9. Young people are also searching for satisfying relationships with their peers, including a close relationship with one special person, whether lover or spouse.
10. Couples in which both partners are relationship-centered tend to be happier than those in which one person is more emotionally involved in the relationship.

Continuity and Change in Development

11. During the transition to adulthood, individuals exhibit both continuity and change.

12. There is considerable stability in personal development, especially in regard to such qualities as introversion-extroversion, anxiety, impulsiveness, hostility, and depression.

13. At the same time, individuals also exhibit varying degrees of personality change because of many factors, including the mellowing that comes with age and experience, the crucial decisions being made in early adulthood, the adaptation to social change, and the increased emphasis on personal growth in contemporary society.

14. There are wide differences among individuals in regard to the degree of personal change during their transition to adulthood, largely because of the greater influence of non-age-graded influences in adulthood and the different priorities individuals place on stability and change in their lives.

15. Finally, there is a tendency for humans to change toward adaptation and health, such that maladjusted adolescents are especially apt to mature as they move into adulthood.

REVIEW QUESTIONS

1. What does it mean for youths to "leave home"?
2. How may parents help adolescents leave home in a mutually satisfying manner?
3. To what extent does going away to college facilitate emotional autonomy?
4. Which youths have the most difficulty leaving home?
5. What is meant by "emotional autonomy"?
6. What are some ways youths may prepare for economic independence?
7. How would you distinguish beween healthy and unhealthy intimate relationships?
8. Why are people in the 18–25-year-old group so prone to loneliness?
9. In what ways are people most likely to change as they make the transition into adulthood?
10. To what extent are you a different person than you were in high school?

Appendix: Methods of Studying Adolescents

Throughout this book you will find numerous references to research studies. In most cases the description of empirical findings is followed by a name and date in parentheses. This indicates the author or authors of the study cited, together with the publication date. The complete publication data is listed in the references at the end of the book.

For instance, in Chapter 14 on youth and drugs there are frequent references to the study by Johnston, O'Malley, and Bachman (1989). As explained in the chapter, this refers to the annual high school survey and follow-up studies that are funded by the National Institute of Drug Abuse. The data in this particular study are based on the survey of the seniors in the class of 1988 together with follow-up studies of some of the same youths several years later. The findings give us a well-rounded picture of the views and practices regarding drug use among high school students, college students, and other post-high school youth. Although these investigators are well aware that the information in their survey is limited to the extent that it is obtained from self-reports, they also have good reason to believe it is reliable because of the careful construction of the questionnaire, the representative sampling of students, and the promise of confidentiality.

Awareness of the different methods used in studying adolescents may help you to put the particular information in proper perspective—that is, under what conditions is it true, how representative is it, and so forth. The purpose of this section is to acquaint you with the various methods of study so that you may become more proficient in understanding the research knowledge in this field.

SCIENTIFIC INQUIRY

Essentially, scientific inquiry has to do with a way of knowing, one that is based on the systematic collection and analysis of data. Yet researchers do not go out simply looking for facts. They usually have a particular purpose in mind, expressed succinctly in a *hypothesis*. The latter may be defined as a testable idea or a statement of expected results. For example, when Margaret Mead went to the Samoan Islands, she was intent on investigating a particular idea—namely, "Adolescent girls in Samoa will behave differently from American girls because of the cultural differences"—a hypothesis later confirmed by her findings.

Another important aspect of research concerns is who is studied, which has to do with *sampling*. Because it is not feasible to study all members of the population of interest, researchers usually select a sample of subjects as a basis for understanding the population as a whole. Both the size and selection of the sample are important, and the larger and more representative the sample the better. A *random sample* is one in which every member of the population has an equal chance of being included; this is usually preferable because it provides a more objective basis of knowledge. However, because of practical considerations, researchers often use other sampling techniques, such as the *representative sample*, which is based on selected variables such as age, sex, and social class. For instance, the 22nd Annual Gallup Poll of the Public's Attitudes toward the Public Schools (Elam, 1990)—which was cited in chapter 8—is based on a modified probability sample of the U.S. population. Although this sample includes only 1,594 adults 18 years and older, the proportion of people in each group—such classifications as age, sex, type of school, and type of community—roughly approximates the proportion of these people in the population as a whole. Thus, their views are considered to be representative of the public's attitudes toward public schools.

The particular characteristics, events, or behaviors of the sample being studied are called *variables*. A variable may refer to any influence that may change or vary to a greater or lesser degree, such as age or social class. The relationships between variables being investigated depend on the type of study. As we explain shortly, in correlational studies the aim is simply to determine whether there is any relationship between two variables, and, if so, the strength of this relationship. By contrast, in experimental studies the aim is to discover the *causal* relationships between two or more variables, such as family size and academic achievement. At the same time, one must be careful in interpreting the findings from both types of studies because the interaction between any two variables may be affected by still other variables, whether included in the study or not.

METHODS OF STUDY

Sometimes people speak of the scientific method as if there were only one such method, which is misleading. Actually, there are a variety of procedures and research designs available, each with its own particular strengths and weaknesses. We explain briefly some of the most commonly used methods: observation, the case study, survey research, correlational studies, experimental studies, and ex post facto studies. These methods have been arranged along a naturalistic-control dimension, according to the degree to which observations are obtained in a naturalistic as opposed to a highly controlled, experimental approach.

Observation

Observation is a primary source of psychological knowledge that can be used in several ways. In the first place, it may be a fruitful source of hypotheses and clues for further research. Charles Darwin, Sigmund Freud, and Jean Piaget all gained valuable clues for their work through intensive observations of others, including their own children. Observation is also a valuable means of collecting data on adolescent behavior and can be done in a relatively open-ended or highly structured way.

In *naturalistic observation*, the aim is to observe adolescents in those settings in which a given behavior normally occurs. For example, peer interaction could be observed on the playground, in the cafeteria, in the school hallway, or in the classroom before class begins. The cardinal rule in naturalistic observation is to stay out of the way of the behavior being observed. *Systematic observation* involves more carefully defined categories of behavior, coding schemes, and more than one observer to offset observer bias. One of the oldest forms of observation is self-observation in the form of diaries and logs. A novel approach, cited in Chapter 7 involved adolescents carrying around electronic pagers for a week. For an entire week, high school students were asked to record what they were doing at various times of the day when they were interrupted by the beeper. One of the main findings was that adolescents spent a much greater amount of time with their peers than with adults (Czikszentmihalyi and Larson, 1984).

Investigators who find it necessary to take a more active role in gathering data may adopt the *participant observer approach*. For example, Margaret Mead said that in her Samoan study she found it best to spend her days as an active participant in the community and then to use her evenings writing up the interviews and observations of the Samoan girls. In Piaget's case, an interest in the qualitative aspects of cognitive development led him to use a clinical method that incorporated many features of the participant-observer approach. Piaget characteristically presented the child or adolescent with a mental task, observed the individual's performance, and then questioned the subject in order to discover the underlying thought processes. Although Piaget's approach has been criticized for not being sufficiently scientific, it has been extraordinarily productive in gaining new understanding of cognitive processes.

The Case-Study Method

This is an approach to understanding adolescent development through an in-depth study of a single individual. Here the researcher exercises considerable control over the study through the choice of the subject, sources of information used, aspects of development included, and interpretation of the data. We have included several abbreviated case studies in this book, such as those in the chapter on psychological disorders. More extensive use of the case study method can be found in Nancy Ralston and Patience Thomas's book *The Adolescent: Case Studies for Analysis* (New York: Chandler Publishing Company, 1974).

Another version of the case-study approach is the use of first-person accounts of adolescents. The author has collected a number of such accounts and has used selective excerpts to illustrate various aspects of adolescent development throughout this book. A more extensive use of first-person accounts can be found in George Goethals and Dennis Klos's book *Experiencing Youth: First-Person Accounts,* 2nd edition (Boston: Little, Brown, and Company, 1976).

Still another approach is the use of retrospective autobiographical accounts of adolescence. Pertinent examples used in this book include Margaret Mead's reflections on her own adolescence, Erik Erikson's account of his adolescence, and various other accounts found in Norman Kiell's book *The Universal Experience of Adolescence* (Boston: Beacon Press, 1967).

Survey Research

Stanley Hall, one of the first investigators to adopt scientific methods for the study of adolescence, pioneered in the use of survey research. Essentially, this involves the use of questionnaires and interviews to learn something about a large number of people. Questions may be asked about opinions, attitudes, beliefs, values, preferences, and practices. It is customary, especially in pencil-and-paper questionnaires, to ask standardized questions, that is, to ask all people the same questions in the same form. Although interviews are more time-consuming, they also provide more flexibility of responses. The interviewer may explain a question that is unclear, include open-ended questions when desired, and elicit a more thorough explanation from the subject than can be obtained through the use of a questionnaire.

Investigators often combine these two strategies. For instance, the Annual Gallup Poll of the Public's Attitudes toward the Public Schools (Elam, 1990) draws on personal, in-depth interviews as well as questionnaire data as a basis for its survey findings. Also, by comparing the results from one year to the next, the investigators may observe consistent patterns and changes in public opinion across time. A major advantage of the survey method is the use of standardized questions to query a large number of people on a variety of topics. A disadvantage is that it assumes a subject's responses are "true" when this may not be so in every case. Some people may simply give the responses they feel they are expected to give or, occasionally out of fear, they may deliberately give a deceptive response.

Correlational Studies

In this approach, investigators attempt to demonstrate that there is a statistical correlation or relationship between two or more variables, such as IQ and school grades. The characteristics being investigated are simply observed or measured to see whether there is any relationship between the variables, and, if so, to determine the strength of that relationship. However, it is important to keep in mind that a correlation does not imply causality, merely that some sort of relationship exists between two or more groups of data.

Numerically, correlations may vary between $+1.00$ (a perfect positive correlation) through 0 (no correlation at all) to -1.00 (a perfect inverse correlation). In most cases, the actual correlation takes the form of numbers between 0 and 1, such as .22 or .57. The larger this number, the stronger is the relationship between the two sets of data. Correlations may also be either positive or negative, that is, inverse. A positive correlation exists whenever a change in one set of data is reflected in a similar change in the other. For instance, there is generally a positive relationship between students' class attendance and their course grade. By contrast, an inverse correlation is one in which a change in one variable or set of data is accompanied by an opposite change in the other variable. For example, there is an inverse relationship between students' course grades and the number of hours spent on a part-time job in excess of 15 hours a week, as explained in Chapter 9.

Experimental Studies

In experimental studies, the aim is to show that there is a *causal* relationship between two or more variables. In order to do this, the experimenter manipulates some variables, known as the independent or experimental variables, and then observes the effect on the subjects' responses, measured in terms of the dependent variables. Experiments are often done in a highly controlled environment, such as the "lab" experiment. But in the case of the "field" experiment, the study is conducted in the natural setting in which the behavior of interest normally occurs, such as the school, neighborhood, or work setting. Most experimental designs include a comparison between two groups—an experimental group and a control group—in order to ensure that the effect measured is a function of the experimental variable rather than some characteristics of the subjects involved. Also, pre- and post-testing of both groups further ensures that any differences between the results of these two groups are a result of the experimental treatment rather than extraneous influences. For example, Treblico (1984) studied the effect of career education on career maturity among high school students in schools that had some type of career education (experimental group) and students in schools without such programs (control group). He found that students generally achieved greater career maturity when they had participated in some type of career education. Furthermore, the more innovative the career education program and the greater support it had in the community, the greater the gains in career maturity experienced by the students.

The extent to which experimental results are significant depends on statistical tests, often expressed in terms of the p value, with p standing for "probability." For instance, if the experimental results are significant at the .05

level of confidence, this means that the experimenters can safely say that the chances of such results occurring by chance alone would be only five in one hundred times. Results at the .01 and .001 level are even more impressive. In all these instances, there is a high probability that the experimental effect was produced by the independent variable.

Ex Post Facto Designs

These are the easiest and most often used research designs. In this approach, the effects of certain events are studied after they have occurred (ex post facto literally means "after the fact"). Even though such studies may resemble other experimental research designs in many ways, they differ in one important respect, in that the treatment is based on selection rather than manipulation. An example would be Rumberger's study (1983) of high school dropouts discussed in Chapter 8. Rumberger gathered a great deal of data from a wide variety of high school dropouts aged 14 to 21. His findings show that the dropout rate varies widely according to many factors, such as age, sex, race, and other socioeconomic variables, with many inner city schools in poor neighborhoods having dropout rates in the 50 percent bracket.

CROSS-SECTIONAL AND LONGITUDINAL STUDIES

There are several other experimental procedures used in studying adolescents, which differ mainly in the time span involved. Researchers interested in measuring age-related changes in development may prefer to use the cross-sectional method, the longitudinal method, or a sequential design that combines both methods.

Cross-Sectional Method

The cross-sectional method is frequently used because it is a relatively inexpensive way of detecting developmental change over a short period of time. In this approach individuals of different ages are studied at about the same time and age, and then age-related changes in development are inferred from the differences among groups. An example would be the study of adolescent sexual attitudes and practices by Laurie Zabin (1984) and her colleagues, as discussed in Chapter 11. Data was gathered from over three thousand junior and senior high school students in four inner-city schools. Then the researchers discussed the sexual attitudes and practices among their subjects on the basis of certain population characteristics such as age, sex, and race.

A major drawback of this approach is that we can never be certain the changes associated with a given age group are primarily a function of that age or due partly to other characteristics of the group selected, such as their intelligence, family background, or values.

Longitudinal Method

By contrast, a longitudinal study has the advantage of following the same individuals over a given period of time, thus increasing the probability that the changes observed are caused primarily by developmental factors. In this approach, the researchers observe the same group of individuals (known as a *cohort*) over a period of time, and make repeated observations or measurements of the subjects at selected intervals of time. An example would be Jack Block's (1981) longitudinal study of personality development. Block observed several hundred individuals for more than twenty years, beginning when the subjects were in junior high school, then in their late teens, in their thirties, and again in middle age. One of his major findings was that there is a high degree of stability in personality development between adolescence and adulthood. However, as you'll discover in the discussion of this issue in Chapter 16, some traits tend to be more stable than others and some individuals exhibit more continuity of personality development than do others over the years.

A major limitation of such studies is that they are time-consuming and difficult to complete. Another problem is the difficulty of maintaining the original sample size, and the distorting effects caused by subjects dropping out. Then too, subjects may become "test-wise" through familiarization with the testing procedure. Finally, there is always the possibility that some of the findings attributed to development may be the result of social and historical factors, such as social change.

Combined Cross-Sectional/Longitudinal Method

There are also research strategies that combine the cross-sectional and longitudinal approaches, thereby minimizing the disadvantages of each method. Here, the researchers take a cross-sectional sample of two or more different age groups (cohorts) and then test them sequentially on two or more occasions.

For instance, Dale Blyth (1983) and his colleagues were interested in finding out the effects of having to change schools at different ages, as seen in the impact on students' self-esteem. To accomplish this goal, the researchers obtained data from students at different grade levels in the Milwaukee schools during the same period (cross-sectional approach) and then tracked them over a five-year period (longitudinal approach). Some of these students were in schools organized around a 6-3-3 pattern, which meant they changed schools twice during their education, while others were in schools using an 8-4 pattern, which meant they changed schools only once. One of their major findings, as discussed in Chapter 10, is that changing schools generally has a negative impact on students' self-esteem, especially when school change coincides with the beginning of puberty, as is often the case with students in the 6-3-3 system. The use of this combined method enabled researchers to draw more comprehensive observations than use of the cross-sectional sample or longitudinal approach alone provide.

References

ACHENBACH, T. M., AND EDELBROCK, C. S. (1981). *Behavioral problems and competencies reported by parents of normal and disturbed children aged four through sixteen.* Monographs of the Society for Research in Child Development 46, 1.

ADAMS, V. (1981). "The sibling bond: A lifelong love/hate dialectic." *Psychology Today,* June 1981.

AGNEW, R., AND HUGULEY, S. (1989). "Adolescent violence toward parents." *Journal of Marriage and the Family* 51, 3, 699–711.

ALEXANDER, S.J. (1984). "Improving sex education programs for young adolescents: Parents' views." *Family Relations* 33, 251–257.

ALTROCCHI, J. (1980). *Abnormal Behavior.* New York: Harcourt Brace Jovanovich.

AMATO, P.R. (1990). "Dimensions of the family environment as perceived by children: A multidimensional scaling analysis." *Journal of Marriage and the Family,* August 1990, 613–620.

AMATO, P.R. (1987). "Family processes in one-parent, stepparent, and intact families: The child's point of view." *Journal of Marriage and the Family* 49, 327–337.

AMERICAN PSYCHIATRIC ASSOCIATION (1987). *Diagnostic and Statistical Manual of Mental Disorders* (DSM-III-R), 3d ed. rev. Washington, D.C.: American Psychiatric Association.

ANDERSON, C. S. (1982). "The search for a school climate: A review of the research." *Review of Educational Research,* Fall 1982, 368–420.

ANDERSON, S. A. AND W. M. FLEMING (1986). "Late adolescents' homeleaving strategies: Predicting ego identity and college adjustment." *Adolescence,* Summer 1986, 453–59.

APTER, D., AND VIHKO, R. (1977). "Serum pregnenolone, progesterone, 17-hydroxy-progesterone, testosterone, and 5-dehydrotestosterone during female puberty." *Journal of Clinical Endocrinology and Metabolism* 45, 1039–1048.

ARCHER, S. L. (1985a). "Career and/or family: The identity process for adolescent girls." *Youth and Society* 16, 3, 289–314.

ARCHER, S.L. (1985b). "Reflections on earlier life decisions: Implications for adult functioning." Paper presented at the biennial meeting of the Society for Research in Child Development, Toronto.

ARCHER, S. L. (1982). "The lower age boundaries for identity development." *Child Development* 53, 1551–1556.

ARIETI, S. (1981). *Understanding and Helping the Schizophrenic.* New York: Simon and Schuster.

ARLIN, P.K. (1975). "Cognitive development in adulthood: A fifth stage?" *Developmental Psychology* 11, 602–606.

AULT-RICHE, M., AND ROSENTHAL, D. (1986). "Family therapy with symptomatic adolescents: An integrated model." In G.K. Leigh and G.W. Peterson, eds., *Adolescents in Families.* Cincinnati: South-Western Publishing Co.

AUSUBEL, D.P., MONTEMAYOR, R. AND SVAJIAN, P. (1977). *Theory and Problems of Adolescent Development,* 2nd ed. New York: Grune and Stratton.

BACHMAN, J.G., O'MALLEY, P.M., AND JOHNSTON, J. (1978). *Youth in Transition: Adolescence to Adulthood: Change and Stability in the Lives of Young Men,* vol. 6. Ann Arbor, MI: Institute for Social Research.

BAHR, H.M., AND MARTIN, T.K. (1983). "And thy neighbor as thyself.: Self-esteem and faith in people as correlates of religiosity and family solidarity among middletown high school students." *Journal for the Scientific Study of Religion,* June 1983, 132–144.

BALTES, P.B. (1979). "Life-span developmental psychology: Some converging observations on history and theory." In P.B. Baltes and O.G. Brim eds. *Life-span Development and Behavior,* vol. 2. New York: Academic Press.

BANDURA, A. (1986). *Social Foundations of Thought and Action.* Englewood Cliffs, NJ: Prentice-Hall.

BANE, M.J. (1979). "Marital disruption and the lives of children." In G. Levinger and O.C. Moles, eds. *Divorce and Separation.* New York: Basic Books.

BARENBOIM, C. (1985). "Person perception and interpersonal behavior." Paper presented at the biennial meeting of the Society for Research in Child Development, Toronto.

BARON, R.A., AND BYRNE, D. (1984). *Social Psychology,* 4th ed. Boston: Allyn and Bacon.

BASKETT, L.M., AND JOHNSTON, S.M. (1982). "The young child's interaction with parents versus siblings." *Child Development* 53, 643–650.

BASS, E., AND DAVIS, L. (1988). *The Courage to Heal.* New York: Harper and Row.

BATSON, C D., AND VENTIS, W.L. (1982). *Religious Experience.* New York: Oxford University Press.

BATTEN, J.D. (1990). *Expectations and Possibilities.* Santa Monica, CA: Hay House.

BAUMASTER, R.F. (1986). *Public Self and Private Self.* New York: Springer-Verlag.

BECK, A.T., AND YOUNG, J.E. (1978). "College blues." *Psychology Today,* September 1978.

BELL, A.P., WEINBERG, M.S., AND HAMMERSMITH, S.K. (1981). *Sexual Preference—Its Development in Men and Women.* Bloomington, IN: Indiana University Press.

BELL-SCOTT, P., AND MCKENRY, P.C. (1986). "Black adolescents and their families." In G.K. Leigh, and Peterson, eds. *Adolescents in Families.* Cincinnati: South-Western Publishing Co.

BENIN, M.H., AND EDWARDS, D.A. (1990). "Adolescents' chores: The difference between dual- and single-earner families." *Journal of Marriage and the Family,* May 1990, 361–373.

BERKOW, R., M.D., ed. (1987). *The Merck Manual of Diagnosis and Therapy,* 15th ed. Rahway, NJ: Merck Sharp & Dohme Research Laboratories.

BERMAN, P.W. (1980). "Are women more responsive than men to the young? A review of developmental and situational variables." *Psychological Bulletin* 88, 668–695.

BERNARD, H.S. (1981). "Identity formation during late adolescence: A review of some empirical findings." *Adolescence,* Summer 1981, 349–358.

BERNDT, T.J. (1982). "The features and effects of friendship in early adolescence." *Child Development* 53, 1447–1460.

BERNDT, T.J. (1979). "Developmental changes in conformity to peers and parents." *Developmental Psychology* 15, 608–616.

BILLY, J.O.G., AND UDRY, J.R. (1985). "The influence of male and female best friends on adolescent sexual behavior." *Adolescence,* Spring 1985, 21–35.

BLEULER, M.E. (1978). "The long term course of schizophrenic psychoses." In L.C. Wynne, R.L. Cromwell, and S. Matthyse *The Nature of Schizophrenia: New Approaches to Research and Treatment.* New York: John Wiley & Sons.

BLOCK, J.H., BLOCK, J., AND GJERDE, P.F. (1986). "The personality of children prior to divorce." *Child Development* 57, 827–840.

BLOCK, J. (1981). "Some enduring and consequential structures of personality." In A. I. Rabin, et. al. eds. *Further Explorations of Personality.* New York: John Wiley & Sons.

BLOS, P. (1979). *The Adolescent Passage: Developmental Issues.* New York: International Universities Press.

BLUMSTEIN, P., AND SCHWARTZ, P. (1983). *American Couples.* New York: William Morrow and Company, Inc.

BLYTH, D.A., BULCROFT, R., AND SIMMONS, R.G. (1981). "The impact of puberty on adolescents: A longitudinal study." Paper presented at the Annual Meeting of the American Psychological Association, Los Angeles, August 26, 1981.

BLYTH, D., HILL, J., AND THIEL, K. (1982). "Early adolescents' significant others: Grade and gender differences in perceived relationships with familial and non-familial adults and young people." *Journal of Youth and Adolescence* 11, 425–450.

BLYTH, D., SIMMONS, R., AND CARLTON-FORD, S. (1983). "The adjustment of early adolescents to school transitions." *Journal of Early Adolescence* 3, 105–120.

BOOTH, A.D., BRINKERHOFF, B., AND WHITE, L.K. (1984). "The impact of parental divorce on courtship." *Journal of Marriage and the Family* 46, 85–94.

BOOTH, A.D., AND EDWARDS, J.N. (1985). "Age at marriage and marital instability." *Journal of Marriage and the Family,* Feb. 1985, 67–75.

BOOTZIN, R.R., AND ACOCELLA, J.R. (1988). *Abnormal Psychology,* 5th ed. New York: Random House.

BRIM, O.G. JR, AND KAGAN, J. (1980). *Constancy and Change in Human Development.* Cambridge, MA: Harvard University Press.

BRODY, C.J., AND STEELMAN, L.C. (1985). "Sibling structure and parental sex-typing of children's household tasks." *Journal of Marriage and the Family* 47, 265–273.

BROOKS-GUNN, J., AND FURSTENBERG, F. (1989). "Adolescent sexual behavior." *American Psychologist* 44, 2, 249–257.

BROOKS-GUNN, J., AND RUBLE, D.N. (1982). "The development of menstrual-related beliefs and behavior during adolescence." *Child Development* 53, 1567–1577.

BROWN, D. (1987). "The status of Holland's theory of vocational choice." *The Career Development Quarterly* 36, 13–23.

BRUCH, H. (1978). *The Golden Cage: The Enigma of Anorexia Nervosa.* Cambridge: Harvard University Press.

BUIS, J.M., AND THOMPSON, D.N. (1986). "Imaginary audience and personal fable: A brief review." *Adolescence* 24, 96, 773–781.

BULLOUGH, V.L. (1981). "Age at menarche: A misunderstanding." *Science,* 1981, 213, 365–366.

BURMAN, B., JOHN, R.S., AND MARGOLIN, G. (1987). "Effects of marital and parent-child relations on children's adjustment." *Journal of Family Psychology* 1, 91–108.

CARNEGIE FOUNDATION FOR THE ADVANCEMENT OF TEACHING (1987). *National Survey of Public School Teachers.* Washington, D.C. Linda Nielsen.

CALIFORNIA STATE DEPARTMENT OF EDUCATION (1990). *Toward a State of Esteem: The final report of the California Task Force to Promote Self-Esteem and Personal and Social Responsibility.* Sacramento.

CASH, T.F., WINSTEAD, B.A., AND JANDA, L.H. (1986). "The Great American Shape-Up." *Psychology Today,* April 1986, 30–37.

CAVAN, R., AND FERDINAND, T. (1981). *Juvenile Delinquency,* 4th ed. Philadelphia: Lippincott.

CHERLIN, A., AND MCCARTHY, J. (1985). "Remarried couple households: Data from the June 1980 current population survey." *Journal of Marriage and the Family,* 47, 23–30.

CHIAM, H. (1987). "Changes in self-concept during adolescence. *Adolescence,* 85", 69–76.

COBLINER, W.G. (1988). "The exclusion of intimacy in the sexuality of the contemporary college-age population." *Adolescence* 23, 99–113.

COHLER, B.J., AND BOXER, A.M. (1984). "Middle adulthood: Settling into the world-person, time and context." In D. Offer and M. Sabshin, eds., *Normality and the Life Cycle.* New York: Basic Books.

COLBY, A., KOHLBERG, L., GIBBS, J., AND LIEBERMAN, M. (1983). "A Longitudinal Study of Moral Judgment." Monographs of the Society for Research in Child Development, 48, Serial No. 200.

COLE, S. (1981). *Working Kids on Working.* New York: Lothrop, Lee, and Shepard.

COLEMAN, J.S., HOFFER, T. AND KILGORE, S. (1981). *Public and Private Schools: A Report to the National Center for Education Statistics by the National Opinion Research Center.* University of Chicago Press, March 1981.

COLEMAN, M., GANONG, L.H., AND ELLIS, P. (1985) "Family structure and dating behavior of adolescents." *Adolescence,* Fall 1985, 537–543.

COLLINS, W. A. (1987). *Research on the Transition to Adolescence.* Unpublished manuscript, University of Minnesota.

COOPER, C.R., GROTEVANT, H.D., MOORE, M.S., AND CONDON, S.M. (1982). "Family support and conflict; Both foster adolescent identity and role taking." Paper presented at the meeting of the American Psychiatric Association, Washington. DC.

COOPER, K.J. (1991). "Study: Seniors' illegal drug use falls." *The Philadelphia Inquirer,* Jan. 25, 1991.

COOPER, K.J. (1990). "Trying to get students to do more homework." *The Philadelphia Inquirer,* Nov. 23, 1990.

CORR, J. (1986). "Before adolescence was born." *The Philadelphia Inquirer,* June 11, 1986.

COSTA, P.T., JR AND MCCRAE, R.R. (1980). "Still stable after all these years: Personality as a key to some issues in adulthood and old age." In P.B. Baltes and G. B. Orville, Jr. eds. *Life-span Development and Behavior,* vol. 3. New York: Academic Press.

CROOKS, R., AND BAUR, K. (1990). *Our Sexuality*, 4th ed. Menlo Park, CA: The Benjamin Cummings Publishing Company, Inc.

CSIKSZENTMIHALYI, M., AND LARSON, R. (1984). *Being Adolescent*. New York: Basic Books.

CUTRONA, C. (1982). "Transition to college: Loneliness and the process of social adjustment." In L. Peplau and D. Perlman, eds. *Loneliness: A Sourcebook of Current Theory, Research, and Therapy*. New York: John Wiley and Sons.

DAMON, W., AND HART, D. (1982). "The development of self-understanding from infancy through adolescence." *Child Development* 53, 841–864

DANIELS, D., DUNN, J., FURSTENBURG, F.F., AND PLOMIN, R. (1985). "Environmental differences within the family and adjustment differences within pairs of adolescent siblings." *Child Development* 56, 764–774.

DARRACH, B., AND NORRIS, J. (1984). "An American tragedy." *Life*, Aug. 1984, 58–74.

DAVIS, K.E. (1985). "Near and dear: Friendship and love compared." *Psychology Today,* February 1985, 22–30.

DAVIS, S.J. (1990). "The 1990–91 job outlook in brief." *Occupational Outlook Quarterly*. U.S. Department of Labor, Bureau of Labor Statistics, Spring 1990, Washington, DC: U.S. Government Printing Office.

DAVIS, S.M., AND HARRIS, M.B. (1982). "Sexual knowledge, sexual interests, and sources of sexual information of rural and urban adolescents from three cultures." *Adolescence* 17

DAVISON, G.C., AND NEALE, J.M. (1982). *Abnormal Psychology*, 3d ed. New York: John Wiley and Sons.

DAWSON, D.A. (1986). "The effects of sex education on adolescent behavior." *Family Planning Perspectives* 18, 162–170.

DE TURCK, M.A., AND MILLER, G.R. (1983). "Adolescent perception of parental message strategies." *Journal of Marriage and the Family* 45, 543–552.

DEAN, R.A. (1982). "Youth: Moonies' target population." *Adolescence,* 1982, 567–574.

DELAMATER, J., AND MACCORQUODALE, P. (1979). *Premarital Sexuality*. Madison, WI: University of Wisconsin Press.

DEVAUS, D.A. (1983). "The relative importance of parents and peers for adolescent religious orientation: An Australian study." *Adolescence,* Spring 1983, 147–158.

DIEGMUELLER, K. (1987). "The violent killings of youths: An adolescent fact of death." *Insight* 3, 18–20.

DIENSTBIER, R.A., KAHLE, L.R., WILLIS, K.A., AND TUNNELL, G.B. (1980). "The impact of moral theories on cheating: Studies of emotion attribution and schema activation." *Motivation and Emotion* 4, 193–216.

DIESENHOUSE, S. (1990) "A rising tide of violence leaves more youths in jail." *The New York Times*, Sunday, July 8, 1990, 4-E.

DISKIN, C. (1988), "Teen suicide programs may do ill, study finds." *Philadelphia Inquirer*, Dec. 26, 1988, 2-a.

DOANE, J., WEST, K., GOLDSTEIN, M.J., RODNICK, E., AND JONES, E. (1981). "Parental communication deviance and effective style as predictors of subsequent schizophrenia spectrum disorders in vulnerable adolescents." *Archives of General Psychiatry* 38, 679–685.

DREYER, P. (1982). "Sexuality during adolescence," in B. Wolman, ed., *Handbook of Developmental Psychology*. Englewood Cliffs, NJ: Prentice-Hall.

DUBOW, E.F. AND LUSTER, T. (1990). "Adjustment of children born to teenage mothers: The contribution of risk and protective factors." *Journal of Marriage and the Family*, May 1990, 393–404.

DUDLEY, R. L., AND DUDLEY, M. G. (1984). "Transmission of religious values from parents to adolescents." *Book of Abstracts: Annual Meeting 1984,* Society for the Scientific Study of Religion, Chicago, IL.

DULIT, E. (1972). "Adolescent thinking à la Piaget: the formal stage." *Journal of Youth and Adolescence* 1, 281–301.

DUNN, J. (1984). "Sibling studies and the developmental impact of critical incidents." In P.B. Baltes and O.G. Brim, eds. *Life-Span Development and Behavior* vol. 6, Orlando, FL: Academic Press.

DUNPHY, D. C. (1980). "Peer group socialization." In R. Muuss, ed., *Adolescent Behavior and Society*, 3d ed. New York: Random House.

DUNPHY, D. C. (1963). "The social structure of urban adolescent peer groups." *Sociometry* 26, 230–246.

EAGLY, A. H. (1983). "Gender and social influence: A social psychological analysis." *American Psychologist* 38, 971–981.

EGELAND, J. A., AND HOSTETTER, A. M. (1983). "Amish study, I: Affective disorders among the Amish." *American Journal of Psychiatry* 140, 56–61.

EISENBERGER, R., AND MASTERSON, F. A. (1983). Required high effort increases subsequent persistence and reduces cheating." *Journal of Personality and Social Psychology* 44, 593–599.

ELAM, S.M. (1990). "The 22nd annual Gallup Poll of the public's attitudes toward the public schools." *Phi Delta Kappan*, September, 41–45.

ELIFSON, K.W., PETERSON, D. M., AND HADAWAY, C. K. (1983). "Religion and delinquency: A contextual analysis." *Criminology* 21, 505–527.

ELKIND, D. (1984). *The Hurried Child*. Reading, MA: Addison-Wesley.

ELKIND, D. (1978). *"Understanding the young adolescent."* *Adolescence* 13, 127–134.

ELLIS, G. J. (1986). "Societal and parental predictors of parent-adolescent conflict." In G.K. Leigh and G.W. Peterson, eds., *Adolescents in Families*. Cincinnati, OH: South-Western Publishing Co.

ENRIGHT, R. D., LAPSLEY, D. K., AND SLUKLA, D. G. (1979). "Adolescent egocentrism in early and late adolescence." *Adolescence* 14, 56, 687–695.

ERIKSON, E. H. (1980a). "Youth and the life cycle." In R. E. Muuss, ed., *Adolescent Behavior and Society*, 3d ed. New York: Random House.

ERIKSON, E. H. (1980b). *Identity and the Life Cycle*. New York: W. W. Norton and Company, Inc.

ERIKSON, E. H. (1975). *Life History and the Historical Moment*. New York: W. W. Norton and Company, Inc.

ERIKSON, E. H. (1968). *Identity: Youth and Crisis*. New York: W. W. Norton and Company, Inc.

FALBO, T., AND POLIT, D. F. (1986). "A quantitative review of the only-child literature: Research evidence and theory development." *Psychological Bulletin* 100, 176–189.

FASSINGER, R. (1985). "A causal model of college women's career choice." *Journal of Vocational Behavior* 27, 123–153.

FAUST, M. S. (1983). "Alternative constructions of adolescent growth." In J. Brooks-Gunn and A.C. Petersen, eds., *Girls at Puberty: Biological, Psychological, and Social Perspectives*. New York: Plenum Press.

FELDMAN, R. S. (1985). *Social Psychology*. New York: McGraw-Hill.

FINKELHOR, D. (1984). *Child Sexual Abuse*. New York: Free Press.

FISCHER, J. L. (1980). "Reciprocity, agreement, and family style in family systems with a disturbed and nondisturbed adolescent." *Journal of Youth and Adolescence* 9, 391–406.

FLAVELL, J. (1985). *Cognitive Development* 2d ed. Englewood Cliffs, NJ: Prentice-Hall.

FLAVELL, J. H. (1981). "Monitoring social-cognitive enterprises: Something else that may develop in the area of social cognition." In J. H. Flavell and L. Ross, eds., *Social Cognitive Development*. New York: Cambridge University Press.

FODERARO, L. W. (1990). "Flash points." *New York Times*, Education Life, supplement, Summer 1990.

FORREST J. AND SILVERMAN, J. (1989). "What public school teachers teach about preventing pregnancy, AIDS and sexually transmitted diseases." *Family Planning Perspectives*, 21, 65–72.

FORREST, J.D., AND SINGH, S. (1990). "The sexual and reproductive behavior of American women, 1982–1988." *Family Planning Perspectives* 22, 5, 206–215.

FOX, M. F., AND HESSE-BIBER, S. (1984). *Women at Work*. Palo Alto, CA: Mayfield

FRANK, S.J., AVERY, C.B., AND LAMAN, M.S. (1988). "Young adults' perceptions of their relationships with their parents: Individual differences in connectedness, competence, and emotional autonomy." *Developmental Psychology*, September, 729–737.

FREEMAN, D. (1983). *Margaret Mead and Samoa*. Cambridge: Harvard University Press.

FREEMAN, R., AND WISE, D. eds. (1982). *The Youth Labor Market Problem: Its Nature, Causes, and Consequences*. Chicago: University of Chicago Press

FREIBERG, P. (1991). "Self-esteem gender gap widens in adolescence." *The APA Monitor*, April, 29.

FREUD, A. (1969). "Adolescence as a developmental disturbance." In G. Kaplan and S. Lobovici, eds., *Adolescence: Psychosocial Perspectives*. New York: Basic Books.

FREUD, A. (1958). "Adolescence." In R. S. Eissler et al., eds., *The Psychoanalytic Study of the Child*. New York: International Universities Press, vol. 13.

FREUD, S. (1964). *New Introductory Lectures on Psychoanalysis*. Trans. James Strachey. New York: W. W. Norton and Company, Inc.

FRISCH, R. E. (1983). "Fatness, puberty, and fertility." In J. Brooks-Gunn and A. C. Petersen, eds., *Girls at Puberty: Biological, Psychological, and Social Perspectives*. New York: Plenum.

FULLER, J.R., AND LaFOUNTAIN, M.J. (1987). "Performance-enhancing drugs in sport: A different form of drug abuse." *Adolescence* 22, 969–976.

FURSTENBURG, F.F., JR., LEVINE, J.A., AND BROOKS-GUNN, J. (1990). "The children of teenage mothers: Patterns of early childbearing in two generations." *Family Planning Perspectives*, March/April 1990, 54–61.

FURSTENBERG, J.J., BROOKS-GUNN, J., AND MORGAN, S.P. (1987). *Adolescent Mothers in Later Life*. New York: Cambridge University Press.

GALLUP, A. M. (1987). "The 19th Annual Gallup Poll of the public's attitudes toward the public schools." *Phi Delta Kappan*, September 1987.

GALLUP, A. M. (1986). "The 18th Annual Gallup Poll of the public's attitudes toward the public schools." *Phi Delta Kappan*, September 1986, 43–59.

GALLUP, A. M. (1985). "The 17th Annual Gallup Poll of the public's attitudes toward the public schools." *Phi Delta Kappan*, September 1985, 35–47.

GALLUP, G.G., JR., AND SUAREZ, S.D. (1986). "Self-awareness and the emergence of mind in humans and other primates." In J. Suls and A.G. Greenwald, eds., *Psychological Perspectives on the Self*, vol 3. Hillsdale, NJ: Erlbaum.

GALVIN, K.M., AND BROMMEL, B.J. (1982). *Family Communication: Cohesion and Change*. Glenview, IL: Scott Foresman.

GARBARINO, J. (1985). *Adolescent Development*. Columbus, OH: Charles E. Merrill.

GARBARINO, J., AND ASP, C.E. (1981). *Successful Schools and Competent Students*. Lexington, MA: Lexington Books.

GARBARINO, J., SEBES, J., AND SCHELLENBACH, C. (1985). "Families at Risk for Destructive Parent-Child Relations in Adolescence." In Laurence Steinberg, *Adolescence*. New York: Alfred A. Knopf.

GAWIN, F.H., AND KLEBER, H.D. (1986). "Abstinence symptomatology and psychiatric diagnosis." *Archives of General Psychiatry* 43, 107–113.

GILLIAM, D. (1983). "Why do we insist on rushing kids into growing up?" *The Philadelphia Inquirer*, Sept. 27, 1983.

GILLIGAN, C. (1982). *In a Different Voice*. Cambridge: Harvard University Press.

GLASER, R., AND TAKANISHI, R. (1986). "Introduction: Creating a knowledge base for education: Psychology's contribution and prospects." *American Psychologist* 10, 1025–1028.

GOETHALS, GEORGE, AND KLOS, DENNIS. (1976) *Experiencing Youth: First-Person Accounts*, 2d ed. Boston: Little, Brown, and Company. 1976

GOLEMAN, D. (1986). "What colleges have learned about suicide." *The New York Times*, Feb. 23, 1986, 22-E.

GOLEMAN, D. (1980). "Leaving home: Is there a right time to go?" *Psychology Today*, August, 55–61.

GOODLAD, J. (1984). *A Place Called School*. New York: McGraw-Hill.

GOODWIN, M.P., AND ROSCOE, B. (1990). "Sibling violence and agonistic interactions among middle adolescents." *Adolescence*, Summer 1990, 451–467.

GORDON, T. (1988). *P.E.T., Parent Effectiveness Training*. New York: New American Library.

GORMAN, M.E. (1984). "Using the Eden Express to teach introductory psychology." *Teaching of Psychology* 11, 39–40.

GRABE, M. (1981). "School size and the importance of school activities." *Adolescence* 16, 61, 21–31.

GRANT, W. V., AND SNYDER, T.D., (1984). *Digest of Education Statistics 1983–84*. Washington, D.C.: U. S. Government Printing Office.

GRATTAN, T.C. (1990). *Civilized America. vol. 2*. London: Bradbury and Evans, 1859. In F.P. Rice, *The Adolescent*, 6th ed. Boston: Allyn and Bacon, Inc.

GREELEY, A.M. (1981). "The state of the nation's happiness." *Psychology Today*, Jan. 1981.

GREENBERG, J. (1982). "Suicide linked to brain chemical deficit." *Science News* 121, 355.

GREENBERGER, E., AND STEINBERG, L. (1986). *When Teenagers Work*. New York: Basic Books.

GREIF, G. L. (1985). "Single fathers rearing children." *Journal of Marriage and the Family* 47, 185–191.

GROSS, D.M., AND SCOTT, S. (1990). "Proceeding with caution." *Time*, July 16, 1990.

GROTEVANT, H.D., AND COOPER, C.R. (1985). "Patterns of interaction in family relationships and the development of identity exploration in adolescence." *Child Development* 56, 415–428.

GROTEVANT, H.D., AND THORBECKE, W.L. (1982). "Sex differences in styles of occupational identity formation in late adolescence." *Developmental Psychology* 18, 396–405.

GURMAN, A.S. (1983). "Family therapy research and the 'new epistemology.'" *Journal of Marital and Family Therapy* 9, 3, 227–234.

HAAS, L. (1981). "Domestic Role Sharing in Sweden." *Journal of Marriage and the Family* 43, 957–967.

HADAWAY, C. K., ELIFSON, K. W., AND PETERSON, D. M. (1984). "Religious involvement and drug use among urban adolescents." *Journal for the Scientific Study of Religion*, June 1984, 109–128.

HALEY, J. (1980). *Leaving Home*. New York: McGraw-Hill.

HALL, G. S. (1967). *Life and Confessions of a Psychologist*. 1923; in N. Kiell, *The Universal Experience of Adolescence*. Boston: Beacon Press.

HALL, G. S. (1904). *Adolescence*. 2 vol. New York: D. Appleton and Company.

HAMMACHEK, D.E. (1985). "The self's development and ego growth: Conceptual analysis and implications for counselors. *Journal of Counseling and Development* 64, 136–142.

HANKS, M., AND ECKLAND, B. K. (1978) "Adult voluntary association and adolescent socialization." *Sociological Quarterly* 19, 3, 481–490.

HARBISON, G. (1990). "A chance to be taller." *Time*, Jan. 8. p. 70.

HARTER, S. (1983). "Developmental perspectives on the self-system." In P. H. Mussen, ed., *Handbook of Child Psychology*, vol. 4. New York: John Wiley and Sons.

HARTUP, W. W. (1983). "The peer system." In P. H. Mussen, ed., *Carmichael's Manual of Child Psychology*, 4th ed., vol. 4. New York: John Wiley and Sons, Inc.

The Harvard Medical School Health Letter (1985). "AIDS: Update." Part 1, November 1985; Part 2, December 1985.

The Harvard Medical School Health Letter (1981). April.

HASKELL, M. R., AND YABLONSKY, L. (1982). *Juvenile Delinquency*, 3d ed. Boston: Houghton Mifflin.

HASS, A. (1979). *Teenage Sexuality*. New York: Macmillan.

HASSETT, J. (1981). "But that would be wrong . . ." *Psychology Today*, November 1981, 34–50.

HAVIGHURST, R. J. (1972). *Developmental Tasks and Education*, 3d ed. New York: David McKay Co., Inc.

HAYES, D., ed. (1987). *Risking the Future: Adolescent Sexuality, Pregnancy, and Childbearing*, vol. 1. Washington, D.C.: Academy Press.

HESS, D. (1990). "Toughen laws on child labor, panel is urged." *The Philadelphia Inquirer*, June 9, p. 15-A.

HETHERINGTON, E.M. (1981). "Children and divorce." In R. Henderson, ed., *Parent-Child Interaction: Theory, Research, and Prospects*. New York: Academic Press.

HETHERINGTON, E. M., HAGAN, M.S., AND ANDERSON, E. R. (1988). "Family transitions: A child's perspective." *American Psychologist*.

HILL, J. (1980). "The family." In M. Johnson, ed., *Toward Adolescence: The Middle School Years* (Seventy-ninth Yearbook of the Society for the Study of Education). Chicago: University of Chicago Press.

HILL, J., HOMBECK, G., MARLOW, L., GREEN, T., AND LYNCH, M. (1985). "Menarcheal status and parent-child relations in families of seventh-grade girls." *Journal of Youth and Adolescence* 14, 301–316.

HIRSCHFELD, R. M. A., AND CROSS, C. K. (1982). "Epidemiology of affective disorders: Psychosocial risk factors." *Archives of General Psychiatry* 39, 35–46.

HOFFMAN, M. L. (1980). "Moral development in adolescence." In J. Adelson, ed., *Handbook of Adolescent Psychology*. New York: John Wiley and Sons.

HOLLAND, J. (1985). *Making Vocational Choices: A Theory of Vocational Personalities and Work Environments*, 2d. ed. Englewood Cliffs, NJ: Prentice Hall.

HOLMES, L. D. (1986). *Quest for the Real Samoa*. South Hadly, MA: Bergin and Garvey.

HOWARD, K. I., KOPTA, S. M., KRAUSE, M. S. , AND ORLINSKY, D. E. (1986). "The dose-effect relationship in psychotherapy." *American Psychologist*, February 1986, 159–164.

HUNTER, F., AND YOUNISS, J. (1982). "Changes in functions of three relations during adolescence." *Developmental Psychology* 18, 806–811.

HUSTON, T. L., RUGGIERO, M, CONNER, R., AND GEIS, G. (1981). "Bystander intervention into crime: A study based on naturally occurring episodes." *Social Psychology Quarterly* 44, 14–23.

INSEL, P. M., AND ROTH, W. T. (1985). *Core Concepts in Health*, 4th ed. Palo Alto, CA: Mayfield.

ISTVAN, J., AND MATARAZZO, J. D. (1984). "Tobacco, alcohol, and caffeine use: A review of their inter-relationships." *Psychological Bulletin* 95, 301–326.

JOHNSTON, L.D., AND O'MALLEY, P.M. (1986). "Why do the nation's students use drugs and alcohol? Self-reported reasons from nine national surveys." *Journal of Drug Issues* 16, 29–66.

JOHNSTON, L. D., O'MALLEY, P.M., AND BACHMAN, J.G. (1989). "Drug Use, Drinking, and Smoking: National Survey Results from High School, College, and Young Adult Populations 1975–1988." Washington, DC: National Institute on Drug Abuse, U.S. Government Printing Office.

JONES, E., M.D. (1953). *The Life and Work of Sigmund Freud*, vol. 1. New York: Basic Books.

JONES-WITTERS, P., AND WITTERS, W.L. (1983). *Drugs and Society*. Monterey, CA: Wadsworth Health Science.

JURICH, A.P., AND JONES, W.C. (1986). "Divorce and the experience of adolescents." In G.K. Leigh and G.W. Peterson, eds., *Adolescents in Families*. Cincinnati: South-Western Publishing Co.

JURICH, A.P., POLSON, C.J.; JURICH, J.A., AND BATES, R.A. (1985). "Family factors in the lives of drug users and abusers." *Adolescence*, Spring 1985, 143–159.

KAHN, S., ZIMMERMAN, G., CZIKSZENTMIHALYI, M., AND GETZELS, J.W. (1985). "Relations between identity in young adulthood and intimacy in midlife." *Journal of Personality and Social Psychology* 49, 1316–1322.

KAHOE, R. D. AND MEADOW, M. J. (1981). "A developmental perspective on religious orientation dimensions." *Journal of Religion and Health*, 20, 8–17.

KALLEBERG, A.L., AND ROSENFELD, R.A. (1990). "Work in the family and in the labor market: A cross-national reciprocal analysis." *Journal of Marriage and the Family*, May 1990, 331–346.

KANDEL, D. (1980). "Stages in adolescent involvement in drug use." In R.E. Muuss, ed., *Adolescent Behavior and Society* 3d ed. New York: Random House.

KELLY, C., AND GOODWIN, G.C. (1983). "Adolescents' perception of three styles of parental control." *Adolescence*, Fall 1983, 567–571.

KENNEDY, S. (1984). "Youth programs stress non-alcoholic activities." *The Philadelphia Inquirer*, May 28, 1984, 8-A.

KERR, B.A. (1983). "Raising the career aspirations of gifted girls." *Vocational Guidance Quarterly* 32, 37–43.

KESSLER, G.R., IBRAHIM, F.A., AND KAHN, H. (1986). "Character development in adolescents." *Adolescence*, Spring 1986, 1–9.

KETT, J. F. (1977). *Rites of Passage: Adolescence in America 1790 to the Present*. New York: Basic Books.

KIDWELL, J.S. (1981). "Number of siblings, sibling spacing, sex, and birth order: Their effects on perceived parent-adolescent relationships." *Journal of Marriage and the Family*, May 1981, 330–335.

KIELL, NORMAN. (1967). *The Universal Experience of Adolescence.* Boston: Beacon Press.

KINGSTON, P.W., AND NOCK, S.L. (1985). "Consequences of the family work day." *Journal of Marriage and the Family* 47, 619–629.

KISKER, E. E. (1985). "Teenagers talk about sex, pregnancy and contraception." *Family Planning Perspectives*, March/April 1985, 83–90.

KLEIN, J.R., AND LITT, I.F. (1983). "Menarche and dysmenorrhea." In J. Brooks-Gunn and A.C. Peterson, eds., *Girls at Puberty: Biological, Psychological, and Social Perspectives.* New York: Plenum Press

KNESS, D. (1983). "Clothing deprivation feelings of three adolescent ethnic groups." *Adolescence*, 18, 659–674.

KNOX, D. AND WILSON, K. (1983). "Dating problems of university students." *College Student Journal*, 17, 225–228.

KOHLBERG, L. (1984). *The Psychology of Moral Development*, vol. 2. San Francisco: Harper and Row.

KRAUTHAMMER, C. (1990). "Education: Doing bad and feeling good." *Time*, Feb. 5, 1990, 78.

KRONICK, D. (1978). "An examination of psychosocial aspects of learning disabled adolescents." *Learning Disability Quarterly* 1, 4, 86–93.

KRUSKEMPER, H.L. (1986). *Anabolic Steroids.* New York, Academic Press.

KUHN, D. (1979). "The significance of Piaget's formal operations stage in education." *Journal of Education* 161, 34–50.

KUIPER, N.A., AND ROGERS, T.B. (1979). "Encoding of personal information: Self-other differences." *Journal of Personality and Social Psychology* 37, 499–514.

KULKA, R. A., AND WEINGARTEN, H. (1979). "The long-term effects of parental divorce in childhood on adult adjustment." *Journal of Social Issues* 33, 4, 50–78.

LABOUVIE-VIEF, G. (1982). "Dynamic development and mature autonomy: A theoretical prologue." *Human Development*, 25, 161–191.

LAMB, D.H. AND REEDER, G.H. (1986). "Reliving golden days." *Psychology Today*, June, 22–30.

LARSON, L. E. (1980). "The influence of parents and peers during adolescence: The situation hypothesis revisited." In R. E. Muuss, ed., *Adolescent Behavior and Society*, 3d. ed. New York: Random House.

LATANE, B., AND DARLEY, J. (1970). *The Unresponsive Bystander: Why Doesn't He Help?* New York: Appleton-Century-Crofts.

LEE, C. C. (1985). "Successful rural black adolescents: A psychological profile." *Adolescence*, Spring 1985, 130–142.

LEIGH, G. K., AND PETERSON, G. W. (1986). *Adolescents in Families.* Cincinnati: South-Western Publishing Company.

LEO, J. (1990). "The trouble with self-esteem." *U. S. News & World Report*, April 2.

LEO, J. (1987). "When the date turns to rape." *Time*, March 23, p. 77.

LEO, J. (1984). "The revolution is over." *Time*, April 9, 74–83.

LERNER, B. (1985). "Self-esteem and excellence: The choice and the paradox." *American Educator* 9, 4, 10–16.

LEVINSON, D. DARROW, C.N., KLEIN, E.B., LEVINSON, M.H., & McKEE, B. (1978). *The Seasons of a Man's Life.* New York: Alfred Knopf.

LEVITZ-JONES, E. M., AND ORLOFSKY, J. L. (1985). "Separation-individuation and intimacy capacity in college women." *Journal of Personality and Social Psychology* 49, 156–169.

LEWIN, T. (1984). "A new push to raise women's pay." *New York Times*, Jan. 1, p. 15.

LEWIN-EPSTEIN, N. (1981). *Youth Employment during High School.* Washington, D. C.: National Center for Education Statistics, U. S. Government Printing Office.

LEWINE, R. R. J. (1981). "Sex differences in schizophrenia: Timing or subtypes?" *Psychological Bulletin* 90, 432–444.

LEWIS, C. (1981). "How adolescents approach decisions: Changes over grades seven to twelve and policy implications." *Child Development* 52, 538–544.

LIPTSITZ, J. S. (1986). "Latchkey kids." *Monitor* 17, 12, p.6.

LIPSITZ, J. S. (1984). *Successful Schools for Young Adolescents.* New Brunswick, NJ: Transaction Books.

LIVSON, N., AND PESKIN. H. (1980). "Perspectives on adolescence from longitudinal research." In J. Adelson, ed., *Handbook of Adolescent Psychology.* New York: John Wiley and Sons, 1980.

LOCHMAN, J.E. AND CURRY, J.F. (1986). "Effects of social problem-solving training and self-instruction training with aggressive boys." *Journal of Clinical Child Psychology*, 15, 159–164.

LONG, L. (1989). "How education can help latchkey children." *Education Digest*, March 1989, 53–57.

LONG, T. AND LONG, L. (1983). *Latchkey Children.* New York: Penguin.

LONG, T. E., AND HADDEN, J. K. (1983). "Religious conversion and the concept of socialization: Integrating the brainwashing and drift models." *Journal for the Scientific Study of Religion*, March 1983, 1–14.

McADOO, H. P. (1982). "Stress absorbing systems in black families." *Family Relations* 31, 479–488.

McALLISTER, E. W. C. (1985). "Religious attitudes of women college students: A follow-up study." *Adolescence*, Winter 1985, 797–804.

McCOMBS, A., AND FOREHAND, R. (1989). "Adolescent school performance following parental divorce: Are there family factors that can enhance success?" *Adolescence*, Winter 1989, 871–880.

McCRARY, E. (1984). "Loneliness, danger and anxiety: The lot of many a latchkey child." *The Philadelphia Inquirer*, June 4, p. 20-BN.

McGEE, E. A. (1982). *Too Little, Too Late.* New York: Ford Foundation.

McLAUGHLIN, S. D., GRADY, W. R., BILLY, J. O. G., LANDALE, N. S., AND WINGES, L. D. (1986). "The effects of the sequencing of marriage and first birth during adolescence." *Family Planning Perspectives.* January/February 1986, 12–18.

MACCOBY, E. E., AND MARTIN, J. A. (1983). "Socialization in the context of the family: Parent-child interaction." In P. H. Mussen, ed., *Handbook of Child Psychology*, 4th ed., vol. 4. New York: John Wiley and Sons.

MALOVICH, N.J., AND STAKE, J.E. (1990). "Sexual harassment on campus: Individual differences in attitudes and beliefs." *Journal of Women Quarterly*, March 1990.

MARCIA, J. (1980). "Identity in adolescence." In J. Adelson, ed., *Handbook of Adolescent Psychology.* New York: John Wiley and Sons.

MARLATT, G.A. AND GORDON, J. R. (1985). *Relapse Prevention: Maintenance Strategies in the Treatment of Addictive Behaviors.* New York: Guilford Press.

MASTERS, W. H., JOHNSON, V. E., AND KOLODNY, R. C. (1988). *Masters and Johnson on Sex and Human Loving*. Glenview, IL: Scott, Foresman.

MEACHAM, J. A., AND SANTILLI, N. R. (1982). "Interstage relationships in Erikson's theory: Identity and intimacy." *Child Development* 52, 1461–1467.

MEAD, M. (1978). *Culture and Commitment*. Garden City, NY: Doubleday.

MEAD, M. (1972). *Blackberry Winter*. New York: William Morrow and Company, Inc.

MEAD, M. (1953). *Growing up in New Guinea*. New York: New American Library.

MEAD, M. (1950). *Coming of Age in Samoa*. New York: New American Library.

MEADOW, M. J., AND KAHOE, R. D. (1984). *Psychology of Religion*. New York: Harper and Row.

MIJUSKOVIC, B. (1986). "Loneliness: Counseling adolescents." *Adolescence* 21, 941–950.

MILLER, B. (1990). "Gender differences in spouse caregiver strain: Socialization and role expectations." *Journal of Marriage and the Family*, May 1990, 311–321.

MILLER, P. Y., AND SIMON, W. (1980). "The development of sexuality in adolescence." In J. Adelson, ed., *Handbook of Adolescent Psychology*. New York: John Wiley and Sons.

MINNETT, A. M., VANDELL, D. L., AND SANTROCK, J. W. (1983). "The effects of sibling status on sibling interaction: Influence of birth order, age, spacing, sex of the child, and sex of the sibling." *Child Development* 54, 1064–1072.

MINUCHIN, P. P., AND SHAPIRO, E. K. (1983). "The school as a context for social development." in P. H. Mussen ed., *Carmichael's Manual of Child Psychology*, 4th ed. New York: John Wiley and Sons.

MINUCHIN, S., AND FISHMAN, H.C. (1981). *Family Therapy Techniques*. Cambridge: Harvard University Press.

MISCHEL, W. (1986). *Introduction to Personality*, 4th ed. New York: Holt, Rinehart and Winston.

MONEY, J. (1987). "Sin, sickness, or status? Homosexual gender identity and psychoneuroendocrinology." *American Psychologist* 42, 384–399.

MONEY, J. (1980). *Love and Love Sickness: The Science of Sex, Gender Difference and Pair-Bonding*. Baltimore: Johns Hopkins University Press.

MONTEMAYOR, R., AND EISEN, M. (1977). "The development of self-conceptions from childhood to adolescence." *Developmental Psychology* 13, 314–319.

MONTEMAYOR, R., AND HANSON, E. (1985). "A naturalistic view of conflict between adolescents and their parents and siblings." *Journal of Early Adolescence* 5, 23–30.

MORRISON, A., GJERDE, P., AND BLOCK, J. H. (1984). "A prospective study of divorce and its relation to family functioning." Paper presented at the biennial meeting of the Society for Research in Child Development, Detroit, April 1983. In John W. Santrock, *Adolescence*. Dubuque, Iowa: William C. Brown.

MORTIMER, J. T., AND KUMKA, D. (1982). "A further examination of the 'occupational linkage hypothesis.'" *The Sociological Quarterly* 23, 3–16.

MOSHER, W. D. (1990). "Contraceptive practice in the United States, 1982–1988." *Family Planning Perspectives*, September/October 1990, 198–205.

MORASH, M.A. (1980). "Working class membership and the adolescent identity crisis." *Adolescence*, 15 (58), 313–320.

MUEHLENHARD, C. L., AND COOK, S. W. (1988). "Men's self-reports of unwanted sexual activity." *The Joy of Sex Research* 24, 58–72.

MURPHY, K. AND WELCH, F. (1989). "Wage premiums for college graduates: Recent growth and possible explanations." *Educational Researcher*, 18, (4), 17–26.

MUUSS, R. E. (1988). *Theories of Adolescence*, 5th ed. New York: Random House.

MUUSS, R. E. (1986). "Adolescent Eating Disorder: Bulimia." *Adolescence*, Summer 1986, 257–267.

NATIONAL COMMISSION ON EXCELLENCE IN EDUCATION (1983). *A Nation at Risk: The Imperative for Educational Reform*. Washington, D.C.: U.S. Department of Education.

NATRIELLO, G., AND DORNBUSH, S.M. (1983). "Bringing behavior back in: The effects of student characteristics and behaviors on the classroom behavior of teachers." *American Educational Research Journal*, Spring 1983, 28–43.

NEEDLE, R.H., SU, S.S., AND DOHERTY, W.J. (1990). "Divorce, remarriage, and adolescent substance use: A prospective longitudinal study." *Journal of Marriage and the Family* 52, 1, 157–169.

NEIMARK, E. D. (1982). "Adolescent thought: Transition to formal operations." In B.B. Wolman, ed., *Handbook of Developmental Psychology*. Englewood Cliffs, NJ: Prentice-Hall.

NEW YORK TIMES (1976). June 13.

NEWMAN, J. (1985). "Adolescents: Why they can be so obnoxious." *Adolescence*, Fall 1985, 635–646.

NEWTON, D. E. (1982). "The status of programs in human sexuality: A preliminary study." *The High School Journal* 6, 232–239.

NICOL, S.E., AND GOTTESMAN, I.I. (1983). "Clues to the genetics and neurobiology of schizophrenia." *American Scientist* 71, 398–404.

NORMAN, J., AND HARRIS, M.W. (1981). *The Private Life of the American Teenager*. New York: Rawson, Wade.

O'BRIEN, R., AND COHEN, S., M.D. (1984). *The Encyclopedia of Drug Abuse*. New York: Facts on File Publications.

OFFER, D., OSTROV, E., AND HOWARD, K.I. (1981). *The Adolescent*. New York: Basic Books.

OFFER, D., OSTROV, E., HOWARD, K.I., AND ATKINSON, R. (1988). *The Teenage World: Adolescents' Self-Image in Ten Countries*. New York: Plenum Medical Book Company.

OGLE, L.T., ed. (1990). *The Condition of Education 1990*. Washington, D.C.: National Center for Education Statistics, U.S. Department of Education. U.S. Government Printing Office.

OLMEDO, E. L. (1981). "Testing linguistic minorities." *American Psychologist* 36, 1078–1085.

On Campus (1985). "Teen suicide: The alarming statistics." Published by the American Federation of Teachers, Washington, D.C. February 1985, p.7.

O'NEILL, C. (1983). "Families threaten, hit, hurt one another." *Family Therapy News* 14, 4, 1–2.

OPENSHAW, D. K., AND THOMAS, D.L. (1986). "The adolescent self and the family." In G.K. Leigh and G.W. Peterson, *Adolescents in Families*. Cincinnati: South-Western Publishing Co.

OPPENHEIMER, M. (1982). "What you should know about herpes." *Seventeen Magazine*, October 1982, 154–155, 170.

O'REILLY, D. (1990). "I deserve it." *The Philadelphia Inquirer*, Dec. 21, 1990, 1-D, 8-D.

ORTMAN, P.E. (1988). "Adolescents' perception of and feelings about control and responsibility in their lives." *Adolescence* 23, 92, 913–924.

OSTROW, R.J. (1982). "Report says legal drugs are the worst killers." *The Philadelphia Inquirer*, Nov. 10, p. 13-A.

PARDECK, J.A., AND PARDECK, J.T. (1990). "Family factors

related to adolescent autonomy." *Adolescence* 25, 98, 311–319.

PARISH, J., AND PARISH, T.S. (1983). "Children's self-concept as related to family structure and family concept." *Adolescence*, Fall 1983, 649–658.

PARKE, R.D., AND SAWIN, D.B. (1979). "Children's privacy in the home: Developmental, ecological, and child-rearing determinants." *Environment and Behavior* 11, 1, 87–104.

PASSER, M. W., AND SEESE, M. (1983). "Life stress and athletic injury: Examination of positive versus negative events and three moderator variables." *Journal of Human Stress.* 9, 11–16.

PAUL, E. L., AND WHITE, K. M. (1990). "The development of intimate relationships in late adolescence." *Adolescence*, Summer 1990, 375–400.

PEIRCE, N. (1987). "Teenagers should be forced to work less." *The Philadelphia Inquirer*, October 31, p. 9-A.

PERRY, C. L., TELCH, M. J., KILLEN, J., BURKE, A., AND MACCOBY, N. (1983). "High school smoking prevention: The relative efficacy of varied treatments and instructions." *Adolescence*, 18, 561–566.

PETER, J. B., BRYSON, Y., AND LOVETT, M. A. (1982). "Genital herpes: Urgent questions, elusive answers." *Diagnostic Medicine*, March/April 1982, 71–74, 76–88.

PETERSEN, A. C., AND TAYLOR, B. (1980). "The biological approach to adolescence." In J. Adelson, ed., *Handbook of Adolescent Psychology*. New York: John Wiley and Sons.

PHARES, E. J. (1988). *Introduction to Personality*, 2d. ed. Glenview, IL.: Scott, Foresman.

PHILLIPS, D.P. (1981). "Newsline." *Psychology Today*, January 1981.

PIAGET, J. (1980). "Intellectual evolution from adolescence to adulthood." In R.E. Muuss, ed., *Adolescent Behavior and Society: A Book of Readings*, 3d ed. New York: Random House, 1980.

PLISKO, V. W., AND STERN, J.D., eds. (1985). *The Condition of Education*, 1985 ed. Washington, D.C.: National Order for Education Statistics, U.S. Government Printing Office.

POLIT-O'HARA, D., AND KAHN, J.R. (1985). "Communication and contraceptive practices in adolescent couples." *Adolescence*, Spring 1985, 33–43.

POLOVY, P. (1980). "A study of moral development and personality relationships in adolescents and young adult Catholic students." *Journal of Clinical Psychology*, 36 (3), 752–757.

POPE, H., AND MUELLER, C.W. (1979). "The intergenerational transmission of marital instability." In G. Levinger and O.C. Moles, eds., *Divorce and Separation*. New York: Basic Books.

PRESCOTT, P. (1981). *The Child Savers*. New York: Alfred A. Knopf.

PUTNAM, F. (1982). "Traces of Eve's faces." *Psychology Today*, October 1982.

RALSTON, N., AND THOMAS, P. (1974). *The Adolescent: Case Studies for Analysis*. New York: Chandler Publishing Co.

RAPEE, R. (1986). "Differential response to hyperventilation in panic disorder and generalized anxiety disorder." *Journal of Abnormal Psychology* 95, 24–28.

RATHUS, S.A., AND NEVID, J.S. (1991). *Abnormal Psychology*. Englewood Cliffs, NJ: Prentice Hall.

RENNER, J. W., AND STAFFORD, D.G. (1976). "The operational levels of secondary school students." In J. W. Renner, D. G. Stafford, et al., *Research, Teaching, and Learning with the Piaget Model*. Norman, OK.: University of Oklahoma Press.

RICH, C.L., SHERMAN, M., AND FOWLER, R.C. (1990). "San Diego suicide study: The adolescents." *Adolescence*, winter 1990, 855–865.

ROARK, A.C. (1986). "Study finds no drift to right among college students." *The Philadelphia Inquirer*, Nov. 3, 1986, 3-A.

ROAZEN, P. (1976). *Erik H. Erikson*. New York: The Free Press.

ROBERTS, A.R. (1982). "Adolescent runaways in suburbia: A new typology." *Adolescence* 17, 379–396.

ROBERTSON, J.F., AND SIMONS, R.L. (1989). "Family factors, self-esteem, and adolescent depression." *Journal of Marriage and the Family*, Feb. 1989, 125–138.

ROBINS, L.N., HELZER, J.E., WEISSMAN, M.M., ORVASCHEL, H., GRUENBERG, E., BURKE, J.D.,JR., AND REGIER, D.A. (1984). "Lifetime prevalence of specific psychiatric disorders in three sites." *Archives of General Psychiatry* 41, 10, 949–958.

ROGERS, C. (1980). *A Way of Being*. Boston: Houghton Mifflin.

ROLL, S., AND MILLEN, L. (1979). "The friend as represented in the dreams of late adolescents: Friendship without rose-colored glasses." *Adolescence* 14, 54, 255–275.

ROSCOE, B., DIANA, M.S., AND BROOKS, R.H. (1987). "Early middle, and late adolescents' views on dating and factors influencing partner selection." *Adolescence*, Spring 1987, 59–68.

ROSCOE, B. AND PETERSON, K. (1984). "Older adolescents: A self-report of engagement in developmental tasks." *Adolescence*, Summer 1984, 391–396.

ROSE, K.J. (1988). *The Body in Time*. New York: John Wiley and Sons.

ROTHMAN, K. M. (1984). "Multivariate analysis of the relationship of person concerns to adolescent ego identity status." *Adolescence*, Fall 1984, 713–727.

RUBENSTEIN, C. (1983). "The modern art of courtly love." *Psychology Today*, July, 40–49.

RUBENSTEIN, C. (1981). "Survey report: Money and self-esteem, relationships, secrecy, envy, satisfaction." *Psychology Today*, May, 29–44.

RUBENSTEIN, C., SHAVER, P., AND PEPLAU, L.A. (1982). "Loneliness." In N. Jackson, ed., *Personal Growth and Behavior, 82/83.* Guilford, CT: Dushkin Publishing Group.

RUBLE, D. N., AND BROOKS-GUNN, J. (1982). "The experience of menarche." *Child Development* 53, 1557–1566.

RUBY, T. AND LAW, R. (1982). "School dropouts—They are not what they seem to be." *Children and Youth Services Review*, 3, 279–291.

RUMBERGER, R.W. (1983). "Dropping out of high school: The influence of race, sex, and family background." *American Education Research Journal*, Summer 1983, 199–220.

RUST, J.O, AND McCRAW, A. (1984). "Influence of masculinity-femininity on adolescent self-esteem and peer acceptance." *Adolescence*, Summer 1984, 359–366.

RUTTER, M. (1983). "School effects on pupil progress: Research findings and policy implications." *Child Development* 54, 1–29.

RUTTER, M., AND GARMEZY, N. (1983). "Developmental Psychopathology." In P.H. Mussen and E.M. Hetherington, eds., *Handbook in Child Psychology*, 4th ed., vol. 4. New York: John Wiley and Sons.

RUTTER, M., AND GILLER, H. (1983). *Juvenile Delinquency*. Baltimore: Penguin Books.

ST CLAIR, S., AND DAY, H.D. (1979). "Ego identity status and values among high school females." *Journal of Youth and Adolescence* 8, 3, 317–326.

SAMET, N. AND KELLY, E.W. (1987). "The relationship of steady dating to self-esteem and sex role identity among adolescents." *Adolescence*, Spring 1987, 231–245.

SANIK, M. M., AND STAFFORD, K. (1985). "Adolescents' contribution to household production: Male and female differences." *Adolescence*, Spring 1985, 207–215.

SANTROCK, J.W., SITTERLE, K.A., AND WARSHAK, R.A. (1988). "Parent-child relationships in stepfather families." In P. Bronstein and P. Cowan, eds., *Fatherhood Today*. New York: John Wiley and Sons.

SANTROCK, J.W., AND WARSHAK, R.A. (1986). "Development, relationships, and legal considerations in father custody families." In M.E. Lamb, ed., *The Father's Role: Applied Perspectives*. New York: John Wiley and Sons.

SAUER, L.E., AND FINE, M.A. (1988). "Parent-child relationships in stepparent families." *Journal of Family Psychology* 1, 434–451.

SCHILL, W.J., MCCARTIN, R., AND MEYER, K. (1985). "Youth employment: Its relationship to academic and family variables." *Journal of Vocational Behavior*, April 1985, 155–163.

SCHLAEFLI, A., REST, J., AND THOMAS, S. (1985). "Does moral education improve moral judgment: A meta-analysis of intervention studies using the defining issues test." *Journal of Educational Research* 55, 319–352.

SCHMID, R. E. (1985). "Survey finds 4 women in 5 try sex before marriage." *The Philadelphia Inquirer*, April 13, 1985. 2-A.

SCHREIBER, F. (1974). *Sybil*. New York: Warner.

SCHULENBERG, J. E., VONDRACEK, F. W., AND CROUTER, A. C. (1984). "The influence of the family on vocational development." *Journal of Marriage and the Family*, February 1984, 129–143.

SCOTT, E. M. (1978). "Young drug abusers and non-abusers: A comparison." *International Journal of Offender Therapy and Comparative Criminology* 22, 2, 105–114.

SCOTT-JONES, D., AND CLARK, M. (1986). "The school experiences of black girls: The interaction of gender, race, and socioeconomic status." *Phi Delta Kappan*, March 1986, 520–526.

SEBALD, H. (1989). "Adolescents' peer orientation: Changes in the support system during the past three decades." *Adolescence*, Winter 1989, 936–946.

SEBALD, H. (1986). "Adolescents' shifting orientation toward parents and peers: A curvilinear trend over recent decades." *Journal of Marriage and the Family*. Feb. 1986, 5–13.

SEDLACK, M., WHEELER, C. W., PULLIN, D. C., AND CUSICK, P. A. (1986). *Selling Students Short*. New York: Teachers College Press of Columbia University.

SELIGMAN, M.E.P. (1988). "Boomer Blues." *Psychology Today*, October, pp. 50–55.

SELMAN, R. L. (1980) *The Growth of Interpersonal Understanding*. New York: Academic Press.

SELMAN, R.L., BEARDSLEE, W., SCHULTZ, L., KRUPA, M., AND PODOREFSKY, D. (1986). "Assessing adolescent interpersonal negotiation strategies: Toward the integration of structural and functional models." *Developmental Psychology* 22, 450–459.

SELTZER, V. C. (1989). *The Psychosocial Worlds of the Adolescent*. New York: John Wiley.

SHAIN, L., AND FARBER, B. A. (1989). "Female identity development and self-reflection in late adolescence." *Adolescence*, Summer 1989, 381–392.

SHARABANY, R., GERSHONI, R., AND HOFMAN, J. (1981). "Girlfriend, boyfriend: Age and sex differences in intimate friendship." *Developmental Psychology* 17, 800–808.

SHELTON, C. M., AND MCADAMS, D. P. (1990). "In search of an everyday morality: The development of a measure." *Adolescence* Winter 1990, 923–940.

SHIGETOMI, D. C., HARTMANN, D. P., AND GELFAND, D. M. (1981) "Sex differences in children's altruistic behavior and reputation for helpfulness." *Developmental Psychology* 17, 377–386.

SIFFORD, D. (1983) "Cults: Educating children is the best prevention." *The Philadelphia Inquirer*, Oct. 10, 1983, 4-C.

SIMMONS, R. G., BURGESON, R., CARLTON-FORD, S., AND BLYTH, D. A. (1987). "The impact of cumulative change in early adolescence." *Child Development* 58, 1235–1243.

SIMMONS, R. G., BURGESON, R., AND REEF, M. J. (1987). "Cumulative change at entry into adolescence." In M. Gunnar, ed., *Development during the Transition to Adolescence*, vol. 21, Hillsdale, NJ: Erlbaum.

SIMPSON, J. A., CAMPBELL, B., AND BERSCHEID, E. (1986). "The association between love and marriage: Kephard (1967) twice revisited." *Personality and Social Psychology Bulletin* 12, 363–372.

SINGER, M., AND ISRALOWITZ. R. (1983). "Probation: A model for coordinating youth services." *Juvenile and Family Court Journal* 1, 35–41.

SMILGIS, M. (1987). "The big chill: Fear of AIDs." *Time*, Feb. 16, 1987, 50–55.

SMOLOWE, J. (1990). "When jobs clash." *Time*, September 3, 1990, 82–84.

SNYDER, J., AND PATTERSON, G. R. (1987). "Family interaction and delinquent behavior." In H. C. Quay, ed., *Handbook of Juvenile Delinquency*. New York: John Wiley.

SNYDER, M. (1984). "When belief creates reality." In L. O. Berkowitz, ed., *Advances in experimental Social Psychology*, vol. 18. New York: Academic Press.

SORENSON, R. C. (1973) *Adolescent Sexuality in Contemporary America*. New York: World Publishing Company.

SPRECHER, S., MCKINNEY, K., WALSH, R, AND ANDERSON, C. (1988). "A revision of the Reiss premarital sexual permissiveness scale." *Journal of Marriage and the Family*. 50, 821–828.

STANLEY, A. (1990). "Child warriors." *Time*, June 18. 1990, 30–52.

STAPLES, R. (1985). "Changes in black family structure: The conflict between family ideology and structural conditions." *Journal of Marriage and the Family* 47, 1005–1013.

STEINBERG, L. (1988). "Reciprocal relation between parent-child distance and pubertal maturation." *Developmental Psychology* 24, 122–128.

STEINBERG, L. (1986). "Latchkey children and susceptibility to peer pressure: An ecological analysis." *Developmental Psychology*, 22, 433–439.

STEINBERG, L., GREENBERGER, E., GARDUQUE, L., RUGGIERO, M., AND VAUX, A. (1982). "Effects of working on adolescent development." *Developmental psychology* 18, 385–395.

STERN, M., NORTHMAN, J.E., AND VAN SLYCK, M.R. (1984). "Father absence and adolescent 'problem behaviors': Alcohol consumption, drug use, and sexual activity." *Adolescence*, Summer 1984, 301–312.

STERNBERG, R.J. (1987). "Intelligence." In R.J. Sternberg and E.S. Smith, eds., *The Psychology of Human Thought*. New York: Cambridge University Press.

STERNBERG, R.J. (1985). *Beyond IQ*. Cambridge: Cambridge University Press.

STERNBERG, R.J., AND NIGRO, G. (1980). "Developmental patterns in the solution of verbal analogies." *Child Development* 51, 27–38.

STIVERS, C. (1988). "Parent-adolescent communication and its relationship to adolescent depression and suicide proneness." *Adolescence*, Summer 1988, 291–295.

STORY, M.D. (1982). "A comparison of university student experiences with various sexual outlets in 1974 and 1980." *Adolescence*, Winter 1982, 737–747.

STOTT, D. (1982). *Delinquency*. New York, SP Medical and Scientific Books.

SUDAK, H., M.D. (1984). *Suicide, In the Young*, Stoneham, MA: Butterworth Publishers.

SULLIVAN, H.S. (1953) *The Interpersonal Theory of Psychiatry*. New York, W. W. Norton and Company.

SULLIVAN, J.F. (1988). "Anti-suicide fight praised in Jersey." *New York Times*, May 29, 1988, 39.

SULLIVAN, K. AND SULLIVAN, A. (1980). "Adolescent-parent separation." *Developmental Psychology*, 16 (2), 93–99.

SUPER, D.E. (1985). "Coming of age in Middletown: Careers in the making." *American Psychologist*, April 1985, 405–414.

SUPER, D.E. (1980). "A life-span life-space approach to career development." *Journal of Vocational Behavior* 16, 3, 282–298.

SWOPE, G.W. (1980). "Kids and cults: Who joins and why?" *Media And Methods* 16, 18–21.

TAKOOSHIAN, H., AND BODINGER, H. (1982). "Bystander indifference to street crime." In L. Savitz and N. Johnson, eds., *Contemporary Criminology*. New York: John Wiley and Sons.

TANNER, J.M. (1978). *Fetus into Man: Physical Growth from Conception to Maturity*. Cambridge: Harvard University Press.

TANNER, J.M. (1973). "Growing up." *Scientific American*, September 1973.

TAUBE, C.A., AND BARRETT, S.A. eds. (1985). *Mental Health, United States, 1985*. Department of Health and Human Services Publication No., (ADM) 85–1378, National Institute of Mental Health, Washington, DC.

TEDESCO, L.A., AND GAIER, E.L. (1988). "Friendship bonds in adolescence." *Adolescence* 89, 127–136.

THIRER, J., AND WRIGHT S.D. (1985) "Sport and social status for adolescent males and females." *Sociology of Sport Journal* 2 (1985) 164–171.

THORNBURG, H.D. (1986). "Adolescent delinquency and families." In G.K. Leigh and G.W. Peterson, eds., *Adolescents in Families*. Cincinnati: South-Western Publishing Co.

THORNBURG, H.D. (1981). "Sources of sex education among early adolescents." *Journal of Early Adolescence*, 1, 171–184.

THORNE, C.R., AND DEBLASSIE, R.R. (1985). "Adolescent substance abuse." *Adolescence*, Summer 1985, 335–347.

TOBLER, M.S. (1986). "Metanalysis of 143 adolescent drug prevention programs: Quantitative outcome results of program participants compared to a control or comparison group." *Journal of Drug Issues* 16, 537–567.

TOLER, A. (1983). "A perception of quality of life of college students and their faculty." *Adolescence* 18, (1983), 585–594.

TOUFEXIS, A. (1989). "Shortcut to the Rambo look." *Time*, Jan. 30, 1989.

TOUFEXIS, A. (1988). "Dark days, darker spirits." *Time*, Jan. 11, 1988.

TREBLICO, G. R. (1984). "Career education and career maturity." *Journal of Vocational behavior*, October 1984, 191–202.

TRICKETT, E. (1978). "Toward a social-ecological conception of adolescent socialization: Normative data on contrasting types of public school classrooms." *Child Development* 49, 408–414.

TROTTER, R.J. (1986). "Three heads are better than one." *Psychology Today*, August 1986, 60.

TUCKER, M.B., AND TAYLOR, R.J. (1989). "Demographic correlates of relationship status among black Americans." *Journal of Marriage and the Family* 51, 3, 655–665.

TURANSKI, J.J. (1982). "Reaching and treating youth with alcohol-related problems: A comprehensive approach." *Alcohol Health and Research World* 7, 3–9.

TWENTYMAN, C.T., ROHRBECK, C.H., AND AMISH, P.A. (1988). "A cognitive-behavioral model of child abuse." In S. Sanders, ed., *Violent Individuals and Families*. Springfield, IL: Charles Thomas.

TYGART, C. (1988). "Public school vandalism: Toward a synthesis of theories and transition to paradigm analysis." *Adolescence* 23, 187–200.

Uniform Crime Reports for the United States, 1989. Federal Bureau of Investigation. Washington, D.C.: Government Printing Office, 1989.

U.S. BUREAU OF THE CENSUS. *Statistical Abstract of the United States: 1990*, 110th ed. Washington, D.C.: U.S. Government Printing Office, 1990.

U.S. BUREAU OF THE CENSUS. *Statistical Abstract of the United States, 1984*, 104th ed. Washington, D.C.: U.S. Government Printing Office, 1984.

U.S. DEPARTMENT OF LABOR (1982). "Dramatic new occupational inroads scored by women." Washington, DC: U.S. Government Printing Office, November 1982.

U.S. DEPARTMENT OF LABOR, BUREAU OF LABOR STATISTICS, *Occupational Outlook Handbook*, 1990–1991 Edition. Washington, D.C.: U.S. Government Printing Office, 1990.

U.S. News and World Report (1982). "America's cults gaining ground again." July 5, 1982, 37–41.

VELDMAN, D.J., AND SANFORD, J.P. (1984). The influence of class ability level on student achievement and classroom behavior." *American Educational Research Journal*, Fall 1984, 629–644.

VIOLATO, C., AND WILEY, A.J. (1990). "Images of adolescence in English/Literature: The Middle Ages to the modern period." *Adolescence*, Summer 1990, 253–264.

VONNEGUT, M. (1975). *The Eden Express: A Personal Account of Schizophrenia*. New York: Praeger, 1975.

WALLERSTEIN, J. S. (1989). *Second Chances: Men, Women and Children a Decade after Divorce*. New York: Ticknor and Fields.

WALLERSTEIN, J. S. (1984). "Children of divorce: Preliminary report of a ten-year followup of young children." *American Journal of Orthopsychiatry* 54, 444–458.

WALLERSTEIN, J. S., AND KELLY, J. B. (1980). *Surviving the Breakup: How Children and Parents Cope with Divorce*. New York: Basic Books.

WALLIS, C. (1985). "Chlamydia: The silent epidemic." *Time*. February 4, 1985.

WATERMAN, A. (1985). *Identity in Adolescence*. San Francisco: Jossey-Bass.

WATT, N., ANTHONY, J., WYNNE, L., AND ROLF, J. (1984). *Children at Risk for Schizophrenia: A Longitudinal Perspective*. New York: Cambridge University Press.

WEHR, S. H., AND KAUFMAN, M. E. (1987). "The effects of assertive training on performance in highly anxious adolescents." *Adolescence* 85, 195–205.

WEIL, A., M.D., AND ROSEN, W. (1983). *Chocolate to Morphine*. Boston: Houghton Mifflin.

WEINER, I. B. (1980). Psychopathology in adolescence." In J. Adelson, ed., *Handbook of Adolescent Psychology*. New York: John Wiley and Sons.

WEISS, R. S.   (1984). "The impact of marital dissolution on income and consumption in single-parent households." *Journal of Marriage and the Family* 46, 115–127.

WEITHORN, L.A. AND CAMPBELL, S.   (1982). "The competency of children and adolescents to make informed treatment decisions." *Child Development*, 53, 1589–1598.

WELTE, J. W., AND ABEL, E. L.   (1989). "Homicide: Drinking by the victim." *Journal of Studies on Alcohol* 50, 197–201.

WESTENDORP, F., BRINK, K. L., ROBERTSON, M. K. AND ORTIZ, I. E.   (1986). "Variables which differentiate placement of adolescents into juvenile justice or mental health systems." *Adolescence*, Spring 1986, 23–37.

WHITE, G. L., JR., MURDOCK, R. T., RICHARDSON, G. E., ELLIS, G. D., AND SCHMIDT, L. J.   (1990). "Development of a tool to assess suicide risk factors in urban adolescence." *Adolescence*. Fall 1990, 655–666.

WHITE, J.   (1991). *Drug Dependence*. Englewood Cliffs, NJ: Prentice-Hall.

WOODROOF, J. T.   (1985). "Premarital sexual behavior and religious adolescents." *Journal for the Scientific Study of Religion*, December 1985, 343–366.

WRIGHT, S. A.   (1984). "Post-involvement attitudes of voluntary defectors from controversial new religious movements." *Journal for the Scientific Study of Religion*, June 1984, 172–182.

WYATT, K., AND GEIS, M.   (1978). "Level of formal thought and organizational memory strategies." *Developmental Psychology* 14, 433–434.

YANKELOVICH, D.   (1981). *New Rules*. New York: Bantam Books.

YOGEV, A., AND RODITI, H.   (1987). "School counselors as gatekeepers: Guidance in poor versus affluent neighborhoods." *Adolescence* 22, 625–639.

YUSSEN, S. R.   (1977). "Characteristics of moral dilemmas written by adolescents." *Developmental Psychology* 13, 162–163.

ZABIN, L. S., AND CLARK, S. D., JR.   (1981). "Why they delay: A study of teenage family planning clinic patients." *Family Planning Perspectives*. September/October, 1981.

ZABIN, L. S., HIRSH, M. B., SMITH, E. A. AND HARDY, J. B.   (1984). "Adolescent sexual attitudes and behavior: Are they consistent?" *Family Planning Perspectives*, July/August 1984, 181–186.

ZELNIK, M., AND KIM, Y. J.,   (1982). "Sex education and its association with teenage sexual activity, pregnancy, and contraceptive use." *Family Planning Perspectives* 14, 117–126.

ZELNIK, M., AND SHAH, F. K.   (1983). "First intercourse among young Americans." *Family Planning Perspectives*, March/April 1983, 64–70.

ZERN, D. S.   (1985). "The expressed preference of different ages of adolescents for assistance in the development of moral values." *Adolescence*, Summer 1985, 405–423.

ZIMBARDO, P., PILKONIS, P., AND NORWOOD, R.   (1974). *The Silent Prison of Shyness*. Glenview, IL: Scott, Foresman and Company.

Glossary

abortion: The spontaneous or medically induced removal of the contents of the uterus during pregnancy.

abstinence: Abstaining from alcoholic drinks.

abuse: Mistreatment in some way, such as physical or sexual abuse.

accommodation: According to Piaget, the changes in one's existing cognitive structures in the process of adapting to an unfamiliar environment.

acting-out behavior: Behavior in which individuals unconsciously relieve their anxiety or unpleasant tensions through expressing them in overt behavior.

adjustment disorder: Maladaptive reaction to a particular stressful situation that results in impaired functioning and symptoms beyond a normal response to such stress; can be expected to decrease when the stress passes.

adolescence: The period of rapid growth between childhood and adulthood, including psychosocial as well as physical growth.

adolescent identity crisis: The characteristic struggle accompanying the adolescent's search for a revised personal identity.

adolescent sexual abuse: Sexual violation, such as forcing a youth to comply with sexual acts under threat or force.

adoption: The voluntary and legal act of taking a child of other parents as a member of one's own family.

adrenocorticotropic hormone (ACTH): Hormone secreted by the pituitary gland that stimulates the adrenal gland.

adult-adolescent communication: The verbal exchange of opinions, attitudes, and feelings between adolescents and adults, often modified by nonverbal behavior.

age-graded influences: Events and experiences that commonly occur at a given stage of life.

aggression: Behavior that intends to cause pain or harm to others.

AIDS (acquired immune deficiency syndrome): A sexually transmitted disease that is communicated through blood products and is ultimately fatal.

alcohol: A colorless, volatile liquid that is the intoxicating element of beer, wine, and whiskey.

alienation: The feeling of psychological distance from other people, society, and oneself, often because of a hostile environment.

alimony: Court-ordered allowance paid to an individual by his or her spouse after a legal separation or divorce.

ambivalence: Having simultaneously conflicting feelings toward a person or thing, such as love and hate.

amenorrhea: The absence of menstruation.

amnesia: Partial or total loss of memory caused by repression, shock, or brain injury.

amphetamines: A widely used groups of stimulants that reduce fatigue and help maintain a high level of efficiency for short periods of time.

androgyny (psychological): The combination of desirable traits from both male and female sex roles, in contrast to the stereotyped masculine and feminine roles.

anorexia nervosa: An eating disorder characterized by a severe loss of appetite and weight.

anthropologist: A person who specializes in the study of the physical and cultural characteristics and institutions of humans.

antipsychotic drugs: Drugs used to relieve symptoms such as extreme agitation, hallucinations, and delusions in psychotic patients.

antisocial behavior: Behavior that violates the basic principles of society; unsociable behavior.

antisocial personality: An individual who violates social norms without evidence of guilt, sometimes known as a sociopath or psychopath.

anxiety: A vague unpleasant feeling of apprehension, warning of impending danger.

anxiety disorder: A psychological disorder characterized by symptoms of inappropriate or excessive anxiety or by attempts to escape from such anxiety.

apprenticeship: A period of training that prepares individuals for the skilled trades like carpentry.

asceticism: An unconscious defensive maneuver by which adolescents may deny their sexual urges and avoid pleasurable associations with sex.

assimilation: According to Piaget, the incorporation of new information into one's existing cognitive structures.

authoritative parenting: Combining warmth and acceptance with moderate parental control and extensive verbal give-and-take.

autonomous decision making: The ability to make important life decisions with a minimum of assistance from others and without an undue need for approval.

autonomous religious orientation: The most mature stage of personal religious development, characterized by greater independence of thought and concern for others than in earlier stages of religious development.

autonomy: The condition of being independent or self-determining.

barbiturates: Any of a group of barbituric acid derivatives used in medicine as sedatives and hypnotics.

bar mitzvah: "Son of the commandment," a Jewish boy who has arrived at the age of religious responsibility—13 years; the ceremony celebrating this event.

bat mitzvah: A Jewish girl who, in Conservative and Reformed congregations, undergoes a ceremony analogous to that of a bar mitzvah; the ceremony celebrating this event.

behavioral autonomy: The ability to perform age-appropriate tasks in a relatively independent manner.

bipolar disorder: An affective or mood disorder involving periods of extreme elation and depression.

birth control: Control of how many children a women will have and when she has them, through the use of contraceptives or fertility-awareness techniques such as the rhythm method.

birth order: The individual's order of birth within a family, which may affect his or her personality because of differential parental treatment.

body image: The mental picture we have of our bodies, often including how we feel about our bodies.

born-again religious experience: A decisive conversion experience based on personal religious faith.

bulimia: An eating disorder characterized by excessive overeating or uncontrolled binge eating followed by self-induced vomiting.

bystander effect: The finding that people are much less likely to help in an emergency when they are with others than when they are alone.

career: A sequence of jobs or occupations; a purposeful life pattern of work.

career education: Helping people to develop a sense of direction and make responsible career choices, including academic and supervised work-study programs.

career inventories: Standardized instruments for helping individuals to identify compatible career goals.

career maturity: The extent to which individuals are progressing toward a career identity, as measured in the Career Maturity Inventory.

career outlook: Projected trends in regard to careers and job openings in the workplace.

career-oriented programs: Certificate and degree programs that prepare people for a particular career.

child labor laws: Laws that regulate adolescents' participation in the workplace.

chlamydia: Inflammation of the urethral tube.

circumcision: Surgical removal of the foreskin from the penis.

cliques: According to Dunphy, small groups that meet mostly for personal sharing.

clitorus: A highly sensitive part of the female's external genitals, its only known purpose being sexual pleasure.

cocaine: A stimulant derived from coca leaves, which, though legally classified as a narcotic drug, induces intense euphoric effects for a short period of time.

cofigurative cultural pattern: The pattern of socialization characterizing societies with moderate social change in which youths learn primarily from their peers.

cognitive: Pertaining to information processing, including perception, memory, and thinking.

cognitive development: Changes in the way of thinking accompanying maturation and experience.

cognitive-disequilibrium model: According to Kohlberg, the concept that growth in the moral understanding comes through the progressive reorganization of moral reasoning as a result of confronting new information and situations one does not fully understand.

cognitive maturity: The ability to think in an adult manner.

cohabitation: Unmarried couples living together, sharing bed and board.

companionship: The relationship between two or more people who associate closely with each other in some way, such as those who work or live together.

compliance: The act or tendency to give in readily to others' requests.

compulsory education: Required attendance at school because of compulsory attendance laws by the state.

concrete operational stage: According to Piaget, the third stage of cognitive development, in which the child can think in terms of basic concepts like time and number, roughly 7 to 11 years of age.

conduct disorders: Childhood and adolescent disorders involving antisocial behavior.

confirmation: A Christian ceremony in which a person is admitted to full membership in a church, having affirmed vows made at baptism. Also, a Jewish ceremony in which young people reaffirm their belief in the basic spiritual and ethical concepts of Judaism.

conformity: Change in one's attitude or behavior in regard to social norms because of real or imagined pressure from others.

conservation: The recognition that a substance's properties such as weight and mass remain the same despite changes in its appearance; according to Piaget, such knowledge occurs in the concrete operational stage.

continuity: The state or quality of being continuous or connected.

contraceptive: Birth-control devices, such as birth-control pills.

conventional morality: According to Kohlberg, the second major level of moral development, in which one's moral judgment is based on internalized, socially acceptable moral standards.

correlation: The degree to which two sets of measures are associated with each other; a statistical measure of relationship.

courtship: The process of social dating between members of the opposite sex, especially when the ultimate goal is marriage.

crack: A concentrated form of cocaine that is more potent and addictive then other forms of cocaine, primarily because it is inhaled.

cross-sex typed: Possessing low levels of traits regarded as appropriate for one's biological sex and high levels of personal characteristics associated with the opposite sex.

crowds: According to Dunphy, larger-size groups that meet primarily for organized social activities.

cult: A nontraditional or unorthodox religious system, with beliefs and customs usually centered around the teachings of a charismatic leader or set of principles.

cultural diversity: Groups of people from a wide variety of ethnic, racial, and cultural backgrounds.

cultural relativism: The view that differences in personality, behavior, and social institutions are due primarily to variations in cultures.

culture: The ideas, customs, arts, and skills that characterize people during a given period of history.

curriculum: A fixed program of studies for graduation from high school or college.

curvilinear: Consisting of or enclosed by a curved line or lines.

custody: The legal arrangement following a divorce specifying which parent the children and adolescents will reside with until they reach legal age.

cyclothymia: A mild, persistent bipolar disorder, involving recurring cycles of mania and depression.

cynicism: The attitude or belief that people are motivated in all their actions only by selfishness.

dating: The practice by which individuals of opposite sexes agree to meet at a specific time and place—either alone or in a group—for a social engagement.

delinquent behavior: Socially deviant behavior by youth under the legal age.

demography: The statistical science dealing with the density, distribution, and vital statistics of populations.

depersonalization: The sense of not being intimately attached to one's body.

depressants: A diverse group of drugs that reduce the activity of the central nervous system.

depression: An emotional state of dejection, with feelings of worthlessness, sadness, and pessimism about the future.

deprogramming: The systematic attempt to reorient former cult members through an intensive teaching and counseling process.

development: The relatively enduring changes in people's capacities and behavior as they grow older, because of the biological growth process and the person's interaction with the environment.

developmental stages: Periods of development when individuals are especially ready to learn some things more than others.

developmental tasks: Capabilities, skills, and attitudes that must be acquired in growing up, especially during critical periods when there is a readiness for learning them.

dichotomy: A division or sharp distinction between two groups.

discretionary powers: The freedom or authority to make decisions.

discrimination: Negative or unfair treatment of people on the basis of such things as their age, sex, or race.

disengaged families: Families characterized by emotionally distant relationships with each other.

disengagement: Withdrawal from social involvement.

displacement: Unconsciously redirecting threatening ideas or impulses onto less threatening objects.

disqualification of communication: Invalidation by family members of their own messages by disguising their true emotions and contradicting themselves.

divorce: The legal dissolution of marriage, usually accompanied by emotional, social, and financial adjustments.

drug abuse: The chronic or excessive ue of any drug, especially when this jeopardizes one's health or interferes with one's psychosocial adjustment.

drug dependence: Defined by the World Health Organization as a "state arising from repeated administration of a drug on a periodic or continuous basis." Drug dependence is subdivided by types, e.g., cocaine type. See also *physical dependence* and *psychological dependence*.

drug, psychoactive: Any substance that alters mood, perception, or consciousness; drugs such as heroin are sometimes referred to as "hard" drugs because of the harsher penalties associated with their use in contrast to the "soft" drugs like alcohol and marijuana.

dual-income families: Families in which both parents are employed in the workplace.

dyslexia: Impairment of the ability to read, often because of a genetic defect or brain injury.

dysmenorrhea: Pain or discomfort before or during menstruation.

dysthymia: A mood disorder involving a mild, persistent depression over an extended period of time.

early adolescence: The early period of adolescent development around the onset of puberty and afterwards, about 10 to 13 years of age.

early adult transition: According to Levinson, the transitional stage between adolescence and adulthood, the initial stage of adulthood.

early maturers: Adolescents who reach their physical maturity earlier than average for their sex.

egalitarian sex roles: Sex roles based on the democratic assumption that men and women should have equal social, political, and economic rights.

ego: According to Freud, the managerial part of personality that strives for adaptation to reality.

ego-defense mechanisms: Automatic, unconscious behavior that protects us from the awareness of anxiety.

egocentrism: According to Piaget, the inadequate differentation of one's thoughts and feelings from those of others, especially evident in the stage of preoperational thought and again in the early phases of formal thought at adolescence.

Electra/Complex: The unconscious tendency of a daughter to be attached to her father and hostile toward her mother.

emotional autonomy: The ability to rely on one's own inner reserves of self-esteem and self-confidence in relation to others.

emotional divorce: The emotional alienation between marriage partners.

empathic listening: Listening and telling people what you've heard them say to you in an accurate, nonjudgmental way.

empathy: The ability to share another's emotions as one's own.

enmeshed families: Families characterized by excessively close emotional relationships with each other.

environment: All the conditions and influences surrounding and affecting the development of individuals.

equilibration: According to Piaget, the inherent regulatory process that facilitates cognitive growth through maintaining a functional balance between assimilation and accommodation.

equilibrium: The state of balance between two opposing forces.

estrogen: A class of hormones that produce female secondary sexual characteristics and affect the menstrual cycle. Estrogen also occurs in lesser amounts in males.

ethnic group: A group that may be distinguished from other groups by its customs, characteristics, and common history.

exceptional students: Students whose special talents or limitations affect their academic functioning significantly more than the average student is affected by his/her gifts or limitations.

expressive role: The expected behaviors associated with caring for the young and fostering their emotional and social development.

externalizers: According to Achenbach, individuals whose psychological conflicts are manifested in external, behavioral problems such as aggression.

extracurricular activities: Activities outside the regular program of studies but under the supervision of the school, such as sports or dramatics.

extrinsic career values: Value placed on a career mostly because of external rewards, such as money or status, rather than the work activity itself.

extrinsic religious orientation: Motivation of religious beliefs and practices primarily by any number of human needs, such as fears and guilt.

family: A group of people related by blood, marriage, or adoption who share a common household.

family as social system: The view that each family member's behavior and development affects all the other members' behavior and development.

family cohesion: The degree of emotional bonding between family members, including the sense of mutual trust and cooperation.

family dissension: The presence of a high degree of emotional conflicts and quarreling within a family.

family therapy: Counseling for the entire family on the assumption that the disturbance of one family member reflects problems in the whole family's interactions.

fixation: Continuing a kind of gratification after one has passed through the psychosexual stage at which this was appropriate.

follicle-stimulating hormone (FSH): Hormone secreted by the pituitary gland that stimulates the follicles and ova in the ovaries and sperm in the testes.

formal operational stage: According to Piaget, the fourth and final stage of cognitive development, in which the adolescent can think in an abstract, logical manner, beginning about 11 or 12 years of age.

friendship: An informal, affectionate relationship between two or more individuals.

Gallup Poll: One of many opinion polls conducted by the Gallup Poll organization in Princeton, New Jersey.

gangs: Groups that are formally organized, have an identifiable leadership, associate regularly, and engage in illegal activities.

gender noncomformity: A lack of comformity to stereotypic masculine and feminine behaviors.

genital herpes: A sexually transmitted disease that, in addition to the discomfort of the symptoms, may lead to serious medical complications.

global esteem: One's characteristic level of self-worth or self-esteem.

Gonadotrophin-releasing hormone (GnRH):   A chemical released by the hypothalamus to control the secretion of luteinizing hormone (LH) and follicle-stimulating hormone (FSH).

gonorrhea: An infectious bacterial disease usually transmitted through sexual intercourse.

group: Two or more persons who share a common interest or goal.

group therapy: All those forms of therapy in which a leader meets with a group of clients, including preexisting groups such as families and those consisting of strangers.

growth spurt: The period of rapid physical growth preceding sexual maturation during adolescence. See *pubescence*.

hallucinogens: Drugs that produce sensations such as distortions of time, space, sound, color, and other bizarre effects.

helping behavior: Actions intended to benefit people in need that have no apparent selfish motivation.

hemorrhage: The escape of large quantities of blood from a blood vessel.

heroin: A drug derived from opium taken mostly for its psychological effects, one of the most addictive and destructive of all illicit drugs.

heteronomous morality: The understanding of right and wrong based on external authority.

heterosexual cliques: Small groups composed of adolescents of both sexes.

heterosexuality: Preference for sex partners of the opposite sex.

Holland's Self-Directed Search: A self-scoring vocational inventory that may assist people in choosing a compatible career.

homosexuality: Emotional and sexual preference for sex partners of the same sex.

hormones: Glandular secretions into the bloodstream which are active in bringing about bodily and sexual maturation during adolescence.

hurried child syndrome: The tendency for chil-

dren and adolescents to grow up faster today because of the increased social pressure to do so.

hymen: The tissue that partially covers the vaginal opening.

hypnotic: A drug that depresses the central nervous system and induces sleep.

hypothalamus: A small structure in the brain that monitors changes in the body's activities such as eating and sleeping and plays a major role in regulating the emotions.

hypothetical: Conditional thinking based on that which is assumed or supposed; involving hypotheses.

hypothetical reasoning: Conditional reasoning based on what is assumed or supposed.

hypothetical-deductive reasoning: Reasoning from known principles or assumptions.

"I" message: The expression of one's feelings about another person's behavior in a nonjudgmental way.

id: According to Freud, the unconscious reservoir of instinctual impulses that supplies the psychic energy for the personality.

ideal self: The self one would like to be.

identification: The unconscious process of attributing characteristics to ourselves which we perceive in others we admire.

identity: According to Erikson, the developmental task of adolescence in which the sense of self is redefined to incorporate one's uniqueness and self-chosen values.

identity achievement: According to Erikson, the successful attainment of personal identity by those who have faced and resolved their adolescent identity crisis.

identity confusion: Sense of confusion over one's personal identity or who one is.

identity crisis: According to Erikson, the characteristic struggle of adolescence consisting of the individual's search for personal identity and the attendant danger of identity confusion.

identity foreclosure: The identity status associated with the avoidance of the adolescent identity crisis, resulting in premature commitments.

identity moratorium: The identity status that accompanies a prolonged adolescent identity crisis in which few, if any, commitments are made.

identity status: The various ways adolescents attempt to resolve their identity crisis, including achievement, foreclosure, moratorium, and confusion.

illegal drugs: Drugs whose over-the-counter sale and possession are prohibited by law.

imaginary audience: According to Piaget, the adolescent's heightened self-consciousness and preoccupation with the anticipated reactions of others.

incongruent (paradoxical) communication: Mixed signals sent by family members.

indoctrination: Systematic instruction involving a set of beliefs or ideas.

information-processing approach: A systematic, psychological approach to cognition in which the human mind is viewed as a complex system for gathering, interpreting, and using information.

inhalants: Any of a group of substances inhaled to alter subjective state, such as plastic (model) cement; sometimes designated as "abused volatile substances."

instrumental hedonism: The understanding of right and wrong based on the satisfaction of one's own interests and needs.

instrumental role: The expected behaviors deemed necessary for survival in a competitive society.

intact families: Families in which adolescents are living with both of their biological parents.

intellectualization: Reducing anxiety by analyzing threatening issues in an emotionally detached way.

intellectually gifted: Students who have an above-average intelligence as measured on a standardized intelligence test, such as an IQ of 130 or more.

intelligence: The capacity for acquiring and applying knowledge.

intelligence quotient (IQ): A measure of intelligence, calculated as a ratio of one's mental age to one's chronological age (in children) or by comparing one's test scores to those of a standardized sample (in adults).

intelligence test: A standardized test designed to assess one's intelligence or capacity for learning.

internalizers: Individuals whose psychological conflicts are manifested primarily in internal symptoms like depression.

intimacy: Interpersonal closeness between two or more persons, such as friends or lovers, which may or may not involve sexual intimacy.

intrinsic career values: Value placed on a career mostly for the work activity itself.

intrinsic religious orientation: The endeavor to internalize and practice one's religious beliefs.

introversion/extroversion: A trait dimension on which people who describe themselves as quiet and introspective are designated as introverts and those who see themselves as active and sociable are extroverts.

job: A set of tasks to be performed within an organization, usually associated with a particular position.

juvenile court: An integral part of the juvenile justice system, usually for juvenile offenders referred by the police.

juvenile delinquency: Illegal behavior committed by youth under the legal age, which is 18 in many states.

juvenile delinquent: Generally, someone under the legal age who has engaged in illegal behavior; technically, a person convicted of such a violation in juvenile court.

juvenile justice: The concept that youthful offend-ers who have not reached legal age should be treated by rules and principles different than the legal system that applies to adults.

LSD: One of the psychedelic drugs taken mostly for its consciousness-expanding properties.

latchkey teens: Teenagers who are left on their own after school because both parents are at work.

late adolescence: The later period of adolescence, including the late teens and possibly the early twenties.

late maturers: Adolescents who reach their physical maturity later than average for their sex.

latency: The long, quiet period in psychosexual development from age six to puberty, in which no major unconscious drives press for satisfaction.

learning climate: A general term, like school climate, that refers to the combined influence of a variety of factors affecting learning, such as classroom size and teacher-student interactions.

learning disabilities: Specific learning deficits exhibited by individuals with normal or near-normal intelligence who have severe difficulties in understanding or using spoken or written language.

leaving home: Separation from one's family of origin, including emotional autonomy as well as moving out of the family house.

Lithium: Lithium carbonate, a chemical salt used to help regulate moods in the bipolar disorder.

loneliness: The state of unhappiness at being alone accompanied by a longing for companionship.

love: A deep and tender feeling of affection for or attachment to a person or persons.

luteinizing hormone: Hormone secreted by the pituitary gland that stimulates the development of the ova, estrogen, and progesterone in females and the sperm and testosterone in males.

mainstreaming: Educational policy of integrating students with special needs into classrooms and social interaction with regular students.

major depression: A prominent and relatively persistent state of depression manifested in poor appetite, insomnia, restlessness or apathy, fatigue, feelings of worthlessness, and recurrent thoughts of death.

maladjustment: The condition of being unable to cope with or adjust to the circumstances of one's life.

malnutrition: Faulty or inadequate nutrition.

marijuana: A derivative of the Cannabis plant which is usually smoked for its relaxing and disinhibiting effects.

marker events: Significant events in one's personal life, such as graduation and getting a job.

masturbation: The self-manipulation of one's sex organ to produce pleasure.

maturation: Unfolding of the biological growth process, resulting from genetic predispositions but also affected by the environment.

median: A measurement that falls in the exact middle of a distribution of scores; half the scores fall above this number and half fall below.

menarche: The developmental onset of menstruation or the girl's first menstrual period.

menstrual cycle: A biological cycle that prepares the lining of the uterus for the possible arrival of a fertilized egg, which usually begins in early adolescence and repeats itself about every twenty eight to thirty five days.

menstruation: The part of the menstrual cycle in which the bloody lining of the uterus is discharged through the vagina.

methadone: One of the narcotic drugs that produces physiological effects similar to those of morphine and heroin but is less habit-forming.

methaqualone: A sedative hypnotic drug that produces effects similar to those of the barbiturates.

midadolescence: The middle period of adolescence, involving the mid-teens, about 14 to 16 years of age.

middle schools: Schools organized around the characteristic needs of early adolescents.

midlife crisis: The period of self-assessment accompanying the realization that one's physical life is half over, beginning about the mid- to late thirties.

miscarriage: The spontaneous premature termination of a pregnancy; spontaneous abortion.

modeling: Observing and emulating the behavior of others.

moral: Pertaining to the distinction between right and wrong in conduct or character.

moral behavior: The conformity of behavior to commonly accepted standards of right and wrong.

moral development: The process by which people come to adopt the standards of right and wrong transmitted by their families and culture, including cognitive, emotional, and behavioral aspects.

moral dilemmas: Hypothetical situations in which one must choose between two unequally unpleasant moral alternatives.

moral reasoning: Thought or deliberation in regard to what is right and wrong.

morphine: An opiate that produces sedative effects through depressing the nervous system; used medically primarily for the relief of pain.

multiple personality: One of the dissociative disorders in which the individual alternates between two or more distinct personalities.

narcissism: Excessive interest in one's own appearance or importance; psychoanalysis—arrest or regression to the initial stage of psychosexual development in which the self is an object of erotic pleasure.

narcissistic personality disorder: A disorder characterized by an undue sense of self-importance, often accompanied by a sense of inferiority.

narcotic: Medically, any drug that produces sleep or relieves pain; legally, any drug regulated by federal narcotic laws.

nocturnal emission: The spontaneous ejaculation of semen during an erotic dream, popularly known as a "wet dream."

non–age-graded influences: Events and experiences that are unique to the individual rather than associated with a given stage of life.

observational learning: Learning by observing and imitating the behavior of others.

obsession: A thought or image that an individual may consider irrational but that recurs repeatedly, compelling the person to dwell on it.

obsessive-compulsive disorder: A preoccupation with unacceptable ideas that appear without external stimuli, accompanied by the urge to engage in repetitive activity to ward off their imaginary threats.

Occupational Outlook Handbook: A resource for career choice, revised and published every two years by the Department of Labor Statistics.

Oedipus complex: The unconscious tendency of a son to be attached to his mother and hostile toward his father.

opiates: A group of drugs that are derivatives of, or are pharmacologically related to, products from the opium poppy and are used medically primarily for the relief of pain.

oral-genital sex: Mouth-to genital contact to create sexual pleasure.

out-of-wedlock birth: Birth to an unmarried woman.

ovary (pl. ovaries): The female sex gland that produces ova (eggs) and sex hormones.

PCP: One of the psychedelic drugs that has widely varying effects on the central nervous system, including symptoms resembling those of an acute schizophrenic disturbance.

panic attack: Acute feelings of apprehension accompanied by disabling symptoms such as dizziness and nausea.

paradox: A statement contrary to common belief.

parent effectiveness training (PET): Systematic skills training for parents in regard to matters of communication and discipline.

parent-adolescent conflicts: Disagreements and conflicts between parents and their adolescents that often arise in the course of parental supervision of adolescents.

parenting style: The manner in which parents attempt to influence their adolescent's psychological and social development.

peer arena therapy: A form of group therapy focusing on peer interactions in which the adolescent's difficulties originally experienced with peers may be reexperienced and resolved in a protected setting guided by a therapist.

peer groups: Groups of people about the same age and social status who share common interests.

peers: People in one's life who are about the same age, grade, and social class.

penis: The male sexual organ consisting of the internal root and external shaft and glans.

permissive indifferent parenting: Unresponsiveness and neglect toward one's adolescents.

permissive indulgent parenting: Emphasizing acceptance and responsiveness toward one's adolescents, rarely placing limits on their behavior.

personal control: Achieved control over one's life, largely synonymous with perceived control.

personal fable: According to Piaget, the adolescent's exaggerated sense of personal uniqueness.

personal identity: The sense of who one is as distinct from others.

personality: The distinctive patterns of thought, emotions, and behavior that characterize an individual's adaptation to the situations of his or her life.

personality disorder: An inflexible and maladaptive pattern of behavior that causes significant impairment in social and occupational functioning.

personality-occupational types: According to Holland, the concept that people seek out those occupations most compatible with their interests and personalities.

perspective: A specific point of view in understanding or judging ideas, things, or events.

perspective taking: The ability to reflect on one's thoughts and feelings from other people's perspectives.

phallic stage: The third stage of psychosexual development, in which the child's genital area becomes the primary source of physical pleasure.

pharmacology: The science dealing with the properties of drugs and their effects on living organisms.

phobia: A persistent and irrational fear of a specific object or activity, accompanied by a compelling desire to avoid it.

physical dependence: Physiological adaption of the body to the presence of a drug, such that the body reacts with predictable symptoms if the drug is abruptly withdrawn.

popularity: Being very well liked by one's friends and acquaintances.

postconventional morality: According to Kohlberg, the highest level of moral development, in which one's moral judgment is based on abstract moral principles.

postfigurative cultural pattern: The pattern of socialization characterizing societies with little social change, in which youths learn primarily from their elders.

precocious puberty: The onset of sexual maturation before age 8 in girls and age 10 in boys.

preconventional morality: According to Kohlberg, the lowest level of moral development, in which one's moral judgment is based on external rewards and punishment.

predatory crimes: Crimes against people, such as aggravated assaults, forcible rapes, and murder.

prefigurative cultural pattern: The pattern of socialization characterizing societies with rapid social change, in which youths must learn many things for themselves.

prejudice: An unjustifiable attitude, usually negative, toward members of a group.

premarital intercourse: The act of sexual intercourse before marriage.

premarital pregnancy: Pregnancy in an unmarried woman.

premature adulthood: Behavior in an adult manner before one is ready to assume the responsibilities of adulthood.

pre-operational stage: According to Piaget, the second stage of cognitive development, in which the child acquires language and symbolic functions but uses these in a perception-bound way, roughly 2 to 7 years of age.

probation: The suspension of a sentence of a person convicted but not yet imprisoned on condition of continued good behavior and reporting to a probation officer.

progesterone: The hormone produced by the ovaries that causes the uterine lining to thicken.

property crimes: Criminal acts against property, such as burglary, theft, and vandalism.

prosocial behavior: Actions intended to benefit others that have no apparent selfish motivation.

psychedelic: Mind-altering group of drugs producing a mental state of great calm and intensely pleasurable perception.

psychoanalysis: The theory of psychosexual development and therapy developed by Sigmund Freud, in which human behavior is based on the dynamic interaction of unconscious desires, conflicts, anxiety, and defenses.

psychological dependence: A felt need for a drug and its effects brought about by habitual use, sometimes known as "habituation."

psychological disorders: Conditions characterized by painful symptoms or personal distress and significant impairment in one or more areas of functioning.

psychopathology: The science dealing with the causes and development of psychological disorders; psychological maladjustment.

psychosocial: Pertaining to the psychological development of the individual in relation to his or her environment.

psychosocial moratorium: Erikson's concept of modern adolescence as a socially approved delay in development granted to those who are not ready to assume adult commitments.

psychotherapy: A helping process in which a

trained therapist performs activities that will facilitate a change in the client's attitudes and behavior, either in a one-to-one or group setting.

psychotic disturbance: A psychosis, a major psychological disorder characterized by loss of contact with reality and loss of control over feelings and actions.

psychotomimetic: Mimicking a psychosis, i.e., producing hallucinations, sensory illusions, and bizarre thoughts.

puberty: Technically, the attainment of sexual maturity or reproductive powers. More generally, the entire process of glandular and bodily changes accompanying sexual maturation.

pubescence: The period of rapid physical growth preceding sexual maturity in adolescence, sometimes called the "growth spurt."

pubic hair: Hair growth in the region of the sex organs.

rape: Sexual intercourse that occurs without consent under actual or threatened force.

reciprocal determinism: The mutual influences among personal factors, environmental factors, and behavior.

reference groups: Groups to which adolescents look for approval and support.

rehabilitation: Treatment that aims to restore individuals to a normal or optimum of health or psychological health.

reinforcement: Any influence or event that strengthens the behavior associated with it (classical conditioning) or preceding it (operant conditioning).

religion: A system of belief, worship, code of ethics, and conduct involving belief in divine or superhuman powers.

religious observance: Refers to a variety of matters, such as group membership, authority, beliefs, ceremonies, and practices that characterize organized religion.

remarried families: Families in which one or both parents have been previously divorced.

repression: Unconscious process of excluding unacceptable ideas or feelings from consciousness.

rites of passage: Ceremonial acts marking the passage from one developmental or cultural stage to another, with the initiation into adulthood sometimes called "puberty rites."

role: The set of behaviors that are expected of people in various positions.

rudimentary: Incompletely developed.

runaways: Youth under the legal age who leave home without parental permission.

satellization theory: Ausubel's theory that socialization is accomplished through a process of initial dependence upon parents (satellization) and eventual breaking away from parents (desatellization).

schizophrenia: A group of disorders characterized by distortions in thought and speech, hallucinations, delusions, blunted emotions, bizarre behavior, and social withdrawal.

school environment: All those conditions and surroundings that effect the student's experiences in school.

school phobia: A persistent and irrational fear of school, accompanied by a compelling desire to avoid it.

scrotum: The pouch of skin of the external male genitals that enclose the testicles.

seasonal affective disorder (SAD): A mood disorder characterized by depression during the winter months.

secondary schools: Those coming next in sequence after elementary schools, e.g., middle schools and high schools.

secular trend: The tendency toward earlier maturation in recent decades, largely because of improved nutrition.

sedatives: A group of drugs that depress the activity of the central nervous system, including the barbiturates and minor tranquilizers, sometimes referred to as "downers."

self-concept: The overall image we have of ourselves including all those perceptions of "I" and "me," together with the feelings, beliefs, and values associated with them.

self-disclosure: The voluntary disclosure of one's deeper thoughts and feelings to others.

self-efficacy: The sense of personal mastery in a particular situation.

self-esteem: The individual's personal judgment of his or her own self-worth; the sense of personal worth associated with one's self-concept.

self-image: The self I see myself to be.

self-reported delinquency: A measure of delinquent behavior obtained through questionnaires involving anonymous answers.

semen: A white-colored fluid ejaculated through the penis that contains sperm mixed with other seminal fluids.

sensori-motor stage: According to Piaget, the earliest stage of cognitive development consisting mostly of trial-and-error learning through use of the senses and muscles, roughly birth to 2 years of age.

set: Psychological makeup or behavior of a drug user: if a good result is expected, it is more likely to occur.

setting: The circumstances in which a drug is taken.

sex education: Teaching the attitudes, information, and skills needed to become sexually competent, including a formal program of sex education in the school.

sex-typed: Possessing traits or characteristics that are regarded as appropriate for one's biological sex.

sexual intercourse: Sexual activity involving the

penetration of the female vagina by the male penis, characteristically accompanied by pelvic thrusting and orgasm for one or both partners.

sexual revolution: The social trend toward more liberal sexual attitudes and behaviors, especially during the 1960s and 1970s.

sexual values: The value aspects of sexuality involved in decision making.

sexual victimization: Forcing a victim to comply with sexual acts under duress or force, such as rape.

sexually transmitted diseases: Infections transmitted primarily by sexual intercourse.

shyness: The tendency to avoid contact or familiarity with others.

sibling rivalry: Competitiveness and conflict between the adolescents in a given family.

siblings: Brothers or sisters.

single-parent families: Families composed of one or more children or adolescents living with only one parent.

sleeper effect: The adolescent's experience of delayed but eventual surfacing of pent-up emotions associated with the parental divorce.

social acceptance: Being liked and accepted by one's peers.

social change: Changes in the structure of society, its institutions, and social patterns.

social cognition: The way individuals think about themselves, their relationships with others, and their participation in groups and the larger society.

social comparison: The general process by which adolescents evaluate their attitudes, beliefs, emotions, and behaviors by comparing them with those of their peers.

social learning theory: The view that learning and the environment play a primary role in human behavior.

social perspective taking: The ability to become aware of other people's viewpoints and to take these into consideration along with one's own views in dealing with people.

social roles: The appropriate attitudes and behaviors expected by society.

social selves: The impressions we think others have of us, derived from our social roles and interactions.

socialization: The process of social interaction through which people acquire the behavior, roles, and norms of a society or group.

socioeconomic background: Classification according to one's parent's education, income, social status, and style of life.

sociopathic: Lacking an adequate sense of right and wrong.

somatic complaints: Complaints about one's physical well-being.

sperm: The male reproductive cell.

split loyalty: Loyalty to one parent at the expense of disloyalty to the other parent.

spouse: A marriage partner.

stage theory: A view of development that emphasizes the emergence of qualitative changes in the organism's capacities and thus a readiness for learning certain behaviors at some stages of development more than others.

standardized achievement tests: Achievement tests based on large samples and established norms.

status offense: Behavior that is illegal primarily because it is committed by someone under the legal age, such as curfew, alcohol, and drug violations.

stepparent: The person who has married one's parent after the death or divorce of the other parent.

stepparent families: Families consisting of one parent who has custody of the children and a stepparent by marriage.

stereotyped sex roles: Widely shared generalizations about male and female behaviors that exaggerate the actual differences between the sexes.

steroids: Synthetic male hormones that increase muscle mass, strength, and performance.

stimulants: A group of drugs that stimulate the activity of the central nervous system, such as cocaine and the amphetamines.

stress: Our response to stimulus events that disturb our equilibrium and tax our ability to cope.

storm and stress hypothesis: The idea that adolescence is generally a period of conflict and emotional turmoil.

Strong-Campbell Interest Inventory: A vocational inventory that may assist individuals in choosing a compatible career.

sublimation: Unconsciously channeling socially unacceptable urges into acceptable behaviors.

suicide: The act of taking one's life intentionally.

superego: According to Freud, the moral agency of personality which includes the conscience and ego ideal.

sympathetic distress: Occurs when feelings of empathy are accompanied by a sense of compassion and a desire to help someone in need.

syphilis: An infectious disease transmitted by sexual intercourse, which if left untreated may lead to the degeneration of bones, heart, and nerve tissue.

testicle (pl. testes): Male sex gland inside the scrotum that produces sperm and sex hormones.

testosterone: A major male sex hormone produced by the testes.

throwaways: Youth who feel they have no alternative but to leave home because they are told to leave or are victims of sexual abuse or violence.

thyroid-stimulating hormone (TSH): Hormone secreted by the pituitary gland that stimulates the thyroid gland.

tobacco: Products prepared from the leaves of the

tobacco plant, containing nicotine, the substance believed to cause tobacco dependence.

traditional sex roles: The expected behaviors associated with the traditionally masculine and feminine roles.

traditional sex-typed: Possessing high levels of traits regarded as appropriate for one's biological sex and low levels of traits associated with the opposite sex.

tranquilizer: A group of drugs that produce sedative and antianxiety effects.

underresponsible communication: Failure by family members to claim ownership of their messages.

undifferentiated sexual identity: Perception of oneself as neither masculine nor feminine in sex-role orientation.

unethical: that which violates established norms of right and wrong.

unisexual cliques: Small groups composed of adolescents of the same sex.

universal ethical principles: The understanding of right and wrong based on general moral principles such as the respect for individual rights.

uterus: Pear-shaped organ inside the female's pelvis

connecting the vagina with the fallopian tubes; the normal site in which the fetus develops.

vagina: The stretchable canal in the female that opens at the vulva and extends about four inches into the pelvis.

value behavior inconsistency: The conflict between values acquired at home and behavior in a manner more acceptable to peers.

victimless crimes: Criminal acts such as disorderly conduct, gambling, and drug abuse violations in which the person arrested is the primary victim.

virgin: A person who has not experienced sexual intercourse.

vocational identity: According to Don Super, a way of thinking about oneself in relation to the kind of life work desired.

voluntary marriage: The view adopted by marriage partners who agree to stay married only as long as they remain "in love."

vulva: The external genitals of the female, including the labia majora, labia minora, clitoris, and urinary and vaginal openings.

work: Generally taken to mean economic employment.

workplace: Working environment outside the home.

Photo Credits

Name Index

Subject Index

Date Due